W9-BCX-425

A Concordance of
The Poetry in English of
Gerard Manley Hopkins

Edited by

Alfred Borrello

Chairman, Division of Liberal Arts
Mercer County Community College

Programmed by

James Anderson

Angelo Triandafilou

The Scarecrow Press, Inc.
Metuchen, N. J. 1969

SBN 8108-0258-9

To

J. and M.

and

Philip and Mary Borrello
my beloved parents.

Table of Contents

A Concordance to the Poems in English of Gerard Manley Hopkins

Introduction

This concordance is the product of a cooperative venture of the Division of Liberal Arts and the Division of Business of Mercer County Community College. It had its genesis in the school's Advanced Computor Field Projects Course and is the work of two members of that class, Messrs. James Anderson and Angelo Triandafilou who, after consulting with me on a suitable author, planned the computor program and solved the many problems that the language of a poet such as Hopkins presents. Though these problems seemed at times to doom the project to failure, the gentlemen persevered and completed the task which you now see. It should prove invaluable to any serious student of Hopkins.

The details of its production are interesting and give some insight into the complexities in developing a concordance such as this. It was produced by using the school's own computor, an IBM 1401 system, and was financed by the College with the approval of Dean John Hanley, the Dean of Administration, whose interest and help in the project was unfailing.

The following units of the system were used: 1) One 1401 central processing unit (CPU) model E6 with scan, column binary, sense switches, direct seek, and advanced programming features; 2) one 1401 printer; 3) one 1402 card read-punch; 4) two 1311 disc drives; 5) three on-line 7330 tape drives; 6) one 1407 console printer.

The following input/output devices were used: 1) a 1407 console printer for error and operator messages; 2) 1402 card read-punch to read input card file; 3) three 7330 tape drives--(four reels of tape were used: the created word file; sort scratch tape one; sort scratch tape two; and sorted word file. The sorted word file was condensed and the revised version was written on a sort scratch tape, one which then became the appendix 2 tape); 4) one 1311 disc drive; (one disc drive pack was used)--for poetry line file; 5) one 1403 printer for listing words omitted from the concordance, the manuscript body, and the appendices.

An enormous amount of time was spent on developing the logistics of the program. The key punching process alone required some seventy hours. Each word in every line then had to be placed on a tape file and the entire line on a disc file. This process involved five hours; the word-tape sorting, two hours; the concordance-body printing, three hours; the appendices tape sort, run twice, two and one-half hours. Finally, the debugging process required some three hundred hours, including some that the young men had intended to use enjoying their class prom.

The text used was the fourth edition of the collected poems published by Oxford University Press (1967) since it contains all of Hopkins' known poems and fragments. The excellent introduction to this work proved invaluable.

Of necessity, this concordance has several peculiarities. Since the printing was done by an unmodified IBM printer no punctuation is indicated save for the hyphen and the period. The absence of certain types of punctuation (e.g., the accent mark) can create difficulties. These difficulties can be solved by consulting the text of the poem in the Oxford edition. This is normally required in any event, since much of Hopkins' meaning emerges from the context in which his eccentricities appear.

These eccentricities led to numerous conferences before final decisions were made concerning how they were to be treated in the program. As a help, it was decided to retain the tradition of computer produced concordances and omit certain words. The decision to omit words was easier than was choice of the words to be omitted. Fortunately, there are certain precedents for such omissions. It seemed pointless to fill page after page with words which in themselves give no genuine clue to Hopkins' choice of language. We found those precedents established in other concordances (notably Stephen Maxwell Parrish's Concordance to the Poetry of Matthew Arnold, 1959). A list of the words we ultimately decided to omit is given in Appendix II.

Other problems arose. Some poems have titles, others do not. It was decided that identification of each poem be limited to the number assigned to it in the fourth edition. When desirable, the number of the stanza is given as well as the number of the line. When the poem consists of one stanza, the stanza count is left blank, i.e., in the typical identification "1, 4, 2" the first number on the left indicates the number of the poem, the second: the stanza, the third: the line.

Since Hopkins uses a large number of compound words of his own making, it was considered advisable that each compound and its parts be indexed. e.g. "Red-Mountain-Barren" is indexed as four words: a) Red-Mountain-Barren, b) Red, c) Mountain, d) Barren. Some words which we decided to omit are indexed, however, when they appear as part of a compound word. e.g. in "Rock-a-bye," the "a" appears in the concordance. The hyphens in these words created another difficulty. When records are sorted on a computor, hyphens fall into sequence before letters. Thus, the word "rock-hard" appears before the word "rocked." In one instance, Hopkins uses a number "8,000." Because of the peculiarities of the machine, numerical data falls into sequence after words. "8,000," therefore is the last notation.

Other problems arose as the program developed, notably the treatment of variant lines. All such lines are included and listed as additional lines in the poem. e.g. Poem 122 (p. 164 of the Oxford edition) lists two variant lines. For the purposes of this concordance they are identified as lines 12 and 13 of the poem. When a line of poetry is exactly ninety-nine positions long, the counters appear on a second line preceeded only by a row of periods. Multiple duplicate lines appearing beneath a given word indicate that the word appears more than once in that line. (The line is listed for each appearance of the word even when the word appears more than once within one line.) In several instances, exceptionally long lines had to be treated as two lines for the purposes of this concordance. (See: p. 97 of the Oxford text for one of these.)

Finally, Appendix I gives an alphabetized list of Hopkins' vocabulary and the number of times each word appears in his poetry. This index shows that Hopkins uses some 6,787 words; plus the 128 words not indexed, or a total of 6,915 words. The total is a bit inflated by inclusion of the many compound words indexed, nevertheless, the list may be used with confidence to study the extent of his vocabulary and to compare it with that of other poets.

This confidence is strengthened when one considers the steps taken to insure that no errors appear. Each of the punched cards was checked for accuracy and the machine itself was programmed to reject errors. But it would be foolhardy to claim that absolutely no errors remain. We trust, however, that the machine has done its labor with absolute accuracy and thoroughness despite any possible human failings on the part of myself or the programmers, or in its reproduction for publication.

Appendix II lists the words Hopkins used in order of the frequency of their use. It is interesting to note the large number of words used only once (4,196). Of the remaining words 1,228 are used only twice.

Number of Words	Number of Times Used
4,196	1
1,028	2
469	3
244	4
188	5
120	6
70	7
58	8
42	9
50	10
27	11

(cont.) Number of Words	Number of Times Used
28	12
26	13
23	14
19	15
19	16
14	17
17	18
8	19
10	20
9	21
6	22
10	23
8	24
5	25
8	26
5	27
5	28
6	29
2	30
5	31
4	32
2	33
5	34
2	35
1	36
4	37
2	38
1	39
3	40
1	41
3	42
3	43
1	44
1	45
1	46
1	48
1	49
1	50
1	53
2	55
1	58
1	59
1	62
2	64
1	69
1	72
1	76
1	80
1	83
1	84
1	87

Number of Words	Number of Times Used
1	89
2	99
1	100
1	101
1	167
1	171
1	239
1	245
1	505

Acknowledgements

There are many individuals who must be thanked for the help they gave in this project. In addition to Dean Hanley, whose encouragement was unfailing, I cannot omit thanking our President, Dr. Richard K. Greenfield, and our Dean of Faculty, Dr. John J. Cadden, who provided the ambient in which such a project could be conceived and brought to reality.

My thanks must also be extended to Mr. Jack Mars, the acting Chairman of the Business Division, who quickly recognized the value of this project for forging the beginning of inter-disciplinary cooperation in our school. I must also thank Mr. Robert A. Angell, the instructor of the course, who welcomed my suggestions and helped and encouraged the Messrs. Anderson and Triandafilou. My special thanks must go to Mr. James Rohe, the Systems Analyst, who gave unstintingly of his time and patience to see this project through to its success; Susan Busch, Jacqueline Smith and Catherine Lorbeck, the keypunchers; my secretaries, Mrs. Madlynne Pastor and Mrs. Carol Cieslikowski; and Mr. Thomas Hurley for the help he gave in compiling the statistics.

I cannot close without acknowledging the debt of gratitude I owe to Dr. Paul Doyle, who, as my one-time professor and now, fortunately for me, my friend, has never ceased to encourage me in this and all the projects I have undertaken.

Trenton, New Jersey
October, 1968

A. Borrello

Word	Poem	Stan.	Line
A			
His charge through the champ-white water-in-a-wallow	40		47
I plod wondering a-wanting just for lack	45		6
Of answer the eagerer a-wanting Jessy or Jack	45		7
With-a-fountains shining-shot furls	71		19
Tatter-tangled and dingle-a-dangled	138		25
To the all-a-leaf of the treetop	138		38
Mortal my mate bearing my rock-a-heart	153		1
A-wanting			
I plod wondering a-wanting just for lack	45		6
Of answer the eagerer a-wanting Jessy or Jack	45		7
Abandoned			
Abandoned by her saints turnd black and blasted	102	2	13
Abel			
Abel is Cains brother and breasts they have sucked the same	28	20	8
Abeles			
Wind-beat whitebeam airy Abeles set on a flare	31	1	6
Abide			
Too near thee and thou must abide	106		3
Abides			
Death with a sovereignty that heeds but hides bodes but abides	28	31	8
Abject			
I cease the mourning and the abject fast	14	1	8
Abode			
Houses that make abode beside the lake	81	6	6
Abolished			
He hath abolished the old drouth	8		1
Abound			
For these make all the virtues to abound	13		13
About			
So glassy white about the sky	3		16
And rise and go about my works again	14	1	9
Contends about its many creeds	23		32
She to the black-about air to the breaker the thickly	28	24	5
About mans beating heart	60		50
When wholesome spirits rustle about	78		27
Were limnd about with radiance rare	78		60
And some of those who stand about	81	7	18
About herself she is most sensitive	94		21
In skeins about the brakes	98	10	3
Most like the silver plighted tuft about	102	1	74
The river wound about it as a waist	107	4	2

Word	Poem	Stan.	Line
About (cont.)			
Which Wordsworth would have dwelt on about the place	107	4	16
When eyes that cast about in heights of Heaven	113		1
Beside them about the hedges hearing him	113		8
As wishing all about us sweet	139		1
Had swarthed about with lion-brown	144		3
Days and days came round about	145		23
It will not well so she would bring about	151		3
How when this bloom this honeysuckle that rides the air so rich about thee	152		23
From thy hand out swayed about	155		3
Are earthworld airworld waterworld thorough hurled all by turn and turn about	159		18
Long where we leave him froliclavish while he looks about him laughs swims	159		42
Above			
There is a massy pile above the waste	1	1	1
In bows above my head as falsified	12	2	4
Eclipsing parapet yet above the wall	12	2	7
I cannot buoy my heart above	18		5
Above it cannot entrance win	18		6
Love it grows darker here and thou art above	20		5
If I shall overtake thee at last above	20		16
In acres all above the wood	21		35
O breath of it bathes great heaven above	27		46
Gnashed but thou art above thou Orion of light	28	21	5
Furred snows charged tuft above tuft tower	29	1	31
Around up above what wind-walks what lovely behaviour	37		2
Throstle above her nested	41		20
Above me round me lie	60		118
Lifts them a little way above	81		38
The angel listed us above	81		119
Above them down the draught of air	83		12
Above	98	21	1
The proper sweet re-attributing above	113		11
That sweetness re-attributing above	113		12
Nor fruit above	127		8
Abreast			
March kind comrade abreast him	47		19
Abroad			
And look abroad on sunny clusters	78		134
Lowly Alice lookd abroad	109	17	1
Abrupt			
Of own of abrupt self there so thrusts on so throngs the ear	44		8
Abundant			
Next to meadows abundant pierced with flowers	98	12	2
Abysmal			
The abysmal ocean hoards of strange and rare	2		55

Word	Poem	Stan.	Line
Abysses			
And still the abysses infinite	· 23		25
Acanthus			
Broad-fluted nor with shafts acanthus-crownd	1	7	3
Acanthus-crownd			
Broad-fluted nor with shafts acanthus-crownd	1	7	3
Accents			
Firm accents strike her fine and scrolled ear	136		21
Accept			
Thou who canst best accept the certainty	13		5
Acceptance			
Acceptance round his mistress mouth	83		8
Accepted			
Those charms accepted of my inmost thought	12	1	9
Accepting			
My all-accepting fixed eye	130		6
Accessories			
With fickle spots of sadness accessories	125		47
Accidents			
And save by darting accidents forget	14	1	10
Accumulated			
Dimmd in the long accumulated dust	1	12	6
Aches			
Holds till hand aches and wonders what is there	151		8
Achieve			
Stirred for a bird the achieve of the mastry of the thing	36		77
Aching			
But come thou balm to aching soul	78		11
Acknowledging			
As acknowledging thy stress	155		6
Acorn			
Sucks close the acorn as the hand and glove	101		3
The hand draws off the glove the acorn-cup	101		9
Acorn-cup			
The hand draws off the glove the acorn-cup	101		9
Acquaintance			
And bred acquaintance of unused towns	107	2	2
Acre			
In the acre of Gethsemane	6		16
Meet in one acre of one land	8		11
The blue wheat-acre is underneath	138		18
Acres			
In acres all above the wood	21		35
Across			
Anon across their swimming splendour strook	2		15
Is this made plain what have I come across	14	3	10
Meal-drift moulded ever and melted across skies	37		4
Across my foundering deck shone	72		18
Let incense hang across the room	78		19
Rolls across the labouring willows	79		4

Word	Poem	Stan.	Line
Across (cont.)			
Ply fold on fold across his dangerous eyes	102	1	20
Thus he ties spiders web across his sight	102	3	28
Such spiders web he ties across his sight	102	3	34
I know it knowing not across from those	119		7
The words came from a court across the way	136		23
Flinty kindcold element let break across his limbs	159		41
Act			
Brute beauty and valour and act oh air pride plume here	36		8
Sweetly then and of free act	78		89
Sees the right thing to do and does not act	94		20
Acts			
Two tedious acts were past	53		29
Acts in Gods eye what in Gods eye he is	56		11
Adamantine			
Would brandle adamantine heaven with ride and jar did	47		46
Adazzle			
With swift slow sweet sour adazzle dim	37		9
Add			
Will add a footrest there to stand	81	7	42
Adder			
The cold whip-adder unespied	106		1
Adela			
Selvaggia Orinda and Adela and the rest	125		44
Admire			
I admire thee master of the tides	28	31	1
For all to see and to admire	131		4
O I admire and sorrow the hearts eye grieves	157		1
Admired			
She was admired the spirit of hell	145		17
Adored			
Be adored among men	28	9	1
Mastery but be adored but be adored king	28	10	8
Mastery but be adored but be adored king	28	10	8
Adown			
Adown the clattering gullies swept the rain	1	13	2
Their filmy tails adown whose length there showd	2		104
Advance			
8000 furlongs in advance	83		16
Adversity			
Shes framed to triumph in adversity	94		23
Advise			
Soul self come poor jackself I do advise	69		9
Aeolis			
Of glassy-clear aeolis metal-lustred	2		69
Aeons			
While ages and while aeons run	23		20

Word	Poem	Stan.	Line
Aerial			
Splendid with phantasies aerial	1	8	2
And flockbells off the aerial	40		6
Aether			
Melting into aether rare	78		74
Afar			
Afar in corridors with pained strain	1	13	7
Affection			
Is very capable of strong affection	94		13
Affined			
Affined well to that sweet solitude	107	1	15
Afflicted			
I heard her say poor poor afflicted soul	111		11
Afflictive			
The sun whose vast afflictive heat	81	2	2
Afflicts			
Afflicts no less what yet I hope may blow	17		6
Aflash			
And crush-silk poppies aflash	138		21
Afoot			
Are afoot heaven-vault fast purpling portends and what first lightning	152		63
Afresh			
Thy doing and dost thou touch me afresh	28	1	7
After			
After the sandfield and the unveined glare	5		29
After the sunset I would lie	15		42
And after it almost unmade what with dread	28	1	6
O unteachably after evil but uttering truth	28	18	5
What most I may eye after be in at the end	39		10
Him after an hour of wintry waves	41		68
After-comers cannot guess the beauty been	42		19
This very very day came down to us after a boon he on	47		5
Days after so I in a sort deserve to	47		26
And none reck of world after this bids wear	57		13
It fancies feigns deems dears the artist after his art	63		6
Who could forgive without grudge after	78		57
Like shuttles fleet the clouds and after	98	3	1
And after that sad sorrow	110		4
What would be a birthday letter that after the birthday came	128		4
Its the day that makes the charm no after-words could succeed	128		7
Time was next whitest after Marys own	136		4
Well after all ah but hark	138		10
And after that off the bough	138		39
After that in perfect hush	145		58
Next after sweet success I am not left even this	152		92
While blind mens eyes shall thirst after daylight			

Word	Poem	Stan.	Line
After (cont.)			
draughts of daylight	152		109
After-comers			
After-comers cannot guess the beauty been	42		19
After-words			
Its the day that makes the charm no after-words could succeed	128		7
Aftercast			
In one fair fall but for times aftercast	157		7
Afterdraught			
Now her afterdraught gullies him too down	41		60
Afternoon			
Then through the afternoon the summer beam	1	12	1
Again			
Amongst come-back-again things things with a revival things with a recovery	152		134
Against			
Trench right the tide that ramps against the shore	34		2
They rain against our much-thick and marsh air	39		7
Where selfwrung selfstrung sheathe-and shelterless thoughts against thoughts in groans grind	61		14
Thy wring-world right foot rock lay a lionlimb against me scan	64		6
Sir Christ against this multitude I strain	81	7	12
The fruit against the wall	105		12
My thought was there to rest against the trees	125		8
Are shut against the canvassing of art	126		6
On one that went against me whereas I had warned her	152		37
Against the wild and wanton work of men	157		36
Age			
Or sunderd from my sight in the age that is	13		3
Could count on prediluvian age	15		10
This in drudgery day-labouring-out lifes age	38		4
An age is now since passed since parted with the reversal	44		3
Age and ages evils hoar hair	58		11
My cries heave herds-long huddle in a main a chief-woe world-sorrow on an age-old anvil wince and sing	65		5
Manwolf worse and their packs infest the age	70		20
Age gasp whose breath is our memento mori	76		7
To that first golden age of gospel times	136		5
Age-old			
My cries heave herds-long huddle in a main a chief-woe world-sorrow on an age-old anvil wince and sing	65		5
Ages			
This to remotest ages was to be	1	8	8
And silver damasqud plates obscurd in ages crust	1	12	9

Word	Poem	Stan.	Line
While ages and while aeons run	23		20
Age and ages evils hoar hair	58		11
Aggrandise			
There God to aggrandise God to glorify	45		8
Ago			
The monks left long ago since which no more	1	15	4
What was its season then how long ago	27		14
Jews killed Jesus long ago	145		52
Aid			
She lends in aid of work and will	139		3
Aidenn			
And where thou dwellest in deep-groved Aidenn	26		23
Aim			
The widow of an insight lost she lives with aim	77		7
Air			
The Zenith melted to a rose of air	2		23
Of something drifting thro delighted air	2		28
Swirling out bloom till all the air is blind	2		89
A little sickness in the air	4		3
Your parched nostrils snuff Egyptian air	5		27
Below me in the bearing air	15		30
And silence and a gulf of air	15		40
Or bat with tender and air-crisping wings	19		2
I thought the air must cut and strain	21		36
You went into the partless air	25		30
For the infinite air is unkind	28	13	4
With the burl of the fountains of air buck and the flood of the wave	28	16	8
She to the black-about air to the breaker the thickly	28	24	5
O look at all the fire-folk sitting in the air	32	1	2
That cordial air made those kind people a hood	34		5
All the air thing wear that build this world of wales	34		10
Of the rolling level underneath him steady air and striding	36		2
Brute beauty and valour and act oh air pride plume here	36		8
They rain against our much-thick and marsh air	40		7
Now he shoots short up to the round air	41		64
Yet ah this air I gather and I release	44		9
Let him oh with his air of angels then lift me lay me only ill	45		9
With the sweetest air that said still plied and pressed	47		3
Pillowy air he treads a time and hangs	50		10
Tall suns tingeing or treacherous the tainting of the earths air	59		5
Wild air world-mothering air	60		1
Wild air world-mothering air	60		1
This air which by lifes law	60		13

Word	Poem	Stan.	Line
Air (cont.)			
As if with air the same	60		36
Her life as life does air	60		45
How air is azured	60		74
Whereas did air not make	60		94
Of Gods love o live air	60		122
World-mothering air air wild	60		124
World-mothering air air wild	60		124
Cloud-puffball torn tufts tossed pillows flaunt forth then chevy on an air	72		1
To whom the common earth and air	78		59
To drift in air the circled earth	78		69
In breezy belts of upper air	78		73
And all in lone air stood the sun	78		76
Of the air-blended diadem	78		115
Breathes in the mysterious air	78		128
That meet in mid-air and be so	78		139
High up the balanced stony air	81	4	2
Above them down the draught of air	83		12
Breaking the air of spring	98	3	7
The liberties of air	98	29	4
The sparky air	98	33	1
He shook with racing notes the standing air	98	38	1
One star by daylight from the strong blue air	102	3	10
Springs in the floating air and the skies swim	113		6
Falling along the breakless pool of air	122		9
Which drives the stony air to utterance	122		18
And daylight and sweet air	133		14
The liberties of air	135		22
The air smells strong of sweetbriar in the park	135		24
To the point of silence in the air	135		32
Spent Pegasus down the stark-precipitous air	136		8
When the air was sweet-and-sour of the flown fineflour of	142		4
Like air he changed in choice	148		18
How when this bloom this honeysuckle that rides the air so rich about thee	152		23
Their crutches shall cast from them on heels of air departing	152		128
Out on the giant air tell summer no	154		3
By rafts and rafts of flake leaves light dealt so painted on the air	159		25
Air-blended			
Of the air-blended diadem	78		115
Air-crisping			
Or bat with tender and air-crisping wings	19		2
Airs			
To the shrouds they took they shook in the hurling and horrible airs	28	15	8
Come then your ways and airs and looks locks maidengear gallantry and gaiety and grace	59		14

Word	Poem	Stan.	Line
Winning ways airs innocent maiden manners sweet looks loose locks long locks love-locks gaygear going gallant girlgrace	59		15
Laying like airs fine flood	60		51
Airwards			
Airwards disturbd and the scarce troubled sea	2		110
Airworld			
Are earthworld airworld waterworld thorough hurled all by turn and turn about	159		18
Airy			
Triumph of airy grace and perfect harmony	1	7	9
Wind-beat whitebeam airy abeles set on a flare	31	1	6
My aspens dear whose airy cages quelled	42		1
The gold-wisp the airy-grey	48		3
The airy empire at his will	78		78
There they did appeal therefore airy vengeances	152		62
Airy-grey			
The gold-wisp the airy-grey	48		3
Akin			
And to those stones become akin	81	3	2
Alarms			
Alarms of wars the daunting wars the death of it	50		6
Alas			
And they are purer but alas not solely	16		5
Three hundred souls o alas on board	40		2
To dearest him that lives alas away	67		8
Alas I rave where calm is due	81		70
That I was so near laughter alas now	102	1	33
Alas but I am all at fault	120		24
Albeit			
When the fierce skies are blue to black albeit	81	2	5
Ale			
Not honour it ale like goldy foam	29	1	35
Alert			
Denis whose motionable alert most vaulting wit	143		1
Alfonso			
That in Majorca Alfonso watched the door	73		14
Alice			
Lowly Alice sat in her bower	109	16	1
Lowly Alice lookd abroad	109	17	1
And Alice they call me	109	19	2
Alien			
Alien from yours as heaven from nadir-fires	78		4
Now coming from the alien eaves	81		3
To alien eaves you fled and went	81		5
Alight			
Mounts then to alight disarming no one dreams	49		13
Alighted			
All as the moth calld underwing alighted	108		1

Word	Poem	Stan.	Line
Alive			
Most dead-alive upon those days	81	2	7
Tis marvel she is yet alive	81		10
Alive or dead my girl is carried in it endlessly	152		27
All			
By conqurors rude of honor and not all	1	8	4
Into the cooling gloom till slowly all	1	12	5
Now all things rosy turnd the west had grown	2		19
With spiked quills all of intensest hue	2		44
Swirling out bloom till all the air is blind	2		89
A glorious wanton all the wrecks in showers	2		93
Is all the winter bird dare try	3		14
Drops out and all our day is done	3		32
Are all the manna-bushes in the land	5		21
Unbakes my pores and streams and makes all fresh	5		32
Blaze for him all this while	5		36
Christ at all hazards fruit hath shewed	7		10
And rivers run where all was dry	8		2
God comes all sweetness to your Lenten lips	11		2
Lo God shall strengthen all the feeble knees	11		14
All mine yet common to my every peer	12	1	8
The window-circles these may all be sought	12	1	11
And all like me may boast impeached not	12	1	13
So that the masons levels courses all	12	2	2
For these make all the virtues to abound	13		13
Into all seasons though no winter cast	14	1	5
And so though each have one while I have all	16		12
And fail or scatter all away	18		2
And other science all gone out of date	19		11
Hear yet my paradox love when all is given	20		13
In all our western shires was rare	21		23
In acres all above the wood	21		35
All down the stair-way of the copse	21		45
From there where all surrenders come	22		7
But not the hand that wrought them all	23		8
Upon Christ throw all away	24		5
Where winter-while is all forgot	25		14
From all the pain of the pasts unrest	26		12
To thee we tender the beauties all	26		21
We all we thro the length of our days	26		34
But roped with always all the way down from the tall	28	4	6
Make mercy in all of us out of us all	28	10	7
Make mercy in all of us out of us all	28	10	7
For all his dreadnought breast and braids of thew	28	16	5
Have you make words break from me here all alone	28	18	3
To bathe in his fall-gold mercies to breathe in his all-fire glances	28	23	8

Word	Poem	Stan.	Line
Ground of being and granite of it past all	28	31	6
The all of water an ark	28	32	2
And all the landscape under survey	30	4	1
For all they shine so high in heaven	30	5	3
And mazy sands all water-wattled	30	6	3
And all is seared with trade bleared smeared with toil	31	1	6
And for all this nature is never spent	31	1	9
O look at all the fire-folk sitting in the air	32	1	2
Ah well it is all a purchase all is a prize	32	1	8
Ah well it is all a purchase all is a prize	32	1	8
Christ home Christ and his mother and all his hallows	32	1	14
The descending blue that blue is all in a rush	33		7
What is all this juice and all this joy	33		9
What is all this juice and all this joy	33		9
I remember a house where all were good	34		1
All over as a bevy of eggs the mothering wing	34		6
All the air thing wear that build this world of wales	34		10
With a flood or a fall low lull-off or all roar	35		3
For rose-moles all in stipple upon trout that swim	37		3
And all trades their gear and tackle and trim	37		6
All things counter original spare strange	37		7
Down all that glory in the heavens to gleam our Saviour	38		6
With all down darkness wide his wading light	40		4
Some asleep unawakened all unwarned eleven fathoms fallen	41		3
Royal and all her royals wore	41		33
All hands for themselves the cry ran then	41		41
All under channel to bury in a beach her	41		48
Doffs all drives full for righteousness	41		55
He was all of lovely manly mould	41		73
Look foot to forelock how all things suit he	41		76
Unchrist all rolled in ruin	41		95
Fresh till doomfire burn all	41		118
Grass and greenworld all together	42		18
All things rising all things sizing	42		25
All things rising all things sizing	42		25
Caps clears and clinches all	42		44
This ecstasy all through mothering earth	42		45
All felled felled are all felled	43		3
All felled felled are all felled	43		3
But a prick will make no eye at all	43		15
He haunted who of all men most sways my spirits to peace	44		11
Or love or pity or all that sweet notes not his might nursle	45		6
With yellowy moisture mild nights blear-all black	46		3

Word	Poem	Stan.	Line
All (cont.)			
All in this case bathed in high hallowing grace	47		11
Run all your race o brace sterner that strain	47		14
When limber liquid youth that to all I teach	48		22
Nothing else is like it no not all so strains	48		29
Us fresh youth fretted in a bloomfall all portending	48		30
Eye all in fellowship	49		4
This all this beauty blooming	49		5
This all this freshness fuming	49		6
A wilder beast from west than all were more	50		7
All while her patience morselled into pangs	50		12
Felix Randal the farrier o is he dead then my duty all ended	52		1
Fatal four disorders fleshed there all contended	53		4
Being anointed and all though a heavenlier heart began some	53		6
Tendered to him ah well God rest him all road ever he offended	53		8
How far from then forethought of all thy more boisterous years	53		12
Life all laced in the others	54		2
Now the night come all	54		10
For wrung all on loves rack	54		17
Keeps grace that keeps all his goings graces	57		10
Thy river and oer gives all to rack or wrong	58		8
To its own best being and its loveliness of youth it is an everlastingness of o it is an all youth	59		13
To its own best being and its loveliness of youth it is an everlastingness of o it is an all youth	59		13
Birth milk and all the rest	60		21
Let all Gods glory through	60		30
Towards all our ghostly good	60		48
More makes when all is done	60		71
With blackness bound and all	60		98
Evening strains to be times vast womb-of-all home-of-all hearse-of-all night	61		2
Evening strains to be times vast womb-of-all home-of-all hearse-of-all night	61		2
Evening strains to be times vast womb-of-all home-of-all hearse-of-all night	61		2
Astray or aswarm all throughther in throngs self steeped and pashed quite	61		6
Disremembering dismembering all now heart you round me right	61		7
Off her once skeined stained veined variety upon all on two spools part pen pack	61		11
Now her all in two flocks two folds black white right wrong reckon but reck butmind	61		12
Our law says love what are loves worthiest			

Word	Poem	Stan.	Line
were all known	62		8
Yea wish that though wish all Gods better beauty grace	62		12
Yes why do we all seeing of a soldier bless him bless	63		1
And fain will find as sterling all as all is smart	63		7
And fain will find as sterling all as all is smart	63		7
He of all can reeve a rope best there he bides in bliss	63		10
Now and seeing somewhere some man do all that man can do	63		11
Nay in all that toil that coil since seems I kissed the rod	64		10
Wretch under a comfort serves in a whirl-wind all	65		11
England whose honour o all my heart woos wife	66	1	5
Remove not but in all removes I can	66	1	9
Purple eyes and seas of liquid leaves all day	68		8
Thirsts all-in-all in all a world of wet	69		8
Thirsts all-in-all in all a world of wet	69		8
Thirsts all-in-all in all a world of wet	69		8
Thirsts all-in-all in all a world of wet	69		8
Tom heart-at-ease Tom navvy he is all for his meal	70		4
Little I reck ho lacklevel in if all had bread	70		9
What country is honour enough in all us lordly head	70		10
Of earths glory earths ease all no one nowhere	70		16
In him all quail to the wallowing o the plough s cheek crimsons curls	71		13
Both are in an unfathomable all is in an enormous dark	72		12
Is any of him at all so stark	72		15
I am all at once what Christ is since he was what I am and	72		22
Earth all out who with trickling increment	73		10
Disappointment all I endeavour end	75	1	3
When strangely loom all shapes that be	78		31
And the waked stars are all alone	78		34
Who knowing all the sins and sores	78		53
And all in lone air stood the sun	78		76
All the welkin overhead	78		96
All a sevenfold-single gem	78		116
There is a day of all the year	81	7	8
They all come here and stand before me clear	81	7	10
And all in one say crucify	81	7	14
And all into the Duomo ran	81		88
Twas said of none but all men knew	81		91
But all the while it seemd to me	81		112
My love and all was sweet and well	81		121

Word	Poem	Stan.	Line
All (cont.)			
For more with him who gives thee all	81		150
For all the miles that they were sped	81		158
Has danced with her and all the while	83		23
See one bow each yet not the same to all	91		6
What were worth nothing if all compliment	94		6
And cannot see at all with others eyes	94		26
Theyre out of date Lent sermons all the year	96	5	2
Of falling water this and all of these	98	2	3
Of all the golden press	98	27	2
To all the starry press	98	28	6
Well I know not but all things seem to-night	102	1	10
Thou Jacinth nor have skill of all thy virtues	102	1	62
Floris thou late-found all-heal	102	1	63
Like knocking thunder all round Britains welkin	102	2	3
Where all the virtues were illustrated	102	2	9
To spread the compass on the all-starrd sky	102	3	8
To turn the compass on the all-starrd sky	102	3	23
And gives for tropes his judgment all away	102	3	29
And gives for tropes his judgment all away	102	3	35
All quests save the recital of their greatness	104		3
Their clarions from all corners of the field	104		4
They draw all coverts cut the fields and suck	104		12
The treasure from all cities	104		13
Or never been at all	105		15
Their changing feet in flicker all the time	107	1	13
Beyond the river all the meadows round	107	4	10
I hope that all the places on our trip	107	4	27
All as the moth calld underwing alighted	108		1
Lord William is king of all this land	109	27	3
Fie she said unto them all	109	28	1
If he were king of all this land	109	28	3
Than all the crowns to me	109	38	4
Whose all-belated leaves yield up themselves	111		2
Ah surely all who have written will profess	117		8
Alas but I am all at fault	120		24
Of the wood-sorrel and all things sensitive	122		11
As the wood-sorrel and all things sensitive	122		14
Lined all with solk of juicy red	124		16
Crept all along a hill upon our left	125		3
I betterd all our path with sanguine eyes	125		17
Flatterys all out of place where praise is true	125		35
But this distemperd court will change it all	125		63
Which says at least then go while all is fresh	125		64
All time at once and span the distant goals	126		4
Only the dahlias blow and all is autumn here	128		10
My all-accepting fixed eye	130		6
While all things else may stir and range	130		7
All else may whirl or dive or fly	130		8
For all to see and to admire	131		4
All glory be ascribed to	133		3

Word	Poem	Stan.	Line
All insufficiencies	133		8
All slumbered whom our rud red tiles	135		1
And all within the house were sound as posts	135		17
Her weeds all mark her maiden though to wed	136		17
All over some such words as these though dark	136		29
And all round not to be found	138		5
Well after all ah but hark	138		10
To the all-a-leaf of the treetop	138		38
As wishing all about us sweet	139		1
Repent he sinned and all his sins be freed	140		6
Of crumbling fore-foundering thundering all-surfy seas in seen	141		5
His locks like all a ravel-ropes-end	144		5
Since all the make of man	148		7
Not of all my eyes see wandering on the world	149	1	1
All is from wreck here there to rescue one	150		6
And breathes the blots off all with sighs on sighs	151		6
All of her glorious gainings unaware	151		10
Have all things ready in his room	152		10
Is all all sheared away thus then I sweat for fear	152		24
Is all all sheared away thus then I sweat for fear	152		24
In all her beauty and sunlight to it is a pit den darkness	152		54
In all her body I say no place was like her eyes	152		56
Now be my pride then perfect all one piece henceforth	152		70
I all my being have hacked in half with her neck one part	152		93
Must all day long taste murder what do now then do	152		98
Deed-bound I am one deed treads all down here cramps all doing what do not yield	152		100
Deed-bound I am one deed treads all down here cramps all doing what do not yield	152		100
Brave all and take what comes as here this rabble is come	152		102
While sick men shall cast sighs of sweet health all despairing	152		108
Not all but we were framed to fail and die	153		6
Is comforts carol of all or woes worst smart	153		8
All day long I like fountain flow	155		2
Not that but thus far all with frailty blest	157		6
Creatures all heft hope hazard interest	157		8
Fast furled and all foredrawn to no or yes	157		28
Roots and rocks is danced and dandled all in froth and waterblowballs down	159		7
Are earthworld airworld waterworld thorough hurled all by turn and turn about	159		18

Word	Poem	Stan.	Line
All (cont.)			
Rose here he feasts lovely all is no more off with down he dings	159		28
All lie tumbled-to then with loop-locks	159		31
And come where lies a coffer burly all of blocks	159		36
All-a-leaf			
To the all-a-leaf of the treetop	138		38
All-accepting			
My all-accepting fixed eye	130		6
All-belated			
Whose all-belated leaves yield up themselves	111		2
All-fire			
To bathe in his fall-gold mercies to breathe in his all-fire glances	28	23	8
All-heal			
Floris thou late-found all-heal	102	1	63
All-in-all			
Thirsts all-in-all in all a world of wet	69		8
All-starrd			
To spread the compass on the all-starrd sky	102	3	8
To turn the compass on the all-starrd sky	102	3	23
All-surfy			
Of crumbling fore-foundering thundering all-surfy seas in seen	141		5
Allow			
Allow at least it has one term and part	102	3	5
Allows			
That piecemeal peace is poor peace what pure peace allows	51		5
Allows the sound of bells in Hamlets round	81	4	6
Alls			
The bald and bold blinking gold when alls done	143		4
How alls to one thing wrought	148		1
Almoner			
Nay more than almoner	60		42
Almost			
And after it almost unmade what with dread	28	1	6
There was a meadow level almost you traced	107	4	1
And said I like this it is almost isled	107	4	25
You have made me quote almost the dismalest proverb I know	128		18
Alms			
Buy then bid then what prayer patience alms vows	32	1	9
The sweet alms self is her	60		43
Aloft			
Though aloft on turf or perch or poor low stage	39		5
On things aloof aloft	60		91
Alone			
Have you make words break from me here all alone	28	18	3

Word	Poem	Stan.	Line
Home at heart heavens sweet gift then leave let that alone	62		11
And the waked stars are all alone	78		34
Which to pure souls alone may be	78		142
Now like the bird that shapes alone	81		6
This heart is warm to you alone	81		129
Of him that looks yet not in that alone	91		3
But Im alone for my loves gone	95		8
Alone upon the hill-top heaven oer him	107	1	8
Yet Id not say it is her face alone	125		61
In a wide world of defiance Caradoc lives alone	152		71
Along			
Pourtrayd along the frieze with Titans brood	1	7	4
Lay along the grasses green	4		22
Along the sanctuary side	22		20
I move along lifes tomb-decked way	23		39
Sometimes a lantern moves along the night	40		1
With along them cragiron under and cold furls	71		18
Glimmerd along the square-cut steep	92		1
Told off their leaves along the piercing gale	98	5	2
One and then one along their walks and kept	107	1	12
Falling along the breakless pool of air	122		9
Crept all along a hill upon our left	125		3
Gallop along the meadow grass	130		26
Those goldnails and their gaylinks that hang along a lime	142		5
That leans along the loins of hills where a candycoloured where a gluegold-brown	159		5
Aloof			
On things aloof aloft	60		91
Or like a lark to glide aloof	78		65
Folds off aloof that signal is and proof	81	6	3
Alp			
Youll dare the Alp youll dart the skiff	30	1	5
Altar			
Upon his altar and with rarest store	1	2	8
The altar-tapers flard in gusts in vain	1	13	5
Now in our altar-vessels stored	6		19
Thou knowest the walls altar and hour and night	28	2	5
Altar-tapers			
The altar-tapers flard in gusts in vain	1	13	5
Altar-vessels			
Now in our altar-vessels stored	6		19
Altars			
And on a thousand altars laid	6		9
Alter			
Perfect not alter it	60		89
Alterd			
Leaves spent new seasons alterd sky	15		2
From Paris unlookd for alterd spent	81		24
You hear and alterd do not hear	81		41

Word	Poem	Stan.	Line
Altogether			
They were else-minded then altogether the men	28	25	5
Alway			
Henceforth let your souls alway	24		29
Now beginning and alway	129		8
Always			
As I markd not always died	4		28
But roped with always all the way down from the tall	28	4	6
Always the time remembereth	81		61
And headed always downwards with less sounding	112		2
Had always doomed her down to this	145		3
Second this fiery strain not always o no no	152		78
Amain			
Upon the mouldring terraces amain	1	13	4
While the sun streams forth amain	78		103
Amansstrength			
Churlsgrace too child of amansstrength how it hangs or hurls	71		16
Amaze			
It does amaze me when the clicking hour	102	1	1
Amazed			
Men are amazed to watch me pass	25		3
Amber			
Whose ken through amber of dark eyes	78		51
Does into amber splendours fail	78		100
Amend			
Christ minds Christs interest what to avow or amend	40		12
Amends			
And I must take your amends cry pardon and then be dumb	128		20
American			
American-outward-bound	28	12	2
American-outward-bound			
American-outward-bound	28	12	2
Amethyst			
Broiders the nets with fans of amethyst	2		66
Amidst			
They tell its story thus amidst the heat	1	2	1
And melts amidst another cield on high	1	6	8
Plashes amidst the billowy apple-trees	2		87
When thou at the random grim forge powerful amidst peers	52		13
Amidst the sistering planets till she comes	103		14
Amiss			
Conceiving whom I must conceive amiss	13		2
Among			
Others with fingers white would comb among	2		112
A moaning voice among the reeds	23		36
Be adored among men	28	9	1

Word	Poem	Stan.	Line
Drowned and among our sholas	28	34	2
Among strangers father and mother dear	66	1	2
Among his brothers three	109	23	2
Among the lilies and thy good domain	123		6
Amongst			
Amongst Castilian barrens mountain-bound	1	1	2
Amongst come-back-again things things with a revival things with a recovery	152		134
Ancient			
Or ancient mounds that cover bones	15		37
Ancles			
Earthless dews on ancles sleek	78		16
And			
When drop-of-blood-and-foam-dapple	42		37
Tongue true vaunt-and tauntless	48		15
Where selfwrung selfstrung sheathe-and shelterless thoughts against thoughts in groans grind	61		14
When the air was sweet-and-sour of the flown fineflour of	142		4
His cheeks the forth-and-flaunting sun	144		2
Andromeda			
Now times Andromeda on this rock rude	50		1
Anew			
This sweet deserter lists herself anew	102	1	65
Angel			
Frowning and forefending angel-warder	48		17
An angel came the judgment done	81		104
The angel lifted us above	81		119
Nor angel insight can	148		5
Angel-warder			
Frowning and forefending angel-warder	48		17
Angels			
Let him oh with his air of angels then lift me lay me only Ill	45		9
Of it angels fall they are towers from heaven a story	76		3
To what the chords of angels are	78		46
Caught from angels wings in heaven	78		110
Who say that angels in your ear	81		122
Far from its head an angels hoverings	89		8
Hang as still as hawk or hawkmoth as the stars or as the angels there	159		26
Anointed			
Being anointed and all though a heavenlier heart began some	52		6
Anon			
Anon across their swimming splendour strook	2		15
Lies in her lap which she anon sweeps off	111		9
Would it were summer-time anon she sang	111		12
Answer			
Of answer the eagerer a-wanting Jessy or Jack	46		7

Word	Poem	Stan.	Line
Answer (cont.)			
The heaven-enforced answer comes	81		144
Yea to myself I answer make	81		145
Two made answer in one breath	109	26	1
Answering			
No answering voice comes from the skies	23		2
Antinous			
But hapless youth Antinous the while	1	11	5
Antipodes			
They are antipodes apart	83		24
Antique			
An antique chaunt and in an unknown tongue	2		131
Anvil			
With an anvil-ding	28	10	1
My cries heave herds-long huddle in a main a chief-woe world-sorrow on an age-old anvil wince and sing	65		5
Anvil-ding			
With an anvil-ding	28	10	1
Any			
I must feed fancy show me any one	14	2	1
Could mould if any tears there were	18		14
Is set in any orchard no	25		10
How to keep is there any any is there none such nowhere known some bow or brooch or braid or brace lace latch or catch or key to keep	58		1
How to keep is there any any is there none such nowhere known some bow or brooch or braid or brace lace latch or catch or key to keep	58		1
Is any of him at all so stark	72		15
When skies are hard as any stone	81		8
The spell of woe if any could	81		79
Is fond of flattery as any she	94		15
From any hedgerow any copse	98	18	1
From any hedgerow any copse	98	18	1
Can I do any harm	125		18
By any lauded statue nor again	125		30
Anywhere any more joy to be in	138		33
Suck any sense from that who can	147		3
Any instant falls means me and I do not repent	152		64
Anything			
Is it anything true does it grow upon ground	27		2
Is anything a milk to the mind so so sighs deep	149	1	2
Anywhere			
Anywhere in the sunlight	138		9
Anywhere any more joy to be in	138		33
Apart			
Apart betwixt ten thousand petalld lips	2		21
The appealing of the passion is tenderer in			

Word	Poem	Stan.	Line
prayer apart	28	26	14
Your signal when apart we stood	81		17
They are antipodes apart	83		24
The stranded keel and kelson warp apart	101		11
He has his portion God who stretchd apart	126		2
Apart wide and new-nestle at heaven most high	149	1	6
Apollo			
Apollo views the smitten python writhe and die	1	11	9
Appal			
Vacant creations lamps appal	23		12
Appareld			
Being a stoled appareld star	81		42
Appeal			
And louched low grass heaven that dost appeal	57		2
There they did appeal therefore airy vengeances	152		62
Appealing			
The appealing of the passion is tenderer in prayer apart	28	26	14
Appear			
And more on each hand thicken and appear	2		30
And scarcely does appear	105		4
As void as those the gentle downs appear	107	1	3
And pressed violets in the folds appear	119		4
I will appear looking such charity	140		3
Appeard			
Appeard not for the present till	92		8
Appearing			
Hovers off the jay-blue heavens appearing	28	26	3
Apple			
Plashes amidst the billowy apple-trees	2		87
Bloom lights the orchard-apple	42		38
Apple-trees			
Plashes amidst the billowy apple-trees	2		87
Appledurcombe			
Now it overvaults appledurcombe	41		29
Apples			
With green-white apples on the bough	124		20
Apply			
And to my palm the point apply	81	7	49
Apprehend			
With twice as fine a sense to apprehend them	102	1	12
Approve			
Which ends those only strains that I approve	19		10
Approved			
Who say that had I known I had approved thee	13		12
A hore of an approved device	81	7	35
April			
Late in the green weeks of April	81		21
Gold gallant flowers much looked at in April-weather	98	16	2
Our sex should be born in April perhaps or			

Word	Poem	Stan.	Line
April (cont.)			
the lily-time	128		13
And where cold daffodils in April are	135		29
April-weather			
Gold gallant flowers much looked at in April-weather	98	16	2
Apt			
The flower of beauty fleece of beauty too too apt to ah to fleet	59		11
Tho apt to throw it in a strange direction	94		14
Arba			
At Kirjath-arba go	5		58
Arc			
Then while the rain-born arc glows higher	78		123
These rather are the arc where beauty shines	102	3	3
Arcadia			
That not Arcadia knew nor haemony	107	1	17
Arcadian			
He was a shepherd of the Arcadian mood	107	1	16
Arch			
Breathe arch and original breath	28	25	2
To me so arch-especial a spirit as heaves in Henry Purcell	45		2
Arch-especial			
To me so arch-especial a spirit as heaves in Henry Purcell	45		2
Arched			
Deeply in the arched lustres	78		133
Arches			
Down roughcast down dazzling whitewash wherever an elm arches	72		3
Arching			
When the rainbow arching high	78		107
Arcs			
Plunge orbd in rainbow arcs and trample and tread	2		78
Argent			
With arm and fin the argent bubbles streamd	2		109
Swolln is the wind that in argent billows	79		3
Argued			
I argued Ill	127		12
Arise			
Save by two stars more crowding lights arise	2		32
Come up arise and slay	5		18
It melts new lights arise as fair	78		118
Ark			
The all of water an ark	28	32	2
Arm			
With arm and fin the argent bubbles streamd	2		109
What stroke has Caradocs right arm dealt what done	152		32

Word	Poem	Stan.	Line
Arms			
And damasqud arms and foliagd carving piled	1	10	2
O for now charms arms what bans off bad	48		34
Hard as hurdle arms with a broth of goldfish flue	71		1
It is hardly a proper treat for a birthday to rest in her arms	128		12
Arose			
Arose in gloom a solemn mockery	1	8	6
Till a lioness arose breasting the babble	28	17	7
Around			
Around the water-nymphs in fretted falls	2		50
How soldiers platting thorns around Christs head	7		4
Around up above what wind-walks what lovely behaviour	38		2
Was around them bound them or wound them with her	41		43
Questioning winds around the hills	78		44
Around it balances the level sea	98	4	2
Round a ring around a ring	138		14
Aroused			
The blame bear who aroused me what I have done violent	152		66
Array			
Returning thanks might offer such array	89		4
Arrival			
And seal of his seraph-arrival and these thy daughters	28	23	5
Art			
Of art best follow nature in a maze	1	6	5
And art and beauty title now too full	1	15	6
Where art thou friend whom I shall never see	13		1
Love it grows darker here and thou art above	20		5
And thou art silent whilst thy world	23		31
To show thee that thou art and near	23		44
Then to behold thee as thou art	23		53
Thou art lightning and love I found it a winter and warm	28	9	6
Hast thy dark descending and most art merciful then	28	9	8
Gnashed but thou art above thou Orion of light	28	21	5
It fancies feigns deems dears the artist after his art	63		6
Thou art indeed just lord if I contend	74	1	1
Take courage this shall need no further art	81	7	33
Leaps up before my vision thou art gone	98	33	2
O why art thou so wan she said	109	31	1
And art thou come from English land	109	31	3
Are shut against the canvassing of art	126		6
Make me pure Lord thou art holy	129		6
The ruins of rifled once a world of art	153		4

Word	Poem	Stan.	Line
Art (cont.)			
With thy might that thou art mild	155		16
But thou bidst and just thou art	155		21
Arthur			
Yet Arthur is a bowman his three-heeled timberll hit	143		3
Arthurs			
But droppd its coil of woes Arthurs Britain	102	2	7
Artist			
It fancies feigns deems dears the artist after his art	63		6
Arts			
What taught the humanities and the round of arts	107	2	6
As			
He raisd the convent as a monstrous grate	1	4	1
The stretching palace lay as handle fixd	1	4	4
In shoals of bloom as in unpeopled skies	2		31
And was as tho some sapphire molten-blue	2		45
To mantle-oer the tail such as is shed	2		49
Soon as when summer of his sister spring	2		84
Or driving vermeil-rain and as he lists	2		91
As poets sing or that it is a pain	2		121
As I walkd a stilly wood	4		5
Summer was as full of flame	4		25
As I markd not always died	4		28
Give us the tale of bricks as heretofore	5		49
And faint as though to die	5		60
Shall shake her fruit as libanus	6		28
That men must wonder as I pass	10		3
As public is my greater privacy	12	1	7
In bows above my head as falsified	12	2	4
Of Gods dear pleadings have as yet not moved thee	13		10
With such malign conjuctions as before	14	2	6
At hopes so evil-heavend as mine are	14	2	14
Let me be to thee as the circling bird	19		1
As silken garden-poppies do	21		7
The bats wings lisping as they flew	21		19
Yet as he changed his mighty stops	21		43
As erst upon chaotic floods	23		21
One word as when a mother speaks	23		50
Then to behold thee as thou art	23		53
Yet made its market here as well	25		32
Maid yet mother as may hath been	26		20
For thou as she wert the one fair daughter	26		25
That was unto Judah as may and brought her	26		31
Who to us are as dew unto grass and tree	26		38
I steady as a water in a well to a poise to a pane	28	4	5
Or rather rather then stealing as spring	28	10	3
Whether at once as once at a crash Paul	28	10	5

Word	Poem	Stan.	Line
Or as austin a lingering-out sweet skill	28	10	6
O father not under thy feathers nor ever as guessing	28	12	5
Is it love in her of the being as her lover had been	28	25	3
Not a dooms-day dazzle in his coming nor dark as he came	28	33	6
More brightening her rare-dear Britain as his reign rolls	28	34	6
Nothing is so beautiful as spring	33		1
Fetched fresh as I suppose off some sweet wood	34		4
All over as a bevy of eggs the mothering wing	34		6
As a skates heel sweeps smooth on a bow-bend the hurl and gliding	36		5
For skies of couple-colour as a brinded cow	37		2
Majestic as a stallion stalwart very-violet-sweet	38		10
As a dare-gale skylark scanted in a dull cage	39		1
As half she had righted and hoped to rise	41		37
As sheer down the ship goes	41		59
And brown-as-dawning-skinned	41		78
To me so arch-especial a spirit as heaves in Henry Purcell	45		2
Falls light as ten years long taught how to and why	47		8
By it heavens befall him as a heart Christs darling dauntless	48		14
Yields tender as a pushed peach	48		23
Take as for tool not toy meant	49		13
Ah as the heart grows older	54		5
As kingfishers catch fire dragonflies draw flame	56		1
As tumbled over rim in roundy wells	56		2
Yonder what high as that we follow now we follow	59		31
Great as no goddesss	60		27
As if with air the same	60		36
Her life as life does air	60		45
And fain will find as sterling all as all is smart	63		7
And fain will find as sterling all as all is smart	63		7
As I am mine their sweating selves but worse	67		14
At God knows when to God knows what whose smiles not wrung see you unforeseen times rather as skies	69		12
Hard as hurdle arms with a broth of goldfish flue	71		1
Though as a beechbole firm finds his as at a rollcall rank	71		9
Though as a beechbole firm finds his as at a			

Word	Poem	Stan.	Line
As (cont.)			
rollcall rank	71		9
Alien from yours as heaven from nadir-fires	78		4
And death falls gently as the snow	78		26
Melt as from a heavenly chrism	78		62
It melts new lights arise as fair	78		118
Fair but of fairness as a vision dreamd	80		1
White-faced as one in sad assay to fly	80		8
As though they were not from within	81	3	4
And numbs and starves as between icy wharves	81	3	6
Thus crucified as I did crucify	81	7	52
When skies are hard as any stone	81		8
Your comfort is as sharp as swords	81		32
Your comfort is as sharp as swords	81		32
You should have been with me as near	81		43
As halves of sweet-pea-blossom are	81		44
As the last pleiad yea behind	81		46
Tis falsely given as love in men	81		49
As a self-embraced sweet thought	85		3
As a self-caressd sweet thought	85		4
He playd his wings as though for flight	87		1
As wrecks of mined embers will	92		13
Her face was such as being diapered	93	2	3
Is fond of flattery as any she	94		15
Yes for a time they held as well	101		1
Together as the criss-crossd shelly cup	101		2
Sucks close the acorn as the hand and glove	101		3
As water moulded to the duct it runs in	101		4
As keel locks close to kelson	101		5
Double as sharp meaning and forcible	102	1	11
With twice as fine a sense to apprehend them	102	1	12
As ever I remember in my life	102	1	13
Lodge his eyes fast but yet as easy and light	102	1	21
As the laid gossamers of Michaelmas	102	1	22
I find I am as ready with my tears	102	1	34
As the fine morsels of a dwindling cloud	102	1	35
My cousin will not love you as I love	102	1	60
And sucks the light as full as Gideons fleece	103		11
And sucks the light as full as Gideons fleece	103		11
And as she dwindles shreds her smock of gold	103		13
As void as clouds that house and harbour none	107	1	1
As void as clouds that house and harbour none	107	1	1
As void as those the gentle downs appear	107	1	3
As void as those the gentle downs appear	107	1	3
His sheep seemd to come from it as they stept	107	1	11
Then sought such leafy shelter as it yields	107	3	16
The river wound about it as a waist	107	4	2
With parallel shafts as upward-parted ashes	107	4	5
Their highest sprays were drawn as fine as lashes	107	4	6
Their highest sprays were drawn as fine as			

Word	Poem	Stan.	Line
lashes	107	4	6
All as the moth calld underwing alighted	108		1
To colour as smooth and fresh as cheeks of roses	108		4
To colour as smooth and fresh as cheeks of roses	108		4
As wedded you must be	109	8	4
His three brothers are each as tall	109	21	3
And each as fair as he	109	21	4
And each as fair as he	109	21	4
As she lay weeping at the night	109	29	1
It is as cold as death without	109	29	3
It is as cold as death without	109	29	3
He gave her kisses cold as ice	109	39	1
Now comes as low beneath	115		4
As Devonshire letters earlier in the year	119		1
As when a soul laments which hath been blest	119		9
As struck with rings of sound the close-shut palms	122		10
As might have struck and shook the close-shut palms	122		13
As the wood-sorrel and all things sensitive	122		14
But sing contented as the dove	124		3
Quite as ladies go	125		27
But the lily is past as I say and the rose is not in its prime	128		14
As it fell upon a day	131		1
As sure as heaven it is	133		6
As sure as heaven it is	133		6
And all within the house were sound as posts	135		17
Think you want daffodils and follow as far	135		30
As where the little hurling sound	135		31
She high at the housetop sitting as they say	136		13
All over some such words as these though dark	136		29
As wishing all about us sweet	139		1
Poetry to it as a tree whose boughs break in the sky	149	1	3
They waste they wither worse they as they run	150		3
Work which to see scarce so much as begun	150		7
Her glass is blest but she as good as blind	151		7
Her glass is blest but she as good as blind	151		7
With dreadful distillation of thoughts sour as blood	152		97
Brave all and take what comes as here this rabble is come	152		102
As long as men are mortal and God merciful	152		115
As long as men are mortal and God merciful	152		115
Or they go rich as roseleaves hence that loathsome came hither	152		129
As sure as what is most sure sure as that spring primroses	152		132

Word	Poem	Stan.	Line
As (cont.)			
As sure as what is most sure sure as that spring primroses	152		132
As sure as what is most sure sure as that spring primroses	152		132
Shall new-dapple next year sure as to-morrow morning	152		133
As acknowledging thy stress	155		6
On my being and as seeing	155		7
As well the sister sits would well the wife	157		14
Hang as still as hawk or hawkmoth as the stars or as the angels there	159		26
Hang as still as hawk or hawkmoth as the stars or as the angels there	159		26
Hang as still as hawk or hawkmoth as the stars or as the angels there	159		26
Hang as still as hawk or hawkmoth as the stars or as the angels there	159		26
Ascend			
Left hand off land I hear the lark ascend	35		5
Ascendancy			
In the ascendancy of rainbows horns	84		2
Ascribed			
All glory be ascribed to	133		3
Ash			
In silk-ash kept from cooling	49		17
And the beadbonny ash that sits over the burn	55		12
Fall to the residuary worm worlds wildfire leave but ash	72		20
Which between ash-tops suffers loss	121		5
Fairyland silk-beech scrolled ash packed sycamore wild wychelm hornbeam fretty overstood	159		24
Ash-tops			
Which between ash-tops suffers loss	121		5
Ashboughs			
Say it is ashboughs whether on a December day and furled	149	1	4
Ashes			
Beauty now for ashes wear	24		19
With parallel shafts as upward-parted ashes	107	4	5
Ashiness			
And Tantalean slaty ashiness	117		5
Aside			
And to put graver sins aside	96	1	3
Ask			
Never ask if meaning it wanting it warned of it men go	28	8	8
Ask of her the mighty mother	42		13
Miss Storys character too much you ask	94		1
You ask why cant Clarissa hold her tongue	96	4	1
What I did ask then was a circle of rose-red			

Word	Poem	Stan.	Line
sealing-wax	128		15
Ask whom he serves or not	148		23
Askd			
The more she askd the more he spoke	109	36	1
But what indeed is askd of me	118		1
This was not askd but what instead	118		7
Asked			
And I have asked to be	9		5
Asking			
Times tasking it is fathers that asking for ease	28	26	11
Asks			
But bid for patience is patience who asks	68		2
Who asks not life but only place to die	80		9
Aslant			
Gazes aslant his shoulder viewing nigh	1	11	6
Asleep			
Feasts when we shall fall asleep	28	35	9
Some asleep unawakened all unwarned eleven fathoms fallen	41		3
Aspect			
Bad Saturn with a swart aspect	83		18
Aspens			
My aspens dear whose airy cages quelled	43		1
And bared is the aspens silky skirting	79		6
Assault			
Be at every assault fresh foiled worse flung deeper disappointed	152		89
Assaulting			
Or a jaunting vaunting vaulting assaulting trumpet telling	141		7
Assay			
White-faced as one in sad assay to fly	80		8
Assignd			
No love prescriptive love with place assignd	102	3	13
Assured			
Else I am well assured I should offend	14	3	5
Assyrian			
Like an Assyrian prince with buds unsheathd	2		62
Astern			
A mile astern lay the blue shores away	2		5
Astrain			
And the midriff astrain with leaning of laced with fires of stress	28	2	8
Astral			
Circlet of astral flowerets diademd	2		61
Astray			
Astray or aswarm all throughther in throngs self in self steeped and pashed quite	61		6
Somewhere we slipt astray you cannot doubt	125		15
Astrew			
Storm flakes were scroll-leaved flowers lily showers sweet heaven was astrew in them	28	21	8

Word	Poem	Stan.	Line
Astrologic			
That reads or holds the astrologic lore	14	2	2
Asunder			
To the stars lovely-asunder	28	5	2
Aswarm			
Astray or aswarm all throughther in throngs self steeped and pashed quite	61		6
At			
Your spouse not laboured-at nor spun	22		28
Tom heart-at-ease Tom navvy he is all for his meal	70		4
Atlantic			
No Atlantic squall overwrought her	41		16
Atmosphere			
Mother my atmosphere	60		115
Attain			
Might so attain their heritage	15		12
Attain the windy levels of the sky	121		4
Attempted			
Time past she has been attempted and pursued	50		5
Attentive			
Which makes us eye-attentive to the eye	125		42
Attire			
She was dressed in silk attire	131		3
Attributes			
With attributes we deem are meet	23		14
Attributing			
The proper sweet re-attributing above	113		11
That sweetness re-attributing above	113		12
Attuneable			
Earnest earthless equal attuneable vaulty voluminous stupendous	61		1
Attuning			
Milky and dark with an attuning stress	107	4	13
Aureoles			
Upwards at once and win their aureoles	126		8
Austin			
Or as Austin a lingering-out sweet skill	28	10	6
Authentic			
The authentic cadence was discovered late	19		9
Autumn			
But from the mountain glens in autumn late	1	13	1
Which I may tell at autumn-time	4		15
Autumn-time no earlier came	4		26
The autumn yellow feather in the boughs	105		5
Only the dahlias blow and all is autumn here	128		10
Autumn-time			
Which I may tell at autumn-time	4		15
Autumn-time no earlier came	4		26
Avenge			
His injury shell avenge with raging shame	82		6

Word	Poem	Stan.	Line
Avoid			
O in turns of tempest me heaped there me frantic to avoid thee and flee	64		8
Avow			
Christ minds Christs interest what to avow or amend	39		12
Away			
A mile astern lay the blue shores away	2		5
The rosy isles so that I stole away	2		140
And fail or scatter all away	18		2
Which praying fails to do away	18		12
Love it is evening now and thou away	20		4
And put away my sun	21		11
Upon Christ throw all away	24		5
Earth throws winters robes away	24		17
And lives at last were washing away	28	15	7
Away in the loveable west	28	24	1
Away from counter court or school	29	1	2
Away from counter court or school	29	1	38
The dappled die-away	48		1
Back beauty keep it beauty beauty beauty from vanishing away	58		2
Where whatevers prized and passes of us everything thats fresh and fast flying of us seems to us sweet of us and swiftly away with done away with undone	59		8
Where whatevers prized and passes of us everything thats fresh and fast flying of us seems to us sweet of us and swiftly away with done away with undone	59		8
To dearest him that lives alas away	67		8
Rare patience roots in these and these away	68		5
A hearts-clarion away griefs gasping joyless days dejection	72		17
Winks away its ring of green	86		2
Heaven comfort sends but harry it away	89		5
And gives for tropes his judgment all away	102	3	29
And gives for tropes his judgment all away	102	3	35
Here at the very furthest reach away	107	4	19
I hear a noise of waters drawn away	112		1
Flung rider and wings away though these were none	136		9
Is all all sheared away thus then I sweat for fear	152		24
It stooped and flashed and fell and ran like water away	152		52
Awful			
Have at the awful overtaking	41		113
Awhile			
You jaded let be call off thoughts awhile	69		10
Awoke			
I awoke in the midsummer not-to-call night in			

Word	Poem	Stan.	Line
Awoke (cont.)			
the white and the walk of the morning	137		1
Ay			
These daredeaths ay this crew in	41		94
Ay sweet to taste beside this woe	81	7	7
Not hope not pray despair ay that brazen de-spair out	152		101
Aye			
Than changeful pomp of courts is aye more wonderful	1	15	9
Azure			
An azure ridge or clouds of violet glowd	2		105
Paves the clouds on the swept azure	79		10
Barterd for an azure dye	86		3
With the ready azure and high carmine think	93	2	2
Shall see the azure turn expressionless	117		4
Azured			
How air is azured	60		74
Azuring			
And azuring-over greybell makes	42		41
Azuring-over			
And azuring-over greybell makes	42		41
Azurous			
And the azurous hung hills are his world-wielding shoulder	37		9
Babble			
Till a lioness arose breasting the babble	28	17	7
Why hear him hear him babble and drop down to his next	38		10
Babes			
Mothers are doubtless happier for their babes	123		1
Babyhood			
Who breathe from groundlong babyhood to hoary	76		6
Back			
What time the baffled Frank swept back pursud	1	14	8
Ebbd back beneath its snowy lids unseen	2		18
And when he turned it back again	21		38
And then lay back to sleep	21		53
Startle the poor sheep back is the shipwrack then a harvest does tempest carry the grain for thee	28	30	8
Our king back oh upon English souls	28	34	4
I muse at how its being puts blissful back	45		2
Back beauty keep it beauty beauty beauty from vanishing away	58		2
Give beauty back beauty beauty beauty back to God beautys self and beautys giver	59		19
Give beauty back beauty beauty beauty back to God beautys self and beautys giver	59		19
He leans to it harry bends look back elbow and liquid waist	71		12

Word	Poem	Stan.	Line
Forwards she leans with hollowing back stock-still	99		1
At once the senses give the music back	113		10
To keep the loaded bolt from plunging back	135		6
Stepped from the stool drew back from the barrow of dark maenefa the mountain	137		4
Amongst come-back-again things things with a revival things with a recovery	152		134
Bid joy back have at the harvest keep hope pale	154		4
Backed			
And the sea flint-flake black-backed in the regular blow	28	13	5
Backward			
Backward are laid her pretty black-fleeced ears	99		13
Backwheels			
In backwheels though bound home	47		43
Bad			
O for now charms arms what bans off bad	47		34
Nature bad base and blind	53		40
Bad saturn with a swart aspect	83		18
A bad verse in the middle then	95		5
Bad I am but yet thy child	155		13
Baffle			
More Christ and baffle death	60		67
Baffled			
What time the baffled frank swept back pursud	1	14	8
Baffling			
Wisest my heart breeds dark heavens baffling ban	66	1	11
Bala			
Bala	90		7
In the van between ffestiniog and bala	96	1	5
Balance			
To the nests nook I balance and buoy	138		43
Balanced			
High up the balanced stony air	81	4	2
Then clouds come like ill-balanced crags	81	7	1
Shake the balanced daffodils	98	7	2
Jarrd down the balanced storm the bleeding heavens	102	2	4
Balances			
Around it balances the level sea	98	4	2
Bald			
The bald and bold blinking gold when alls done	143		4
Baldbright			
A beetling baldbright cloud thorough England	41		24
Bales			
Bounden bales or a hoard of bullion	41		9
Ball			
That like this sleek and seeing ball	43		14
A blear and blinding ball	60		97

Word	Poem	Stan.	Line
Ball (cont.)			
Of nerve the clammy ball was dry	81		98
Ballad			
With a ballad with a ballad a rebound	146		3
With a ballad with a ballad a rebound	146		3
Balls			
And danced the balls of dew that stood	21		34
Balm			
But come thou balm to aching soul	78		11
Ban			
Wisest my heart breeds dark heavens baffling ban	66	1	11
Band			
We shall be sheaved with one band	8		14
Lock with my right then knot a barken band	81	7	45
Bands			
Sheaved in cruel bands bruised sore	6		5
Why should their foolish bands their hopeless hearses	89		1
And in grey bands the sun should lie still born	90		3
Though self-made bands at last may true love bind	102	3	19
They have held his eyes with blindfold bands	109	13	1
Banes			
By many blows and banes but now hears roar	49		6
May but call on your banes to more carouse	157		30
Bank			
And she beat the bank down with her bows and the ride of her keel	28	14	5
On meadow and river and wind-wandering weed-winding bank	43		8
Bankrupt			
My bankrupt heart has no more tears to spend	14	3	4
Banks			
Wood banks and brakes wash wet like lakes	42		42
Sir life upon thy cause see banks and brakes	75	1	8
On Chebars banks and why they went	78		49
Like scalded banks toppd once with principal flowers	102	2	14
Beyond the banks wete steep a brush of trees	107	4	3
In spring our river-banks are topt	124		17
Never never never in their blue banks again	152		47
And lapped in shining hair roll to the banks edge then	152		50
Down the bettling banks like water in water-falls	152		51
Bannd			
And count the rosy cross with bannd disas-trous things	89		9
Banned			
Banned by the land of their birth	28	21	2

Word	Poem	Stan.	Line
Banner			
Be under her banner and live for her honour	156		3
Under her banner I'll live for her honour	156		4
Under her banner we live for her honour	156		5
To follow a banner and fight for honour	156		9
We follow her banner we fight for her honour	156		10
But under her banner I live for her honour	156		14
Under her banner we march for her honour	156		15
If under her banner I fall for her honour	156		19
Under her banner we fall for her honour	156		20
Banquet			
We scarcely call that banquet food	6		31
Bans			
O for now charms arms what bans off bad	47		34
Bar			
On tangled shoals that bar the brook a crowd	2		96
Barbarous			
Summer ends now now barbarous in beauty the stooks rise	37		1
Bare			
The boughs the boughs are bare enough	3		1
Is bare now nor can foot feel being shod	31	1	8
To thriftless reave both our rich round world bare	57		12
Whose glory bare would blind	60		108
In wide the worlds weal rare gold bold steel bare	70		17
Delightfully the bright wind boisterous ropes wrestles beats earth bare	72		5
The hanging snows rush down and bare	81	4	4
Breathe oer my bare nerve rather I desire	81	5	5
Bare the condition of a realm at riot	82		4
There is no parting or bare interstice	98	22	4
Right rooting in the bare butts wincing navel in the sight of the sun	143		5
Till walk the world he can with bare his feet	159		35
Barebill			
With gorgons gear and barebill thongs and fangs	49		14
Bared			
And bared is the aspens silky skirting	79		6
Barely			
Barely a sigh to thought of hopes forgone	14	3	9
And barely to escape the curse	81		170
Bargain			
To the bargain of its hate to throw	145		20
Barken			
Lock with my right then knot a barken band	81	7	45
Barley			
And barley turn to weed and wild	114		5
Barn			
These are indeed the barn withindoors house	32	1	12

Word	Poem	Stan.	Line
Barrack			
A bugler boy from barrack it is over the hill	47		1
Barrd			
And with coffin-black he barrd the green	4		11
Barred			
I took of vine a cross-barred rod or rood	20		8
That nest within close-barred doors	78		54
Her barred fingers claspd upon her eyes	111		6
Barrel			
Underneath their glassy barrel of a fairy green	141		6
Barrelled			
Rope-over thigh knee-nave and barrelled shank	71		3
Barren			
With barren rigour and a frigid gloom	1	1	8
It seems for grandeur barren left and dull	1	15	8
To man that needs would worship block or barren stone	62		7
Barrens			
Amongst Castilian barrens mountain-bound	1	1	2
Barriers			
Or wring their barriers in bursts of fear or rage	38		8
Barrow			
Stepped from the stool drew back from the barrow of dark maenefa the mountain	137		4
Or ringlet-race on burling barrow brown	157		12
Barrowy			
Stand at stress each limbs barrowy brawn his thew	71		6
Bars			
Formed bars of stone beyond in stiffend state	1	4	3
Bars or hells speel thwarts this to hoard unheard	66	1	12
Through other bars it used to thrill	81		15
Oer passes bleak oer perilous bars	83		3
Barter			
Who can but barter slender sums	81		146
Barterd			
Barterd for an azure dye	86		3
Base			
Thou hast a base and brickish skirt there sours	43		5
Nature bad base and blind	53		40
Basilisk			
Morn does not now new-basilisk his stare	99		17
Basket			
I bear a basket lined with grass	10		1
And at the basket that I bear	10		4
I bear a basket lined with grass	25		1
With the basket I bear	25		4
A basket broad of woven white rods	98	19	1
Basks			
Our ruins of wrecked past purpose there she			

Word	Poem	Stan.	Line
basks	68		7
Bason			
And in a bason brings the blocks	81	7	21
Bass			
What bass is our viol for tragic tones	76		8
Bat			
Or bat with tender and air-crisping wings	19		2
Bath			
This bath of blue and slake	60		95
She brims her bath in cold or heat	139		2
Bathe			
To bathe in his fall-gold mercies to breathe in his all-fire glances	28	23	8
Bathed			
All in this case bathed in high hallowing grace	46		11
Her white weed-bathed knees are shut together	99		2
Bathes			
O breath of it bathes great heaven above	27		46
Bathing			
Bathing it is summers sovereign good	159		13
Bats			
The bats wings lisping as they flew	21		19
Battering			
Didst fettle for the great grey drayhorse his bright and battering sandal	52		14
Battle			
Of battle once upon St Lawrence day	1	2	2
Battled			
That battled gods for heaven brilliant-hued	1	7	5
Battling			
Battling with God is now my prayer	18		16
Bay			
And gaind thro growing dusk the stirless bay	2		141
What none would have known of it only the heart being hard at bay	28	7	8
Yet did the dark side of the bay of thy blessing	28	12	7
Bright sun lanced fire in the heavenly bay	41		21
To keep at bay	58		10
The furthest reach this side on that the bay	107	4	20
Bays			
Or else their cooings came from bays of trees	98	2	1
Beach			
All under channel to bury in a beach her	41		48
Beacon			
Tarpeian-fast but a blown beacon of light	28	29	8
A beacon an eternal beam flesh fade and mortal trash	72		19
Bead			
That brow and bead of being	47		39
That bead the plain did ever havering church-tower	100		6

Word	Poem	Stan.	Line
Beadbonny			
And the beadbonny ash that sits over the burn	55		12
Beakleaved			
Only the beakleaved boughs dragonish damask the toolsmooth bleak light black	61		9
Beam			
Then through the afternoon the summer beam	1	12	1
The breakers rolled on her beam with ruinous shock	28	14	6
What hinders are you beam-blind yet to a fault	45		12
A beacon an eternal beam flesh fade and mortal trash	72		19
Beam-blind			
What hinders are you beam-blind yet to a fault	45		12
Beaming			
Foamfalling is not fresh to it rainbow by it not beaming	152		55
Beams			
Rich beams till death or distance buys them quite	39		8
Their harness beams like scythes in morning grass	104		6
And are they thus the fine the fingering beams	157		9
Bean			
And the piece thats like a bean	86		4
Bear			
When he has made us bear his leaf	6		30
Bear him to heaven on easeful wings	7		15
I bear a basket lined with grass	10		1
And at the basket that I bear	10		4
I bear a basket lined with grass	25		1
With the basket I bear	25		4
Confirmed beauty will not bear a stress	117		1
They brought their hundredweights to bear	145		51
The blame bear who aroused me what I have done violent	152		66
O but I bear my burning witness though	157		35
Bearer			
Stood capital eminent gonfalon bearer	98	28	5
Bearing			
Below me in the bearing air	15		30
Beautys bearing or muse of mounting vein	46		10
Stone palsy cancer cough lung-wasting womb-not-bearing	152		113
Mortal my mate bearing my rock-a-heart	153		1
Bears			
Within her wears bears cares and combs the same	77		6
Beast			
Christs lily and beast of the waste wood	28	20	6
A wilder beast from west than all were more	49		7
Beat			

Word	Poem	Stan.	Line
Hung like a wreck that flames not billows beat	1	3	4
The driving storm at hour of vespers beat	1	13	3
And beat upon my whorled ear	22		2
And she beat the bank down with her bows and the ride of her keel	28	14	5
Burden in winds burly and beat of endragoned seas	28	26	16
Wind-beat whitebeam airy abeles set on a flare	32	1	6
Downs forefalls beat to the burial	41		7
That beat and breathe in power	48		11
Beat heave and the strong mountain tire	81	5	2
Ruinous heart-beat wandering death	81		53
O heart have done you beat you beat so high	135		35
O heart have done you beat you beat so high	135		35
What beauty beat behind	148		12
Warm beat with cold beat company shall I	153		2
Warm beat with cold beat company shall I	153		2
Beating			
Blue-beating and hoary-glow height or night still higher	28	26	5
About mans beating heart	60		50
Beats			
Delightfully the bright wind boisterous ropes wrestles beats earth bare	72		5
But vastness blurs and time beats level enough the resurrection	72		16
Beauties			
To thee we tender the beauties all	26		21
Beautiful			
Nothing is so beautiful as spring	32		1
Marbled river boisterously beautiful between	159		6
Beauty			
And scarcely traces where one beauty strays	1	6	7
And art and beauty title now too full	1	15	6
None besides me this bye-ways beauty try	12	2	9
Beauty now for ashes wear	24		19
Brute beauty and valour and act oh air pride plume here	35		8
He fathers-forth whose beauty is past change	36		10
Summer ends now now barbarous in beauty the stooks rise	37		1
Men go by me whom either beauty bright	39		5
Is strung by duty is strained to beauty	41		77
After-comers cannot guess the beauty been	42		19
That neighbour-nature thy grey beauty is grounded	43		6
This all this beauty blooming	48		5
Back beauty keep it beauty beauty beauty from vanishing away	58		2
Back beauty keep it beauty beauty beauty from vanishing away	58		2

Word	Poem	Stan.	Line
Beauty (cont.)			
Back beauty keep it beauty beauty beauty from vanishing away	58		2
Back beauty keep it beauty beauty beauty from vanishing away	58		2
The flower of beauty fleece of beauty too too apt to ah to fleet	59		11
The flower of beauty fleece of beauty too too apt to ah to fleet	59		11
Them beauty-in-the-ghost deliver it early now long before death	59		18
Give beauty back beauty beauty beauty back to God beautys self and beautys giver	59		19
Give beauty back beauty beauty beauty back to God beautys self and beautys giver	59		19
Give beauty back beauty beauty beauty back to God beautys self and beautys giver	59		19
Give beauty back beauty beauty beauty back to God beautys self and beautys giver	59		19
To what serves mortal beauty dangerous does set dancing blood the o-seal-that-so feature flung prouder form	62		1
What do then how meet beauty merely meet it own	62		10
Yea wish that though wish all Gods better beauty grace	62		12
Beauty it may be is the meet of lines	102	3	1
These rather are the arc where beauty shines	102	3	3
Say beauty lies but in the meet of lines	102	3	21
Confirmed beauty will not bear a stress	117		1
Why theres an interest and sweet soul in beauty	125		41
For a beauty-bow to his hat	144		16
The Christ-ed beauty of her mind	145		15
What beauty beat behind	148		12
In all her beauty and sunlight to it is a pit den darkness	152		54
Mays beauty massacre and wisped wild clouds grow	154		2
Immortal beauty is death with duty	156		18
Beauty-bow			
For a beauty-bow to his hat	144		16
Beauty-in-the-ghost			
Them beauty-in-the-ghost deliver it early now long before death	59		18
Beautys			
Beautys bearing or muse of mounting vein	46		10
With not her either beautys equal or	49		2
Give beauty back beauty beauty beauty back to God beautys self and beautys giver	59		19
Give beauty back beauty beauty beauty back to God beautys self and beautys giver	59		19

Word	Poem	Stan.	Line
And Beautys dearest veriest vein is tears	157		4
Beckoned			
Beckoned me beside him	53		13
By there comes a listless stranger beckoned by the noise	159		14
Become			
And to those stones become akin	81	3	2
Bed			
Low lie his mates now on watery bed	40		57
Groom and grace you bride your bed	51		2
Sure s bed now low be it lustily he his low lot feel	70		5
No running in the river-bed	81		161
Comes to the bed	102	1	17
So waste in tears over this bed of sweetness	102	1	38
Crept trembling out of bed	135		4
The cart road with a shallowy bed	135		26
And bridegroom waits and ready are bower and bed	136		18
Bedded			
And they were bedded till daylight	109	1	3
Beds			
Fair beds they seemd of water-lily flakes	2		13
In beds in gardens in thick plots I stand	5		37
Bee			
Thats built for by the bee	148		36
Beech			
Fairyland silk-beech scrolled ash packed sycamore wild wychelm hornbeam fretty overstood	159		24
Beechbole			
Though as a beechbole firm finds his as at a rollcall rank	71		9
Bees			
Stars like golden bees	98	25	3
Beetle			
A bush-browed beetle-browed billow is it	141		3
Beetle-browed			
A bush-browed beetle-browed billow is it	141		3
Beetling			
A beetling baldbright cloud thorough England	41		24
Down the beetling banks like water in water-falls	152		51
Befal			
What would befal the godless flock	92		7
Befall			
By it heavens befall him as a heart Christs darling dauntless	47		14
Before			
Before the sepulchre there stood a gate	1	4	6
More wondrous to have borne such hope before	1	15	7
Sudden death before me stood	4		6

Word	Poem	Stan.	Line
Before (cont.)			
With such malign conjuctions as before	14	2	6
But now before the pot can glow	15		13
Before me the hurtle of hell	28	3	2
Though felt before though in high flood yet	28	7	7
Before-time-taken dearest prized and priced	28	22	6
In Eden Garden have get before it cloy	33		11
Before it cloud Christ Lord and sour with sinning	33		12
Them beauty-in-the-ghost deliver it early now long before death	59		18
She stood before a light not hers and seemd	80		3
They all come here and stand before me clear	81	7	10
Before that rock my seat he stands	81	7	15
To wash before the multitude	81	7	23
Before the mountain no not one	81		143
And saw the men before the flood	93	1	2
Leaps up before my vision thou art gone	98	33	2
Yet there came one who sent his flock before him	107	1	7
Before he went to sea	109	1	4
She stood before them in the glen	109	25	1
I thought before I gather strength	118		13
For a letter comes at last shall I say before Christmas is come	128		19
Before or behind or far or at hand	138		7
Before the Spring was done	144		4
A growing burnish brighter than before	151		4
Before-time-taken			
Before-time-taken dearest prized and priced	28	22	6
Began			
For he began at once and shook	21		29
Being anointed and all though a heavenlier heart began some	52		6
Heard unheeded leaves me a lonely began	66	1	13
That night the judgment day began	81		90
Begged			
My late being there begged of me overflowing	47		6
Begin			
White to begin with immaculate white	27		33
Let charity thus begin at home	81		124
Now begin on Christmas day	129		9
Beginning			
A strain of the earths sweet being in the beginning	32		10
Be beginning since no nothing can be done	58		9
So be beginning be beginning to despair	58		13
So be beginning be beginning to despair	58		13
Be beginning to despair to despair	58		15
Now beginning and alway	129		8

Word	Poem	Stan.	Line
Begun			
And let him prove my passion was begun	14	2	4
So from the dawn was ill begun	21		9
And now the marriage feast begun	22		26
But grant my penitence begun	81		137
In copying well what you have best begun	125		21
Work which to see scarce so much as begun	150		7
Behaviour			
Around up above what wind-walks what lovely behaviour	38		2
Behind			
Slim-pointed sea-gull plumes and droop behind	2		80
The steep-up roof at last behind the small	12	2	6
Behind where where was a where was a place	28	3	3
Hurling the haven behind	28	13	2
Grasp God throned behind	28	31	7
As the last pleiad yea behind	81		46
Or if he leave the west behind	83		5
Be hid behind	127		20
Before or behind or far or at hand	138		7
What beauty beat behind	148		12
His sweetest nectar hides behind	148		42
Her glass drinks light she darkles down behind	151		9
Behold			
Behold at Elim wells on every hand	5		23
Behold we have the joy in harvest	6		2
Then to behold thee as thou art	23		53
Beholder			
These things these things were here and but the beholder	37		11
Being			
Your scarce-sheathed bones are weary of being bent	11		13
What none would have known of it only the heart being hard at bay	28	7	8
Gush flush the man the being with it sour or sweet	28	8	5
Do you mother of being in me heart	28	18	4
Is it love in her of the being as her lover had been	28	25	3
Ground of being and granite of it past all	28	31	6
Is bare now nor can foot feel being shod	31	1	8
A strain of the earths sweet being in the beginning	32		10
Being mighty a master being a father and fond	34		14
Being mighty a master being a father and fond	34		14
Being pure we lifes pride and cared-for crown	35		11
Is it only its being brighter	42		9
To touch her being so slender	43		13
I muse at how its being puts blissful back	45		2
My late being there begged of me overflowing	47		6

Word	Poem	Stan.	Line
Being (cont.)			
That brow and bead of being	47		39
Her flower her piece of being doomed dragon food	49		4
Being anointed and all though a heavenlier heart began some	53		6
Deals out that being indoors each one dwells	57		6
To its own best being and its loveliness of youth it is an everlastingness of o it is an all youth	59		13
Fire-featuring heaven for earth her being has unbound her dapple is at an end	61		5
Our redcoats our tars both these being the greater part	63		2
Me were I pleading plead nor do I I weary of idle a being but by where wars are rife	66	2	7
Being a stoled appareld star	81		42
Her face was such as being diapered	93	2	3
Boughs being pruned birds preened show more fair	96	7	1
Being not forgotten for primroses note	107	3	19
What being in rank-old nature should earlier have that breath been	141		1
Being to her virtue clinching-blind	145		18
But being lifted immortal of immortal brightness	152		58
I all my being have hacked in half with her neck one part	152		93
On my being and as seeing	155		7
Beings			
On beings dread and vacant maze	23		30
Though down his beings bent	148		17
Bela			
Is not some little Bela set	81		142
Belated			
Whose all-belated leaves yield up themselves	111		2
Belie			
And coldly do belie the thought of thee	117		12
Believe			
To make believe my mood was mock o I might think so	152		41
Hark hearer hear what I do lend a thought now make believe	159		1
Believes			
But having that believes it greater still	94		10
Believes herself religious and is not	94		29
Bell			
Withouten instrument or conch or bell	2		128
And listen to the passing bell	23		40
Maiden could obey so be a bell to ring of it and	28	30	7
Cuckoo-echoing bell-swarmed lark-charmed			

Word	Poem	Stan.	Line
rook-racked river-rounded	43		2
A bell at midnight woke the town	81		87
Bell-swarmed			
Cuckoo-echoing bell-swarmed lark-charmed rook-racked river-rounded	43		2
Bellbright			
With dare and with downdolphinry and bellbright bodies huddling out	159		17
Belled			
With belled fire and the moth-soft milky way	28	26	6
Only the belled foxgloves lispd together	107	1	6
Belleisle			
News from belleisle even such a sweetness blows	119		6
Bellerophon			
And Paul is Tarsus true Bellerophon	136		10
Bellisle			
Bellisle that is a fabling name but we	116		1
Bellows			
At length the bellows shall not blow	15		15
Bells			
Though no high-hung bells or din	28	35	1
Stones ring like each tucked string tells each hung bells	56		3
To hear the sheep-bells dimly die	78		71
Allows the sound of bells in hamlets round	81	4	6
From Oxford comes the throng and hum of bells	98	3	6
And to their feet the narrow bells gave rhyme	107	1	14
Gave the much music of our Oxford bells	107	2	8
Belong			
For lips and hearts they belong to thee	26		37
Below			
Is set upon your boughs below	10		10
Below me in the bearing air	15		30
The wild woman-kind below	28	16	2
The dapple-eared lily below thee that country and town did	43		3
Of mile-long reaches of our road below us	125		7
Heaven turned its starlight eyes below	145		46
Belts			
In breezy belts of upper air	78		73
Belvedere			
I walk my breezy belvedere	15		25
Bend			
As a skates heel sweeps smooth on a bow-bend the hurl and gliding	36		5
Of us we do bid God bend to him even so	68		11
Bends			
He leans to it Harry bends look back elbow and liquid waist	71		12

Word	Poem	Stan.	Line
Beneath			
Wherein beneath the cornice horsemen rode	1	7	7
Ebbd back beneath its snowy lids unseen	2		18
And silver films beneath with pearly mist	2		67
You would not house beneath my own	81		4
Now comes as low beneath	115		4
Benediction			
Then came the benediction	81		99
Benefits			
But since I have no scope for benefits	102	1	55
Bent			
Your scarce-sheathed bones are weary of being bent	11		13
Because the Holy Ghost over the bent	31	2	13
Her will was bent at God for that	145		37
Though down his beings bent	148		17
Bereft			
Of mazy shape and hue but now bereft	1	8	3
What would the world be once bereft	55		13
Berg			
So like a berg of hyaline	3		17
Beryl			
Clustering entrancingly in beryl lakes	2		14
In beryl-covered fens so dim	3		26
Beryl-covered			
In beryl-covered fens so dim	3		26
Beside			
Beckoned me beside him	53		13
And in the dews beside his nest	78		91
Houses that make abode beside the lake	81	6	6
Ay sweet to taste beside this woe	81	7	7
The ringed blindworm hard beside	106		4
That was beside the sea	109	15	2
Besides his brothers three	109	20	2
Beside his brothers three	109	21	2
Beside his brothers three	109	22	4
Beside them about the hedges hearing him	113		8
Ah no and she who sits beside	120		14
Besides			
None besides me this bye-ways beauty try	12	2	9
Bespoken			
But he scores it in scarlet himself on his own bespoken	28	22	5
Best			
Of art best follow nature in a maze	1	6	5
Thou who canst best accept the certainty	13		5
No better serves me now save best no other	16		13
We lash with the best or worst	28	8	2
Best	28	24	9
Mans sprit will be flesh-bound when found at best	38		12
Of the best we boast our sailors are	40		75

Word	Poem	Stan.	Line
Best in graceless growth thou hast confounded	43		7
You father what you buy me I like best	46		2
Shares their best gifts surely fall how things will	47		4
To its own best being and its loveliness of youth it is an everlastingness of o it is an all youth	59		13
He of all can reeve a rope best there he bides in bliss	63		10
I never saw those fields whereon their best	119		11
Ill meant yet true I best should flatter then	125		20
In copying well what you have best begun	125		21
The best ideal is the true	133		1
Worst will the best what worm was here we cry	157		31
That he hies to a pool neighbouring sees it is the best	159		22
Bestowing			
Boon in my bestowing	47		7
Bethlehem			
But the Bethlehem star may lead me	129		3
Bethlem			
Bethlem or Nazareth	60		65
Bethlems			
New Bethlems and he born	60		63
Betimes			
The lock of clouds betimes and hangs the day	98	31	3
Betray			
And what if she my confidence betray	94		4
Betrayd			
A threads of light betrayd the hill	92		9
Better			
No better serves me now save best no other	16		13
Yea wish that though wish all Gods better beauty grace	62		12
And yet I know it would be better so	81	7	6
Diamonds are better cut who pare repair	96	7	5
But late is better than never you see you have managed so	128		17
Reason selfdisposal choice of better or worse way	152		94
Betterd			
I betterd all our path with sanguine eyes	125		17
Between			
His charnelhouse-grate ribs between	4		10
Between the tower-top and the ground	15		29
Towery city and branchy between towers	44		1
And numbs and starves as between icy wharves	81	3	6
In the van between ffestiniog and bala	96	1	5
Tingling between dusk and silver	98	1	4
No truth between you three	109	28	2

Word	Poem	Stan.	Line
Between (cont.)			
Which between ash-tops suffers loss	121		5
Moonless darkness stands between	129		1
Marbled river boisterously beautiful between	159		6
Betweenpie			
Betweenpie mountains lights a lovely mile	69		13
Betweens			
Betweens I heard the water still	21		44
Betweenwhiles			
Betweenwhiles but she sees herself not him	151		12
Betwixt			
The cloisters crossd with equal courts betwixt	1	4	2
Apart betwixt ten thousand petalld lips	2		21
Girdles goes home betwixt	60		4
Beuno			
Lord Beuno comes tonight	152		7
Bevy			
All over as a bevy of eggs the mothering wing	33		6
Sees the bevy of them how the boys	159		16
Beyond			
Formed bars of stone beyond in stiffend state	1	4	3
Beyond the hurst with such a hue	21		6
Oh till thou givest that sense beyond	23		43
Beyond saying sweet past telling of tongue	28	9	5
That bird beyond the remembering his free fells	38		3
Undenizened beyond bound	70		15
But with his other foot three miles beyond	100		4
Beyond and one within the lookers eye	102	3	6
A rainbow also shapes itself beyond	107	3	6
Beyond the banks wete steep a brush of trees	107	4	3
Beyond the river all the meadows round	107	4	10
Beyond the world the streams are full	130		24
Beyond Magdalen and by the bridge on a place called there the plain	142		1
But from beyond seas Erin France and Flanders everywhere	152		125
His looks the souls own letters see beyond	157		15
What need I strain my heart beyond my ken	157		34
Bid			
And bid to catch him ere the drop of day	20		2
Buy then bid then what prayer patience alms vows	31	1	9
But bid for patience is patience who asks	68		2
Of us we do bid God bend to him even so	68		11
To rise you bid me with the lark	96	6	1
Bid your para goodnight sweet exhibition	97		8
Bid joy back have at the harvest keep hope pale	154		4
Bides			
He of all can reeve a rope best there he bides in bliss	63		10

Word	Poem	Stan.	Line
Bird (cont.)			
Cuckoo bird and open ear wells heart-springs delightfully sweet	146		2
Birds			
Them birds build but not I build no but strain	75	1	11
Boughs being pruned birds preened show more fair	96	7	1
Birth			
Night to a myriad worlds gives birth	23		9
Till a maid in Davids house had birth	26		30
Since its birth and its bloom and its breathing its last	27		17
Banned by the land of their birth	28	21	2
But here was heart-throe birth of a brain	28	29	7
Tells Mary her mirth till Christs birth	41		46
Birth milk and all the rest	60		21
My spirit hath a birth	78		3
Birthday			
I thought that you would have written my birthday came and went	128		1
What would be a birthday letter that after the birthday came	128		4
What would be a birthday letter that after the birthday came	128		4
Think this my birthday falls in saddening time of year	128		9
It is hardly a proper treat for a birthday to rest in her arms	128		12
Biscay			
Or rearing billow of the biscay water	40		17
Bit			
Smiled blushed and bit his lip	53		19
Bite			
I bite my hands my looks I shroud	81		65
Bitten			
I know of the bored and bitten rocks	120		20
Bitter			
Sweet flowers I carry sweets for bitter	10		6
Therefore how bitter and learnt how late the truth	17		14
Carries treats of sweet for bitter	25		6
Bitter would have me taste my taste was me	67		10
Bitterer			
Heart go and bleed at a bitterer vein for the	28	30	3
Bitterness			
The bitterness of death was past	81		120
Into the bitterness of sin	92		6
Black			
But through black branches rarely drest	3		20
And with coffin-black he barrd the green	4		11
With a subtle web of black	4		20
And the sea flint-flake black-backed in the			

Word	Poem	Stan.	Line
regular blow	28	13	5
She to the black-about air to the breaker the thickly	28	24	5
And though the last lights off the black west went	30	1	11
But what black Boreas wrecked her he	40		23
With yellowy moisture mild nights blear-all black	45		3
Only the beakleaved boughs dragonish damask the toolsmooth bleak light black	61		9
Ever so black on it our tale o our oracle let life waned ah let life wind	61		10
Now her all in two flocks two folds black white right wrong reckon but reck but mind	61		12
What hours o what black hours we have spent	67		2
Sheer off disseveral a star death blots black out nor mark	72		14
When the fierce skies are blue to black albeit	81	2	5
Her nostril glistens and her wet black eye	99		5
Her finger-long new horns are cappd with black	99		7
Backward are laid her pretty black-fleeced ears	99		13
Abandoned by her saints turnd black and blasted	102	2	13
Gilds with some sparky fancies his black night	102	3	30
Black-about			
She to the black-about air to the breaker the thickly	28	24	5
Black-backed			
And the sea flint-flake black-backed in the regular blow	28	13	5
Black-fleeced			
Backward are laid her pretty black-fleeced ears	99		13
Blackest			
Deep calls to deep and blackest night	23		27
Blackness			
With blackness bound and all	60		98
Blacks			
And a few leaves not lily-white but charactered over with blacks	128		16
Blade			
The blood-gush blade-gash	138		22
Still the scarlet swings and dances on the blade	152		44
Blade-Gash			
The blook-gush blade-gash	138		22
Blades			
Blades of Milan in circles rangd grew rust	1	12	8
Does lay men low with one blades sudden blow	81	2	3
And leaves the blades whereer he will veer	98	1	3
Blady			
Ill take in hand the blady stone	81	7	48

Word	Poem	Stan.	Line
Blame			
The blame bear who aroused me what I have done violent	152		66
Blast			
The Simon Peter of a soul to the blast	28	28	7
Blast bole and bloom together	40		15
And reel no blast the fretful fire	81	5	4
And like a self-outwitted blast	81		74
Into his hollowd palm should moan the blast	90		2
Blasted			
Abandoned by her saints turnd black and blasted	102	2	13
Blasts			
Doors slammd to the blasts continually more low	1	13	8
But if the rain-blasts be unbound	3		7
Blaze			
Blaze for him all this while	5		36
The shearing rays contract me with their blaze	81	2	6
Blazon			
In blazon gilt and images of bronze	102	2	10
In gilt and blazon and bronze statuary	102	2	11
In gilt and blazon and maild shapes of bronze	102	2	12
Or bring more or more blazon mans distress	150		4
Blazoned			
With blazoned groins and crowned with hues of majesty	1	6	9
And blazoned in however bold the name	76		10
Blazonry			
With golden fillets and rich blazonry	1	7	6
Bleached			
His bleached both and woolwoven wear	159		29
Bleak			
Shine and blue-bleak embers ah my dear	36		12
How it does my heart good visiting at that bleak hill	47		21
Only the beakleaved boughs dragonish damask the toolsmooth bleak light black	61		9
Oer passes bleak oer perilous bars	83		3
Blear			
The sour scythe cringe and the blear share come	28	11	8
With yellowy moisture mild nights blear-all black	45		3
A blear and blinding ball	60		97
Blear-all			
With yellowy moisture mild nights blear-all black	45		3
Bleared			
And all is seared with trade bleared smeared with toil	31	1	6
Bleat			
My cry is like a bleat a few	81		66

Word	Poem	Stan.	Line
There was no bleat of ewe no chime of wether	107	1	5
Bleats			
Epistles while the running pastoral bleats	107	4	22
Bleed			
Heart go and bleed at a bitterer vein for the	28	30	3
Intolerable tears I bleed	81		67
Bleeding			
And bleeding saw thus hung from room to room	1	10	8
Lay bleeding to Madrid the last they bore	1	15	2
Jarrd down the balanced storm the bleeding heavens	102	2	4
Bleeds			
And zeal is flushed and pity bleeds	23		34
Blended			
Of the air-blended diadem	78		115
Bless			
For I greet him the days I meet him and bless when I understand	28	5	8
Yes why do we all seeing of a soldier bless him bless	63		1
Yes why do we all seeing of a soldier bless him bless	63		1
Of virtues I most warmly bless	96	1	1
What I know of thee I bless	155		5
Blessed			
How to name it blessed it	25		25
For souls that might have blessed the time	133		9
Blessed be everything	135		16
Blessing			
Yet did the dark side of the bay of thy bless-ing	28	12	7
Blest			
That was blest in it once though now it is not	27		9
As when a soul laments which hath been blest	119		9
Her glass is blest but she as good as blind	151		7
Not that but thus far all with frailty blest	157		6
Blight			
It is the blight man was born for	54		14
Blind			
Swirling out bloom till all the air is blind	2		89
More powerless than the blind or lame	15		20
What hinders are you beam-blind yet to a fault	45		12
Nature bad base and blind	53		40
Whose glory bare would blind	60		108
By groping round my comfortless than blind	69		6
Being to her virtue clinching-blind	145		18
Her glass is blest but she as good as blind	151		7
While blind mens eyes shall thirst after day-light draughts of daylight	152		109
Blindfold			
They have held his eyes with blindfold bands	109	13	1

Word	Poem	Stan.	Line
Blinding			
Giddies the soul with blinding daze	23		28
A blear and blinding ball	60		97
Gilds with some sparky fancies blinding night	102	3	36
Blindness			
Blindness a learned fool and well-bred churl	102	3	32
Blinds			
Blinds her but she that weather sees one thing one	28	19	5
Blindworm			
The ringed blindworm hard beside	106		4
Blinking			
The bald and bold blinking gold when alls done	143		4
Bliss			
That thou hadst borne proportion in my bliss	13		6
Not out of his bliss	28	6	1
Springs universal bliss	41		34
He of all can reeve a rope best there he bides in bliss	63		10
My winter world that scarcely breathes that bliss	77		13
But chaptered in the chief of bliss	145		2
Blissful			
I muse at how its being puts blissful back	45		2
Block			
To man that needs would worship block or barren stone	62		7
The outgoings of the vale does block	92		11
Helpd by the darkness of a block of copse	107	3	14
Blocks			
And in a bason brings the blocks	81	7	21
Towards wastes where round the ice-blocks tilt and fret	88		7
Towards those wastes where the ice-blocks tilt and fret	88		11
And come where lies a coffer burly all of blocks	159		36
Blood			
An intense line of throbbing blood-light shook	2		16
Thro silver gloomd to a blood-vivid clot	2		107
But even our saviours and our blood	6		32
Ah dip in blood the palmtree pen	25		37
When drop-of-blood-and-foam-dapple	41		37
The deathdance in his blood	60		52
To what serves mortal beauty dangerous does set dancing blood the o-seal-that-so feature flung prouder form	62		1
Bones built in me flesh filled blood brimmed the curse	67		11
From hands now clammy with strange blood	81	7	25
Now stars of blood	98	26	2
So late there is no force in sap or blood	105		11

Word	Poem	Stan.	Line
The blood-gush blade-gash	138		22
With dreadful distillation of thoughts sour as blood	152		97
Blood-gush			
The blood-gush blade-gash	138		22
Blood-light			
An intense line of throbbing blood-light shook	2		16
Blood-vivid			
Thro silver gloomd to a blood-vivid clot	2		107
Bloods			
Whose bloods I reck no more of no more rank with hers	152		103
Bloody			
Or tender pinks with bloody Tyrian dye	2		47
And every saint of bloody hour	145		44
In bloody letters lessons of earnest of revenge	152		35
Bloom			
And held a cross of flowers in purple bloom	1	10	6
In shoals of bloom as in unpeopled skies	2		31
Swirling out bloom till all the air is blind	2		89
And thickend like that drifted bloom the flock	2		99
And broke into bloom upon Nazareth hill	27		11
Since its birth and its bloom and its breathing its last	27		17
Look March-bloom like on mealed-with-yellow sallows	31	1	11
Blast bole and bloom together	40		15
Bloom lights the orchard-apple	41		38
Breathing bloom of a chastity in mansex fine	47		16
Bloom breathe that one breath more	60		92
How when this bloom this honeysuckle that rides the air so rich about thee	152		23
By her bloom fast by her fresh her fleeced bloom	152		83
By her bloom fast by her fresh her fleeced bloom	152		83
Bloomfall			
Us fresh youth fretted in a bloomfall all portending	47		30
Blooming			
This all this beauty blooming	48		5
Blooms			
With garnet wreaths and blooms of rosy-budded fire	2		26
The floating blooms and with tide flowing quenchd	2		139
The glassy peartree leaves and blooms they brush	32		6
His brightest blooms lie there unblown	148		41
Blossom			
With rosy foam and pelting blossom and mists	2		90
But the blossom the blossom there who can it be	27		27

Word	Poem	Stan.	Line
Blossom (cont.)			
But the blossom the blossom there who can it be	27		27
What was the colour of that blossom bright	27		32
And bird and blossom swell	41		23
As halves of sweet-pea-blossom are	81		44
Of standing to the blossom-hitting shower	107	3	4
Blossom-hitting			
Of standing to the blossom-hitting shower	107	3	4
Blot			
Blot the perpetual festival of day	89		2
Their heads together in a stormy blot	90		6
Blotless			
The unquestiond readings of a blotless book	16		6
Blots			
Sheer off disseveral a star death blots black out nor mark	72		14
And breathes the blots off all with sighs on sighs	151		6
Blow			
A stealthy wind crept round seeking to blow	2		137
And a few lilies blow	9		4
None in Caesars gardens blow	10		8
At length the bellows shall not blow	15		15
Afflicts no less what yet I hope may blow	17		6
None in Caesars garden blow	25		8
When was the summer that saw the bud blow	27		15
And the sea flint-blake black-backed in the regular blow	28	13	5
He was pitched to his death at a blow	28	16	4
And the blow bore from land	40		19
Does lay men low with one blades sudden blow	81	2	3
Only the dahlias blow and all is autumn here	128		10
Perhaps we struck no blow Gwenvrewi lives perhaps	152		40
Blowing			
Of the cold wind blowing	132		3
Blown			
To an orbd rose which by hot pantings blown	2		20
Tarpeian-fast but a blown beacon of light	28	29	8
Life this wildworth blown so sweet	40		93
Nor night is blown with flame-rings everywhere	99		18
Blowpipe			
Spur live and lancing like the blowpipe flame	77		2
Blows			
By many blows and banes but now hears roar	49		6
News from Belleisle even such a sweetness blows	119		6
Blue			
A mile astern lay the blue shores away	2		5
And was as tho some sapphire molten-blue	2		45
And pencilled blue so daintily	3		18
Into the flat blue mist the sun	3		31

Word	Poem	Stan.	Line
Hovers off the jay-blue heavens appearing	28	26	3
Blue-beating and hoary-glow height or night still higher	28	26	5
The descending blue that blue is all in a rush	32		7
The descending blue that blue is all in a rush	32		7
Shine and blue-bleak embers ah my dear	35		12
And you were a liar o blue March day	40		20
Cluster of bugle blue eggs thin	41		21
The glass-blue days are those	60		83
Blue be it this blue heaven	60		86
Blue be it this blue heaven	60		86
This bath of blue and slake	60		95
Of a mastering heaven utterly blue	79		2
When the fierce skies are blue to black albeit	81	2	5
At last up the blue element	87		6
One star by daylight from the strong blue air	102	3	10
The blue with brighter places not remote	107	3	20
Dry up the blue and be not slaked thereby	117		7
And my blue eyes again for me	120		23
The sky is blue and the winds pull	130		22
With white strokes and strains of the blue	138		17
The blue wheat-acre is underneath	138		18
No more than red and blue	148		33
Mells blue and snowwhite through them a fringe and fray	149	1	9
Mells blue and snowwhite through their fringe and fray	149	2	5
Never never never in their blue banks again	152		47
O now while skies are blue now while seas are salt	152		106
Blue-beating			
Blue-beating and hoary-glow height or night still higher	28	26	5
Blue-bleak			
Shine and blue-bleak embers ah my dear	35		12
Bluebell			
Once jostling thick the bluebell sheaves	81		13
Bluebells			
In lakes of bluebells pieced with primroses	98	9	3
Were eyes of central primrose bluebells ran	98	10	2
And each drew bluebells up and for relief	107	3	17
The bluebells up whose crystal-ending rods in their natural sods	112		8
Of bluebells sheaved in May	144		10
A juice rides rich through bluebells in vine leaves	157		3
Bluer			
And bluer grey the flocks of trees look in the plain	105		8
Bluff			
Them broad in bluff hide his frowning feet lashed raced	71		17

Word	Poem	Stan.	Line
Blurrd			
Of dewy gorse blurrd with the gossamer fine	2		40
Blurs			
But vastness blurs and time beats level enough the Resurrection	72		16
Blushed			
Smiled blushed and bit his lip	53		19
Blustering			
With a south-westerly wind blustering with a tide rolls reels	141		4
Board			
Three hundred souls o alas on board	40		2
Boards			
And he boards her in oh such joy	40		70
Boast			
And all like me may boast impeached not	12	1	13
Carrier-witted I am bold to boast	28	3	7
Of the best we boast our sailors are	40		75
Boasting			
And boasting I have fairer things than these	2		86
Boatman			
But the boatman on the green	131		5
Boded			
Ravens for prosperously-boded curses	89		3
Bodes			
Death with a sovereignty that heeds but hides bodes but abides	28	31	8
Bodies			
Out of hallowed bodies bred	51		4
With dare and with downdolphinry and bell-bright bodies huddling out	159		17
Body			
Which lightening oer the body rosy-pale	2		72
Breathe body of lovely death	28	25	4
His body swayd upon tiptoes	87		3
Save in the body of the rains	130		20
The body of Margaret Clitheroe	145		21
In all her body I say no place was like her eyes	152		56
Boisterous			
How far from then forethought of all thy more boisterious years	52		12
Delightfully the bright wind boisterious ropes wrestles beats earth bare	72		5
Boisterously			
Marbled river boisterously beautiful between	159		6
Bold			
Carrier-witted I am bold to boast	28	3	7
The heart rears wings bold and bolder	37		13
Now the other was brass-bold	53		25
In wide the worlds weal rare gold bold steel bare	70		17

Word	Poem	Stan.	Line
And blazoned in however bold the name	76		10
With what bold grace	102	1	64
But I was ignorantly bold	118		5
The bald and bold blinking gold when alls done	143		4
Boldboys			
Men boldboys soon to be men	40		13
Bolder			
The heart rears wings bold and bolder	37		13
Both thought and thew now bolder	48		8
Bole			
Blast bole and bloom together	40		15
Bolt			
To keep the loaded bolt from plunging back	135		6
Bolts			
I put the door to with the bolts unpinned	135		11
Bone			
Ah touched in your bower of bone	28	18	1
Mans mounting spirit in his bone-house mean house dwells	38		2
And press it down on either side a bone	81	7	50
Penance shall clothe me to the bone	81		135
Bone-house			
Mans mounting spirit in his bone-house mean house dwells	39		2
Boned			
Who have watched his mould of man big-boned and hardy-handsome	52		2
Bones			
For where the martyrs bones were thickest trod	1	5	8
Your scarce-sheathed bones are weary of being bent	11		13
Or ancient mounds that cover bones	15		37
Thou hast bound bones and veins in me fastened me flesh	28	1	5
For a rainbow footing it nor he for his bones risen	38		14
Bones this sinew and will not waken	40		83
With darksome devouring eyes my bruised bones and fan	64		7
Bones built in me flesh filled blood brimmed the curse	67		11
But man we scaffold of score brittle bones	76		5
Their cheeks moved and the bones therein	92		3
Deaths bones fell in with sudden clank	92		12
Bonfire			
Footfretted in it million-fueled natures bonfire burns on	72		9
Boniface			
It hurls hurls off boniface down	40		31
Bonnet			
A windpuff-bonnet of fawn-froth	55		5

Word	Poem	Stan.	Line
Bonniest			
But quench her bonniest dearest to her her clearest-selved spark	72		10
Book			
In the most murderous passage of his book	14	2	11
The unquestiond readings of a blotless book	16		6
Boon			
Of heaven what boon to buy you boy or gain	46		12
This very very day came down to us after a boon he on	47		5
Boon in my bestowing	47		7
Boons			
Those dearer more divine boons whose haven the heart is	152		131
Boots			
Over finger-teasing task his twiny boots	159		33
Borders			
Stars float from the borders of the main	98	20	1
Bore			
The richest gift St Lawrence ever bore	1	2	6
Lay bleeding to Madrid the last they bore	1	15	2
Are spatterd we desire the yoke we bore	5		53
And the blow bore from land	40		19
Too proud too proud what a press she bore	40		32
Wondering why my master bore it	40		97
Boreas			
But what black boreas wrecked her he	40		22
Bored			
I know of the bored and bitten rocks	120		20
Bores			
Its dearest changed to bores	114		16
Born			
When a sister born for each strong month-brother	26		1
Now burn new born to the world	28	33	1
My people and born own nation	40		86
There boy bugler born he tells me of Irish	47		2
It is the blight man was born for	54		14
New Bethlems and he born	60		63
Who born so comes to be	60		68
But sleep again ere day be born	78		24
Then while the rain-born arc glows higher	78		123
And in grey bands the sun should lie still born	90		3
So those who born in thee	123		4
Our sex should be born in April perhaps or the lily-time	128		13
Borne			
More wondrous to have borne such hope before	1	15	7
Your hands have borne the tent-poles on you plod	5		7
That thou hadst borne proportion in my bliss	13		6

Word	Poem	Stan.	Line
Boroughs			
The bright boroughs the circle-citadels there	31	1	3
Borrow			
And fain in the springtime surcease would borrow	26		11
Bossd			
Tuggd the bossd smooth-lippd giant strombus-shell	2		57
Bough			
With green-white apples on the bough	124		20
For brier bough furrow or green ground	138		6
And after that off the bough	138		39
Boughs			
The boughs the boughs are bare enough	3		1
The boughs the boughs are bare enough	3		1
Is set upon your boughs below	10		10
Look look a may-mess like on orchard boughs	31	1	10
Your round me roaming end and under be my boughs	50		2
Only the beakleaved boughs dragonish damask the toolsmooth bleak light black	61		9
Boughs being pruned birds preened show more fair	96	7	1
The autumn yellow feather in the boughs	105		5
Poetry to it as a tree whose boughs break in the sky	149	1	3
To have havoc-pocked so see the hung-heavenward boughs	157		32
Bound			
Amongst Castilian barrens mountain-bound	1	1	2
One bound oer dripping gold a turquoise-gemmd	2		60
Then I saw that he had bound	4		18
Bound for the harbour and your crew	21		14
And may has come hair-bound in flowers	26		13
Thou hast bound bones and veins in me fastened me flesh	28	1	5
American-outward-bound	28	12	2
And ever if bound here hardest home	29	1	33
Mans spirit will be flesh-bound when found at best	38		12
I think where from and bound I wonder where	39		3
Was around them bound them or wound them with her	40		43
In backwheels though bound home	47		43
To his own selfbent so bound so tied to his turn	57		11
With blackness bound and all	60		98
Undenizened beyond bound	70		15
They have bound his feet they have bound his hands	109	13	3
They have bound his feet they have bound his			

Word	Poem	Stan.	Line
Bound (cont.)			
hands			
Deed-bound I am one deed treads all down here cramps all doing what do not yield	152		100
Bound on what thou hadst forbid	155		10
Bounden			
Bounden bales or a hoard of bullion	40		9
Bow			
Take Canaan with your sword and with your bow	5		56
As a skates heel sweeps smooth on a bow-bend the hurl and gliding	36		5
Bow swung finds tongue to fling out broad its name	56		4
How to keep is there any any is there none such nowhere known some bow or brooch or braid or brace lace latch or catch or key to keep	58		1
Melted in the dizzy bow	78		140
To bow but little and worship not	81		141
See one bow each yet not the same to all	91		6
Flying a bow	98	6	3
For a beauty-bow to his hat	144		16
Bow-bend			
As a skates heel sweeps smooth on a bow-bend the hurl and gliding	36		5
Bowd			
And where the brow in first descending bowd	107	1	9
Of burden came and bowd my head	118		11
Bower			
Ah touched in your bower of bone	28	18	1
Lowly Alice sat in her bower	109	16	1
And bridegroom waits and ready are bower and bed	136		18
Ranked round the bower	159		51
Bowl			
To halve the bowl of Penmaen pool	29	1	12
Bowman			
Yet Arthur is a bowman his three-heeled timberll hit	143		3
Bows			
In bows above my head as falsified	12	2	4
And she beat the bank down with her bows and the ride of her keel	28	14	5
Box			
Break the box and shed the nard	24		1
Boy			
A boy feels when the poet he pores upon	14	3	13
Innocent mind and Mayday in girl and boy	33		13
He has lost count what came next poor boy	40		71
Of heaven what boon to buy you boy or gain	46		12
A bugler boy from barrack it is over the hill	47		1
There boy bugler born he tells me of Irish	47		2

Word	Poem	Stan.	Line
Ran revel in the elder boy	53		9
But half the pains he spends upon his boy	97		4
Boys			
Our boys plays brought on	53		6
Of it must be boys from the town	159		12
Sees the bevy of them how the boys	159		16
Brace			
Run all your race o brace sterner that strain	46		14
How to keep is there any any is there none such nowhere known some bow or brooch or braid or brace lace latch or catch or key to keep	58		1
Low-covered pass and brace the woodland clods	112		6
Braes			
Are the groins of the braes that the brook treads through	55		10
Braggart			
Of braggart bugles cry it in	28	35	2
Whose braggart scutcheon whose complaisant crest	98	32	1
Brags			
The thunder brags in joints and sparkling jags	81	7	3
Braid			
How to keep is there any any is there none such nowhere known some bow or brooch or braid or brace lace latch or catch or key to keep	58		1
Braids			
The Glaucus cleped others small braids enclusterd	2		68
For all his dreadnought breast and braids of thew	28	16	5
Brain			
But here was heart-throe birth of a brain	28	29	7
Cleaves not my brain burns not my feet	81	2	4
Phrenzy but edged and clear of brain	81		52
Brains			
And did the children of his brains enjoy	97		3
Brakes			
Wood banks and brakes wash wet like lakes	41		42
Sir life upon thy cause see banks and brakes	75	1	8
In skeins about the brakes	98	10	3
Of the brakes of lilies	98	19	4
Brambles			
With bills of rime the brambles shew	3		4
Branch			
An olive-branch whence richly reek	78		15
A branch of walnut leaves and that	120		6
Branches			
But through black branches rarely drest	3		20
Five ways the precious branches torn	6		14

Word	Poem	Stan.	Line
Branchy			
Towery city and branchy between towers	44		1
Of some branchy bunchy bushybowered wood	159		3
Brand			
But be the war within the brand we wield	73		6
Brandle			
Would brandle adamantine heaven with ride and jar did	47		46
Brands			
They have taken out their long brands	109	14	1
Brass			
My heaven is brass and iron my earth	18		9
Now the other was brass-bold	53		25
Brass-bold			
Now the other was brass-bold	53		25
Brave			
With a ropes end round the man handy and brave	28	16	3
Brave all and take what comes as here this rabble is come	152		102
Bravest			
Holiest loveliest bravest	40		110
Brawling			
To the men in the tops and the tackle rode over the storms brawling	28	19	8
Brawn			
Stand at stress each limbs barrowy brawn his thew	71		6
Brazen			
My prayers must meet a brazen heaven	18		1
Not hope not pray despair ay that brazen despair out	152		101
Bread			
At morn we found the heavenly bread	6		8
He is with you in the breaking of the bread	20		18
God giver of breath and bread	28	1	2
Little I reck ho lacklevel in if all had bread	70		9
To gentle manna and simple bread	81		175
Breadth			
But each a hands breadth further than the next	91		7
Break			
Then saw I sudden from the waters break	2		74
Break the box and shed the nard	24		1
Night roared with the heart-break hearing a heart-broke rabble	28	17	5
Have you make words break from me here all alone	28	18	3
Our make and making break are breaking down	34		13
And then my heart goes near to break	81	6	7
I will break free from the Jews company	81	7	36
I need not love I need not break	81		138
And hedges break and lose the kine	114		2

Word	Poem	Stan.	Line
Poetry to it as a tree whose boughs break in the sky	149	1	3
Flinty kindcold element let break across his limbs	159		41
Breaker			
She to the black-about air to the breaker the thickly	28	24	5
Breakers			
The breakers rolled on her beam with ruinous shock	28	14	6
Breaking			
He is with you in the breaking of the bread	20		18
Our make and making break are breaking down	34		13
The wind comes breaking here and there with laughter	98	3	3
Breaking the air of spring	98	3	7
The breaking leaves of gold are curld upon her lips	98	14	3
Breakless			
Falling along the breakless pool of air	122		9
Breaks			
Ill wait till morn eternal breaks	23		54
Buckle and the fire that breaks from thee then a billion	36		9
Pointed with pierced lights and breaks of rays	98	24	2
Like a cuppd chestnut damaskd with dark breaks	99		12
Drops the fruit out the duct runs dry or breaks	101		10
So late the hoar green chestnut breaks a bud	105		9
Breast			
Lies in the breast of the young year-mother	26		3
And the promise of summer within her breast	26		16
To thy breast to thy rest to thy glory divine	27		48
For all his dreadnought breast and braids of thew	28	16	5
Finger of a tender of o of a feathery delicacy the breast of the	28	30	6
World broods with warm breast and with ah bright wings	31	1	14
Welcome in womb and breast	60		20
Unseen the heroic breast not outward-steeled	73		7
To cool his plumy throbbing breast	78		92
Are measured outwards from my breast	130		2
This garland of their gambol flashes in his breast	159		19
Breasted			
Star-eyed strawberry-breasted	41		19
Breasting			
Till a lioness arose breasting the babble	28	17	7
Breasts			
The breasts desponding sob I quell	23		38

Word	Poem	Stan.	Line
Breasts (cont.)			
Abel is Cains brother and breasts they have sucked the same	28	20	8
Breath			
Only with utterance of sweet breath they sung	2		130
You striped in secret with breath-taking whips	11		3
The windpipe when he sucked his breath	21		37
Nostrils your careless breath that spend	22		17
At the touch of her wandering wondering breath	26		6
O breath of it bathes great heaven above	27		46
God giver of breath and bread	28	1	2
Breathe arch and original breath	28	25	2
The-last-breath penitent spirits the uttermost mark	28	32	6
Now he wrings for breath with the deathgush brown	40		61
Resign them sign them seal them send them motion them with breath	59		16
Men here may draw like breath	60		66
Bloom breathe that one breath more	60		92
Age gasp whose breath is our memento mori	76		7
Silence holds breath upon her throne	78		33
At once I struggle with my breath	81		58
Two made answer in one breath	109	26	1
And breath upon it that is her face is this	125		58
And breathed delightful breath	133		10
What being in rank-old nature should earlier have that breath been	141		1
And breath immortal thronged that show	145		45
Breath-taking			
You striped in secret with breath-taking whips	11		3
Breathe			
Breathe Easter now you serged fellowships	11		7
Pluck the harp and breathe the horn	24		11
To bathe in his fall-gold mercies to breathe in his all-fire glances	28	23	8
Breathe arch and original breath	28	25	2
Breathe body of lovely death	28	25	4
That beat and breathe in power	48		11
Now but to breathe its praise	60		15
Bloom breathe that one breath more	60		92
Who breathe from groundlong babyhood to hoary	76		6
Breathe oer my bare nerve rather I desire	81	5	5
They breathe not who are late to run	81		148
Breathe in such ether or the quickly elms	100		7
Breathed			
Comforting smell breathed at very entering	33		3
Breathed round the rack of ribs the scooped flank lank	71		2
And breathed delightful breath	133		10

Word	Poem	Stan.	Line
Breathes			
Breathes once and quenched faster that it came	77		3
My winter world that scarcely breathes that bliss	77		13
Breathes in the mysterious air	78		128
And breathes the blots off all with sighs on sighs	151		6
Breathing			
Since its birth and its bloom and its breathing its last	27		17
Only the breathing temple and fleet	40		92
Breathing bloom of a chastity in mansex fine	47		16
Their clouds with breathing edges white	130		23
Bred			
Sydney Fletcher bristol-bred	41		57
Out of hallowed bodies bred	51		4
This by despair bred hangdog dull by rage	70		19
Blindness a learned fool and well-bred churl	102	3	32
A learned fool indeed and well-bred churl	102	3	38
And bred acquaintance of unused towns	107	2	2
What shall I do for the land that bred me	156		1
Breed			
Times eunuch and not breed one work that wakes	75	1	12
Breeds			
Wisest my heart breeds dark heavens baffling ban	66	1	11
Breeze			
While the breeze by rank and measure	79		9
And keeps the breeze and clears the seas	83		13
Plays to the breeze where now are fled her fears	99		15
To these Castara is rain or breeze or spring	125		54
Breezy			
I walk my breezy belvedere	15		25
In breezy belts of upper air	78		73
Bremen			
On Saturday sailed from Bremen	28	12	1
Brickish			
Thou hast a base and brickish skirt there sours	43		5
Bricks			
Give us the tale of bricks as heretofore	5		49
Bride			
And poverty be thou the bride	22		25
Groom and grace you bride your bed	51		2
Then she seems sweet who seems his bride	120		16
Then sweetest seems the seeming bride	120		18
Bridegroom			
And bridegroom waits and ready are bower and bed	136		18
Bridge			
Beyond Magdalen and by the bridge on a place			

Word	Poem	Stan.	Line
Bridge (cont.)			
called there the plain	142		1
Bridging			
Bridging the slender difference of two stars	103		3
Brief			
Then lull then leave off fury had shrieked no lingering let me be fell force I must be brief	65		6
Then lull then leave off fury had shrieked no lingering let me be fell force I must be brief	65		6
Rupture running sores what more in brief in burden	152		114
Brier			
For brier bough furrow or green ground	138		6
Bright			
Eye-greeting doves bright-counter to the rook	16		3
My eyes hold yet the rinds and bright	25		33
What was the colour of that blossom bright	27		32
World broods with warm breast and with ah bright wings	31	1	14
The bright boroughs the circle-citadels there	32	1	3
The shocks this piece-bright paling shuts the spouse	32	1	13
Men go by me whom either beauty bright	39		5
Bright sun lanced fire in the heavenly bay	40		21
Didst fettle for the great grey drayhorse his bright and battering sandal	52		14
Delightfully the bright wind boisterious ropes wrestles beats earth bare	72		5
And gather in like hurdles bright	98	29	3
He drops his bright roots in the waterd sward	100		2
Slight with such violet their bright-maskd green	100		9
Warnd by the bright procession of the stars	102	1	59
Bright hues long lookd at thin dissolve and fly	117		2
Bright-lifting with a little-lasting smile	125		57
Hampstead was never bright and whatever miss cullys charms	128		11
And gather in like hurdles bright	135		21
And bright iconium eastwards reach my rhymes	136		6
But ah bright forelock cluster that you are	157		17
Bright-counter			
Eye-greeting doves bright-counter to the rook	16		3
Bright-lifting			
Bright-lifting with a little-lasting smile	125		57
Bright-maskd			
Slight with such violet their bright-maskd green	100		9
Brighten			
Fairer than this one to brighten our day	26		8

Word	Poem	Stan.	Line
Brightening			
More brightening her rare-dear Britain as his reign rolls	28	34	6
Brighter			
Shew brighter shaken in penmaen pool	29	1	20
Is it only its being brighter	41		9
The blue with brighter places not remote	107	3	20
A growing burnish brighter than before	151		4
Brightest			
His brightest blooms lie there unblown	148		41
Brightness			
But being lifted immortal of immortal brightness	152		58
Brilliance			
Flares his wet brilliance in the dintless heaven	98	34	2
Brilliant			
That battled gods for heaven brilliant-hued	1	7	5
The vast of heaven stung with brilliant stars	98	21	2
Gem-fleeced at morn so brilliant is the weather	99		4
Brilliant-hued			
That battled gods for heaven brilliant-hued	1	7	5
Brim			
Its brindled wharves and yellow brim	3		28
God shall oer-brim the measures you have spent	11		9
Brim in a flash full hither than last or first	28	8	6
Brimmed			
Bones built in me flesh filled blood brimmed the curse	67		11
Brims			
She brims her bath in cold or heat	139		2
And with heavenfallen freshness down from moorland still brims	159		39
Brinded			
For skies of couple-colour as a brinded cow	37		2
Brindled			
Its brindled wharves and yellow brim	3		28
Brine			
The rash smart sloggering brine	28	19	4
With brine and shine and whirling wind	40		79
Bring			
And bring your offerings to a grateful God	5		11
Bring in the glistery straw	5		46
Yet know not how our gifts to bring	23		17
Hither bring pearl opal sard	24		3
The praise of the lips and the hearts of us bring to thee	26		35
Bring me palm with pearled knops	98	18	2
And primrose bring and make a sheaf	98	18	3
And bring a crown for thee	109	23	4

Word	Poem	Stan.	Line
Bring (cont.)			
Or bring more or more blazon mans distress	150		4
It will not well so she would bring about	151		3
Bringing			
O this is bringing tears may swarm	25		35
Bringing heads of daffodillies	98	16	1
Brings			
From wastes of rock he brings	7		11
And in a bason brings the blocks	81	7	21
Field-flown the departed day no morning brings	153		9
Brink			
Oh morning at the brown brink eastward springs	30	1	12
Bristol			
Sydney Fletcher Bristol-bred	40		56
Bristol-bred			
Sydney Fletcher Bristol-bred	40		56
Britain			
More brightening her rare-dear Britain as his reign rolls	28	34	6
But droppd its coil of woes Arthurs Britain	102	2	7
Britains			
Like knocking thunder all round Britains welkin	102	2	3
Brittle			
But man we scaffold of score brittle bones	76		5
A brittle sheen runs upward like a cliff	98	6	2
And on their brittle green quils	98	7	1
With sulphur-colourd lilies brittle in stalk	98	12	3
Broad			
Broad-fluted nor with shafts acanthus-crownd	1	7	3
In some broad palmy mead and saintly smiled	1	10	5
Bow swung finds tongue to fling out broad its name	56		4
Them broad in bluff hide his frowning feet lashed raced	71		17
In wandering until broad light of day	80		6
A basket broad of woven white rods	98	19	1
Bud shelling or broad-shed	138		24
Broad-fluted			
Broad-fluted nor with shafts acanthus-crownd	1	7	3
Broad-shed			
Bud shelling or broad-shed	138		24
Broiders			
Broiders the nets with fans of amethyst	2		66
Broidery			
Had gotten him a wreath of sweet spring-broidery	2		101
Broke			
And broke into bloom upon Nazareth hill	27		11
Night roared with the heart-break hearing a heart-broke rabble	28	17	5
Sickness broke him impatient he cursed at			

Word	Poem	Stan.	Line
first but mended	52		5
Broken			
Slumberd at last in one sweet deep heart-broken close	2		135
By speech so sweetly broken up and gone	125		31
Bronze			
In blazon gilt and images of bronze	102	2	10
In gilt and blazon and bronze statuary	102	2	11
In gilt and blazon and maild shapes of bronze	102	2	12
Bronzen			
Their pansy-dark or bronzen locks were strung	2		53
Brooch			
How to keep is there any any is there none such nowhere known some bow or brooch or brace lace latch or catch or key to keep	58		1
Brood			
Pourtrayd along the frieze with titans brood	1	7	4
He comes to brood and sit	50		11
Broods			
And still the unbroken silence broods	23		19
World broods with warm breast and with ah bright wings	30	1	14
These should have starvd with the green broods of spring	105		14
Brook			
On tangled shoals that bar the brook a crowd	2		96
The clogged brook runs with choking sound	3		9
A row of ripples in the brook	21		31
Are the groins of the braes that the brook treads through	55		10
They said we could not miss a pushing brook	125		5
I knew the brook that parts in two	135		25
Brooks			
Fresh brooks to salt sand-teasing waters shoaly	16		4
While rushy rains shall fall or brooks shall fleet from fountains	152		107
Broth			
Turns and twindles over the broth	55		6
Hard as hurdle arms with a broth of goldish flue	71		1
Brother			
He has a sin of mine he its near brother	16		9
When a sister born for each strong month-brother	26		1
Abel is Cains brother and breasts they have sucked the same	28	20	8
Then up and spake the third brother	109	27	1
Towards my brother every other	155		23
Brothers			
How lovely the elder brothers	53		1

Word	Poem	Stan.	Line
Brothers (cont.)			
Brothers and sisters are in Christ not near	66	1	3
He saw his brothers three	109	7	2
Beside his brothers three	109	20	2
Beside his brothers three	109	21	2
His three brothers are each as tall	109	21	3
Beside his brothers three	109	22	4
Among his brothers three	109	23	2
But saw his brothers three	109	24	4
Father mother brothers sisters friends	159		49
Brought			
The day that brought my lasting pain	21		10
That was unto Judah as may and brought her	26		31
Our boys plays brought on	53		6
And brought the sense of gentle fellowship	107	2	4
They brought their hundredweights to bear	145		51
Brow			
Warm on his brow lo where is another	26		7
That brow and bead of being	47		39
The shepherds brow fronting forked lightning owns	76		1
And where the brow in first descending bowd	107	1	9
With yellow flags will suit his brow	124		18
Hover-float to the hedge brow	138		40
Browed			
A bush-browed beetle-browed billow is it	141		3
A bush-browed beetle-browed billow is it	141		3
Brown			
Oh morning at the brown brink eastward springs	30	1	12
Now he wrings for breath with the deathgush brown	40		61
And brown-as-dawning-skinned	40		78
This darksome burn horseback brown	55		1
Her hues a various brown with creamy lakes	99		11
Had swarthed about with lion-brown	144		3
Or ringlet-race on burling barrow brown	157		12
That leans along the loins of hills where a candycoloured where a gluegold-brown	159		5
Brown-as-dawning-skinned			
And brown-as-dawning-skinned	40		78
Brows			
Droopd oer the brows like hectors casque and swayd	2		42
Earth brows of such care care and dear concern	57		14
The seraph brows of Galahad	78		42
Browzed			
Whose gaps and hollows are not browzed upon	107	1	2
Bruise			
To bruise them dearer yet the rebellious wills	68		10
Bruised			

Word	Poem	Stan.	Line
Bruised			
Sheaved in cruel bands bruised sore	6		5
With darksome devouring eyes my bruised bones and fan	64		7
Brush			
The glassy peartree leaves and blooms they brush	32		6
They watched the brush of the swift stringy drops	107	3	13
Beyond the banks wete steep a brush of trees	107	4	3
At highest when he seems to brush the clouds	122		4
Brute			
Brute beauty and valour and act oh air pride plume here	36		8
Bubbles			
With bubbles bugle-eyed struggle and stick	2		95
With arm and fin the argent bubbles streamd	2		109
Buck			
With the burl of the fountains of air buck and the flood of the wave	28	16	8
Buckle			
Buckle and the fire that breaks from thee then a billion	36		9
Bud			
And planets bud whereer we turn our mazed eyes	2		33
When was the summer that saw the bud blow	27		15
So late the hoar green chestnut breaks a bud	105		9
Bud shelling or broad-shed	138		24
Budded			
With garnet wreaths and blooms of rosy-budded fire	2		26
Buds			
Like an Assyrian prince with buds unsheathd	2		62
Not set because their buds not spring	10		11
Is it a wonder if the buds are slow	17		3
Not set because their buds not spring	25		11
The ends of the crisp buds she chips	98	14	1
With the multitude of the lily-buds	98	19	3
With the warmd and the waterd buds	98	19	7
Than we in the east dare look for buds disclose	119		2
Bugle			
With bubbles bugle-eyed struggle and stick	2		95
The bugle moon by daylight floats	3		15
And storms bugle his fame	28	11	4
Cluster of bugle blue eggs thin	41		21
Bugle-eyed			
With bubbles bugle-eyed struggle and stick	2		95
Bugler			
A bugler boy from barrack it is over the hill	47		1
There boy bugler born he tells me of Irish	47		2

Word	Poem	Stan.	Line
Bugles			
Of braggart bugles cry it in	28	35	2
Build			
But men and masters plan and build	15		6
Build his church and deck his shrine	24		7
All the air thing wear that build this world of wales	33		10
Them birds build but not I build no but strain	75	1	11
Them birds build but not I build no but strain	75	1	11
Built			
Bones built in me flesh filled blood brimmed the curse	67		11
Built thoroughfare heaven-roysterers in gay-gangs they throng they glitter in marches	72		2
Thats built for by the bee	148		36
Who built these walls made known	148		37
Built of chancequarried selfquained hoar-husked rocks	159		37
Bulk			
Must see the eagles bulk renderd in mists	88		3
Bulky			
Circled the safe flanks of the bulky hills	125		10
Bullion			
Bounden bales or a hoard of bullion	40		9
Bunchy			
Of some branchy bunchy bushybowered wood	159		3
Buoy			
I cannot buoy my heart above	18		5
To the nests nook I balance and buoy	138		43
Burden			
The easy burden of yore	5		54
Burden in winds burly and beat of endragoned seas	28	26	16
Of burden came and bowd my head	118		11
Rupture running sores what more in brief in burden	152		114
Burial			
Downs forefalls beat to the burial	40		7
Burl			
With the burl of the fountains of air buck and the flood of the wave	28	16	8
Burling			
Or ringlet-race on burling barrow brown	157		12
Burly			
Burden in winds burly and beat of endragoned seas	28	26	16
Upon my forehead hit the burly wind	135		12
And come where lies a coffer burly all of blocks	159		36
Burn			
Now burn new born to the world	28	33	1
Fresh till doomfire burn all	40		118

Word	Poem	Stan.	Line
This darksome burn horseback brown	55		1
And the beadbonny ash that sits over the burn	55		12
Burning			
And slendering to his burning rim	3		30
O but I bear my burning witness though	157		35
Burnish			
A growing burnish brighter than before	151		4
I can scour thee fresh burnish thee sheathe thee in thy dark lair these drops	152		46
Burnishd			
And fretted clouds with burnishd rim	78		101
Burns			
Some candle clear burns somewhere I come by	45		1
Footfretted in it million-fueled natures bonfire burns on	72		9
Cleaves not my brain burns not my feet	81	2	4
Burr			
Great butter-burr leaves floord the slope corpse ground	107	4	9
Burst			
Will mouthed to flesh-burst	28	8	4
In summer in a burst of summertime	142		2
Bursts			
Or wring their barriers in bursts of fear or rage	38		8
Bury			
All under channel to bury in a beach her	40		48
Bush			
A bush-browed beetle-browed billow is it	141		3
Bush-browed			
Bush-browed beetle-browed billow is it	141		3
Bushes			
Are all the manna-bushes in the land	5		21
Thick-fleeced bushes like a heifers ear	98	11	1
Out-fleeced bushes like a spaniels ear	98	11	2
Bushybowered			
Of some branchy bunchy bushybowered wood	159		3
Business			
Who like me knowing his nature to the heart home natures business	152		76
Busy			
Robberys hand is busy to	40		90
Butcher			
So be it thou steel thou butcher	152		45
Butmind			
Now her all in two flocks two folds black white right wrong reckon but reck butmind	61		12
Butter			
Great butter-burr leaves floord the slope corpse ground	107	4	9
Butter-burr			
Great butter-burr leaves floord the slope corpse			

Word	Poem	Stan.	Line
Butter-burr (cont.)			
ground	107	4	9
Butterflies			
Two tongues like butterflies	98	12	7
Butts			
Right rooting in the bare butts wincing navel in the sight of the sun	143		5
Buy			
Buy then bid then what prayer patience alms vows	31	1	9
But tell me child your choice what shall I buy	46		1
You father what you buy me I like best	46		2
Of heaven what boon to buy you boy or gain	46		12
Buys			
Rich beams till death or distance buys them quite	39		8
By			
Of us the wimpled-water-dimpled not-by-morning-matched face	59		10
Bye			
None besides me this bye-ways beauty try	12	2	9
Bye-ways			
None besides me this bye-ways beauty try	12	2	9
Bygones			
I might let bygones be our curse	40		88
Byplay			
Turn most on tender byplay	53		16
Cadair			
Come plant the staff by cadair cliff	29	1	7
Cadence			
The authentic cadence was discovered late	19		9
Caerwys			
You came by Caerwys sir	152		2
I came by Caerwys	152		3
Caesars			
None in Caesars gardens blow	10		8
None in Caesars garden blow	25		8
Cage			
As a dare-gale skylark scanted in a dull cage	38		1
Cages			
My aspens dear whose airy cages quelled	42		1
Cains			
Abel is Cains brother and breasts they have sucked the same	28	20	8
Caked			
Mid feverd fumes and slime and caked clot	78		8
Call			
The gross flock call them quails	5		16
Most wide ye are who call this gust simoom	5		26
We scarcely call that banquet food	6		31
Save Christ to Christ I look on Christ I call	16		14

Word	Poem	Stan.	Line
My prayers I scarcely call to pray	18		4
Love o my God to call thee love and love	19		14
Ears and the call of the tall nun	28	19	7
Jacks call and cue at last	53		30
You jaded let be call off thoughts awhile	69		10
A silver scarce-call-silver gloss	98	17	1
With potent lips call down cemented towers	104		5
How shall I call my love she said	109	4	3
Lord William they call me	109	5	2
And Alice they call me	109	19	2
I awoke in the midsummer not-to-call night in the white and the walk of the morning	137		1
Call no such maiden mine the deeper grows her dearness	152		18
Call me Englands fames fond lover	156		11
May but call on your banes to more carouse	157		30
Calld			
I calld them and I thought them then	81		164
All as the moth calld underwing alighted	108		1
Called			
Had called the seasons changeful moods	23		23
Of the month by men called virginal	26		22
I came where called and eyed him	53		14
Nor can you long be what you now are called fair	58		6
And called to come at mealtime she would not	136		33
Beyond magdalen and by the bridge on a place called there the plain	142		1
Calling			
Sister a sister calling	28	19	1
Was calling o Christ Christ come quickly	28	24	7
Since proud it calls the calling manly gives a guess	63		4
Calls			
Deep calls to deep and blackest night	23		27
The cross to her she calls Christ to her Christens her wild-worst	28	24	8
With delight calls to mind	41		30
Since proud it calls the calling manly gives a guess	63		4
Cuckoo calls cuckoo up the wood	81		22
When cuckoo calls and I may hear	98	37	1
But then her tether calls her she falls off	103		12
Calm			
Alas I rave where calm is due	81		70
I cannot calm I cannot heed	81		72
Calvary			
To hero of calvary Christs feet	28	8	7
Calvarys			
For us by calvarys distress	6		17
Came			
When chiefs and monarchs came their gifts to lay	1	2	7

Word	Poem	Stan.	Line
Came (cont.)			
Came midst the drizzle telling how last night	1	14	2
And thro their parting lids there came and went	2		11
Autumn-time no earlier came	4		26
But they came from the south	25		13
That came when a line of kings did cease	26		26
She was first of a five and came	28	20	1
Not a dooms-day dazzle in his coming nor dark as he came	28	33	6
Came equipped deadly-electric	40		23
He has lost count what came next poor boy	40		71
This very very day came down to us after a boon he on	47		5
Came I say this day to it to a first communion	47		8
I came where called and eyed him	53		14
Crying what I do is me for that I came	56		8
A mother came to mould	60		104
Breathes once and quenched faster than it came	77		3
Then came the benediction	81		99
An angel came the judgment done	81		104
Or else their cooings came from bays of trees	98	2	1
They came	98	12	1
Yet there came one who sent his flock before him	107	1	7
Sylvester came they went by cumnor hill	107	3	9
Sounds reachd him Richard came Sylvester smiled	107	4	24
Came running over the lea	109	17	4
And she came out to see	109	24	2
When you came forth for me	109	33	4
When I came forth for thee	109	34	2
Who came from further than the stars	115		3
Of burden came and bowd my head	118		11
I thought that you would have written my birthday came and went	128		1
What would be a birthday letter that after the birthday came	128		4
The words came from a court across the way	136		23
Days and days came round about	145		23
You came by caerwys sir	152		2
I came by caerwys	152		3
Round and round they came and flashed towards heaven	152		60
Or they go rich as roseleaves hence that loathsome came hither	152		129
Campion			
Rough-robin or five-lipped campion clear	144		15
Canaan			
Take Canaan with your sword and with your bow	5		56

Word	Poem	Stan.	Line
Cancer			
Stone palsy cancer cough lung-wasting womb-not-bearing	152		113
Candle			
Some candle clear burns somewhere I come by	45		1
Mend first and vital candle in close hearts vault	45		10
The moon dwindled and thinned to the fringe of a fingernail held to the candle	137		2
With tears to put her candle out	145		24
Candlemas			
Candlemas lady day	41		5
Candles			
By shine of candles three	109	1	2
Candour			
But candour never hurt the dearest friend	94		8
Candycoloured			
That leans along the loins of hills where a candycoloured where a gluegold-brown	159		5
Cannon			
O welcome there their steel or cannon	156		17
Cant			
Talks of self-sacrifice yet cant forgive	94		22
You ask why cant Clarissa hold her tongue	96	4	1
Canvas			
And canvas and compass the whorl and the wheel	28	14	7
Canvass			
To canvass the retirement of the lark	113		2
Canvassing			
Are shut against the canvassing of art	126		6
Cap			
His cap shall be shining fur	124		13
Capable			
Is very capable of strong affection	94		13
Capes			
They seem to fold the hills with golden capes	104		11
Capital			
Stood capital eminent gonfalon bearer	98	28	5
Cappd			
Her finger-long new horns are cappd with black	99		7
Capped			
Word last how a lush-kept plush-capped sloe	28	8	3
Caps			
Caps clears and clinches all	41		44
Caps occasion with an intellectual fit	143		2
Capsize			
This was that fell capsize	40		36
Captain			
Marcus hare high her captain	40		44

Word	Poem	Stan.	Line
Captivity			
The screen of my captivity	81	6	2
Caradoc			
In a wide world of defiance Caradoc lives alone	152		71
Caradocs			
What stroke has Caradocs right arm dealt what done	152		32
Care			
The music that I care to hear	22		4
There eyes them heart wants care haunts foot follows kind	39		13
Kept to her care-drowned and wrapped in	40		45
With your fresh thoughts care for can you	54		4
Earth brows of such care care and dear concern	57		14
Earth brows of such care care and dear concern	57		14
O then weary then why should we tread o why are we so haggard at the heart so care-coiled care-killed so fagged so fashed so cogged so cumbered	59		26
O then weary then why should we tread o why are we so haggard at the heart so care-coiled care-killed so fagged so fashed so cogged so cumbered	59		26
When the thing we freely forfeit is kept with fonder a care	59		27
Fonder a care kept than we could have kept it kept	59		28
Far with fonder a care and we we should have lost it finer fonder	59		29
A care kept where kept do but tell us where kept where	59		30
In both care but share care	70		18
In both care but share care	70		18
You hear nor care of love and pain	81		35
In sordidness of care and crime	133		11
Care-coiled			
O then weary then why should we tread o why are we so haggard at the heart so care-coiled care-killed so fagged so fashed so cogged so cumbered	59		26
Care-drowned			
Kept to her care-drowned and wrapped in	40		45
Care-killed			
O then weary then why should we tread o why are we so haggard at the heart so care-coiled care-killed so fagged so fashed so cogged so cumbered	59		26
Cared			
Being pure we lifes pride and cared-for crown	34		11

Word	Poem	Stan.	Line
Carrion			
Not ill not carrion comfort despair not feast on thee	64		1
Carry			
Sweet flowers I carry sweets for bitter	10		6
Startle the poor sheep back is the shipwrack then a harvest does tempest carry the grain for thee	28	30	8
Cart			
The jading and jar of the cart	28	26	10
The cart road with a shallowy bed	135		26
Carved			
Trenched with tears carved with cares	28	15	3
Carving			
And damasqud arms and foliagd carving piled	1	10	2
Case			
All in this case bathed in high hallowing grace	46		11
Cased			
Pierce her she hangs upon the flame-cased sun	103		10
Casements			
Of colour in high casements face to face	1	6	3
Casque			
Droopd oer the brows like Hectors casque and swayd	2		42
Cast			
Into all seasons though no winter cast	14	1	5
That dares to cast its searching sight	23		29
He was to cure the extremity where he had cast her	28	27	6
And cast by conscience out spendsavour salt	45		14
I cast for comfort I can no more get	69		5
And swarter still the rolling pines should cast	90		5
When eyes that cast about in heights of heaven	113		1
No piece matched those eyes kept most part much cast down	152		57
While sick men shall cast sighs of sweet health all despairing	152		108
Their crutches shall cast from them on heels of air departing	152		128
Castara			
Why should I go because Castara goes	125		38
But why then should Castara weigh with me	125		40
To these Castara is rain or breeze or spring	125		54
To these Castara is dew is dawn is day	125		55
To say I go because Castara goes	125		60
Much cause to go because Castara goes	125		65
Castaras			
That this is true of tis Castaras self	125		62
Castilian			
Amongst Castilian barrens mountain-bound	1	1	2
Cataract			
To quench the fine-drawn cataract	78		90

Word	Poem	Stan.	Line
Catch			
And bid to catch him ere the drop of day	20		2
As kingfishers catch fire dragonflies draw flame	56		1
How to keep is there any any is there none such nowhere known some bow or brooch or braid or brace lace latch or catch or key to keep	58		1
Catch sunlight and one strain of stupid praise	98	32	2
Catches			
Falling flakes to the throng that catches and quails	28	24	6
Caught			
I caught this morning mornings minion kingdom of daylights dauphin dapple-dawn-drawn falcon in his riding	36		1
Caught on the dank-ytressed trees	78		106
Caught from angels wings in heaven	78		110
She caught the crying of those three	145		29
Cause			
I know the sadness but the cause know not	2		125
Spring not cause world is wintering	10		12
Grows less and less sweet to him and knows no cause	14	3	14
Sir life upon thy cause see banks and brakes	75	1	8
I know I may my cause with words	81		30
And if it is why there is cause enough	125		59
Much cause to go because Castara goes	125		65
Cavernous			
And then goes out into the cavernous dark	103		16
Cease			
I cease the mourning and the abject fast	14	1	8
That came when a line of kings did cease	26		26
Ceaseless			
The motes in ceaseless eddy shine and fall	1	12	4
Cell			
But both will share one cell this was good news Gwenvrewi	152		14
Cells			
Yet both droop deadly sometimes in their cells	38		7
Cemented			
With potent lips call down cemented towers	104		5
Censers			
What relish shall the censers send	22		19
Central			
A fortress or true faith and central stand	1	5	3
Were eyes of central primrose bluebells ran	98	10	2
And spins her skirts out while her central star	103		7
Centre			
Would not put out some tiny golden centre	98	22	6
Rounds its still-purpling centre-darks of cloud	98	30	6

Word	Poem	Stan.	Line
Centre (cont.)			
The mouthed centre of a violet	102	1	75
And I must have the centre in my heart	102	3	7
Centre-darks			
Rounds its still-purpling centre-darks of cloud	98	30	6
Centreings			
Rounds its still-purpling centreings of cloud	98	30	3
Centres			
That many centres found in many hearts	107	2	5
With centres duly touchd and nestlike spots	107	4	7
Centurion			
Vespillo my centurion hacks out	81	7	19
Ceres			
To golden-girdled Cypris Ceres there	1	11	3
Certainty			
Thou who canst best accept the certainty	13		5
Chaff			
Why that my chaff might fly my grain lie sheer and clear	64		9
Chained			
Christs only charity charmed and chained these two	136		12
Chair			
Three rivals throng her garden chair	83		10
Chalky			
Of wringing tree-tops chalky lanes	78		135
Chamferd			
Enriched posts are chamferd everywhere	96	7	3
Champ			
His charge through the champ-white water-in-a-wallow	40		47
Champ-white			
His charge through the champ-white water-in-a-wallow	40		47
Chance			
How then should Gregory a father have gleaned else from swarmed Rome but God to a nation dealt that days dear chance	62		6
Chancequarried			
Built of chancequarried selfquained hoar-husked rocks	159		37
Changd			
Changd to a flower and there with placid eye	1	11	8
Change			
He fathers-forth whose beauty is past change	36		10
And watches change upon the sea	78		32
But this distemperd court will change it all	125		63
The unchanging register of change	130		5
O lovely ease in change of place	130		27
Is corpse now cannot change my other self this soul	152		95

Word	Poem	Stan.	Line
Changed			
Yet as he changed his mighty stops	21		43
Its dearest changed to bores	114		16
Like air he changed in choice	148		18
Changeful			
Fair relics too the changeful moor had left	1	8	1
Than changeful pomp of courts is aye more wonderful	1	15	9
Had called the seasons changeful moods	23		23
Changeless			
From both of whom a changeless note is heard	19		4
Changing			
Their changing feet in flicker all the time	107	1	13
His pleasure to the changing clime	124		6
His pleasure to the changing clime	124		10
Channel			
His channel under clammy coats	3		11
All under channel to bury in a beach her	40		48
Channelled			
Seems by a divine doom channelled nor do I cry	47		41
Chaotic			
As erst upon chaotic floods	23		21
Chapel			
Thus I come underneath this chapel-side	12	2	1
Chapel-side			
Thus I come underneath this chapel-side	12	2	1
Chapleted			
With lace of rosy weed were chapleted	2		59
Chaplets			
Chaplets for dishevelled hair	24		21
Chaptered			
But chaptered in the chief of bliss	145		2
Character			
Miss storys character too much you ask	94		1
Her character she does not realize	94		25
Charactered			
And a few leaves not lily-white but charactered over with blacks	128		16
Charge			
His charge through the champ-white water-in-a-wallow	40		47
We will charge our flocks that they not feed	98	15	2
Charged			
Furred snows charged tuft above tuft tower	29	1	31
The world is charged with the grandeur of God	30	1	1
Charged steeped sky will not	60		80
Charitable			
Charitable not live this tormented mind	69		3
Charity			
In grace that is charity grace that is love	27		47
Draw me by charity mother of mine	27		49

Word	Poem	Stan.	Line
Charity (cont.)			
Divine charity dear charity	51		7
Divine charity dear charity	51		7
Let charity thus begin at home	81		124
Christs only charity charmed and chained these two	136		12
I will appear looking such charity	140		3
Charitys			
Our hearts charitys hearths fire our thoughts chivalrys throngs Lord	28	34	8
Charless			
And charless wain the wonderous seven	29	1	17
Charm			
Have lost that cheer and charm of earths past prime	34		12
There was a charm would countervail	81		78
Its the day that makes the charm no after-words could succeed	128		7
Charmed			
Cuckoo-echoing bell-swarmed lark-charmed rook-racked river-rounded	43		2
Christs only charity charmed and chained these two	136		12
Charms			
Those charms accepted of my inmost thought	12	1	9
O for now charms arms what bans off bad	47		34
Hampstead was never bright and whatever Miss Cullys charms	128		11
Charnelhouse			
His charnelhouse-grate ribs between	4		10
Charnelhouse-grate			
His charnelhouse-grate ribs between	4		10
Chart			
Doomsday and death whose dateless thought must chart	126		3
Charted			
Because its place is known and charted there	102	3	12
Charter			
Has not a charter that its sap shall last	14	1	4
Chase			
But I must yield the chase or rest and eat	20		11
Chasms			
Of seamen whelmd in chasms of the mid-main	2		120
Chastening			
Let patience with her chastening wand	23		45
Chastity			
Breathing bloom of a chastity in mansex fine	47		16
Chaunt			
An antique chaunt and in an unknown tongue	2		131
Cheap			
Frightful sheer no-man-fathomed hold them cheap	65		8

Word	Poem	Stan.	Line
Chebars			
On chebars banks and why they went	78		49
Check			
The womans wailing the crying of child without check	28	17	6
Chee			
Teevo cheevo cheevio chee	138		1
Cheek			
Cheek and the wimpled lip	48		2
In him all quail to the wallowing o the plough s cheek crimsons curls	71		13
Crisp lips straight nose and tender-slanted cheek	136		16
Cheeks			
Till dimpled joy steals oer its cheeks	23		52
Cheeks right rude of feature	40		49
His tear-tricked cheeks of flame	53		36
Their cheeks moved and the bones therein	92		3
To colour as smooth and fresh as cheeks of roses	108		4
His cheeks the forth-and-flaunting sun	144		2
Cheer			
Have lost that cheer and charm of earths past prime	34		12
Hand rather my heart lo lapped strength stole joy would laugh cheer	64		11
Cheer whom though the hero whose heaven-handling flung me foot trod	64		12
That struggling should not sear him a gift should cheer him	142		8
But more cheer is when may	149	2	4
Cheered			
Peace and food cheered me where four rough ways meet	20		12
Cheering			
For how to the hearts cheering	28	26	1
Cheerless			
Strike churl hurl cheerless wind then heltering hail	154		1
Cheers			
Cheers death would follow	40		46
Cheevio			
Teevo cheevo cheevio chee	138		1
Cheevio when the cry within	138		34
Cheevo			
Teevo cheevo cheevio chee	138		1
Chequers			
Those crooked rough-scored chequers may be pieced	11		4
Cherry			
With silver-surfed cherry	41		40

Word	Poem	Stan.	Line
Chervil			
With fretty chervil look and fresh wind shakes	75	1	10
Chestnut			
Fresh-firecoal chestnut-falls finches wings	36		4
The chestnut-fans are loosely flirting	79		5
Like a cuppd chestnut damaskd with dark breaks	99		12
So late the hoar green chestnut breaks a bud	105		9
Chestnut-falls			
Fresh-firecoal chestnut-falls finches wings	36		4
Chestnut-fans			
The chestnut-fans are loosely flirting	79		5
Chevalier			
Times told lovelier more dangerous o my chevalier	36		10
Chevy			
Cloud-puffball torn tufts tossed pillows flaunt forth then chevy on an air	72		1
Chewd			
They chewd the cud in hollows deep	92		2
Chief			
My cries heave herds-long huddle in a main a chief-woe world-sorrow on an age-old anvil wince and sing	65		5
But chaptered in the chief of bliss	145		2
Chief-woe			
My cries heave herds-long huddle in a main a chief-woe world-sorrow on an age-old anvil wince and sing	65		5
Chiefs			
When chiefs and monarchs came their gifts to lay	1	2	7
Chieftain			
And choose for chieftain one	148		28
Child			
Here playd the virgin mother with her child	1	10	4
And lead me child-like by the hand	23		47
Springs one daughter the sweet child may	26		2
The womans wailing the crying of child without check	28	17	6
Most o maids child thy choice and worthy the winning	32		14
But tell me child your choice what shall I buy	46		1
Thy tears that touched my heart child Felix poor Felix Randal	52		11
Now no matter child the name	54		10
Fold home fast fold thy child	60		126
Churlsgrace too child of amansstrength how it hangs or hurls	71		16
With a two years child at her knee	109	16	2
And mother have no milk for child	114		7
Within her womb the child was quick	145		39

Word	Poem	Stan.	Line
Choke			
And then I choke to tell this out	81	7	16
Should choke sweet virtues glory is times great guilt	136		2
She was with the choke of woe	145		60
Choking			
The clogged brook runs with choking sound	3		9
Choose			
Can something hope wish day come not choose not to be	64		4
I choose one but when I desire	81	7	22
Choose one for hell and one for heaven	81		106
And choose for chieftain one	148		28
Chords			
Or stretchd chords tuneable on turtles shell	2		129
To what the chords of angels are	78		46
Chose			
And if I chose a love to wed	109	10	1
Perhaps it was for this she chose the place	111		15
Chrism			
Melt as from a heavenly chrism	78		62
Christ			
Christ our sacrifice is made	6		10
Christ at all hazards fruit hath shewed	7		10
No but for Christ who hath foreknown and loved thee	13		14
Save Christ to Christ I look on Christ I call	16		14
Save Christ to Christ I look on Christ I call	16		14
Save Christ to Christ I look on Christ I call	16		14
Upon Christ throw all away	24		5
Christ Jesus our Lord her God and her Son	27		29
Thy terror o Christ o God	28	2	4
And cipher of suffering Christ	28	22	2
Was calling o Christ Christ come quickly	28	24	7
Was calling o Christ Christ come quickly	28	24	7
The cross to her she calls Christ to her Christens her wild-worst	28	24	8
Ipse the only one Christ king head	28	27	5
The Christ of the Father compassionate fetched in the storm of his strides	28	32	8
Christ home Christ and his mother and all his hallows	31	1	14
Christ home Christ and his mother and all his hallows	31	1	14
Before it cloud Christ Lord and sour with sinning	32		12
Christ minds Christs interest what to avow or amend	39		12
But to Christ Lord of thunder	40		108
Forth Christ from cupboard fetched how fain I or feet	47		10
Realm both Christ is heir to and there reigns	47		32

Word	Poem	Stan.	Line
Christ for Christ plays in ten thousand places	56		12
Christ for Christ plays in ten thousand places	56		12
Be Christ our Saviour still	60		54
More Christ and baffle death	60		67
Mark Christ our king he knows war served this soldiering through	63		9
And cry o Christ-done deed so God-made-flesh does too	63		13
Were I come oer again cries Christ it should be this	63		14
Brothers and sisters are in Christ not near	66	1	3
I am all at once what Christ is since he was what I am and	72		22
On Christ they do and on the martyr may	73		5
Is this from Christ to be shut out	81	1	2
But yet they say Christ comes at the last day	81	1	6
Sir Christ against this multitude I strain	81	7	12
For love and greater glory of Christ	118		4
The Christ-ed beauty of her mind	145		15
Christ lived in Margaret Clitheroe	145		28
Hope holds to Christ the minds own mirror out	151		1
Theres none but truth can stead you Christ is truth	157		20
Christ-done			
And cry o Christ-done deed so God-made-flesh does too	63		13
Christ-ed			
The Christ-ed beauty of her mind	145		15
Christens			
The cross to her she calls Christ to her Christens her wild-worst	28	24	8
Christian			
I find another Christian here	25		42
Christians			
The pang of Tartarus Christians hold	81	1	1
Christmas			
For a letter comes at last shall I say before Christmas is come	128		19
Now begin on Christmas day	129		9
Christs			
How soldiers platting thorns around Christs head	7		4
Of the gospel proffer a pressure a principle Christs gift	28	4	8
To hero of Calvary Christs feet	28	8	7
Christs lily and beast of the waste wood	28	20	6
Christ minds Christs interest what to avow or amend	39		12
Tells Mary her mirth till Christs birth	41		46
By it heavens befall him as a heart Christs darling dauntless	47		14

Word	Poem	Stan.	Line
Christs (cont.)			
Just such slips of soldiery Christs royal ration	47		28
And hold at Christs employment	48		14
Christs only charity charmed and chained these two	136		12
Christus			
I try the Christus oer again	81	7	11
Chrysolite			
Sapphire Jacinth Chrysolite	78		119
Church			
Build his church and deck his shrine	24		7
That bead the plain did ever havering church-tower	100		6
Church-tower			
That bead the plain did ever havering church-tower	100		6
Churl			
Blindness a learned fool and well-bred churl	102	3	32
A learned fool indeed and well-bred churl	102	3	38
Strike churl hurl cheerless wind then heltering hail	154		1
Churlsgrace			
Churlsgrace too child of amansstrength how it hangs or hurls	71		16
Churning			
And churning in the mill	21		46
Cield			
And melts amidst another cield on high	1	6	8
Cinquefoil			
Stigma signal cinquefoil token	28	22	7
Cipher			
And cipher of suffering Christ	28	22	2
Circle			
But most in a half-circle watchd the sun	2		116
The bright boroughs the circle-citadels there	31	1	3
And each a dinted circle the grass was red	107	4	11
What I did ask then was a circle of rose-red sealing-wax	128		15
Circle-citadels			
The bright boroughs the circle-citadels there	31	1	3
Circled			
To drift in air the circled earth	78		69
Circled the safe flanks of the bulky hills	125		10
Circles			
Blades of Milan in circles rangd grew rust	1	12	8
The window-circles these may all be sought	12	1	11
Circlet			
Circlet of astral flowerets diademd	2		61
Circling			
Let me be to thee as the circling bird	19		1
Citadels			
The bright boroughs the circle-citadels there	31	1	3

Word	Poem	Stan.	Line
Cite			
Ill cite no further what the initiate know	119		10
Cithern			
With heavenly cithern from high choir	78		13
Cities			
The treasure from all cities	104		13
City			
No I should love the city less	15		21
I see the city pigeons veer	15		27
Towery city and branchy between towers	43		1
The city tires to death	133		12
Clad			
Grant that close-folded peace that clad	78		41
I am warmly clad	132		4
Clammy			
His channel under clammy coats	3		11
From hands now clammy with strange blood	81	7	25
Of nerve the clammy ball was dry	81		98
The more some monstrous hand gropes with clammy fingers there	152		20
Clammyish			
Fast or they in clammyish lashtender combs creep	149	1	5
Clank			
Deaths bones fell in with sudden clank	92		12
Clarion			
Now ringing clarion-clear to whence it rose	2		134
A hearts-clarion away griefs gasping joyless days dejection	72		17
Clarion-clear			
Now ringing clarion-clear to whence it rose	2		134
Clarions			
Their clarions from all corners of the field	104		4
Clarissa			
You ask why cant Clarissa hold her tongue	96	4	1
Claspd			
Her barred fingers claspd upon her eyes	111		6
Clasped			
Clutched hands through clasped knees	53		21
A cusp still clasped him a fluke yet fanged him entangled him not quit utterly	137		5
Classic			
This was no classic temple orderd round	1	7	1
Clattering			
Adown the clattering gullies swept the rain	1	13	2
Claude			
The skill of dreamy claude and Titians mellow gloom	1	10	9
Clay			
To plash with cool feet the clay juicy soil	5		50
Yea iron is mingled with my clay	18		10
Nor tears nor tears this clay uncouth	18		13

Word	Poem	Stan.	Line
Clay (cont.)			
But frail clay nay but foul clay here it is the heart	63		3
But frail clay nay but foul clay here it is the heart	63		3
Clayfields			
Nor close the clayfields sharded sores	114		14
Clear			
Of glassy-clear aeolis metal-lustred	2		69
Now ringing clarion-clear to whence it rose	2		134
A singing bird in morning clear	21		41
Some candle clear burns somewhere I come by	45		1
Why that my chaff might fly my grain lie sheer and clear	64		9
Not of clear skies but storm to be	81	6	4
They all come here and stand before me clear	81	7	10
Phrenzy but edged and clear of brain	81		52
Rough-robin or five-lipped campion clear	144		15
Clearest			
But quench her bonniest dearest to her her clearest-selved spark	72		10
Clearest-selved			
But quench her bonniest dearest to her her clearest-selved spark	72		10
Clears			
Caps clears and clinches all	41		44
And keeps the breeze and clears the seas	83		13
Cleave			
Southern dean or Lancashire clough or devon cleave	159		4
Cleaves			
Cleaves not my brain burns not my feet	81	2	4
And cleaves I struggle and am dumb	81	7	28
Cleped			
The glaucus cleped others small braids enclusterd	2		68
Clicking			
It does amaze me when the clicking hour	102	1	1
Cliff			
Come plant the staff by cadair cliff	29	1	7
But his eye no cliff no coast or	40		66
A brittle sheen runs upward like a cliff	98	6	2
Cliffs			
Showerd the cliffs and every fret and spire	2		25
O the mind mind has mountains cliffs of fall	65		7
Like flame they gather on our cliffs at evening	104		7
Clime			
Where winter is the clime forgot	10		14
His pleasure to the changing clime	124		6
His pleasure to the changing clime	124		10

Word	Poem	Stan.	Line
Clinches			
Caps clears and clinches all	41		44
Clinching			
Being to her virtue clinching-blind	145		18
Clinching-blind			
Being to her virtue clinching-blind	145		18
Cling			
Will on the moulding strike and cling	130		10
Clings			
Come when night clings to what is hers	78		21
In hollows of her form the shadow clings	99		8
Clings on the stroke of death that I can smile	102	1	2
Clitheroe			
Must deal with Margaret Clitheroe	145		7
Is a shroud for Margaret Clitheroe	145		14
The body of Margaret Clitheroe	145		21
Christ lived in Margaret Clitheroe	145		28
To the death with Margaret Clitheroe	145		35
To the murder of Margaret Clitheroe	145		47
Gods daughter Margaret Clitheroe	145		54
It is over Margaret Clitheroe	145		61
Clods			
Low-covered pass and brace the woodland clods	112		6
Clogged			
The clogged brook runs with choking sound	3		9
Cloister			
Under the cloister-light of greenhouse vines	84		6
Cloister-light			
Under the cloister-light of greenhouse vines	84		6
Cloisterd			
A cloisterd convent first the proudest home	1	1	6
Cloistering			
Fruit-cloistering hyacinth-warding woods	81		163
Cloisters			
The cloisters crossd with equal courts betwixt	1	4	2
Close			
Slumberd at last in one sweet deep heart-broken close	2		135
The darkness did not close that night	21		3
Mend first and vital candle in close hearts vault	45		10
Grant that close-folded peace that clad	78		41
That nest within close-barred doors	78		54
The stars were packed so close that night	98	29	1
Are still her neck is creased in close-ply rings	99		10
Sucks close the acorn as the hand and glove	101		3
As keel locks close to kelson	101		5
That tears and laughter are hung close together	102	1	16
Close-rooted in the downward-hollowing fields	107	3	15
Nor close the clayfields sharded sores	114		14

Word	Poem	Stan.	Line
Close (cont.)			
As struck with rings of sound the close-shut palms	122		10
As might have struck and shook the close-shut palms	122		13
Close-barred			
That nest within close-barred doors	78		54
Close-folded			
Grant that close-folded peace that clad	78		41
Close-ply			
Are still her neck is creased in close-ply rings	99		10
Close-rooted			
Close-rooted in the downward-hollowing fields	107	3	15
Close-shut			
As struck with rings of sound the close-shut palms	122		10
As might have struck and shook the close-shut palms	122		13
Closer			
Closer because faint morning stirs	78		22
Closes			
Of flowers that counting closes	98	19	6
Clot			
Thro silver gloomd to a blood-vivid clot	2		107
Mid feverd fumes and slime and caked clot	78		8
Clothe			
We guess we clothe thee unseen king	23		13
Penance shall clothe me to the bone	81		135
Clothes			
And lily-coloured clothes provide	22		27
Cloud			
Of filmy globes and rosy floating cloud	2		97
Before it cloud Christ Lord and sour with sinning	32		12
A beetling baldbright cloud thorough England	40		24
Cloud-puffball torn tufts tossed pillows flaunt forth then chevy on an air	72		1
Under the cloud-festooned roof	78		66
On to ledges of grey cloud	78		80
And with weeping cloud is spread	78		95
My tears are but a cloud of rain	81		36
Say oer it hangs a water-cloud	81		56
Rounds its still-purpling centreings of cloud	98	30	3
Rounds its still-purpling centre-darks of cloud	98	30	6
As the fine morsels of a dwindling cloud	102	1	35
He sat and wrought his outline on a cloud	107	1	10
Cloud-festooned			
Under the cloud-festooned roof	78		66
Cloud-puffball			
Cloud-puffball torn tufts tossed pillows flaunt forth then chevy on an air	72		1

Word	Poem	Stan.	Line
Clouds			
An azure ridge or clouds of violet glowd	2		105
My window shows the travelling clouds	15		1
And sheep-flock clouds like worlds of wool	29	1	18
Of silk-sack clouds has wilder wilful-wavier	37		3
Till the lifted clouds were nigh	78		72
And fretted clouds with burnishd rim	78		101
Paves the clouds on the swept azure	79		10
Then clouds come like ill-balanced crags	81	7	1
Like shuttles fleet the clouds and after	98	3	1
The lock of clouds betimes and hangs the day	98	31	3
Covers with shallow silver the lock of clouds	98	31	5
There was no crease or gather in the clouds	102	2	6
As void as clouds that house and harbour none	107	1	1
Of streams and clouds like meshd and parted moss	121		2
Of water clouds like parted moss	121		3
At highest when he seems to brush the clouds	122		4
Their clouds with breathing edges white	130		23
Mays beauty massacre and wisped wild clouds grow	154		2
Clough			
Southern dean or Lancashire clough or Devon cleave	159		4
Cloy			
In Eden garden have get before it cloy	32		11
Cluster			
Cluster of bugle blue eggs thin	41		21
But ah bright forelock cluster that you are	157		17
Clusterd			
Clusterd in troops and halod by the light	2		36
Clustering			
Clustering entrancingly in beryl lakes	2		14
Clusters			
And look abroad on sunny clusters	78		134
Clutched			
Clutched hands through clasped knees	53		21
Coal			
Flashing like flecks of coal	60		100
Coast			
But his eye no cliff no coast or	40		66
Coat			
Her silky coat is sheeny like a hill	99		3
Coated			
Stand shock and silver-coated	98	13	2
Coats			
His channel under clammy coats	3		11
Cobbled			
Through the cobbled foam-fleece what could he do	28	16	7
Cocooning			
Shakes its cocooning mists and so she comes	103		8

Word	Poem	Stan.	Line
Coffer			
And come where lies a coffer burly all of blocks	159		36
Coffin			
And with coffin-black he barrd the green	4		11
Coffin-black			
And with coffin-black he barrd the green	4		11
Cogged			
O then weary then why should we tread o why are we so haggard at the heart so care-coiled care-killed so fagged so fashed so cogged so cumbered	59		26
Coifed			
Of a coifed sisterhood	28	20	2
Coil			
Nay in all that toil that coil since seems I kissed the rod	64		10
But droppd its coil of woes Arthurs Britain	102	2	7
Coiled			
O then weary then why should we tread o why are we so haggard at the heart so care-coiled care-killed so fagged so fashed so cogged so cumbered	59		26
O then weary then why should we tread o why are we so haggard at the heart so care-coiled care-killed so fagged so fashed so cogged so cumbered	59		26
Coils			
Coils keeps and teases simple sight	22		12
Coinage			
Thus we shall profit while gold coinage still	96	7	7
Cold			
With loathd cold fishes far from man or what	2		124
With draught of thin and pursuant cold so nips	11		6
The furnace shall at last be cold	15		16
See how spring opens with disabling cold	17		1
They fought with Gods cold	28	17	1
The grey lawns cold where gold where quick-gold lies	31	1	5
They say who saw one sea-corpse cold	40		72
With along them cragiron under and cold furls	71		18
This outer cold my exile from of old	81	1	3
The cold whip-adder unespied	106		1
It is as cold as death without	109	29	3
He gave her kisses cold as ice	109	39	1
Of the cold wind blowing	132		3
And where cold daffodils in April are	135		29
She brims her bath in cold or heat	139		2
Warm beat with cold beat company shall I	153		2
Colder			
It will come to such sights colder	54		6

Word	Poem	Stan.	Line
Coldly			
And coldly do belie the thought of thee	117		12
Coldness			
The stabbing coldness of rebuff	83		28
Collapsing			
Then faild the tongue the poor collapsing frame	1	3	3
Colomb			
That has it and she is fairer than Colomb	125		43
Colossal			
If a wuthering of his palmy snow-pinions scatter a colossal smile	44		13
Colour			
Of colour in high casements face to face	1	6	3
But watching while the colour grew	21		12
What was the colour of that blossom bright	27		32
For skies of couple-colour as a brinded cow	36		2
When every colour glows	60		84
No colour in the overhead	81		160
To colour as smooth and fresh as cheeks of roses	108		4
That make my eyes sore and cross-colour things	125		46
Colourd			
With sulphur-colourd lilies brittle in stalk	98	12	3
And long the trees were colourd but the oer-head	107	4	12
Coloured			
And lily-coloured clothes provide	22		27
Careless these in coloured wisp	159		30
Colouring			
We found were dabbled with a colouring growth	98	9	2
Colours			
The waxen colours weep and run	3		29
And marching to false colours those few strokes	102	1	69
Columnar			
Gods counsel columnar-severe	145		1
Columnar-severe			
Gods counsel columnar-severe	145		1
Columns			
Flush thro their heaving columns when they halt	104		10
Comb			
Others with fingers white would comb among	2		112
In coop and in comb the fleece of his foam	55		3
Combating			
The keener to come at the comfort for feeling the combating keen	28	25	8
Combes			
Lovely the woods waters meadows combes vales	33		9
Combs			
And it crowds and it combs to the fall	28	4	4

Word	Poem	Stan.	Line
Combs (cont.)			
But the combs of a smother of sand night drew her	28	14	3
His crisp combs and that comes those ways we know	68		14
Within her wears bears cares and combs the same	77		6
Fast or they in clammyish lashtender combs creep	149	1	5
Come			
Come by the flesh-pots you shall sit unshod	5		9
Come up arise and slay	5		18
Ye weary come into the shade	6		26
Where no storms come	9		6
Thus I come underneath this chapel-side	12	2	1
You see that I have come to passions end	14	3	1
Is this made plain what have I come across	14	3	10
Love come down to me if thy name be love	20		6
From there where all surrenders come	22		7
So fresh that come in fasts divine	22		16
And May has come hair-bound in flowers	26		13
I shall come home to thee mother of mine	27		25
The sour scythe cringe and the blear share come	28	11	8
Was calling o Christ come quickly	28	24	7
The keener to come at the comfort for feeling the combating keen	28	25	8
Reach me a fancy come faster	28	27	2
Come plant the staff by cadair cliff	29	1	7
Come swing the sculls on penmaen pool	29	1	8
Then come who pine for peace or pleasure	29	1	37
She had come from a cruise training seamen	40		12
Some candle clear burns somewhere I come by	45		1
Come you indoors come home your fading fire	45		9
Come you indoors come home your fading fire	45		9
To own my heart I yield you do come sometimes but	50		4
He comes with work to do he does not come to coo	50		10
Now the night come all	53		10
It will come to such sights colder	54		6
Come then your ways and airs and looks locks maidengear gallantry and gaiety and grace	59		14
Were I come oer again cries Christ it should be this	63		14
Can something hope wish day come not choose not to be	64		4
Soul self come poor jackself I do advise	69		9
But come thou balm to aching soul	78		11
Come when night clings to what is hers	78		21
Come because then most thinly lies	78		35
My several moans come distant in their tones	81	3	3

Word	Poem	Stan.	Line
To come to me from the underground	81	4	7
Then clouds come like ill-balanced crags	81	7	1
They all come here and stand before me clear	81	7	10
And I come laden from such floods	98	19	5
Come out of space or suddenly engenderd	103		4
No they are come their horn is lifted up	104		1
At morn they come upon our lands like rains	104		8
His sheep seemd to come from it as they stept	107	1	11
Sylvester come Sylvester you may trust	107	3	1
The shining slates and houses come and see	107	3	7
When I come home from sea	109	5	4
Come with you from over the sea	109	7	4
Come with me from over the sea	109	8	2
The crown has come to thee	109	9	4
That this has come to thee	109	14	4
And he will come to thee	109	19	4
He would have come for me	109	28	4
And art thou come from English land	109	31	3
Or come from over the sea	109	31	4
I am not come from English land	109	32	1
If I were come from paradise	109	32	3
O death death he is come	115		1
The king of glory will come in	115		10
Who is it how come to this forgotten land	122		19
We have come four do you think	125		14
Come Daphnis	125		36
Good Valerian I will come	125		37
For a letter comes at last shall I say before Christmas is come	128		19
And called to come at mealtime she would not	136		33
Brave all and take what comes as here this rabble is come	152		102
Come	152		105
Amongst come-back-again things things with a revival things with a recovery	152		134
Thee God I come from to Thee go	155		1
And come where lies a coffer burly all of blocks	159		36
Come-back-again			
Amongst come-back-again things things with a revival things with a recovery	152		134
Comers			
After-comers cannot guess the beauty been	42		19
Comes			
A press of winged things comes down this way	5		15
God comes all sweetness to your lenten lips	11		2
No answering voice comes from the skies	23		2
He comes with work to do he does not come to coo	50		10
He comes to brood and sit	50		11

Word	Poem	Stan.	Line
Comes (cont.)			
Who born so comes to be	60		68
His crisp combs and that comes those ways we know	68		14
But yet they say Christ comes at the last day	81	1	6
The heaven-enforced answer comes	81		144
The wind comes breaking here and there with laughter	98	3	3
From Oxford comes the throng and hum of bells	98	3	6
Comes to the bed	102	1	17
Shakes its cocooning mists and so she comes	103		8
Amidst the sistering planets till she comes	103		14
Lord William comes hunting tomorrow morning	109	19	3
Now comes as low beneath	115		4
That comes again to the woodland tree	124		4
The hatred comes with a good grace from you	125		34
For a letter comes at last shall I say before Christmas is come	128		19
Lord Beuno comes tonight	152		7
Brave all and take what comes as here this rabble is come	152		102
Than sewers with sacred oils mankind that mob comes	152		104
By there comes a listless stranger beckoned by the noise	159		14
Comet			
I am like a slip of comet	103		1
Comfort			
The keener to come at the comfort for feeling the combating keen	28	25	8
Each be others comfort kind	51		5
My tongue had taught thee comfort touch had quenched thy tears	52		10
Theres comfort then theres salt	53		39
Not ill not carrion comfort despair not feast on thee	64		1
Wretch under a comfort serves in a whirl-wind all	65		11
I cast for comfort I can no more get	69		5
Elsewhere leave comfort root-room let joy size	69		11
Your comfort is as sharp as swords	81		32
Heaven comfort sends but Harry it away	89		5
And in this darksome world what comfort can I find	152		80
Down this darksome world comfort where can I find	152		81
Comfortable			
The comfortable gloom	5		28
Comforter			
Comforter where where is your comforting	65		3

Word	Poem	Stan.	Line
Comforting			
Comforting smell breathed at very entering	33		3
Comforter where where is your comforting	65		3
Comfortless			
Comfortless unconfessed of them	28	30	4
By groping round my comfortless than blind	69		6
Comforts			
Is comforts carol of all or woes worst smart	153		8
Coming			
Not a dooms-day dazzle is his coming nor dark as he came	28	33	6
Now coming from the alien eaves	81		3
Commander			
Her commander and thou too and thou this way	40		51
Commands			
I give commands for water for my hands	81	7	17
Common			
All mine yet common to my every peer	12	1	8
I have found my music in a common word	19		5
To whom the common earth and air	78		59
Commonweal			
Thousands of thorns thoughts swings though commonweal	70		8
Your will is law in that small commonweal	150		11
Communion			
Came I say this day to it to a first communion	47		8
Companion			
Let what there needs be done stay with him one companion	152		12
Company			
Far off a nereid company and shake	2		75
Our company thronged the hall	53		11
I will break free from the Jews company	81	7	36
With a golden company	109	6	4
Warm beat with cold beat company shall I	153		2
Comparison			
That here will serve me for camparison	14	3	11
Compass			
At corners flank the stretching compass round	1	1	4
And canvas and compass the whorl and the wheel	28	14	7
Went forth to compass mysteries	78		52
And could not compass it	95		4
Where the stint compass of a skylarks wings	98	22	5
To spread the compass on the all-starrd sky	102	3	8
To turn the compass on the all-starrd sky	102	3	23
Compassion			
And kind compassion at his lifes last need	140		4
Compassionate			
The Christ of the father compassionate fetched in the storm of his strides	28	32	8

Word	Poem	Stan.	Line
Complaisant			
Whose braggart scutcheon whose complaisant crest	98	32	1
Complete			
Complete thy creature dear o where it fails	33		13
Compliment			
What were worth nothing if all compliment	94		6
Compulsion			
By visual compulsion till I hide	12	2	5
Comrade			
March kind comrade abreast him	47		19
Concavity			
Of its concavity	121		6
Conceive			
Conceiving whom I must conceive amiss	13		2
For so conceived so to conceive thee is done	28	29	6
Where she shall yet conceive	60		61
Conceived			
For so conceived so to conceive thee is done	28	29	6
Tis so conceived in his lineament	102	1	49
Tis so conceived in his true lineament	102	1	50
Conceiving			
Conceiving whom I must conceive amiss	13		2
Concern			
Earth brows of such care care and dear concern	57		14
Concerned			
The eurydice it concerned thee o Lord	40		1
Conch			
Withouten instrument or conch or bell	2		128
Concording			
Or take it thus that the concording stars	122		7
Condition			
In its condition no the tropic tree	14	1	3
Bare the condition of a realm at riot	82		4
Confess			
Thou heardst me truer than tongue confess	28	2	3
Confidante			
When tis the confidante that sets the task	94		2
Confidence			
And what if she my confidence betray	94		4
Confined			
Love by prenatal serfdom still confined	102	3	15
Confirmed			
Confirmed beauty will not bear a stress	117		1
Confound			
Of those who strove Gods gospel to confound	1	1	7
Confounded			
Best in graceless growth thou hast confounded	43		7
Confront			
And hosts confront with flags unfurled	23		33
Confused			
And so my trust confused struck and shook	16		7

Word	Poem	Stan.	Line
Conjecture			
Who made conjecture nearest far	78		45
Conjuctions			
With such malign conjuctions as before	14	2	6
Conquest			
Could crowd career with conquest while there went	73		12
Conqurors			
By conqurors rude of honor and not all	1	8	4
Conscience			
And cast by conscience out spendsavour salt	45		14
Considerate			
God lover of souls swaying considerate scales	33		12
Considered			
She not considered whether or no	145		33
Consolation			
Then though I should tread tufts of consolation	47		25
Sits without consolation marking not	111		4
Constancy			
Upraisd and emblem of that fiery constancy	1	3	8
Consumes			
Death or distance soon consumes them wind	39		9
Consuming			
Give God while worth consuming	48		7
Contagious			
I have drawn heat from this contagious sun	103		18
Contend			
Thou art indeed just Lord if I contend	74	1	1
Contended			
Fatal four disorders fleshed there all contended	52		4
Contends			
Contends about its many creeds	23		32
Content			
Most ill-content this least least thing I do	102	1	57
Contented			
Go then I am contented here to lie	5		55
Like a contented wind or gentle shocks	98	2	2
Though ill-contented precious precious floris	102	1	56
But sing contented as the dove	124		3
Contentment			
She leans on him with such contentment fond	157		13
Continence			
He praised the lovely lot of continence	136		28
Continent			
Yet God that hews mountain and continent	73		9
Continually			
Doors slammd to the blasts continually more low	1	13	8
Contract			
The shearing rays contract me with their blaze	81	2	6
Controlld			
Controlld them to a grey-green temperateness	107	4	14

Word	Poem	Stan.	Line
Convent			
A cloisterd convent first the proudest home	1	1	6
He raisd the convent as a monstrous grate	1	4	1
Fling to the convent wicket fast	81		75
Coo			
The wood but not a dove would coo	21		21
He comes with work to do he does not come to coo	50		10
Cooings			
Or else their cooings came from bays of trees	98	2	1
Cool			
To plash with cool feet the clay juicy soil	5		50
When grey showers gather and gusts are cool	29	1	26
To cool his plumy throbbing breast	78		92
Cooling			
Into the cooling gloom till slowly all	1	12	5
In silk-ash kept from cooling	48		17
Coop			
In coop and in comb the fleece of his foam	55		3
Coped			
Once encounter in here coped and poised powers	43		4
Copse			
Of foliage fallen in the copse	3		12
The copse was never more than grey	21		2
All down the stair-way of the copse	21		45
The peacockd copse were known to fill	81		14
That lick the shelly leaves which floor the copse	84		4
From any hedgerow any copse	98	18	1
Helpd by the darkness of a block of copse	107	3	14
Work through a coverd copse whose hollow rounding	112		3
Copses			
The violet moves and copses rock	98	3	4
Copying			
In copying well what you have best begun	125		21
In copying how	125		22
In copying your sweet silence	125		24
Coral			
With coral shells thick-pearled cords whateer	2		54
Corded			
And the corn is corded and shoulders its sheaf	138		19
Cordial			
That cordial air made those kind people a hood	33		5
Cords			
With coral shells thick-pearled cords whateer	2		54
Corn			
And never turned to corn	7		8
With corn that they shall laugh and sing	8		17

Word	Poem	Stan.	Line
And seven ears crown the lodged corn	114		6
And the corn is corded and shoulders its sheaf	138		19
Corner			
To grace them spires are shaped with corner squinches	96	7	2
Scarce worth discovery in some corner seen	103		2
Corners			
At corners flank the stretching compass round	1	1	4
Their clarions from all corners of the field	104		4
Cornicd			
He rangd long corridors and cornicd halls	1	10	1
Cornice			
Wherein beneath the cornice horsemen rode	1	7	7
Pendant in formal line from cornice tall	1	12	7
Coronals			
The dainty onyx-coronals deflowers	2		92
Coronet			
I have wrongd it of its coronet and now	102	1	51
Corpse			
They say who saw one sea-corpse cold	40		72
Great butter-burr leaves floord the slope corpse ground	107	4	9
Is corpse now cannot change my other self this soul	152		95
Corpses			
He hides our corpses dropping by the way	5		5
Correspond			
Only the inmate does not correspond	33		11
Corridors			
He rangd long corridors and cornicd halls	1	10	1
Afar in corridors with pained strain	1	13	7
Corruption			
Enough corruption was the worlds first woe	157		33
Corse			
To newborn prince and royal corse inanimate	1	4	9
And the poor corse impale with it and fray	89		7
Cost			
Stop not now to count the cost	24		2
Cot			
No tumbler woke and shook the cot	135		13
Cottages			
Down-splinterd rocks crushd cottages drear sight	1	14	5
Cough			
Stone palsy cancer cough lung-wasting womb-not-bearing	152		113
Council			
She pleased the queen and council so	145		34
Counsel			
Gods counsel columnar-severe	145		1

Word	Poem	Stan.	Line
Count			
Could count on prediluvian age	15		10
Stop not now to count the cost	24		2
He has lost count what came next poor boy	40		71
And count the rosy cross with bannd disastrous things	89		9
Countenance			
Master more may than gaze gaze out of countenance	62		4
Counter			
Eye-greeting doves bright-counter to the rook	16		3
Away from counter court or school	29	1	2
Away from counter court or school	29	1	38
All things counter original spare strange	36		7
That still makes counter-roundels in the pond	107	3	5
Counter-roundels			
That still makes counter-roundels in the pond	107	3	5
Counterfeit			
This downy counterfeit upon my lip	102	1	5
Counterfoiling			
Her showy leaves staid watchet counterfoiling	108		5
Counterpart			
I dreamed my counterpart it seemd	81		86
Man my mate and counterpart	155		24
Countervail			
There was a charm would countervail	81		78
Counting			
Of flowers that counting closes	98	19	6
Countless			
Is cries countless cries like dead letters sent	67		7
Country			
Since country is so tender	42		12
The dapple-eared lily below thee that country and town did	43		3
What country is honour enough in all us lordly head	70		10
While the upgazing country seems	78		125
What put taught graces on his country lip	107	2	3
The country song of willow the poor soul	111		13
A wonder in the country and a landmark	125		4
But country and flag the flag I am under	156		7
County			
In the ruddied county of the days upbringing	98	28	4
Couple			
For skies of couple-colour as a brinded cow	36		2
Couple-colour			
For skies of couple-colour as a brinded cow	36		2
Courage			
Take courage this shall need no further art	81	7	33
Course			
Why it seemed of course seemed of right it should	33		8

Word	Poem	Stan.	Line
Courses			
So that the masons levels courses all	12	2	2
Court			
Away from counter court or school	29	1	2
Away from counter court or school	29	1	38
But this distemperd court will change it all	125		63
The words came from a court across the way	136		23
Courtesies			
The mint of current courtesies the forge	102	2	8
Courts			
The cloisters crossd with equal courts betwixt	1	4	2
Than changeful pomp of courts is aye more wonderful	1	15	9
Cousin			
My cousin will not love you as I love	102	1	60
The skylark is my cousin and he	138		12
Cover			
Which the tides cover in their overflow	2		2
Or ancient mounds that cover bones	15		37
Might cover the neighbour downs with a span of singing	98	28	2
Do cover from the starry spread	135		2
That the hanging honeysuck the dogeared hazels in the cover	159		9
Coverd			
Work through a coverd copse whose hollow rounding	112		3
Covered			
In beryl-covered fens so dim	3		26
Low-covered pass and brace the woodland clods	112		6
Coverlid			
Her sober simple coverlid underplighted	108		3
Covers			
The veil that covers mysteries	78		36
Covers with shallow silver that unsets	98	31	2
Covers with shallow silver the lock of clouds	98	31	5
Coverts			
They draw all coverts cut the fields and suck	104		12
Cow			
For skies of couple-colour as a brinded cow	36		2
Crackd			
While his crackd flesh lay hissing on the grate	1	3	2
Cradock			
The woeful cradock o the woeful word then what	152		48
Cragiron			
With along them cragiron under and cold furls	71		18
Crags			
Then clouds come like ill-balanced crags	81	7	1
Cramps			
Deed-bound I am one deed treads all down here cramps all doing what do not yield	152		100

Word	Poem	Stan.	Line
Crash			
Whether at once as once at a crash paul	28	10	5
In a flash at a trumpet crash	72		21
Crawl			
The hoarse leaves crawl on hissing ground	3		5
Creamy			
Her hues a various brown with creamy lakes	99		11
Crease			
There was no crease or gather in the clouds	102	2	6
Creased			
Which with its lined and creased flank	92		10
Are still her neck is creased in close-ply rings	99		10
Creases			
Of yestertempests creases in pool and rutpeel parches	72		6
Creating			
To my creating thought would neither hear	66	1	6
Creation			
The roll the rise the carol the creation	77		12
Creations			
Vacant creations lamps appal	23		12
Creature			
Complete thy creature dear o where it fails	33		13
Creatures			
Creatures all heft hope hazard interest	157		8
Credit			
And Ill pretend the credit given of yore	14	2	3
Creeds			
Contends about its many creeds	23		32
Creep			
See love I creep and thou on wings dost ride	20		3
Durance deal with that steep or deep here creep	65		10
Fast or they in clammyish lashtender combs creep	149	1	5
Crept			
A stealthy wind crept round seeking to blow	2		137
Crept all along a hill upon our left	125		3
Crept trembling out of bed	135		4
Cressetedeast			
Let him easter in us be a dayspring to the dimness of us be a crimson-cressetedeast	28	34	5
Crest			
This was their manner one translucent crest	2		38
The sumptuous ridge-crest leave to poise and ride	12	2	8
Whose braggart scutcheon whose complaisant crest	98	32	1
Crew			
Bound for the harbour and your crew	21		14
These daredbaths ay this crew in	40		94

Word	Poem	Stan.	Line
By a grey eyes heed steered well one crew fall to	71		5
Cried			
Or is it that she cried for the crown then	28	25	7
You cried but I have served thee well	81		107
I yield I would have cried at last	81		117
I cried with my desire	135		10
Cries			
This means you need not fear the storms the cries	14	3	2
Were I come oer again cries Christ it should be this	63		14
My cries heave herds-long huddle in a main a chief-woe world-sorrow on an age-old anvil wince and sing	65		5
My cries heave herds-long huddle in a main a chief-woe world-sorrow on an age-old anvil wince and sing	65		5
Is cries countless cries like dead letters sent	67		7
Is cries countless cries like dead letters sent	67		7
Meantime some tongue cries what teryth what thou poor fond father	152		22
Crime			
In sordidness of care and crime	133		11
Crimson			
Speared open lustrous gashes crimson-white	2		8
The waves were rosy-lippd the crimson glare	2		24
To shew the crimson streams that inward shine	2		71
Thro crimson-golden floods pass swallowd into fire	2		83
Where yonder crimson fireball sits	3		23
A crimson east that bids for rain	21		8
Let him easter in us be a dayspring to the dimness of us be a crimson-cressetedeast	28	34	5
Mantling passion in a grandeur crimson grandeur	152		69
Crimson-cressetedeast			
Let him easter in us be a dayspring to the dimness of us be a crimson-cressetedeast	28	34	5
Crimson-golden			
Thro crimson-golden floods pass swallowd into fire	2		83
Crimson-white			
Speard open lustrous gashes crimson-white	2		8
Crimsonings			
When the rose ran in crimsonings down the cross-wood	27		35
Crimsons			
In him all quail to the wallowing o the plough s cheek crimsons curls	71		13

Word	Poem	Stan.	Line
Cringe			
The sour scythe cringe and the blear share come	28	11	8
Cripples			
While cripples are while lepers dancers in dismal limbdance	152		111
Crisp			
His crisp combs and that comes those ways we know	68		14
The ends of the crisp buds she chips	98	14	1
Crisp lips straight nose and tender-slanted cheek	136		16
Will crisp itself or settle and spin	145		10
Forward falling forehead frowning lips crisp	159		32
Crispd			
Crispd up and starchy from a short half-hour	107	3	3
Crisping			
Or bat with tender and air-crisping wings	19		2
Crisps			
In crisps of curl off wild winch whirl and pour	34		7
Criss			
Together as the criss-crossd shelly cup	101		2
Criss-crossd			
Together as the criss-crossd shelly cup	101		2
Crocodiles			
Fawning fawning crocodiles	145		22
Crooked			
Those crooked rough-scored chequers may be pieced	11		4
Cross			
And held a cross of flowers in purple bloom	1	10	6
I took of vine a cross-barred rod or rood	20		8
When the rose ran in crimsonings down the cross-wood	27		35
The cross to her she calls Christ to her Christens her wild-worst	28	24	8
Thus I shall make a cross and int	81	7	41
And count the rosy cross with bannd disastrous things	89		9
That make my eyes sore and cross-colour things	125		46
Cross-barred			
I took of vine a cross-barred rod or rood	20		8
Cross-colour			
That make my eyes sore and cross-colour things	125		46
Cross-wood			
When the rose ran in crimsonings down the cross-wood	27		35
Crossbridle			
Wag or crossbridle in a wind lifted windlaced	71		14

Word	Poem	Stan.	Line
Crossd			
The cloisters crossd with equal courts betwixt	1	4	2
Together as the criss-crossd shelly cup	101		2
Crosses			
To crosses meant for Jesus you whom the east	11		5
Crouch			
Crouch lay knee by earth low under	40		109
Crowd			
Crowd down upon a stream and jostling thick	2		94
On tangled shoals that bar the brook a crowd	2		96
Could crowd career with conquest while there went	73		12
Crowded			
So those mermaidens crowded to my rock	2		98
Crowded let his table be	24		26
Crowding			
Save by two stars more crowding lights arise	2		32
Crowds			
The making and the melting crowds	15		3
And it crowds and it combs to the fall	28	4	4
Crown			
From crown to tail-fin floating fringed the spine	2		41
Or is it that she cried for the crown then	28	25	7
Being pure we lifes pride and cared-for crown	34		11
The crown has come to thee	109	9	4
The crown should be unto her head	109	10	3
The crown shall be for me	109	15	4
If he wear the crown upon his head	109	23	1
If he wear a crown upon his head	109	23	3
And bring a crown for thee	109	23	4
Is that the kings crown on your head	109	35	1
And have you a crown for me	109	35	2
If it were a crown of paradise	109	35	3
I have a crown for thee	109	37	4
And seven ears crown the lodged corn	114		6
Crownals			
And foliagd crownals pointing how the ways	1	6	4
He where the crownals droopd himself reviled	1	10	7
Crownd			
A pious work with threefold purpose crownd	1	1	5
Broad-fluted nor with shafts acanthus-crownd	1	7	3
Crowned			
With blazoned groins and crowned with hues of majesty	1	6	9
Crowning			
I see the crowning of their towers	15		7
There shall her crowning be	109	39	4
Crowns			
Than all the crowns to me	109	38	4
Crucified			
Lovescape crucified	28	23	4

Word	Poem	Stan.	Line
Crucified (cont.)			
Thus crucified as I did crucify	81	7	52
Just like Jesus crucified	145		50
Crucify			
And all in one say crucify	81	7	14
For he whom I send forth to crucify	81	7	31
Thus crucified as I did crucify	81	7	52
Cruel			
Sheaved in cruel bands bruised sore	6		5
Cruise			
She had come from a cruise training seamen	40		12
Crumbled			
From one frail horn that crumbled to the plain	107	3	11
Crumbling			
Of crumbling fore-foundering thundering all-surfy seas in seen	141		5
Crush			
And they who crush the oil	5		52
And crush-silk poppies aflash	138		21
When she felt the kill-weights crush	145		55
Crush-silk			
And crush-silk poppies aflash	138		21
Crushd			
Down-splinterd rocks crushd cottages drear sight	1	14	5
Yea crushd my heart and made me dumb	118		12
Crushed			
Crushed them or water and drowned them or rolled	28	17	3
Crushed why do men then now not reck his rod	30	1	4
Word went she should be crushed out flat	145		38
Crushes			
Crushes and tears the rare enjewelling	2		85
Crust			
And silver damasqud plates obscurd in ages crust	1	12	9
The can must be so sweet the crust	22		15
Squandering ooze to squeezed dough crust dust stanches starches	72		7
That shall unglue the crust of sin	81		133
Crutches			
What sights shall be when some that swung wretches on crutches	152		127
Their crutches shall cast from them on heels of air departing	152		128
Cry			
They shrive themselves and cry good service to our God	1	5	9
Of braggart bugles cry it in	28	35	2
All hands for themselves the cry ran then	40		41

Word	Poem	Stan.	Line
Seems by a divine doom channelled nor do I cry	47		41
And cry o Christ-done deed so God-made-flesh does too	63		13
In me or most weary cry I can no more I can	64		3
I cry o rocks and mountain make me room	81	7	5
Lord but they cry so loud and what am I	81	7	13
And I cry out for wounded love	81		33
My cry is like a bleat a few	81		66
Are heard that cry she does repent	81		123
I can send up an Esaus cry	81		126
And I must take your amends cry pardon and then be dumb	128		20
Cheevio when the cry within	138		34
Worst will the best what worm was here we cry	157		31
Crying			
The womans wailing the crying of child without check	28	17	6
Crying what I do is me for that I came	56		8
She caught the crying of those three	145		29
Crystal			
The bluebells up whose crystal-ending rods in their natural sods	112		8
Crystal-ending			
The bluebells up whose crystal-ending rods in their natural sods	112		8
Crystalline			
With growths of myriad feelers crystalline	2		70
Cuckoo			
Cuckoo-echoing bell-swarmed lark-charmed rook-racked river-rounded	43		2
Cuckoo calls cuckoo up the wood	81		22
Cuckoo calls cuckoo up the wood	81		22
When cuckoo calls and I may hear	98	37	1
Cuckoo bird and open ear wells heart-springs delightfully sweet	146		2
Cuckoo-echoing			
Cuckoo-echoing bell-swarmed lark-charmed rook-racked river-rounded	43		2
Cuckoocall			
And magic cuckoocall	41		43
Cud			
They chewd the cud in hollows deep	92		2
Cue			
Jacks call and cue at last	53		30
Cullys			
Hampstead was never bright and whatever Miss Cullys charms	128		11
Cumber			
But foul and cumber not	78		9

Word	Poem	Stan.	Line
Cumbered			
O then weary then why should we tread o why are we so haggard at the heart so care-coiled care-killed so fagged so fashed so cogged so cumbered	59		26
Cumbrous			
The incapable and cumbrous shame	15		18
Cumnor			
Sylvester came they went by Cumnor hill	107	3	9
Cup			
Together as the criss-crossd shelly cup	101		2
The hand draws off the glove the acorn-cup	101		9
Cupboard			
Forth Christ from cupboard fetched how fain I of feet	47		10
Cuppd			
Like a cuppd chestnut damaskd with dark breaks	99		12
Curb			
Lord now curb him for ever o daring o deep insight	152		73
Curded			
That onewhere curded onewhere sucked or sank	71		7
Cure			
He was to cure the extremity where he had cast her	28	27	6
Curfew			
It is the shut the curfew sent	22		6
Curl			
In crisps of curl off wild winch whirl and pour	34		7
Curld			
The breaking leaves of gold are curld upon her lips	98	14	3
Curls			
In him all quail to the wallowing o the plough s cheek crimsons curls	71		13
Current			
Is worth and current with a lessend mill	96	7	8
The mint of current courtesies the forge	102	2	8
Curse			
I might let bygones be our curse	40		88
Bones built in me flesh filled blood brimmed the curse	67		11
And barely to escape the curse	81		170
Weeping even now I curse myself remembering	102	1	44
Cursed			
Sitting eastnortheast in cursed quarter the wind	28	13	6
Sickness broke him impatient he cursed at first but mended	52		5
Curses			
Ravens for prosperously-boded curses	89		3

Word	Poem	Stan.	Line
Left not a rood with curses unimpregnate	102	2	5
Cursing			
And hate the ill-visaged cursing tars	114		10
Curves			
With shining-hilted curves that they may stay	112		7
Cusp			
A cusp still clasped him a fluke yet fanged him entangled him not quit utterly	137		5
Customary			
These names these faces they are customary	125		51
Cut			
I thought the air must cut and strain	21		36
Glimmerd along the square-cut steep	92		1
Diamonds are better cut who pare repair	96	7	5
They draw all coverts cut the fields and suck	104		12
Cyclads			
Those cyclads made that thickend on my sight	2		37
Cypris			
To golden-girdled Cypris Ceres there	1	11	3
Dabbled			
We found were dabbled with a colouring growth	98	9	2
Daffodil			
For orience of the daffodil	81		12
Daffodillies			
Bringing heads of daffodillies	98	16	1
Daffodils			
Shake the balanced daffodils	98	7	2
And where cold daffodils in April are	135		29
Think you want daffodils and follow as far	135		30
Dahlias			
Only the dahlias blow and all is autumn here	128		10
Daintily			
And rencilled blue so daintily	3		18
Dainty			
With the dainty-delicate fretted fringe of fingers	2		64
The dainty onyx-coronals deflowers	2		92
Dandy-hung dainty head	138		26
Dainty-delicate			
With the dainty-delicate fretted fringe of fingers	2		64
Daisies			
I spy the nearest daisies through the dark	135		23
Dale			
That more he shuns our special dale	21		24
Thy lovely dale down thus and thus bids reel	57		7
Dallies			
He dallies yet and yet with me	110		6
Damask			
Only the beakleaved boughs dragonish damask the toolsmooth bleak light black	61		9

Word	Poem	Stan.	Line
Damaskd			
Like a cuppd chestnut damaskd with dark breaks	99		12
Damasqud			
And damasqud arms and foliagd carving piled	1	10	2
And silver damasqud plates obscurd in ages crust	1	12	9
Dame			
Dame at our door	28	34	1
Damp			
In a hollow lush and damp	4		7
Damson			
Kiss my hand to the dappled-with-damson west	28	5	5
Dance			
Like shiverd rubies dance or sheen of sapphire hail	2		73
Danced			
And danced the balls of dew that stood	21		34
Has danced with her and all the while	83		23
Roots and rocks is danced and dandled all in froth and waterblowballs down	159		7
Dancers			
While cripples are while lepers dancers in dismal limbdance	152		111
Dances			
Dances for sad footsteps slow	24		22
Still the scarlet swings and dances on the blade	152		44
Dancing			
To what serves mortal beauty dangerous does set dancing blood the o-seal-that-so feature flung prouder form	62		1
Dandled			
They could tell him for hours dandled the to and fro	28	16	6
That dandled a sandalled	42		6
And the sunlight sidled like dewdrops like dandled diamonds	144		17
Roots and rooks is danced and dandled all in froth and waterblowballs down	159		7
Dandy			
Dandy-hung dainty head	138		26
Dandy-hung			
Dandy-hung dainty head	138		26
Danger			
Not danger electrical horror then further it finds	28	26	13
Dangerous			
Times told lovelier more dangerous o my chevalier	35		10
To what serves mortal beauty dangerous does set dancing blood the o-seal-that-so feature			

Word	Poem	Stan.	Line
flung prouder form	62	1	1
Ply fold on fold across his dangerous eyes	102		20
Dangerously			
Undone done with soon done with and yet dearly and dangerously sweet	59		9
Dangled			
Tatter-tangled and dingle-a-dangled	138		25
Dank			
Down that dank rock oer which their lush long tresses weep	2		115
And from dank feathers wring the drops	3		8
Caught on the dank-ytressed trees	78		106
Dank-ytressed			
Caught on the dank-ytressed trees	78		106
Dantes			
How Shakespeares England weds with Dantes Italy	98	35	2
Daphnis			
Come Daphnis	125		36
Dapple			
I caught this morning mornings minion kingdom of daylights dauphin dapple-dawn-drawn falcon in his riding	36		1
When drop-of-blood-and-foam-dapple	41		37
The dapple-eared lily below thee that country and town did	43		3
Fire-featuring heaven for earth her being has unbound her dapple is at an end	61		5
Shall new-dapple next year sure as to-morrow morning	152		133
Dapple-dawn-drawn			
I caught this morning mornings minion kingdom of daylights dauphin dapple-dawn-drawn falcon in his riding	36		1
Dapple-eared			
The dapple-eared lily below thee that country and town did	43		3
Dappled			
Kiss my hand to the dappled-with-damson west	28	5	5
Glory be to God for dappled things	36		1
The dappled die-away	48		1
Degged with dew dappled with dew	55		9
Dappled with diminishd trees	98	8	2
Dappled-with-damson			
Kiss my hand to the dappled-with-damson west	28	5	5
Dare			
Is all the winter bird dare try	3		14
Youll dare the Alp youll dart the skiff	29	1	5

Word	Poem	Stan.	Line
Dare (cont.)			
As a dare-gale skylark scanted in a dull cage	38		1
How dare I paint miss story to miss may	94		3
Than we in the east dare look for buds disclose	119		2
I dare not taste the thickening salt	120		26
With dare and with downdolphinry and bell-bright bodies huddling out	159		17
Dare-gale			
As a dare-gale skylark scanted in a dull cage	38		1
Dared			
Dropped eyes and dared not look	53		32
To dream I dared so much for thee	118		6
Daredeaths			
These daredeaths ay this crew in	40		94
Dares			
That dares to cast its searching sight	23		29
Daring			
Might we not think the sweet and daring rises	122		2
Lord now curb him for ever o daring o deep insight	152		73
Dark			
Their pansy-dark or bronzen locks were strung	2		53
Be shelled eyes with double dark	22		9
Hast thy dark descending and most art merciful then	28	9	8
Yet did the dark side of the bay of thy blessing	28	12	7
She drove in the dark to leeward	28	14	1
Lower than death and the dark	28	32	4
Not a dooms-day dazzle in his coming nor dark as he came	28	33	6
Wisest my heart breeds dark heavens baffling ban	66	1	11
I wake and feel the fell of dark not day	67		1
Eyes in their dark can day or thirst can find	69		7
Both are in an unfathomable all is in an enormous dark	72		12
Whose ken through amber of dark eyes	78		51
With me tis rising in the dark	96	6	2
While phosphor risen upon the shallowing dark	98	28	3
In more precision now of light and dark	98	30	1
Like a cuppd chestnut damaskd with dark breaks	99		12
And then goes out into the cavernous dark	103		16
Milky and dark with an attuning stress	107	4	13
I spy the nearest daisies through the dark	135		23
All over some such words as these though dark	136		29
Stepped from the stool drew back from the barrow of dark maenefa the mountain	137		4

Word	Poem	Stan.	Line
God lighten your dark heart but no	145		27
I can scour thee fresh burnish thee sheathe thee in thy dark lair these drops	152		46
Discovering you dark tramplers tyrant years	157		2
Dark or daylight on and on here he will then here he will the fleet	159		40
Darkend			
Here in some darkend landscape Paris fair	1	11	1
Darkened			
Thee may-hope of our darkened ways	26		40
Darker			
Love it grows darker here and thou art above	20		5
To deaths more silent darker spell	23		42
Darkles			
Her glass drinks light she darkles down behind	151		9
Darkness			
A faithful guard of inner darkness fixd	1	4	7
The darkness did not close that night	21		3
If still in darkness not in fear	23		48
With all down darkness wide his wading light	39		4
Doff darkness homing nature knows the rest	46		6
Of now done darkness I wretch lay wrestling with my God my God	64		15
Light and darkness from him flings	78		68
Helpd by the darkness of a block of copse	107	3	14
Moonless darkness stands between	129		1
In the staring darkness	132		1
In all her beauty and sunlight to it is a pit den darkness	152		54
Darks			
Rounds its still-purpling centre-darks of cloud	98	30	6
Darksome			
From darksome darksome penmaen pool	29	1	32
From darksome darksome penmaen pool	29	1	32
This darksome burn horseback brown	55		1
With darksome devouring eyes my bruised bones and fan	64		7
And in this darksome world what comfort can I find	152		80
Down this darksome world comfort where can I find	152		81
Darling			
By it heavens befall him as a heart Christs darling dauntless	47		14
Dart			
Youll dare the Alp youll dart the skiff	29	1	5
Darting			
And save by darting accidents forget	14	1	10
Dashed			
Hideous dashed down leaving earth a winter withering	152		84

Word	Poem	Stan.	Line
Date			
And other science all gone out of date	19		11
Theyre out of date lent sermons all the year	96	5	2
Dated			
New-dated from the terms that reappear	12	1	1
Dated due to season	41		4
Dateless			
Doomsday and death whose dateless thought must chart	126		3
Dates			
It dates from day	28	7	1
Daughter			
Springs one daughter the sweet child may	26		2
For thou as she wert the one fair daughter	26		25
Gods daughter Margaret Clitheroe	145		54
No man has such a daughter the fathers of the world	152		17
Daughters			
And seal of his seraph-arrival and these thy daughters	28	23	5
I have tall daughters dear that heed my hand	158		2
Daunting			
Alarms of wars the daunting wars the death of it	50		6
Dauntless			
By it heavens befall him as a heart Christs darling dauntless	47		14
Dauphin			
I caught this morning mornings minion kingdom of daylights dauphin dapple-dawn-drawn falcon in his riding	36		1
Davids			
Till a maid in Davids house had birth	26		30
Dawn			
So from the dawn was ill begun	21		9
From lifes dawn it is drawn down	28	20	7
I caught this morning mornings minion kingdom of daylights dauphin dapple-dawn-drawn falcon in his riding	36		1
The heightening dawn with milky orience	98	30	2
Dawn that the pebbly low-down east	98	31	1
Dawn that low-down pebbly east	98	31	4
To these castara is dew is dawn is day	125		55
Dawning			
And brown-as-dawning-skinned	40		78
Day			
Of battle once upon St Lawrence day	1	2	2
And it was at the setting of the day	2		6
Drops out and all our day is done	3		32
He slew the Egyptian yesterday to-day	5		3
He feeds me with his manna every day	5		13
And bid to catch him ere the drop of day	20		2

Word	Poem	Stan.	Line
But day passed into day	21		4
But day passed into day	21		4
The day that brought my lasting pain	21		10
Summoning men from speechless day	23		41
Know ye this is Easter day	24		6
Decks herself for Easter day	24		18
Let in joy this Easter day	24		24
Make each morn an Easter day	24		30
Fairer than this one to brighten our day	26		8
With joy for to-day and hope for to-morrow	26		15
It dates from day	28	7	1
And frightful a nightfall folded rueful a day	28	15	5
Not a dooms-day dazzle in his coming nor dark as he came	28	33	6
This in drudgery day-labouring-out lifes age	38		4
And you were a liar o blue march day	40		20
Day and night I deplore	40		85
Grace that day grace was wanted	40		115
Candlemas lady day	41		5
This very very day came down to us after a boon he on	47		5
Came I say this day to it to a first communion	47		8
In scarlet or somewhere of some day seeing	47		38
Can something hope wish day come not choose not to be	64		4
Life death does end and each day dies with sleep	65		12
I wake and feel the fell of dark not day	67		1
Purple eyes and seas of liquid leaves all day	68		8
Eyes in their dark can day or thirst can find	69		7
And on the fighter forge his glorious day	73		4
But sleep again ere day be born	78		24
In wandering until broad light of day	80		6
But yet they say Christ comes at the last day	81	1	6
The lightnings leap the day of doom	81	7	4
There is a day of all the year	81	7	8
That night the judgment day began	81		90
He meets upon midsummer day	83		27
Blot the perpetual festival of day	89		2
If that were true it could not live a day	97		2
The lock of clouds betimes and hangs the day	98	31	3
That early sperses and high hangs the day	98	31	6
And stumbling swears he walks by light of day	102	3	31
And stumbling swears he walks by light of day	102	3	37
On such a season of the day and year	107	1	4
To these castara is dew is dawn is day	125		55
Its the day that makes the charm no after-words could succeed	128		7
Now begin on Christmas day	129		9
As it fell upon a day	131		1
Young Thecla scanned the dazzling streets one day	136		14

Word	Poem	Stan.	Line
Day (cont.)			
She looked she listened Paul taught long that day	136		24
To-day the sky is two and two	138		16
A day off shearing day	144		12
A day off shearing day	144		12
Say it is ashboughs whether on a December day and furled	149	1	4
Must all day long taste murder what do now then do	152		98
With the uproll and the downcarol of day and night delivering	152		118
Field-flown the departed day no morning brings	153		9
All day long I like fountain flow	155		2
That fleeted else like day-dissolved dreams	157		11
Day-dissolved			
That fleeted else like day-dissolved dreams	157		11
Day-labouring-out			
This in drudgery day-labouring-out lifes age	38		4
Daylight			
The bugle moon by daylight floats	3		15
In the gardens of God in the daylight divine	27		6
In the gardens of God in the daylight divine	27		12
In the gardens of God in the daylight divine	27		18
In the gardens of God in the daylight divine	27		24
In the gardens of God in the daylight divine	27		30
In the gardens of God in the daylight divine	27		36
In the gardens of God in the daylight divine	27		42
One star by daylight from the strong blue air	102	3	10
And they were bedded till daylight	109	1	3
And daylight and sweet air	133		14
While blind mens eyes shall thirst after day-light draughts of daylight	152		109
While blind mens eyes shall thirst after day-light draughts of daylight	152		109
Dark or daylight on and on here he will then here he will the fleet	159		40
Daylights			
I caught this morning mornings minion kingdom of daylights dauphin dapple-dawn-drawn falcon in his riding	36		1
Days			
In forty days reachd heaven from earth	6		24
Chilling remembrance of my days of old	17		5
We all we thro the length of our days	26		34
For I greet him the days I meet him and bless when I understand	28	5	8
Dress his days to a dexterous and starlight order	47		20
Days after so I in a sort deserve to	47		26
An our days Gods own Galahad though this			

Word	Poem	Stan.	Line
childs drift	47		40
The glass-blue days are those	60		83
How then should Gregory a father have gleaned else from swarmed Rome but God to a nation dealt that days dear chance	62		6
A hearts-clarion away griefs gasping joyless days dejection	72		17
Most dead-alive upon those days	81	2	7
In the ruddied county of the days upbringing	98	28	4
I think it is seven days she said	109	16	3
And kindred to my lamentable days	125		52
Days and days came round about	145		23
Days and days came round about	145		23
But here here is a workman from his days task sweats	152		42
Dayspring			
Let him Easter in us be a dayspring to the dimness of us be a crimson-cressetedeast	28	34	5
Daystar			
What must make our daystar	60		106
Daze			
Giddies the soul with blinding daze	23		28
Dazzle			
Not a dooms-day dazzle in his coming nor dark as he came	28	33	6
Dazzling			
Down roughcast down dazzling whitewash wherever an elm arches	72		3
Young Thecla scanned the dazzling streets one day	136		14
Deacon			
His deacon dirvan warm twice over must the welcome be	152		13
Dead			
Lord of living and dead	28	1	4
Dead to the kentish knock	28	14	4
Do deal Lord it with living and dead	28	27	7
Felix Randal the farrier o is he dead then my duty all ended	52		1
Is cries countless cries like dead letters sent	67		7
Most dead-alive upon those days	81	2	7
In whose dead lake even a voice may make	81	4	3
They are not dead who die they are but lost who live	98	40	1
Her jailor with his vigil-organ dead	99		16
Ere you set sail the king was dead	109	9	3
And John shall lie where winds are dead	114		9
I prove it what then when these lines are dead	117		11
Alive or dead my girl is carried in it endlessly	152		27
Dead-alive			
Most dead-alive upon those days	81	2	7

Word	Poem	Stan.	Line
Deadly			
Yet both droop deadly sometimes in their cells	38		7
Came equipped deadly-electric	40		23
Deadly-electric			
Came equipped deadly-electric	40		23
Deadning			
An endless round of deadning solitude	1	14	6
Deaf			
Or deaf ears shall desire that lipmusic thats lost upon them	152		110
Deal			
Which makes me when with men I deal	15		19
Do deal Lord it with living and dead	28	27	7
Thy plea with him who dealt nay does now deal	57		6
Durance deal with that steep or deep here creep	65		10
Must deal with Margaret Clitheroe	145		7
Deals			
Deals triumph and immortal years	51		12
Deals out that being indoors each one dwells	56		6
Dealt			
Swings the stroke dealt	28	6	4
Thy plea with him who dealt nay does now deal	57		6
How then should Gregory a father have gleaned else from swarmed Rome but God to a nation dealt that days dear chance	62		6
What stroke has Caradocs right arm dealt what done	152		32
By rafts and rafts of flake leaves light dealt so painted on the air	159		25
Dean			
This dry dean now no longer dry nor dumb but moist and musical	152		117
Southern dean or Lancashire clough or devon cleave	159		4
What is the delightful dean	159		46
Dear			
Of Gods dear pleadings have as yet not moved thee	13		10
More brightening her rare-dear Britain as his reign rolls	28	34	6
Complete thy creature dear o where it fails	33		13
Shine and blue-bleak embers ah my dear	35		12
My aspens dear whose airy cages quelled	42		1
Have fair fallen o fair fair have fallen so dear	44		1
Divine charity dear charity	51		7
Else but in dear and dogged man ah the heir	57		10
Earth brows of such care care and dear concern	57		14
Be thou then o thou dear	60		114
How then should Gregory a father have gleaned else from swarmed Rome but God to a			

Word	Poem	Stan.	Line
nation dealt that days dear chance	62		6
Among strangers father and mother dear	66	1	2
Duly dear Lord my prize is won	81		109
This flower this floris this dear majesty	102	1	39
Meadows to them inexplicably dear	119		8
Dear grace and girder of mine and me	134		2
Makes welcome death does dear forgetfulness	150		8
I have tall daughters dear that heed my hand	158		2
Dearer			
Much dearer to mankind	60		107
To bruise them dearer yet the rebellious wills	68		10
Those dearer more divine boons whose haven the heart is	152		131
Dearest			
Before-time-taken dearest prized and priced	28	22	6
There lives the dearest freshness deep down things	30	1	10
To dearest him that lives alas away	67		8
But quench her bonniest dearest to her her clearest-selved spark	72		10
But candour never hurt the dearest friend	94		8
Its dearest changed to bores	114		16
And beautys dearest veriest vein is tears	157		4
Dearly			
Dearly thou canst be kind	53		41
There dearly then dearly	53		42
There dearly then dearly	53		42
Dearly thou canst be kind	53		43
Undone done with soon done with and yet dearly and dangerously sweet	59		9
Dearness			
Call no such maiden mine the deeper grows her dearness	152		18
Dears			
It fancies feigns deems dears the artist after his art	63		6
Dearth			
And never thirst or dearth	5		48
So hardend is it in this dearth	18		11
Death			
But opend twice in life and death to state	1	4	8
Sudden death before me stood	4		6
Death said I what do you here	4		12
Death was vanishd from the glade	4		17
Death to mark them in the spring	4		32
The music must be death	21		39
And lifes first germs from death had won	23		24
Fang or flood goes death on drum	28	11	3
He was pitched to his death at a blow	28	16	4
Breathe body of lovely death	28	25	4
Death with a sovereignty that heeds but hides bodes but abides	28	31	8

Word	Poem	Stan.	Line
Death (cont.)			
Lower than death and the dark	28	32	4
Rich beams till death or distance buys them quite	39		8
Death or distance soon consumes them wind	39		9
Death teeming in by her portholes	40		38
Cheers death would follow	40		46
What death half lifts the latch of	48		19
Alarms of wars the daunting wars the death of it	50		6
Them beauty-in-the-ghost deliver it early now long before death	59		18
More Christ and baffle death	60		67
Life death does end and each day dies with sleep	65		12
Sheer off disseveral a star death blots black out nor mark	72		14
And death falls gently as the snow	78		26
Ruinous heart-beat wandering death	81		53
The bitterness of death was past	81		120
Clings on the stroke of death that I can smile	102	1	2
To not ungentle death now forth I run	103		19
It is as cold as death without	109	29	3
O death death he is come	115		1
O death death he is come	115		1
Thy ribbed ports o death	115		5
Doomsday and death whose dateless thought must chart	126		3
The city tires to death	133		12
Pressed to death he plants the year	145		4
To the death with Margaret Clitheroe	145		35
Makes welcome death does dear forgetfulness	150		8
Immortal beauty is death with duty	156		18
Deathdance			
The deathdance in his blood	60		52
Deathgush			
Now he wrings for breath with the deathgush brown	40		61
Deaths			
To deaths more silent darker spell	23		42
Ruck and wrinkle drooping dying deaths worst winding sheets tombs and worms and tumbling to decay	58		12
Ruck and wrinkle drooping dying deaths worst winding sheets tombs and worms and tumbling to decay	58		12
And I that die these deaths that feed this flame	76		12
Gather the sooty plumage from deaths wings	89		6
Deaths bones fell in with sudden clank	92		12
Debt			
Freely forgives the monstrous debt	81		151

Word	Poem	Stan.	Line
Yea a debt to pay thee yet	155		19
Decay			
Ruck and wrinkle drooping dying deaths worst winding sheets tombs and worms and tumbling to decay	58		12
Decaying			
And yield a song to the decaying year	105		2
December			
Say it is ashboughs whether on a December day and furled	149	1	4
Deck			
To deck and make most lordly evermore	1	2	9
While he was washing from on deck	21		54
Build his church and deck his shrine	24		7
And they could not and fell to the deck	28	17	2
Across my foundering deck shone	72		18
Decked			
I move along lifes tomb-decked way	23		39
Decks			
Decks herself for Easter day	24		18
Raced down decks round messes of mortals	40		39
Decreased			
You vigil-keepers with low flames decreased	11		8
Decree			
I am gall I am heartburn Gods most deep decree	67		9
Deed			
And cry o Christ-done deed so God-made-flesh does too	63		13
And features in flesh what deed he each must do	71		10
Or ever did for my sake some good deed	140		2
Deed-bound I am one deed treads all down here cramps all doing what do not yield	152		100
Deed-bound I am one deed treads all down here cramps all doing what do not yield	152		100
Deed-bound			
Deed-bound I am one deed treads all down here cramps all doing what do not yield	152		100
Deem			
With attributes we deem are meet	23		14
Deemed			
Was deemed dreamed who	60		28
Deems			
It fancies feigns deems dears the artist after his art	63		6
Deep			
Were veind and streakd with dusk-deep lazuli	2		46
Swimming and languishd green upon the deep	2		114
Slumberd at last in one sweet deep heart-broken close	2		135
Made headway in the frothy deep	21		51

Word	Poem	Stan.	Line
Deep (cont.)			
Deep calls to deep and blackest night	23		27
Deep calls to deep and blackest night	23		27
And where thou dwellest in deep-groved Aidenn	26		23
There lives the dearest freshness deep down things	30	1	10
Deep deeper than divined	51		6
O is there no frowning of these wrinkles ranked wrinkles deep	58		3
Durance deal with that steep or deep here creep	65		10
I am gall I am heartburn Gods most deep decree	67		9
They chewd the cud in hollows deep	92		2
Deep shame it were to be discoverd so	102	1	42
The river spans it with so deep a hip	107	4	26
Is anything a milk to the mind so so sighs deep	149	1	2
Lord now curb him for ever o daring o deep insight	152		73
Deep-groved			
And where thou dwellest in deep-groved aidenn	26		23
Deepening			
The deepening intensity	78		114
Deeper			
Deep deeper than divined	51		6
Call no such maiden mine the deeper grows her dearness	152		18
Be at every assault fresh foiled worse flung deeper disappointed	152		89
Deeply			
Deeply surely I need to deplore it	40		96
Deeply in the arched lustres	78		133
Deeps			
Risn from the deeps to gaze on sun and heaven	2		35
Spins to the widow-making unchilding unfathering deeps	28	13	8
Defeat			
Philip took oath while glory or defeat	1	2	3
Defeat thwart me oh the sots and thralls of lust	75	1	6
Defiance			
In a wide world of defiance Caradoc lives alone	152		71
Deflowers			
The dainty onyx-coronals deflowers	2		92
Deft			
In a neighbour deft-handed are you that liar	45		13
Deft-handed			
In a neighbour deft-handed are you that liar	45		13
Degged			
Degged with dew dappled with dew	55		9

Word	Poem	Stan.	Line
Degree			
Your name and your degree	109	4	2
That was of low degree	109	10	2
With one of low degree	109	12	4
That is of low degree	109	18	4
And thou of low degree	109	27	4
Is tasteless nothing and in my degree	117		10
With wealth that mocks his high degree	124		22
Degrees			
Rounded it thinning skywards by degrees	107	4	4
Dejection			
A hearts-clarion away griefs gasping joyless days dejection	72		17
Delay			
And more must in yet longer lights delay	67		4
Delicacy			
Finger of a tender of o of a feathery delicacy the breast of the	28	30	6
Delicate			
With the dainty-delicate fretted fringe of fingers	2		64
Delicious			
Delicious kindness he is patient patience fills	68		13
Delight			
Than the most are must delight her	41		10
With delight calls to mind	41		30
The fine delight that fathers thought the strong	77		1
Delighted			
Of something drifting thro delighted air	2		28
Delightful			
And breathed delightful breath	133		10
Their young delightful hour do feature down	157		10
What is the delightful dean	159		46
Delightfully			
Delightfully the bright wind boisterous ropes wrestles beats earth bare	72		5
Cuckoo bird and open ear wells heart-springs delightfully sweet	146		2
Deliver			
Stroke and a stress that stars and storms deliver	28	6	5
And with sighs soaring soaring sighs deliver	59		17
Them beauty-in-the-ghost deliver it early now long before death	59		18
Delivering			
With the uproll and the downcarol of day and night delivering	152		118
Dell			
And pledged purply in a half-lit dell	112		11
Delve			
When we delve or hew	42		10
When we hew or delve	42		18

Word	Poem	Stan.	Line
Delves			
Down in dim woods the diamond delves the elves-eyes	31	1	4
Den			
Wring thy rebel dogged in den	28	9	3
In all her beauty and sunlight to it is a pit den darkness	152		54
Denial			
And will not take denial	110		7
Denis			
Denis whose motionable alert most vaulting wit	143		1
Dense			
The dense and the driven passion and frightful sweat	28	7	5
Dented			
Most dented lay Sylvester reading Keats	107	4	21
Departed			
Field-flown the departed day no morning brings	153		9
Departing			
That shapes in half-light his departing rings	19		3
Their crutches shall cast from them on heels of air departing	152		128
Depend			
You may depend that ere a week was fled	97		5
Deplore			
Day and night I deplore	40		85
Deeply surely I need to deplore it	40		96
Depths			
To know the dusk depths of the ponderous sea	2		122
Descend			
To hear his strain descend less loud	78		79
The time save when her tears which still descend	111		5
Descending			
Hast thy dark descending and most art merciful then	28	9	8
The descending blue that blue is all in a rush	32		7
And where the brow in first descending bowd	107	1	9
Descried			
And find it will not therefore be descried	102	3	11
Desert			
Our prayer seems lost in desert ways	23		5
Deserter			
This sweet deserter lists herself anew	102	1	65
Deserve			
Days after so I in a sort deserve to	47		26
Deserving			
To me God knows deserving no such thing	33		2
Desirable			
This was the prized the desirable sight un-			

Word	Poem	Stan.	Line
sought presented so easily	137		6
Desire			
Are spatterd we desire the yoke we bore	5		53
But I desire the wilderness	15		23
Desire not to be rinsed with wine	22		14
What by your measure is the heaven of desire	28	26	7
You there are master do your own desire	45		11
Breathe oer my bare nerve rather I desire	81	5	5
I choose one but when I desire	81	7	22
I cried with my desire	135		10
Or deaf ears shall desire that lipmusic thats lost upon them	152		110
Desired			
I have desired to go	9		1
I have desired desired to pass	130		28
I have desired desired to pass	130		28
Desires			
Hence sensual gross desires	78		1
Desirous			
To the often takings of desirous winds	111		3
Despair			
It rounds and rounds despair to drowning	55		8
And wisdom is early to despair	58		8
So be beginning be beginning to despair	58		13
Be beginning to despair to despair	58		15
Be beginning to despair to despair	58		15
Despair despair despair despair	58		16
Despair despair despair despair	58		16
Despair despair despair despair	58		16
Despair despair despair despair	58		16
Not ill not carrion comfort despair not feast on thee	64		1
This by despair bred hangdog dull by rage	70		19
Not hope not pray despair ay that brazen despair out	152		101
Not hope not pray despair ay that brazen despair out	152		101
Despairing			
While sick men shall cast sighs of sweet health all despairing	152		108
Despatch			
Let him ride her pride in his triumph despatch and have done with his doom there	28	27	8
Your offering with despatch of	48		21
Despatches			
Despatches with no flinching but will flesh o can flesh	152		77
Desperate			
With fiercer weepings of these desperate eyes	14	3	6
O Deutschland double a desperate name	28	20	3
Despise			
That gave you vantage when you would despise	14	3	3

Word	Poem	Stan.	Line
Despise (cont.)			
Things that she likes seems often to despise	94		17
Desponding			
The breasts desponding sob I quell	23		38
Destined			
The destined lover whom his stars	83		1
Deutschland			
The Deutschland on Sunday and so the sky keeps	28	13	3
O Deutschland double a desperate name	28	20	3
Device			
A hope of an approved device	81	7	35
Devilish			
That no recorded devilish thing was done	14	2	8
Devon			
Southern dean or Lancashire clough or Devon cleave	159		4
Devonshire			
As Devonshire letters earlier in the year	119		1
Devouring			
With darksome devouring eyes my bruised bones and fan	64		7
Dew			
The field is soppd with merciful dew	8		3
These drops which be they stars or dew	10		18
Up till that mornings fall of dew	21		27
And danced the balls of dew that stood	21		34
Which is it star or dew	25		18
Who to us are as dew unto grass and tree	26		38
Degged with dew dappled with dew	55		9
Degged with dew dappled with dew	55		9
Her mild-white throat and folded dew-lap slack	99		9
To these Castara is dew is dawn is day	125		55
Dew-lap			
Her milk-white throat and folded dew-lap slack	99		9
Dewbell			
The dewbell in the mallows mouth	25		15
Dewdrop			
The dewdrop on the larkspurs mouth	10		15
Dewdrops			
And the sunlight sidled like dewdrops like dandled diamonds	144		17
Dews			
Earthless dews on ancles sleek	78		16
And in the dews beside his nest	78		91
Dewy			
Of dewy gorse blurrd with the gossamer fine	2		40
Dewy fields in the morning under the sun	98	13	1
Dexterous			
Dress his days to a dexterous and starlight order	47		20
Diadem			
Of the air-blended diadem	78		115

Word	Poem	Stan.	Line
Diademd			
Circlet of astral flowerets diademd	2		61
Diamond			
Down in dim woods the diamond delves the elves-eyes	31	1	4
This Jack joke poor potsherd patch matchwood immortal diamond	72		23
Is immortal diamond	72		24
Diamonds			
Diamonds are better cut who pare repair	96	7	5
And the sunlight sidled like dewdrops like dandled diamonds	144		17
Diapered			
Her face was such as being diapered	93	2	3
Diapers			
Of finishd diapers that fills the eye	1	6	6
Dick			
By him and rips out rockfire homeforth sturdy dick	70		3
Die			
Apollo views the smitten python writhe and die	1	11	9
And faint as though to die	5		60
That I shall live I shall not die	8		7
With free long looking ere I die	15		44
The dappled die-away	48		1
And I that die these deaths that feed this flame	76		12
To hear the sheep-bells dimly die	78		71
Who asks not life but only place to die	80		9
I die I die I do not live	81		69
I die I die I do not live	81		69
They are not dead who die they are but lost who live	98	40	1
Not all but we were framed to fail and die	153		6
Die-away			
The dappled die-away	48		1
Died			
As I markd not always died	4		28
Drawn to the life that died	28	23	2
Dies			
Our hymn in the vast silence dies	23		6
Life death does end and each day dies with sleep	65		12
Dies off in hyacinthed ground	135		33
Diet			
She kept her love-thoughts on most lenten diet	82		7
Difference			
Bridging the slender difference of two stars	103		3
Dight			
The rim with ruby fringes dight	78		120
Dim			
In beryl-covered fens so dim	3		26

Word	Poem	Stan.	Line
Dim (cont.)			
Whats yonder grizzled dyphwys dim	29	1	9
Down in dim woods the diamond delves the elves-eyes	31	1	4
With swift slow sweet sour adazzle dim	36		9
Made sweeter not made dim	60		111
I told you that she turned her mirror dim	151		11
Diminishd			
Dappled with diminishd trees	98	8	2
Diminishes			
He heightens worth who guardedly diminishes	96	7	4
Dimly			
To hear the sheep-bells dimly die	78		71
Dimmd			
Dimmd in the long accumulated dust	1	12	6
Dimness			
Let him Easter in us be a dayspring to the dimness of us be a crimson-cressetedeast	28	34	5
Dimpled			
Till dimpled joy steals oer its cheeks	23		52
Of us the wimpled-water-dimpled not-by-morning-matched face	59		10
Dimpling			
The languent smooth with dimpling drops and flash	2		103
Din			
Though no high-hung bells or din	28	35	1
Ding			
With an anvil-ding	28	10	1
Dingle			
Tatter-tangled and dingle-a-dangled	138		25
Dingle-a-dangled			
Tatter-tangled and dingle-a-dangled	138		25
Dings			
Rose here he feasts lovely all is no more off with down he dings	159		28
Dint			
And with sharp flint will part my feet and dint	81	7	43
Dinted			
And each a dinted circle the grass was red	107	4	11
Dintless			
Flares his wet brilliance in the dintless heaven	98	34	2
Dip			
Ah dip in blood the palmtree pen	25		37
Or drove with a divers dip	53		20
Sweetness from the hour and dip	78		132
Dippd			
Tresses dippd in rainbow fire	78		14
Direction			
Tho apt to throw it in a strange direction	94		14

Word	Poem	Stan.	Line
Directly			
Gaze on and fall directly forth on life	157		16
Dirvan			
His deacon dirvan warm twice over must the welcome be	152		13
Disabling			
See how spring opens with disabling cold	17		1
Disallow			
Maskd with such violet disallow their green	100		10
Disappointed			
Be at every assault fresh foiled worse flung deeper disappointed	152		89
Disappointment			
The sceptic disappointment and the loss	14	3	12
Let me though see no more of him and not disappointment	47		36
Disappointment all I endeavour end	75	1	3
Disarming			
Mounts then to alight disarming no one dreams	49		13
Disarray			
Swung down at a disarray	144		8
Disaster			
Disaster there but may he not rankle and roam	47		42
Disastrous			
And count the rosy cross with bannd disastrous things	89		9
Discharge			
Thence the discharge of it there its swelling to be	28	7	6
Discharging			
Gross mind discharging fouled laughter	78		58
Disclose			
Than we in the east dare look for buds disclose	119		2
Discloses			
Turning and pacing so by slips discloses	108		2
Discontent			
These are my very text of discontent	125		50
Discord			
Since trampled Spain by royal discord torn	1	15	1
Discoverd			
With not to be discoverd gold	15		14
Be discoverd to my sight	78		17
Then was discoverd in the pathless sky	80		7
Discoverd everywhere	98	24	3
Deep shame it were to be discoverd so	102	1	42
Discovered			
The authentic cadence was discovered late	19		9
Discovering			
Discovering you dark tramplers tyrant years	157		2
Discovery			
Scarce worth discovery in some corner seen	103		2

Word	Poem	Stan.	Line
Dishevelled			
Chaplets for dishevelled hair	24		21
Dismal			
He seemd a dismal mirky stamp	4		8
It seemd so hard and dismal thing	4		31
Why if it be so for the dismal morn	90		1
While cripples are while lepers dancers in dismal limbdance	152		111
Dismalest			
You have made me quote almost the dismalest proverb I know	128		18
Dismay			
The lorn moon pale with piteous dismay	80		4
Dismembering			
Disremembering dismembering all now heart you round me right	61		7
Disobedient			
Which once were disobedient	93	1	3
Disorders			
Fatal four disorders fleshed there all contended	52		4
Disparadised			
Have willd to be disparadised	118		3
Dispel			
Dispel the doubt and dry the tear	23		46
Dispense			
Since God has let dispense	60		40
Dispenses			
And rosing part on part dispenses green	100		3
Disposes			
Even so my thought the rose and grey disposes	108		7
Disquiet			
With levelld lashes stilling their disquiet	82		2
Disregarded			
Prayer go disregarded	47		47
Disremembering			
Disremembering dismembering all now heart you round me right	61		7
Disseveral			
Sheer off disseveral a star death blots black out nor mark	72		14
Dissolve			
Bright hues long lookd at thin dissolve and fly	117		2
Dissolved			
That fleeted else like day-dissolved dreams	157		11
Distance			
Rich beams till death or distance buys them quite	39		8
Death or distance soon consumes them wind	39		9
Distance	98	8	1
Distanced			
With such a violet slight their distanced green	100		8

Word	Poem	Stan.	Line
Distant			
My several moans come distant in their tones	81	3	3
All time at once and span the distant goals	126		4
Distemperd			
But this distemperd court will change it all	125		63
Distillation			
With dreadful distillation of thoughts sour as blood	152		97
Distills			
And where is he who more and more distills	68		12
Distinction			
And ill love my distinction near or far	14	2	12
Distress			
For us by Calvarys distress	6		17
Or bring more or more blazon mans distress	150		4
Distressed			
But uncumbered meadow-down is not distressed	38		13
Disturbd			
Airwards disturbd and the scarce troubled sea	2		110
Dither			
Makes dither makes hover	159		10
Dive			
All else may whirl or dive or fly	130		8
Divers			
Or drove with a divers dip	53		20
Divide			
For only try by gazing to divide	102	3	9
Divided			
Parted me leaf and leaf divided me eyelid and eyelid of slumber	137		7
Divine			
With form divine a fiery chivalry	1	7	8
I never saw her so divine	3		19
So fresh that come in fasts divine	22		16
In the gardens of God in the daylight divine	27		6
In the gardens of God in the daylight divine	27		12
In the gardens of God in the daylight divine	27		18
In the gardens of God in the daylight divine	27		24
In the gardens of God in the daylight divine	27		30
In the gardens of God in the daylight divine	27		36
In the gardens of God in the daylight divine	27		42
To thy breast to thy rest to thy glory divine	27		48
Has one fetch in her she rears herself to divine	28	19	6
There and your sweetest sendings ah divine	47		13
Seems by a divine doom channelled nor do I cry	47		41
Divine charity dear charity	51		7
And hide it though she does one may divine	94		11
Those dearer more divine boons whose haven the heart is	152		131

Word	Poem	Stan.	Line
Divined			
Deep deeper than divined	51		6
Divinely			
Lies divinely still at rest	78		98
Diving			
Some diving merrily downward drove and gleamd	2		108
Dizzy			
Melted in the dizzy bow	78		140
Doff			
Doff darkness homing nature knows the rest	46		6
Doffs			
Doffs all drives full for righteousness	40		55
Dog			
Dog he did give tongue	53		34
Dogeared			
That the hanging honeysuck the dogeared hazels in the cover	159		9
Doggd			
Such heathenish misadventure doggd one sin	102	2	15
Dogged			
Wring thy rebel dogged in den	28	9	3
Else but in dear and dogged man ah the heir	57		10
Dogrose			
The furl of fresh-leaved dogrose down	144		1
Dogs			
Such heathenish misadventure dogs one sin	102	2	16
Doing			
Thy doing and dost thou touch me afresh	28	1	7
There needs but little doing	152		11
Deed-bound I am one deed treads all down here cramps all doing what do not yield	152		100
Domain			
Among the lilies and thy good domain	123		6
Dominant			
I have found the dominant of my range and state	19		13
Done			
Drops out and all our day is done	3		32
That no recorded devilish thing was done	14	2	8
It is the waste done in unreticent youth	17		10
Your parley was not done and there	25		29
Let him ride her pride in his triumph despatch and have done with his doom there	28	27	8
For so conceived so to conceive thee is done	28	29	6
Be beginning since no nothing can be done	58		9
Where whatevers prized and passes of us everything thats fresh and fast flying of us seems to us sweet of us and swiftly away with done away with undone	59		8
Undone done with soon done with and yet dearly and dangerously sweet	59		9

Word	Poem	Stan.	Line
Undone done with soon done with and yet dearly and dangerously sweet	59		9
More makes when all is done	60		71
And cry o Christ-done deed so God-made-flesh does too	63		13
Of now done darkness I wretch lay wrestling with my God my God	64		15
An angel came the judgment done	81		104
So I go out my little sweet is done	103		17
Loose on the stem has done its summering	105		13
When this was done and I could look	135		7
O heart have done you beat you beat so high	135		35
The bald and bold blinking gold when alls done	143		4
Before the Spring was done	144		4
Let what there needs be done stay with him one companion	152		12
What stroke has Caradocs right arm dealt what done	152		32
What work what harms done there is no harm done none yet	152		39
What work what harms done there is no harm done none yet	152		39
The blame bear who aroused me what I have done violent	152		66
I have like a lion done lionlike done	152		67
I have like a lion done lionlike done	152		67
Doom			
The goal was a shoal of a fourth the doom to be drowned	28	12	6
Let him ride her pride in his triumph despatch and have done with his doom there	28	27	8
Seems by a divine doom channelled nor do I cry	47		41
The lightnings leap the day of doom	81	7	4
The sea took pity it interposed with doom	158		1
Doomed			
Her flower her piece of being doomed dragon food	49		4
Had always doomed her down to this	145		3
Doomfire			
Fresh till doomfire burn all	40		118
Dooms			
Not a dooms-day dazzle in his coming nor dark as he came	28	33	6
Dooms-day			
Not a dooms-day dazzle in his coming nor dark as he came	28	33	6
Doomsday			
Doomsday and death whose dateless thought must chart	126		3
Door			
Where stands no host at door or hearth	23		11

Word	Poem	Stan.	Line
Door (cont.)			
Dame at our door	28	34	1
That in Majorca Alfonso watched the door	73		14
Open the door to me	109	29	4
When she had made the door wide	109	30	3
Then at the door what work there was good lack	135		5
I put the door to with the bolts unpinned	135		11
Doors			
Doors slammd to the blasts continually more low	1	13	8
That nest within close-barred doors	78		54
Be ye lift up ye everlasting doors	115		9
Doric			
With massy pillars of the Doric mood	1	7	2
Dorothea			
Dorothea or was your writ	25		27
Dorothy			
Nor fruit nor flowers nor Dorothy	10		24
Fruit nor flower nor Dorothy	25		24
Double			
Be shelled eyes with double dark	22		9
O Deutschland double a desperate name	28	20	3
Double-natured name	28	33	2
Double and higher than his wont	78		111
Double as sharp meaning and forcible	102	1	11
Making them double-musical and they	112		5
Double-musical			
Making them double-musical and they	112		5
Double-natured			
Double-natured name	28	33	2
Doublet			
Round this unsexing doublet while I set	102	1	4
Doubt			
Dispel the doubt and dry the tear	23		46
From God and man is hell no doubt	81	1	4
Somewhere we slipt astray you cannot doubt	125		15
Doubtless			
Doubtless the voice now falln now spent	81		2
Mothers are doubtless happier for their babes	123		1
Dough			
Selfyeast of spirit a dull dough sours I see	67		12
Squandering ooze to squeezed dough crust dust stanches starches	72		7
Dove			
The wood but not a dove would coo	21		21
But sing contended as the dove	124		3
Doves			
Eye-greeting doves bright-counter to the rook	16		3
Flake-doves sent floating forth at a farm-yard scare	32	1	7

Word	Poem	Stan.	Line
Dovewinged			
My heart but you were dovewinged I can tell	28	3	6
Down			
But further down the valley left and right	1	14	4
Down-splinterd rocks crushd cottages drear sight	1	14	5
Crowd down upon a stream and jostling thick	2		94
Down that dank rock oer which their lush long tresses weep	2		115
A press of winged things comes down this way	5		15
Love come down to me if thy name be love	20		6
All down the stair-way of the copse	21		45
When the rose ran in crimsonings down the cross-wood	27		35
Hard down with a horror of height	28	2	7
But roped with always all the way down from the tall	28	4	6
And she beat the bank down with her bows and the ride of her keel	28	14	5
From lifes dawn it is drawn down	28	20	7
The down-dugged ground-hugged grey	28	26	2
There lives the dearest freshness deep down things	31	1	10
Down in dim woods the diamond delves the elves-eyes	32	1	4
Our make and making break are breaking down	35		13
No wonder of it sheer plod makes plough down sillion	36		11
Down all that glory in the heavens to glean our Saviour	38		6
Why hear him hear him babble and drop down to his nest	39		10
But uncumbered meadow-down is not distressed	39		13
With all down darkness wide his wading light	40		4
It hurls hurls off Boniface Down	41		31
Raged down decks round messes of mortals	41		39
As sheer down the ship goes	41		59
Now her afterdraught gullies him too down	41		60
This very very day came down to us after a boon he on	48		5
His rollrock highroad roaring down	56		2
Thy lovely dale down thus and thus bids reel	58		7
Down no waving off of these most mournful messengers still messengers sad and stealing messengers of grey	59		4
Down roughcast down dazzling whitewash wherever an elm arches	72		3
Down roughcast down dazzling whitewash wherever an elm arches	72		3

Word	Poem	Stan.	Line
Down (cont.)			
And down the welkin gushing free	78		85
The hanging snows rush down and bare	81	4	4
Shouldering down valleys smokes the gloom	81	7	2
And press it down on either side a bone	81	7	50
You met me I had hastend down	81		89
Above them down the draught of air	83		12
And tangles on a down of France	83		14
I must hunt down the prize	88		1
Dawn that the pebbly low-down east	98	31	1
Dawn that low-down pebbly east	98	31	4
Thy impalpable oppression pin him down	102	1	19
Jarrd down the balanced storm the bleeding heavens	102	2	4
With potent lips call down cemented towers	104		5
Down upon ground fell she	109	39	2
Had let such music down without impediment	122		8
Spent Pegasus down the stark-precipitous air	136		8
And down the furrow dry	138		27
But down drop if it says stop	138		37
The furl of fresh-leaved dogrose down	144		1
Swung down at a disarray	144		8
Had always doomed her down to this	145		3
Though down his beings bent	148		17
Her glass drinks light she darkles down behind	151		9
Down the beetling banks like water in waterfalls	152		51
No piece matched those eyes kept most part much cast down	152		57
Loyal to his own soul laying his own law down no law nor	152		72
Down this darksome world comfort where can I find	152		81
Hideous dashed down leaving earth a winter withering	152		84
Deed-bound I am one deed treads all down here cramps all doing what do not yield	152		100
Their young delightful hour do feature down	157		10
Roots and rocks is danced and dandled all in froth and waterblowballs down	159		7
Rose here he feasts lovely all is no more off with down he dings	159		28
And with heavenfallen freshness down from moorland still brims	159		39
Down-dugged			
The down-dugged ground-hugged grey	28	26	2
Down-splinterd			
Down-splinterd rocks crushd cottages drear sight	1	14	5
Downcarol			
With the uproll and the downcarol of day and			

Word	Poem	Stan.	Line
night delivering	152		118
Downdolphinry			
With dare and with downdolphinry and bell-bright bodies huddling out	159		17
Downright			
At downright no or yes	40		54
Downs			
Downs forefalls beat to the burial	40		7
Might cover the neighbour downs with a span of singing	98	28	2
As voids as those the gentle downs appear	107	1	3
But what drew shepherd Richard from his downs	107	2	1
Downward			
Some diving merrily downward drove and gleamd	2		108
Close-rooted in the downward-hollowing fields	107	3	15
Downward-hollowing			
Close-rooted in the downward-hollowing fields	107	3	15
Downwards			
And headed always downwards with less sounding	112		2
Downy			
This downy counterfeit upon my lip	102	1	5
Dragon			
Her flower her piece of being doomed dragon food	49		4
Dragonflies			
As kingfishers catch fire dragonflies draw flame	56		1
Dragonish			
Only the beakleaved boughs dragonish damask the toolsmooth bleak light black	61		9
Dragons			
There rid the dragons root out there the sin	150		10
Drain			
To mans last dust drain fast towards mans first slime	35		14
Draining			
And water draining through and through	21		20
Draught			
With draught of thin and pursuant cold so nips	11		6
Above them down the draught of air	83		12
Draughts			
While blind mens eyes shall thirst after day-light draughts of daylight	152		109
Draw			
Pure fasted faces draw unto this feast	11		1
Draw me by charity mother of mine	27		49
As kingfishers catch fire dragonflies draw			

Word	Poem	Stan.	Line
Draw (cont.)			
flame	56		1
My lung must draw and draw	60		14
My lung must draw and draw	60		14
Men here may draw like breath	60		66
They draw all coverts cut the fields and suck	104		12
Drawer			
Once in a drawer of Indian wood	81		80
Drawn			
Where in a newly-drawn green litter	10		5
Which in newly drawn green litter	25		5
From lifes dawn it is drawn down	28	20	7
Drawn to the life that died	28	23	2
I caught this morning mornings minion kingdom of daylights dauphin dapple-dawn-drawn falcon in his riding	36		1
I caught this morning mornings minion kingdom of daylights dauphin dapple-dawn-drawn falcon in his riding	36		1
To quench the fine-drawn cataract	78		90
I have drawn heat from this contagious sun	103		18
Their highest sprays were drawn as fine as lashes	107	4	6
I hear a noise of waters drawn away	112		1
Draws			
The hand draws off the glove the acorn-cup	101		9
Tampering with those sweet bines draws them out strains them strains them	152		21
Drayhorse			
Didst fettle for the great grey drayhorse his bright and battering sandal	52		14
Dread			
On beings dread and vacant maze	23		30
And after it almost unmade what with dread	28	1	6
Dreaded			
Your footing now to the much-dreaded dust	107	3	2
Dreadful			
But mine is dreadful leaping pain	81		51
With dreadful distillation of thoughts sour as blood	152		97
Fallers in dreadful frothpits waterfearers wild	152		112
Dreadnought			
For all his dreadnought breast and braids of thew	28	16	5
Dream			
I had a dream a wondrous thing	4		1
But we dream we are rooted in earth dust	28	11	5
To dream I cared so much for thee	118		6
Dreamd			
Fair but of fairness as a vision dreamd	80		1

Word	Poem	Stan.	Line
I dreamd my counterpart it seemd	81		86
Dreamed			
Was deemed dreamed who	60		28
Upon you dreamed	81		85
Dreams			
Mounts then to alight disarming no one dreams	49		13
Touched from heaven in sweet dreams	78		126
That fleeted else like day-dissolved dreams	157		11
Dreamy			
The skill of dreamy Claude and Titians mellow gloom	1	10	9
Drear			
Down-splinterd rocks crushd cottages drear sight	1	14	5
Drenchd			
Lingerd then raised the washing waves and drenchd	2		138
Has drenchd the molten sunset hour	78		94
Drenched			
The drenched hair of slabby weeds that swung	2		113
Dress			
Dress hoar-hallowed shrines unvisited	40		91
Dress his days to a dexterous and starlight order	47		20
You folded did you not your dress	81		81
He shall have summer sweets and dress	124		5
Dressed			
She was dressed in silk attire	131		3
Drest			
But through black branches rarely drest	3		20
Drew			
In starry water-meads they drew	10		17
But the combs of a smother of sand night drew her	28	14	3
But what drew shepherd Richard from his downs	107	2	1
And each drew bluebells up and for relief	107	3	17
Stepped from the stool drew back from the barrow of dark Maenefa the mountain	137		4
Drift			
Fast but mined with a motion a drift	28	4	3
Meal-drift moulded ever and melted across skies	37		4
An our days Gods own Galahad though this childs drift	47		40
To drift in air the circled earth	78		69
Drifted			
And thickend like that drifted bloom the flock	2		99
Drifting			
Of something drifting thro delighted air	2		28

Word	Poem	Stan.	Line
Drilled			
The shapen flags and drilled holes of sky	12	2	11
Drink			
Who would drink water from a stony rock	5		20
Strike timbrels sing eat drink be full of mirth	5		43
My more than meat and drink	60		11
That I may drink that ecstacy	78		141
Drinks			
Her glass drinks light she darkles down behind	151		9
Dripping			
One bound oer dripping gold a turquoise-gemmd	2		60
Driven			
The dense and the driven passion and frightful sweat	28	7	5
Because the music from his bill forth-driven	113		3
Drives			
Doffs all drives full for righteousness	41		55
Which drives the stony air to utterance	122		18
Driving			
The driving storm at hour of vespers beat	1	13	3
Of driving vermeil-rain and as he lists	2		91
Drizzle			
Came midst the drizzle telling how last night	1	14	2
Drond			
Louder the monks drond out Gregorians slow	1	13	6
Droop			
Slim-pointed sea-gull plumes and droop behind	2		80
Yet both droop deadly sometimes in their cells	39		7
They seem to press and droop and stare	135		20
Droopd			
He where the crownals droopd himself reviled	1	10	7
Droopd oer the brows like Hectors casque and swayd	2		42
Drooping			
Grains from his drooping head	7		13
Ruck and wrinkle drooping dying deaths worst winding sheets tombs and worms and tumbling to decay	58		12
Drop			
And bid to catch him ere the drop of day	20		2
Why hear him hear him babble and drop down to his nest	39		10
When drop-of-blood-and-foam dapple	42		37
A drop of shade rolls over field and flock	98	3	2
Shape on the under side and size and drop	111		7
But down drop if it says stop	138		37

Word	Poem	Stan.	Line
Drop-of-blood-and-foam-dapple			
When drop-of-blood-and-foam-dapple	42		37
Droppd			
But droppd its coil of woes Arthurs Britain	102	2	7
Dropped			
Dropped eyes and dared not look	54		32
Dropping			
He hides our corpses dropping by the way	5		5
Drops			
The languent smooth with dimpling drops and flash	2		103
And from dank feathers wring the drops	3		8
Drops out and all our day is done	3		32
Grapes grew and drops of wine were shed	7		5
These drops which be they stars or dew	10		18
In the first signals of the several drops	84		3
When the wind drops you hear the skylarks sing	98	3	5
He drops his bright roots in the waterd sward	100		2
Drops the fruit out the duct runs dry or breaks	101		10
That piece themselves into a race of drops	102	1	36
They watched the brush of the swift stringy drops	107	3	13
He drops upon the wind again	130		13
I can scour thee fresh burnish thee sheathe thee in thy dark lair these drops	152		46
He drops towards the river unseen	159		15
Drouth			
He hath abolished the old drouth	8		1
Drove			
Some diving merrily downward drove and gleamd	2		108
She drove in the dark to leeward	28	14	1
Or drove with a divers dip	54		20
Drowned			
The goal was a shoal of a fourth the doom to be drowned	29	12	6
Crushed them or water and drawned them or rolled	29	17	3
Drowned and among our shoals	29	34	2
Kept to her care-drowned and wrapped in	41		45
Drowned o pity and indignation manshape that shone	72		13
Drowning			
It rounds and rounds despair to drowning	56		8
Drowsy			
Glazed water vaulted oer a drowsy stone	98	39	1
Drudgery			
This in drudgery day-labouring-out lifes age	39		4

Word	Poem	Stan.	Line
Drum			
Fang or flood goes death on drum	28	11	3
Heaved drum on drum but hands also	145		6
Heaved drum on drum but hands also	145		6
Dry			
Those whose dry plot for moisture gapes	6		11
The rivn vine leafless lifeless dry	6		22
And rivers run where all was dry	8		2
Dispel the doubt and dry the tear	23		46
Dry were her sad eyes that would fain have streamd	80		2
Of nerve the clammy ball was dry	81		98
Drops the fruit out the duct runs dry or breaks	101		10
Like Pharohs ears of windy harvest dry	117		6
Dry up the blue and be not slaked thereby	117		7
My root is dry	127		4
And down the furrow dry	138		27
This dry dean now no longer dry nor dumb but moist and musical	152		117
This dry dean now no longer dry nor dumb but moist and musical	152		117
Duct			
As water moulded to the duct it runs in	101		4
Drops the fruit out the duct runs dry or breaks	101		10
Due			
Dated due to season	42		4
Alas I rave where calm is due	81		70
Dugged			
The down-dugged ground-hugged grey	28	26	2
Dull			
It seems for grandeur barren left and dull	1	15	8
As a dare-gale skylark scanted in a dull cage	39		1
Selfyeast of spirit a dull dough sours I see	67		12
This by despair bred hangdog dull by rage	70		19
Duly			
Duly dear Lord my prize is won	81		109
With centres duly touchd and nestlike spots	107	4	7
Dumb			
Where the green swell is in the havens dumb	9		7
Shape nothing lips be lovely-dumb	22		5
And cleaves I struggle and am dumb	81	7	28
Yea crushd my heart and made me dumb	118		12
And I must take your amends cry pardon and then be dumb	128		20
This dry dean now no longer dry nor dumb but moist and musical	152		117
Duomo			
And all into the Duomo ran	81		88
Durance			
Durance deal with that steep or deep here	65		10

Word	Poem	Stan.	Line
creep	65		10
During			
During the eastering of untainted morns	84		1
Dusk			
Were veind and streakd with dusk-deep lazuli	2		46
To know the dusk depths of the ponderous sea	2		122
And gaind thro growing dusk the stirless bay	2		141
Tingling between dusk and silver	98	1	4
Dusk-deep			
Were veind and streakd with dusk-deep lazuli	2		46
Dust			
Dimmd in the long accumulated dust	1	12	6
But we dream we are rooted in earth dust	28	11	5
To mans last dust drain fast towards mans first slime	35		14
Squandering ooze to squeezed dough crust dust stanches starches	72		7
Your footing now to the much-dreaded dust	107	3	2
Duty			
In mankinds medley a duty-swerver	41		53
Is strung by duty is strained to beauty	41		77
Felix Randal the farrier o is he dead then my duty all ended	52		1
Immortal beauty is death with duty	156		18
Duty-swerver			
In mankinds medley a duty-swerver	41		53
Dwarf			
There was a wood of dwarf and soured oaks	125		2
Dwarfs			
A freezing runnel sobs and dwarfs	81	3	7
Dwellest			
And where thou swellest in deep-groved Aidenn	26		23
Dwells			
I knew not why but know that sadness dwells	2		118
Mans mounting spirit in his bone-house mean house dwells	39		2
Deals out that being indoors each one dwells	56		6
Dwelt			
And a sweet sadness dwelt on everyone	2		117
Which Wordsworth would have dwelt on about the place	107	4	16
Dwindled			
Dwindled to infancy	60		19
The moon dwindled and thinned to the fringe of a fingernail held to the candle	137		2
Dwindles			
And as she dwindles shreds her smock of gold	103		13
Dwindling			
As the fine morsels of a dwindling cloud	102	1	35
Dye			
Or tender pinks with bloody tyrian dye	2		47

Word	Poem	Stan.	Line
Dye (cont.)			
Barterd for an azure dye	86		3
Dying			
Ruck and wrinkle drooping dying deaths worst winding sheets tombs and worms and tumbling to decay	58		12
Dyphwys			
Whats yonder grizzled dyphwys dim	30	1	9
Eager			
But then I make an eager shift to see	81	6	5
Eagerer			
Of answer the eagerer a-wanting Jessy or Jack	46		7
Eagles			
Must see the eagles bulk renderd in mists	88		3
Ear			
And beat upon my whorled ear	22		2
The ear it strikes like lightnings to hear him sing	33		5
On ear and ear two noises too old to end	35		1
On ear and ear two noises too old to end	35		1
Of own of abrupt self there so thrusts on so throngs the ear	45		8
Who say that angels in your ear	81		122
Thick-fleeced bushes like a heifers ear	98	11	1
Out-fleeced bushes like a spaniels ear	98	11	2
Rather to ear than eye shews where they stray	112		4
With ear-caressing speech where is the tongue	122		17
Firm accents strike her fine and scrolled ear	136		21
The ear in milk lush the sash	138		20
Cuckoo bird and open ear wells heart-springs delightfully sweet	146		2
Ear-caressing			
With ear-caressing speech where is the tongue	122		17
Eared			
The dapple-eared lily below thee that country and town did	44		3
Earlier			
Autumn-time no earlier came	4		26
Months earlier since I had our sweet reprieve and ransom	53		7
As Devonshire letters earlier in the year	119		1
What being in rank-old nature should earlier have that breath been	141		1
Earlier or you fail at our force and lie	153		3
Earliest			
Waste her earliest stars earlstars stars principal overbend us	61		4

Word	Poem	Stan.	Line
The place in the east with earliest milky morn	98	30	5
Earlstars			
Waste her earliest stars earlstars stars principal overbend us	61		4
Early			
And wisdom is early to despair	58		8
Them beauty-in-the-ghost deliver it early now long before death	59		18
Or ever the early stirrings of skylark	98	28	1
That early sperses and high hangs the day	98	31	6
Earnest			
Earnest earthless equal attuneable vaulty voluminous stupendous	61		1
And grave past girlhood earnest in her eyes	136		20
The earnest-hearted maiden sat and heard	136		32
In bloody letters lessons of earnest of revenge	152		35
Monuments of my earnest records of my revenge	152		36
Your feast of that most in you earnest eye	157		29
Earnest-hearted			
The earnest-hearted maiden sat and heard	136		32
Ears			
Ears and the call of the tall nun	28	19	7
Then let the march tread our ears	51		9
Stir in my ears speak there	60		121
Backward are laid her pretty black-fleeced ears	99		13
Then often the ears in a new fashion hark	113		7
And seven ears crown the lodged corn	114		6
Like Pharohs ears of windy harvest dry	117		6
Or deaf ears shall desire that lipmusic thats lost upon them	152		110
Earth			
Eighth wonder of the earth in size in store	1	15	5
But earth has never felt the snow	3		2
Spread oer the swart face of this prodigal earth	5		45
In forty days reachd heaven from earth	6		24
My heaven is brass and iron my earth	18		9
We see the glories of the earth	23		7
Empty though it be on earth	24		8
Earth throws winters robes away	24		17
And like the storm-months smote the earth	26		29
But we dream we are rooted in earth dust	28	11	5
Surf snow river and earth	28	21	4
Heaven and earth are word of worded by	28	28	6
And hurles for him o half hurls earth for him off under his feet	37		14
Crouch lay knee by earth low under	40		109
This ecstasy all through mothering earth	41		45

Word	Poem	Stan.	Line
Earth (cont.)			
Earth sweet earth sweet landscape with leaves throng	58		1
Earth sweet earth sweet landscape with leaves throng	58		1
Earth brows of such care care and dear concern	58		14
Earth is the fairer for	60		93
Fire-featuring heaven for earth her being has unbound her dapple is at an end	61		5
Delightfully the bright wind boisterous ropes wrestles beats earth bare	72		5
Earth hears no hurtle then from fiercest fray	73		8
Earth all out who with trickling increment	73		10
Right offspring of your grimy mother earth	78		2
And that grief masters joy on earth	78		55
To whom the common earth and air	78		59
To drift in air the circled earth	78		69
Mix oer the not unmoved earth	78		130
And a grey heaven does the hushd earth house	105		7
The earth and heaven so little known	130		1
Of greenery and old earth gropes for grasps at steep	149	2	6
Hideous dashed down leaving earth a winter withering	152		84
Like the thing that never knew the earth never off roots	159		27
Upon this only gambolling and echoing-of-earth note	159		45
Earthless			
Earnest earthless equal attuneable vaulty voluminous stupendous	61		1
Earthless dews on ancles sleek	78		16
Earths			
It was made of earths mould but it went from mens eyes	27		3
A strain of the earths sweet being in the beginning	33		10
Have lost that cheer and charm of earths past prime	35		12
And what is earths eye tongue or heart else where	58		9
Tall suns tingeing or treacherous the tainting of the earths air	59		5
Of earths glory earths ease all no one nowhere	70		16
Of earths glory earths ease all no one nowhere	70		16
Of greenery it is old earths groping towards the steep	149	1	10

Word	Poem	Stan.	Line
Earthworld			
Are earthworld airworld waterworld thorough hurled all by turn and turn about	159		18
Ease			
Give myrrhy-threaded golden folds of ease	11		12
Times tasking it is fathers that asking for ease	28	26	11
Tom heart-at-ease Tom Navvy he is all for his meal	70		4
Of earths glory earths ease all no one nowhere	70		16
Yet leaves him in ungirdled ease	83		15
O lovely ease in change of place	130		27
Easeful			
Bear him to heaven on easeful wings	7		15
Easily			
The heart guesses easily is it the same	27		21
This was the prized the desirable sight unsought presented so easily	137		6
East			
But these were found in the east and south	10		13
To crosses meant for Jesus you whom the east	11		5
A crimson east that bids for rain	21		8
The place in the east with earliest milky morn	98	30	5
Dawn that the pebbly low-down east	98	31	1
Dawn that low-down pebbly east	98	31	4
Than we in the east dare look for buds disclose	119		2
And justify the east and west	130		4
Easter			
On Easter morn the tree was forth	6		23
Breathe Easter now you serged fellowships	11		7
Know ye this is Easter day	24		6
Know ye not tis Easter morn	24		12
Decks herself for Easter day	24		18
Let in joy this Easter day	24		24
Make each morn an Easter day	24		30
Let him Easter in us be a dayspring to the dimness of us be a crimson-cressetedeast	28	34	5
Eastering			
During the Eastering of untainted morns	84		1
Eastern			
Twice lovely tinted eastern turned Greek	136		15
Eastnortheast			
Sitting eastnortheast in cursed quarter the wind	28	13	6
Eastward			
Oh morning at the brown brink eastward springs	31	1	12

Word	Poem	Stan.	Line
Eastwards			
And bright iconium eastwards reach my rhymes	136		6
Easy			
From easy runnels the rich-pieced land	5		39
The easy burden of yore	5		54
Lodge his eyes fast but yet as easy and light	102	1	21
Eat			
Strike timbrels sing eat drink be full of mirth	5		43
But I must yield the chase or rest and eat	20		11
Unpalateable fruits to eat	81		167
Eaten			
The lawless honey eaten of old	92		4
Eaves			
Now coming from the alien eaves	81		3
To alien eaves you fled and went	81		5
Ebb			
Waylay her at ebb past Penmaen pool	30	1	24
Ebbd			
Ebbd back beneath its snowy lids unseen	2		18
Echod			
Then passd the wind and sobbd with mountain-echod woe	1	13	9
Echoing			
Through the echoing timber does so rinse and wring	33		4
Cuckoo-echoing bell-swarmed lark-charmed rook-racked river-rounded	44		2
Have here a true one echoing the sound	116		2
Upon this only gambolling and echoing-of-earth note	159		45
Echoing-of-earth			
Upon this only gambolling and echoing-of-earth note	159		45
Eclipse			
By interchange gaspd splendour and eclipse	2		22
Eclipsing			
Eclipsing parapet yet above the wall	12	2	7
Ecstacy			
That I may drink that ecstacy	78		141
Late I fell in the ecstacy	93	1	1
Ecstasy			
In his ecstasy then off off forth on swing	36		4
This ecstasy all through mothering earth	42		45
Keeps a kind of joy in it a zest an edge an ecstasy	152		91
Ed			
The Christ-ed beauty of her mind	145		15
Eddies			
In eddies of the wind he went	87		5

Word	Poem	Stan.	Line
Eddy			
The motes in ceaseless eddy shine and fall	1	12	4
Eden			
In Eden garden have get before it cloy	33		11
Edge			
And lapped in shining hair roll to the banks edge then	152		50
Keeps a kind of joy in it a zest an edge an ecstasy	152		91
Edged			
Phrenzy but edged and clear of brain	81		52
Edges			
Their clouds with breathing edges white	130		23
Effectual			
Or had been effectual to have sown with notes	122		12
Eggs			
Thrushs eggs look little low heavens and thrush	33		3
All over as a bevy of eggs the mothering wing	34		6
Cluster of bugle blue eggs thin	42		21
Egypt			
Egypt the valley of our pleasance there	5		25
Egyptian			
He slew the Egyptian yesterday to-day	5		3
Your parched nostrils snuff Egyptian air	5		27
My national old Egyptian reed gave way	20		7
Eighth			
Eighth wonder of the earth in size in store	1	15	5
El			
Exiled most remote El Khor	81		47
Elbow			
He leans to it Harry bends look back elbow and liquid waist	71		12
Elder			
How lovely the elder brothers	54		1
Ran revel in the elder boy	54		9
Eldering			
Never-eldering revel and river of youth	28	18	7
Elected			
Elected silence sing to me	22		1
Electric			
Came equipped deadly-electric	41		23
Electrical			
Not danger electrical horror then further it finds	28	26	13
Element			
And nursing element	60		10
I can stand pent in the monstrous element	81	5	3
The penetrative element	81		132
At last up the blue element	87		6

Word	Poem	Stan.	Line
Element (cont.)			
And slender element to piece and plot	102	3	25
Flinty kindcold element let break across his limbs	159		41
Elemented			
So strangely elemented is my minds weather	102	1	15
Elements			
Piecing the elements out by plan and plot	102	3	18
The slender elements to piece and plot	102	3	26
By heady elements for no man knows	103		5
Eleven			
Some asleep unawakened all unwarned eleven fathoms fallen	41		3
Elim			
Behold at Elim wells on every hand	5		23
Elm			
Down roughcast down dazzling whitewash wherever an elm arches	72		3
The vexd elm-heads are pale with the view	79		1
Elm-heads			
The vexd elm-heads are pale with the view	79		1
Elms			
Breathe in such ether or the quickly elms	100		7
Elmy			
And not from purple Wales only nor from elmy England	152		124
Eloquent			
Which only makes you eloquent	22		8
Else			
Else I am well assured I should offend	14	3	5
They were else-minded then altogether the men	28	25	5
In mould or mind or what not else makes rare	40		6
Nothing else is like it no not all so strains	48		29
And what is earths eye tongue or heart else where	58		9
Else but in dear and dogged man ah the heir	58		10
How then should Gregory a father have gleaned else from swarmed Rome but God to a nation dealt that days dear chance	62		6
Or this or else I do not love	81		114
Or else their cooings came from bays of trees	98	2	1
Too late or else much much too soon	105		16
While all things else may stir and range	130		7
All else may whirl or dive or fly	130		8
Or what is else there is your world within	150		9
Or else a funeral and yet tis not a funeral	152		25
That fleeted else like day-dissolved dreams	157		11
Else-minded			
They were else-minded then altogether the men	28	25	5

Word	Poem	Stan.	Line
Elsewhere			
Nor elsewhere can thy sweetness unendear	12	1	5
Somewhere elsewhere there is ah well where one	59		6
Elsewhere leave comfort root-room let joy size	69		11
Elves			
Down in dim woods the diamond delves the elves-eyes	32	1	4
Embers			
Shine and blue-bleak embers ah my dear	36		12
As wrecks of mined embers will	92		13
Emblem			
Upraisd an emblem of that fiery constancy	1	3	8
Embraced			
As a self-embraced sweet thought	85		3
Eminent			
Stood capital eminent gonfalon bearer	98	28	5
Empire			
The airy empire at his will	78		78
Employment			
And hold at Christs employment	48		14
Empty			
Yet like a lighted empty hall	23		10
Empty though it be on earth	24		8
Enclusterd			
The glaucus clepted others small braids enclusterd	2		68
Encounter			
Once encounter in here coped and poised powers	44		4
Encrimsoning			
Where the eye fixd fled the encrimsoning spot	2		9
End			
The end	2		144
You see that I have come to passions end	14	3	1
With a ropes end round the man handy and brave	28	16	3
On ear and ear two noises too old to end	35		1
What most I may eye after be in at the end	40		10
To mend her we end her	43		17
Your round me roaming end and under be my boughs	51		2
Fire-featuring heaven for earth her being has unbound her dapple is at an end	61		5
With our evening is over us our night whelms whelms and will end us	61		8
Life death does end and each day dies with sleep	65		12
Disappointment all I endeavour end	75	1	3
His locks like all a ravel-ropes-end	144		5

Word	Poem	Stan.	Line
End (cont.)			
Spend me or end me what God shall send me	156		13
Endears			
This seeing the sick endears them to us too it endears	53		9
This seeing the sick endears them to us too it endears	53		9
I plead familiarness endears	81		26
Endeavour			
Disappointment all I endeavour end	75	1	3
Ended			
Felix Randal the farrier o is he dead then my duty all ended	53		1
And these are spent and ended quite	130		21
Ending			
That sweets sweeter ending	48		31
Ending in sweet uncertainty	78		121
The bluebells up whose crystal-ending rods in their natural sods	112		8
Endless			
An endless round of deadning solitude	1	14	6
Endlessly			
Alive or dead my girl is carried in it endlessly	152		27
Endragoned			
Burden in winds burly and beat of endragoned seas	28	26	16
Ends			
Which ends those only strains that I approve	19		10
Summer ends now now barbarous in beauty the stooks rise	38		1
The ends of the crisp buds she chips	98	14	1
Endured			
Idle for ever to waft her or wind her with these she endured	28	14	8
Enduring			
A thing that weeps enduring long	81		50
Enemy			
Wert thou my enemy o thou my friend	75	1	4
Enforced			
The heaven-enforced answer comes	81		144
Engaged			
Or thorn-engaged impaled and pent	81		19
Engemming			
With flowing tracery engemming rays	1	6	2
Engenderd			
Come out of space or suddenly engenderd	103		4
England			
A beetling baldbright cloud thorough England	41		24
England whose honour o all my heart woos wife	66	1	5
How Shakespeares England weds with Dantes Italy	98	35	2

Word	Poem	Stan.	Line
And not from purple Wales only nor from Elmy England	152		124
Englands			
Call me Englands fames fond lover	156		11
English			
Our king back oh upon English souls	28	34	4
Mother to an English sire he	48		3
Then will you wed with an English lady	109	8	3
And art thou come from English land	109	31	3
I am not come from English land	109	32	1
Enjewelling			
Crushes and tears the rare enjewelling	2		85
Enjoy			
And did the children of his brains enjoy	97		3
Enjoyment			
This pride of primes enjoyment	49		12
Enormous			
Both are in an unfathomable all is in an enormous dark	72		12
The smouldering enormous winter welkin may	149	1	8
The smouldering enormous winter welkin eye	149	2	3
Enough			
The boughs the boughs are bare enough	3		1
What country is honour enough in all us lordly head	70		10
But vastness blurs and time beats level enough the resurrection	72		16
Mercy is left enough for one	81		105
Not win if this be not enough	83		26
Has wit enough but less than female tact	94		19
Some are pretty enough and some are poor indeed	98	15	4
And if it is why there is cause enough	125		59
Enough corruption was the worlds first woe	157		33
Enough now since the sacred matter that I mean	159		43
Enriched			
Enriched posts are chamferd everywhere	96	7	3
Enrolld			
Enrolld and sexing with our ruder files	102	1	67
Enrolld and sexed with our ruder files	102	1	68
Entangled			
A cusp still clasped him a fluke yet fanged him entangled him not quit utterly	137		5
Enter			
You have your wish enter these walls one said	20		17
Entering			
Comforting smell breathed at very entering	34		3
Entrance			
Above it cannot entrance win	18		6

Word	Poem	Stan.	Line
Entrancingly			
Clustering entrancingly in Beryl lakes	2		14
Envied			
Stretches the envied fruit with fatal smile	1	11	2
Epistles			
Epistles while the running pastoral bleats	107	4	22
Equal			
The cloisters crossd with equal courts betwixt	1	4	2
With not her either beautys equal or	50		2
Earnest earthless equal attuneable vaulty voluminous stupendous	61		1
Equipped			
Came equipped deadly-electric	41		23
Ere			
I mark the flowers ere the prime	4		14
Ere I had further question made	4		16
With free long looking ere I die	15		44
Which should ere now have led my feet to the field	17		9
And bid to catch him ere the drop of day	20		2
The spirit hovered ere the sun	23		22
But sleep again ere day be born	78		24
You may depend that ere a week was fled	97		5
Ere you set sail the king was dead	109	9	3
Erin			
But from beyond seas Erin France and Flanders everywhere	152		125
Erst			
As erst upon chaotic floods	23		21
Esaus			
I can send up an Esaus cry	81		126
Escape			
And barely to escape the curse	81		170
Escorial			
Unmindful of their grace the Escorial	1	8	5
Especial			
The sweet especial scene	43		22
Sweet especial rural scene	43		24
To me so arch-especial a spirit as heaves in Henry Purcell	45		2
Espial			
Fear hindrance and espial	110		3
Essence			
The essence neer forgot the fold	81		82
Estates			
Lay open thine estates	115		7
Esteemd			
And I esteemd the sandal good	81		83
Etc			
And your two etc	101		12

Word	Poem	Stan.	Line
Eternal			
Ill wait till morn eternal breaks	23		54
Prayer shall fetch pity eternal	41		119
A beacon an eternal beam flesh fade and mortal trash	72		19
The immortals of the eternal ring	145		30
Ether			
Breathe in such ether or the quickly elms	100		7
Eucharist			
That left to the Lord of the Eucharist I here lie by	48		44
Eunuch			
Times eunuch and not breed one work that wakes	75	1	12
Eurydice			
The Eurydice it concerned thee o Lord	40		1
Eve			
Him morning noon and eve	60		62
I walk towards eve our walks again	81		54
Even			
But even our Saviours and our blood	6		32
Oh even for the weakness of the plea	13		8
That less is heavens higher even yet	14	1	12
Even your unpassiond eyelids might be wet	14	1	14
Even than this my thankless lore	15		22
Not vault them the million of rounds of thy mercy not reeve even them in	28	12	8
Then even in weariest wintry hour	30	1	29
It is even seen times something server	41		52
Where we even where we mean	43		16
Of us we do bid God bend to him even so	68		11
In whose dead lake even a voice may make	81	4	3
With loops of veins not of an even pink	93	2	4
Weeping even now I curse myself remembering	102	1	44
Even to the tillage of the sweetest spot	102	3	16
Even so my thought the rose and grey disposes	108		7
News from belleisle even such a sweetness blows	119		6
Next after sweet success I am not left even this	152		92
Not now to name even	152		130
Evening			
It seemd an evening in the spring	4		2
Love it is evening now and thou away	20		4
In tufts of evening sky so soon	25		22
There evening noon and morn	60		64
Evening strains to be times vast womb-of-all home-of-all hearse-of-all night	61		2
With our evening is over us our night whelms whelms and will end us	61		8

Word	Poem	Stan.	Line
Evening (cont.)			
Like flame they gather on our cliffs at evening	104		7
Event			
Those years and years by of world without event	73		13
Ever			
The richest gift St Lawrence ever bore	1	2	6
Must you be gorged with proof did ever sand	5		41
And the ever-fretting shirt of punishment	11		11
No influential heaven ever wore	14	2	7
O father not under thy feathers nor ever as guessing	28	12	5
Idle for ever to waft her or wind her with these she endured	28	14	8
The treasure never eyesight got nor was ever guessed what for the hearing	28	26	8
And ever if bound here hardest home	30	1	33
Meal-drift moulded ever and melted across skies	38		4
And looks love ever in a lad	48		35
When will you ever peace wild wooddove shy wings shut	51		1
Fast you ever fast bind	52		8
Tendered to him ah well God rest him all road ever he offended	53		8
Ever so black on it our tale o our oracle let life waned ah let life wind	61		10
And there for ever grovel	78		7
Or ever the early stirrings of skylark	98	28	1
That bead the plain did ever havering church-tower	100		6
As ever I remember in my life	102	1	13
Or ever he set his foot to the land	109	7	1
To him who ever thought with love of me	140		1
Or ever did for my sake some good deed	140		2
Lord now curb him for ever o daring o deep insight	152		73
Ever-fretting			
And the ever-fretting shirt of punishment	11		11
Everlasting			
Be ye lift up ye everlasting doors	115		9
Everlastingness			
To its own best being and its loveliness of youth it is an everlastingness of o it is an all youth	59		13
Evermore			
To deck and make most lordly evermore	1	2	9
Every			
Showerd the cliffs and every fret and spire	2		25
He feeds me with his manna every day	5		13
Behold at Elim wells on every hand	5		23

Word	Poem	Stan.	Line
All mine yet common to my every peer	12	1	8
And every praised sequence of sweet strings	19		7
Every inch a tar	41		74
See not a hair is not an eyelash not the least lash lost every hair	59		20
In every least things life	60		8
My meal at every wink	60		12
When every colour glows	60		84
Heaven and every field are still	85		2
Spannd with shadow every one	98	8	3
And every heart think loathingly	114		15
I am the midst of every zone	130		3
And every saint of bloody hour	145		44
Be at every assault fresh foiled worse flung deeper disappointed	152		89
Towards my brother every other	155		23
Everyone			
And a sweet sadness dwelt on everyone	2		117
In his heart said everyone	109	15	3
Everything			
Growth in everything	42		16
Where whatevers prized and passes of us everything thats fresh and fast flying of us seems to us sweet of us and swiftly away with done away with undone	59		8
Blessed be everything	135		16
Everywhere			
From too much fragrance everywhere	4		4
Now he gasps now he gazes everywhere	41		65
Nestling me everywhere	60		2
Enriched posts are chamferd everywhere	96	7	3
Discoverd everywhere	98	24	3
Nor night is blown with flame-rings everywhere	99		18
But from beyond seas Erin France and Flanders everywhere	152		125
Evil			
At hopes so evil-heavend as mine are	14	2	14
O unteachably after evil but uttering truth	28	18	5
My evil words thorny with pain	81		27
Evil-heavend			
At hopes so evil-heavend as mine are	14	2	14
Evils			
Age and ages evils hoar hair	59		11
Ewe			
There was no bleat of ewe no chime of wether	107	1	5
Except			
Except for sin	127		7
Excess			
At once perceived with excess	118		10

Word	Poem	Stan.	Line
Exhibition			
Bid your papa goodnight sweet exhibition	97		8
Exile			
This outer cold my exile from of old	81	1	3
Exiled			
Exiled most remote El Khor	81		47
Explanation			
Now yields you with some sighs our explanation	77		14
Exploit			
Honour is flashed off exploit so we say	73		1
Express			
And scarlet wear the spirit of war there express	63		8
Expressed			
Nor mouth had no nor mind expressed	55		12
Expressionless			
Shall see the azure turn expressionless	117		4
Exquisite			
Are you turned for an exquisite smart	28	18	2
Some good and so he does leave patience exquisite	50		8
Lit with exquisite tints seven	78		109
Extremes			
Her Perseus linger and leave her to her extremes	50		9
Extremity			
He was to cure the extremity where he had cast her	28	27	6
Exultation			
To remember and exultation	42		47
Eye			
Of finishd diapers that fills the eye	1	6	6
Changd to a flower and there with placid eye	1	11	8
Where the eye fixd fled the encrimsoning spot	2		9
A quivering pennon then for eye too keen	2		17
The one peculiar of their pleasured eye	12	2	13
Eye-greeting doves bright-counter to the rook	16		3
There was single eye	28	28	2
What most I may eye after be in at the end	40		10
But his eye no cliff no coast or	41		66
But a prick will make no eye at all	43		15
Have an eye to the sakes of him quaint moonmarks to his pelted plumage under	45		10
Or to-fro tender trambeams truckle at the eye	46		4
Eye all in fellowship	49		4
Acts in Gods eye what in Gods eye he is	57		11
Acts in Gods eye what in Gods eye he is	57		11
And what is earths eye tongue or heart			

Word	Poem	Stan.	Line
elsewhere	58		9
Fronting my froward eye	60		119
Mark you how the peacocks eye	86		1
Which yet is in the eye or in the thought	91		9
Her nostril glistens and her wet black eye	99		5
Beyond and one within the lookers eye	102	3	6
Rather to ear than eye shews where they stray	112		4
Which makes us eye-attentive to the eye	125		42
Which makes us eye-attentive to the eye	125		42
My all-accepting fixed eye	130		6
Where shake shadow is suns-eye-ringed	138		42
The smouldering enormous winter welkin eye	149	2	3
O I admire and sorrow the hearts eye grieves	157		1
Your feast of that most in you earnest eye	157		29
Eye-attentive			
Which makes us eye-attentive to the eye	125		42
Eye-greeting			
Eye-greeting doves bright-counter to the rook	16		3
Eyed			
With bubbles bugle-eyed struggle and stick	2		95
Star-eyed strawberry-breasted	42		19
I came where called and eyed him	54		14
Eyelash			
See not a hair is not an eyelash not the least lash lost every hair	59		20
That each eyelash or hair	60		3
Eyelid			
Parted me leaf and leaf divided me eyelid and eyelid of slumber	137		7
Parted me leaf and leaf divided me eyelid and eyelid of slumber	137		7
Eyelids			
Even your unpassioned eyelids might be wet	14	1	14
Eyes			
And planets bud whereer we turn our mazed eyes	2		33
By other eyes and other suitors move	12	1	12
With fiercer weepings of these desperate eyes	14	3	6
Be shelled eyes with double dark	22		9
Flowers do ope their heavenward eyes	24		15
My eyes hold yet the rinds and bright	25		33
With eyes that smile thro the tears of the hours	26		14
The gladdest thing that our eyes have seen	26		18
It was made of earths mould but it went from mens eyes	27		3
Down in dim woods the diamond delves the			

Word	Poem	Stan.	Line
Eyes (cont.)			
elves-eyes	32	1	4
I walk I lift up I lift up heart eyes	38		5
And eyes heart what looks what lips yet gave you a	38		7
That interests our eyes and who goes there	40		2
There eyes them heart wants care haunts foot follows kind	40		13
Dropped eyes and dared not look	54		32
Lovely in limbs and lovely in eyes not his	57		13
With darksome devouring eyes my bruised bones and fan	64		7
Purple eyes and seas of liquid leaves all day	68		8
Eyes in their dark can day or thirst can find	69		7
By a grey eyes heed steered well one crew fall to	71		5
Whose ken through amber of dark eyes	78		51
Dry were her sad eyes that would fain have streamd	80		2
With hope with shut eyes fixedly	81	7	51
She schools the flighty pupils of her eyes	82		1
And cannot see at all with others eyes	94		26
Were eyes of central primrose bluebells ran	98	10	2
Ply fold on fold across his dangerous eyes	102	1	20
Lodge his eyes fast but yet as easy and light	102	1	21
They have held his eyes with blindfold bands	109	13	1
Her barred fingers claspd upon her eyes	111		6
When eyes that cast about in heights of heaven	113		1
And my blue eyes again for me	120		23
Nor locks nor eyes shall win again	120		25
I betterd all our path with sanguine eyes	125		17
That make my eyes sore and cross-colour things	125		46
And grave past girlhood earnest in her eyes	136		20
Heaven turned its starlight eyes below	145		46
Not of all my eyes see wandering on the world	149	1	1
And turns to wash it from her welling eyes	151		5
Her eyes oh and her eyes	152		53
Her eyes oh and her eyes	152		53
In all her body I say no place was like her eyes	152		56
No piece matched those eyes kept most part much cast down	152		57
While blind mens eyes shall thirst after daylight draughts of daylight	152		109
Eyesight			
The treasure never eyesight got nor was			

Word	Poem	Stan.	Line
ever guessed what for the hearing	28	26	8
Ezekiels			
Shewn to Ezekiels opend sight	78		48
Fabian			
She markd where I and Fabian met	120		1
For Fabian that suspects her not	120		4
Fable			
And here the faithful waver the faithless fable and miss	28	6	8
Fabled			
Near by is Pauls free Tarsus fabled where	136		7
Fabling			
Bellisle that is a fabling name but we	116		1
Face			
Of colour in high casements face to face	1	6	3
Of colour in high casements face to face	1	6	3
Spread oer the swart face of this prodigal earth	5		45
With light on her face like the waves at play	26		4
The frown of his face	28	3	1
That lace the face of Penmaen pool	30	1	28
Mannerly-hearted more than handsome face	47		9
Of us the wimpled-water-dimpled not-by-morning-matched face	59		10
Worlds loveliest mens selves self flashes off frame and face	62		9
They swathe and lace the shroud-plaits oer my face	81	5	6
Her face was such as being diapered	93	2	3
I must not turn the lantern on his face	102	1	25
Since on the face it is unsafe to look	102	1	47
She loves his face she knows the spot	120		2
A something in her face of guile	120		10
And breath upon it that is her face is this	125		58
Yet Id not say it is her face alone	125		61
Faced			
White-faced as one in sad assay to fly	80		8
Faces			
Pure fasted faces draw unto this feast	11		1
To the father through the features of mens faces	57		14
These names these faces they are customary	125		51
And faces fit for leisure gaze	133		13
Fade			
A beacon an eternal beam flesh fade and mortal trash	72		19
Faded			
Rich Titians faded in the straying gleam	1	12	3
And James shall hate his faded red	114		11
Fading			
Come you indoors come home your fading fire	46		9

Word	Poem	Stan.	Line
Fagged			
O then weary then why should we tread o why are we so haggard at the heart so care-coiled care-killed so fagged so fashed so cogged so cumbered	59		26
O then weary then why should we tread o why are we so haggard at the heart so care-coiled care-killed so fagged so fashed so cogged so cumbered	59		26
Fail			
Where springs not fail	9		2
And fail or scatter all away	18		2
Does into amber splendours fail	78		100
I storm and shock you so I fail	81		73
That shall not fail in winter-time	124		8
Earlier or you fail at our force and lie	153		3
Not all but we were framed to fail and die	153		6
Faild			
Then faild the tongue the poor collapsing frame	1	3	3
Failing			
Was a rose or failing that	144		14
Fails			
My soul does loathe it and my spirit fails	5		14
Which praying fails to do away	18		12
Complete thy creature dear o where it fails	34		13
Failure			
For poor loves failure than his hopeless rise	14	3	7
Fain			
And fain in the springtime surcease would borrow	26		11
Forth Christ from cupboard fetched how fain I of feet	48		10
And fain will find as sterling all as all is smart	63		7
Dry were her sad eyes that would fain have streamd	80		2
And fain would follow I who led	81		172
Faint			
And faint as though to die	5		60
Closer because faint morning stirs	78		22
Fainter			
And fainter finer trickle far	78		81
Fair			
Fair relics too the changeful moor had left	1	8	1
Here in some darkend landscape Paris fair	1	11	1
Fair beds they seemd of water-lily flakes	2		13
Goshen is green and fair	5		30
I am so light I am so fair	10		2
I am so light and fair	25		2
For thou as she wert the one fair daughter	26		25
With richness the racing lambs too have fair			

Word	Poem	Stan.	Line
their fling	33		8
Have fair fallen o fair fair have fallen so dear	45		1
Have fair fallen o fair fair have fallen so dear	45		1
Have fair fallen o fair fair have fallen so dear	45		1
Nor can you long be what you now are called fair	59		6
It melts new lights arise as fair	78		118
Fair but of fairness as a vision dreamd	80		1
Boughs being pruned birds preened show more fair	96	7	1
And is so fair to see	109	20	4
And each as fair as he	109	21	4
Have told me I am fair to see	124		24
Are never known for fair	133		16
In one fair fall but for times aftercast	157		7
Fairer			
And boasting I have fairer things than these	2		86
Fairer than this one to brighten our day	26		8
Earth is the fairer for	60		93
The fairer waxed he	109	36	2
That has it and she is fairer than Colomb	125		43
Fairer these are the flaring shows unlovely	125		45
Fairly			
Snowflake thats fairly mixed	60		6
Fairness			
Fair but of fairness as a vision dreamd	80		1
Fairy			
In frank in fairy Penmaen pool	30	1	16
Underneath their glassy barrel of a fairy green	141		6
Into fairy trees wildflowers woodferns	159		50
Fairyland			
Fairyland silk beech scrolled ash-packed sycamore wild wychelm hornbeam fretty overstood	159		24
Faith			
The sculpturd image of such faith would be	1	3	7
A fortress of true faith and central stand	1	5	3
The pride of faith and home of sternest piety	1	8	9
Faithful			
A faithful guard of inner darkness fixd	1	4	7
And here the faithful waver the faithless fable and miss	28	6	8
Faithless			
And here the faithful waver the faithless fable and miss	28	6	8
Falcon			
I caught this morning mornings minion king-dom of daylights dauphin dapple-dawn-drawn			

Word	Poem	Stan.	Line
Falcon (cont.)			
falcon in his riding	36		1
Fall			
Of those gilt webs that languishd in a fall	1	8	7
The motes in ceaseless eddy shine and fall	1	12	4
Their fall was fuller of regret	4		30
The vigorous horizontals each way fall	12	2	3
Knowing them well I can but see the fall	16		10
Up till that mornings fall of dew	21		27
And it crowds and it combs to the fall	28	4	4
Joy fall to thee father Francis	28	23	1
To bathe in his fall-gold mercies to breathe in his all-fire glances	28	23	8
Of the yore-flood of the years fall	28	31	2
Feasts when we shall fall asleep	28	35	9
With a flood or a fall low lull-off or all roar	35		3
Fall gall themselves and gash gold-vermilion	36		13
Shares their best gifts surely fall how things will	48		4
For love he leans forth needs his neck must fall on kiss	63		12
O the mind mind has mountains cliffs of fall	65		7
By a grey eyes heed steered well one crew fall to	71		5
Fall to the residuary worm worlds wildfire leave but ash	72		20
Of it angels fall they are towers from heaven a story	76		3
The fall is oer told off the leaves	81		9
I fall I tear and shower the weed	81		64
And feeds new leaves upon the winds of fall	105		10
What have we seen her head sheared from her shoulders fall	152		49
While rushy rains shall fall or brooks shall fleet from fountains	152		107
If under her banner I fall for her honour	156		19
Under her banner we fall for her honour	156		20
In one fair fall but for times aftercast	157		7
Gaze on and fall directly forth on life	157		16
Fall-gold			
To bathe in his fall-gold mercies to breathe in his all-fire glances	28	23	8
Fallen			
Of foliage fallen in the copse	3		12
For the fallen rise and the stricken spring to thee	26		39
Some asleep unawakened all unwarned eleven fathoms fallen	41		3
Have fair fallen o fair fair have fallen so dear	45		1
Have fair fallen o fair fair have fallen so			

Word	Poem	Stan.	Line
dear	45		1
Fallers			
Fallers in dreadful frothpits waterfearers wild	152		112
Falling			
Falling flakes to the throng that catches and quails	28	24	6
The sun on falling waters writes the text	91		8
Of falling water this and all of these	98	2	3
Falling along the breakless pool of air	122		9
Forward falling forehead frowning lips crisp	159		32
Falln			
Doubtless the voice now falln now spent	81		2
Fallow foam-fallow hanks falln off their ranks	144		7
Fallow			
Landscape plotted and pieced fold fallow and plough	37		5
Fallow foam-fallow hanks falln off their ranks	144		7
Fallow foam-fallow hanks falln off their ranks	144		7
Fallowbootfellow			
Tom then Toms fallowbootfellow piles pick	70		.2
Fallows			
The unenduring fallows of the heaven	122		6
Falls			
Around the water-nymphs in fretted falls	2		50
Flesh falls within sight of us we though our flower the same	28	11	6
Fresh-firecoal chestnut-falls finches wings	37		4
Falls light as ten years long taught how to and why	47		8
Flutes and low to the lake falls home	56		4
And death falls gently as the snow	78		26
But then her tether calls her she falls off	103		12
And for the tinklings on the falls and swells	107	2	7
A noise of falls I am possessed by	121		1
Think this my birthday falls in saddening time of year	128		9
Following falls and falls of rain	142		3
Following falls and falls of rain	142		3
Any instant falls means me and I do not repent	152		64
False			
And marching to false colours those few strokes	102	1	69
Falsely			
Tis falsely given as love in men	81		49
Falsified			
In bows above my head as falsified	12	2	4

Word	Poem	Stan.	Line
Falter			
His sick stars falter more he may	83		25
Fame			
And storms bugle his fame	28	11	4
They stand they shine in the sun fame has foregone	104		2
Her fame to keep her fame to recover	156		12
Her fame to keep her fame to recover	156		12
Fames			
Call me Englands fames fond lover	156		11
Familiar			
More sweet-familiar grows my love to thee	12	1	2
Familiar and so hated by the sick	125		48
Hated and too familiar to the sick	125		49
Familiarness			
I plead familiarness endears	81		26
Fan			
Some carried the sea-fan some round the head	2		58
With darksome devouring eyes my bruised bones and fan	64		7
Than fan or hood or strawy plait	120		8
Fancied			
Must be that fancied it	148		4
Fancies			
It fancies feigns deems dears the artist after his art	63		6
Gilds with some sparky fancies his black night	102	3	30
Gilds with some sparky fancies his black night	102	3	36
Fanciful			
This is too much the father nay the mother fanciful	152		29
Fancy			
I must feed fancy show me any one	14	2	1
Reach me a fancy come faster	28	27	2
Fang			
Fang or flood goes death on drum	28	11	3
And find a flint a fang of ice	81	7	37
Fanged			
A cusp still clasped him a fluke yet fanged him entangled him not quit utterly	137		5
Fangs			
With gorgons gear and barebill thongs and fangs	50		14
Fans			
Broiders the nets with fans of amethyst	2		66
Off him but meaning motion fans fresh our wits with wonder	45		14
The chestnut-fans are loosely flirting	79		5

Word	Poem	Stan.	Line
Fantastic			
So grown fantastic in his piety	1	3	5
Far			
Far off a nereid company and shake	2		75
With loathd cold fishes far from man or what	2		124
Or far-off promise of a time to be	13		4
And Ill love my distinction near or far	14	2	12
How far from then forethought of all thy more boisterous years	53		12
Far with fonder a care and we we should have lost it finer fonder	59		29
Who made conjecture nearest far	78		45
And fainter finer trickle far	78		81
Tho far or sick or heavy or still	81		18
And you are gone so heavenly far	81		34
So far but I have yet within	81		131
Not furtherd far my travelld feet	81		157
Not so far from the pole	88		8
Not so far from the pole	88		12
Far from its head an angels hoverings	89		8
Not so far outward in the sea	120		21
Think you want daffodils and follow as far	135		30
Before or behind or far or at hand	138		7
Not that but thus far all with frailty blest	157		6
Far-off			
Or far-off promise of a time to be	13		4
Farmyard			
Flake-doves sent floating forth at a farm-yard scare	32	1	7
Farrier			
Felix Randal the farrier o is he dead then my duty all ended	53		1
Fashed			
O then weary then why should we tread o why are we so haggard at the heart so care-coiled care-killed so fagged so fashed so cogged so cumbered	59		26
Fashion			
Then often the ears in a new fashion hark	113		7
Fast			
Sphered so fast sweet soul we see	10		23
I cease the mourning and the abject fast	14	1	8
Sphered so fast sweet soul we see	25		23
Fast but mined with a motion a drift	28	4	3
Tarpeian-fast but a blown beacon of light	28	28	8
To mans last dust drain fast towards mans first slime	35		14
Their ransom their rescue and first fast last friend	40		14
Fast foundering own generation	41		87
Fast you ever fast bind	52		8
Fast you ever fast bind	52		8

Word	Poem	Stan.	Line
Fast (cont.)			
Where whatevers prized and passes of us everything thats fresh and fast flying of us seems to us sweet of us and swiftly away with done away with undone	59		8
Fold home fast fold thy child	60		126
Man how fast his firedint his mark on mind is gone	72		11
The point fast in and my left hand	81		44
Fling to the convent wicket fast	81		75
His lips moved fast in sense too thick	81		100
My fast-lodged tongue to her the gift	81		116
And straight showers parallel should follow fast	90		4
Lodge his eyes fast but yet as easy and light	102	1	21
That his fast-flowing hours with sandy silt	136		1
Fast or they in clammyish lashtender combs creep	149	1	5
Are afoot heaven-vault fast purpling portends and what first lightning	152		63
By her bloom fast by her fresh her fleeced bloom	152		83
Happy the father mother of these too fast	157		5
Fast furled and all foredrawn to no or yes	157		28
Fast he opens last he off wrings	159		34
Fast-flowing			
That his fast-flowing hours with sandy silt	136		1
Fast-lodged			
My fast-lodged tongue to her the gift	81		116
Fasted			
Pure fasted faces draw unto this feast	11		1
Fasten			
Why fasten that upon her	42		7
Fastened			
Thou hast bound bones and veins in me fastened me flesh	28	1	5
Never fleets more fastened with the tenderest truth	59		12
Faster			
Reach me a fancy come faster	28	27	2
Breathes once and quenched faster than it came	77		3
Fasts			
So fresh that come in fasts divine	22		16
Fatal			
Stretches the envied fruit with fatal smile	1	11	2
Fatal four disorders fleshed there all contended	53		4
And loves a fatal fault to patronize	94		18
Father			
Sun-flushed until it seemd their father sea	2		100

Word	Poem	Stan.	Line
Father and fondler of heart thou hast wrung	28	9	7
O father not under thy feathers nor ever as guessing	28	12	5
Joy fall to thee Father Francis	28	23	1
The Christ of the Father compassionate fetched in the storm of his strides	28	32	8
Being mighty a master being a father and fond	34		14
You father what you buy me I like best	47		2
To the father through the features of mens faces	57		14
How then should Gregory a father have gleaned else from swarmed Rome but God to a nation dealt that days dear chance	62		6
How then should Gregory a father have gleaned else from swarmed Rome but God to a nation dealt that days dear chance	62		6
Among strangers father and mother dear	66	1	2
On seeing her children say goodnight to their father	97		7
Thy father thou shalt see	109	16	4
And father be overworn	114		8
He spoke of God the Father and his Son	136		25
The child is father to the man	147		1
The child is father to the man	147		4
The man is father to the child	147		6
The child is father to the man	147		7
Meantime some tongue cries what teryth what thou poor fond father	152		22
This is too much the father nay the mother fanciful	152		29
Father be thou reconciled	155		14
Happy the father mother of these too fast	157		5
Father mother brothers sisters friends	159		49
Fatherd			
Or fatherd by the sunderd south	83		6
Fathers			
Times tasking it is fathers that asking for ease	28	26	11
He fathers-forth whose beauty is past change	37		10
The fine delight that fathers thought the strong	77		1
No man has such a daughter the fathers of the world	152		17
Fathers-forth			
He fathers-forth whose beauty is past change	37		10
Fathomed			
Frightful sheer no-man-fathomed hold them cheap	65		8
Fathoms			
Some asleep unawakened all unwarned eleven fathoms fallen	41		3

Word	Poem	Stan.	Line
Fault			
This fault in one I found that in another	16		11
What hinders are you beam-blind yet to a fault	46		12
Ah nature framed in fault	53		38
And loves a fatal fault to patronize	94		18
Alas but I am all at fault	120		24
This fault-not-found-with good	148		31
Fault-not-found-with			
This fault-not-found-with good	148		31
Favour			
And five-lived and leaved favour and pride	28	23	6
Favourable			
Forward-like but however and like favourable heaven heard these	48		48
Favoured			
Of favoured make and mind and health and youth	157		18
Favouring			
And favouring virgin freshness yet	139		6
Favourite			
The swallow favourite of the gale	130		9
Fawn			
A windpuff-bonnet of fawn-froth	56		5
Fawn-froth			
A windpuff-bonnet of fawn-froth	56		5
Fawning			
Fawning fawning crocodiles	145		22
Fawning fawning crocodiles	145		22
Fealty			
And still thou bindst me to fresh fealty	12	1	3
Fear			
And fear no iron rod	5		12
This means you need not fear the storms the cries	14	3	2
With not a thing to make me fear	21		40
If still in darkness not in fear	23		48
Or wring their barriers in bursts of fear or rage	39		8
Not mood in him nor meaning proud fire or sacred fear	45		5
Young John then fear then joy	54		8
Fear hindrance and espial	110		3
Is all all sheared away thus then I sweat for fear	152		24
Feard			
Lately I feard	102	1	6
Feared			
I only feared the wet for you	21		13
Fearful			
And for that fearful hour life is more thin	81	3	5

Word	Poem	Stan.	Line
Fearing			
Till fearing ravage worse than in his flight	1	14	7
Fears			
Because she fears her fingers will be stung	96	4	2
Plays to the breeze where now are fled her fears	99		15
I here forbid my thoughts to fool themselves with fears	152		30
Feast			
Pure fasted faces draw unto this feast	11		1
And now the marriage feast begun	22		26
What was the feast followed the night	28	29	3
Feast of the one woman without stain	28	29	5
Not Ill not carrion comfort despair not feast on thee	64		1
Your feast of that most in you earnest eye	157		29
Feasting			
Looks laid for feasting and for rest	3		24
With a feasting in her honour	42		8
Feasts			
Feasts when we shall fall asleep	28	35	9
Her feasts follow reason	42		3
Rose here he feasts lovely all is no more off with down he dings	159		28
Feather			
One scarlet feather trailing to the wind	2		81
Flesh and fleece fur and feather	42		17
The autumn yellow feather in the boughs	105		5
Feathers			
And from dank feathers wring the drops	3		8
O father not under thy feathers nor ever as guessing	28	12	5
Feathery			
Finger of a tender of o of a feathery delicacy the breast of the	28	30	6
The knot of feathery locks upon her head	99		14
Feature			
Cheeks right rude of feature	41		49
It is the forged feature finds me it is the rehearsal	45		7
To what serves mortal beauty dangerous does set dancing blood the o-seal-that-so feature flung prouder form	62		1
Their young delightful hour do feature down	157		10
Features			
To the father through the features of mens faces	57		14
And features in flesh what deed he each must do	71		10
Her mould of features mated well	145		16
Featuring			
Fire-featuring heaven for earth her being			

Word	Poem	Stan.	Line
Featuring (cont.)			
has unbound her dapple is at an end	61		5
Fed			
Her homes and fields that folded and fed me	156		2
Fee			
That has both gold and fee	109	9	2
Shewn him both gold and fee	109	11	2
Because of gold and fee	109	12	2
Feeble			
Lo God shall strengthen all the feeble knees	11		14
Feed			
I must feed fancy show me any one	14	2	1
And I that die these deaths that feed this flame	76		12
We will charge our flocks that they not feed	98	15	2
Feeds			
He feeds me with his manna every day	5		13
And feeds new leaves upon the winds of fall	105		10
Feel			
But feel the long success of sin	18		8
O feel-of-primrose hands o feet	22		21
Over again I feel thy finger and find thee	28	1	8
Is bare now nor can foot feel being shod	30	1	8
To with no tongue to plead no heart to feel	57		3
I wake and feel the fell of dark not day	67		1
Sure s bed now low be it lustily he his low lot feel	70		5
And hard men feel a softening touch	78		30
And feel no blast the fretful fire	81	5	4
Some knelt some stood I seemd to feel	81		93
Feel-of-primrose			
O feel-of-primrose hands o feet	22		21
Feelers			
With growths of myriad feelers crystalline	2		70
Feeling			
The keener to come at the comfort for feeling the combating keen	28	25	8
Some pageant which takes tears and I must foot with feeling that	152		26
Lifes quick this kind this keen self-feeling	152		96
Feels			
A boy feels when the poet he pores upon	14	3	13
Feet			
The trumpet waxes loud tired are your feet	5		8
To plash with cool feet the clay juicy soil	5		50
Which should ere now have led my feet to the field	17		9
O feel-of-primrose hands o feet	22		21
Where seek thee with unsandalled feet	23		18
To hero of Calvary Christs feet	28	8	7
And hurls for him o half hurls earth for him off under his feet	37		14

Word	Poem	Stan.	Line
Forth Christ from cupboard fetched how fain I of feet	48		10
Them broad in bluff hide his frowning feet lashed raced	71		17
Cleaves not my brain burns not my feet	81	2	4
And with sharp flint will part my feet and dint	81	7	43
Not furtherd far my travelld feet	81		157
Their changing feet in flicker all the time	107	1	13
And to their feet the narrow bells gave rhyme	107	1	14
They have bound his feet they have bound his hands	109	13	3
Till walk the world he can with bare his feet	159		35
Feigns			
It fancies feigns deems dears the artist after his art	63		6
Felicitous			
No not uncomforted lovely-felicitous providence	28	30	5
Felix			
Felix Randal the farrier o is he dead then my duty all ended	53		1
Thy tears that touched my heart child Felix poor Felix Randal	53		11
Thy tears that touched my heart child Felix poor Felix Randal	53		11
Fell			
Fell on the palace and the lust of rabble rude	1	14	9
The winged fowls took part part fell in thorn	7		7
And they could not and fell to the deck	28	17	2
This was that fell capsize	41		36
Witnessed so fortune fell	54		4
Of a pool so pitchblack fell-frowning	56		7
Then lull then leave off fury had shrieked no lingering let me be fell force I must be brief	65		6
I wake and feel the fell of dark not day	67		1
Something I said I swooned and fell	81		118
Deaths bones fell in with sudden clank	92		12
Late I fell in the ecstacy	93	1	1
Down upon ground fell she	109	39	2
A standing fell	112		9
As it fell upon a day	131		1
It stooped and flashed and fell and ran like water away	152		52
Fell-frowning			
Of a pool so pitchblack fell-frowning	55		7
Felled			
Felled and furled them the hearts of oak	41		5

Word	Poem	Stan.	Line
Felled (cont.)			
All felled felled are all felled	43		3
All felled felled are all felled	43		3
All felled felled are all felled	43		3
Fellowship			
Eye all in fellowship	49		4
And brought the sense of gentle fellowship	107	2	4
Fellowships			
Breathe Easter now you serged fellowships	11		7
Fells			
Fells or flanks of the voel a vein	28	4	7
That bird beyond the remembering his free fells	39		3
Felt			
But earth has never felt the snow	3		2
Springs the stress felt	28	6	2
Though felt before though in high flood yet	28	7	7
When she felt the kill-weights crush	145		55
Female			
Has wit enough but less than female tact	94		19
Fenced			
For us the vine was fenced with thorn	6		13
Fens			
In beryl-covered fens so dim	3		26
Fern			
Wiry heathpacks flitches of fern	56		11
Fertile			
Had been more fertile and had sown with notes	122		5
Fervent			
Than treble-fervent more of other men	14	1	13
Festival			
Blot the perpetual festival of day	89		2
Festooned			
Under the cloud-festooned roof	78		66
Fetch			
Has one fetch in her she rears herself to divine	28	19	6
Prayer shall fetch pity eternal	41		119
Fetched			
The Christ of the Father compassionate fetched in the storm of his strides	28	32	8
Fetched fresh as I suppose off some sweet wood	34		4
Forth Christ from cupboard fetched how fain I of feet	48		10
Fettle			
Didst fettle for the great grey drayhorse his bright and battering sandal	53		14
Fever			
My tempests there my fire and fever fussy	76		14

Word	Poem	Stan.	Line
Feverd			
Mid feverd fumes and slime and caked clot	78		8
Few			
And a few lilies blow	9		4
Nor first from heaven and few know this	28	6	3
Five notes or seven late and few	81		23
My cry is like a bleat a few	81		66
And marching to false colours those few strokes	102	1	69
And a few leaves not lily-white but charactered over with blacks	128		16
Ffestiniog			
In the van between Ffestiniog and Bala	96	1	5
Fickle			
Whatever is fickle freckled who knows how	37		8
With fickle spots of sadness accessories	125		47
Fie			
Fie you are not Lord William she said	109	26	3
O fie that this should be	109	26	4
Fie she said unto them all	109	28	1
Field			
The field where he has planted us	6		27
The field is soppd with merciful dew	8		3
Which should ere now have led my feet to the field	17		9
Should tongue that time now trumpet now that field	73		3
Heaven and every field are still	85		2
A drop of shade rolls over field and flock	98	3	2
Whose silver skins lie level and thick in field	102	1	23
Their clarions from all corners of the field	104		4
Over field and tree	109	17	2
And field-flowers make the fields forlorn	114		3
Field-flown the departed day no morning brings	153		9
Where is the field I must play the man on	156		16
Field-flowers			
And field-flowers make the fields forlorn	114		3
Field-flown			
Field-flown the departed day no morning brings	153		9
Fields			
To fields where flies no sharp and sided hail	9		3
Dewy fields in the morning under the sun	98	13	1
To spill oer fields of lilies so could I	102	1	37
To fields of light millions of travelling rays	103		9
They draw all coverts cut the fields and suck	104		12
Close-rooted in the downward-hollowing fields	107	3	15
Of sheep from the high fields and other wild	107	4	23

Word	Poem	Stan.	Line
Fields (cont.)			
And field-flowers make the fields forlorn	114		3
I never saw those fields whereon their best	119		11
Her homes and fields that folded and fed me	156		2
Fierce			
Hung in the swaying of the fierce melee	1	2	4
When the fierce skies are blue to black albeit	81	2	5
Fiercer			
With fiercer weepings of these desperate eyes	14	3	6
Fiercest			
Earth hears no hurtle then from fiercest fray	73		8
Fiery			
Upraisd an emblem of that fiery constancy	1	3	8
Legates might rush zeal-rampant fiery	1	5	5
With form divine a fiery chivalry	1	7	8
Wiry and white-fiery and whirlwind-swivelled snow	28	13	7
Second this fiery strain not always o no no	152		78
Fig			
Handle the fig suck the full-sappd vine-shoot	5		38
Fight			
To follow a banner and fight for honour	156		9
We follow her banner we fight for her honour	156		10
Fighter			
And on the fighter forge his glorious day	73		4
Files			
Sexing and ranking with our ruder files	102	1	66
Enrolld and sexing with our ruder files	102	1	67
Enrolld and sexed with our ruder files	102	1	68
Filial			
They kiss the rod with filial submission	97		9
Fill			
And have your fill of meat	5		10
To sing scarce heard and singing fill	78		77
The peacockd copse were known to fill	81		14
I have filld that hard to fill is	98	19	2
Met a new shower and saw the rainbow fill	107	3	10
Filld			
I have filld that hard to fill is	98	19	2
Filled			
Bones built in me flesh filled blood brimmed the curse	67		11
Filleted			
And the water warbles over into filleted with glassy grassy quicksilvery shives and shoots	159		38
Fillets			
With golden fillets and rich blazonry	1	7	6
Fills			
Of finishd diapers that fills the eye	1	6	6
Delicious kindness he is patient patience fills	68		13

Word	Poem	Stan.	Line
Who knew the inner spirit that fills	78		43
Film			
Of tremulous film more subtle than the vest	2		39
Films			
And silver films beneath with pearly mist	2		67
Filmy			
Of filmy globes and rosy floating cloud	2		97
Their filmy tails adown whose length there showd	2		104
Filth			
Scoor you from teeming filth some sickly hovel	78		6
Fin			
From crown to tail-fin floating fringed the spine	2		41
A tinted fin on either shoulder hung	2		52
With arm and fin the argent bubbles streamd	2		109
Finches			
Fresh-firecoal chestnut-falls finches wings	37		4
Find			
Then find in the horizon-round	15		31
And find the uncreated light	22		10
I find another Christian here	25		42
Find me a place by thee mother of mine	27		7
Over again I feel thy finger and find thee	28	1	8
Some find me a sword some	28	11	1
And fain will find as sterling all as all is smart	63		7
Eyes in their dark can day or thirst can find	69		7
And find a flint a fang of ice	81	7	37
But now are fled and hard to find	81		45
No flowers to find no place to halt	81		159
Shall when his star is zenithd find	83		7
I find I am as ready with my tears	102	1	34
And find it will not therefore be descried	102	3	11
So takes the sister sense can find no mark	113		4
Would he not find	127		18
You look again and cannot find	130		19
And I should find him there	135		34
You spoil the plot I find my true love by	135		36
And in this darksome world what comfort can I find	152		80
Down this darksome world comfort where can I find	152		81
Finding			
Five the finding and sake	28	22	1
Finds			
Not danger electrical horror then further it finds	28	26	13
And flowers finds soonest	42		12
It is the forged feature finds me it is the rehearsal	45		7

Word	Poem	Stan.	Line
Finds (cont.)			
Bow swung finds tongue to fling out broad its name	56		4
Though as a beechbole firm finds his as at a rollcall rank	71		9
There is the shilling that finds me willing	156		8
Fine			
Of dewy gorse blurrd with the gossamer fine	2		40
To its own fine function wild and self-instressed	47		7
Breathing bloom of a chastity in mansex fine	48		16
Laying like airs fine flood	60		51
The fine delight that fathers thought the strong	77		1
To quench the fine-drawn cataract	78		90
With twice as fine a sense to apprehend them	102	1	12
As the fine morsels of a dwindling cloud	102	1	35
Their highest sprays were drawn as fine as lashes	107	4	6
Firm accents strike her fine and scrolled ear	136		21
The motion of that mans heart is fine	142		6
And are they thus the fine the fingering beams	157		9
Fine-drawn			
To quench the fine-drawn cataract	78		90
Fineflour			
When the air was sweet-and-sour of the flown fineflour of	142		4
Finer			
Far with fonder a care and we we should have lost it finer fonder	59		29
And fainter finer trickle far	78		81
Finger			
Over again I feel thy finger and find thee	28	1	8
Finger of a tender of o of a feathery delicacy the breast of the	28	30	6
O his nimble finger his gnarled grip	41		80
Her finger-long new horns are cappd with black	99		7
Over finger-teasing task his twiny boots	159		33
Finger-long			
Her finger-long new horns are cappd with black	99		7
Finger-teasing			
Over finger-teasing task his twiny boots	159		33
Fingergaps			
Round the four fingergaps	60		78
Fingering			
And are they thus the fine the fingering beams	157		9

Word	Poem	Stan.	Line
Fingernail			
The moon dwindled and thinned to the fringe of a fingernail held to the candle	137		2
Fingers			
With the dainty-delicate fretted fringe of fingers	2		64
Others with fingers white would comb among	2		112
By that window what task what fingers ply	46		5
Because she fears her fingers will be stung	96	4	2
Runs his fingers through the wheat	98	1	2
Her barred fingers claspd upon her eyes	111		6
I see her riving fingers tear	120		5
The last thing Margarets fingers sew	145		13
The more some monstrous hand gropes with clammy fingers there	152		20
Finishd			
No finishd proof was this of Gothic grace	1	6	1
Of finishd diapers that fills the eye	1	6	6
Fire			
With garnet wreaths and blooms of rosy-budded fire	2		26
Thro crimson-golden floods pass swallowd into fire	2		83
And with fire in him forge thy will	28	10	2
To bathe in his fall-gold mercies to breathe in his all-fire glances	28	23	8
With belled fire and the moth-soft milky way	28	26	6
A released shower let flash to the shire not a lightning of fire hard-hurled	28	33	8
Our hearts charitys hearths fire our thoughts chivalrys throngs lord	28	34	8
O look at all the fire-folk sitting in the air	32	1	2
Buckle and the fire that breaks from thee then a billion	36		9
Bright sun lanced fire in the heavenly bay	41		21
Not mood in him nor meaning proud fire or sacred fear	45		5
Come you indoors come home your fading fire	46		9
As kingfishers catch fire dragonflies draw flame	57		1
His fire the sun would shake	60		96
Fire-featuring heaven for earth her being has unbound her dapple is at an end	61		5
My tempests there my fire and fever fussy	76		14
Sweet fire the sire of muse my soul needs this	77		9
Tresses dippd in rainbow fire	78		14
And feel no blast the fretful fire	81	5	4
The vital fire does suddenly retire	81	7	24
I saw the stars like flash of fire	135		8

Word	Poem	Stan.	Line
Fire-featuring			
Fire-featuring heaven for earth her being has unbound her dapple is at an end	61		5
Fire-folk			
O look at all the fire-folk sitting in the air	32	1	2
Fireball			
Where yonder crimson fireball sits	3		23
Firecoal			
Fresh-firecoal chestnut-falls finches wings	37		4
Fired			
Who fired France for Mary without spot	44		14
Firedint			
Man how fast his firedint his mark on mind is gone	72		11
Fires			
And the midriff astrain with leaning of laced with fires of stress	28	2	8
Alien from yours as heaven from nadir-fires	78		4
Firm			
Though as a beechbole firm finds his as at a rollcall rank	71		9
Firm accents strike her fine and scrolled ear	136		21
Firmament			
Keen glimpses of the inner firmament	2		12
Unswerving through the firmament	78		50
First			
A cloisterd convent first the proudest home	1	1	6
For us was gatherd the first-fruits	6		3
And lifes first germs from death had won	23		24
Nor first from heaven and few know this	28	6	3
Brim in a flash full hither then last or first	28	8	6
She was first of a five and came	28	20	1
To mans last dust drain fast towards mans first slime	35		14
Their ransom their rescue and first fast last friend	40		14
Mend first and vital candle in close hearts vault	46		10
He swung to his first poised purport of reply	47		4
Came I say this day to it to a first communion	48		8
Sickness broke him impatient he cursed at first but mended	53		5
In the first signals of the several drops	84		3
Who first knew moonlight by the hunters moon	105		17
And where the brow in first descending bowd	107	1	9
To that first golden age of gospel times	136		5
Are afoot heaven-vault fast purpling portends			

Word	Poem	Stan.	Line
and what first lightning	152		63
Enough corruption was the worlds first woe	157		33
First-fruits			
For us was gatherd the first-fruits	6		3
Fishes			
With loathd cold fishes far from man or what	2		124
Fit			
Fit for flowers water-pierced and rilly	98	15	6
And faces fit for leisure gaze	133		13
Caps occasion with an intellectual fit	143		2
Fits			
In fits of music till sunset	78		87
Five			
Five ways the precious branches torn	6		14
Food for five thousand on the thorns he shed	7		12
How many leaves had it five they were then	27		38
Five like the senses and members of men	27		39
Five is their number by nature but now	27		40
She was first of a five and came	28	20	1
Five the finding and sake	28	22	1
And five-lived and leaved favour and pride	28	23	6
Five and twenty years have run	28	35	5
A turn of seven notes or five	81		7
Five notes or seven late and few	81		23
The sweetest sonnet five or six times read	117		9
Rough-robin or five-lipped campion clear	144		15
Five-lipped			
Rough-robin or five-lipped campion clear	144		15
Five-lived			
And five-lived and leaved favour and pride	28	23	6
Fix			
Bids him this way his gazes fix	120		15
Fixd			
The stretching palace lay as handle fixd	1	4	4
A faithful guard of inner darkness fixd	1	4	7
Where the eye fixd fled the encrimsoning spot	2		9
Fixed			
To hold me quite fixed in the selfsame plight	81	7	46
My all-accepting fixed eye	130		6
Fixedly			
With hope with shut eyes fixedly	81	7	51
Flag			
But country and flag the flag I am under	156		7
But country and flag the flag I am under	156		7
Flags			
The shapen flags and drilled holes of sky	12	2	11
And hosts confront with flags unfurled	23		33
With yellow flags will suit his brow	124		18
Flake			
And the sea flint-flake black-backed in the			

Word	Poem	Stan.	Line
Flake (cont.)			
regular blow	28	13	5
For lettering of the lambs fleece ruddying of the rose-flake	28	22	8
Flake-doves sent floating forth at a farm-yard scare	32	1	7
By rafts and rafts of flake leaves light dealt so painted on the air	159		25
Flake-doves			
Flake-doves sent floating forth at a farm-yard scare	32	1	7
Flakes			
Fair beds they seemd of water lily flakes	2		13
But what a wild flush on the flakes of it stood	27		34
Storm flakes were scroll-leaved flowers lily showers sweet heaven was astrew in them	28	21	8
Falling flakes to the throng that catches and quails	28	24	6
Flame			
Summer was as full of flame	4		25
To flash from the flame to the flame then tower from the grace to the grace	28	3	8
To flash from the flame to the flame then tower from the grace to the grace	28	3	8
The flange and the rail flame	28	11	2
Miracle-in-Mary-of-flame	28	33	4
It will flame out like shining from shook foil	31	1	2
His tear-tricked cheeks of flame	54		36
As kingfishers catch fire dragonflies draw flame	57		1
And I that die these deaths that feed this flame	76		12
Spur live and lancing like the blowpipe flame	77		2
Nor night is blown with flame-rings every-where	99		18
Pierce her she hangs upon the flame-cased sun	103		10
Like flame they gather on our cliffs at evening	104		7
Flame-rash rudred	138		23
Flame-cased			
Pierce her she hangs upon the flame-cased sun	103		10
Flame-rash			
Flame-rash rudred	138		23
Flame-rings			
Nor night is blown with flame-rings every-where	99		18

Word	Poem	Stan.	Line
Flames			
Hung like a wreck that flames not billows beat	1	3	4
You vigil-keepers with low flames decreased	11		8
Sky peakd with tiny flames	98	25	5
Flanders			
But from beyond seas Erin France and Flanders everywhere	152		125
Flange			
The flange and the rail flame	28	11	2
Flank			
At corners flank the stretching compass round	1	1	4
Breathed round the rack of ribs the scooped flank lank	71		2
Which with its lined and creased flank	92		10
Flanks			
Fells or flanks of the voel a vein	28	4	7
Circled the staff flanks of the bulky hills	125		10
Flard			
The altar-tapers flard in gusts in vain	1	13	5
Flare			
Wind-beat whitebeam airy abeles set on a flare	32	1	6
They plough our vales you see the unsteady flare	104		9
Flares			
Flares his wet brilliance in the dintless heaven	98	34	2
Flaring			
Fairer these are the flaring shows unlovely	125		45
Flash			
The languent smooth with dimpling drops and flash	2		103
To flash from the flame to the flame then tower from the grace to the grace	28	3	8
Brim in a flash full hither then last or first	28	8	6
A released shower let flash to the shire not a lightning of fire hard-hurled	28	33	8
In a flash at a trumpet crash	72		21
I saw the stars like flash of fire	135		8
Flashed			
Honour is flashed off exploit so we say	73		1
It stooped and flashed and fell and ran like water away	152		52
Round and round they came and flashed towards heaven	152		60
Flashes			
Worlds loveliest mens selves self flashes off frame and face	62		9
This garland of their gambol flashes in his breast	159		19

Word	Poem	Stan.	Line
Flashing			
Flashing like flecks of coal	60		100
Flat			
Into the flat blue mist the sun	3		31
Word went she should be crushed out flat	145		38
Flats			
No rains shall fresh the flats of sea	114		13
Flatter			
Ill meant yet true I best should flatter then	125		20
Flattery			
Is fond of flattery as any she	94		15
What if I hated flattery	125		32
Flatterys			
Flatterys all out of place where praise is true	125		35
Flaunt			
Cloud-puffball torn tufts tossed pillows flaunt forth then chevy on an air	72		1
Flaunting			
His cheeks the forth-and-flaunting sun	144		2
Flawed			
And wordy warrants are flawed through	25		38
Flecks			
Flashing like flecks of coal	60		100
Fled			
Where the eye fixd fled the encrimsoning spot	2		9
And fled with a fling of the heart to the heart of the host	28	3	5
To alien eaves you fled and went	81		5
But now are fled and hard to find	81		45
You may depend that ere a week was fled	97		5
Plays to the breeze where now are fled her fears	99		15
Fledged			
From wings swan-fledged a wheel of watery light	2		76
Flee			
O in turns of tempest me heaped there me frantic to avoid thee and flee	64		8
Fleece			
Through the cobbled foam-fleece what could he do	28	16	7
For lettering of the lambs fleece ruddying of the rose-flake	28	22	8
Flesh and fleece fur and feather	42		17
In coop and in comb the fleece of his foam	56		3
The flower of beauty fleece of beauty too too apt to ah to fleet	59		11
And sucks the light as full as Gideons fleece	103		11
Fleeced			
Thick-fleeced bushes like a heifers ear	98	11	1

Word	Poem	Stan.	Line
Out-fleeced bushes like a spaniels ear	98	11	2
Sky fleeced with the milky way	98	23	2
Gem-fleeced at morn so brilliant is the weather	99		4
Backward are laid her pretty black-fleeced ears	99		13
By her bloom fast by her fresh her fleeced bloom	152		83
Fleeces			
Or wind-long fleeces on the flock	144		11
Fleeciest			
The fleeciest frailest-flixed	60		5
Fleet			
Only the breathing temple and fleet	41		92
The flower of beauty fleece of beauty too too apt to ah to fleet	59		11
The wind that passes by so fleet	98	1	1
Like shuttles fleet the clouds and after	98	3	1
While rushy rains shall fall or brooks shall fleet from fountains	152		107
Dark or daylight on and on here he will then here he will the fleet	159		40
Fleeted			
That fleeted else like day-dissolved dreams	157		11
Fleets			
Never fleets more fastened with the tenderest truth	59		12
Fleming			
Upon the stubborn fleming and the rod	1	5	6
Flesh			
While his crackd flesh lay hissing on the grate	1	3	2
From flesh-flowers of the rock but more were wreathd	2		63
Come by the flesh-pots you shall sit unshod	5		9
Of leaves of greenest flesh	5		34
Thou hast bound bones and veins in me fastened me flesh	28	1	5
Will mouthed to flesh-burst	28	8	4
Flesh falls within sight of us we though our flower the same	28	11	6
Mans sprit will be flesh-bound when found at best	39		12
Flesh and fleece fur and feather	42		17
Of her flesh he took flesh	60		55
Of her flesh he took flesh	60		55
Not flesh but spirit now	60		58
And cry o Christ-done deed so God-made-flesh does too	63		13
Bones built in me flesh filled blood brimmed the curse	67		11
And features in flesh what deed he each			

Word	Poem	Stan.	Line
Flesh (cont.)			
must do	71		10
A beacon and eternal beam flesh fade and mortal trash	72		19
And those strokes once that gashed flesh or galled shield	73		2
And soul is subtle and flesh weak	77		37
Despatches with no flinching but will flesh o can flesh	152		77
Despatches with no flinching but will flesh o can flesh	152		77
Flesh-bound			
Mans sprit will be flesh-bound when found at best	39		12
Flesh-burst			
Will mouthed to flesh-burst	28	8	4
Flesh-flowers			
From flesh-flowers of the rock but more were wreathd	2		63
Flesh-pots			
Come by the flesh-pots you shall sit unshod	5		9
Fleshed			
The heaven-flung heart-fleshed maiden-furled	28	33	3
Fatal four disorders fleshed there all contended	53		4
Fletcher			
Sydney Fletcher Bristol-bred	41		56
Flew			
The bats wings lisping as they flew	21		19
Flicker			
Their changing feet in flicker all the time	107	1	13
Flickering			
Flickering with sunny spokes and left and right	2		77
At last the bird is found a flickering shape and slim	113		9
Flies			
To fields where flies no sharp and sided hail	9		3
Flight			
Till fearing ravage worse than in his flight	1	14	7
He playd his wings as though for flight	87		1
Of the flown skylark and his traverse flight	122		3
Flighty			
She schools the flighty pupils of her eyes	82		1
Flinching			
Despatches with no flinching but will flesh o can flesh	152		77
Fling			
And fled with a fling of the heart to the heart of the host	28	3	5
With richness the racing lambs too have fair their fling	33		8

Word	Poem	Stan.	Line
Bow swung finds tongue to fling out broad its name	57		4
Then would I fling me up to sip	78		131
Fling to the convent wicket fast	81		75
Flings			
Light and darkness from him flings	77		68
Flint			
And the sea flint-flake black-backed in the regular blow	28	13	5
And find a flint a fang of ice	81	7	37
And with sharp flint will part my feet and dint	81	7	43
Flint-flake			
And the sea flint-flake black-backed in the regular blow	28	13	5
Flints			
Of small and sugar flints I knew	135		27
Flinty			
Part found no root upon the flinty road	7		9
Flinty kindcold element let break across his limbs	159		41
Flirting			
The chestnut-fans are loosely flirting	79		5
Flitches			
Wiry heathpacks flitches of fern	56		11
Flits			
And tho the silver seed that flits	83		11
Flixed			
The fleeciest frailest-flixed	60		5
Float			
Stars float from the borders of the main	98	20	1
Hover-float to the hedge brow	138		40
I should be wronging longer leaving it to float	159		44
Floated			
And gathering floated where the gaze was not	2		10
Floating			
With a thin floating veil of water hoar	2		4
From crown to tail-fin floating fringed the spine	2		41
Of filmy globes and rosy floating cloud	2		97
The floating blooms and with tide flowing quenchd	2		139
Flake-doves sent floating forth at a farm-yard scare	32	1	7
Springs in the floating air and the skies swim	113		6
Floats			
The bugle moon by daylight floats	3		15
Flock			
Then like a flock of sea-fowl mounting higher	2		82
And thickend like that drifted bloom the flock	2		99

Word	Poem	Stan.	Line
Flock (cont.)			
The gross flock call them quails	5		16
A shelter for this flock	5		22
And sheep-flock clouds like worlds of wool	30	1	18
What would befal the godless flock	92		7
A drop of shade rolls over field and flock	98	3	2
Yet there came one who sent his flock before him	107	1	7
Or wind-long fleeces on the flock	144		11
Flockbells			
And flockbells off the aerial	41		6
Flocks			
Rural rural keeping folk flocks and flowers	44		8
Now her all in two flocks two folds black white right wrong reckon but reck but mind	61		12
We will charge our flocks that they not feed	98	15	2
He rises from the flocks of villages	100		5
And bluer grey the flocks of trees look in the plain	105		8
Flood			
Though felt before though in high flood yet	28	7	7
Fang or flood goes death on drum	28	11	3
With the burl of the fountains of air buck and the flood of the wave	28	16	8
Of the yore-flood of the years fall	28	31	2
With a flood or a fall low lull-off or all roar	35		3
Laying like airs fine flood	60		51
And saw the men before the flood	93	1	2
Floods			
Thro crimson-golden floods pass swallowd into fire	2		83
As erst upon chaotic floods	23		21
And I come laden from such floods	98	19	5
Floodtide			
If floodtide teeming thrills her full	30	1	22
Floor			
Scourged upon the threshing-floor	6		6
That lick the shelly leaves which floor the copse	84		4
Floord			
Great butter-burr leaves floord the slope corpse ground	107	4	9
Floris			
My signalling tears might ring up Floris now	102	1	7
Sleep Floris while I rob you tighten o sleep	102	1	18
Turns the lantern on Floris hand	102	1	27
This flower this Floris this dear majesty	102	1	39
Worse than when Floris found me in the garden	102	1	43
Ah Floris Floris let me speak this little	102	1	53
Ah Floris Floris let me speak this little	102	1	53

Word	Poem	Stan.	Line
Though ill-contented precious precious Floris	102	1	56
Floris she will not hit thy sum of worth	102	1	61
Floris thou late-found all-heal	102	1	63
Flow			
Let it flow for heavenly mirth	24		10
Through her and from her flow	60		32
All day long I like fountain flow	155		2
Flower			
Changd to a flower and there with placid eye	1	11	8
I gather points of lote-flower from an isle	5		33
Fruit not flower nor Dorothy	25		24
Flesh falls within sight of us we though our flower the same	28	11	6
Her flower her piece of being doomed dragon food	50		4
The flower of beauty fleece of beauty too too apt to ah to fleet	59		11
And the flower strips	98	14	2
This flower this Floris this dear majesty	102	1	39
The temperd soil where only her flower is found	102	3	4
If it were a flower of paradise	109	34	3
Flowerets			
Circlet of astral flowerets diademd	2		.61
Flowers			
And held a cross of flowers in purple bloom	1	10	6
From flesh-flowers of the rock but more were wreathd	2		63
On the flowers that were seen	4		9
I mark the flowers ere the prime	4		14
Many trees and flowers round	4		19
And the flowers that he had tied	4		27
Sweet flowers I carry sweets for bitter	10		6
Nor fruit nor flowers nor Dorothy	10		24
Flowers do ope their heavenward eyes	24		15
And may has come hair-bound in flowers	26		13
Storm flakes were scroll-leaved flowers lily showers sweet heaven was astrew in them	28	21	8
And flowers finds soonest	42		12
Rural rural keeping folk flocks and flowers	44		8
No flowers to find no place to halt	81		159
Next to meadows abundant pierced with flowers	98	12	2
Fit for flowers water-pierced and rilly	98	15	6
Gold gallant flowers much looked at in April-weather	98	16	2
Of flowers that counting closes	98	19	6
Like scalded banks toppd once with principal flowers	102	2	14
And field-flowers make the fields forlorn	114		3

Word	Poem	Stan.	Line
Flowing			
With flowing tracery engemming rays	1	6	2
The floating blooms and with tide flowing quenchd	2		139
That his fast-flowing hours with sandy silt	136		1
Flown			
Of the flown skylark and his traverse flight	122		3
When the air was sweet-and-sour of the flown fineflour of	142		4
Field-flown the departed day no morning brings	153		9
Flue			
Hard as hurdle arms with a broth of goldish flue	71		1
Fluke			
A cusp still clasped him a fluke yet fanged him entangled him not quit utterly	137		5
Flung			
The heaven-flung heart-fleshed maiden-furled	28	33	3
But Harry in his hands he has flung	54		35
To what serves mortal beauty dangerous does set dancing blood the o-seal-that-so feature flung prouder form	62		1
Cheer whom though the hero whose heaven-handling flung me foot trod	64		12
Flung rider and wings away though these were none	136		9
Be at every assault fresh foiled worse flung deeper disappointed	152		89
Flush			
But what a wild flush on the flakes of it stood	27		34
Gush flush the man the being with it sour or sweet	28	8	5
Flush thro their heaving columns when they halt	104		10
Flushd			
Sun-flushd until it seemd their father sea	2		100
Flushed			
And zeal is flushed and pity bleeds	23		34
That guilt is hushed by hearts are flushed by and melt	28	6	6
Flushes			
The whole landscape flushes on a sudden at a sound	146		5
Fluted			
Broad-fluted nor with shafts acanthus-crownd	1	7	3
Flutes			
Flutes and low to the lake falls home	56		4
Fly			
What the heart is which like carriers let fly	47		5
Why that my chaff might fly my grain lie			

Word	Poem	Stan.	Line
sheer and clear	64		9
White-faced as one in sad assay to fly	80		8
Bright hues long lookd at thin dissolve and fly	117		2
All else may whirl or dive or fly	130		8
Flying			
Where whatevers prized and passes of us everything thats fresh and fast flying of us seems to us sweet of us and swiftly away with done away with undone	59		8
Flying a bow	98	6	3
Foam			
The satin-purfled smooth to foam and spread	2		79
With rosy foam and pelting blossom and mists	2		90
Through the cobbled foam-fleece what could he do	28	16	7
Not honour it ale like goldy foam	30	1	35
When drop-of-blood-and-foam-dapple	42		37
In coop and in comb the fleece of his foam	56		3
Foam-tuft fumitory	138		30
Fallow foam-fallow hanks falln off their ranks	144		7
Foam-fallow			
Fallow foam-fallow hanks falln off their ranks	144		7
Foam-fleece			
Through the cobbled foam-fleece what could he do	28	16	7
Foam-tuft			
Foam-tuft fumitory	138		30
Foamfalling			
Foamfalling is not fresh to it rainbow by it not beaming	152		55
Foil			
It will flame out like shining from shook foil	31	1	2
Foiled			
Be at every assault fresh foiled worse flung deeper disappointed	152		89
Foiling			
Her showy leaves with gentle watchet foiling	108		6
Fold			
Landscape plotted and pieced fold fallow and plough	37		5
Fold home fast fold thy child	60		126
Fold home fast fold thy child	60		126
The essence neer forgot the fold	81		82
Ply fold on fold across his dangerous eyes	102	1	20
Ply fold on fold across his dangerous eyes	102	1	20
They seem to fold the hills with golden capes	104	1	11

Word	Poem	Stan.	Line
Folded			
And frightful a nightfall folded rueful a day	28	15	5
Of a fresh and following folded rank	43		4
Grant that close-folded peace that clad	77		41
You folded did you not your dress	81		81
Her milk-white throat and folded dew-lap slack	99		9
Her homes and fields that folded and fed me	156		2
Folds			
Give myrrhy-threaded golden folds of ease	11		12
Now her all in two flocks two folds black white right wrong reckon but reck but mind	61		12
Folds off aloof that signal is and proof	81	6	3
The shallow folds of the wood	98	9	1
And pressed violets in the folds appear	119		4
Foliagd			
And foliagd crownals pointing how the ways	1	6	4
And damasqud arms and foliagd carving piled	1	10	2
Foliage			
Of foliage fallen in the copse	3		12
Folk			
O look at all the fire-folk sitting in the air	32	1	2
Rural rural keeping folk flocks and flowers	44		8
Follow			
Of art best follow nature in a maze	1	6	5
Cheers death would follow	41		46
Her feasts follow reason	42		3
Yonder what high as that we follow now we follow	59		31
Yonder what high as that we follow now we follow	59		31
And fain would follow I who led	81		172
And straight showers parallel should follow fast	90		4
Lead shepherd now we follow shepherd lead	98	15	7
Wilt thou follow me my true love	109	37	1
Wilt thou follow me my true love	109	37	3
O I will follow thee my true love	109	38	1
Think you want daffodils and follow as far	135		30
To follow a banner and fight for honour	156		9
We follow her banner we fight for her honour	156		10
Followed			
What was the feast followed the night	28	29	3
Following			
Of a fresh and following folded rank	43		4
Ran through it following which we should have sight	125		6
Following falls and falls of rain	142		3
Follows			
There eyes them heart wants care haunts			

Word	Poem	Stan.	Line
Foot (cont.)			
Thy wring-world right foot rock lay a lion-limb against me scan	64		6
Cheer whom though the hero whose heaven-handling flung me foot trod	64		12
That mammocks mighty foot but no way sped	70		12
Head and foot shoulder and shank	71		4
But with his other foot three miles beyond	100		4
Or ever he set his foot to the land	109	7	1
Some pageant which takes tears and I must foot with feeling that	152		26
Footfretted			
Footfretted in it million-fueled natures bonfire burns on	72		9
Footing			
For a rainbow footing it nor he for his bones risen	39		14
Your footing now to the much-dreaded dust	107	3	2
Footrest			
Will add a footrest there to stand	81	7	42
Footsteps			
Dances for sad footsteps slow	24		22
Footway			
The footway Stephen said	135		28
For			
Being pure we lifes pride and cared-for crown	35		11
Forbid			
I here forbid my thoughts to fool themselves with fears	152		30
Bound on what thou hadst forbid	155		10
Forcd			
Of forcd persuasion issue oer the free	1	5	7
Force			
Then lull then leave off fury had shrieked no lingering let me be fell force I must be brief	65		6
So late there is no force in sap or blood	105		11
Earlier or you fail at our force and lie	153		3
Forced			
They rose at last and forced her from the spot	136		34
Forcible			
Double as sharp meaning and forcible	102	1	11
Forcibly			
So forcibly he sung	21		32
Fore			
Of crumbling fore-foundering thundering all-surfy seas in seen	141		5
Fore-foundering			
Of crumbling fore-foundering thundering all-surfy seas in seen	141		5

Word	Poem	Stan.	Line
Forecast			
Not kind to freeze me with forecast	134		1
No wisdom can forecast by gauge or guess	157		26
Foredrawn			
Fast furled and all foredrawn to no or yes	157		28
Forefalls			
Downs forefalls beat to the burial	41		7
Forefending			
Frowning and forefending angel-warder	48		17
Foregone			
They stand they shine in the sun fame has foregone	104		2
Forehead			
On a pastoral forehead of Wales	28	24	2
Upon my forehead hit the burly wind	135		12
Forward falling forehead frowning lips crisp	159		32
Foreign			
O have you here a foreign lady	109	7	3
O I have here no foreign lady	109	8	1
Foreknown			
No but for Christ who hath foreknown and loved thee	13		14
Forelock			
Look foot to forelock how all things suit he	41		76
But ah bright forelock cluster that you are	157		17
Forepangs			
More pangs will schooled at forepangs wilder wring	65		2
Forethought			
How far from then forethought of all thy more boisterous years	53		12
Forfeit			
When the thing we freely forfeit is kept with fonder a care	59		27
Forge			
And with fire in him forge thy will	28	10	2
When thou at the random grim forge powerful amidst peers	53		13
And on the fighter forge his glorious day	73		4
That forge her title of inheritance	102	1	70
The mint of current courtesies the forge	102	2	8
Forged			
It is the forged feature finds me it is the rehearsal	45		7
Forget			
Forget the waking trumpet the long law	5		44
And save by darting accidents forget	14	1	10
Wave with the meadow forget that there must	28	11	7
Forgetfulness			
Makes welcome death does dear forgetfulness	150		8
Forgive			
Who could forgive without grudge after	77		57

Word	Poem	Stan.	Line
Forgive (cont.)			
I would remember love forgive	81		71
Talks of self-sacrifice yet cant forgive	94		22
Forgiven			
I did repent I am forgiven	81		110
Forgives			
Freely forgives the monstrous debt	81		151
Forgiving			
But no forgiving voice replies	23		4
Forgone			
Barely a sigh to thought of hopes forgone	14	3	9
Forgot			
Where winter is the clime forgot	10		14
Where winter-while is all forgot	25		14
The essence neer forgot the fold	81		82
But is not that my grievance you promised and you forgot	128		6
Forgotten			
Being not forgotten for primroses note	107	3	19
Who is it how come to this forgotten land	122		19
Forked			
The shepherds brow fronting forked lightning owns	76		1
Forlorn			
The choicest remnants thence such home forlorn	1	15	3
And field-flowers make the fields forlorn	114		3
Form			
With form divine a fiery chivalry	1	7	8
God three-numbered form	28	9	2
To what serves mortal beauty dangerous does set dancing blood the o-seal-that-so feature flung prouder form	62		1
In hollows of her form the shadow clings	99		8
Formal			
Pendant in formal line from cornice tall	1	12	7
Formed			
Formed bars of stone beyond in stiffend state	1	4	3
Formerly			
But where was it formerly which is the spot	27		8
Forms			
Forms and warms the life within	42		22
Forsaken			
Slumber in these forsaken	41		82
His thoughts on her forsaken that she seems	50		11
Forsook			
When Henry heart-forsook	54		31
Forth			
On Easter morn the tree was forth	6		23
Flake-doves sent floating forth at a farmyard scare	32	1	7
In his ecstasy then off off forth on swing	36		4

Word	Poem	Stan.	Line
He fathers-forth whose beauty is past change	37		10
Forth Christ from cupboard fetched how fain I of feet	48		10
For love he leans forth needs his neck must fall on kiss	63		12
Cloud-puffball torn tufts tossed pillows flaunt forth then chevy on an air	72		1
Went forth to compass mysteries	77		52
While the sun streams forth amain	77		103
For he whom I send forth to crucify	81	7	31
To not ungentle death now forth I run	103		19
When you came forth for me	109	33	4
When I came forth for thee	109	34	2
Because the music from his bill forth-driven	113		3
His cheeks the forth-and-flaunting sun	144		2
Gaze on and fall directly forth on life	157		16
Forth-and-flaunting			
His cheeks the forth-and-flaunting sun	144		2
Forth-driven			
Because the music from his bill forth-driven	113		3
Fortress			
A fortress of true faith and central stand	1	5	3
Fortune			
Witnessed so fortune fell	54		4
Forty			
In forty days reachd heaven from earth	6		24
Forward			
Then a lurch forward frigate and men	41		40
Forward-like but however and like favourable heaven heard these	48		48
Forward she leans with hollowing back stock-still	99		1
Forward falling forehead frowning lips crisp	159		32
Forward-like			
Forward-like but however and like favourable heaven heard these	48		48
Fought			
They fought with Gods cold	28	17	1
Me or me that fought him O which one is it each one	64		13
Foul			
But frail clay nay but foul clay here it is the heart	63		3
But foul and cumber not	77		9
Fouled			
Gross mind discharging fouled laughter	77		58
Found			
At morn we found the heavenly bread	6		8
Part found no root upon the flinty road	7		9
But these were found in the east and south	10		13

Word	Poem	Stan.	Line
Found (cont.)			
And for those virtues I in thee have found	13		11
This fault in one I found that in another	16		11
I have found my music in a common word	19		5
I have found the dominant of my range and state	19		13
I did not mean to sleep but found	21		15
And a spring-time joy have found	24		16
The rose in a mystery where is it found	27		1
Thou art lightning and love I found it a winter and warm	28	9	6
Mans sprit will be flesh-bound when found at best	39		12
Yet found unstinted place for mirth	77		56
I found the ways were sown with salt	81		155
We found were dabbled with a colouring growth	98	9	2
Worse than when Floris found me in the garden	102	1	43
Floris thou late-found all-heal	102	1	63
The temperd soil where only her flower is found	102	3	4
That many centres found in many hearts	107	2	5
At last the bird is found a flickering shape and slim	113		9
And all round not to be found	138		5
This fault-not-found-with good	148		31
One once that was found wanting when good weighed	157		24
Foundered			
Where she foundered one stroke	41		4
Foundering			
Fast foundering own generation	41		87
Across my foundering deck shone	72		18
Of crumbling fore-foundering thundering all-surfy seas in seen	141		5
Fountain			
All day long I like fountain flow	155		2
Fountains			
With the burl of the fountains of air buck and the flood of the wave	28	16	8
Since sacred fountains to the sun	28	35	6
With-a-fountains shining-shot furls	71		19
While rushy rains shall fall or brooks shall fleet from fountains	152		107
Founts			
Then laverd founts and posturd stone he mixd	1	4	5
Four			
A sombre length of grey four towers placed	1	1	3
Peace and food cheered me where four rough ways meet	20		12

Word	Poem	Stan.	Line
Fatal four disorders fleshed there all contended	53		4
Round the four fingergaps	60		78
And thrice and four times and again	98	37	2
We have come four do you think	125		14
Several times I saw them thrice or four times turning	152		59
Fourth			
The goal was a shoal of a fourth the doom to be drowned	28	12	6
Fowl			
Then like a flock of sea-fowl mounting higher	2		82
Not that the sweet-fowl song-fowl needs no rest	39		9
Not that the sweet-fowl song-fowl needs no rest	39		9
Fowls			
The winged fowls took part part fell in thorn	7		7
Foxgloves			
Only the belled foxgloves lispd together	107	1	6
Fragrance			
From too much fragrance everywhere	4		4
In the quick fragrance of tall rolling pines	84		5
Frail			
How these two shame this shallow and frail town	35		9
But frail clay nay but foul clay here it is the heart	63		3
From one frail horn that crumbled to the plain	107	3	11
But in pale water frail water wild rash and reeling water	152		120
Frailest			
The fleeciest frailest-flixed	60		5
Frailest-flixed			
The fleeciest frailest-flixed	60		5
Frailty			
Not that but thus far all with frailty blest	157		6
Frame			
Then faild the tongue the poor collapsing frame	1	3	3
Worlds loveliest mens selves self flashes off frame and face	62		9
Framed			
Ah nature framed in fault	54		38
Shes framed to triumph in adversity	94		23
Not all but we were framed to fail and die	153		6
France			
Who fired France for Mary without spot	44		14
And tangles on a down of France	83		14
But from beyond seas Erin France and Flanders everywhere	152		125

Word	Poem	Stan.	Line
Frances			
Thus Frances sighed at home while Luke	21		50
Francis			
Joy fall to thee Father Francis	28	23	1
Frank			
What time the baffled Frank swept back pursud	1	14	8
In Frank in fairy Penmaen pool	29	1	16
Frantic			
O in turns of tempest me heaped there me frantic to avoid thee and flee	64		8
Fray			
Earth hears no hurtle then from fiercest fray	73		8
Or fray a granite from the precipice	81	7	38
And the poor corse impale with it and fray	89		7
Mells blue and snowwhite through them a fringe and fray	149	1	9
Mells blue with snowwhite through their fringe and fray	149	2	5
Freckled			
Whatever is fickle freckled who knows how	37		8
Free			
Of forcd persuasion issue oer the free	1	5	7
Then free and kind the wilderness	15		36
With free long looking ere I die	15		44
That bird beyond the remembering his free fells	39		3
And down the welkin gushing free	77		85
Sweetly then and of free act	77		89
I will break free from the Jews company	81	7	36
New love is free love or true love tis not	102	3	20
New love is free love or true love tis not	102	3	27
And risen sons yet are the childless free	123		2
Near by is Pauls free Tarsus fabled where	136		7
Not free in this because	148		13
His powers seemed free to play	148		14
Freed			
To the sight of him who freed me	129		4
Repent he sinned and all his sins be freed	140		6
Freely			
When the thing we freely forfeit is kept with fonder a care	59		27
Freely forgives the monstrous debt	81		151
Freeze			
Not kind to freeze me with forecast	134		1
Freezing			
A freezing runnel sobs and dwarfs	81	3	7
Freighted			
For did she pride her freighted fully on	41		8
Frenzied			
My frenzied working is not understood	81	7	26

Word	Poem	Stan.	Line
Frequenting			
Frequenting there while moon shall wear and wend	35		4
Fresh			
Unbakes my pores and streams and makes all fresh	5		32
And still thou bindst me to fresh fealty	12	1	3
Fresh brooks to salt sand-teasing waters shoaly	16		4
So fresh that come in fasts divine	22		16
Fetched fresh as I suppose off some sweet wood	34		4
His rash-fresh re-winded new-skeined score	35		6
Fresh-firecoal chestnut-falls finches wings	37		4
Fresh till doomfire burn all	41		118
Of a fresh and following folded rank	43		4
Off him but meaning motion fans fresh our wits with wonder	45		14
Us fresh youth fretted in a bloomfall all portending	48		30
With your fresh thoughts care for can you	55		4
Where whatevers prized and passes of us everything thats fresh and fast flying of us seems to us sweet of us and swiftly away with done away with undone	59		8
He does take fresh and fresh	60		56
He does take fresh and fresh	60		56
Those lovely lads once wet-fresh windfalls of wars storm	62		5
With fretty chervil look and fresh wind shakes	75	1	10
To colour as smooth and fresh as cheeks of roses	108		4
No rains shall fresh the flats of sea	114		13
Which says at least then go while all is fresh	125		64
The furl of fresh-leaved dogrose down	144		1
I can scour thee fresh burnish thee sheathe thee in thy dark lair these drops	152		46
Foamfalling is not fresh to it rainbow by it not beaming	152		55
By her bloom fast by her fresh her fleeced bloom	152		83
Be at every assault fresh foiled worse flung deeper disappointed	152		89
Fresh-firecoal			
Fresh-firecoal chestnut-falls finches wings	37		4
Fresh-leaved			
The furl of fresh-leaved dogrose down	144		1
Freshest			
There sweetest freshest shadowiest	159		23

Word	Poem	Stan.	Line
Freshly			
Ill lay them by and freshly turn instead	117		13
Freshness			
There lives the dearest freshness deep down things	31	1	10
This all this freshness fuming	49		6
And favouring virgin freshness yet	139		6
And with heavenfallen freshness down from moorland still brims	159		39
Fret			
Showerd the cliffs and every fret and spire	2		25
Quartz-fret or sparks of salt	60		101
Towards wastes where round the ice-blocks tilt and fret	88		7
Towards those wastes where the ice-blocks tilt and fret	88		11
Fretful			
And feel no blast the fretful fire	81	5	4
Frets			
A gold-water Pactolus frets	3		27
Fretted			
Around the water-nymphs in fretted falls	2		50
With the dainty-delicate fretted fringe of fingers	2		64
Us fresh youth fretted in a bloomfall all portending	48		30
And fretted clouds with burnishd rim	77		101
Fretting			
And the ever-fretting shirt of punishment	11		11
Fretty			
With fretty chervil look and fresh wind shakes	75	1	10
Fairyland silk-beech scrolled ash packed sycamore wild wychelm hornbeam fretty overstood	159		24
Friend			
Where art thou friend whom I shall never see	13		1
Their ransom their rescue and first fast last friend	40		14
Wert thou my enemy o thou my friend	75	1	4
But candour never hurt the dearest friend	94		8
The kings friend told the thing that was hid	109	12	1
Friends			
To the sweet living of my friends I look	16		2
So is it with my friends I note to hear	119		5
Father mother brothers sisters friends	159		49
Frieze			
Pourtrayd along the frieze with Titans brood	1	7	4
With oil of gladness for sackcloth and frieze	11		10
Frigate			
Then a lurch forward frigate and men	41		40

Word	Poem	Stan.	Line
Frightful			
The dense and the driven passion and frightful sweat	28	7	5
And frightful a nightfall folded rueful a day	28	15	5
Frightful sheer no-man-fathomed hold them cheap	65		8
Frigid			
With barren rigour and a frigid gloom	1	1	8
Fringe			
With the dainty-delicate fretted fringe of fingers	2		64
The moon dwindled and thinned to the fringe of a fingernail held to the candle	137		2
Mells blue and snowwhite through them a fringe and fray	149	1	9
Mells blue with snowwhite through their fringe and fray	149	2	5
Fringed			
From crown to tail-fin floating fringed the spine	2		41
Fringes			
The rim with ruby fringes dight	77		120
Fro			
They could tell him for hours dandled the to and fro	28	16	6
Or to-fro tender trambeams truckle at the eye	46		4
Frocks			
That frocks an oar in Penmaen pool	29	1	36
Froliclavish			
Long where we leave him froliclavish while he looks about him laughs swims	159		42
Fronting			
Fronting my froward eye	60		119
The shepherds brow fronting forked lightning owns	76		1
Fronts			
Fronts Venus his ill-launched hope	83		19
Frost			
Frost-furred our ivies are and rough	3		3
Frost-furred			
Frost-furred our ivies are and rough	3		3
Froth			
A windpuff-bonnet of fawn-froth	56		5
Roots and rocks is danced and dandled all in froth and waterblowballs down	159		7
Frothpits			
Fallers in dreadful frothpits waterfearers wild	152		112
Frothy			
Made headway in the frothy deep	21		51

Word	Poem	Stan.	Line
Froward			
Fronting my froward eye	60		119
Frown			
The frown of his face	28	3	1
Frowning			
Frowning and forefending angel-warder	48		17
Of a pool so pitchblack fell-frowning	56		7
O is there no frowning of these wrinkles ranked wrinkles deep	59		3
Them broad in bluff hide his frowning feet lashed raced	71		17
Forward falling forehead frowning lips crisp	159		32
Fruit			
Stretches the envied fruit with fatal smile	1	11	2
Terrible fruit was on the tree	6		15
Shall shake her fruit as Libanus	6		28
Christ at all hazards fruit hath shewed	7		10
Nor fruit nor flowers nor Dorothy	10		24
Fruit nor flower nor Dorothy	25		24
Fruit-cloistering hyacinth-warding woods	81		163
Drops the fruit out the duct runs dry or breaks	101		10
The fruit against the wall	105		12
Nor fruit above	127		8
Or paring of paradisaical fruit lovely in waning but lustreless	137		3
Fruit-cloistering			
Fruit-cloistering hyacinth-warding woods	81		163
Fruits			
For us was gatherd the first-fruits	6		3
Unpalateable fruits to eat	81		167
Fueled			
Footfretted in it million-fueled natures bonfire burns on	72		9
Fulfil			
And thy purpose to fulfil	155		18
Fulfilld			
And happy promises fulfilld	15		8
Full			
And art and beauty title now too full	1	15	6
Then they thus ranged gan make full plaintively	2		126
Summer was as full of flame	4		25
Handle the fig suck the full-sappd vine-shoot	5		38
Strike timbrels sing eat drink be full of mirth	5		43
Brim in a flash full hither then last or first	28	8	6
If floodtide teeming thrills her full	29	1	22
Doffs all drives full for righteousness	41		55
Then is my misery full indeed	81		68
And sucks the light as full as Gideons fleece	103		11
Now while the full-leaved hursts unalterd			

Word	Poem	Stan.	Line
stand	105		3
His steady wheel quite to the full again	107	3	12
Beyond the world the streams are full	130		24
Full-leaved			
Now while the full-leaved hursts unalterd stand	105		3
Full-sappd			
Handle the fig suck the full-sappd vine-shoot	5		38
Fuller			
Their fall was fuller of regret	4		30
Fully			
For did she pride her freighted fully on	41		8
Fumes			
Mid feverd fumes and slime and caked clot	78		8
Fuming			
This all this freshness fuming	49		6
Fumitory			
Foam-tuft fumitory	138		30
Function			
To its own fine function wild and self-instressed	47		7
Funeral			
Or else a funeral and yet tis not a funeral	152		25
Or else a funeral and yet tis not a funeral	152		25
Fur			
Flesh and fleece fur and feather	42		17
His cap shall be shining fur	124		13
Furl			
The furl of fresh-leaved dogrose down	144		1
Furled			
The heaven-flung heart-fleshed maiden-furled	28	33	3
Felled and furled them the hearts of oak	41		5
Say it is ashboughs whether on a December day and furled	149	1	4
Fast furled and all foredrawn to no or yes	157		28
Furlongs			
8000 furlongs in advance	83		16
Furls			
With along them cragiron under and cold furls	71		18
With-a-fountains shining-shot furls	71		19
Furnace			
The furnace shall at last be cold	15		16
Furred			
Frost-furred our ivies are and rough	3		3
Furred snows charged tuft above tuft tower	29	1	31
Furrow			
Yawnd like long furrow in the heart	77		64
For brier bough furrow or green ground	138		6
And down the furrow dry	138		27
Furrows			
From furrows of the poor and stinting weald	17		13

Word	Poem	Stan.	Line
Further			
But further down the valley left and right	1	14	4
Ere I had further question made	4		16
Not danger electrical horror then further it finds	28	26	13
Take courage this shall need no further art	81	7	33
But each a hands breadth further than the next	91		7
Who came from further than the stars	115		3
Ill cite no further what the initiate know	119		10
Furtherd			
Not furtherd far my travelld feet	81		157
Furthest			
Here at the very furthest reach away	107	4	19
The furthest reach this side on that the bay	107	4	20
Fury			
Then lull then leave off fury had shrieked no lingering let me be fell force I must be brief	65		6
Fussy			
My tempests there my fire and fever fussy	76		14
Futility			
I reasond the futility	81		113
Gaiety			
Come then your ways and airs and looks locks maidengear gallantry and gaiety and grace	59		14
Gain			
Of heaven what boon to buy you boy or gain	47		12
Gaind			
And gaind thro growing dusk the stirless bay	2		141
Gainings			
All of her glorious gainings unaware	151		10
Galahad			
An our days Gods own Galahad though this childs drift	48		40
The seraph brows of Galahad	78		42
Galaxy			
Now quicken sheathed in the yellow galaxy	98	22	3
Gale			
As a dare-gale skylark scanted in a dull cage	39		1
Too late lost gone with the gale	41		35
Told off their leaves along the piercing gale	98	5	2
The swallow favourite of the gale	130		9
Gales			
And they the prey of the gales	28	24	4
Galilee			
Of his going in Galilee	28	7	2
Galilees			
It is Galilees growth it grew at Gods will	27		10
Gall			
Fall gall themselves and gash gold-vermilion	36		13

Word	Poem	Stan.	Line
Gardens (cont.)			
In the gardens of God in the daylight divine	27		6
In the gardens of God in the daylight divine	27		12
In the gardens of God in the daylight divine	27		18
In the gardens of God in the daylight divine	27		24
In the gardens of God in the daylight divine	27		30
In the gardens of God in the daylight divine	27		36
In the gardens of God in the daylight divine	27		42
Garland			
This garland of their gambol flashes in his breast	159		19
Garlanded			
Tom garlanded with squat and surly steel	70		1
Nor mind nor mainstrength gold go garlanded	70		13
Garnered			
For learning stored and garnered	81		169
Garnering			
In harvest and in garnering	8		15
Garnet			
With garnet wreaths and blooms of rosy-budded fire	2		26
Gash			
Fall gall themselves and gash gold-vermilion	36		13
The blood-gush blade-gash	138		22
Gashed			
And those strokes once that gashed flesh or galled shield	73		2
Gashes			
Speard open lustrous gashes crimson-white	2		8
Gasp			
Age gasp whose breath is our memento mori	76		7
Gaspd			
By interchange gaspd splendour and eclipse	2		22
Gasping			
A hearts-clarion away griefs gasping joyless days dejection	72		17
Gasps			
Now he gasps now he gazes everywhere	41		65
Gate			
Before the sepulchre there stood a gate	1	4	6
Gates			
Lift up your heads o gates	115		8
Gather			
I gather points of lote-flower from an isle	5		33
On thistles that men look not grapes to gather	7		2
Gather gladness from the skies	24		13
Other I gather in measure her minds	28	26	15
When grey showers gather and gusts are cool	29	1	26
Yet ah this air I gather and I release	44		9
Gather the sooty plumage from deaths wings	89		6
And gather in like hurdles bright	98	29	3

Word	Poem	Stan.	Line
There was no crease or gather in the clouds	102	2	6
Like flame they gather on our cliffs at evening	104		7
I thought before I gather strength	118		13
And gather in like hurdles bright	135		21
Gatherd			
For us was gatherd the first-fruits	6		3
Gathering			
And gathering floated where the gaze was not	2		10
Gathers			
It gathers to a greatness like the ooze of oil	31	1	3
Gauge			
No wisdom can forecast by gauge or guess	157		26
Gave			
That gave you vantage when you would despise	14	3	3
My national old Egyptian reed gave way	20		7
And eyes heart what looks what lips yet gave you a	38		7
Gave Gods infinity	60		18
And to their feet the narrow bells gave rhyme	107	1	14
Gave the much music of our Oxford bells	107	2	8
He gave her kisses cold as ice	109	39	1
Gay			
Built thoroughfare heaven-roysterers in gay-gangs they throng they glitter in marches	72		2
There was a lady very gay	131		2
Gay-gangs			
Built thoroughfare heaven-roysterers in gay-gangs they throng they glitter in marches	72		2
Gaygear			
Winning ways airs innocent maiden manners sweet looks loose locks long locks love-locks gaygear going gallant girlgrace	59		15
Winning ways airs innocent maiden manners sweet looks loose locks long locks love-locks gaygear going gallant girlgrace	59		15
Gaylinks			
Those goldnails and their gaylinks that hang along a lime	142		5
Gaze			
And gathering floated where the gaze was not	2		10
Risn from the deeps to gaze on sun and heaven	2		35
Had she a quince in hand yet gaze	10		19
Surround the peak from which we gaze	23		26
Master more may than gaze gaze out of countenance	62		4
Master more may than gaze gaze out of countenance	62		4
Then may I upwards gaze and see	77		113
And faces fit for leisure gaze	133		13

Word	Poem	Stan.	Line
Gaze (cont.)			
Gaze on and fall directly forth on life	157		16
Gazed			
I gazed unhinderd mermaids six or seven	2		34
Gazes			
Gazes aslant his shoulder viewing nigh	1	11	6
Now he gasps now he gazes everywhere	41		65
Bids him this way his gazes fix	120		15
Gazing			
For only try by gazing to divide	102	3	9
Gear			
And all trades their gear and tackle and trim	37		6
With gorgons gear and barebill thongs and fangs	50		14
Gem			
All a sevenfold-single gem	77		116
Gem-fleeced at morn so brilliant is the weather	99		4
Gem-fleeced			
Gem-fleeced at morn so brilliant is the weather	99		4
Gemmd			
One bound oer dripping gold a turquoise-gemmd	2		60
General			
Their special-general title to thy love	12	1	14
Generation			
Fast foundering own generation	41		87
Generations			
Generations have trod have trod have trod	31	1	5
Gennesareth			
Woke thee with a we are perishing in the weather of Gennesareth	28	25	6
Gentle			
To gentle manna and simple bread	81		175
Like a contented wind or gentle shocks	98	2	2
As void as those the gentle downs appear	107	1	3
And brought the sense of gentle fellowship	107	2	4
Her showy leaves with gentle watchet foiling	108		6
Gently			
And death falls gently as the snow	77		26
Germs			
And lifes first germs from death had won	23		24
Gertrude			
But Gertrude Lily and Luther are two of a town	28	20	5
Get			
In Eden garden have get before it cloy	33		11
Kind love both give and get only what word	66	1	10
I cast for comfort I can no more get	69		5
And now I get some precious slips	81		84

Word	Poem	Stan.	Line
Says get you get you a lady to wed	109	9	1
Says get you get you a lady to wed	109	9	1
Why get thee gone then tell thy mother I want her	152		16
Gethsemane			
In the acre of Gethsemane	6		16
Ghost			
Because the Holy Ghost over the bent	31	1	13
What heart heard of ghost guessed	55		13
Them beauty-in-the-ghost deliver it early now long before death	59		18
Ghostly			
Towards all our ghostly good	60		48
Ghosts			
Or listening thought of linen-winded ghosts	135		18
Giant			
Tuggd the bossd smooth-lippd giant strombus-shell	2		57
Our passion-plunged giant risen	28	32	7
Of just majestical and giant groans	76		4
Out on the giant air tell summer no	154		3
Giants			
The triple-hummocked giants stool	29	1	10
Giddies			
Giddies the soul with blinding daze	23		28
Gideons			
And sucks the light as full as Gideons fleece	103		11
Gift			
The richest gift St Lawrence ever bore	1	2	6
Philip supposing that the gift most meet	1	3	6
Of the Gospel proffer a pressure a principle Christs gift	28	4	8
Home at heart heavens sweet gift then leave let that alone	62		11
Give him the gift I cannot tell	81		111
My fast-lodged tongue to her the gift	81		116
That struggling should not sear him a gift should cheer him	142		8
Gifts			
When chiefs and monarchs came their gifts to lay	1	2	7
Yet know not how our gifts to bring	23		17
Shares their best gifts surely fall how things will	48		4
Gilded			
His gilded rowels	98	26	1
Gilds			
Gilds with some sparky fancies his black night	102	3	30
Gilds with some sparky fancies blinding night	102	3	36

Word	Poem	Stan.	Line
Gilt			
Of those gilt webs that languishd in a fall	1	8	7
In blazon gilt and images of bronze	102	2	10
In gilt and blazon and bronze statuary	102	2	11
In gilt and blazon and maild shapes of bronze	102	2	12
Girder			
Dear Grace and girder of mine and me	134		2
Girdled			
To golden-girdled Cypris Ceres there	1	11	3
Girdles			
Girdles goes home betwixt	60		4
Girl			
Innocent mind and mayday in girl and boy	33		13
What is it Gwen my girl why do you hover and haunt me	152		1
Alive or dead my girl is carried in it endlessly	152		27
Girlgrace			
Winning ways airs innocent maiden manners sweet looks loose locks long locks lovelocks gaygear going gallant girlgrace	59		15
Girlhood			
And grave past girlhood earnest in her eyes	136		20
Girth			
The girth of it and the wharf of it and the wall	28	31	4
Spreading still its sunned girth	77		70
Girthed			
Not Goshen wasteful wide huge-girthed Nile	5		31
Give			
Give us the tale of bricks as heretofore	5		49
Give myrrhy-threaded golden folds of ease	11		12
Give God while worth consuming	49		7
Dog he did give tongue	54		34
Give beauty back beauty beauty back to God beautys self and beautys giver	59		19
Kind love both give and get only what word	66	1	10
I give commands for water for my hands	81	7	17
I plead and you will give your tears	81		28
Give him the gift I cannot tell	81		111
Give us our green lots in another mead	98	15	5
Is to give regimen to the imperfect wind	102	3	24
I give you my love and I give you my land	109	5	3
I give you my love and I give you my land	109	5	3
If I give thee kisses three	109	37	2
Give me thy kisses three	109	38	2
At once the senses give the music back	113		10
Must I give tongue again	125		23
Given			
And Ill pretend the credit given of yore	14	2	3
Hear yet my paradox love when all is given	20		13
Tis falsely given as love in men	81		49

Word	Poem	Stan.	Line
His tale and telling has been given to me	107	1	18
Giver			
God giver of breath and bread	28	1	2
Give beauty back beauty beauty beauty back to God beautys self and beautys giver	59		19
Gives			
Into my hand he gives a host for prey	5		17
Night to a myriad worlds gives birth	23		9
Thy river and oer gives all to rack or wrong	58		8
Since proud it calls the calling manly gives a guess	63		4
For more with him who gives thee all	81		150
And gives for tropes his judgment all away	102	3	29
And gives for tropes his judgment all away	102	3	35
Givest			
Oh till thou givest that sense beyond	23		43
Glacier			
Some ice that locks the glacier to the rocks	81	7	20
Glad			
And Im very glad	132		5
I am so very o so very glad	138		31
Gladdest			
The gladdest thing that our eyes have seen	26		18
Glade			
Death was vanishd from the glade	4		17
Gladness			
With oil of gladness for sackcloth and frieze	11		10
Gather gladness from the skies	24		13
Glance			
Mens wits to the things that are what good means where a glance	62		3
Glances			
To bathe in his fall-gold mercies to breathe in his all-fire glances	28	23	8
Glare			
The waves were rosy-lippd the crimson glare	2		24
Sickend and thickend by the glare and sand	5		19
After the sandfield and the unveined glare	5		29
Glass			
The glass-blue days are those	60		83
Her glass is blest but she as good as blind	151		7
Her glass drinks light she darkles down behind	151		9
Glass-blue			
The glass-blue days are those	60		83
Glassy			
Of glassy-clear aeolis metal-lustred	2		69
So glassy white about the sky	3		16
The glassy peartree leaves and blooms they brush	33		6
They webbd the sky with glassy light	87		2

Word	Poem	Stan.	Line
Glassy (cont.)			
Underneath their glassy barrel of a fairy green	141		6
And the water warbles over into filleted with glassy grassy quicksilvery shives and shoots	159		38
Glassy-clear			
Of glassy-clear aeolis metal-lustred	2		69
Glaucus			
The Glaucus cleped others small braids enclusterd	2		68
Glazed			
Glazed water vaulted oer a drowsy stone	98	39	1
Gleam			
Rich Titians faded in the straying gleam	1	12	3
Gleamd			
With painting gleamd the rich pilasterd walls	1	10	3
Some diving merrily downward drove and gleamd	2		108
Glean			
Down all that glory in the heavens to glean our Saviour	38		6
Gleaned			
How then should Gregory a father have gleaned else from swarmed Rome but God to a nation dealt that days dear chance	62		6
Glee			
What can it be this glee the good you have there of your own	28	18	8
Glen			
She stood before them in the glen	109	25	1
Glens			
But from the mountain glens in autumn late	1	13	1
Glide			
Or like a lark to glide aloof	77		65
With waved passes there shall glide	106		2
Glides			
For the listenr for the lingerer with a love glides	28	32	3
Gliding			
As a skates heel sweeps smooth on a bow-bend the hurl and gliding	36		5
Glimmerd			
Glimmerd along the square-cut steep	92		1
Glimpses			
Keen glimpses of the inner firmament	2		12
Glistens			
Her nostril glistens and her wet black eye	99		5
Glistery			
Bring in the glistery straw	5		46
Glitter			
Built thoroughfare heaven-roysterers in gay-			

Word	Poem	Stan.	Line
gangs they throng they glitter in marches	72		2
Globe			
Mantles the guilty globe	60		39
Globes			
Of filmy globes and rosy floating cloud	2		97
Gloom			
With barren rigour and a frigid gloom	1	1	8
Arose in gloom a solemn mockery	1	8	6
The skill of dreamy Claude and Titians mellow gloom	1	10	9
Into the cooling gloom till slowly all	1	12	5
The comfortable gloom	5		28
Now Carisbrook keep goes under in gloom	41		28
And sober lustres take the gloom	77		20
Shouldering down valleys smokes the gloom	81	7	2
Now more precisely touched in light and gloom	98	30	4
Gloomd			
Thro silver gloomd to a blood-vivid clot	2		107
Glories			
We see the glories of the earth	23		7
Glorify			
There God to aggrandise God to glorify	46		8
Glorious			
A glorious wanton all the wrecks in showers	2		93
And on the fighter forge his glorious day	73		4
All of her glorious gainings unaware	151		10
Glory			
Philip took oath while glory or defeat	1	2	3
To thy breast to thy rest to thy glory divine	27		48
Glow glory in thunder	28	5	4
Thou hadst glory of this nun	28	29	4
Glory be to God for dappled things	37		1
Down all that glory in the heavens to glean our Saviour	38		6
Let all Gods glory through	60		30
Gods glory which would go	60		31
Whose glory bare would blind	60		108
Of earths glory earths ease all no one nowhere	70		16
The horror and the havoc and the glory	76		2
The king of glory will come in	115		10
For love and greater glory of Christ	118		4
All glory be ascribed to	133		3
Should choke sweet virtues glory is times great guilt	136		2
Gloss			
A silver scarce-call-silver gloss	98	17	1
Glove			
Sucks close the acorn as the hand and glove	101		3
The hand draws off the glove the acorn-cup	101		9
Glow			
But now before the pot can glow	15		13
Glow glory in thunder	28	5	4
Blue-beating and hoary-glow height or night			

Word	Poem	Stan.	Line
Glow (cont.)			
still higher	28	26	5
Mote-like in thy mighty glow	155		4
Glowd			
An azure ridge or clouds of violet glowd	2		105
Glowless			
The moonlight-mated glowless glowworms shine	98	36	1
Glows			
When every colour glows	60		84
Then while the rain-born arc glows higher	77		123
Glowworms			
The moonlight-mated glowless glowworms shine	98	36	1
Glue			
Or sweet the golden glue	148		35
Gluegold			
That leans along the loins of hills where a candycoloured where a gluegold-brown	159		5
Gluegold-brown			
That leans along the loins of hills where a candycoloured where a gluegold-brown	159		5
Gnarled			
O his nimble finger his gnarled grip	41		80
Gnarls			
With the gnarls of the nails in thee niche of the lance his	28	23	3
Gnashed			
Gnashed but thou art above thou Orion of light	28	21	5
Go			
Go then I am contented here to lie	5		55
At Kirjath-arba go	5		58
I have desired to go	9		1
And rise and go about my works again	14	1	9
Never ask if meaning it wanting it warned of it men go	28	8	8
Heart go and bleed at a bitterer vein for the	28	30	3
Men go by me whom either beauty bright	40		5
Prayer go disregarded	48		47
Gods glory which would go	60		31
Nor mind nor mainstrength gold go garlanded	70		13
No let that go I have said goodnight to shame	102	1	45
So I go out my little sweet is done	103		17
Or if I go she stays meanwhile	120		28
Quite as ladies go	125		27
Why should I go because Castara goes	125		38
To say I go because Castara goes	125		60
Which says at least then go while all is fresh	125		64
Much cause to go because Castara goes	125		65
Says go on then I go on	138		35

Word	Poem	Stan.	Line
God (cont.)			
To God beautys self and beautys giver	59		19
Since God has let dispense	60		40
So God was God of old	60		103
So God was God of old	60		103
How then should Gregory a father have gleaned else from swarmed Rome but God to a nation dealt that days dear chance	62		6
And cry o Christ-done deed so God-made-flesh does too	63		13
Of now done darkness I wretch lay wrestling with my God my God	64		15
Of now done darkness I wretch lay wrestling with my God my God	64		15
Of us we do bid God bend to him even so	68		11
At God knows when to God knows what whose smiles not wrung see you unforeseen times rather as skies	69		12
At God knows when to God knows what whose smiles not wrung see you unforeseen times rather as skies	69		12
Yet God that hews mountain and continent	73		9
From God and man is hell no doubt	81	1	4
Make it to God I am not spent	81		130
He has his portion God who stretchd apart	126		2
Man is most low God is most high	133		5
He spoke of God the Father and His Son	136		25
God lighten your dark heart but no	145		27
Her will was bent at God for that	145		37
As long as men are mortal and God merciful	152		115
Thee God I come from to Thee go	155		1
Spend me or end me what God shall send me	156		13
None good but God a warning waved to	157		23
God-made-flesh			
And cry o Christ-done deed so God-made-flesh does too	63		13
Goddesss			
Great as no goddesss	60		27
Godhead			
Low-latched in leaf-light housel his too huge godhead	48		12
Godless			
What would befal the godless flock	92		7
Gods			
Of those who strove Gods gospel to confound	1	1	7
That battled Gods for heaven brilliant-hued	1	7	5
Of Gods dear pleadings have as yet not moved thee	13		10
Seek Gods house in happy throng	24		25
It is Galilees growth it grew at Gods will	27		10
They fought with Gods cold	28	17	1
Till a lifebelt and Gods will	41		62

Word	Poem	Stan.	Line
An our days Gods own Galahad though this childs drift	48		40
Acts in Gods eye what in Gods eye he is	57		11
Acts in Gods eye what in Gods eye he is	57		11
Gave Gods infinity	60		18
Let all Gods glory through	60		30
Gods glory which would go	60		31
Both Gods and Marys son	60		72
Of Gods love o live air	60		122
Yea wish that though wish all Gods better beauty grace	62		12
I am gall I am heartburn Gods most deep decree	67		9
Gods counsel columnar-severe	145		1
Gods son these they did not know	145		53
Gods daughter Margaret Clitheroe	145		54
Goes			
Fang or flood goes death on drum	28	11	3
That interests our eyes and who goes there	40		2
Now Carisbrook keep goes under in gloom	41		28
As sheer down the ship goes	41		59
Selves goes itself myself it speaks and spells	57		7
Girdles goes home betwixt	60		4
And then my heart goes near to break	81	6	7
And then goes out into the cavernous dark	103		16
Why should I go because Castara goes	125		38
To say I go because Castara goes	125		60
Much cause to go because Castara goes	125		65
Goes marching thro my mind what sense is this it has none	152		28
Going			
Of his going in Galilee	28	7	2
Winning ways airs innocent maiden manners sweet looks loose locks long locks love-locks gaygear going gallant girlgrace	57		15
Goings			
Keeps grace that keeps all his goings graces	56		10
Gold			
One bound oer dripping gold a turquoise-gemmd	2		60
A gold-water Pactolus frets	3		27
With not to be discoverd gold	15		14
To bathe in his fall-gold mercies to breathe in his all-fire glances	28	23	8
The grey lawns cold where gold where quickgold lies	32	1	5
Fall gall themselves and gash gold-vermilion	36		13
The gold-wisp the airy-grey	49		3
Nor mind nor mainstrength gold go garlanded	70		13
In wide the worlds weal rare gold bold steel bare	70		17
Thus we shall profit while gold coinage still	96	7	7

Word	Poem	Stan.	Line
Gold (cont.)			
The breaking leaves of gold are curld upon her lips	98	14	3
A pure gold lily but by the pure gold lily	98	15	1
A pure gold lily but by the pure gold lily	98	15	1
Gold gallant flowers much looked at in April-weather	98	16	2
Stars like gold tufts	98	25	2
And as she dwindles shreds her smock of gold	103		13
That has both gold and fee	109	9	2
Shewn him both gold and fee	109	11	2
Because of gold and fee	109	12	2
The bald and bold blinking gold when alls done	143		4
Gold-vermilion			
Fall gall themselves and gash gold-vermilion	36		13
Gold-water			
A gold-water Pactolus frets	3		27
Gold-wisp			
The gold-wisp the airy-grey	49		3
Golden			
With golden fillets and rich blazonry	1	7	6
To golden-girdled Cypris Ceres there	1	11	3
Thro crimson-golden floods pass swallowd into fire	2		83
Give myrrhy-threaded golden folds of ease	11		12
But you shall walk the golden street	22		23
More golden than the world of lights	83		2
Would not put out some tiny golden centre	98	22	6
The sky minted into golden sequins	98	25	1
Stars like golden bees	98	25	3
Stars like golden rowels	98	25	4
Of all the golden press	98	27	2
They seem to fold the hills with golden capes	104		11
Then he set sail in a golden ship	109	6	3
With a golden company	109	6	4
And stained and knots of golden thread	124		14
To that first golden age of gospel times	136		5
Or sweet the golden glue	148		35
Golden-girdled			
To golden-girdled Cypris Ceres there	1	11	3
Goldengrove			
Over goldengrove unleaving	55		2
Goldish			
Hard as hurdle arms with a broth of goldish flue	71		1
Goldnails			
Those goldnails and their gaylinks that hang along a lime	142		5
Goldy			
Not honour it ale like goldy foam	30	1	35

Word	Poem	Stan.	Line
Gone			
And other science all gone out of date	19		11
Now her mallow-row is gone	25		21
Hope was twelve hours gone	28	15	4
Too late lost gone with the gale	41		35
When shrovetide two years gone	54		5
Man how fast his firedint his mark on mind is gone	72		11
And you are gone so heavenly far	81		34
But Im alone for my loves gone	95		8
Leaps up before my vision thou art gone	98	33	2
Now one word more and then I am gone indeed	102	1	58
One has gone to the kings steward	109	11	1
She has gone with him to paradise	109	39	3
By speech so sweetly broken up and gone	125		31
You to be gone and I lag last	134		3
Till the longing is less and the good gone	138		36
Why get thee gone then tell thy mother I want her	152		16
Gonfalon			
Stood capital eminent gonfalon bearer	98	28	5
Good			
They shrive themselves and cry good service to our God	1	5	9
That seed which the good sower once did sow	17		7
What can it be this glee the good you have there of your own	28	18	8
O world wide of its good	28	20	4
I remember a house where all were good	34		1
Though grief yield them no good	41		106
With that world of good	42		27
How it does my heart good visiting at that bleak hill	48		21
Some good and so he does leave patience exquisite	51		8
Towards all our ghostly good	60		48
Mens wits to the things that are what good means where a glance	62		3
And I esteemd the sandal good	81		83
Tune it to words of good intent	81		127
O what will you now good servingman	109	18	1
Among the lilies and thy good domain	123		6
The hatred comes with a good grace from you	125		34
Good Valerian I will come	125		37
Then at the door what work there was good lack	135		5
Till the longing is less and the good gone	138		36
Or ever did for my sake some good deed	140		2
For good grows wild and wide	148		25
This fault-not-found-with good	148		31

Word	Poem	Stan.	Line
Grace			
No finishd proof was this of Gothic grace	1	6	1
Triumph of airy grace and perfect harmony	1	7	9
Unmindful of their grace the Escorial	1	8	5
Suiting its grace with him or her	25		26
Sweet unto God and the sweetness is grace	27		45
In grace that is charity grace that is love	27		47
In grace that is charity grace that is love	27		47
To flash from the flame to the flame then tower from the grace to the grace	28	3	8
To flash from the flame to the flame then tower from the grace to the grace	28	3	8
So at home time was to his truth and grace	41		99
Grace that day grace was wanted	41		115
Grace that day grace was wanted	41		115
All in this case bathed in high hallowing grace	47		11
Groom and grace you bride your bed	52		2
Keeps grace that keeps all his going graces	57		10
Come then your ways and airs and looks locks maidengear gallantry and gaiety and grace	59		14
But mothers each new grace	60		22
And plays in grace her part	60		49
Yea wish that though wish all Gods better beauty grace	62		12
To grace them spires are shaped with corner squinches	96	7	2
With what bold grace	102	1	64
Making the shadow sweeter a spiritual grace	107	4	15
The hatred comes with a good grace from you	125		34
Dear grace and girder of mine and me	134		2
Gracefully			
But has not learnt to take it gracefully	94		16
Graceless			
Best in graceless growth thou has confounded	44		7
Graces			
Keeps grace that keeps all his going graces	57		10
What put taught graces on his country lip	107	2	3
Grafted			
We are so grafted on his wood	6		33
Grain			
Startle the poor sheep back is the shipwrack then a harvest does tempest carry the grain for thee	28	30	8
Startle the poor sheep back is the shipwrack then a harvest does tempest carry the grain for thee	28	30	8
Why that my chaff might fly my grain lie sheer and clear	64		9
Grains			
Grains from his drooping head	7		13

Word	Poem	Stan.	Line
Grandeur			
It seems for grandeur barren left and dull	1	15	8
The world is charged with the grandeur of God	31	1	1
Mantling passion in a grandeur crimson grandeur	152		69
Mantling passion in a grandeur crimson grandeur	152		69
Granite			
Ground of being and granite of it past all	28	31	6
Or fray a granite from the precipice	81	7	38
Grant			
Grant that close-folded peace that clad	77		41
But grant my penitence begun	81		137
Granted			
Heard have heard and granted	41		114
Not granted only o on that path you pace	47		13
Grapes			
Who tread the grapes are splayd with stripes of gore	5		51
We shout with them that tread the grapes	6		12
On thistles that men look not grapes to gather	7		2
Grapes grew and drops of wine were shed	7		5
Grasp			
Grasp God throned behind	28	31	7
Grasps			
Of greenery and old earth gropes for grasps at steep	149	2	6
Grass			
I bear a basket lined with grass	10		1
I bear a basket lined with grass	25		1
Who to us are as dew unto grass and tree	26		38
Grass and greenworld all together	42		18
And louched low grass heaven that dost appeal	58		2
Their harness beams like scythes in morning grass	104		6
And each a dinted circle the grass was red	107	4	11
Who lies on grass and pores upon the sky	117		3
Gallop along the meadow grass	130		26
Grasses			
Lay along the grasses green	4		22
Grassy			
And the water warbles over into filleted with glassy grassy quicksilvery shives and shoots	159		38
Grate			
While his crackd flesh lay hissing on the grate	1	3	2
He raisd the convent as a monstrous grate	1	4	1
His charnelhouse-grate ribs between	4		10
We hear our hearts grate on themselves it			

Word	Poem	Stan.	Line
kills	68		9
Grateful			
And bring your offerings to a grateful God	5		11
Grave			
Warm-laid grave of a womb-life grey	28	7	3
And grave past girlhood earnest in her eyes	136		20
Graver			
And to put graver sins aside	96	1	3
Graves			
From tears shed over childrens graves	123		3
Great			
O breath of it bathes great heaven above	27		46
Wings so some great stormfowl whenever he has walked his while	45		11
Didst fettle for the great grey drayhorse his bright and battering sandal	53		14
Great as no goddesss	60		27
Having the infinitely great	81		152
Great butter-burr leaves floord the slope corpse ground	107	4	9
Should choke sweet virtues glory is times great guilt	136		2
Great Thecla the plumed passionflower	145		42
Greater			
As public is my greater privacy	12	1	7
Our redcoats our tars both these being the greater part	63		2
But having that believes it greater still	94		10
For love and greater glory of Christ	118		4
Greatness			
It gathers to a greatness like the ooze of oil	31	1	3
All quests save the recital of their greatness	104		3
Greece			
Rivalled insight be rival Italy or Greece	44		13
Greek			
Twice lovely tinted eastern turned Greek	136		15
Green			
Swimming and languishd green upon the deep	2		114
The miles profound of solid green and be	2		123
And with coffin-black he barrd the green	4		11
Lay along the grasses green	4		22
Goshen is green and fair	5		30
Where the green swell is in the havens dumb	9		7
Where in a newly-drawn green litter	10		5
Which in newly drawn green litter	25		5
Hack and rack the growing green	43		11
Late in the green weeks of April	81		21
Winks away its ring of green	86		2
Must see the green seas roll	88		9
And on their brittle green quils	98	7	1
In the green spots of that wood	98	10	1
Give us our green lots in another mead	98	15	5

Word	Poem	Stan.	Line
Green (cont.)			
And rosing part on part dispenses green	100		3
With such a violet slight their distanced green	100		8
Slight with such violet their bright-maskd green	100		9
Maskd with such violet disallow their green	100		10
So late the hoar green chestnut breaks a bud	105		9
These should have starvd with the green broods of spring	105		14
Controlld them to a grey-green temperateness	107	4	14
With green-white apples on the bough	124		20
But the boatman on the green	131		5
For brier bough furrow or green ground	138		6
Underneath their glassy barrel of a fairy green	141		6
Green-white			
With green-white apples on the bough	124		20
Greenery			
Of greenery it is old earths groping towards the steep	149	1	10
Of greenery and old earth gropes for grasps at steep	149	2	6
Greenest			
Of leaves of greenest flesh	5		34
Greenhouse			
Under the cloister-light of greenhouse vines	84		6
Greenness			
That thrive in the loamy greenness of this place	122		15
Greenworld			
Grass and greenworld all together	41		18
Greet			
For I greet him the days I meet him and bless when I understand	28	5	8
Greeting			
Eye-greeting doves bright-counter to the rook	16		3
Rapturous loves greeting of realer of rounder replies	37		8
Gregorians			
Louder the monks drond out Gregorians slow	1	13	6
Gregory			
How then should Gregory a father have gleaned else from swarmed Rome but God to a nation dealt that days dear chance	62		6
Grew			
Blades of Milan in circles rangd grew rust	1	12	8
Grapes grew and drops of wine were shed	7		5

Word	Poem	Stan.	Line
Grieving			
Margaret are you grieving	55		1
Grim			
When thou at the random grim forge powerful amidst peers	53		13
Grimy			
In grimy vasty vault	60		102
Right offspring of your grimy mother earth	78		2
Grind			
Hailropes hustle and grind their	41		26
Where selfwrung selfstrung sheathe-and shelterless thoughts against thoughts in groans grind	61		14
Grip			
O his nimble finger his gnarled grip	41		80
Grizzled			
Whats yonder grizzled dyphwys dim	30	1	9
Groans			
Where selfwrung selfstrung sheathe-and shelterless thoughts against thoughts in groans grind	61		14
Of just majestical and giant groans	76		4
Groins			
With blazoned groins and crowned with hues of majesty	1	6	9
Are the groins of the braes that the brook treads through	56		10
Groom			
Groom and grace you bride your bed	52		2
Gropes			
Of greenery and old earth gropes for grasps at steep	149	2	6
The more some monstrous hand gropes with clammy fingers there	152		20
Groping			
By groping round my comfortless than blind	69		6
Of greenery it is old earths groping towards the steep	149	1	10
Gross			
The gross flock call them quails	5		16
Hence sensual gross desires	77		1
Gross mind discharging fouled laughter	77		58
Ground			
The hoarse leaves crawl on hissing ground	3		5
Between the tower-top and the ground	15		29
Take a lesson from the ground	24		14
Is it anything true does it grow upon ground	27		2
The down-dugged ground-hugged grey	28	26	2
Ground of being and granite of it past all	28	31	6
With heavens lights high hung round or mother-ground	70		11
Great butter-burr leaves floord the slope			

Word	Poem	Stan.	Line
corpse ground	107	4	9
Down upon ground fell she	109	39	2
And one to each of us is holy ground	116		3
Dies off in hyacinthed ground	135		33
For brier bough furrow or green ground	138		6
Off trundled timber and scoops of the hill-side ground hollow hollow hollow ground	146		4
Off trundled timber and scoops of the hill-side ground hollow hollow hollow ground	146		4
Ground-hugged			
The down-dugged ground-hugged grey	28	26	2
Grounded			
That neighbour-nature thy grey beauty is grounded	44		6
Groundlong			
Who breathe from groundlong babyhood to hoary	76		6
Grounds			
O grounds of hell make room	115		2
Grove			
The towers musical quiet-walled grove	12	1	10
Leave it with its grove hard by	98	15	3
Groved			
And where thou dwellest in deep-groved Aidenn	26		23
Grovel			
And there for ever grovel	78		7
Grow			
Is it anything true does it grow upon ground	27		2
Now I grow numb my tongue strikes on the gum	81	7	27
The weighty weeks without hands grow	145		5
Mays beauty massacre and wisped wild clouds grow	154		2
Growing			
And gaind thro growing dusk the stirless bay	2		141
Hack and rack the growing green	43		11
A growing burnish brighter than before	151		4
Grown			
So grown fantastic in his piety	1	3	5
Now all things rosy turnd the west had grown	2		19
Hope had grown grey hairs	28	15	1
Grown wicked in the wicked wars	114		12
Grows			
More sweet-familiar grows my love to thee	12	1	2
Grows less and less sweet to him and knows no cause	14	3	14
Love it grows darker here and thou art above	20		5
Ah as the heart grows older	55		5
But when she sights the sun she grows and sizes	103		6

Word	Poem	Stan.	Line
Grows (cont.)			
For good grows wild and wide	148		25
The times are nightfall look their light grows less	150		1
Call no such maiden mine the deeper grows her dearness	152		18
Growth			
It is Galilees growth it grew at Gods will	27		10
Growth in everything	41		16
Best in graceless growth thou hast confounded	43		7
We found were dabbled with a colouring growth	98	9	2
Growths			
With growths of myriad feelers crystalline	2		70
Grudge			
Who could forgive without grudge after	77		57
Guard			
A faithful guard of inner darkness fixd	1	4	7
Guardedly			
He heightens worth who guardedly diminishes	96	7	4
Guess			
We guess we clothe thee unseen king	23		13
After-comers cannot guess the beauty been	42		19
Since proud it calls the calling manly gives a guess	63		4
Something we guess or know some spirits start	126		7
No wisdom can forecast by gauge or guess	157		26
Guessed			
The treasure never eyesight got nor was ever guessed what for the hearing	28	26	8
What heart heard of ghost guessed	54		13
Guesses			
The heart guesses easily is it the same	27		21
Guessing			
O father not under thy feathers nor ever as guessing	28	12	5
Guile			
Where Phoebus weeps for him whom Zephyrs guile	1	11	7
A something in her face of guile	120		10
And speeds uncheckd her murderous guile	120		30
Guilt			
That guilt is hushed by hearts are flushed by and melt	28	6	6
Should choke sweet virtues glory is times great guilt	136		2
Guilty			
Mantles the guilty globe	60		39
Guilty of silence	125		26
Guinevere			
O Guinevere	102	2	1

Word	Poem	Stan.	Line
Gulf			
And silence and a gulf of air	15		40
Gulfs			
The recurb and the recovery of the gulfs sides	28	31	3
Gull			
Slim-pointed sea-gull plumes and droop behind	2		80
Gullies			
Adown the clattering gullies swept the rain	1	13	2
Now her afterdraught gullies him too down	41		60
Gum			
Now I grow numb my tongue strikes on the gum	81	7	27
Gurgled			
Marking the spot when they have gurgled oer	2		3
Gurgled where they had sunk melodiously	2		111
Gurgling			
White loomd my rock the water gurgling oer	2		142
To pause then from his gurgling bill	77		83
Gush			
Gush flush the man the being with it sour or sweet	28	8	5
The blood-gush blade-gash	138		22
Gushing			
And down the welkin gushing free	77		85
Gust			
Most wide ye are who call this gust Simoom	5		26
She listened how the sea-gust shook	21		52
Gusts			
The altar-tapers flard in gusts in vain	1	13	5
His lusty hands in gusts of scented wind	2		88
When grey showers gather and gusts are cool	30	1	26
Gusty			
And silver-shot with gusty light	79		8
Gwen			
What is it Gwen my girl why do you hover and haunt me	152		1
Gwenvrewi			
But both will share one cell this was good news Gwenvrewi	152		14
Perhaps we struck no blow Gwenvrewi lives perhaps	152		40
With no now no Gwenvrewi I must miss her most	152		85
Hack			
Hack and rack the growing green	43		11
Hacked			
I all my being have hacked in half with her neck one part	152		93
Hacks			
Vespillo my centurion hacks out	81	7	19

Word	Poem	Stan.	Line
Haemony			
That not Arcadia knew nor haemony	107	1	17
Haggard			
O then weary then why should we tread o why are we so haggard at the heart so care-coiled care-killed so fagged so cogged so cumbered	59		26
Haggle			
O hideous vice to haggle yet	81		149
Hail			
Like shiverd rubies dance or sheen of sapphire hail	2		73
To fields where flies no sharp and sided hail	9		3
Who would not shelter from the hail	81		76
Strike churl hurl cheerless wind then heltering hail	154		1
Hailropes			
Hailropes hustle and grind their	41		26
Hair			
The drenched hair of slabby weeds that swung	2		113
Chaplets for dishevelled hair	24		21
And May has come hair-bound in flowers	26		13
Age and ages evils hoar hair	59		11
See not a hair is not an eyelash not the least lash lost every hair	59		20
See not a hair is not an eyelash not the least lash lost every hair	59		20
Is hair of the head numbered	59		21
That each eyelash or hair	60		3
More sweetly shades her stolen hair	120		7
And lapped in shining hair roll to the banks edge then	152		50
Hair-bound			
And May has come hair-bound in flowers	26		13
Hairs			
Hope had grown grey hairs	28	15	1
Half			
But most in a half-circle watchd the sun	2		116
That shapes in half-light his departing rings	19		3
And hurls for him o half hurls earth for him off under his feet	38		14
As half she had righted and hoped to rise	41		37
What death half lifts the latch of	49		19
But half the pains he spends upon his boy	97		4
Her lids half-meshing shelter from the sky	99		6
Crispd up and starchy from a short half-hour	107	3	3
And pledged purply in a half-lit dell	112		11
And half mislike her loveless kiss	120		13
I all my being have hacked in half with her neck one part	152		93

Word	Poem	Stan.	Line
Half-circle			
But most in a half-circle watchd the sun	2		116
Half-hour			
Crispd up and starchy from a short half-hour	107	3	3
Half-light			
That shapes in half-light his departing rings	19		3
Half-lit			
And pledged purply in a half-lit dell	112		11
Half-meshing			
Her lids half-meshing shelter from the sky	99		6
Hall			
Yet like a lighted empty hall	23		10
Our company thronged the hall	54		11
There the hall rung	54		33
Hallowed			
Dress hoar-hallowed shrines unvisited	41		91
Out of hallowed bodies bred	52		4
Hallowing			
All in this case bathed in high hallowing grace	47		11
Hallows			
Christ home Christ and His mother and all His hallows	32	1	14
Halls			
He rangd long corridors and cornicd halls	1	10	1
Halod			
Clusterd in troops and halod by the light	2		36
Halt			
No flowers to find no place to halt	81		159
Flush thro their heaving columns when they halt	104		10
Halve			
To halve the bowl of Penmaen pool	29	1	12
Halves			
As halves of sweet-pea-blossom are	81		44
Hamlets			
Allows the sound of bells in hamlets round	81	4	6
Hampstead			
Hampstead was never bright and whatever Miss Cullys charms	128		11
Hand			
And more on each hand thicken and appear	2		30
Into my hand he gives a host for prey	5		17
Behold at Elim wells on every hand	5		23
So trickle from your hand	5		42
And a quince in hand not one	10		9
Had she a quince in hand yet gaze	10		19
But not the hand that wrought them all	23		8
My hand upon my lips I lay	23		37
And lead me child-like by the hand	23		47
I kiss my hand	28	5	1
Kiss my hand to the dappled-with-damson west	28	5	5

Word	Poem	Stan.	Line
Hand (cont.)			
Left hand off land I hear the lark ascend	35		5
Home was hard at hand	41		18
Of ruinous shrine no hand or worse	41		89
Robberys hand is busy to	41		90
Head heart hand heel and shoulder	49		10
Where you can lift your hand	60		76
And her hand leaves his light	60		112
Hand rather my heart lo lapped strength stole joy would laugh cheer	64		11
He hand to mouth he lives and voids with shame	75		9
Now known and hand at work now never wrong	77		8
The point fast in and my left hand	80	7	44
Ill take in hand the blady stone	80	7	48
Who knelt were for the lords right hand	81		94
See on one hand	100		1
Sucks close the acorn as the hand and glove	101		3
The hand draws off the glove the acorn-cup	101		9
No Ill not hazard it only his hand	102	1	26
Turns the lantern on Floris hand	102	1	27
Now let me see you you large princely hand	102	1	46
Yet this could be no others hand than his	102	1	48
Now I am minded to take pipe in hand	105		1
If it be a white rose in his hand	109	22	1
Is it a lily in your hand	109	33	1
Before or behind or far or at hand	138		7
Her hand from heaven to turn a mill	139		4
That he will out of hand and heartily	140		5
Holds till hand aches and wonders what is there	151		8
The more some monstrous hand gropes with clammy fingers there	152		20
When ts light I quenched its rose times one rich rose my hand	152		82
From thy hand out swayed about	155		3
I have tall daughters dear that heed my hand	158		2
Handed			
In a neighbour deft-handed are you that liar	46		13
Handle			
The stretching palace lay as handle fixd	1	4	4
Handle the fig suck the full-sappd vine-shoot	5		38
Unchilld I handle stinging snow	80	2	1
Handling			
Cheer whom though the herd whose heaven-handling flung me foot trod	64		12
Hands			
His lusty hands in gusts of scented wind	2		88
Your hands have borne the tent-poles on you plod	5		7

Word	Poem	Stan.	Line
O feel-of-primrose hands o feet	22		21
All hands for themselves the cry ran then	41		41
Clutched hands through clasped knees	54		21
But Harry in his hands he has flung	54		35
I give commands for water for my hands	80	7	17
From hands now clammy with strange blood	80	7	25
I bit my hands my looks I shroud	80		65
But each a hands breadth further than the next	91		7
They have bound his feet they have bound his hands	109	13	3
The weighty weeks without hands grow	145		5
Heaved drum on drum but hands also	145		6
She held her hands to like in prayer	145		48
Handsome			
Mannerly-hearted more than handsome face	47		9
Who have watched his mould of man big-boned and hardy-handsome	53		2
Handy			
With a ropes end round the man handy and brave	28	16	3
Hang			
God with honour hang your head	52		1
Let incense hang across the room	77		19
Hang of a treble size	88		4
Those goldnails and their gaylinks that hang along a lime	142		5
Hang as still as hawk or hawkmoth as the stars or as the angels there	159		26
Hangdog			
This by despair bred hangdog dull by rage	70		19
Hanging			
The hanging snows rush down and bare	81	4	4
That the hanging honeysuck the dogeared hazels in the cover	159		9
Hangs			
Pillowy air he treads a time and hangs	50		10
Churlsgrace too child of amansstrength how it hangs or hurls	71		16
Say oer it hangs a water-cloud	81		56
The lock of clouds betimes and hangs the day	98	31	3
That early sperses and high hangs the day	98	31	6
Pierce her she hangs upon the flame-cased sun	103		10
Hanker			
Therewith to hanker for the small	81		153
Hanks			
Fallow foam-fallow hanks falln off their ranks	144		7
Hapless			
But hapless youth Antinous the while	1	11	5

Word	Poem	Stan.	Line
Happd			
They have happd him with the sand and stone	109	15	1
Happier			
Of if they try it I am happier then	12	2	10
My happier world wherein	60		116
Mothers are doubtless happier for their babes	123		1
Happiness			
And I can teach him happiness	124		7
Happy			
The happy leafing it is so with me	14	1	6
And happy promises fulfilld	15		8
Seek gods house in happy throng	24		25
Happy the father mother of these too fast	157		5
Harbour			
Bound for the harbour and your crew	21		14
As void as clouds that house and harbour none	107	1	1
Hard			
Hard by a royal palace and a royal tomb	1	1	9
It seemd so hard and dismal thing	4		31
Hard down with a horror of height	28	2	7
What none would have known of it only the heart being hard at bay	28	7	8
A released shower let flash to the shire not a lightning of fire hard-hurled	28	33	8
Home was hard at hand	41		18
Patience hard thing the hard thing but to pray	68		1
Patience hard thing the hard thing but to pray	68		1
Hard as hurdle arms with a broth of goldish flue	71		1
And hard men feel a softening touch	77		30
When skies are hard as any stone	81		8
But now are fled and hard to find	81		45
It was a hard thing to undo this knot	91		1
It was a hard thing to undo this knot	91		10
Leave it with its grove hard by	98	15	3
I have filld that hard to fill is	98	19	2
The ringed blindworm hard beside	106		4
Hard-hurled			
A released shower let flash to the shire not a lightning of fire hard-hurled	28	33	8
Hardend			
So hardend is it in this dearth	18		11
Hardest			
And ever if bound here hardest home	29	1	33
Hardly			
It is hardly a proper treat for a birthday to rest in her arms	128		12
Hardy			
Who have watched his mould of man big-boned and hardy-handsome	53		2

Word	Poem	Stan.	Line
Hardy-handsome			
Who have watched his mould of man big-boned and hardy-handsome	53		2
Hare			
Marcus hare high her captain	41		44
Hark			
Hark the molten melody	77		86
Then often the ears in a new fashion hark	113		7
Well after all ah but hark	138		10
Hark hearer hear what I do lend a thought now make believe	159		1
Harm			
Can I do any harm	125		18
What work what harms done there is no harm done none yet	152		39
Harmonies			
Whence spring the jewelld harmonies	77		138
We tuned to one key and made their harmonies	98	2	4
Harmony			
Triumph of airy grace and perfect harmony	1	7	9
Harms			
What work what harms done there is no harm done none yet	152		39
Harness			
Their harness beams like scythes in morning grass	104		6
Harp			
Pluck the harp and breathe the horn	24		11
Harry			
But Harry in his hands he has flung	54		35
He leans to it Harry bends look back elbow and liquid waist	71		12
Heaven comfort sends but harry it away	89		5
Harshness			
I can hear the harshness	132		2
Harvest			
Behold we have the joy in harvest	6		2
In harvest and in garnering	8		15
Startle the poor sheep back is the shipwrack then a harvest does tempest carry the grain for thee	28	30	8
Like Pharohs ears of windy harvest dry	117		6
Bid joy back have at the harvest keep hope pale	154		4
Hastend			
You met me I had hastend down	81		89
Hat			
For a beauty-bow to his hat	144		16
Hate			
And then I hate the most that lore	15		33
And hate the ill-visaged cursing tars	114		10

Word	Poem	Stan.	Line
Hate (cont.)			
And James shall hate his faded red	114		11
To the bargain of its hate to throw	145		20
Hated			
What if I hated flattery	125		32
Familiar and so hated by the sick	125		48
Hated and too familiar to the sick	125		49
Hatred			
The hatred comes with a good grace from you	125		34
Haunt			
What is it Gwen my girl why do you hover and haunt me	152		1
Haunted			
He haunted who of all men most sways my spirits to peace	44		11
Haunts			
There eyes them heart wants care haunts foot follows kind	40		13
Haven			
Hurling the haven behind	28	13	2
Remember us in the roads the heaven-haven of the reward	28	34	3
In unimperilld haven is wreckd	83		20
Those dearer more divine boons whose haven the heart is	152		131
Havens			
Where the green swell is in the havens dumb	9		7
Havering			
That bead the plain did ever havering church-tower	100		6
Having			
Having the infinitely great	81		152
But having that believes it greater still	94		10
Havoc			
Strokes of havoc unselve	43		21
The horror and the havoc and the glory	75		2
To have havoc-pocked so see the hung-heavenward boughs	157		32
Havoc-pocked			
To have havoc-pocked so see the hung-heavenward boughs	157		32
Hawk			
Hang as still as hawk or hawkmoth as the stars or as the angels there	159		26
Hawkmoth			
Hang as still as hawk or hawkmoth as the stars or as the angels there	159		26
Hawling			
And the inboard seas run swirling and hawling	28	19	3

Word	Poem	Stan.	Line
Hazard			
No Ill not hazard it only his hand	102	1	26
Creatures all heft hope hazard interest	157		8
Hazards			
Christ at all hazards fruit hath shewed	7		10
Haze			
From a haze of sapphire light	77		18
Hazels			
That the hanging honeysuck the dogeared hazels in the cover	159		9
Head			
Some carried the sea-fan some round the head	2		58
Where the upper mill-stone roofd his head	6		7
How soldiers platting thorns around Christs head	7		4
Grains from his drooping head	7		13
In bows above my head as falsified	12	2	4
My head to hear he might have strung	21		30
Ipse the only one Christ King head	28	27	5
Toil has shed round your head	28	35	15
Head heart hand heel and shoulder	49		10
God with honour hang your head	52		1
Is hair of the head numbered	59		21
What country is honour enough in all us lordly head	70		10
Head and foot shoulder and shank	71		4
Far from its head an angels hoverings	89		8
There would not be a whole place in his head	97		6
The knot of feathery locks upon her head	99		14
And long the trees were colourd but the oer-head	107	4	12
The crown should be unto her head	109	10	3
If he wear the crown upon his head	109	23	1
If he wear a crown upon his head	109	23	3
Is that the kings crown on your head	109	35	1
Of burden came and bowd my head	118		11
Dandy-hung dainty head	138		26
Head of a rebel	152		33
What have we seen her head sheared from her shoulders fall	152		49
Headed			
And headed always downwards with less sounding	112		2
Heads			
The vexd elm-heads are pale with the view	79		1
Their heads together in a stormy blot	90		6
Bringing heads of daffodillies	98	16	1
Lift up your heads o gates	115		8
Headstrong			
Hies headstrong to its wellbeing of a self-wise self-will	48		24

Word	Poem	Stan.	Line
Headway			
Made headway in the frothy deep	21		51
Heady			
By heady elements for no man knows	103		5
Heal			
Yet it is now too late to heal	15		17
Floris thou late-found all-heal	102	1	63
Health			
While sick men shall cast sighs of sweet health all despairing	152		108
Of favoured make and mind and health and youth	157		18
Heaped			
O in turns of tempest me heaped there me frantic to avoid thee and flee	64		8
Hear			
Hear yet my paradox love when all is given	20		13
And I could hear the tiniest sound	21		17
My head to hear he might have strung	21		30
To me was terrible to hear	21		42
The music that I care to hear	22		4
The ear it strikes like lightnings to hear him sing	33		5
Left hand off land I hear the lark ascend	35		5
Why hear him hear him babble and drop down to his nest	39		10
Why hear him hear him babble and drop down to his nest	39		10
To my creating thought would neither hear	66	1	6
We hear our hearts grate on themselves it kills	68		9
To hear the sheep-bells dimly die	77		71
To hear his strain descend less loud	77		79
Would I could hear the other Pilates shout	80	1	5
I hear the multitude tramp by	80	7	29
At last I hear the voice well known	81		1
At last I hear the voice I knew	81		25
You hear nor care of love and pain	81		35
You hear and alterd do not hear	81		41
You hear and alterd do not hear	81		41
The others heard I could not hear	81		101
Herclots preachings Ill no longer hear	96	5	1
When the wind drops you hear the skylarks sing	98	3	5
When cuckoo calls and I may hear	98	37	1
I hear a noise of waters drawn away	112		1
So is it with my friends I note to hear	119		5
I can hear the harshness	132		2
Hark hearer hear what I do lend a thought now make believe	159		1
We are there when we hear a shout	159		8

Word	Poem	Stan.	Line
Heard			
From both of whom a changeless note is heard	19		4
Betweens I heard the water still	21		44
Your passing steps I never heard	21		48
And truth is heard with tears impearled	23		35
Word that heard and kept thee and uttered thee outright	28	29	8
He thought he heard say	41		50
Heard have heard and granted	41		114
Heard have heard and granted	41		114
Forward-like but however and like favourable heaven heard these	48		48
What heart heard of ghost guessed	55		13
Heard unheeded leaves me a lonely began	66	1	13
To sing scarce heard and singing fill	77		77
The others heard I could not hear	81		101
Are heard that cry she does repent	81		123
She heard the hunt the morrow morning	109	24	1
She heard but knockings three	109	29	2
I heard her say poor poor afflicted soul	111		11
The earnest-hearted maiden sat and heard	136		32
Heardest			
Thou heardst me truer than tongue confess	28	2	3
Hearer			
Hark hearer hear what I do lend a thought now make believe	159		1
Hearers			
Themselves live singing and their hearers kill	96	2	2
Hearing			
Night roared with the heart-break hearing a heart-broke rabble	28	17	5
The treasure never eyesight got nor was ever guessed what for the hearing	28	26	8
Beside them about the hedges hearing him	113		8
Hears			
By many blows and banes but now hears roar	50		6
Earth hears no hurtle then from fiercest fray	73		8
Hearse			
Evening strains to be times vast womb-of-all home-of-all hearse-of-all night	61		2
Hearse-of-all			
Evening strains to be times vast womb-of-all home-of-all hearse-of-all night	61		2
Hearses			
Why should their foolish bands their hopeless hearses	89		1
Hearst			
And the prayer thou hearst me making	41		112

Word	Poem	Stan.	Line
Heart			
Slumberd at last in one sweet deep heart-broken close	2		135
My bankrupt heart has no more tears to spend	14	3	4
I cannot buoy my heart above	18		5
Speak whisper to my watching heart	23		49
The heart guesses easily is it the same	27		21
Mary the Virgin well the heart knows	27		22
The swoon of a heart that the sweep and the hurl of thee trod	28	2	6
And fled with a fling of the heart to the heart of the host	28	3	5
And fled with a fling of the heart to the heart of the host	28	3	5
My heart but you were dovewinged I can tell	28	3	6
What none would have known of it only the heart being hard at bay	28	7	8
Father and fondler of heart thou hast wrung	28	9	7
Night roared with the heart-break hearing a heart-broke rabble	28	17	5
Night roared with the heart-break hearing a heart-broke rabble	28	17	5
Do you mother of being in me heart	28	18	4
Of the sodden-with-its-sorrowing heart	28	26	12
Ah there was a heart right	28	28	1
But here was heart-throe birth of a brain	28	29	7
Heart go and bleed at a bitterer vein for the	28	30	3
The heaven-flung heart-fleshed maiden-furled	28	33	3
Rebuffed the big wind my heart in hiding	36		6
I walk I lift up I lift up heart eyes	38		5
And eyes heart what looks what lips yet gave you a	38		7
The heart rears wings bold and bolder	38		13
There eyes them heart wants care haunts foot follows kind	40		13
What the heart is which like carriers let fly	47		5
By it heavens befall him as a heart Christs darling dauntless	48		14
How it does my heart good visiting at that bleak hill	48		21
Head heart hand heel and shoulder	49		10
To own my heart I yield you do come sometimes but	51		4
Being anointed and all though a heavenlier heart began some	53		6
Thy tears that touched my heart child Felix poor Felix Randal	53		11
His heart up at the strain	54		27
When Henry heart-forsook	54		31
Ah as the heart grows older	55		5
What heart heard of ghost guessed	55		13

Word	Poem	Stan.	Line
To with no tongue to plead no heart to feel	58		3
And what is earths eye tongue or heart else where	58		9
O then weary then why should we tread o why are we so haggard at the heart so care-coiled care-killed so fagged so fashed so cogged so cumbered	59		26
About mans beating heart	60		50
Disremembering dismembering all now heart you round me right	61		7
Home at heart heavens sweet gift then leave let that alone	62		11
But frail clay nay but foul clay here it is the heart	63		3
Hand rather my heart lo lapped strength stole joy would laugh cheer	64		11
England whose honour o all my heart woos wife	66	1	5
Wisest my heart breeds dark heavens baffling ban	66	1	11
This night what sights you heart saw ways you went	67		3
My own heart let me more have pity on let	69		1
Tom heart-at-ease Tom Navvy he is all for his meal	70		4
Yawnd like long furrow in the heart	77		64
And then my heart goes near to break	80	6	7
Whispers if thou have warmth at heart	80	7	32
Ruinous heart-beat wandering death	81		53
This heart is warm to you alone	81		129
Her choice in roses knows by heart	83		22
Where my heart lists	88		2
And wear it thus a pectoral by my heart	102	1	31
And I must have the centre in my heart	102	3	7
In his heart said everyone	109	15	3
And every heart think loathingly	114		15
Yea crushd my heart and made me dumb	118		12
My heart irregularly shook	135		9
O heart have done you beat you beat so high	135		35
That here personal tells off these heart-song powerful peals	141		2
The motion of that mans heart is fine	142		6
God lighten your dark heart but no	145		27
Cuckoo bird and open ear wells heart-springs delightfully sweet	146		2
Learn how the heart is hence	148		6
And more and more times laces round and round my heart	152		19
My heart where have we been what have we seen my mind	152		31
What is virtue valour only the heart valiant	152		74
Who like me knowing his nature to the heart			

Word	Poem	Stan.	Line
by and melt	28	6	6
For how to the hearts cheering	28	26	1
Jesu hearts light	28	29	1
Our hearts charitys hearths fire our thoughts chivalrys throngs lord	28	34	8
Felled and furled them the hearts of oak	41		5
Mend first and vital candle in close hearts vault	46		10
Told tales with what hearts stress	54		23
Nowhere natural hearts ivy patience masks	68		6
We hear our hearts grate on themselves it kills	68		9
A hearts-clarion away griefs gasping joyless days dejection	72		17
When waking hearts can pardon much	77		29
And pride is nerveless and hearts meek	77		38
That many centres found in many hearts	107	2	5
O I admire and sorrow the hearts eye grieves	157		1
Hearts-clarion			
A hearts-clarion away griefs gasping joyless days dejection	72		17
Heartsore			
Seldomer heartsore that treads through prickproof thick	70		7
Heat			
They tell its story thus amidst the heat	1	2	1
The sun whose vast afflictive heat	81	2	2
I have drawn heat from this contagious sun	103		18
She brims her bath in cold or heat	139		2
Heathenish			
Such heathenish misadventure doggd one sin	102	2	15
Such heathenish misadventure dogs one sin	102	2	16
Heathpacks			
Wiry heathpacks flitches of fern	56		11
Heave			
My cries heave herds-long huddle in a main a chief-woe world—sorrow on an age-old anvil wince and sing	65		5
Beat heave and the strong mountain tire	80	5	2
Heaved			
Heaved drum on drum but hands also	145		6
Heaven			
That battled Gods for heaven brilliant-hued	1	7	5
Risn from the deeps to gaze on sun and heaven	2		35
In forty days reachd heaven from earth	6		24
Bear him to heaven on easeful wings	7		15
No influential heaven ever wore	14	2	7
My prayers must meet a brazen heaven	18		1
My heaven is brass and iron my earth	18		9
I must oertake thee at once and under heaven	20		15

Word	Poem	Stan.	Line
Heaven (cont.)			
O breath of it bathes great heaven above	27		46
Nor first from heaven and few know this	28	6	3
Storm flakes were scroll-leaved flowers lily showers sweet heaven was astrew in them	28	21	8
What by your measure is the heaven of desire	28	26	7
Heaven and earth are word of worded by	28	28	6
The heaven-flung heart-fleshed maiden-furled	28	33	3
Remember us in the roads the heaven-haven of the reward	28	34	3
For all they shine so high in heaven	29	1	19
Of heaven what boon to buy you boy or gain	47		12
Would brandle adamantine heaven with ride and jar did	48		46
Forward-like but however and like favourable heaven heard these	48		48
And louched low grass heaven that dost appeal	58		2
Blue be it this blue heaven	60		86
Fire-featuring heaven for earth her being has unbound her dapple is at an end	61		5
Cheer whom though the hero whose heaven-handling flung me foot trod	64		12
Built thoroughfare heaven-roysterers in gay-gangs they throng they glitter in marches	72		2
Of it angels fall they are towers from heaven a story	75		3
Alien from yours as heaven from nadir-fires	77		4
Where liquid heaven sapphire-pale	77		99
Caught from angels wings in heaven	77		110
Touchd from heaven in sweet dreams	77		126
Of a mastering heaven utterly blue	79		2
Choose one for hell and one for heaven	81		106
The heaven-enforced answer comes	81		144
Heaven and every field are still	85		2
Heaven comfort sends but harry it away	89		5
The vast of heaven stung with brilliant stars	98	21	2
Flares his wet brilliance in the dintless heaven	98	34	2
And a grey heaven does the hushd earth house	105		7
Alone upon the hill-top heaven oer him	107	1	8
Heaven make the time be short she said	109	3	1
Heaven make it sweet to you she said	109	3	3
When eyes that cast about in heights of heaven	113		1
The unenduring fallows of the heaven	122		6
The earth and heaven so little known	130		1
As sure as heaven it is	133		6
Nor I nor heaven would have it be	134		4

Word	Poem	Stan.	Line
Heavens (cont.)			
thrush	33		3
Down all that glory in the heavens to glean our Saviour	38		6
By it heavens befall him as a heart Christs darling dauntless	48		14
Home at heart heavens sweet gift then leave let that alone	62		11
Wisest my heart breeds dark heavens baffling ban	66	1	11
With heavens lights high hung round or mother-ground	70		11
The wrought rim of heavens font	77		112
Jarrd down the balanced storm the bleeding heavens	102	2	4
Heavenward			
Flowers do ope their heavenward eyes	24		15
To have havoc-pocked so see the hung-heavenward boughs	157		32
Heaves			
To me so arch-especial a spirit as heaves in Henry Purcell	45		2
Heaving			
Flush thro their heaving columns when they halt	104		10
Heavy			
Tho far or sick or heavy or still	81		18
Heavyheaded			
This side that side hurling a heavyheaded hundredfold	59		24
Hectors			
Droopd oer the brows like Hectors casque and swayd	2		42
Hedge			
Hover-float to the hedge brow	138		40
Hedgerow			
From any hedgerow any copse	98	18	1
Hedges			
Beside them about the hedges hearing him	113		8
And hedges break and lose the kine	114		2
Heed			
By a grey eyes heed steered well one crew fall to	71		5
I cannot calm I cannot heed	81		72
I have tall daughters dear that heed my hand	158		2
Heeds			
Death with a sovereignty that heeds but hides bodes but abides	28	31	8
Heel			
As a skates heel sweeps smooth on a bow-bend the hurl and gliding	36		5
Head heart hand heel and shoulder	49		10

Word	Poem	Stan.	Line
Heeled			
Yet Arthur is a bowman his three-heeled timberll hit	143		3
Heels			
Their crutches shall cast from them on heels of air departing	152		128
Heft			
Creatures all heft hope hazard interest	157		8
Heifers			
Thick-fleeced bushes like a heifers ear	98	11	1
Height			
There on a long and squared height	15		41
Hard down with a horror of height	28	2	7
Blue-bearing and hoary-glow height or night still higher	28	26	5
Her fond yellow hornlight wound to the west her wild hollow hoarlight hung to the height	61		3
Heightening			
The heightening dawn with milky orience	98	30	2
Heightens			
He heightens worth who guardedly diminishes	96	7	4
Heights			
When eyes that cast about in heights of heaven	113		1
Heir			
Realm both Christ is heir to and there reigns	48		32
Else but in dear and dogged man ah the heir	58		10
Held			
And held a cross of flowers in purple bloom	1	10	6
Yes for a time they held as well	101		1
They have held his eyes with blindfold bands	109	13	1
The moon dwindled and thinned to the fringe of a fingernail held to the candle	137		2
She held her hands to like in prayer	145		48
Helen			
Did Helen steal my love from me	95		1
It might be Helen Jane or Kate	95		6
Hell			
Before me the hurtle of hell	28	3	2
Not that hell knows redeeming	41		116
Squander the hell-rook ranks Sally to molest him	48		18
What hell hopes soon the snatch of	49		20
From God and man is hell no doubt	81	1	4
Choose one for hell and one for heaven	81		106
O grounds of hell make room	115		2
She was admired the spirit of hell	145		17
Hell-rook			
Squander the hell-rook ranks Sally to molest him	48		18

Word	Poem	Stan.	Line
Hells			
Bars or hells spell thwarts this to hoard unheard	66	1	12
Help			
And I not help nor word now of success	150		5
Help me sir and so I will	155		20
Helpd			
Helpd by the darkness of a block of copse	107	3	14
Helps			
He says his science helps him not to look	14	2	13
Heltering			
Strike churl hurl cheerless wind then heltering hail	154		1
Hempen			
With hempen strands in spray	144		6
Hence			
Hence sensual gross desires	77		1
Learn how the heart is hence	148		6
Or they go rich as roseleaves hence that loathsome came hither	152		129
Henceforth			
Henceforth let your souls alway	24		29
Now be my pride then perfect all one piece henceforth	152		70
Henry			
To me so arch-especial a spirit as heaves in Henry Purcell	45		2
Henry by the wall	54		12
When Henry heart-forsook	54		31
Herclots			
Herclots preachings Ill no longer hear	96	5	1
Herds			
My cries heave herds-long huddle in a main a chief-woe world-sorrow on an age-old anvil wince and sing	65		5
My cries heave herds-long huddle in a main a chief-woe world-sorrow on an age-old anvil wince and sing	65		5
Herds-long			
My cries heave herds-long huddle in a main a chief-woe world-sorrow on an age-old anvil wince and sing	65		5
Hereafter			
Me live to my sad self hereafter kind	69		2
Heresy			
Of the outward sentence low lays him listed to a heresy here	45		4
Heretic			
While from the pulpit in a heretic land	1	5	1
Heretofore			
Give us the tale of bricks as heretofore	5		49

Word	Poem	Stan.	Line
Heritage			
Might so attain their heritage	15		12
Love by monition heritage or lot	102	3	14
Hero			
To hero of Calvary Christs feet	28	8	7
Pride rose price hero of us high-priest	28	34	7
Save my hero o hero savest	41		111
Save my hero o hero savest	41		111
Cheer whom though the hero whose heaven-handling flung me foot trod	64		12
Heroic			
Unseen the heroic breast not outward-steeled	73		7
Hew			
When we delve or hew	43		10
When we hew or delve	43		18
Hews			
Yet God that hews mountain and continent	73		9
Hid			
The kings friend told the thing that was hid	109	12	1
Be hid behind	127		20
Once I turned from thee and hid	155		9
Hide			
By visual compulsion till I hide	12	2	5
Them broad in bluff hide his frowning feet lashed raced	71		17
And hide it though she does one may divine	94		11
Hideous			
O hideous vice to haggle yet	81		149
Hideous dashed down leaving earth a winter withering	152		84
Hides			
He hides our corpses dropping by the way	5		5
Death with a sovereignty that heeds but hides bodes but abides	28	31	8
His sweetest nectar hides behind	148		42
Hiding			
Rebuffed the big wind my heart in hiding	36		6
Hies			
Hies headstrong to its wellbeing of a self-wise self-will	48		24
That he hies to a pool neighbouring sees it is the best	159		22
High			
Of colour in high casements face to face	1	6	3
And melts amidst another cield on high	1	6	8
Though felt before though in high flood yet	28	7	7
Pride rose prince hero of us high-priest	28	34	7
Though no high-hung bells or din	28	35	1
For all they shine so high in heaven	29	1	19
High there how he rung upon the rein of a wimpling wing	36		3

Word	Poem	Stan.	Line
High (cont.)			
Marcus hare high her captain	41		44
All in this case bathed in high hallowing grace	47		11
Yonder what high as that we follow now we follow	59		31
She holds high motherhood	60		47
With heavens lights high hung round or mother-ground	70		11
With heavenly cithern from high choir	77		13
When the rainbow arching high	77		107
High up the balanced stony air	81	4	2
With the ready azure and high carmine think	93	2	2
That early sperses and high hangs the day	98	31	6
Of sheep from the high fields and other wild	107	4	23
With wealth that mocks his high degree	124		22
Man is most low God is most high	133		5
O heart have done you beat you beat so high	135		35
She high at the housetop sitting as they say	136		13
Apart wide and new-nestle at heaven most high	149	1	6
High-hung			
Though no high-hung bells or din	28	35	1
High-priest			
Pride rose prince hero of us high-priest	28	34	7
Higher			
Then like a flock of sea-fowl mounting higher	2		82
That less is heavens higher even yet	14	1	12
Blue-beating and hoary-glow height or night still higher	28	26	5
Double and higher than his wont	77		111
Then while the rain-born arc glows higher	77		123
Highest			
Their highest sprays were drawn as fine as lashes	107	4	6
At highest when he seems to brush the clouds	122		4
Highroad			
His rollrock highroad roaring down	56		2
Hill			
And broke into bloom upon Nazareth hill	27		11
A bugler boy from barrack it is over the hill	48		1
How it does my heart good visiting at that bleak hill	48		21
Hill	85		1
A thread of light betrayd the hill	92		9
Her silky coat is sheeny like a hill	99		3
Alone upon the hill-top heaven oer him	107	1	8
Sylvester came they went by cumnor hill	107	3	9
Crept all along a hill upon our left	125		3

Word	Poem	Stan.	Line
Hill-top			
Alone upon the hill-top heaven oer him	107	1	8
Hills			
And the azurous hung hills are his world-wielding shoulder	38		9
Questioning winds around the hills	77		44
They seem to fold the hills with golden capes	104		11
Circled the safe flanks of the bulky hills	125		10
That leans along the loins of hills where a candycoloured where a gluegold-brown	159		5
Hillside			
Off trundled timber and scoops of the hill-side ground hollow hollow hollow ground	146		4
Hilted			
With shining-hilted curves that they may stay	112		7
Hinders			
What hinders are you bean-blind yet to a fault	46		12
Hindrance			
Fear hindrance and espial	110		3
Hip			
The river spans it with so deep a hip	107	4	26
Hissing			
While his crackd flesh lay hissing on the grate	1	3	2
The hoarse leaves crawl on hissing ground	3		5
Hit			
Floris she will not hit thy sum of worth	102	1	61
Upon my forehead hit the burly wind	135		12
Yet Arthur is a bowman his three-heeled timberll hit	143		3
Hither			
Hither bring pearl opal sard	24		3
Brim in a flash full hither then last or first	28	8	6
Or they go rich as roseleaves hence that loathsome came hither	152		129
Hitherto			
And I had thought so hitherto	21		26
Hitting			
Of standing to the blossom-hitting shower	107	3	4
Ho			
Little I reck ho lacklevel in if all had bread	70		9
Hoar			
With a thin floating veil of water hoar	2		4
Hoar messmate hobs and nobs with him	29	1	11
Dress hoar-hallowed shrines unvisited	41		91
Age and ages evils hoar hair	59		11
So late the hoar green chestnut breaks a bud	105		9
Built of chancequarried selfquained hoar-husked rocks	159		37

Word	Poem	Stan.	Line
Hoar-hallowed			
Dress hoar-hallowed shrines unvisited	41		91
Hoar-husked			
Built of chancequarried selfquained hoar-husked rocks	159		37
Hoard			
Bounden bales or a hoard of bullion	41		9
Bars or hells speel thwarts this to hoard unheard	66	1	12
Hoards			
The abysmal ocean hoards of strange and rare	2		55
Hoarlight			
Her fond yellow hornlight wound to the west her wild hollow hoarlight hung to the height	61		3
Hoarse			
The hoarse leaves crawl on hissing ground	3		5
Hoary			
Blue-beating and hoary-glow height or night still higher	28	26	5
Who breathe from groundlong babyhood to hoary	75		6
Hoary-glow			
Blue-beating and hoary-glow height or night still higher	28	26	5
Hobs			
Hoar messmate hobs and nobs with him	29	1	11
Hold			
My eyes hold yet the rinds and bright	25		33
And hold at Christs employment	49		14
He had no work to hold	54		26
Frightful sheer no-man-fathomed hold them cheap	65		8
The pang of Tartarus Christians hold	80	1	1
To hold me quite fixed in the selfsame plight	80	7	46
You ask why cant Clarissa hold her tongue	96	4	1
Hold him	102	1	24
Holds			
That reads or holds the astrologic lore	14	2	2
That holds no promise of success	15		34
She holds high motherhood	60		47
Silence holds breath upon her throne	77		33
Hope holds to Christ the minds own mirror out	151		1
Holds till hand aches and wonders what is there	151		8
Holes			
The shapen flags and drilled holes of sky	12	2	11
Holier			
You see but with a holier mind	81		40

Word	Poem	Stan.	Line
Holiest			
Holiest loveliest bravest	41		110
Holiness			
Something of thy holiness	155		8
Hollow			
In a hollow lush and damp	4		7
Her fond yellow hornlight wound to the west her wild hollow hoarlight hung to the height	61		3
Work through a coverd copse whose hollow rounding	112		3
Off trundled timber and scoops of the hill-side ground hollow hollow hollow ground	146		4
Off trundled timber and scoops of the hill-side ground hollow hollow hollow ground	146		4
Off trundled timber and scoops of the hill-side ground hollow hollow hollow ground	146		4
Hollowd			
Into his hollowd palm should moan the blast	90		2
Hollowing			
Forward she leans with hollowing back stock-still	99		1
Close-rooted in the downward-hollowing fields	107	3	15
Hollows			
They chewd the cud in hollows deep	92		2
In hollows of her form the shadow clings	99		8
Whose gaps and hollows are not bronzed upon	107	1	2
Holy			
Does it smell sweet too in that holy place	27		44
Because the Holy Ghost over the bent	31	1	13
And one to each of us is holy ground	116		3
Make me pure Lord thou art holy	129		6
The holy three in one	133		4
Here to this holy well shall pilgrimages be	152		123
Home			
A cloisterd convent first the proudest home	1	1	6
The pride of faith and home of sternest piety	1	8	9
The choicest remnants thence such home forlorn	1	15	3
Thus Frances sighed at home while Luke	21		50
I shall come home to thee mother of mine	27		25
And ever if bound here hardest home	29	1	33
Christ home Christ and his mother and all his hallows	32	1	14
Home was hard at hand	41		18
So at home time was to his truth and grace	41		99
Come you indoors come home your fading fire	46		9
In backwheels though bound home	48		43
Flutes and low to the lake falls home	56		4

Word	Poem	Stan.	Line
Home (cont.)			
Girdles goes home betwixt	60		4
Fold home fast fold thy child	60		126
Evening strains to be times vast womb-of-all home-of-all hearse-of-all night	61		2
Home at heart heavens sweet gift then leave let that alone	62		11
Let charity thus begin at home	81		124
When are you home my love she said	109	2	1
When are you home from sea	109	2	2
You may look for me home my love he said	109	2	3
When I come home from sea	109	5	4
That Ive got a home	132		6
Who like me knowing his nature to the heart home natures business	152		76
Home-of-all			
Evening strains to be times vast womb-of-all home-of-all hearse-of-all night	61		2
Homeforth			
By him and rips out rockfire homeforth sturdy Dick	70		3
Homes			
Her homes and fields that folded and fed me	156		2
Homing			
Doff darkness homing nature knows the rest	47		6
Honest			
Sweet soul not scorning honest sweat	139		5
Honey			
The lawless honey eaten of old	92		4
Honeysuck			
That the hanging honeysuck the dogeared Hazels in the cover	159		9
Honeysuckle			
How when this bloom this honeysuckle that rides the air so rich about thee	152		23
Honor			
By conqurors rude of honor and not all	1	8	4
Honour			
Not honour it ale like goldy foam	29	1	35
With a feasting in her honour	42		8
God with honour hang your head	52		1
England whose honour o all my heart woos wife	66	1	5
What country is honour enough in all us lordly head	70		10
Honour is flashed off exploit so we say	73		1
Be under her banner and live for her honour	156		3
Under her banner Ill live for her honour	156		4
Under her banner we live for her honour	156		5
To follow a banner and fight for honour	156		9
We follow her banner we fight for her honour	156		10

Word	Poem	Stan.	Line
But under her banner I live for her honour	156		14
Under her banner we march for her honour	156		15
If under her banner I fall for her honour	156		19
Under her banner we fall for her honour	156		20
Honouring			
Honouring an uncontrolled royal wrathful nature	152		68
Hood			
That cordial air made those kind people a hood	34		5
Than fan or hood or strawy plait	120		8
We are leafwhelmed somewhere with the hood	159		2
Hope			
More wondrous to have borne such hope before	1	15	7
Afflicts no less what yet I hope may blow	17		6
With joy for to-day and hope for to-morrow	26		15
Thee may-hope of our darkened ways	26		40
Hope had grown grey hairs	28	15	1
Hope had mourning on	28	15	2
Hope was twelve hours gone	28	15	4
Can something hope wish day come not choose not to be	64		4
I have a hope if so it be	80	7	34
A hope of an approved device	80	7	35
With hope with shut eyes fixedly	80	7	51
Fronts Venus his ill-launched hope	83		19
I hope that all the places on our trip	107	4	27
Hope holds to Christ the minds own mirror out	151		1
To hunger and not have yet hope on for to storm and strive and	152		88
Not hope not pray despair ay that brazen despair out	152		101
Bid joy back have at the harvest keep hope pale	154		4
Creatures all heft hope hazard interest	157		8
Hoped			
As half she had righted and hoped to rise	41		37
Hopeless			
For poor loves failure than his hopeless rise	14	3	7
Why should their foolish bands their hopeless hearses	89		1
Hopes			
At hopes so evil-heavend as mine are	14	2	14
Barely a sigh to thought of hopes forgone	14	3	9
Those sweet hopes quell whose least me quickenings lift	48		37
What hell hopes soon the snatch of	49		20
That hopes that makesbelieve the men must be no less	63		5

Word	Poem	Stan.	Line
Hopes (cont.)			
My hopes and my unworthiness	118		9
Horizon			
Then find in the horizon-round	15		31
Horizon-round			
Then find in the horizon-round	15		31
Horizontals			
The vigorous horizontals each way fall	12	2	3
Horn			
Pluck the harp and breathe the horn	24		11
No they are come their horn is lifted up	104		1
From one frail horn that crumbled to the plain	107	3	11
Hornbeam			
Fairyland silk-beech scrolled ash packed sycamore wild wychelm hornbeam fretty overstood	159		24
Hornlight			
Her fond yellow hornlight wound to the west her wild hollow hoarlight hung to the height	61		3
Horns			
Her injurys looks off by both horns of shore	50		3
In the ascendancy of rainbows horns	84		2
Her finger-long new horns are cappd with black	99		7
Horoscope			
But in the others horoscope	83		17
Horrible			
To the shrouds they took they shook in the hurling and horrible airs	28	15	8
Horror			
Hard down with a horror of height	28	2	7
Not danger electrical horror then further it finds	28	26	13
The horror and the havoc and the glory	76		2
Horseback			
This darksome burn horseback brown	56		1
Horsemen			
Wherein beneath the cornice horsemen rode	1	7	7
Horses			
And watch until our horses and the men	125		9
Host			
Into my hand he gives a host for prey	5		17
Where stands no host at door or hearth	23		11
And fled with a fling of the heart to the heart of the host	28	3	5
Hosts			
And hosts confront with flags unfurled	23		33
Hot			
To an orbd rose which by hot pantings blown	2		20
In hot sands perilous	56		4

Word	Poem	Stan.	Line
Hour			
The driving storm at hour of vespers beat	1	13	3
In the worst hour thats measured by the sun	14	2	5
Thou knowest the walls altar and hour and night	28	2	5
Then even in weariest wintry hour	29	1	29
Him after an hour of wintry waves	41		68
Has drenchd the molten sunset hour	77		94
Sweetness from the hour and dip	77		132
And for that fearful hour life is more thin	80	3	5
It does amaze me when the clicking hour	102	1	1
Crispd up and starchy from a short half-hour	107	3	3
And every saint of bloody hour	145		44
For a quarter of an hour or so	145		59
Their young delightful hour do feature down	157		10
Hourglass			
In an hourglass at the wall	28	4	2
Hours			
They do not waste their meted hours	15		5
With eyes that smile thro the tears of the hours	26		14
Hope was twelve hours gone	28	15	4
They could tell him for hours dandled the to and fro	28	16	6
What hours o what black hours we have spent	67		2
What hours o what black hours we have spent	67		2
Hours I mean years mean life and my lament	67		6
Do in spare hours more thrive than I that spend	74	1	7
That his fast-flowing hours with sandy silt	136		1
And you unhouse and house the lord	22		24
Seek Gods house in happy throng	24		25
Till a maid in Davids house had birth	26		30
These are indeed the barn withindoors house	32	1	12
I remember a house where all were good	34		1
Mans mounting spirit in his bone-house mean house dwells	39		2
Mans mounting spirit in his bone-house mean house dwells	39		2
That plumes to peace thereafter and when peace here does house	51		9
You would not house beneath my own	81		4
No house of rimmon may I take	81		140
And a grey heaven does the hushd earth house	105		7
As void as clouds that house and harbour none	107	1	1
And all within the house were sounds as			

Word	Poem	Stan.	Line
Hours (cont.)			
posts	135		17
Housed			
But she who had housed them thither	41		42
Housel			
Low-latched in leaf-light housel his too huge godhead	48		12
Houseless			
Then sweetest seems the houseless shore	15		35
Houses			
Houses that make abode beside the lake	80	6	6
The shining slates and houses come and see	107	3	7
Housetop			
She high at the housetop sitting as they say	136		13
Hovel			
Scoop you from teeming filth some sickly hovel	77		6
Hover			
Hover-float to the hedge brow	138		40
They touch they tabour on it hover on it here there hurled	149	2	1
What is it Gwen my girl why do you hover and haunt me	152		1
Makes dither makes hover	159		10
Hover-float			
Hover-float to the hedge brow	138		40
Hovered			
The spirit hovered ere the sun	23		22
Hoverings			
Far from its head an angels hoverings	89		8
Hovers			
Hovers off the jay-blue heavens appearing	28	26	3
Huddle			
My cries heave herds-long huddle in a main a chief-woe world-sorrow on an age-old anvil wince and sing	65		5
Huddling			
With dare and with downdolphinry and bell-bright bodies huddling out	159		17
Hue			
Of mazy shape and hue but now bereft	1	8	3
With spiked quills all of intensest hue	2		44
Beyond the hurst with such a hue	21		6
Each hue so rarely wrought that where	77		117
Twixt real hue and phantasy	77		122
Hued			
That battled Gods for heaven brilliant-hued	1	7	5
Hued sunbeam will transmit	60		88
Hues			
With blazoned groins and crowned with hues			

Word	Poem	Stan.	Line
of majesty	1	6	9
Most like those hues that in the prism	77		61
Her hues a various brown with creamy lakes	99		11
Bright hues long lookd at thin dissolve and fly	117		2
Huge			
Not Goshen wasteful wide huge-girthed nile	5		31
Low-latched in leaf-light housel his too huge godhead	48		12
Huge-girthed			
Not Goshen wasteful wide huge-girthed nile	5		31
Hugged			
The down-dugged ground-hugged grey	28	26	2
Hum			
From Oxford comes the throng and hum of bells	98	3	6
Humanities			
What taught the humanities and the round of arts	107	2	6
Hummocked			
The triple-hummocked giants stool	29	1	10
Hundred			
Two hundred souls in the round	28	12	4
Three hundred souls o alas on board	41		2
Hundredfold			
This side that side hurling a heavyheaded hundredfold	59		24
Hundredweights			
They brought their hundredweights to bear	145		51
Hung			
Hung in the swaying of the fierce melee	1	2	4
Hung like a wreck that flames not billows beat	1	3	4
And bleeding saw thus hung from room to room	1	10	8
A tinted fin on either shoulder hung	2		52
Though no high-hung bells or din	28	35	1
And the azurous hung hills are his world-wielding shoulder	38		9
He hung on the imps success	54		24
Stones ring like each tucked string tells each hung bells	57		3
Her fond yellow hornlight wound to the west her wild hollow hoarlight hung to the height	61		3
May who neer hung there nor does long our small	65		9
With heavens lights high hung round or mother-ground	70		11
Yet when my unset tresses hung loose-traced	102	1	3
That tears and laughter are hung close			

Word	Poem	Stan.	Line
Hung (cont.)			
together	102	1	16
Dandy-hung dainty head	138		26
To have havoc-pocked so see the hung-heavenward boughs	157		32
Hung-heavenward			
To have havoc-pocked so see the hung-heavenward boughs	157		32
Hunger			
One spot and hunger to be there	15		32
That neer need hunger Tom Tom seldom sick	70		6
To hunger and not have yet hope on for to storm and strive and	152		88
Hungered			
Then next I hungered love when here they say	20		9
Hunt			
I must hunt down the prize	88		1
She heard the hunt the morrow morning	109	24	1
Hunters			
Who first knew moonlight by the hunters moon	105		17
Hunting			
And hunting winds and the long-lying snow	17		2
Lord William comes hunting tomorrow morning	109	19	3
Hurdle			
Hard as hurdle arms with a broth of goldfish flue	71		1
Hurdles			
And gather in like hurdles bright	98	29	3
And gather in like hurdles bright	135		21
Hurl			
The swoon of a heart that the sweep and the hurl of thee trod	28	2	6
As a skates heel sweeps smooth on a bow-bend the hurl and gliding	36		5
Strike churl hurl cheerless wind then heltering hail	154		1
Hurled			
A released shower let flash to the shire not a lightning of fire hard-hurled	28	33	8
They touch they tabour on it hover on it here there hurled	149	2	1
Are earthworld airworld waterworld thorough hurled all by turn and turn about	159		18
Hurling			
Hurling the haven behind	28	13	2
To the shrouds they took they shook in the hurling and horrible airs	28	15	8
This side that side hurling a heavyheaded hundredfold	59		24

Word	Poem	Stan.	Line
As where the little hurling sound	135		31
Hurls			
And hurls for him o half hurls earth for him off under his feet	38		14
And hurls for him o half hurls earth for him off under his feet	38		14
It hurls hurls off Boniface down	41		31
It hurls hurls off Boniface down	41		31
Churlsgrace too child of amansstrength how it hangs or hurls	71		16
Hurried			
Nocturns I thought were hurried through	81		92
Hurst			
Beyond the hurst with such a hue	21		6
Hursts			
Now while the full-leaved hursts unalterd stand	105		3
Hurt			
But candour never hurt the dearest friend	94		8
Hurtle			
Before me the hurtle of hell	28	3	2
Earth hears no hurtle then from fiercest fray	73		8
Hush			
There is one yes I have one hush there	59		2
After that in perfect hush	145		58
Hushd			
And a grey heaven does the hushd earth house	105		7
Hushed			
That guilt is hushed by hearts are flushed by and melt	28	6	6
Husked			
Built of chancequarried selfquained hoar-husked rocks	159		37
Hussy			
Man Jack the man is just his mate a hussy	76		11
Hustle			
Hailropes hustle and grind their	41		26
Hutch			
Palate the hutch of tasty lust	22		13
Hyacinth			
Fruit-cloistering hyacinth-warding woods	81		163
Hyacinth-warding			
Fruit-cloistering hyacinth-warding woods	81		163
Hyacinthed			
Dies off in hyacinthed ground	135		33
Hyacinths			
Of hyacinths	112		10
Hyaline			
So like a berg of hyaline	3		17

Word	Poem	Stan.	Line
Hymn			
Our hymn in the vast silence dies	23		6
Hypocrite			
When when peace will you peace Ill not play hypocrite	51		3
I			
So I am victor now I swear to pay	1	2	5
So I am victor now I swear to pay	1	2	5
Rowing I reachd a rock the sea was low	2		1
Then looking on the waters I was ware	2		27
I gazed unhinderd mermaids six or seven	2		34
Then saw I sudden from the waters break	2		74
And boasting I have fairer things than these	2		86
I knew not why but know that sadness dwells	2		118
I know the sadness but the cause know not	2		125
The rosy isles so that I stole away	2		140
Whence oft I watch but see those mermaids now no more	2		143
I never saw her so divine	3		19
I see long reefs of violets	3		25
I had a dream a wondrous thing	4		1
As I walkd a stilly wood	4		5
Death said I what do you here	4		12
I mark the flowers ere the prime	4		14
Which I may tell at autumn-time	4		15
Ere I had further question made	4		16
Then I saw that he had bound	4		18
As I markd not always died	4		28
I gather points of lote-flower from an isle	5		33
In beds in gardens in thick plots I stand	5		37
I water with my foot	5		40
Go then I am contented here to lie	5		55
Sure this is Nile I sicken I know not why	5		59
Sure this is Nile I sicken I know not why	5		59
I read the story rather	7		3
That I shall live I shall not die	8		7
That I shall live I shall not die	8		7
But I shall when the shocks are stored	8		8
We meet together you and I	8		10
And I will turn my looks to you	8		12
I have desired to go	9		1
And I have asked to be	9		5
I bear a basket lined with grass	10		1
I am so light I am so fair	10		2
I am so light I am so fair	10		2
That men must wonder as I pass	10		3
And at the basket that I bear	10		4
Sweet flowers I carry sweets for bitter	10		6
Lilies I shew you lilies none	10		7
Thus I come underneath this chapel-side	12	2	1
By visual compulsion till I hide	12	2	5
Or if they try it I am happier then	12	2	10

Word	Poem	Stan.	Line
And I have only set the same to pen	12	2	14
Where art thou friend whom I shall never see	13		1
Conceiving whom I must conceive amiss	13		2
That I have taken to plead with if the sound	13		9
And for those virtues I in thee have found	13		11
Who say that had I known I had approved thee	13		12
Who say that had I known I had approved thee	13		12
I never promised such persistency	14	1	2
I cease the mourning and the abject fast	14	1	8
I must feed fancy show me any one	14	2	1
You see that I have come to passions end	14	3	1
Else I am well assured I should offend	14	3	5
Else I am well assured I should offend	14	3	5
But now I am so tired I soon shall send	14	3	8
But now I am so tired I soon shall send	14	3	8
Is this made plain what have I come across	14	3	10
The whole world passes I stand by	15		4
I see the crowning of their towers	15		7
And I perhaps if my intent	15		9
The labours I should then have spent	15		11
Which makes me when with men I deal	15		19
No I should love the city less	15		21
But I desire the wilderness	15		23
I walk my breezy belvedere	15		25
I see the city pigeons veer	15		27
I mark the tower swallows run	15		28
And then I hate the most that lore	15		33
After the sunset I would lie	15		42
With free long looking ere I die	15		44
To the sweet living of my friends I look	16		2
Knowing them well I can but see the fall	16		10
This fault in one I found that in another	16		11
And so though each have one while I have all	16		12
Save Christ to Christ I look on Christ I call	16		14
Save Christ to Christ I look on Christ I call	16		14
Afflicts no less what yet I hope may blow	17		6
That I may win with late-learnt skill uncouth	17		12
My prayers I scarcely call to pray	18		4
I cannot buoy my heart above	18		5
I reckon precedents of love	18		7
I have found my music in a common word	19		5
And know infallibly which I preferred	19		8
Which ends those only strains that I approve	19		10
I have found the dominant of my range and state	19		13
Love I was shewn upon the mountain-side	20		1
See love I creep and thou on wings dost ride	20		3
I took of vine a cross-barred rod or rood	20		8
Then next I hungered love when here they say	20		9
But I must yield the chase or rest and eat	20		11
To see thee I must see thee to love love	20		14
I must oertake thee at once and under heaven	20		15

Word	Poem	Stan.	Line
I (cont.)			
If I shall overtake thee at last above	20		16
And soon I saw it shewing new	21		5
I only feared the wet for you	21		13
I did not mean to sleep but found	21		15
I had slept a little and was chill	21		16
And I could hear the tiniest sound	21		17
And I had thought so hitherto	21		26
And now I wish that it were true	21		28
I thought the air must cut and strain	21		36
Betweens I heard the water still	21		44
But that sweet sound which I preferred	21		47
Your passing steps I never heard	21		48
The music that I care to hear	22		4
My hand upon my lips I lay	23		37
The breasts desponding sob I quell	23		38
I move along lifes tomb-decked way	23		39
I bear a basket lined with grass	25		1
I am so light and fair	25		2
With the basket I bear	25		4
That a quince I pore upon	25		19
I find another Christian here	25		42
I shall look on thy loveliness mother of mine	27		13
I shall keep time with thee mother of mine	27		19
I shall come home to thee mother of mine	27		25
I shall worship his wounds with thee mother of mine	27		37
Over again I feel thy finger and find thee	28	1	8
I did say yes	28	2	1
I whirled out wings that spell	28	3	4
My heart but you were dovewinged I can tell	28	3	6
Carrier-witted I am bold to boast	28	3	7
I am soft sift	28	4	1
I steady as a water in a well to a poise to a pane	28	4	5
I kiss my hand	28	5	1
For I greet him the days I meet him and bless when I understand	28	5	8
For I greet him the days I meet him and bless when I understand	28	5	8
For I greet him the days I meet him and bless when I understand	28	5	8
Thou art lightning and love I found it a winter and warm	28	9	6
I was under a roof here I was at rest	28	24	3
I was under a roof here I was at rest	28	24	3
Other I gather in measure her minds	28	26	15
But how shall I make me room there	28	27	1
I admire thee master of the tides	28	31	1
I remember a house where all were good	34		1
Fetched fresh as I suppose off some sweet wood	34		4

Word	Poem	Stan.	Line
Left hand off land I hear the lark ascend	35		5
I caught this morning mornings minion king-dom of daylights dauphin dapple-dawn-drawn falcon in his riding	36		1
I walk I lift up I lift up heart eyes	38		5
I walk I lift up I lift up heart eyes	38		5
I walk I lift up I lift up heart eyes	38		5
I think where from and bound I wonder where	40		3
I think where from and bound I wonder where	40		3
What most I may eye after be in at the end	40		10
I cannot and out of sight is out of mind	40		11
Day and night I deplore	41		85
I might let bygones be our curse	41		88
Deeply surely I need to deplore it	41		96
May is Marys month and I	42		1
Yet ah this air I gather and I release	44		9
Yet ah this air I gather and I release	44		9
Some candle clear burns somewhere I come by	46		1
I muse at how its being puts blissful back	46		2
I plod wondering a-wanting just for lack	46		6
But tell me child your choice what shall I buy	47		1
You father what you buy me I like best	47		2
Came I say this day to it to a first communion	48		8
Forth Christ from cupboard fetched how fain I of feet	48		10
When limber liquid youth that to all I teach	48		22
Then though I should tread tufts of consolation	48		25
Days after so I in a sort deserve to	48		26
Seems by a divine doom channelled nor do I cry	48		41
That left to the Lord of the Eucharist I here lie by	48		44
Recorded only I have put my lips on pleas	48		45
To own my heart I yie'd you do come sometimes but	51		4
I to him turn with tears	52		10
Months earlier since I had our sweet reprieve and ransom	53		7
Love-laced what once I well	54		3
I came where called and eyed him	54		14
Crying what I do is me for that I came	57		8
Crying what I do is me for that I came	57		8
I say more the just man justices	57		9
There is one yes I have one hush there	59		2
One yes I can tell such a key I do know such a place	59		7
One yes I can tell such a key I do know such a place	59		7

Word	Poem	Stan.	Line
I (cont.)			
I say that we are wound	60		34
If I have understood	60		46
Were I come oer again cries Christ it should be this	63		14
In me or most weary cry I can no more I can	64		3
In me or most weary cry I can no more I can	64		3
Nay in all that toil that coil since seems I kissed the rod	64		10
Of now done darkness I wretch lay wrestling with my God my God	64		15
Then lull then leave off fury had shrieked no lingering let me be fell force I must be brief	65		6
Then lull then leave off fury had shrieked no lingering let me be fell force I must be brief	65		6
Me were I pleading plead nor do I I weary of idle a being but by where wars are rife	66	1	7
Me were I pleading plead nor do I I weary of idle a being but by where wars are rife	66	1	7
Me were I pleading plead nor do I I weary of idle a being but by where wars are rife	66	1	7
I am in Ireland now now I am at a third	66	1	8
I am in Ireland now now I am at a third	66	1	8
Remove not but in all removes I can	66	1	9
I wake and feel the fell of dark not day	67		1
With witness I speak this but where I say	67		5
With witness I speak this but where I say	67		5
Hours I mean years mean life and my lament	67		6
I am Gall I am heartburn Gods most deep decree	67		9
I am Gall I am heartburn Gods most deep decree	67		9
Selfyeast of spirit a dull dough sours I see	67		12
As I am mine their sweating selves but worse	67		14
I cast for comfort I can no more get	69		5
I cast for comfort I can no more get	69		5
Soul self come poor jackself I do advise	69		9
Little I reck ho lacklevel in if all had bread	70		9
I am all at once what Christ is since he was what I am and	72		22
I am all at once what Christ is since he was what I am and	72		22
Thou art indeed just Lord if I contend	74	1	1
With thee but sir so what I plead is just	74	1	1
Disappointment all I endeavour end	74	1	3
How wouldst thou worse I wonder than thou dost	74	1	5

Word	Poem	Stan.	Line
Do in spare hours more thrive than I that spend	74	1	7
Them birds build but not I build no but strain	74	1	11
And I that die these deaths that feed this flame	75		12
I want the one rapture of an inspiration	76		10
Some of the secrets I would know	77		40
Then may I upwards gaze and see	77		113
Then would I fling me up to sip	77		131
That I may drink that ecstacy	77		141
Would I could hear the other Pilates shout	80	1	5
Unchilld I handle stinging snow	80	2	1
Then I seek out the shadow of stones	80	3	1
Sometimes I see the summit stake	80	4	1
I can stand pent in the monstrous element	80	5	3
Breathe oer my bare nerve rather I desire	80	5	5
But then I make an eager shift to see	80	6	5
I cry o rocks and mountain make me room	80	7	5
And yet I know it would be better so	80	7	6
I try the Christus oer again	80	7	11
Sir Christ against this multitude I strain	80	7	12
Lord but they cry so loud and what am I	80	7	13
And then I choke to tell this out	80	7	16
I give commands for water for my hands	80	7	17
I choose one but when I desire	80	7	22
I choose one but when I desire	80	7	22
Now I grow numb my tongue strikes on the gum	80	7	27
And cleaves I struggle and am dumb	80	7	28
I hear the multitude tramp by	80	7	29
For he whom I send forth to crucify	80	7	31
I have a hope if so it be	80	7	34
I will break free from the Jews company	89	7	36
And I shall shape one to my thought	80	7	40
Thus I shall make a cross and int	80	7	41
And thus I will thrust in my right	80	7	47
Thus crucified as I did crucify	80	7	52
At last I hear the voice well known	81		1
At last I hear the voice I knew	81		25
At last I hear the voice I knew	81		25
I plead familiarness endears	81		26
I plead and you will give your tears	81		28
I plead and ah how much in vain	81		29
I know I mar my cause with words	81		30
I know I mar my cause with words	81		30
So be it I must maim and mar	81		31
And I cry out for wounded love	81		33
I walk towards eve our walks again	81		54
At once I struggle with my breath	81		58
No louder when I was with you	81		60
I fall I tear and shower the weed	81		64

Word	Poem	Stan.	Line
I (cont.)			
I fall I tear and shower the weed	81		64
I bite my hands my looks I shroud	81		65
I bite my hands my looks I shroud	81		65
Intolerable tears I bleed	81		67
I die I die I do not live	81		69
I die I die I do not live	81		69
I die I die I do not live	81		69
Alas I rave where calm is due	81		70
I would remember love forgive	81		71
I cannot calm I cannot heed	81		72
I cannot calm I cannot heed	81		72
I storm and shock you so I fail	81		73
I storm and shock you so I fail	81		73
And I esteemd the sandal good	81		83
And now I get some precious slips	81		84
I dreamd my counterpart it seemd	81		86
You met me I had hastend down	81		89
Nocturns I thought were hurried through	81		92
Some knelt some stood I seemd to feel	81		93
They are the goats who stand said I	81		95
I stood but does she stand or kneel	81		96
I strove to look I lost the trick	81		97
I strove to look I lost the trick	81		97
The others heard I could not hear	81		101
You cried but I have served thee well	81		107
O Lord but I have wrought and striven	81		108
I did repent I am forgiven	81		110
I did repent I am forgiven	81		110
Give him the gift I cannot tell	81		111
I reasond the futility	81		113
Or this or else I do not love	81		114
I inly said but could not move	81		115
I yield I would have cried at last	81		117
I yield I would have cried at last	81		117
Something I said I swooned and fell	81		118
Something I said I swooned and fell	81		118
I can send up an Esaus cry	81		126
Make it to God I am not spent	81		130
So far but I have yet within	81		131
Teach me the way I will repent	81		136
I need not love I need not break	81		138
I need not love I need not break	81		138
No house of rimmon may I take	81		140
Yea to myself I answer make	81		145
I found the ways were sown with salt	81		155
Where you and I were wont to tread	81		156
I calld them and I thought them then	81		164
I calld them and I thought them then	81		164
When you were learner and I read	81		165
What have I more than other men	81		168
I who was wise would be untaught	81		171

Word	Poem	Stan.	Line
And fain would follow I who led	81		172
How shall I search who never sought	81		173
I must hunt down the prize	88		1
Late I fell in the ecstacy	93	1	1
How dare I paint miss story to miss may	94		3
Of virtues I most warmly bless	96	1	1
I own a preference for pride	96	1	4
Your simile I keep	96	3	2
I have filld that hard to fill is	98	19	2
And I come laden from such floods	98	19	5
When cuckoo calls and I may hear	98	37	1
Clings on the stroke of death that I can smile	102	1	2
Round this unsexing doublet while I set	102	1	4
Lately I feard	102	1	6
Well I know not but all things seem to-night	102	1	10
As ever I remember in my life	102	1	13
Laughing or tears I think I could do either	102	1	14
Laughing or tears I think I could do either	102	1	14
Sleep Floris while I rob you tighten o sleep	102	1	18
I must not turn the lantern on his face	102	1	25
Did I say but lately	102	1	32
That I was so near laughter alas now	102	1	33
I find I am as ready with my tears	102	1	34
I find I am as ready with my tears	102	1	34
To spill oer fields of lilies so could I	102	1	37
Weeping even now I curse myself remembering	102	1	44
No let that go I have said goodnight to shame	102	1	45
I have wrongd it of its coronet and now	102	1	51
I outrage it with treasonable kissing	102	1	52
What I do now is but the least least thing	102	1	54
But since I have no scope for benefits	102	1	55
Most ill-content this least least thing I do	102	1	57
Now one word more and then I am gone indeed	102	1	58
My cousin will not love you as I love	102	1	60
I read that the recital of thy sin	102	2	2
And I must have the centre in my heart	102	3	7
I am like a slip of comet	103		1
So I go out my little sweet is done	103		17
I have drawn heat from this contagious sun	103		18
To not ungentle death now forth I run	103		19
Now I am minded to take pipe in hand	105		1
And said I like this it is almost isled	107	4	25
I hope that all the places on our trip	107	4	27
How shall I call my love she said	109	4	3
O I am the kings son he said	109	5	1
I give you my love and I give you my land	109	5	3
I give you my love and I give you my land	109	5	3

Word	Poem	Stan.	Line
I (cont.)			
When I come home from sea	109	5	4
O I have here no foreign lady	109	8	1
And if I chose a love to wed	109	10	1
I think it is seven days she said	109	16	3
I am Lord Williams love she said	109	19	1
I pray you tell to me	109	25	4
And each said I am he	109	26	2
I am not come from English land	109	32	1
If I were come from paradise	109	32	3
Is it a rose I see	109	33	2
I did not pull it in kings garden	109	34	1
When I came forth for thee	109	34	2
If I give thee kisses three	109	37	2
I have a crown for thee	109	37	4
O I will follow thee my true love	109	38	1
I would not make the trial	110		2
I heard her say poor poor afflicted soul	111		11
I hear a noise of waters drawn away	112		1
I prove it what then when these lines are dead	117		11
But I was ignorantly bold	118		5
To dream I dared so much for thee	118		6
Waking I thought and it sufficed	118		8
I thought before I gather strength	118		13
I thought before I gather strength	118		13
So is it with my friends I note to hear	119		5
I know it knowing not across from those	119		7
I never saw those fields whereon their best	119		11
She markd where I and Fabian met	120		1
I see her riving fingers tear	120		5
I know of the bored and bitten rocks	120		20
Alas but I am all at fault	120		24
I dare not taste the thickening salt	120		26
I cannot meet the swallowing main	120		27
Of if I go she stays meanwhile	120		28
A noise of falls I am possessed by	121		1
I think he will not tire of me	124		2
And I can teach him happiness	124		7
And I shall know of sweets for him	124		11
But if I cannot tempt his thought	124		21
The shepherds whom I value not	124		23
Have told me I am fair to see	124		24
True madam I am sorry now to see	125		16
I betterd all our path with sanguine eyes	125		17
Can I do any harm	125		18
If you are silent that I know of none	125		19
Ill meant yet true I best should flatter then	125		20
Must I give tongue again	125		23
Am I so	125		25
What if I hated flattery	125		32
Good Valerian I will come	125		37

Word	Poem	Stan.	Line
Why should I go because Castara goes	125		38
I do not but to please Valerian	125		39
Of which I say there is no joy in them	125		53
To say I go because Castara goes	125		60
Are known but I	127		2
I none can shew	127		6
I do not love	127		10
I argued Ill	127		12
I keep my trust	127		15
I thought that you would have written my birthday came and went	128		1
And with the last post over I knew no letter was sent	128		2
I know what you will tell me neglectful that you were not	128		5
But the lily is past as I say and the rose is not in its prime	128		14
What I did ask then was a circle of rose-red sealing-wax	128		15
You have made me quote almost the dismalest proverb I know	128		18
For a letter comes at last shall I say before Christmas is come	128		19
And I must take your amends cry pardon and then be dumb	128		20
From the self that I have been	129		5
I am the midst of every zone	130		3
I have desired desired to pass	130		28
I can hear the harshness	132		2
I am warmly clad	132		4
You to be gone and I lag last	134		3
Nor I nor heaven would have it be	134		4
When I with never-needed wiles	135		3
When this was done and I could look	135		7
I saw the stars like flash of fire	135		8
I cried with my desire	135		10
I put the door to with the bolts unpinned	135		11
I spy the nearest daisies through the dark	135		23
I knew the brook that parts in two	135		25
Of small and sugar flints I knew	135		27
And I should find him there	135		34
You spoil the plot I find my true love by	135		36
I awoke in the midsummer not-to-call night in the white and the walk of the morning	137		1
I am the little woodlark	138		11
And while I sail must listen I sing	138		15
And while I sail must listen I sing	138		15
I am so very o so very glad	138		31
That I do think there is not to be had	138		32
Says go on then I go on	138		35
To the nests nook I balance and buoy	138		43
I will appear looking such charity	140		3

Word	Poem	Stan.	Line
I (cont.)			
I suffer this she said for thee	145		57
And I not help nor word now of success	150		5
I told you that she turned her mirror dim	151		11
I came by Caerwys	152		3
Why get thee gone then tell thy mother I want her	152		16
Is all all sheared away thus then I sweat for fear	152		24
Some pageant which takes tears and I must foot with feeling that	152		26
I here forbid my thoughts to fool themselves with fears	152		30
On one that went against me whereas I had warned her	152		37
Warned her well she knew I warned her of this work	152		38
To make believe my mood was mock o I might think so	152		41
Wiped I am sure this was it seems not well for still	152		43
I can scour thee fresh burnish thee sheathe thee in thy dark lair these drops	152		46
In all her body I say no place was like her eyes	152		56
Several times I saw them thrice or four times turning	152		59
Any instant falls means me and I do not repent	152		64
I do not and I will not repent not repent	152		65
I do not and I will not repent not repent	152		65
The blame bear who aroused me what I have done violent	152		66
I have like a lion done lionlike done	152		67
And in this darksome world what comfort can I find	152		80
Down this darksome world comfort where can I find	152		81
When ts light I quenched its rose times one rich rose my hand	152		82
With no now no Gwenvrewi I must miss her most	152		85
The turmoil and the torment it has I swear a sweetness	152		90
Next after sweet success I am not left even this	152		92
I all my being have hacked in half with her neck one part	152		93
Deed-bound I am one deed treads all down here cramps all doing what do not yield	152		100
Whose bloods I reck no more of no more rank with hers	152		103

Word	Poem	Stan.	Line
Warm beat with cold beat company shall I	153		2
Thee God I come from to thee go	155		1
All day long I like fountain flow	155		2
What I know of thee I bless	155		5
What I know of thee I bless	155		5
Once I turned from thee and hid	155		9
Sow the wind I would I sinned	155		11
Sow the wind I would I sinned	155		11
I repent of what I did	155		12
I repent of what I did	155		12
Bad I am but yet thy child	155		13
Spare thou me since I see	155		15
I have life left with me still	155		17
Help me sir and so I will	155		20
What shall I do for the land that bred me	156		1
But country and flag the flag I am under	156		7
But under her banner I live for her honour	156		14
Where is the field I must play the man on	156		16
If under her banner I fall for her honour	156		19
O I admire and sorrow the hearts eye grieves	157		1
What need I strain my heart beyond my ken	157		34
O but I bear my burning witness though	157		35
I have tall daughters dear that heed my hand	158		2
Hark hearer hear what I do lend a thought now make believe	159		1
Enough now since the sacred matter that I mean	159		43
I should be wronging longer leaving it to float	159		44
Ice			
Some ice that locks the glacier to the rocks	80	7	20
And find a flint a fang of ice	80	7	37
This ice this lead this steel this stone	81		128
Towards wastes where round the ice-blocks tilt and fret	88		7
Towards those wastes where the ice-blocks tilt and fret	88		11
He gave her kisses cold as ice	109	39	1
Ice-blocks			
Towards wastes where round the ice-blocks tilt and fret	88		7
Towards those wastes where the ice-blocks tilt and fret	88		11
Iconium			
And bright iconium eastwards reach my rhymes	136		6
Icy			
And numbs and starves as between icy wharves	81	3	6

Word	Poem	Stan.	Line
Id			
Yet Id not say it is her face alone	125		61
Ideal			
The best ideal is the true	133		1
Idle			
Idle for ever to waft her or wind her with these she endured	28	14	8
Me were I pleading plead nor do I I weary of idle a being but by where wars are rife	66	1	7
Ignorantly			
But I was ignorantly bold	118		5
Ill			
And Ill pretend the credit given of yore	14	2	3
And Ill love my distinction near or far	14	2	12
So from the dawn was Ill begun	21		9
Ill wait till morn eternal breaks	23		54
Let him oh with his air of angels then lift me lay me only Ill	45		9
When when peace will you peace Ill not play hypocrite	51		3
Not Ill not carrion comfort despair not feast on thee	64		1
And the tide of Ill is out	77		28
Then clouds come like ill-balanced crags	80	7	1
Ill take in hand the blady stone	80	7	48
Fronts Venus his ill-launched hope	83		19
Herclots preachings Ill no longer hear	96	5	1
No Ill not hazard it only his hand	102	1	26
No time to think Ill knot it on this ribbon	102	1	30
To speak so yet Ill speak it for this once	102	1	41
Though ill-contented precious precious Floris	102	1	56
Most ill-content this least least thing I do	102	1	57
And hate the ill-visaged cursing tars	114		10
Ill lay them by and freshly turn instead	117		13
Ill cite no further what the initiate know	119		10
Ill meant yet true I best should flatter then	125		20
I argued ill	127		12
Under her banner Ill live for her honour	156		4
Ill-balanced			
Then clouds come like ill-balanced crags	80	7	1
Ill-content			
Most ill-content this least least thing I do	102	1	57
Ill-contented			
Though ill-contented precious precious Floris	102	1	56
Ill-launched			
Fronts Venus his ill-launched hope	83		19
Ill-visaged			
And hate the ill-visaged cursing tars	114		10
Illumined			
Think of an opening page illumined	93	2	1
Illustrated			
Where all the virtues were illustrated	102	2	9

Word	Poem	Stan.	Line
Im			
But Im alone for my loves gone	95		8
And Im very glad	132		5
Image			
The sculpturd image of such faith would be	1	3	7
Images			
In blazon gilt and images of bronze	102	2	10
Imagining			
Each in his own imagining	23		15
Immaculate			
White to begin with immaculate white	27		33
Mary immaculate	60		24
Immortal			
Deals triumph and immortal years	52		12
This Jack joke poor potsherd patch match- wood immortal diamond	72		23
Is immortal diamond	72		24
Leaves yet the mind a mother of immortal song	76		4
And breath immortal thronged that show	145		45
But being lifted immortal of immortal brightness	152		58
But being lifted immortal of immortal brightness	152		58
Immortal beauty is death with duty	156		.18
Immortals			
The immortals of the eternal ring	145		30
Impale			
And the poor corse impale with it and fray	89		7
Impaled			
Or thorn-engaged impaled and pent	81		19
Impalpable			
Thy impalpable oppression pin him down	102	1	19
Impatient			
Sickness broke him impatient he cursed at first but mended	53		5
Impeached			
And all like me may boast impeached not	12	1	13
Impearled			
And truth is heard with tears impearled	23		35
Impediment			
Had let such music down without impediment	122		8
Impenitent			
Often when winds impenitent	80	5	1
Imperfect			
It is a regimen on the imperfect wind	102	3	17
Is to give regimen to the imperfect wind	102	3	24
Imps			
He hung on the imps success	54		24
In			
Miracle-in-Mary-of-flame	28	33	4
His charge through the champ-white water-			

Word	Poem	Stan.	Line
In(cont.)			
in-a-wallow	41		47
Them beauty-in-the-ghost deliver it early now long before death	59		18
Thirsts all-in-all in all a world of wet	69		8
Inanimate			
To newborn prince and royal corse inanimate	1	4	9
Inboard			
And the inboard seas run swirling and hawling	28	19	3
Incapable			
The incapable and cumbrous shame	15		18
Incense			
Let incense hang across the room	77		19
Inch			
Every inch a tar	41		74
Inches			
Is statuary rated by its inches	96	7	6
Increase			
That warring wasted the lands increase	26		28
Increment			
Earth all out who with trickling increment	73		10
Indeed			
Indeed while such a wonders warm	25		36
These are indeed the barn withindoors house	32	1	12
Thou art indeed just Lord if I contend	74	1	1
Then is my misery full indeed	81		68
Some are pretty enough and some are poor indeed	98	15	4
Now one word more and then I am gone indeed	102	1	58
A learned fool indeed and well-bred churl	102	3	38
But what indeed is askd of me	118		1
Three miles indeed	125		13
Indian			
Once in a drawer of Indian wood	81		80
Indifference			
Is laws indifference	148		8
Indignation			
Drowned o pity and indignation manshape that shone	72		13
Indivisible			
Stars waving their indivisible rays	98	23	1
Indoors			
Come you indoors come home your fading fire	46		9
Deals out that being indoors each one dwells	57		6
Inexplicably			
Meadows to them inexplicably dear	119		8
Infallibly			
And know infallibly which I preferred	19		8
Infancy			
Dwindled to infancy	60		19

Word	Poem	Stan.	Line
Infant			
Soft when she sees her infant start	23		51
Infest			
Manwolf worse and their packs infest the age	70		20
Infinite			
And still th abysses infinite	23		25
For the infinite air is unkind	28	13	4
Infinitely			
Having the infinitely great	81		152
Infinity			
Gave Gods infinity	60		18
Influential			
No influential heaven ever wore	14	2	7
Inheritance			
That forge her title of inheritance	102	1	70
Initiate			
Ill cite no further what the initiate know	119		10
Injury			
His injury shell avenge with raging shame	82		6
Injurys			
Her injurys looks off by both horns of shore	50		3
Inly			
I inly said but could not move	81		115
She inly nourishes a wish to shine	94		12
Inmate			
Only the inmate does not correspond	34		11
Inmost			
Those charms accepted of my inmost thought	12	1	9
Is slightly selfish in her inmost soul	94		28
Inner			
A faithful guard of inner darkness fixd	1	4	7
Keen glimpses of the inner firmament	2		12
Who knew the inner spirit that fills	77		43
Innocent			
Innocent mind and mayday in girl and boy	33		13
Winning ways airs innocent maiden manners sweet looks loose locks long locks lovelocks gaygear going gallant girlgrace	59		15
Insight			
Rivalled insight be rival Italy or Greece	44		13
The widow of an insight lost she lives with aim	76		7
Nor angel insight can	148		5
Lord now curb him for ever o daring o deep insight	152		73
Inspiration			
I want the one rapture of an inspiration	76		10
Instant			
Any instant falls means me and I do not repent	152		64
Instead			
Ill lay them by and freshly turn instead	117		13

Word	Poem	Stan.	Line
Instead (cont.)			
This was not askd but what instead	118		7
Instressed			
His mystery must be instressed stressed	28	5	7
To its own fine function wild and self-instressed	47		7
Instrument			
Withouten instrument or conch or bell	2		128
That was an instrument	148		19
Insufficiencies			
All insufficiencies	133		8
Int			
Thus I shall make a cross and int	80	7	41
Intellectual			
Caps occasion with an intellectual fit	143		2
Intense			
An intense line of throbbing blood-light shook	2		16
Intensest			
With spiked quills all of intensest hue	2		44
Intensity			
The deepening intensity	77		114
Intent			
And I perhaps if my intent	15		9
Tune it to words of good intent	81		127
Interchange			
By interchange gaspd splendour and eclipse	2		22
Interest			
Christ minds Christs interest what to avow or amend	40		12
Why theres an interest and sweet soul in beauty	125		41
Creatures all heft hope hazard interest	157		8
Interests			
That interests our eyes and who goes there	40		2
Interposed			
The sea took pity it interposed with doom	158		1
Interstice			
There is no parting or bare interstice	98	22	4
In them			
Storm flakes were scroll-leaved flowers lily showers sweet heaven was astrew in them	28	21	8
Intolerable			
Intolerable tears I bleed	81		67
Invention			
For who makes rainbows by invention	91		4
Inward			
To shew the crimson streams that inward shine	2		71
Ipse			
Ipse the only one Christ King dead	28	27	5
Ireland			
I am in Ireland now now I am at a third	66	1	8

Word	Poem	Stan.	Line
Irish			
There boy bugler born he tells me of Irish	48		2
Iron			
And fear no iron rod	5		12
My heaven is brass and iron my earth	18		9
Yea iron is mingled with my clay	18		10
Irregularly			
My heart irregularly shook	135		9
Island			
There is an island westerd in the main	98	4	1
Isle			
An isle of roses and another near	2		29
I gather points of lote-flower from an isle	5		33
Isled			
Wound with thee in thee isled	60		125
And said I like this it is almost isled	107	4	25
Isles			
The rosy isles so that I stole away	2		140
Issue			
Of forcd persuasion issue oer the free	1	5	7
Italy			
Rivalled insight be rival Italy or Greece	44		13
How Shakespeares England weds with Dantes Italy	98	35	2
Its			
Of the sodden-with-its-sorrowing heart	28	26	12
Ive			
That Ive got a home	132		6
Ivies			
Frost-furred our ivies are and rough	3		3
Ivy			
Nowhere natural hearts ivy patience masks	68		6
Jacinth			
Sapphire Jacinth chrysolite	77		119
Thou Jacinth nor have skill of all thy virtues	102	1	62
Jacinthine			
Of that Jacinthine thing that where it lingers	2		65
Jack			
Of answer the eagerer a-wanting Jessy or Jack	46		7
My lad and lost in Jack	54		18
This Jack joke poor potsherd patch match-wood immortal diamond	72		23
Man Jack the man is just his mate a hussy	75		11
Jacks			
Jacks call and cue at last	54		30
Jackself			
Soul self come poor Jackself I do advise	69		9
Jaded			
You jaded let be call off thoughts awhile	69		10
Jading			
The jading and jar of the cart	28	26	10

Word	Poem	Stan.	Line
Jagged			
Meanwhile a litter of the jagged leaves	111		8
Jags			
The thunder brags in joints and sparkling jags	80	7	3
Jailor			
Her jailor with his vigil-organ dead	99		16
James			
And James shall hate his faded red	114		11
Jane			
Or was it Jane she is too plain	95		3
It might be Helen Jane or Kate	95		6
Jar			
The jading and jar of the cart	28	26	10
Would brandle adamantine heaven with ride and jar did	48		46
Jarrd			
Jarrd down the balanced storm the bleeding heavens	102	2	4
Jaunting			
Or a jaunting vaunting vaulting assaulting trumpet telling	141		7
Jay			
Hovers off the jay-blue heavens appearing	28	26	3
Jay-blue			
Hovers off the jay-blue heavens appearing	28	26	3
Jessy			
Of answer the eagerer a-wanting Jessy or Jack	46		7
Jesu			
Jesu hearts light	28	29	1
Jesu maids son	28	29	2
Jesus			
To crosses meant for Jesus you whom the east	11		5
Christ Jesus our Lord her God and her Son	27		29
Just like Jesus crucified	145		50
Jews killed Jesus long ago	145		52
Jet			
The pupil plays its liquid jet	86		5
Jewelld			
Whence spring the jewelld harmonies	77		138
Jews			
I will break free from the Jews company	80	7	36
Jews killed Jesus long ago	145		52
John			
Part was picked for John	54		7
Young John then fear then joy	54		8
And John shall lie where winds are dead	114		9
Joints			
The thunder brags in joints and sparkling jags	80	7	3

Word	Poem	Stan.	Line
Joke			
This Jack joke poor potsherd patch match-wood immortal diamond	72		23
Jolt			
Jolt	101		7
Josephs			
In Josephs garden they threw by	6		21
Jostling			
Crowd down upon a stream and jostling thick	2		94
Once jostling thick the bluebell sheaves	81		13
Or like a juicy and jostling shock	144		9
Joy			
Behold we have the joy in harvest	6		2
Till dimpled joy steals oer its cheeks	23		52
And a spring-time joy have found	24		16
Let in joy this Easter day	24		24
With joy for to-day and hope for to-morrow	26		15
And we that joy in this month joy-laden	26		17
And we that joy in this month joy-laden	26		17
Joy fall to thee Father Francis	28	23	1
What is all this juice and all this joy	33		9
And he boards her in oh such joy	41		70
Young John then fear then joy	54		8
Hand rather my heart lo lapped strength stole joy would laugh cheer	64		11
Elsewhere leave comfort root-room let joy size	69		11
And that grief masters joy on earth	77		55
Of which I say there is no joy in them	125		53
Anywhere any more joy to be in	138		33
With a sweet joy of a sweet joy	138		44
With a sweet joy of a sweet joy	138		44
Sweet of a sweet of a sweet joy	138		45
Of a sweet a sweet sweet joy	138		46
Keeps a kind of joy in it a zest an edge an ecstasy	152		91
Bid joy back have at the harvest keep hope pale	154		4
Joy-laden			
And we that joy in this month joy-laden	26		17
Joyless			
A hearts-clarion away griefs gasping joyless days dejection	72		17
Joys			
Of summertime joys	159		21
Jubilee			
Makes the silver jubilee	28	35	4
Showering silver jubilee	28	35	8
This her silver jubilee	28	35	12
Silver but for jubilee	28	35	16
Utter silver jubilee	28	35	20

Word	Poem	Stan.	Line
Judah			
That was unto Judah as may and brought her	26		31
Judge			
To be a judge and ruler over us	5		2
Judgment			
That night the judgment day began	81		90
An angel came the judgment done	81		104
And gives for tropes his judgment all away	102	3	29
And gives for tropes his judgment all away	102	3	35
Juice			
What is all this juice and all this joy	33		9
A juice rides rich through bluebells in vine leaves	157		3
Juicy			
To plash with cool feet the clay juicy soil	5		50
Lined all with silk of juicy red	124		16
Or like a juicy and jostling shock	144		9
Just			
Just seen may be to many unknown men	12	2	12
I plod wondering a-wanting just for lack	46		6
Just such slips of soldiery Christs royal ration	48		28
I say more the just man justices	57		9
Thou art indeed just Lord if I contend	74	1	1
With thee but sir so what I plead is just	74	1	1
Of just majestical and giant groans	75		4
Man Jack the man is just his mate a hussy	75		11
With just such sweet potential skill	81		20
The sun just risen	98	34	1
Just like Jesus crucified	145		50
But thou bidst and just thou art	155		21
Justices			
I say more the just man justices	57		9
Justify			
And justify the east and west	130		4
Kate			
It might be Helen Jane or Kate	95		6
Keats			
Most dented lay Sylvester reading Keats	107	4	21
Keel			
And she beat the bank down with her bows and the ride of her keel	28	14	5
As keel locks close to Kelson	101		5
The stranded keel and kelson warp apart	101		11
Keen			
Keen glimpses of the inner firmament	2		12
A quivering pennon then for eye too keen	2		17
The keener to come at the comfort for feeling the combating keen	28	25	8
Lifes quick this kind this keen self-feeling	152		96

Word	Poem	Stan.	Line
Keener			
The keener to come at the comfort for feeling the combating keen	28	25	8
Keep			
Upon the stir and keep of pride	22		18
I shall keep time with thee mother of mine	27		19
Shrewsbury may see others keep	28	35	10
Now Carisbrook keep goes under in gloom	41		28
How to keep is there any any is there none such nowhere known some bow or brooch or braid or brace lace latch or catch or key to keep	59		1
How to keep is there any any is there none such nowhere known some bow or brooch or braid or brace lace latch or catch or key to keep	59		1
Back beauty keep it beauty beauty beauty from vanishing away	59		2
To keep at bay	59		10
Who could keep silence tho the smart	77		63
Then will he keep in this stay	80	1	7
Your simile I keep	96	3	2
I keep my trust	127		15
To keep the loaded bolt from plunging back	135		6
Bid joy back have at the harvest keep hope pale	154		4
Her fame to keep her fame to recover	156		12
Keepers			
You vigil-keepers with low flames decreased	11		8
Keeping			
Rural rural keeping folk flocks and flowers	44		8
Keeps			
Coils keeps and teases simple sight	22		12
The Deutschland on Sunday and so the sky keeps	28	13	3
Keeps grace that keeps all his goings graces	57		10
Keeps grace that keeps all his goings graces	57		10
Than Purcell tune lets tread to see it does this keeps warm	62		2
And keeps the breeze and clears the seas	83		13
Keeps a kind of joy in it a zest an edge an ecstasy	152		91
Water which keeps thy name for not in rock written	152		119
Kelson			
As keel locks close to kelson	101		5
The stranded keel and kelson warp apart	101		11
Ken			
Whose ken through amber of dark eyes	77		51
What need I strain my heart beyond my ken	157		34
Kentish			
Dead to the Kentish knock	28	14	4

Word	Poem	Stan.	Line
Kept			
Ye have kept your choicest wine	24		9
Word last how a lush-kept plush-capped sloe	28	8	3
Word that heard and kept thee and uttered thee outright	28	29	8
Kept to her care-drowned and wrapped in	41		45
In silk-ash kept from cooling	49		17
When the thing we freely forfeit is kept with fonder a care	59		27
Fonder a care kept than we could have kept it kept	59		28
Fonder a care kept than we could have kept it kept	59		28
Fonder a care kept than we could have kept it kept	59		28
A care kept where kept do but tell us where kept where	59		30
A care kept where kept do but tell us where kept where	59		30
A care kept where kept do but tell us where kept where	59		30
She kept her love-thoughts on most lenten diet	82		7
One and then one along their walks and kept	107	1	12
No piece matched those eyes kept most part much cast down	152		57
Key			
How to keep is there any any is there none such nowhere known some bow or brooch or braid or brace lace latch or catch or key to keep	59		1
One yes I can tell such a key I do know such a place	59		7
We tuned to one key and made their harmonies	98	2	4
Khor			
Exiled most remote El Khor	81		47
Kill			
Themselves live singing and their hearers kill	96	2	2
Who means to wed or means to kill	120		29
When she felt the kill-weights crush	145		55
Kill-weights			
When she felt the kill-weights crush	145		55
Killed			
O then weary then why should we tread o why are we so haggard at the heart so care-coiled care-killed so fagged so fashed so cogged so cumbered	59		26
Jews killed Jesus long ago	145		52
Kills			
We hear our hearts grate on themselves			

Word	Poem	Stan.	Line
Kings			
That came when a line of kings did cease	26		26
O I am the kings son he said	109	5	1
One has gone to the kings steward	109	11	1
The kings friend told the thing that was hid	109	12	1
Did you pull it in the kings garden	109	33	3
I did not pull it in kings garden	109	34	1
Is that the kings crown on your head	109	35	1
Kirjath			
At Kirjath-arba go	5		58
Kirjath-arba			
At Kirjath-arba go	5		58
Kiss			
I kiss my hand	28	5	1
Kiss my hand to the dappled-with-damson west	28	5	5
For love he leans forth needs his neck must fall on kiss	63		12
They kiss the rod with filial submission	97		9
And relish not her loveless kiss	120		11
And half mislike her loveless kiss	120		13
Kissed			
Nay in all that toil that coil since seems I kissed the rod	64		10
Kisses			
If I give thee kisses three	109	37	2
Give me thy kisses three	109	38	2
Sweeter thy kisses my own love	109	38	3
He gave her kisses cold as ice	109	39	1
Kissing			
I outrage it with treasonable kissing	102	1	52
Kneading			
Kneading the mounded mire that stops	3		10
Knee			
Manger maidens knee	28	7	4
Crouch lay knee by earth low under	41		109
Rope-over thigh knee-nave and barrelled shank	71		3
They made him kneel on knee	109	14	2
With a two years child at her knee	109	16	2
She kneeled upon her knee	109	25	2
Knee-nave			
Rope-over thigh knee-nave and barrelled shank	71		3
Kneel			
I stood but does she stand or kneel	81		96
They made him kneel on knee	109	14	2
Kneeled			
She kneeled upon her knee	109	25	2
Knees			
Lo God shall strengthen all the feeble knees	11		14
Clutched hands through clasped knees	54		21

Word	Poem	Stan.	Line
Her white weed-bathed knees are shut together	99		2
Knells			
On mermaids whether that they ring the knells	2		119
Knelt			
Here he knelt then in regimental red	48		9
Some knelt some stood I seemd to feel	81		93
Who knelt were for the lords right hand	81		94
Knew			
I knew not why but know that sadness dwells	2		118
Loathed for a love men knew in them	28	21	1
And knew the who and the why	28	28	4
O if we but knew what we do	43		9
Who knew the inner spirit that fills	77		43
At last I hear the voice I knew	81		25
Twas said of none but all men knew	81		91
Who first knew moonlight by the hunters moon	105		17
That not Arcadia knew nor Haemony	107	1	17
And with the last post over I knew no letter was sent	128		2
I knew the brook that parts in two	135		25
Of small and sugar flints I knew	135		27
Warned her well she knew I warned her of this work	152		38
Like the thing that never knew the earth never off roots	159		27
Knock			
Dead to the Kentish knock	28	14	4
Knocking			
Like knocking thunder all round Britains Welkin	102	2	3
She heard but knockings three	109	29	2
Knops			
Bring me palm with pearled knops	98	18	2
Knopt			
In summer are our orchards knopt	124		19
Knot			
Lock with my right then knot a barken band	80	7	45
It was a hard thing to undo this knot	91		1
It was a hard thing to undo this knot	91		10
The knot of feathery locks upon her head	99		14
No time to think Ill knot it on this ribbon	102	1	30
Knots			
And oaks but these were leaved in sharper knots	107	4	8
And stained and knots of golden thread	124		14
Know			
I knew not why but know that sadness dwells	2		118
To know the dusk depths of the ponderous sea	2		122

Word	Poem	Stan.	Line
such nowhere known some bow or brooch or braid or brace lace latch or catch or key to keep	58		1
Our law says love what are loves worthiest were all known	62		8
Now known and hand at work now never wrong	76		8
At last I hear the voice well known	81		1
The peacockd copse were known to fill	81		14
Because its place is known and charted there	102	3	12
But let me sing that which is known to me	116		4
Are known but I	127		2
The earth and heaven so little known	130		1
Are never known for fair	133		16
Who thinks of Thecla yet her name was known	136		3
Is known to men more than me	138		13
Made known though thick through stone	148		11
Who built these walls made known	148		37
Knows			
Grows less and less sweet to him and knows no cause	14	3	14
Mary the virgin well the heart knows	27		22
To me God knows deserving no such thing	34		2
Whatever is fickle freckled who knows how	35		8
Not that hell knows redeeming	41		116
Doff darkness homing nature knows the rest	47		6
Mark Christ our king he knows war served this soldiering through	63		9
At God knows when to God knows what whose smiles not wrung see you unforeseen times rather as skies	69		12
At God knows when to God knows what whose smiles not wrung see you unforeseen times rather as skies	69		12
Her choice in roses knows by heart	83		22
By heady elements for no man knows	103		5
She loves his face she knows the spot	120		2
Laboured			
Your spouse not laboured-at nor spun	22		28
Laboured-at			
Your spouse not laboured-at nor spun	22		28
Labouring			
This in drudgery day-labouring-out lifes age	39		4
Rolls across the labouring willows	79		4
Labours			
The labours I should then have spent	15		11
Lace			
With lace of rosy weed were chapleted	2		59
That lace the face of Penmaen pool	29	1	28
How to keep is there any any is there none such nowhere known some bow or brooch			

Word	Poem	Stan.	Line
Lace (cont.)			
or braid or brace lace latch or catch or key to keep	59		1
Shivelights and shadowtackle in long lashes lace lance and pair	72		4
They swathe and lace the shroud-plaits oer my face	80	5	6
And lace-leaved lovely	138		29
Lace-leaved			
And lace-leaved lovely	138		29
Laced			
And the midriff astrain with leaning of laced with fires of stress	28	2	8
Life all laced in the others	54		2
Love-laced what once I well	54		3
See his wind-lilylocks-laced	71		15
Now leaved how thick laced they are again	74	1	9
Laces			
And more and more times laces round and round my heart	152		19
Lack			
I plod wondering a-wanting just for lack	46		6
Then at the door what work there was good lack	135		5
Lacklevel			
Little I reck ho lacklevel in if all had bread	70		9
Lad			
And locks love ever in a lad	48		35
My lad and lost in Jack	54		18
Lade			
Lads and men her lade and treasure	41		11
Laden			
And we that joy in this month joy-laden	26		17
And I come laden from such floods	98	19	5
Ladies			
Quite as ladies go	125		27
Lads			
Lads and men her lade and treasure	41		11
Those lovely lads once wet-fresh windfalls of wars storm	62		5
Lady			
Such opposition to the lady-star	14	2	10
Candlemas lady day	42		5
But the lady month may	42		6
O have you here a foreign lady	109	7	3
O I have here no foreign lady	109	8	1
Then will you wed with an English lady	109	8	3
Says get you get you a lady to wed	109	9	1
There was a lady very gay	131		2
Lady-star			
Such opposition to the lady-star	14	2	10

Word	Poem	Stan.	Line
Turns the lantern on Floris hand	102	1	27
Lap			
Her milk-white throat and folded dew-lap slack	99		9
Lies in her lap which she anon sweeps off	111		9
Lapped			
Hand rather my heart lo lapped strength stole joy would laugh cheer	64		11
And lapped in shining hair roll to the banks edge then	152		50
Laps			
Skywards rich rich it laps	60		77
Lapsed			
But when the sun had lapsed to ocean lo	2		136
Large			
It is too large for me what does that mean	102	1	29
Now let me see you you large princely hand	102	1	46
Lark			
Left hand off land I hear the lark ascend	35		5
Cuckoo-echoing bell-swarmed lark-charmed rook-racked river-rounded	44		2
Or like a lark to glide aloof	77		65
To rise you bid me with the lark	96	6	1
To canvass the retirement of the lark	113		2
Lark-charmed			
Cuckoo-echoing bell-swarmed lark-charmed rook-racked river-rounded	44		2
Larkspur			
That was her larkspur row so soon	10		22
Larkspurs			
The dewdrop on the larkspurs mouth	10		15
Lash			
We lash with the best or worst	28	8	2
See not a hair is not an eyelash not the least lash lost every hair	59		20
Lashed			
O at lightning and lashed rod	28	2	2
Them broad in bluff hide his frowning feet lashed raced	71		17
Lashes			
Shivelights and shadowtackle in long lashes lace lance and pair	72		4
With levelld lashes stilling their disquiet	82		2
Their highest sprays were drawn as fine as lashes	107	4	6
Lashtender			
Fast or they in clammyish lashtender combs creep	149	1	5
Last			
Came midst the drizzle telling how last night	1	14	2
Lay bleeding to Madrid the last they bore	1	15	2

Word	Poem	Stan.	Line
Last (cont.)			
Slumberd at last in one sweet deep heart-broken close	2		135
The steep-up roof at last behind the small	12	2	6
Has not a charter that its sap shall last	14	1	4
The furnace shall at last be cold	15		16
If I shall overtake thee at last above	20		16
Since its birth and its bloom and its breathing its last	27		17
Word last how a lush-kept plush-capped sloe	28	8	3
Brim in a flash full hither then last or first	28	8	6
And lives at last were washing away	28	15	7
The-last-breath penitent spirits the uttermost mark	28	32	6
And though the last lights off the black west went	31	1	11
To mans last dust drain fast towards mans first slime	35		14
Their ransom their rescue and first fast last friend	40		14
Jacks call and cue at last	54		30
Not untwist slack they may be these last strands of man	64		2
But yet they say Christ comes at the last day	80	1	6
At last I hear the voice well known	81		1
At last I hear the voice I knew	81		25
As the last pleiad yea behind	81		46
I yield I would have cried at last	81		117
At last up the blue element	87		6
Though self-made bands at last may true love bind	102	3	19
To single Saturn last and solitary	103		15
At last the bird is found a flickering shape and slim	113		9
And with the last post over I knew no letter was sent	128		2
And if you write at last it never can be the same	128		3
For a letter comes at last shall I say before Christmas is come	128		19
You to be gone and I lag last	134		3
They rose at last and forced her from the spot	136		34
And kind compassion at his lifes last need	140		4
The last thing Margarets fingers sew	145		13
And then that last and shortest	153		11
Fast he opens last he off wrings	159		34
Lasting			
The day that brought my lasting pain	21		10
Bright-lifting with a little-lasting smile	125		57
Latch			
What death half lifts the latch of	49		19

Word	Poem	Stan.	Line
Most dented lay Sylvester reading Keats	107	4	21
As she lay weeping at the night	109	29	1
Lay open thine estates	115		7
Ill lay them by and freshly turn instead	117		13
Laying			
Laying like airs fine flood	60		51
Loyal to his own soul laying his own law down no law nor	152		72
Lays			
Of the outward sentence low lays him listed to a heresy here	45		4
Lazuli			
Were veind and streakd with dusk-deep Lazuli	2		46
Lea			
Came running over the lea	109	17	4
Lead			
And lead me child-like by the hand	23		47
This ice this lead this steel this stone	81		128
Of rivers lead thro storms and nights	83		4
But single lead a misdirected life	94		32
Lead shepherd now we follow shepherd lead	98	15	7
Lead shepherd now we follow shepherd lead	98	15	7
But the Bethlehem star may lead me	129		3
Leaf			
When he has made us bear his leaf	6		30
Or where is strength to make the leaf unfold	17		4
Make me a leaf in thee mother of mine	27		43
Low-latched in leaf-light housel his too huge godhead	48		12
With his pulld and plotted leaf	98	18	4
Took primroses their pulld and plotted leaf	107	3	18
Parted me leaf and leaf divided me eyelid and eyelid of slumber	137		7
Parted me leaf and leaf divided me eyelid and eyelid of slumber	137		7
To the all-a-leaf of the treetop	138		38
Leaf-light			
Low-latched in leaf-light housel his too huge godhead	48		12
Leafing			
The happy leafing it is so with me	14	1	6
Leafless			
The rivn vine leafless lifeless dry	6		22
Leafmeal			
Though worlds of wanwood leafmeal lie	55		8
Leafwhelmed			
We are leafwhelmed somewhere with the hood	159		2
Leafy			
Then sought such leafy shelter as it yields	107	3	16
So long to this sweet spot this leafy lean-over	152		116

Word	Poem	Stan.	Line
Leagues			
Leagues leagues of seamanship	41		81
Leagues leagues of seamanship	41		81
Lean			
So long to this sweet spot this leafy lean-over	152		116
Lean-over			
So long to this sweet spot this leafy lean-over	152		116
Leaning			
And the midriff astrain with leaning of laced with fires of stress	28	2	8
Man lives that list that leaning in the will	157		25
Leans			
For love he leans forth needs his neck must fall on kiss	63		12
He leans to it Harry bends look back elbow and liquid waist	71		12
Forward she leans with hollowing back stock-still	99		1
She leans on him with such contentment fond	157		13
That leans along the loins of hills where a candycoloured where a gluegold-brown	159		5
Leap			
The lightnings leap the day of doom	80	7	4
Leaping			
Quelled or quenched in leaves the leaping sun	43		2
But mine is dreadful leaping pain	81		51
Leaps			
Leaps up before my vision thou art gone	98	33	2
Learn			
Learn who the heart is hence	148		6
Learned			
Blindness a learned fool and well-bred churl	102	3	32
A learned fool indeed and well-bred churl	102	3	38
Learner			
When you were learner and I read	81		165
Learning			
For learning stored and garnered	81		169
Learnt			
That I may win with late-learnt skill uncouth	17		12
Therefore how bitter and learnt how late the truth	17		14
And learnt her not to startle at his name	82		8
But has not learnt to take it gracefully	94		16
Leas			
Streaks of shadow thistled leas	77		137
Lease			
O where live well your lease of leisure	29	1	3
Leash			
She puts in leash her paird lips lest surprise	82		3

Word	Poem	Stan.	Line
Least			
Those sweet hopes quell whose least me quickenings lift	48		37
See not a hair is not an eyelash not the least lash lost every hair	59		20
In every least things life	60		8
What I do now is but the least least thing	102	1	54
What I do now is but the least least thing	102	1	54
Most ill-content this least least thing I do	102	1	57
Most ill-content this least least thing I do	102	1	57
Allow at least it has one term and part	102	3	5
Which says at least then go while all is fresh	125		64
Leave			
The sumptuous ridge-crest leave to poise and ride	12	2	8
Her Perseus linger and leave her to her extremes	50		9
O surely reaving peace my lord should leave in lieu	51		7
Some good and so he does leave patience exquisite	51		8
Home at heart heavens sweet gift then leave let that alone	62		11
Then lull then leave off fury had shrieked no lingering let me be fell force I must be brief	65		6
Elsewhere leave comfort root-room let joy size	69		11
Fall to the residuary worm worlds wildfire leave but ash	72		20
Or is he leave the west behind	83		5
Leave it with its grove hard by	98	15	3
Long where we leave him froliclavish while he looks about him laughs swims	159		42
Leaved			
Storm flakes were scroll-leaved flowers lily showers sweet heaven was astrew in them	28	21	8
And five-lived and leaved favour and pride	28	23	6
Now leaved how thick laced they are again	74	1	9
Now while the full-leaved hursts unalterd stand	105		3
And oaks but these were leaved in sharper knots	107	4	8
And lace-leaved lovely	138		29
The furl of fresh-leaved dogrose down	144		1
Leaves			
The hoarse leaves crawl on hissing ground	3		5
Of leaves of greenest flesh	5		34
Leaves spent new seasons alterd sky	15		2
The mist upon the leaves have strewed	21		33
How many leaves had it five they were then	27		38

Word	Poem	Stan.	Line
Leaves (cont.)			
The glassy peartree leaves and blooms they brush	33		6
Quelled or quenched in leaves the leaping sun	43		2
Leaves like the things of man you	55		3
Earth sweet earth sweet landscape with leaves throng	58		1
And her hand leaves his light	60		112
Heard unheeded leaves me a lonely began	66	1	13
Purple eyes and seas of liquid leaves all day	68		8
Leaves yet the mind a mother of immortal song	76		4
The fall is oer told off the leaves	81		9
Yet leaves him in ungirdled ease	83		15
That lick the shelly leaves which floor the copse	84		4
And leaves the blades whereer he will veer	98	1	3
Told off their leaves along the piercing gale	98	5	2
The breaking leaves of gold are curld upon her lips	98	14	3
Lighted the watery-plated leaves	98	17	2
The watery-plated plane-leaves lit	98	17	3
And feeds new leaves upon the winds of fall	105		10
Great butter-burr leaves floord the slope corpse ground	107	4	9
Her showy leaves staid watchet counter-foiling	108		5
Her showy leaves with gentle watchet foiling	108		6
Whose all-belated leaves yield up themselves	111		2
Meanwhile a litter of the jagged leaves	111		8
A branch of walnut leaves and that	120		6
And a few leaves not lily-white but charactered over with blacks	128		16
A juice rides rich through bluebells in vine leaves	157		3
By rafts and rafts of flake leaves light dealt so painted on the air	159		25
Leaving			
Hideous dashed down leaving earth a winter withering	152		84
I should be wronging longer leaving it to float	159		44
Led			
Which should ere now have led my feet to the field	17		9
And fain would follow I who led	81		172
Led Richard with a sweet undoing pain	107	4	17
Ledges			
On to ledges of grey cloud	77		80
Leeward			
She drove in the dark to leeward	28	14	1

Word	Poem	Stan.	Line
Left			
Fair relics too the changeful moor had left	1	8	1
But further down the valley left and right	1	14	4
The monks left long ago since which no more	1	15	4
It seems for grandeur barren left and dull	1	15	8
Flickering with sunny spokes and left and right	2		77
Youve parlour-pastime left and wholl	29	1	34
Left hand off land I hear the lark ascend	35		5
That left to the lord of the Eucharist I here lie by	48		44
Of wet and of wildness let them be left	56		14
O let them be left wildness and wet	56		15
Nay what we had lighthanded left in surly the mere mould	59		22
The point fast in and my left hand	80	7	44
Mercy is left enough for one	81		105
Left not a rood with curses unimpregnate	102	2	5
Crept all along a hill upon our left	125		3
Either left either right	138		8
Next after sweet success I am not left even this	152		92
I have life left with me still	155		17
Legates			
Legates might rush zeal-rampant fiery	1	5	5
Leger			
And sheathe at once his leger wing	130		12
Legion			
And would not have that legion of winged things	7		14
Leisure			
O where live well your lease of leisure	29	1	3
And faces fit for leisure gaze	133		13
Lend			
Lend him a lift from the sea-swill	41		63
Hark hearer hear what I do lend a thought now make believe	159		1
Lends			
She lends in aid of work and will	139		3
Length			
A sombre length of grey four towers placed	1	1	3
Their filmy tails adown whose length there showd	2		104
At length the bellows shall not blow	15		15
We all we thro the length of our days	26		34
Lent			
Once it was scarce perceived lent	81		11
Theyre out of date lent sermons all the year	96	5	2
Lenten			
God comes all sweetness to your lenten lips	11		2
She kept her love-thoughts on most lenten diet	82		7

Word	Poem	Stan.	Line
Lepers			
While cripples are while lepers dancers in dismal limbdance	152		111
Less			
My love is less my love is less for thee	14	1	7
My love is less my love is less for thee	14	1	7
That less is heavens higher even yet	14	1	12
Grows less and less sweet to him and knows no cause	14	3	14
Grows less and less sweet to him and knows no cause	14	3	14
No I should love the city less	15		21
Afflicts no less what yet I hope may blow	17		6
Or less would win mans mind	60		109
That hopes that makesbelieve the men must be no less	63		5
To hear his strain descend less loud	77		79
Has wit enough but less than female tact	94		19
The more he told the less she spoke	109	36	3
And headed always downwards with less sounding	112		2
That are not less in winter-time	124		12
Till the longing is less and the good gone	138		36
The times are nightfall look their light grows less	150		1
Lessend			
And the lessend stars ray not	85		6
Is worth and current with a lessend mill	96	7	8
Lessened			
My love is lessened and must soon be past	14	1	1
Lesson			
Take a lesson from the ground	24		14
Lessons			
In bloody letters lessons of earnest of revenge	152		35
Lest			
She puts in leash her paird lips lest surprise	82		3
Let			
And let him prove my passion was begun	14	2	4
Let me be to thee as the circling bird	19		1
Let patience with her chastening wand	23		45
Let it flow for heavenly mirth	24		10
Let in joy this Easter day	24		24
Crowded let his table be	24		26
Henceforth let your souls alway	24		29
Let him ride her pride in his triumph despatch and have done with his doom there	28	27	8
A released shower let flash to the shire not a lightning of fire hard-hurled	28	33	8
Let him Easter in us be a dayspring to the dimness of us be a crimson-cressetedeast	28	34	5
Let the chime of a rhyme	28	35	19

Word	Poem	Stan.	Line
I might let bygones be our curse	41		88
And one but let be let be	41		102
And one but let be let be	41		102
Let him oh with his air of angels then lift me lay me only Ill	45		9
What the heart is which like carriers let fly	47		5
Let me though see no more of him and not disappointment	48		36
Then let the march tread our ears	52		9
Of wet and of wildness let them be left	56		14
O let them be left wildness and wet	56		15
Let all Gods glory through	60		30
Since God has let dispense	60		40
Ever so black on it our tale o our oracle let life waned ah let life wind	61		10
Ever so black on it our tale o our oracle let life waned ah let life wind	61		10
Home at heart heavens sweet gift then leave let that alone	62		11
Then lull then leave off fury had shrieked no lingering let me be fell force I must be brief	65		6
My own heart let me more have pity on let	69		1
My own heart let me more have pity on let	69		1
You jaded let be call off thoughts awhile	69		10
Elsewhere leave comfort root-room let joy size	69		11
Let incense hang across the room	77		19
Let the warbled sweetness rill	77		84
Let charity thus begin at home	81		124
Let me now	101		6
No let that go I have said goodnight to shame	102	1	45
Now let me see you you large princely hand	102	1	46
Ah Floris Floris let me speak this little	102	1	53
But let me sing that which is known to me	116		4
Had let such music down without impediment	122		8
Small matter of that then let him smother	145		40
Let what there needs be done stay with him one companion	152		12
Let winter wed one sow them in her womb	158		3
Flinty kindcold element let break across his limbs	159		41
Lets			
Than Purcell tune lets tread to see it does this keeps warm	62		2
Letter			
Although the letter said	7		1
And with the last post over I knew no letter was sent	128		2
What would be a birthday letter that after the birthday came	128		4

Word	Poem	Stan.	Line
Letter (cont.)			
For a letter comes at last shall I say before Christmas is come	128		19
Lettering			
For lettering of the lambs fleece ruddying of the rose-flake	28	22	8
Letters			
Is cries countless cries like dead letters sent	67		7
As Devonshire letters earlier in the year	119		1
In bloody letters lessons of earnest of revenge	152		35
His looks the souls own letters see beyond	157		15
Levant			
To watch the low or Levant sun	15		26
Level			
Of the rolling level underneath him steady air and striding	36		2
But vastness blurs and time beats level enough the resurrection	72		16
Around it balances the level sea	98	4	2
Whose silver skins lie level and thick in field	102	1	23
There was a meadow level almost you traced	107	4	1
Levelld			
With levelld lashes stilling their disquiet	82		2
Levels			
So that the masons levels courses all	12	2	2
Attain the windy levels of the sky	121		4
Lewd			
Rife in her wrongs more lawless and more lewd	50		8
Liar			
And you were a liar o blue March day	41		20
In a neighbour deft-handed are you that liar	46		13
Libanus			
Shall shake her fruit as libanus	6		28
Liberties			
The liberties of air	98	29	4
The liberties of air	135		22
Lick			
That lick the shelly leaves which floor the copse	84		4
Lid			
Shot lightning to the stifling lid of night	125		56
Lids			
And thro their parting lids there came and went	2		11
Ebbd back beneath its snowy lids unseen	2		18
Her lids half-meshing shelter from the sky	99		6
Lie			
Go then I am contented here to lie	5		55

Word	Poem	Stan.	Line
After the sunset I would lie	15		42
Low lie his mates now on watery bed	41		57
That left to the lord of the Eucharist I here lie by	48		44
Though worlds of wanwood leafmeal lie	55		8
Above me round me lie	60		118
Why that my chaff might fly my grain lie sheer and clear	64		9
And in grey bands the sun should lie still born	90		3
Whose silver skins lie level and thick in field	102	1	23
And John shall lie where winds are dead	114		9
His brightest blooms lie there unblown	148		41
Earlier or you fail at our force and lie	153		3
All lie tumbled-to then with loop-locks	159		31
Lies			
Lies in the breast of the young year-mother	26		3
The grey lawns cold where gold where quick-gold lies	32	1	5
To seem the stranger lies my lot my life	66	1	1
Come because then most thinly lies	77		35
Lies divinely still at rest	77		98
Say beauty lies but in the meet of lines	102	3	21
Lies in her lap which she anon sweeps off	111		9
Who lies on grass and pores upon the sky	117		3
Where lies your landmark seamark or souls star	157		19
And come where lies a coffer burly all of blocks	159		36
Lieu			
O surely reaving peace my lord should leave in lieu	51		7
Life			
But opend twice in life and death to state	1	4	8
Warm-laid grave of a womb-life grey	28	7	3
Drawn to the life that died	28	23	2
Your wealth of life is some way spent	28	35	14
Life this wildworth blown so sweet	41		93
Forms and warms the life within	42		22
Life all laced in the others	54		2
In every least things life	60		8
Her life as life does air	60		45
Her life as life does air	60		45
Ever so black on it our tale o our oracle let life waned ah let life wind	61		10
Ever so black on it our tale o our oracle let life waned ah let life wind	61		10
Life death does end and each day dies with sleep	65		12
To seem the stranger lies my lot my life	66	1	1
Hours I mean years mean life and my lament	67		6

Word	Poem	Stan.	Line
Life (cont.)			
Sir life upon thy cause see banks and brakes	74	1	8
Mine o thou Lord of life send my roots rain	74	1	13
Who asks not life but only place to die	79		9
And for that fearful hour life is more thin	80	3	5
When life revisits me nerve and vein	80	7	9
But single lead a misdirected life	94		32
As ever I remember in my life	102	1	13
If life within	127		5
We cannot live this life out sometimes we must weary	152		79
I have life left with me still	155		17
Gaze on and fall directly forth on life	157		16
Lifebelt			
Till a lifebelt and gods will	41		62
Lifeless			
The rivn vine leafless lifeless dry	6		22
Lifes			
And lifes first germs from death had won	23		24
I move along lifes tomb-decked way	23		39
From lifes dawn it is drawn down	28	20	7
Being pure we lifes pride and cared-for crown	35		11
This in drudgery day-labouring-out lifes age	39		4
This air which by lifes law	60		13
That in smooth spoons spy lifes masque mirrored tame	75		13
And kind compassion at his lifes last need	140		4
Lifes quick this kind this keen self-feeling	152		96
Lift			
I walk I lift up I lift up heart eyes	38		5
I walk I lift up I lift up heart eyes	38		5
Lend him a lift from the sea-swill	41		63
Let him oh with his air of angels then lift me lay me only Ill	45		9
Those sweet hopes quell whose least me quickenings lift	48		37
Where you can lift your hand	60		76
Lift up your heads o gates	115		8
Be ye lift up ye everlasting doors	115		9
Lifted			
For us was lifted from the roots	6		4
Wag or crossbridle in a wind lifted wind-laced	71		14
Till the lifted clouds were nigh	77		72
The angel lifted us above	81		119
No they are come their horn is lifted up	104		1
But being lifted immortal of immortal brightness	152		58
Lifting			
Bright-lifting with a little-lasting smile	125		57

Word	Poem	Stan.	Line
Lifts			
What death half lifts the latch of	49		19
Lifts them a little way above	81		38
Light			
Plum-purple was the west but spikes of light	2		7
An intense line of throbbing blood-light shook	2		16
Clusterd in troops and halod by the light	2		36
From wings swan-fledged a wheel of watery light	2		76
I am so light I am so fair	10		2
And pierce the yellow waxen light	15		43
That shapes in half-light his departing rings	19		3
From nine oclock till morning light	21		1
And find the uncreated light	22		10
I am so light and fair	25		2
It waned into the world of light	25		31
With light on her face like the waves at play	26		4
Gnashed but thou art above thou Orion of light	28	21	5
Tarpeian-fast but a blown beacon of light	28	28	8
Jesu hearts light	28	29	1
With all down darkness wide his wading light	40		4
Falls light as ten years long taught how to and why	47		8
Low-latched in leaf-light housel his too huge godhead	48		12
Stain light yea mark you this	60		81
And her hand leaves his light	60		112
Only the beakleaved boughs dragonish damask the toolsmooth bleak light black	61		9
From a haze of sapphire light	77		18
Light and darkness from him flings	77		68
And silver-shot with gusty light	78		8
She stood before a light not hers and seemd	79		3
In wandering until broad light of day	79		6
The light was so the wind so loud	81		59
Under the cloister-light of greenhouse vines	84		6
They webbd the sky with glassy light	87		2
A thread of light betrayd the hill	92		9
In more precision now of light and dark	98	30	1
Now more precisely touched in light and gloom	98	30	4
Lodge his eyes fast but yet as easy and light	102	1	21
And stumbling swears he walks by light of day	102	3	31
And stumbling swears he walks by light of day	102	3	37
To fields of light millions of travelling rays	103		9
And sucks the light as full as Gideons fleece	103		11
The times are nightfall look their light grows less	150		1
Her glass drinks light she darkles down			

Word	Poem	Stan.	Line
Light (cont.)			
behind	151		9
When ts light I quenched its rose times one rich rose my hand	152		82
By rafts and rafts of flake leaves light dealt so painted on the air	159		25
Lighted			
Yet like a lighted empty hall	23		10
Lighted the watery-plated leaves	98	17	2
Lighten			
God lighten your dark heart but no	145		27
Lightening			
Which lightening oer the body rosy-pale	2		72
Lighthanded			
Nay what we had lighthanded left in surly the mere mould	59		22
Lightning			
O at lightning and lashed rod	28	2	2
Thou art lightning and love I found it a winter and warm	28	9	6
A released shower let flash to the shire not a lightning of fire hard-hurled	28	33	8
The shepherds brow fronting forked lightning owns	75		1
Shot lightning to the stifling lid of night	125		56
Are afoot heaven-vault fast purpling portends and what first lightning	152		63
Lightnings			
The ear it strikes like lightnings to hear him sing	33		5
The lightnings leap the day of doom	80	7	4
Lights			
Save by two stars more crowding lights arise	2		32
And though the last lights off the black west went	31	1	11
Bloom lights the orchard-apple	42		38
And more must in yet longer lights delay	67		4
Betweenpie mountains lights a lovely mile	69		13
With heavens lights high hung round or mother-ground	70		11
When sick men turn and lights are low	77		25
It melts new lights arise as fair	77		118
More golden than the world of lights	83		2
Pointed with pierced lights and breaks of rays	98	24	2
Lightship			
Nor rescue only rocket and lightship shone	28	15	6
Like			
Hung like a wreck that flames not billows beat	1	3	4
Droopd oer the brows like Hectors casque and swayd	2		42

Word	Poem	Stan.	Line
Like an Assyrian prince with buds unsheathd	2		62
Like shiverd rubies dance or sheen of sapphire hail	2		73
Then like a flock of sea-fowl mounting higher	2		82
And thickend like that drifted bloom the flock	2		99
So like a berg of hyaline	3		17
And all like me may boast impeached not	12	1	13
Yet like a lighted empty hall	23		10
And lead me child-like by the hand	23		47
With light on her face like the waves at play	26		4
And like the storm-months smote the earth	26		29
Five like the senses and members of men	27		39
But it rides time like riding a river	28	6	7
And sheep-flock clouds like worlds of wool	29	1	18
Not honour it ale like goldy foam	29	1	35
It will flame out like shining from shook foil	31	1	2
It gathers to a greatness like the ooze of oil	31	1	3
Look look a may-mess like on orchard boughs	32	1	10
Look March-bloom like on mealed-with-yellow sallows	32	1	11
The ear it strikes like lightnings to hear him sing	33		5
He was but one like thousands more	41		84
Wood banks and brakes wash wet like lakes	42		42
That like this sleek and seeing ball	43		14
You father what you buy me I like best	47		2
What the heart is which like carriers let fly	47		5
Nothing else is like it no not all so strains	48		29
Forward-like but however and like favourable heaven heard these	48		48
Forward-like but however and like favourable heaven heard these	48		48
And many a mark like these	54		22
Leaves like the things of man you	55		3
Stones ring like each tucked string tells each hung bells	57		3
Laying like airs fine flood	60		51
Men here may draw like breath	60		66
Flashing like flecks of coal	60		100
Those limbs like ours which are	60		105
Is cries countless cries like dead letters sent	67		7
The lost are like this and their scourge to be	67		13
Spur live and lancing like the blowpipe flame	76		2
Most like those hues that in the prism	77		61
Yawnd like long furrow in the heart	77		64
Or like a lark to glide aloof	77		65
Then clouds come like ill-balanced crags	80	7	1
Now like the bird that shapes alone	81		6
My passion like a foolish wind	81		37
My cry is like a bleat a few	81		66
And like a self-outwitted blast	81		74

Word	Poem	Stan.	Line
Like (cont.)			
And the piece thats like a bean	86		4
Like a wind-perplexed rose	87		4
Like a contented wind or gentle shocks	98	2	2
Like shuttles fleet the clouds and after	98	3	1
A brittle sheen runs upward like a cliff	98	6	2
Thick-fleeced bushes like a heifers ear	98	11	1
Out-fleeced bushes like a spaniels ear	98	11	2
Two tongues like butterflies	98	12	7
Stars like gold tufts	98	25	2
Stars like golden bees	98	25	3
Stars like golden rowels	98	25	4
And gather in like hurdles bright	98	29	3
Her silky coat is sheeny like a hill	99		3
Like a cuppd chestnut damaskd with dark breaks	99		12
Most like the tuft of plighted silver round	102	1	72
Most like the plighted tuft of silver round	102	1	73
Most like the silver plighted tuft about	102	1	74
Like knocking thunder all round Britains Welkin	102	2	3
Like scalded banks toppd once with principal flowers	102	2	14
I am like a slip of comet	103		1
Their harness beams like scythes in morning grass	104		6
Like flame they gather on our cliffs at evening	104		7
At morn they come upon our lands like rains	104		8
You may quote Wordsworth if you like to me	107	3	8
And said I like this it is almost isled	107	4	25
It were more like to be	109	32	4
It were more like to be	109	34	4
It were more like to be	109	35	4
Like me sat sighing by a sycamore-tree	111		14
Like Pharohs ears of windy harvest dry	117		6
Of streams and clouds like meshd and parted moss	121		2
Of water clouds like parted moss	121		3
I saw the stars like flash of fire	135		8
And gather in like hurdles bright	135		21
Like that poor pocket of pence poor pence of mine	142		9
His locks like all a ravel-ropes-end	144		5
Or like a juicy and jostling shock	144		9
And the sunlight sidled like dewdrops like dandled diamonds	144		17
And the sunlight sidled like dewdrops like dandled diamonds	144		17
Like water soon to be sucked in	145		9
She held her hands to like in prayer	145		48

Word	Poem	Stan.	Line
Just like Jesus crucified	145		50
Like air he changed in choice	148		18
Down the beetling banks like water in waterfalls	152		51
It stooped and flashed and fell and ran like water away	152		52
In all her body I say no place was like her eyes	152		56
I have like a lion done lionlike done	152		67
Who like me knowing his nature to the heart home natures business	152		76
All day long I like fountain glow	155		2
Mote-like in thy mighty glow	155		4
That fleeted else like day-dissolved dreams	157		11
Like the thing that never knew the earth never off roots	159		27
Likeness			
To take his lovely likeness more and more	151		2
Likes			
Things that she likes seems often to despise	94		17
Likest			
That likest in me either that or this	13		7
Lilies			
And a few lilies blow	9		4
Lilies I shew you lilies none	10		7
Lilies I shew you lilies none	10		7
See my lilies lilies none	25		7
See my lilies lilies none	25		7
With sulphur-colourd lilies brittle in stalk	98	12	3
Of the brakes of lilies	98	19	4
To spill oer fields of lilies so could I	102	1	37
Among the lilies and thy good domain	123		6
Lily			
Fair beds they seemd of water-lily flakes	2		13
She pillowing low her lily neck	21		55
And lily-coloured clothes provide	22		27
But Gertrude lily and Luther are two of a town	28	20	5
Christs lily and beast of the waste wood	28	20	6
Storm flakes were scroll-leaved flowers lily showers sweet heaven was astrew in them	28	21	8
The dapple-eared lily below thee that country and town did	44		3
When lily-yellow is the west	81		55
A pure gold lily but by the pure gold lily	98	15	1
A pure gold lily but by the pure gold lily	98	15	1
With the multitude of the lily-buds	98	19	3
A lily if it should be	109	22	2
Is it a lily in your hand	109	33	1
Our sex should be born in April perhaps or the lily-time	128		13
But the lily is past as I say and the rose			

Word	Poem	Stan.	Line
Lily (cont.)			
is not in its prime	128		14
And a few leaves not lily-white but characterеd over with blacks	128		16
Lily-buds			
With the multitude of the lily-buds	98	19	3
Lily-coloured			
And lily-coloured clothes provide	22		27
Lily-time			
Our sex should be born in April perhaps or the lily-time	128		13
Lily-white			
And a few leaves not lily-white but charactered over with blacks	128		16
Lily-yellow			
When lily-yellow is the west	81		55
Lilylocks			
See his wind-lilylocks-laced	71		15
Limbdance			
While cripples are while lepers dancers in dismal limbdance	152		111
Limber			
When limber liquid youth that to all I teach	48		22
Limbs			
Lovely in limbs and lovely in eyes not his	57		13
Those limbs like ours which are	60		105
Stand at stress each limbs barrowy brawn his thew	71		6
Struck off it has written upon lovely limbs	152		34
Flinty kindcold element let break across his limbs	159		41
Lime			
Those goldnails and their gaylinks that hang along a lime	142		5
Limnd			
Were limnd about with radiance rare	77		60
Line			
Pendant in formal line from cornice tall	1	12	7
An intense line of throbbing blood-light shook	2		16
That came when a line of kings did cease	26		26
Lineament			
Tis so conceived in his lineament	102	1	49
Tis so conceived in his true lineament	102	1	50
Lined			
I bear a basket lined with grass	10		1
I bear a basket lined with grass	25		1
Which with its lined and creased flank	92		10
Lined all with silk of juicy red	124		16
Linen			
Or listening thought of linen-winded ghosts	135		18
Linen-winded			
Or listening thought of linen-winded ghosts	135		18

Word	Poem	Stan.	Line
Lines			
O then if in my lagging lines you miss	76		11
Beauty it may be is the meet of lines	102	3	1
Say beauty lies but in the meet of lines	102	3	21
I prove it what then when these lines are dead	117		11
Linger			
Her Perseus linger and leave her to her extremes	50		9
Lingerd			
Lingerd then raised the washing waves and drenchd	2		138
Lingerer			
For the listenr for the lingerer with a love glides	28	32	3
Lingering			
Or as Austin a lingering-out sweet skill	28	10	6
Then lull then leave off fury had shrieked no lingering let me be fell force I must be brief	65		6
Lingering-out			
Or as Austin a lingering-out sweet skill	28	10	6
Lingers			
Of that jacinthine thing that where it lingers	2		65
Linked			
Lo linked heavens with milky ways	10		21
Lion			
Had swarthed about with lion-brown	144		3
I have like a lion done lionlike done	152		67
Lion-brown			
Had swarthed about with lion-brown	144		3
Lioness			
Till a lioness arose breasting the babble	28	17	7
Lionlike			
I have like a lion done lionlike done	152		67
Lionlimb			
Thy wring-world right foot rock lay a lionlimb against me scan	64		6
Lip			
Cheek and the wimpled lip	49		2
Smiled blushed and bit his lip	54		19
This downy counterfeit upon my lip	102	1	5
To manhood on the upper lip they lookd	102	1	71
What put taught graces on his country lip	107	2	3
Lipmusic			
Or deaf ears shall desire that lipmusic thats lost upon them	152		110
Lippd			
The waves were rosy-lippd the crimson glare	2		24
Tuggd the bossd smooth-lippd giant strombus-shell	2		57

Word	Poem	Stan.	Line
Lipped			
Rough-robin or five-lipped campion clear	144		15
Lips			
Apart betwixt ten thousand petalld lips	2		21
And taught my lips to quote this word	8		6
God comes all sweetness to your lenten lips	11		2
A warfare of my lips in truth	18		15
Shape nothing lips be lovely-dumb	22		5
My hand upon my lips I lay	23		37
Man from the lips of him speaketh and saith	26		5
The praise of the lips and the hearts of us bring to thee	26		35
For lips and hearts they belong to thee	26		37
And eyes heart what looks what lips yet gave you a	38		7
Recorded only I have put my lips on pleas	48		45
His lips moved fast in sense too thick	81		100
She puts in leash her paird lips lest surprise	82		3
The breaking leaves of gold are curld upon her lips	98	14	3
With potent lips call down cemented towers	104		5
Crisp lips straight nose and tender-slanted cheek	136		16
Forward falling forehead frowning lips crisp	159		32
Liquid			
When limber liquid youth that to all I teach	48		22
Purple eyes and seas of liquid leaves all day	68		8
He leans to it Harry bends look back elbow and liquid waist	71		12
Where liquid heaven sapphire-pale	77		99
The pupil plays its liquid jet	86		5
Lispd			
Only the belled foxgloves lispd together	107	1	6
Lisping			
The bats wings lisping as they flew	21		19
Lissome			
With lissome scions sweet scions	52		3
List			
Man lives that list that leaning in the will	157		25
Listed			
Of the outward sentence low lays him listed to a heresy here	45		4
Listen			
And listen to the passing bell	23		40
Said listen now to me	109	27	2
And while I sail must listen I sing	138		15
Listened			
She listened how the sea-gust shook	21		52
She looked she listened Paul taught long that day	136		24
Listening			
To where the listening uplands are	77		82

Word	Poem	Stan.	Line
Or listening thought of linen-winded ghosts	135		18
Listenr			
For the listenr for the lingerer with a love glides	28	32	3
Listless			
By there comes a listless stranger beckoned by the noise	159		14
Lists			
Of driving vermeil-rain and as he lists	2		91
Where my heart lists	88		2
This sweet deserter lists herself anew	102	1	65
Lit			
Lit with exquisite tints seven	77		109
The watery-plated plane-leaves lit	98	17	3
And pledged purply in a half-lit dell	112		11
Litter			
Where in a newly-drawn green litter	10		5
Which in newly drawn green litter	25		5
Meanwhile a litter of the jagged leaves	111		8
Little			
A little sickness in the air	4		3
I had slept a little and was chill	21		16
Thrushs eggs look little low heavens and thrush	33		3
Little I reck ho lacklevel in if all had bread	70		9
Lifts them a little way above	81		38
To bow but little and worship not	81		141
Is not some little Bela set	81		142
Ah Floris Floris let me speak this little	102	1	53
So I go out my little sweet is done	103		17
Bright-lifting with a little-lasting smile	125		57
The earth and heaven so little known	130		1
His little pennon is unfurled	130		14
As where the little hurling sound	135		31
I am the little woodlark	138		11
There needs but little doing	152		11
Little-lasting			
Bright-lifting with a little-lasting smile	125		57
Live			
That I shall live I shall not die	8		7
O where live well your lease of leisure	29	1	3
Long live the weeds and the wilderness yet	56		16
Of Gods love o live air	60		122
Me live to my sad self hereafter kind	69		2
Charitable not live this tormented mind	69		3
Spur live and lancing like the blowpipe flame	76		2
I die I die I do not live	81		69
Themselves live singing and their hearers kill	96	2	2
If that were true it could not live a day	97		2
And seals of live carnation which had each	98	12	5
We live to see	98	35	1

Word	Poem	Stan.	Line
Live (cont.)			
They are not dead who die they are but lost who live	98	40	1
We cannot live this life out sometimes we must weary	152		79
Be under her banner and live for her honour	156		3
Under her banner Ill live for her honour	156		4
Under her banner we live for her honour	156		5
But under her banner I live for her honour	156		14
Lived			
And five-lived and leaved favour and pride	28	23	6
He lived on these weeds and waters these walls are what	44		10
Christ lived in Margaret Clitheroe	145		28
Lives			
And lives at last were washing away	28	15	7
There lives the dearest freshness deep down things	31	1	10
To dearest him that lives alas away	67		8
He hand to mouth he lives and voids with shame	75		9
The widow of an insight lost she lives with aim	76		7
There lives the witch shall win my locks	120		22
Perhaps we struck no blow Gwenvrewi lives perhaps	152		40
In a wide world of defiance Caradoc lives alone	152		71
Man lives that list that leaning in the will	157		25
Living			
To the sweet living of my friends I look	16		2
Lord of living and dead	28	1	4
Do deal Lord it with living and dead	28	27	7
Lo			
But when the sun had lapsed to ocean lo	2		136
Lo linked heavens with milky ways	10		21
Lo God shall strengthen all the feeble knees	11		14
Warm on his brow lo where is another	26		7
Hand rather my heart lo lapped strength stole joy would laugh cheer	64		11
Loaded			
To keep the loaded bolt from plunging back	135		6
Loading			
So loading with obstruction that threshold	17		8
Loamy			
That thrive in the loamy greenness of this place	122		15
Loathd			
With loathd cold fishes far from man or what	2		124
Loathe			
My soul does loathe it and my spirit fails	5		14

Word	Poem	Stan.	Line
Loathed			
Loathed for a love men knew in them	28	21	1
Loathingly			
And every heart think loathingly	114		15
Loathsome			
Or they go rich as roseleaves hence that loathsome came hither	152		129
Lock			
Lock with my right then knot a barken band	80	7	45
The lock of clouds betimes and hangs the day	98	31	3
Covers with shallow silver the lock of clouds	98	31	5
Locks			
Their pansy-dark or bronzen locks were strung	2		53
And locks love ever in a lad	48		35
Come then your ways and airs and looks locks maidengear gallantry and gaiety and grace	59		14
Winning ways airs innocent maiden manners sweet looks loose locks long locks love-locks gaygear going gallant girlgrace	59		15
Winning ways airs innocent maiden manners sweet looks loose locks long locks love-locks gaygear going gallant girlgrace	59		15
Some ice that locks the glacier to the rocks	80	7	20
The knot of feathery locks upon her head	99		14
As keel locks close to kelson	101		5
And there she waits with locks unwet	120		3
There lives the witch shall win my locks	120		22
Nor locks nor eyes shall win again	120		25
His locks like all a ravel-ropes-end	144		5
All lie tumbled-to then with loop-locks	159		31
Lodge			
Lodge his eyes fast but yet as easy and light	102	1	21
Lodged			
My fast-lodged tongue to her the gift	81		116
And seven ears crown the lodged corn	114		6
Lodges			
Or never lodges there	21		25
Their rocky lodges then the weather rare	80	4	5
In the lodges of the perishable souls	126		1
Loins			
That leans along the loins of hills where a candycoloured where a gluegold-brown	159		5
Lone			
And all in lone air stood the sun	77		76
Lonely			
Heard unheeded leaves me a lonely began	66	1	13
Long			
He rangd long corridors and cornicd halls	1	10	1
Dimmd in the long accumulated dust	1	12	6
The monks left long ago since which no more	1	15	4

Word	Poem	Stan.	Line
Long (cont.)			
Down that dank rock oer which their lush long tresses weep	2		115
I see long reefs of violets	3		25
Forget the waking trumpet the long law	5		44
With long-superfluous ties for nothing here	12	1	4
There on a long and squared height	15		41
With free long looking ere I die	15		44
And hunting winds and the long-lying snow	17		2
But feel the long success of sin	18		8
What was its season then how long ago	27		14
Who long for rest who look for pleasure	29	1	1
When weeds in wheels shoot long and lovely and lush	33		2
Fails light as ten years long taught how to and why	47		8
Long live the weeds and the wilderness yet	56		16
That canst but only be but dost that long	58		4
Nor can you long be what you now are called fair	59		6
Winning ways airs innocent maiden manners sweet looks loose locks long locks love-locks gaygear going gallant girlgrace	59		15
Winning ways airs innocent maiden manners sweet looks loose locks long locks love-locks gaygear going gallant girlgrace	59		15
Them beauty-in-the-ghost deliver it early now long before death	59		18
My cries heave herds-long huddle in a main a chief-woe world-sorrow on an age-old anvil wince and sing	65		5
May who neer hung there nor does long our small	65		9
Shivelights and shadowtackle in long lashes lace lance and pair	72		4
Nine months she then nay years nine years she long	76		5
Yawnd like long furrow in the heart	77		64
A thing that weeps enduring long	81		50
Her finger-long new horns are cappd with black	99		7
And long the trees were colourd but the oer-head	107	4	12
They have taken out their long brands	109	14	1
Bright hues long lookd at thin dissolve and fly	117		2
Of mile-long reaches of our road below us	125		7
And how long was the way	125		11
She looked she listened Paul taught long that day	136		24
Or wind-long fleeces on the flock	144		11
Jews killed Jesus long ago	145		52

Word	Poem	Stan.	Line
Must all day long taste murder what do now then do	152		98
As long as men are mortal and God merciful	152		115
So long to this sweet spot this leafy lean-over	152		116
All day long I like fountain flow	155		2
Long where we leave him froliclavish while he looks about him laughs swims	159		42
Long-lying			
And hunting winds and the long-lying snow	17		2
Long-superfluous			
With long-superfluous ties for nothing here	12	1	4
Longer			
And more must in yet longer lights delay	67		4
Herclots preachings Ill no longer hear	96	5	1
This dry dean now no longer dry nor dumb but moist and musical	152		117
I should be wronging longer leaving it to float	159		44
Longing			
Till the longing is less and the good gone	138		36
Look			
On thistles that men look not grapes to gather	7		2
He says his science helps him not to look	14	2	13
To the sweet living of my friends I look	16		2
Save Christ to Christ I look on Christ I call	16		14
Quinces look when not one	25		9
I shall look on thy loveliness mother of mine	27		13
Strike you the sight of it look at it loom there	28	27	3
Who long for rest who look for pleasure	29	1	1
Look at the stars look look up at the skies	32	1	1
Look at the stars look look up at the skies	32	1	1
Look at the stars look look up at the skies	32	1	1
O look at all the fire-folk sitting in the air	32	1	2
Look look a May-mess like on orchard boughs	32	1	10
Look look a May-mess like on orchard boughs	32	1	10
Look March-bloom like on mealed-with-yellow sallows	32	1	11
Thrushs eggs look little low heavens and thrush	33		3
Look foot to forelock how all things suit he	41		76
Dropped eyes and dared not look	54		32
Again look overhead	60		73
He leans to it Harry bends look back elbow and liquid waist	71		12
With fretty chervil look and fresh wind shakes	74	1	10
And look abroad on sunny clusters	77		134

Word	Poem	Stan.	Line
Look (cont.)			
I strove to look I lost the trick	81		97
To win a look of violet	86		6
Since on the face it is unsafe to look	102	1	47
And bluer grey the flocks of trees look in the plain	105		8
You may look for me home my love he said	109	2	3
Than we in the east dare look for buds disclose	119		2
You look again and cannot find	130		19
When this was done and I could look	135		7
The times are nightfall look their light grows less	150		1
Lookd			
To manhood on the upper lip they lookd	102	1	71
Lowly Alice lookd abroad	109	17	1
Bright hues long lookd at thin dissolve and fly	117		2
Looked			
Gold gallant flowers much looked at in April-weather	98	16	2
She looked she listened Paul taught long that day	136		24
Lookers			
Beyond and one within the lookers eye	102	3	6
Looking			
Then looking on the waters I was ware	2		27
With free long looking ere I die	15		44
I will appear looking such charity	140		3
Looks			
Looks laid for feasting and for rest	3		24
And I will turn my looks to you	8		12
And eyes heart what looks what lips yet gave you a	38		7
Her injurys looks off by both horns of shore	50		3
Come then your ways and airs and looks locks maidengear gallantry and gaiety and grace	59		14
Winning ways airs innocent maiden manners sweet looks loose locks long locks love-locks gaygear going gallant girlgrace	59		15
Looks from the zenith round the sky	77		108
His very looks in other years	81		62
I bite my hands my looks I shroud	81		65
Of him that looks yet not in that alone	91		3
How looks the night there does not miss a star	98	22	1
When maddest looks the slighted nix	120		19
His looks the souls own letters see beyond	157		15
Long where we leave him froliclavish while he looks about him laughs swims	159		42

Word	Poem	Stan.	Line
Loom			
Strike you the sight of it look at it loom there	28	27	3
When strangely loom all shapes that be	77		31
Loomd			
White loomd my rock the water gurgling oer	2		142
Loop			
All lie tumbled-to then with loop-locks	159		31
Loop-locks			
All lie tumbled-to then with loop-locks	159		31
Looped			
Why raindrop-roundels looped together	29	1	27
Loops			
With loops of veins not of an even pink	93	2	4
Loose			
Winning ways airs innocent maiden manners sweet looks loose locks long locks love-locks gaygear going gallant girlgrace	59		15
Yet when my unset tresses hung loose-traced	102	1	3
Loose on the stem has done its summering	105		13
Loose-traced			
Yet when my unset tresses hung loose-traced	102	1	3
Loosely			
The chestnut-fans are loosely flirting	78		5
Loosend			
Phoebus loosend tresses swim	77		102
Lord			
Is the sweet vintage of our Lord	6		20
See the salvation of the Lord	8		9
And you unhouse and house the Lord	22		24
Christ Jesus our Lord her God and her Son	27		29
Lord of living and dead	28	1	4
Do deal Lord it with living and dead	28	27	7
Our hearts charitys hearths fire our thoughts chivalrys throngs lord	28	34	8
Before it cloud Christ Lord and sour with sinning	31		12
The Eurydice it concerned thee o Lord	41		1
But to Christ Lord of thunder	41		108
Magnify the Lord	42		32
That left to the Lord of the Eucharist I here lie by	48		44
O surely reaving peace my Lord should leave in lieu	51		7
Thou art indeed just Lord if I contend	73	1	1
Mine o thou Lord of life send my roots rain	74	1	13
Lord but they cry so loud and what am I	80	7	13
O Lord but I have wrought and striven	81		108
Duly dear Lord my prize is won	81		109
Lord William they call me	109	5	2

Word	Poem	Stan.	Line
Lord (cont.)			
Says are you not Lord Williams love	109	18	3
I am Lord Williams love she said	109	19	1
Lord William comes hunting tomorrow morning	109	19	3
But how will you Lord William know	109	20	1
Yet how will you Lord William know	109	21	1
In this wise you may know your lord	109	22	3
O where is Lord William my lords she said	109	25	3
Fie you are not Lord William she said	109	26	3
Lord William is king of all this land	109	27	3
Make wide thou o lord of sin	115		6
Make me pure Lord thou are holy	129		6
Make me meek Lord thou wert lowly	129		7
Lord Beuno comes tonight	152		7
Lord now curb him for ever o daring o deep insight	152		73
Lordly			
To deck and make most lordly evermore	1	2	9
What country is honour enough in all us lordly head	70		10
Lords			
Who knelt were for the lords right hand	81		94
O where is Lord William my lords she said	109	25	3
Lore			
That reads or holds the astrologic lore	14	2	2
Even than this my thankless lore	15		22
And then I hate the most that lore	15		33
Lorn			
The lorn moon pale with piteous dismay	79		4
Lose			
And hedges break and lose the kine	114		2
Loss			
The sceptic disappointment and the loss	14	3	12
To trace some traceless loss of thought again	107	4	18
Which between ash-tops suffers loss	121		5
Losses			
By slender losses are undone	81		147
Lost			
Our prayer seems lost in desert ways	23		5
Reck not what the poor have lost	24		4
Have lost that cheer and charm of earths past prime	35		12
Too late lost gone with the gale	41		35
He has lost count what came next poor boy	41		71
O well wept mother have lost son	41		104
My lad and lost in Jack	54		18
See not a hair is not an eyelash not the least lash lost every hair	59		20
Far with fonder a care and we we should have lost it finer fonder	59		29

Word	Poem	Stan.	Line
Love (cont.)			
Love come down to me if thy name be love	20		6
Love come down to me if thy name be love	20		6
Then next I hungered love when here they say	20		9
Hear yet my paradox love when all is given	20		13
To see thee I must see thee to love love	20		14
To see thee I must see thee to love love	20		14
Wherefore we love thee wherefore we sing to thee	26		33
In grace that is charity grace that is love	27		47
Thou art lightning and love I found it a winter and warm	28	9	6
Loathed for a love men knew in them	28	21	1
Is it love in her of the being as her lover had been	28	25	3
For the listenr for the lingerer with a love glides	28	32	3
Or love or pity or all that sweet notes not his might nursle	45		6
And locks love ever in a lad	48		35
Love-laced what once I well	54		3
For fond love and for shame	54		37
Of Gods love o live air	60		122
Our law says love what are loves worthiest were all known	62		8
For love he leans forth needs his neck must fall on kiss	63		12
Kind love both give and get only what word	66	1	10
And I cry out for wounded love	81		33
You hear nor care of love and pain	81		35
The love of women is not so strong	81		48
Tis falsely given as love in men	81		49
I would remember love forgive	81		71
Or this or else I do not love	81		114
My love and all was sweet and well	81		121
I need not love I need not break	81		138
Knowledge is strong but love is sweet	81		154
She kept her love-thoughts on most lenten diet	82		7
Did Helen steal my love from me	95		1
My cousin will not love you as I love	102	1	60
My cousin will not love you as I love	102	1	60
No love prescriptive love with place assignd	102	3	13
No love prescriptive love with place assignd	102	3	13
Love by monition heritage or lot	102	3	14
Love by prenatal serfdom still confined	102	3	15
Though self-made bands at last may true love bind	102	3	19
New love is free love or true love tis not	102	3	20
New love is free love or true love tis not	102	3	20
New love is free love or true love tis not	102	3	20
New love is free love or true love tis not	102	3	27

Word	Poem	Stan.	Line
New love is free love or true love tis not	102	3	27
New love is free love or true love tis not	102	3	27
When are you home my love she said	109	2	1
You may look for me home my love he said	109	2	3
How shall I call my love she said	109	4	3
I give you my love and I give you my land	109	5	3
He yearnd he yearnd to have his love	109	6	1
And if I chose a love to wed	109	10	1
Says are you not Lord Williams love	109	18	3
I am Lord Williams love she said	109	19	1
Because he is my love she said	109	20	3
Her true love she might see	109	30	4
Wilt thou follow me my true love	109	37	1
Wilt thou follow me my true love	109	37	3
O I will follow thee my true love	109	38	1
Sweeter thy kisses my own love	109	38	3
For love and greater glory of Christ	118		4
And undivulged love does overflow	119		12
Who loves me here and has my love	124		1
I do not love	127		10
You spoil the plot I find my true love by	135		36
To him who ever thought with love of me	140		1
Wedlock what the water spousal love	159		47
Love-laced			
Love-laced what once I well	54		3
Love-thoughts			
She kept her love-thoughts on most lenten diet	82		7
Loveable			
Away in the loveable west	28	24	1
Loved			
No but for Christ who hath foreknown and loved thee	13		14
Loveless			
And relish not her loveless kiss	120		11
And half mislike her loveless kiss	120		13
Lovelier			
Times told lovelier more dangerous o my chevalier	36		10
Loveliest			
Holiest loveliest bravest	41		110
Worlds loveliest mens selves self flashes off frame and face	62		9
Loveliness			
I shall look on thy loveliness mother of mine	27		13
To its own best being and its loveliness of youth it is an everlastingness of o it is an all youth	59		13
Lovelocks			
Winning ways airs innocent maiden manners sweet looks loose locks long locks love-locks gaygear going gallant girlgrace	59		15

Word	Poem	Stan.	Line
Lovely			
Shape nothing lips be lovely-dumb	22		5
To the stars lovely-asunder	28	5	2
Breathe body of lovely death	28	25	4
No not uncomforted lovely-felicitous providence	28	30	5
When weeds in wheels shoot long and lovely and lush	33		2
Lovely the woods waters meadows combes vales	34		9
Around up above what wind-walks what lovely behaviour	38		2
He was all of lovely manly mould	41		73
How lovely the elder brothers	54		1
Lovely in limbs and lovely in eyes not his	57		13
Lovely in limbs and lovely in eyes not his	57		13
Thy lovely dale down thus and thus bids reel	58		7
Those lovely lads once wet-fresh windfalls of wars storm	62		5
Betweenpie mountains lights a lovely mile	69		13
O lovely ease in change of place	130		27
Twice lovely tinted eastern turned Greek	136		15
He praised the lovely lot of continence	136		28
Or paring of paradisaical fruit lovely in waning but lustreless	137		3
And lace-leaved lovely	138		29
To take his lovely likeness more and more	151		2
Struck off it has written upon lovely limbs	152		34
Rose here he feasts lovely all is no more off with down he dings	159		28
Lovely-asunder			
To the stars lovely-asunder	28	5	2
Lovely-dumb			
Shape nothing lips be lovely-dumb	22		5
Lovely-felicitous			
No not uncomforted lovely-felicitous providence	28	30	5
Lover			
Is it love in her of the being as her lover had been	28	25	3
God lover of souls swaying considerate scales	34		12
The destined lover whom his stars	83		1
Call me Englands fames fond lover	156		11
Loves			
For poor loves failure than his hopeless rise	14	3	7
Or once or never took loves proper food	20		10
Rapturous loves greeting of realer of rounder replies	38		8
For wrung all on loves rack	54		17
Our law says love what are loves worthiest were all known	62		8
And loves a fatal fault to patronize	94		18

Word	Poem	Stan.	Line
But Im alone for my loves gone	95		8
She loves his face she knows the spot	120		2
Who loves me here and has my love	124		1
Lovescape			
Lovescape crucified	28	23	4
Low			
Doors slammd to the blasts continually more low	1	13	8
Rowing I reachd a rock the sea was low	2		1
Because the sighting wind is low	3		6
You vigil-keepers with low flames decreased	11		8
To watch the low or levant sun	15		26
She pillowing low her lily neck	21		55
Thrushs eggs look little low heavens and thrush	33		3
With a flood or a fall low lull-off or all roar	35		3
Though aloft on turf or perch or poor low stage	39		5
Low lie his mates now on watery bed	41		57
Crouch lay knee by earth low under	41		109
Of the outward sentence low lays him listed to a heresy here	45		4
Low-latched in leaf-light housel his too huge godhead	48		12
Flutes and low to the lake falls home	56		4
And louched low grass heaven that dost appeal	58		2
Sure s bed now low be it lustily he his low lot feel	70		5
Sure s bed now low be it lustily he his low lot feel	70		5
When sick men turn and lights are low	77		25
Does lay men low with one blades sudden blow	80	2	3
Dawn that the pebbly low-down east	98	31	1
Dawn that low-down pebbly east	98	31	4
That was of low degree	109	10	2
With one of low degree	109	12	4
That is of low degree	109	18	4
And thou of low degree	109	27	4
Low-covered pass and brace the woodland clods	112		6
Now comes as low beneath	115		4
Man is most low God is most high	133		5
Low-covered			
Low-covered pass and brace the woodland clods	112		6
Low-down			
Dawn that the pebbly low-down east	98	31	1
Dawn that low-down pebbly east	98	31	4

Word	Poem	Stan.	Line
Low-latched			
Low-latched in leaf-light housel his too huge godhead	48		12
Lower			
Lower than death and the dark	28	32	4
Lowly			
Said who then is this lowly woman	109	11	3
It is for the shame of the lowly woman	109	14	3
Lowly Alice sat in her bower	109	16	1
Lowly Alice lookd abroad	109	17	1
Make me meek Lord thou wert lowly	129		7
Loyal			
Loyal to his own soul laying his own law down no law nor	152		72
Luke			
Thus Frances sighed at home while Luke	21		50
Lull			
With a flood or a fall low lull-off or all roar	35		3
Then lull then leave off fury had shrieked no lingering let me be fell force I must be brief	65		6
Lull-off			
With a flood or a fall low lull-off or all roar	35		3
Lung			
My lung must draw and draw	60		14
Stone palsy cancer cough lung-wasting womb-not-bearing	152		113
Lung-wasting			
Stone palsy cancer cough lung-wasting womb-not-bearing	152		113
Lurch			
Then a lurch forward frigate and men	41		40
Lush			
Down that dank rock oer which their lush long tresses weep	2		115
In a hollow lush and damp	4		7
Word last how a lush-kept plush-capped sloe	28	8	3
When weeds in wheels shoot long and lovely and lush	33		2
The ear in milk lush the sash	138		20
Lush-kept			
Word last how a lush-kept plush-capped sloe	28	8	3
Lust			
Fell on the palace and the lust of rabble rude	1	14	9
Palate the hutch of tasty lust	22		13
Defeat thwart me oh the sots and thralls of lust	74	1	6
Lustily			
Sure s bed now low be it lustily he his low lot feel	70		5
Lustred			
Of glassy-clear aeolis metal-lustred	2		69

Word	Poem	Stan.	Line
Lustreless			
Or paring of paradisaical fruit lovely in waning but lustreless	137		3
Lustres			
And sober lustres take the gloom	77		20
Deeply in the arched lustres	77		133
Lustrous			
Speard open lustrous gashes crimson-white	2		8
Lusty			
His lusty hands in gusts of scented wind	2		88
Luther			
But Gertrude Lily and Luther are two of a town	28	20	5
Lying			
And hunting winds and the long-lying snow	17		2
Madam			
True madam I am sorry now to see	125		16
Maddest			
When maddest looks the slighted nix	120		19
Made			
Those cyclads made that thickend on my sight	2		37
Ere I had further question made	4		16
Who is this Moses who made him we say	5		1
Christ our sacrifice is made	6		10
When he has made us bear his leaf	6		30
Is this made plain what have I come across	14	3	10
And minor sweetness scarce made mention of	19		12
Made headway in the frothy deep	21		51
Yet made its market here as well	25		32
It was made of earths mould but it went from mens eyes	27		3
That cordial air made those kind people a hood	34		5
Made sweeter not made dim	60		111
Made sweeter not made dim	60		111
And cry o Christ-done deed so God-made-flesh does too	63		13
Who made conjecture nearest far	77		45
We tuned to one key and made their harmonies	98	2	4
Though self-made bands at last may true love bind	102	3	19
They made him kneel on knee	109	14	2
Two made answer in one breath	109	26	1
When she had made the door wide	109	30	3
Yea crushd my heart and made me dumb	118		12
You have made me quote almost the dismalest proverb I know	128		18
Of world made marred and mended lost and won	136		26
The world was saved by virgins made the			

Word	Poem	Stan.	Line
Made (cont.)			
mark	136		30
Made known though thick through stone	148		11
Who built these walls made known	148		37
Madrid			
Lay bleeding to Madrid the last they bore	1	15	2
Madrigal			
Why tears is it tears such a melting a Madrigal start	28	18	6
Maenefa			
Stepped from the stool drew back from the barrow of dark Maenefa the mountain	137		4
Maentwrog			
Maentwrog	91		11
Maentwrog	98	2	5
Magdalen			
Beyond Magdalen and by the bridge on a place called there the plain	142		1
Magic			
And magic cuckoocall	42		43
Magnify			
Magnify the Lord	42		32
Magnifying			
Their magnifying of each its kind	42		29
Maid			
Maid yet mother as may hath been	26		20
Salute thee mother the maid-months queen	26		24
Till a maid in Davids house had birth	26		30
Next Mary mother of maid and nun	145		43
And what sways with you maybe this sweet maid	157		22
Maid-months			
Salute thee mother the maid-months queen	26		24
Maiden			
Oh thou proud mother and much proud maiden	26		19
Thee oh maiden most worthy of praise	26		36
Maiden could obey so be a bell to ring of it and	28	30	7
The heaven-flung heart-fleshed maiden-furled	28	33	3
Winning ways airs innocent maiden manners sweet looks loose locks long locks love-locks gaygear going gallant girlgrace	59		15
Her weeds all mark her maiden though to wed	136		17
The earnest-hearted maiden sat and heard	136		32
Call no such maiden mine the deeper grows her dearness	152		18
Maiden-furled			
The heaven-flung heart-fleshed maiden-furled	28	33	3
Maidengear			
Come then your ways and airs and looks locks maidengear gallantry and gaiety and grace	59		14

Word	Poem	Stan.	Line
Make (cont.)			
What must make our daystar	60		106
In whose dead lake even a voice may make	80	4	3
But then I make an eager shift to see	80	6	5
Houses that make abode beside the lake	80	6	6
I cry o rocks and mountain make me room	80	7	5
Thus I shall make a cross and int	80	7	41
Make it to God I am not spent	81		130
Yea to myself I answer make	81		145
Married will make a sweet and matchless wife	94		31
And primrose bring and make a sheaf	98	18	3
Heaven make the time be short she said	109	3	1
Heaven make it sweet to you she said	109	3	3
And make it short to me	109	3	4
I would not make the trial	110		2
And field-flowers make the fields forlorn	114		3
O grounds of hell make room	115		2
Make wide thou o lord of sin	115		6
That make my eyes sore and cross-colour things	125		46
Make me pure lord thou are holy	129		6
Make me meek lord thou were lowly	129		7
Whom want could not make pine pine	142		7
Since all the make of man	148		7
To make believe my mood was mock o I might think so	152		41
Of favoured make and mind and health and youth	157		18
Hark hearer hear what I do lend a thought now make believe	159		1
Makes			
Wherein he makes us stray	5		6
Unbakes my pores and streams and makes all fresh	5		32
Which makes me when with men I deal	15		19
Which makes so small the promise of that yield	17		11
Which only makes you eloquent	22		8
Makes the silver jubilee	28	35	4
No wonder of it sheer plod makes plough down sillion	36		11
In mould or mind or what not else makes rare	40		6
Mark makes in the rivelling snowstorm	41		67
And azuring-over greybell makes	42		41
And makes o marvellous	60		59
More makes when all is done	60		71
Veins violets and tall trees makes more and more	73		11
For who makes rainbows by invention	91		4
That still makes counter-roundels in the pond	107	3	5

Word	Poem	Stan.	Line
Man (cont.)			
Now and seeing somewhere some man do all that man can do	63		11
Not untwist slack they may be these last strands of man	64		2
Frightful sheer no-man-fathomed hold them cheap	65		8
Man how fast his firedint his mark on mind is gone	72		11
But man we scaffold of score brittle bones	75		5
Man Jack the man is just his mate a hussy	75		11
Man Jack the man is just his mate a hussy	75		11
From God and man is hell no doubt	80	1	4
By heady elements for no man knows	103		5
Man is most low God is most high	133		5
The child is father to the man	147		1
The child is father to the man	147		4
The man is father to the child	147		6
The child is father to the man	147		7
Since all the make of man	148		7
What makes the man and what	148		21
The man within that makes	148		22
No man has such a daughter the fathers of the world	152		17
Man my mate and counterpart	155		24
Where is the field I must play the man on	156		16
Man lives that list that leaning in the will	157		25
Managed			
But late is better than never you see you have managed so	128		17
Manger			
Manger maidens knee	28	7	4
Manhood			
This royal manhood tis in me rebellion	102	1	40
To manhood on the upper lip they lookd	102	1	71
Mankind			
Much dearer to mankind	60		107
Than sewers with sacred oils mankind that mob comes	152		104
Mankinds			
In mankinds medley a duty-swerver	40		53
Manly			
He was all of lovely manly mould	40		73
Since proud it calls the calling manly gives a guess	63		4
Manmarks			
Squadroned masks and manmarks treadmire toil there	72		8
Manna			
He feeds me with his manna every day	5		13
Are all the manna-bushes in the land	5		21
To gentle manna and simple bread	81		175

Word	Poem	Stan.	Line
Many (cont.)			
Many trees and flowers round	4		19
Are you sandblind slabs of water many a mile	5		35
Just seen may be to many unknown men	12	2	12
Contends about its many creeds	23		32
How many leaves had it five they were then	27		38
By many blows and banes but now hears roar	50		6
And many a mark like these	54		22
Minds me in many ways	60		16
And many standing round a waterfall	91		5
That many centres found in many hearts	107	2	5
That many centres found in many hearts	107	2	5
But many a silver visionary spark	113		5
Mar			
I know I mar my cause with words	81		30
So be it I must maim and mar	81		31
Marbled			
Marbled river boisterously beautiful between	159		6
March			
Look March-bloom like on mealed-with-yellow sallows	32	1	11
And you were a liar o blue March day	41		20
March kind comrade abreast him	48		19
Then let the march tread our ears	52		9
Under her banner we march for her honour	156		15
March-bloom			
Look March-bloom like on mealed-with-yellow sallows	32	1	11
Marches			
Built thoroughfare heaven-roysterers in gay-gangs they throng they glitter in marches	72		2
Marching			
And marching to false colours those few strokes	102	1	69
Goes marching thro my mind what sense is this it has none	152		28
Marcus			
Marcus hare high her captain	41		44
Margaret			
Margaret are you grieving	55		1
It is Margaret you mourn for	55		15
Must deal with Margaret Clitheroe	145		7
Is a shroud for Margaret Clitheroe	145		14
The body of Margaret Clitheroe	145		21
Christ lived in Margaret Clitheroe	145		28
To the death with Margaret Clitheroe	145		35
To the murder of Margaret Clitheroe	145		47
Gods daughter Margaret Clitheroe	145		54
It is over Margaret Clitheroe	145		61
Margarets			
The last thing Margarets fingers sew	145		13

Word	Poem	Stan.	Line
Mark			
I mark the flowers ere the prime	4		14
Death to mark them in the spring	4		32
I mark the tower swallows run	15		28
Mark the mark is of mans make	28	22	3
Mark the mark is of mans make	28	22	3
The-last-breath penitent spirits the uttermost mark	28	32	6
Mark makes in the rivelling snowstorm	41		67
And many a mark like these	54		22
Stain light yea mark you this	60		81
Mark Christ our king he knows war served this soldiering through	63		9
Man how fast his firedint his mark on mind is gone	72		11
Sheer off disseveral a star death blots black out nor mark	72		14
Mark you how the peacocks eye	86		1
So takes the sister sense can find no mark	113		4
Her weeds all mark her maiden though to wed	136		17
The world was saved by virgins made the mark	136		30
Markd			
As I markd not always died	4		28
She markd where I and Fabian met	120		1
Market			
Yet made its market here as well	25		32
Marking			
Marking the spot when they have gurgled oer	2		3
Sits without consolation marking not	111		4
Marred			
Of world made marred and mended lost and won	136		26
Marriage			
And now the marriage feast begun	22		26
Married			
Married will make a sweet and matchless wife	94		31
Marsh			
They rain against our much-thick and marsh air	40		7
Martinmas			
This weary martinmas would it were summer	111		10
Martyr			
Thou martyr-master in thy sight	28	21	7
On Christ they do and on the martyr may	73		5
Martyr-master			
Thou martyr-master in thy sight	28	21	7
Martyrs			
For where the martyrs bones were thickest trod	1	5	8

Word	Poem	Stan.	Line
Marvel			
Its marvel she is yet alive	81		10
Marvellous			
The marvellous milk was Walsingham way	41		101
And makes o marvellous	60		59
Mary			
Mary the Virgin well the heart knows	27		22
Is Mary the rose then Mary the tree	27		26
Is Mary the rose then Mary the tree	27		26
Miracle-in-Mary-of-flame	28	33	4
Mary sees sympathising	42		26
To offering Mary may	42		36
Tells Mary her mirth till Christs birth	42		46
Who fired France for Mary without spot	44		14
Mary Immaculate	60		24
Is Mary more by name	60		37
Mary mother of us where is your relief	65		4
Next Mary mother of maid and nun	145		43
Marys			
May is Marys month and I	42		1
Both Gods and Marys son	60		72
Time was next whitest after Marys own	136		4
Maskd			
Slight with such violet their bright-maskd green	100		9
Maskd with such violet disallow their green	100		10
Masks			
Nowhere natural hearts ivy patience masks	68		6
Squadroned masks and manmarks treadmire toil there	72		8
Masons			
So that the masons levels courses all	12	2	2
Masque			
That in smooth spoons spy lifes masque mirrored tame	75		13
Massacre			
Mays beauty massacre and wisped wild clouds grow	154		2
Massy			
There is a massy pile above the waste	1	1	1
With massy pillars of the doric mood	1	7	2
Master			
Through him melt him but master him still	28	10	4
A master her master and mine	28	19	2
A master her master and mine	28	19	2
Thou martyr-master in thy sight	28	21	7
Thing that she there then the master	28	27	4
I admire thee master of the tides	28	31	1
Being mighty a master being a father and fond	34		14
Wondering why my master bore it	41		97
You there are master do your own desire	46		11

Word	Poem	Stan.	Line
Master more may than gaze gaze out of countenance	62		4
Masterhood			
Therefore this masterhood	148		29
Mastering			
Thou mastering me	28	1	1
Of a mastering heaven utterly blue	78		2
Masters			
For that staunch saint still praisd his masters name	1	3	1
But men and masters plan and build	15		6
And that grief masters joy on earth	77		55
Mastery			
Mastery but be adored but be adored king	28	10	8
Stirred for a bird the achieve of the mastery of the thing	36		7
And mastery in the mind	49		16
Match			
Rise match your strength with monstrous talmai	56		57
Matched			
Of us the wimpled-water-dimpled not-by-morning-matched face	59		10
No piece matched those eyes kept most part much cast down	152		57
Matchless			
Married will make a sweet and matchless wife	94		31
Matchwood			
This Jack joke poor potsherd patch matchwood immortal diamond	72		23
Mate			
Man Jack the man is just his mate a hussy	75		11
Mortal my mate bearing my rock-a-heart	153		1
Man my mate and counterpart	155		24
Mated			
The moonlight-mated glowless glowworms shine	98	36	1
Her mould of features mated well	145		16
Mates			
Sooner than their mates and yet	4		29
Low lie his mates now on watery bed	41		57
Matter			
Now no matter child the name	55		10
Small matter of that then let him smother	145		40
Enough now since the sacred matter that I mean	159		43
Mawddach			
The mawddach how she trips though throttled	30		21
May			
Thee may-hope of our darkened ways	26		40

Word	Poem	Stan.	Line
May (cont.)			
Look look a may-mess like on orchard boughs	32	1	10
May-hope			
Thee May-hope of our darkened ways	26		40
May-mess			
Look look a May-mess like on orchard boughs	32	1	10
Maybe			
And what sways with you maybe this sweet maid	157		22
Mayday			
Innocent mind and mayday in girl and boy	33		13
Mays			
Mays beauty massacre and wisped wild clouds grow	154		2
Maze			
Of art best follow nature in a maze	1	6	5
On beings dread and vacant maze	23		30
Mazed			
Two mazed shepherds perishd in the tide	1	14	3
And planets bud whereer we turn our mazed eyes	2		33
Mazy			
Of mazy shape and hue but now bereft	1	8	3
And mazy sands all water-wattled	30		23
Me			
Careless of me they sported some would plash	2		102
Sudden death before me stood	4		6
He feeds me with his manna every day	5		13
And you shall meet me with reply	8		13
And still thou bindst me to fresh fealty	12	1	3
This is my park my pleasaunce this to me	12	1	6
And all like me may boast impeached not	12	1	13
None besides me this bye-ways beauty try	12	2	9
That likest in me either that or this	13		7
The happy leafing it is so with me	14	1	6
I must feed fancy show me any one	14	2	1
That here will serve me for comparison	14	3	11
Which makes me when with men I deal	15		19
Below me in the bearing air	15		30
No better serves me now save best no other	16		13
Let me be to thee as the circling bird	19		1
Love come down to me if thy name be love	20		6
Peace and food cheered me where four rough ways meet	20		12
With not a thing to make me fear	21		40
To me was terrible to hear	21		42
Elected silence sing to me	22		1
Pipe me to pastures still and be	22		3
And lead me child-like by the hand	23		47

Word	Poem	Stan.	Line
Men are amazed to watch me pass	25		3
Find me a place by thee mother of mine	27		7
Tell me the name now tell me its name	27		20
Tell me the name now tell me its name	27		20
Shew me thy son mother mother of mine	27		31
Make me a leaf in thee mother of mine	27		43
Draw me by charity mother of mine	27		49
Thou mastering me	28	1	1
Thou hast bound bones and veins in me fastened me flesh	28	1	5
Thou hast bound bones and veins in me fastened me flesh	28	1	5
Thy doing and dost thou touch me afresh	28	1	7
Thou heardst me truer than tongue confess	28	2	3
Before me the hurtle of hell	28	3	2
Some find me a sword some	28	11	1
Have you make words break from me here all alone	28	18	3
Do you mother of being in me heart	28	18	4
But how shall I make me room there	28	27	1
Reach me a fancy come faster	28	27	2
To me God knows deserving no such thing	34		2
Men go by me whom either beauty bright	40		5
And the prayer thou hearst me making	41		112
To me so arch-especial a spirit as heaves in Henry Purcell	45		2
It is the forged feature finds me it is the rehearsal	45		7
Let him oh with his air of angels then lift me lay me only Ill	45		9
Let him oh with his air of angels then lift me lay me only Ill	45		9
But tell me child your choice what shall I buy	47		1
You father what you buy me I like best	47		2
There boy bugler born he tells me of Irish	48		2
My late being there begged of me overflowing	48		6
Let me though see no more of him and not disappointment	48		36
Those sweet hopes quell whose least me quickenings lift	48		37
Your round me roaming end and under be my boughs	51		2
Beckoned me beside him	54		13
Crying what I do is me for that I came	57		8
Nestling me everywhere	60		2
Minds me in many ways	60		16
New self and nobler me	60		69
Above me round me lie	60		118
Above me round me lie	60		118
Disremembering dismembering all now heart you round me right	61		7

Word	Poem	Stan.	Line
Me (cont.)			
In me or most weary cry I can no more I can	64		3
But ah but o thou terrible why wouldst thou rude on me	64		5
Thy wring-world right foot rock lay a lion-limb against me scan	64		6
O in turns of tempest me heaped there me frantic to avoid thee and flee	64		8
O in turns of tempest me heaped there me frantic to avoid thee and flee	64		8
Cheer whom though the hero whose heaven-handling flung me foot trod	64		12
Me or me that fought him o which one is it each one	64		13
Me or me that fought him o which one is it each one	64		13
Then lull then leave off fury had shrieked no lingering let me be fell force I must be brief	65		6
Me were I pleading plead nor do I I weary of idle a being but by where wars are rife	66	1	7
Heard unheeded leaves me a lonely began	66	1	13
Bitter would have me taste my taste was me	67		10
Bitter would have me taste my taste was me	67		10
Bones built in me flesh filled blood brimmed the curse	67		11
My own heart let me more have pity on let	69		1
Me live to my sad self hereafter kind	69		2
Defeat thwart me oh the sots and thralls of lust	74	1	6
Touch me and purify and shew	77		39
Then would I fling me up to sip	77		131
The shearing rays contract me with their blaze	80	2	6
To come to me from the underground	80	4	7
I cry o rocks and mountain make me room	80	7	5
When life revisits me nerve and vein	80	7	9
They all come here and stand before me clear	80	7	10
To hold me quite fixed in the selfsame plight	80	7	46
And carried me with ravishment	81		16
You should have been with me as near	81		43
You met me I had hastend down	81		89
Save me and you were standing near	81		103
But all the while it seemd to me	81		112
Teach me the paces that you went	81		125
Penance shall clothe me to the bone	81		135
Teach me the way I will repent	81		136
Did Helen steal my love from me	95		1
That should have been true to me	95		9
To rise you bid me with the lark	96	6	1

Word	Poem	Stan.	Line
With me tis rising in the dark	96	6	2
Bring me palm with pearled knops	98	18	2
Let me now	101		6
It does amaze me when the clicking hour	102	1	1
It is too large for me what does that mean	102	1	29
This royal manhood tis in me rebellion	102	1	40
Worse than when Floris found me in the garden	102	1	43
Now let me see you you large princely hand	102	1	46
Ah Floris Floris let me speak this little	102	1	53
His tale and telling has been given to me	107	1	18
You may quote Wordsworth if you like to me	107	3	8
You may look for me home my love he said	109	2	3
And make it short to me	109	3	4
Lord William they call me	109	5	2
Come with me from over the sea	109	8	2
And truly tell to me	109	11	4
The crown shall be for me	109	15	4
O what will you now with me	109	18	2
And Alice they call me	109	19	2
I pray you tell to me	109	25	4
Said listen now to me	109	27	2
He would have come for me	109	28	4
Open the door to me	109	29	4
Said open open to me	109	30	2
And why so short with me	109	31	2
When you came forth for me	109	33	4
And have you a crown for me	109	35	2
Wilt thou follow me my true love	109	37	1
Wilt thou follow me my true love	109	37	3
Give me thy kisses three	109	38	2
Than all the crowns to me	109	38	4
He dallies yet and yet with me	110		6
Like me sat sighing by a sycamore-tree	111		14
But let me sing that which is known to me	116		4
But let me sing that which is known to me	116		4
But what indeed is askd of me	118		1
Yea crushd my heart and made me dumb	118		12
And my blue eyes again for me	120		23
Who loves me here and has my love	124		1
I think he will not tire of me	124		2
Have told me I am fair to see	124		24
But why then should Castara weigh with me	125		40
And search me through	127		17
I know what you will tell me neglectful that you were not	128		5
You have made me quote almost the dismalest proverb I know	128		18
But the Bethlehem star may lead me	129		3
To the sight of him who freed me	129		4
Make me pure Lord thou art holy	129		6
Make me meek Lord thou wert lowly	129		7

Word	Poem	Stan.	Line
Me (cont.)			
Not kind to freeze me with forecast	134		1
Dear grace and girder of mine and me	134		2
Parted me leaf and leaf divided me eyelid and eyelid of slumber	137		7
Parted me leaf and leaf divided me eyelid and eyelid of slumber	137		7
Is known to men more than me	138		13
To him who ever thought with love of me	140		1
What is it Gwen my girl why do you hover and haunt me	152		1
Your uncle met the messenger met me and this the message	152		6
On one that went against me whereas I had warned her	152		37
Any instant falls means me and I do not repent	152		64
The blame bear who aroused me what I have done violent	152		66
Who like me knowing his nature to the heart home natures business	152		76
Spare thou me since I see	155		15
I have life left with me still	155		17
Help me sir and so I will	155		20
Me shew mercy from my heart	155		22
What shall I do for the land that bred me	156		1
Her homes and fields that folded and fed me	156		2
There is the shilling that finds me willing	156		8
Call me Englands fames fond lover	156		11
Spend me or end me what God shall send me	156		13
Spend me or end me what God shall send me	156		13
Spend me or end me what God shall send me	156		13
Mead			
In some broad palmy mead and saintly smiled	1	10	5
Give us our green lots in another mead	98	15	5
Meadow			
Wave with the meadow forget that there must	28	11	7
But uncumbered meadow-down is not distressed	39		13
On meadow and river and wind-wandering weed-winding bank	43		8
There was a meadow level almost you traced	107	4	1
Gallop along the meadow grass	130		26
Meadow-down			
But uncumbered meadow-down is not distressed	39		13
Meadows			
Lovely the woods waters meadows combes vales	34		9
Next to meadows abundant pierced with flowers	98	12	2

Word	Poem	Stan.	Line
Beyond the river all the meadows round	107	4	10
Meadows to them inexplicably dear	119		8
Meads			
In starry water-meads they drew	10		17
Meal			
Meal-drift moulded ever and melted across skies	38		4
My meal at every wink	60		12
Tom heart-at-ease Tom Navvy he is all for his meal	70		4
Meal-drift			
Meal-drift moulded ever and melted across skies	38		4
Mealed			
Look March-bloom like on mealed-with-yellow sallows	32	1	11
Mealed-with-yellow			
Look March-bloom like on mealed-with-yellow sallows	32	1	11
Mealtime			
And called to come at mealtime she would not	136		33
Mean			
I did not mean to sleep but found	21		15
The majesty what did she mean	28	25	1
Mans mounting spirit in his bone-house mean house dwells	39		2
Where we even where we mean	43		16
Hours I mean years mean life and my lament	67		6
Hours I mean years mean life and my lament	67		6
It is too large for me what does that mean	102	1	29
Enough now since the sacred matter that I mean	159		43
Meaning			
Never ask if meaning it wanting it warned of it men go	28	8	8
Not mood in him nor meaning proud fire or sacred fear	45		5
Off him but meaning motion fans fresh our wits with wonder	45		14
Double as sharp meaning and forcible	102	1	11
Means			
This means you need not fear the storms the cries	14	3	2
Mens wits to the things that are what good means where a glance	62		3
Who means to wed or means to kill	120		29
Who means to wed or means to kill	120		29
She mends the way she means to go	145		12
Any instant falls means me and I do not			

Word	Poem	Stan.	Line
Means (cont.)			
repent	152		64
Meant			
To crosses meant for Jesus you whom the East	11		5
Take as for tool not toy meant	49		13
And men are meant to share	60		44
Ill meant yet true I best should flatter then	125		20
Meantime			
Meantime some tongue cries what Teryth what thou poor fond father	152		22
Meanwhile			
Meanwhile a litter of the jagged leaves	111		8
Or if I go she stays meanwhile	120		28
Meanwhiles			
By meanwhiles making my play	54		15
Measure			
What by your measure is the heaven of desire	28	26	7
Other I gather in measure her minds	28	26	15
Spend here your measure of time and treasure	30		39
Precious passing measure	41		10
While the breeze by rank and measure	79		9
Measured			
In the worst hour thats measured by the sun	14	2	5
Are measured outwards from my breast	130		2
Measures			
God shall oer-brim the measures you have spent	11		9
Meat			
And have your fill of meat	5		10
My more than meat and drink	60		11
Medalliond			
At red Pompeii on medalliond walls	2		51
Medley			
In mankinds medley a duty-swerver	41		53
Meek			
And pride is nerveless and hearts meek	77		38
Make me meek Lord thou wert lowly	129		7
Meet			
Philip supposing that the gift most meet	1	3	6
We meet together you and I	8		10
Meet in one acre of one land	8		11
And you shall meet me with reply	8		13
My prayers must meet a brazen heaven	18		1
Peace and food cheered me where four rough ways meet	20		12
With attributes we deem are meet	23		14
For I greet him the days I meet him and bless when I understand	28	5	8
Wanting which two when they once meet	38		12

Word	Poem	Stan.	Line
To wend and meet no sin	60		117
What do then how meet beauty merely meet it own	62		10
What do then how meet beauty merely meet it own	62		10
That meet in mid-air and be so	77		139
And passages where we used to meet	81		162
Beauty it may be is the meet of lines	102	3	1
Say beauty lies but in the meet of lines	102	3	21
Said it was not meet the king should wed	109	12	3
Tomorrow meet you o not tomorrow	110		1
I cannot meet the swallowing main	120		27
Meets			
He meets her stintless of her smile	83		21
He meets upon midsummer day	83		27
Melancholy			
Yields to the sultry siege of melancholy	16		8
Melee			
Hung in the swaying of the fierce melee	1	2	4
Mellow			
The skill of dreamy Claude and Titians mellow gloom	1	10	9
When his mellow smile he sees	77		105
Mells			
Mells blue and snowwhite through them a fringe and fray	149	1	9
Mells blue with snowwhite through their fringe and fray	149	2	5
Melodious			
Swelld the sweet strain to a melodious wail	2		133
Melodiously			
Gurgled where they had sunk melodiously	2		111
Melody			
Hark the molten melody	77		86
Melt			
That guilt is hushed by hearts are flushed by and melt	28	6	6
Through him melt him but master him still	28	10	4
Melt as from a heavenly chrism	77		62
Melted			
The Zenith melted to a rose of air	2		23
Meal-drift moulded ever and melted across skies	38		4
Melted in the dizzy bow	77		140
Steel may be melted and rock rent	81		134
Melting			
Now melting upward thro the sloping scale	2		132
The making and the melting crowds	15		3
Why tears is it tears such a melting a madrigal start	28	18	6
Melting into aether rare	77		74

Word	Poem	Stan.	Line
Melts			
And melts amidst another cield on high	1	6	8
It melts new lights arise as fair	77		118
Members			
Five like the senses and members of men	27		39
The members how they sit	148		2
Memento			
Age gasp whose breath is our memento mori	75		7
Memoried			
Swells that are sweeter-memoried than the rose	119		3
Memory			
To thy not-staled uncharted memory	117		14
Men			
On thistles that men look not grapes to gather	7		2
That men must wonder as I pass	10		3
Just seen may be to many unknown men	12	2	12
Than treble-fervent more of other men	14	1	13
But men and masters plan and build	15		6
Which makes me when with men I deal	15		19
Summoning men from speechless day	23		41
Men are amazed to watch me pass	25		3
Of the month by men called virginal	26		22
Five like the senses and members of men	27		39
Never ask if meaning it wanting it warned of it men go	28	8	8
Be adored among men	28	9	1
Take settler and seamen tell men with women	28	12	3
To the men in the tops and the tackle rode over the storms brawling	28	19	8
Loathed for a love men knew in them	28	21	1
They were else-minded then altogether the men	28	25	5
Crushed why do men then now not reck his rod	31	1	4
Men go by me whom either beauty bright	40		5
Lads and men her lade and treasure	41		11
Men boldboys soon to be men	41		13
Men boldboys soon to be men	41		13
Then a lurch forward frigate and men	41		40
He haunted who of all men most sways my spirits to peace	44		11
And men are meant to share	60		44
Men here may draw like breath	60		66
That hopes that makesbelieve the men must be no less	63		5
When sick men turn and lights are low	77		25
And hard men feel a softening touch	77		30
Does lay men low with one blades sudden blow	80	2	3

Word	Poem	Stan.	Line
Tis falsely given as love in men	81		49
Twas said of none but all men knew	81		91
What have I more than other men	81		168
And saw the men before the flood	93	1	2
And watch until our horses and the men	125		9
Is known to men more than me	138		13
While sick men shall cast sighs of sweet health all despairing	152		108
As long as men are mortal and God merciful	152		115
Against the wild and wanton work of men	157		36
Mend			
To mend her we end her	43		17
Mend first and vital candle in close hearts vault	46		10
Mended			
Sickness broke him impatient he cursed at first but mended	53		5
Of world made marred and mended lost and won	136		26
Mends			
She mends the way she means to go	145		12
Mens			
It was made of earths mould but it went from mens eyes	27		3
To the father through the features of mens faces	57		14
Mens wits to the things that are what good means where a glance	62		3
Worlds loveliest mens selves self flashes off frame and face	62		9
While blind mens eyes shall thirst after daylight draughts of daylight	152		109
Mention			
And minor sweetness scarce made mention of	19		12
Mercies			
To bathe in his fall-gold mercies to breathe in his all-fire glances	28	23	8
Merciful			
The field is soppd with merciful dew	8		3
Hast thy dark descending and most art merciful then	28	9	8
As long as men are mortal and God merciful	152		115
Mercy			
Make mercy in all of us out of us all	28	10	7
Not vault them the million of rounds of thy mercy not reeve even them in	28	12	8
With a mercy that outrides	28	32	1
With mercy round and round	60		35
Mercy is left enough for one	81		105
Me shew mercy from my heart	155		22

Word	Poem	Stan.	Line
Mere			
Nay what we had lighthanded left in surly the mere mould	59		22
Merely			
Merely a woman yet	60		25
What do then how meet beauty merely meet it own	62		10
Mermaidens			
So those mermaidens crowded to my rock	2		98
Mermaids			
I gazed unhinderd mermaids six or seven	2		34
On mermaids whether that they ring the knells	2		119
Whence oft I watch but see those mermaids now no more	2		143
Merrily			
Some diving merrily downward drove and gleamd	2		108
Merry			
And thicket and thorp are merry	42		39
Maidens shall weep at merry morn	114		1
Meshd			
Of streams and clouds like meshd and parted moss	121		2
Meshing			
Her lids half-meshing shelter from the sky	99		6
Mess			
Look look a May-mess like on orchard boughs	32	1	10
Message			
Your uncle met the messenger met me and this the message	152		6
Messenger			
Served by messenger	25		28
Some messenger there might have met you from my uncle	152		5
Your uncle met the messenger met me and this the message	152		6
Messengers			
Down no waving off of these most mournful messengers still messengers sad and stealing messengers of grey	59		4
Down no waving off of these most mournful messengers still messengers sad and stealing messengers of grey	59		4
Down no waving off of these most mournful messengers still messengers sad and stealing messengers of grey	59		4
Messes			
Here are sweet messes without price or worth	5		47
Raged down decks round messes of mortals	41		39

Word	Poem	Stan.	Line
Messmate			
Hoar messmate hobs and nobs with him	29	1	11
Met			
You met me I had hastend down	81		89
Met a new shower and saw the rainbow fill	107	3	10
She markd where I and Fabian met	120		1
Some messenger there might have met you from my uncle	152		5
Your uncle met the messenger met me and this the message	152		6
Your uncle met the messenger met me and this the message	152		6
Metal			
Of glassy-clear aeolis metal-lustred	2		69
Metal-lustred			
Of glassy-clear aeolis metal-lustred	2		69
Metaphors			
Shake and unset your morticed metaphors	101		8
Meted			
They do not waste their meted hours	15		5
Methinks			
Methinks my laughter is more perilous	102	1	8
Methinks there is more peril from my laughter	102	1	9
Mi			
No more than re and mi	148		34
Michaelmas			
As the laid gossamers of Michaelmas	102	1	22
Mid			
Of seamen whelmd in chasms of the mid-main	2		120
Mid-numbered he in three of the thunder-throne	28	33	5
Mid feverd fumes and slime and caked clot	77		8
That meet in mid-air and be so	77		139
Mid-air			
That meet in mid-air and be so	77		139
Mid-main			
Of seamen whelmd in chasms of the mid-main	2		120
Mid-numbered			
Mid-numbered he in three of the thunder-throne	28	33	5
Middle			
A bad verse in the middle then	95		5
Midnight			
A bell at midnight woke the town	81		87
They were wedded at midnight	109	1	1
Midriff			
And the midriff astrain with leaning of laced with fires of stress	28	2	8

Word	Poem	Stan.	Line
Midst			
Came midst the drizzle telling how last night	1	14	2
I am the midst of every zone	130		3
Midsummer			
He meets upon midsummer day	83		27
I awoke in the midsummer not-to-call night in the white and the walk of the morning	137		1
Mien			
Withal her mien is modest ways are wise	136		19
Might			
Legates might rush zeal-rampant fiery	1	5	5
Even your unpassiond eyelids might be wet	14	1	14
Might so attain their heritage	15		12
My head to hear he might have strung	21		30
I might let bygones be our curse	41		88
Or love or pity or all that sweet notes not his might nursle	45		6
Why that my chaff might fly my grain lie sheer and clear	64		9
Returning thanks might offer such array	89		4
It might be Helen Jane or Kate	95		6
It might be none of the three	95		7
Might cover the neighbour downs with a span of singing	98	28	2
My signalling tears might ring up Floris now	102	1	7
Her true love she might see	109	30	4
Might we not think the sweet and daring rises	122		2
As might have struck and shook the close-shut palms	122		13
For souls that might have blessed the time	133		9
Some messenger there might have met you from my uncle	152		5
To make believe my mood was mock o I might think so	152		41
That might have spared her were it but for passion-sake	152		86
With thy might that thou art mild	155		16
Mighty			
Yet as he changed his mighty stops	21		43
Being mighty a master being a father and fond	34		14
Ask of her the mighty mother	42		13
That mammocks mighty foot but no way sped	70		12
Mote-like in thy mighty glow	155		4
Milan			
Blades of Milan in circles rangd grew rust	1	12	8
Mild			
Will or mild nights the new morsels of spring	34		7
With yellowy moisture mild nights blear-all black	46		3

Word	Poem	Stan.	Line
Million (cont.)			
The million sorts of unaccounted motes	98	22	2
Million-fueled			
Footfretted in it million-fueled natures bonfire burns on	72		9
Millions			
To fields of light millions of travelling rays	103		9
Mind			
Stanching quenching ocean of a motionable mind	28	31	5
Innocent mind and Mayday in girl and boy	31		13
In mould or mind or what not else makes rare	40		6
I cannot and out of sight is out of mind	40		11
With delight calls to mind	42		30
And mastery in the mind	49		16
Nor mouth had no nor mind expressed	55		12
Or less would win mans mind	60		109
O the mind mind has mountains cliffs of fall	65		7
O the mind mind has mountains cliffs of fall	65		7
Charitable not live this tormented mind	69		3
With this tormented mind tormenting yet	69		4
Nor mind nor mainstrength gold go garlanded	70		13
Man how fast his firedint his mark on mind is gone	72		11
Leaves yet the mind a mother of immortal song	76		4
Gross mind discharging fouled laughter	77		58
You see but with a holier mind	81		40
The Christ-ed beauty of her mind	145		15
The music of his mind	148		10
The music of his mind	148		38
Is anything a milk to the mind so so sighs deep	149	1	2
Goes marching thro my mind what sense is this it has none	152		28
My heart where have we been what have we seen my mind	152		31
Of favoured make and mind and health and youth	157		18
Minded			
They were else-minded then altogether the men	28	25	5
Now I am minded to take pipe in hand	105		1
Minds			
Other I gather in measure her minds	28	26	15
Christ minds Christs interest what to avow or amend	40		12
Minds me in many ways	60		16
So strangely elemented is my minds weather	102	1	15
Hope holds to Christ the minds own mirror			

Word	Poem	Stan.	Line
out	151		1
Mine			
All mine yet common to my every peer	12	1	8
At hopes so evil-heavend as mine are	14	2	14
He has a sin of mine he its near brother	16		9
Find me a place by thee mother of mine	27		7
I shall look on thy loveliness mother of mine	27		13
I shall keep time with thee mother of mine	27		19
I shall come home to thee mother of mine	27		25
Shew me thy son mother mother of mine	27		31
I shall worship his wounds with thee mother of mine	27		37
Make me a leaf in thee mother of mine	27		43
Draw me by charity mother of mine	27		49
A master her master and mine	28	19	2
As I am mine their sweating selves but worse	67		14
Mine o thou Lord of life send my roots rain	74	1	13
But mine is dreadful leaping pain	81		51
Dear grace and girder of mine and me	134		2
Like that poor pocket of pence poor pence of mine	142		9
Call no such maiden mine the deeper grows her dearness	152		18
Mined			
Fast but mined with a motion a drift	28	4	3
As wrecks of mined embers will	92		13
Mingle			
Mingle praises prayer and song	24		27
Riding there did storms not mingle and	41		25
Mingled			
Yea iron is mingled with my clay	18		10
Minion			
I caught this morning mornings minion kingdom of daylights dauphin dapple-dawn-drawn falcon in his riding	36		1
Miniver			
He shall be warm with miniver	124		15
Minor			
And minor sweetness scarce made mention of	19		12
Mint			
The mint of current courtesies the forge	102	2	8
Minted			
The sky minted into golden sequins	98	25	1
Miracle			
Remainder of a miracle	25		34
Miracle-in-mary-of-flame	28	33	4
Miracle-in-mary-of-flame			
Miracle-in-mary-of-flame	28	33	4
Mire			
Kneading the mounded mire that stops	3		10

Word	Poem	Stan.	Line
Mirky			
He seemd a dismal mirky stamp	4		8
Mirror			
Hope holds to Christ the minds own mirror out	151		1
I told you that she turned her mirror dim	151		11
Mirrored			
That in smooth spoons spy lifes masque mirrored tame	75		13
Mirth			
Strike timbrels sing eat drink be full of mirth	5		43
Let it flow for heavenly mirth	24		10
Tells Mary her mirth till Christs birth	42		46
Yet found unstinted place for mirth	77		56
While sheeny tears and sunlit mirth	77		129
Misadventure			
Such heathenish misadventure doggd one sin	102	2	15
Such heathenish misadventure dogs one sin	102	2	16
Misdirected			
But single lead a misdirected life	94		32
Misery			
Then is my misery full indeed	81		68
Mislike			
And half mislike her loveless kiss	120		13
Miss			
And here the faithful waver the faithless fable and miss	28	6	8
O then if in my lagging lines you miss	76		11
Miss Storys character too much you ask	94		1
How dare I paint Miss Story to Miss May	94		3
How dare I paint Miss Story to Miss May	94		3
Miss Story has a moderate power of will	94		9
Miss ms a nightingale tis well	96	3	1
How looks the night there does not miss a star	98	22	1
He sees her o but he must miss	120		9
They said we could not miss a pushing brook	125		5
Hampstead was never bright and whatever Miss Cullys charms	128		11
With no now no Gwenvrewi I must miss her most	152		85
Missd			
Who rising late had missd her painful way	80		5
Missing			
Missing prosperity and praise	133		15
Mist			
And silver films beneath with pearly mist	2		67
Into the flat blue mist the sun	3		31
The mist upon the leaves have strewed	21		33
Mistress			
Acceptance round his mistress mouth	83		8

Word	Poem	Stan.	Light
Mists			
With rosy foam and pelting blossom and mists	2		90
Must see the eagles bulk renderd in mists	88		3
Shakes its cocooning mists and so she comes	103		8
Mix			
Mix oer the not unmoved earth	77		130
Mixd			
Then laverd founts and posturd stone he mixd	1	4	5
Mixed			
Snowflake thats fairly mixed	60		6
Moan			
Into his hollowd palm should moan the blast	90		2
Moaning			
A moaning voice among the reeds	23		36
Moans			
My several moans come distant in their tones	80	3	3
Mob			
Than sewers with sacred oils mankind that mob comes	152		104
Mock			
To make believe my mood was mock o I might think so	152		41
Mockery			
Arose in gloom a solemn mockery	1	8	6
Mocks			
With wealth that mocks his high degree	124		22
Moderate			
Miss Story has a moderate power of will	94		9
Modest			
Withal her mien is modest ways are wise	136		19
Moist			
This dry dean now no longer dry nor dumb but moist and musical	152		117
Moisture			
Those whose dry plot for moisture gapes	6		11
With yellowy moisture mild nights blear-all black	46		3
Moles			
For rose-moles all in stipple upon trout that swim	37		3
Molest			
Squander the hell-rook ranks sally to molest him	48		18
Molten			
And was as tho some sapphire molten-blue	2		45
Hark the molten melody	77		86
Has frenchd the molten sunset hour	77		94
Molten-blue			
And was as tho some sapphire molten-blue	2		45
Monarchs			
When chiefs and monarchs came their gifts			

Word	Poem	Stan.	Line
Who first knew moonlight by the hunters moon	105		17
The moon dwindled and thinned to the fringe of a fingernail held to the candle	137		2
Moonless			
Moonless darkness stands between	129		1
Moonlight			
The moonlight-mated glowless glowworms shine	98	36	1
Who first knew moonlight by the hunters moon	105		17
Moonlight-mated			
The moonlight-mated glowless glowworms shine	98	36	1
Moonmarks			
Have an eye to the sakes of him quaint moonmarks to his pelted plumage under	45		10
Moor			
Fair relics too the changeful moor had left	1	8	1
Moorland			
And with heavenfallen freshness down from moorland still brims	159		39
More			
Doors slammd to the blasts continually more low	1	13	8
The monks left long ago since which no more	1	15	4
More wondrous to have borne such hope before	1	15	7
Than changeful pomp of courts is aye more wonderful	1	15	9
And more on each hand thicken and appear	2		30
Save by two stars more crowding lights arise	2		32
Of tremulous film more subtle than the vest	2		39
From flesh-flowers of the rock but more were wreathd	2		63
Whence oft I watch but see those mermaids now no more	2		143
More sweet-familiar grows my love to thee	12	1	2
Than treble-fervent more of other men	14	1	13
My bankrupt heart has no more tears to spend	14	3	4
More powerless than the blind or lame	15		20
The copse was never more than grey	21		2
That more he shuns our special dale	21		24
To deaths more silent darker spell	23		42
More will wear this wand and then	25		39
More brightening her rare-dear Britain as his reign rolls	28	34	6
Times told lovelier more dangerous o my chevalier	36		10
He was but one like thousands more	41		84
More more than was will yet be	41		103

Word	Poem	Stan.	Line
More (cont.)			
More more than was will yet be	41		103
Well but there was more than this	42		33
Mannerly-hearted more than handsome face	47		9
Let me though see no more of him and not disappointment	48		36
A wilder beast from west than all were more	50		7
Rife in her wrongs more lawless and more lewd	50		8
Rife in her wrongs more lawless and more lewd	50		8
How far from then forethought of all thy more boisterous years	53		12
I say more the just man justices	57		9
Never fleets more fastened with the tenderest truth	59		12
My more than meat and drink	60		11
Is Mary more by name	60		37
Nay more than almoner	60		42
More Christ and baffle death	60		67
More makes when all is done	60		71
Bloom breathe that one breath more	60		92
Master more may than gaze gaze out of countenance	62		4
In me or most weary cry I can no more I can	64		3
More pangs will schooled at forepangs wilder wring	65		2
And more must in yet longer lights delay	67		4
And where is he who more and more distills	68		12
And where is he who more and more distills	68		12
My own heart let me more have pity on let	69		1
I cast for comfort I can no more get	69		5
Veins violets and tall trees makes more and more	73		11
Veins violets and tall trees makes more and more	73		11
Do in spare hours more thrive than I that spend	74	1	7
And for that fearful hour life is more thin	80	3	5
But you so sphered see no more	81		39
For more with him who gives thee all	81		150
What have I more than other men	81		168
More golden than the world of lights	83		2
His sick stars falter more he may	83		25
Boughs being pruned birds preened show more fair	96	7	1
In more precision now of light and dark	98	30	1
Now more precisely touched in light and gloom	98	30	4
Methinks my laughter is more perilous	102	1	8

Word	Poem	Stan.	Line
Methinks there is more peril from my laughter	102	1	9
Now one word more and then I am gone indeed	102	1	58
It were more like to be	109	32	4
It were more like to be	109	34	4
It were more like to be	109	35	4
The more she askd the more he spoke	109	36	1
The more she askd the more he spoke	109	36	1
The more he told the less she spoke	109	36	3
More sweetly shades her stolen hair	120		7
Had been more fertile and had sown with notes	122		5
Past the past no more be seen	129		2
Is known to men more than me	138		13
Anywhere any more joy to be in	138		33
No more than red and blue	148		33
No more than re and mi	148		34
But more cheer is when may	149	2	4
Or bring more or more blazon mans distress	150		4
Or bring more or more blazon mans distress	150		4
To take his lovely likeness more and more	151		2
To take his lovely likeness more and more	151		2
And more and more times laces round and round my heart	152		19
And more and more times laces round and round my heart	152		19
The more some monstrous hand gropes with clammy fingers there	152		20
Whose bloods I reck no more of no more rank with hers	152		103
Whose bloods I reck no more of no more rank with hers	152		103
Rupture running sores what more in brief in burden	152		114
Pilgrims still pilgrims more pilgrims still more poor pilgrims	152		126
Pilgrims still pilgrims more pilgrims still more poor pilgrims	152		126
Those dearer more divine boons whose haven the heart is	152		131
May but call on your hanes to more carouse	157		30
Rose here he feasts lovely all is no more off with down he dings	159		28
Mori			
Age gasp whose breath is our memento mori	76		7
Morn			
Next morn a peasant from the mountain side	1	14	1
At morn we found the heavenly bread	6		8
On Easter morn the tree was forth	6		23

Word	Poem	Stan.	Line
Morn (cont.)			
Ill wait till morn eternal breaks	23		54
Know ye not tis Easter morn	24		12
Make each morn an Easter day	24		30
There evening noon and morn	60		64
When chill woods wake and think of morn	77		23
Why if it be so for the dismal morn	90		1
The place in the east with earliest milky morn	98	30	5
Gem-fleeced at morn so brillant is the weather	99		4
Morn does not now new-basilisk his stare	99		17
At morn they come upon our lands like rains	104		8
Maidens shall weep at merry morn	114		1
Morning			
From nine oclock till morning light	21		1
The morning was so still	21		18
A singing bird in morning clear	21		41
Oh morning at the brown brink eastward springs	31	1	12
I caught this morning mornings minion kingdom of daylights dauphin dapple-dawn-drawn falcon in his riding	36		1
Of us the wimpled-water-dimpled not-by-morning-matched face	59		10
Him morning noon and eve	60		62
Closer because faint morning stirs	77		22
Dewy fields in the morning under the sun	98	13	1
Their harness beams like scythes in morning grass	104		6
Lord William comes hunting tomorrow morning	109	19	3
She heard the hunt the morrow morning	109	24	1
I awoke in the midsummer not-to-call night in the white and the walk of the morning	137		1
Shall new-dapple next year sure as tomorrow morning	152		133
Field-flown the departed day no morning brings	153		9
Mornings			
Up till that mornings fall of dew	21		27
I caught this morning mornings minion kingdom of daylights dauphin dapple-dawn-drawn falcon in his riding	36		1
Morns			
During the eastering of untainted morns	84		1
Morrow			
With joy for to-day and hope for to-morrow	26		15
She heard the hunt the morrow morning	109	24	1
Shall new-dapple next year sure as tomorrow morning	152		133

Word	Poem	Stan.	Line
Morselled			
All while her patience morselled into pangs	50		12
Morsels			
Will or mild nights the new morsels of spring	34		7
As the fine morsels of a dwindling cloud	102	1	35
Mortal			
Each mortal thing does one thing and the same	57		5
To what serves mortal beauty dangerous does set dancing blood the o-seal-that-so feature flung prouder form	62		1
A beacon an eternal beam flesh fade and mortal trash	72		19
As long as men are mortal and god merciful	152		115
Mortal my mate bearing my rock-a-heart	153		1
Mortals			
Raced down decks round messes of mortals	41		39
Morticed			
Shake and unset your morticed metaphors	101		8
Moses			
Who is this Moses who made him we say	5		1
Moss			
Of streams and clouds like meshd and parted moss	121		2
Of water clouds like parted moss	121		3
Most			
To deck and make most lordly evermore	1	2	9
Philip supposing that the gift most meet	1	3	6
But most in a half-circle watchd the sun	2		116
Most wide ye are who call this gust simoom	5		26
In the most murderous passage of his book	14	2	11
And then I hate the most that lore	15		33
Thee oh maiden most worthy of praise	26		36
Hast thy dark descending and most art merciful then	28	9	8
Most o maids child thy choice and worthy the winning	33		14
What most I may eye after be in at the end	40		10
Than the most are must delight her	42		10
He haunted who of all men most sways my spirits to peace	44		11
Turn most on tender byplay	54		16
Down no waving off of these most mournful messengers still messengers sad and stealing messengers of grey	59		4
In me or most weary cry I can no more I can	64		3
I am gall I am heartburn gods most deep decree	67		9
Come because then most thinly lies	77		35
Most like those hues that in the prism	77		61

Word	Poem	Stan.	Line
Most (cont.)			
Most dead-alive upon those days	80	2	7
O here is the most piteous part	80	7	30
Exiled most remote El Khor	81		47
She kept her love-thoughts on most lenten diet	82		7
About herself she is most sensitive	94		21
Of virtues I most warmly bless	96	1	1
Most rarely see unselfishness	96	1	2
A star most spiritual principal preeminent	98	27	1
Most ill-content this least least thing I do	102	1	57
Most like the tuft of plighted silver round	102	1	72
Most like the plighted tuft of silver round	102	1	73
Most like the silver plighted tuft about	102	1	74
Most dented lay Sylvester reading Keats	107	4	21
Man is most low God is most high	133		5
Man is most low God is most high	133		5
Of virtue and vice but most it seemed his sense	136		27
Denis whose motionable alert most vaulting wit	143		1
Apart wide and new-nestle at heaven most high	149	1	6
No piece matched those eyes kept most part much cast down	152		57
With no now no Gwenvrewi I must miss her most	152		85
As sure as what is most sure sure as that spring primroses	152		132
The selfless self of self most strange most still	157		27
The selfless self of self most strange most still	157		27
Your feast of that most in you earnest eye	157		29
Mote			
Mote-like in thy mighty glow	155		4
Mote-like			
Mote-like in thy mighty glow	155		4
Motes			
The motes in ceaseless eddy shine and fall	1	12	4
The million sorts of unaccounted motes	98	22	2
Moth			
With belled fire and the moth-soft milky way	28	26	6
All as the moth calld underwing alighted	108		1
Moth-soft			
With belled fire and the moth-soft milky way	28	26	6
Mother			
Here playd the virgin mother with her child	1	10	4
One word as when a mother speaks	23		50
Lies in the breast of the young year-mother	26		3
Oh thou proud mother and much proud maiden	26		19
Maid yet mother as may hath been	26		20

Word	Poem	Stan.	Line
Salute thee mother the maid-months queen	26		24
Find me a place by thee mother of mine	27		7
I shall look on thy loveliness mother of mine	27		13
I shall keep time with thee mother of mine	27		19
I shall come home to thee mother of mine	27		25
Shew me thy son mother mother of mine	27		31
Shew me thy son mother mother of mine	27		31
I shall worship his wounds with thee mother of mine	27		37
Make me a leaf in thee mother of mine	27		43
Draw me by charity mother of mine	27		49
Do you mother of being in me heart	28	18	4
Christ home Christ and his mother and all his hallows	32	1	14
O well wept mother have lost son	41		104
Ask of her the mighty mother	42		13
Mother to an English sire he	48		3
A mother came to mould	60		104
Mother my atmosphere	60		115
Mary mother of us where is your relief	65		4
Among strangers father and mother dear	66	1	2
With heavens lights high hung round or mother-ground	70		11
Leaves yet the mind a mother of immortal song	76		4
Right offspring of your grimy mother earth	77		2
And mother have no milk for child	114		7
And wreck in ruins of his mother	145		41
Next Mary mother of maid and nun	145		43
Why get thee gone then tell thy mother I want her	152		16
This is too much the father nay the mother fanciful	152		29
Happy the father mother of these too fast	157		5
Father mother brothers sisters friends	159		49
Mother-ground			
With heavens lights high hung round or mother-ground	70		11
Motherhood			
Natures motherhood	42		28
She holds high motherhood	60		47
Mothering			
All over as a bevy of eggs the mothering wing	34		6
This ecstasy all through mothering earth	42		45
Wild air world-mothering air	60		1
World-mothering air air wild	60		124
Mothers			
But mothers each new grace	60		22
Mothers are doubtless happier for their babes	123		1

Word	Poem	Stan.	Line
Motion			
Fast but mined with a motion a drift	28	4	3
Off him but meaning motion fans fresh our wits with wonder	45		14
Resign them sign them seal them send them motion them with breath	59		16
In motion is no weight or pain	130		15
The motion of that mans heart is fine	142		6
Motionable			
Stanching quenching ocean of a motionable mind	28	31	5
Denis whose motionable alert most vaulting wit	143		1
Mould			
Could mould if any tears there were	18		14
It was made of earths mould but it went from mens eyes	27		3
In mould or mind or what not else makes rare	40		6
He was all of lovely manly mould	41		73
Who have watched his mould of man big-boned and hardy-handsome	53		2
Nay what we had lighthanded left in surly the mere mould	59		22
A mother came to mould	60		104
Her mould of features mated well	145		16
Moulded			
Meal-drift moulded ever and melted across skies	38		4
As water moulded to the duct it runs in	101		4
Moulding			
Will on the moulding strike and cling	130		10
Mouldring			
Upon the mouldring terraces amain	1	13	4
Mounded			
Kneading the mounded mire that stops	3		10
Mounds			
Or ancient mounds that cover bones	15		37
Mountain			
Amongst Castilian barrens mountain-bound	1	1	2
But from the mountain glens in autumn late	1	13	1
Then passd the wind and sobbd with mountain-echod woe	1	13	9
Next morn a peasant from the mountain side	1	14	1
Love I was shewn upon the mountain-side	20		1
Yet God that hews mountain and continent	73		9
Beat heave and the strong mountain tire	80	5	2
I cry o rocks and mountain make me room	80	7	5
Before the mountain no not one	81		143
Stepped from the stool drew back from the barrow of dark Maenefa the mountain	137		4

Word	Poem	Stan.	Line
Mountain-bound			
Amongst Castilian barrens mountain-bound	1	1	2
Mountain-echod			
Then passd the wind and sobbd with mountain-echod woe	1	13	9
Mountain-side			
Love I was shewn upon the mountain-side	20		1
Mountains			
O the mind mind has mountains cliffs of fall	65		7
Betweenpie mountains lights a lovely mile	69		13
Mounting			
Then like a flock of sea-fowl mounting higher	2		82
Mans mounting spirit in his bone-house mean house dwells	39		2
Beautys bearing or muse of mounting vein	47		10
Mounts			
Mounts then to alight disarming no one dreams	50		13
Mourn			
It is Margaret you mourn for	55		15
Mournful			
Down no waving off of these most mournful messengers still messengers sad and stealing messengers of grey	59		4
Mourning			
I cease the mourning and the abject fast	14	1	8
Hope had mourning on	28	15	2
Mouth			
He hath put a new song in my mouth	8		4
The dewdrop on the larkspurs mouth	10		15
The dewbell in the mallows mouth	25		15
Nor mouth had no nor mind expressed	55		12
He hand to mouth he lives and voids with shame	75		9
Acceptance round his mistress mouth	83		8
Mouthed			
Will mouthed to flesh-burst	28	8	4
The mouthed centre of a violet	102	1	75
Move			
By other eyes and other suitors move	12	1	12
I move along lifes tomb-decked way	23		39
I inly said but could not move	81		115
Moved			
Of Gods dear pleadings have as yet not moved thee	13		10
His lips moved fast in sense too thick	81		100
Their cheeks moved and the bones therein	92		3
Moves			
Sometimes a lantern moves along the night	40		1
The violet moves and copses rock	98	3	4
Ms			
Miss Ms a nightingale tis well	96	3	1

Word	Poem	Stan.	Line
Much			
From too much fragrance everywhere	4		4
Oh thou proud mother and much proud maiden	26		19
They rain against our much-thick and marsh air	40		7
Much had much to say	42		35
Much had much to say	42		35
Though much the mystery how	60		57
Much dearer to mankind	60		107
When waking hearts can pardon much	77		29
I plead and ah how much in vain	81		29
Miss Storys character too much you ask	94		1
Gold gallant flowers much looked at in April-weather	98	16	2
Too late or else much much too soon	105		16
Too late or else much much too soon	105		16
Gave the much music of our Oxford bells	107	2	8
Your footing now to the much-dreaded dust	107	3	2
To dream I dared so much for thee	118		6
Much cause to go because Castara goes	125		65
Work which to see scarce so much as begun	150		7
This is too much the father nay the mother fanciful	152		29
No piece matched those eyes kept most part much cast down	152		57
Much-dreaded			
Your footing now to the much-dreaded dust	107	3	2
Much-thick			
They rain against our much-thick and marsh air	40		7
Multiply			
They multiply multiply who can tell how	27		41
They multiply multiply who can tell how	27		41
Multitude			
Sir Christ against this multitude I strain	80	7	12
To wash before the multitude	80	7	23
I hear the multitude tramp by	80	7	29
With the multitude of the lily-buds	98	19	3
Murder			
To the murder of Margaret Clitheroe	145		47
Must all day long taste murder what do now then do	152		98
Murderous			
In the most murderous passage of his book	14	2	11
And speeds uncheckd her murderous guile	120		30
Muse			
Muse at that and wonder why	42		2
I muse at how its being puts blissful back	46		2
Beautys bearing or muse of mounting vein	47		10
Sweet fire the sire of muse my soul needs this	76		9

Word	Poem	Stan.	Line
Music			
I have found my music in a common word	19		5
The music must be death	21		39
The music that I care to hear	22		4
And pelt music till nones to spill nor spend	35		8
In fits of music till sunset	77		87
Gave the much music of our Oxford bells	107	2	8
Because the music from his bill forth-driven	113		3
At once the senses give the music back	113		10
Had let such music down without impediment	122		8
The music of his mind	148		10
The music of his mind	148		38
Musical			
The towers musical quiet-walled grove	12	1	10
Making them double-musical and they	112		5
This dry dean now no longer dry nor dumb but moist and musical	152		117
My			
Those cyclads made that thickend on my sight	2		37
So those mermaidens crowded to my rock	2		98
White loomd my rock the water gurgling oer	2		142
My soul does loathe it and my spirit fails	5		14
My soul does loathe it and my spirit fails	5		14
Into my hand he gives a host for prey	5		17
Unbakes my pores and streams and makes all fresh	5		32
I water with my foot	5		40
He hath put a new song in my mouth	8		4
And taught my lips to quote this word	8		6
And I will turn my looks to you	8		12
More sweet-familiar grows my love to thee	12	1	2
This is my park my pleasaunce this to me	12	1	6
This is my park my pleasaunce this to me	12	1	6
As public is my greater privacy	12	1	7
All mine yet common to my every peer	12	1	8
Those charms accepted of my inmost thought	12	1	9
In bows above my head as falsified	12	2	4
Or sunderd from my sight in the age that is	13		3
That thou hadst borne proportion in my bliss	13		6
My love is lessened and must soon be past	14	1	1
My love is less my love is less for thee	14	1	7
My love is less my love is less for thee	14	1	7
And rise and go about my works again	14	1	9
And let him prove my passion was begun	14	2	4
And Ill love my distinction near or far	14	2	12
My bankrupt heart has no more tears to spend	14	3	4
My window shows the travelling clouds	15		1
And I perhaps if my intent	15		9
Even than this my thankless lore	15		22
I walk my breezy Belvedere	15		25

Word	Poem	Stan.	Line
My (cont.)			
To the sweet living of my friends I look	16		2
And so my trust confused struck and shook	16		7
Chilling remembrance of my days of old	17		5
Which should ere now have led my feet to the field	17		9
My prayers must meet a brazen heaven	18		1
My prayers I scarcely call to pray	18		4
I cannot buoy my heart above	18		5
My heaven is brass and iron my earth	18		9
My heaven is brass and iron my earth	18		9
Yea iron is mingled with my clay	18		10
A warfare of my lips in truth	18		15
Battling with God is now my prayer	18		16
I have found my music in a common word	19		5
I have found the dominant of my range and state	19		13
Love o my God to call thee love and love	19		14
My national old Egyptian reed gave way	20		7
Hear yet my paradox love when all is given	20		13
The day that brought my lasting pain	21		10
And put away my sun	21		11
My head to hear he might have strung	21		30
And beat upon my whorled ear	22		2
My hand upon my lips I lay	23		37
My hand upon my lips I lay	23		37
Speak whisper to my watching heart	23		49
See my lilies lilies none	25		7
My eyes hold yet the rinds and bright	25		33
My heart but you were dovewinged I can tell	28	3	6
I kiss my hand	28	5	1
Kiss my hand to the dappled-with-damson west	28	5	5
Rebuffed the big wind my heart in hiding	36		6
Times told lovelier more dangerous o my chevalier	36		10
Shine and blue-bleak embers ah my dear	36		12
My people and born own nation	41		86
Wondering why my master bore it	41		97
Save my hero o hero savest	41		111
My aspens dear whose airy cages quelled	43		1
He haunted who of all men most sways my spirits to peace	44		11
My late being there begged of me over-flowing	48		6
Boon in my bestowing	48		7
How it does my heart good visiting at that bleak hill	48		21
Recorded only I have put my lips on pleas	48		45
Your round me roaming end and under be my boughs	51		2
To own my heart I yield you do come some-			

Word	Poem	Stan.	Line
times but	51		4
O surely reaving peace my lord should leave in lieu	51		7
Felix Randal the farrier o is he dead then my duty all ended	53		1
My tongue had taught thee comfort touch had quenched thy tears	53		10
Thy tears that touched my heart child Felix poor Felix Randal	53		11
By meanwhiles making my play	54		15
My lad and lost in Jack	54		18
My more than meat and drink	60		11
My meal at every wink	60		12
My lung must draw and draw	60		14
Mother my atmosphere	60		115
My happier world wherein	60		116
Fronting my froward eye	60		119
Stir in my ears speak there	60		121
With darksome devouring eyes my bruised bones and fan	64		7
Why that my chaff might fly my grain lie sheer and clear	64		9
Why that my chaff might fly my grain lie sheer and clear	64		9
Hand rather my heart lo lapped strength stole joy would laugh cheer	64		11
Of now done darkness I wretch lay wrestling with my God my God	64		15
Of now done darkness I wretch lay wrestling with my God my God	64		15
My cries heave herds-long huddle in a main a chief-woe world-sorrow on an age-old anvil wince and sing	65		5
To seem the stranger lies my lot my life	66	1	1
To seem the stranger lies my lot my life	66	1	1
And he my peace my parting sword and strife	66	1	4
And he my peace my parting sword and strife	66	1	4
England whose honour o all my heart woos wife	66	1	5
To my creating thought would neither hear	66	1	6
Wisest my heart breeds dark heavens baffling ban	66	1	11
Hours I mean years mean life and my lament	67		6
Bitter would have me taste my taste was me	67		10
My own heart let me more have pity on let	69		1
Me live to my sad self hereafter kind	69		2
By groping round my comfortless than blind	69		6
Across my foundering deck shone	72		18
Wert thou my enemy o thou my friend	74	1	4
Wert thou my enemy o thou my friend	74	1	4

Word	Poem	Stan.	Line
My (cont.)			
Mine o thou Lord of life send my roots rain	74	1	13
My tempests there my fire and fever fussy	75		14
My tempests there my fire and fever fussy	75		14
Sweet fire the sire of muse my soul needs this	76		9
O then if in my lagging lines you miss	76		11
My winter world that scarcely breathes that bliss	76		13
My spirit hath a birth	77		3
The shaken plumage of my spirits wings	77		10
Be discoverd to my sight	77		17
This outer cold my exile from of old	80	1	3
Cleaves not my brain burns not my feet	80	2	4
Cleaves not my brain burns not my feet	80	2	4
My several moans come distant in their tones	80	3	3
Breathe oer my bare nerve rather I desire	80	5	5
They swathe and lace the shroud-plaits oer my face	80	5	6
The screen of my captivity	80	6	2
And then my heart goes near to break	80	6	7
Before that rock my seat he stands	80	7	15
I give commands for water for my hands	80	7	17
Vespillo my centurion hacks out	80	7	19
My frenzied working is not understood	80	7	26
Now I grow numb my tongue strikes on the gum	80	7	27
And I shall shape one to my thought	80	7	40
And with sharp flint will part my feet and dint	80	7	43
The point fast in and my left hand	80	7	44
Lock with my right then knot a barken band	80	7	45
And thus I will thrust in my right	80	7	47
And to my palm the point apply	80	7	49
You would not house beneath my own	81		4
My evil words thorny with pain	81		27
I know I mar my cause with words	81		30
My tears are but a cloud of rain	81		36
My passion like a foolish wind	81		37
At once I struggle with my breath	81		58
I bite my hands my looks I shroud	81		65
I bite my hands my looks I shroud	81		65
My cry is like a bleat a few	81		66
Then is my misery full indeed	81		68
I dreamd my counterpart it seemd	81		86
Duly dear Lord my prize is won	81		109
My fast-lodged tongue to her the gift	81		116
My love and all was sweet and well	81		121
But grant my penitence begun	81		137
Rememberd sweetness for my thought	81		139
Not furtherd far my travelld feet	81		157

Word	Poem	Stan.	Line
How turn my passion-pastured thought	81		174
Where my heart lists	88		2
And what if she my confidence betray	94		4
What if my subject seeing this resent	94		5
Did Helen steal my love from me	95		1
But Im alone for my loves gone	95		8
Leaps up before my vision thou art gone	98	33	2
Yet when my unset tresses hung loose-traced	102	1	3
This downy counterfeit upon my lip	102	1	5
My signalling tears might ring up Floris now	102	1	7
Methinks my laughter is more perilous	102	1	8
Methinks there is more peril from my laughter	102	1	9
As ever I remember in my life	102	1	13
So strangely elemented is my minds weather	102	1	15
And wear it thus a pectoral by my heart	102	1	31
I find I am as ready with my tears	102	1	34
My cousin will not love you as I love	102	1	60
And I must have the centre in my heart	102	3	7
So I go out my little sweet is done	103		17
Even so my thought the rose and grey disposes	108		7
When are you home my love she said	109	2	1
You may look for me home my love he said	109	2	3
How shall I call my love she said	109	4	3
I give you my love and I give you my land	109	5	3
I give you my love and I give you my land	109	5	3
Because he is my love she said	109	20	3
O where is Lord William my lords she said	109	25	3
Wilt thou follow me my true love	109	37	1
Wilt thou follow me my true love	109	37	3
O I will follow thee my true love	109	38	1
Sweeter thy kisses my own love	109	38	3
Is tasteless nothing and in my degree	117		10
My hopes and my unworthiness	118		9
My hopes and my unworthiness	118		9
Of burden came and bowd my head	118		11
Yea crushd my heart and made me dumb	118		12
So is it with my friends I note to hear	119		5
There lives the witch shall win my locks	120		22
And my blue eyes again for me	120		23
Who loves me here and has my love	124		1
My thought was there to rest against the trees	125		8
That make my eyes sore and cross-colour things	125		46
These are my very text of discontent	125		50
And kindred to my lamentable days	125		52

Word	Poem	Stan.	Line
My (cont.)			
My sap is sealed	127		3
My root is dry	127		4
I keep my trust	127		15
I thought that you would have written my birthday came and went	128		1
But is not that my grievance you promised and you forgot	128		6
Think this my birthday falls in saddening time of year	128		9
Are measured outwards from my breast	130		2
My all-accepting fixed eye	130		6
My heart irregularly shook	135		9
I cried with my desire	135		10
Upon my forehead hit the burly wind	135		12
You spoil the plot I find my true love by	135		36
And bright iconium eastwards reach my rhymes	136		6
The skylark is my cousin and he	138		12
Or ever did for my sake some good deed	140		2
Not of all my eyes see wandering on the world	149	1	1
What is it Gwen my girl why do you hover and haunt me	152		1
Some messenger there might have met you from my uncle	152		5
And more and more times laces round and round my heart	152		19
Alive or dead my girl is carried in it endlessly	152		27
Goes marching thro my mind what sense is this it has none	152		28
I here forbid my thoughts to fool themselves with fears	152		30
My heart where have we been what have we seen my mind	152		31
My heart where have we been what have we seen my mind	152		31
Monuments of my earnest records of my revenge	152		36
Monuments of my earnest records of my revenge	152		36
To make believe my mood was mock o I might think so	152		41
Now be my pride then perfect all one piece henceforth	152		70
When ts light I quenched its rose times one rich rose my hand	152		82
I all my being have hacked in half with her neck one part	152		93
Is corpse now cannot change my other self this soul	152		95

Word	Poem	Stan.	Line
Name (cont.)			
Double-natured name	28	33	2
Now no matter child the name	55		10
Bow swung finds tongue to fling out broad its name	57		4
Is Mary more by name	60		37
And blazoned in however bold the name	75		10
And learnt her not to startle at his name	82		8
And what is your true name she said	109	4	1
Your name and your degree	109	4	2
Bellisle that is a fabling name but we	116		1
Who thinks of Thecla yet her name was known	136		3
She told his name times-over three	145		56
Water which keeps thy name for not in rock written	152		119
Not now to name even	152		130
Thy name	152		135
Names			
These names these faces they are customary	125		51
Nard			
Break the box and shed the nard	24		1
Narrow			
And to their feet the narrow bells gave rhyme	107	1	14
Nation			
My people and born own nation	41		86
How then should Gregory a father have gleaned else from swarmed Rome but God to a nation dealt that days dear chance	62		6
National			
My national old Egyptian reed gave way	20		7
Natural			
Nowhere natural hearts ivy patience masks	68		6
The bluebells up whose crystal-ending rods in their natural sods	112		8
Take their peculiar thorns and natural pain	123		5
Nature			
Of art best follow nature in a maze	1	6	5
Five is their number by nature but now	27		40
And for all this nature is never spent	31	1	9
That neighbour-nature thy grey beauty is grounded	44		6
Doff darkness homing nature knows the rest	47		6
And told by nature tower	49		9
Ah nature framed in fault	54		38
Nature bad base and blind	54		40
What being in rank-old nature should earlier have that breath been	141		1
Honouring an uncontrolled royal wrathful nature	152		68
Who like me knowing his nature to the heart			

Word	Poem	Stan.	Line
home natures business	152		76
Natured			
Double-natured name	28	33	2
Natures			
What is sound natures round	28	35	3
At tranquil turns by natures rule	29	1	14
Natures motherhood	42		28
Footfretted in it million-fueled natures bonfire burns on	72		9
Who like me knowing his nature to the heart home natures business	152		76
Nautilus			
Some traild the Nautilus or on the swell	2		56
Nave			
Rope-over thigh knee-nave and barrelled shank	71		3
Navel			
Right rooting in the bare butts wincing navel in the sight of the sun	143		5
Navvy			
Tom heart-at-ease Tom Navvy he is all for his meal	70		4
Nay			
Nay roguish ran the vein	54		28
Thy plea with him who dealt nay does now deal	58		6
Nay what we had lighthanded left in surly the mere mould	59		22
Nay more than almoner	60		42
O how nay do but stand	60		75
But frail clay nay but foul clay here it is the heart	63		3
Nay in all that toil that coil since seems I kissed the rod	64		10
Nine months she then nay years nine years she long	76		5
This is too much the father nay the mother fanciful	152		29
Nay	152		99
Nazareth			
And broke into bloom upon Nazareth hill	27		11
Bethlem or Nazareth	60		65
Nazareths			
New Nazareths in us	60		60
Near			
An isle of roses and another near	2		29
And Ill love my distinction near or far	14	2	12
He has a sin of mine he its near brother	16		9
To show thee that thou art and near	23		44
Proconsul is Sapricius near	25		41
Two thousands of years are near upon past	27		16
Now near by Ventnor town	41		30

Word	Poem	Stan.	Line
Near (cont.)			
Brothers and sisters are in Christ not near	66	1	3
And then my heart goes near to break	80	6	7
You should have been with me as near	81		43
Save me and you were standing near	81		103
That I was so near laughter alas now	102	1	33
Too near thee and thou must abide	106		3
Near by is Pauls free Tarsus fabled where	136		7
A mans voice and a new voice speaking near	136		22
Nearest			
Who made conjecture nearest far	77		45
I spy the nearest daisies through the dark	135		23
Nearness			
They are neighbours but what nearness could not do	136		11
Neck			
She pillowing low her lily neck	21		55
For love he leans forth needs his neck must fall on kiss	63		12
Are still her neck is creased in close-ply rings	99		10
I all my being have hacked in half with her neck one part	152		93
Nectar			
His sweetest nectar hides behind	148		42
Need			
This means you need not fear the storms the cries	14	3	2
Not today we need lament	28	35	13
Deeply surely I need to deplore it	41		96
That neer need hunger Tom Tom seldom sick	70		6
Take courage this shall need no further art	80	7	33
I need not love I need not break	81		138
I need not love I need not break	81		138
And kind compassion at his lifes last need	140		4
What need I strain my heart beyond my ken	157		34
Needed			
When I with never-needed wiles	135		3
Needful			
This needful never spent	60		9
Needs			
Not that the sweet-fowl song-fowl needs no rest	39		9
To man that needs would worship block or barren stone	62		7
For love he leans forth needs his neck must fall on kiss	63		12
Sweet fire the sire of muse my soul needs this	76		9
There needs but little doing	152		11
Let what there needs be done stay with him one companion	152		12

Word	Poem	Stan.	Line
Neer			
May who neer hung there nor does long our small	65		9
That neer need hunger Tom Tom seldom sick	70		6
The essence neer forgot the fold	81		82
Neglectful			
I know what you will tell me neglectful that you were not	128		5
Neighbour			
That neighbour-nature thy grey beauty is grounded	44		6
In a neighbour deft-handed are you that liar	46		13
Might cover the neighbour downs with a span of singing	98	28	2
Neighbour-nature			
That neighbour-nature thy grey beauty is grounded	44		6
Neighbouring			
That he hies to a pool neighbouring sees it is the best	159		11
Neighbours			
They are neighbours but what nearness could not do	136		11
Neight			
And when the silent neight were won	77		75
Nereid			
Far off a nereid company and shake	2		75
Nerve			
Breathe oer my bare nerve rather I desire	80	5	5
When life revisits me nerve and vein	80	7	9
Of nerve the clammy ball was dry	81		98
Nerveless			
And pride is nerveless and hearts meek	77		38
Nest			
Why hear him hear him babble and drop down to his nest	39		10
But his own nest wild nest no prison	39		11
But his own nest wild nest no prison	39		11
That nest within close-barred doors	77		54
And in the dews beside his nest	77		91
Nested			
Throstle above her nested	42		20
Nestle			
Apart wide and new-nestle at heaven most high	149	1	6
Nestlike			
With centres duly touchd and nestlike spots	107	4	7
Nestling			
Nestling me everywhere	60		2
Nests			
To the nests nook I balance and buoy	138		43

Word	Poem	Stan.	Line
Nets			
Broiders the nets with fans of amethyst	2		66
Never			
But earth has never felt the snow	3		2
I never saw her so divine	3		19
And never thirst or dearth	5		48
And never turned to corn	7		8
Where art thou friend whom I shall never see	13		1
I never promised such persistency	14	1	2
Or once or never took loves proper food	20		10
The copse was never more than grey	21		2
Or never lodges there	21		25
Your passing steps I never heard	21		48
Never ask if meaning it wanting it warned of it men go	28	8	8
Never-eldering revel and river of youth	28	18	7
The treasure never eyesight got not was ever guessed what for the hearing	28	26	8
And for all this nature is never spent	31	1	9
Never fleets more fastened with the tenderest truth	59		12
This needful never spent	60		9
Now known and hand at work now never wrong	76		8
How shall I search who never sought	81		173
But candour never hurt the dearest friend	94		8
Prudence she has but wise shell never be	94		24
And thinking that she thinks has never thought	94		30
She never had the wit	95		2
Or never been at all	105		15
And there she never saw the king	109	24	3
I never saw those fields whereon their best	119		11
It never yet so sweetly was put on	125		29
And if you write at last it never can be the same	128		3
Hampstead was never bright and whatever Miss Cullys charms	128		11
But late is better than never you see you have managed so	128		17
Are never known for fair	133		16
When I with never-needed wiles	135		3
The rookery never stirred a wing	135		14
Never never never in their blue banks again	152		47
Never never never in their blue banks again	152		47
Never never never in their blue banks again	152		47
Like the thing that never knew the earth never off roots	159		27
Like the thing that never knew the earth never off roots	159		27
Never-eldering			
Never-eldering revel and river of youth	28	18	7

Word	Poem	Stan.	Line
Never-needed			
When I with never-needed wiles	135		3
New			
He hath put a new song in my mouth	8		4
The words are old the purport new	8		5
New-dated from the terms that reappear	12	1	1
Leaves spent new seasons alterd sky	15		2
And soon I saw it shewing new	21		5
Now burn new born to the world	28	33	1
Of New Years month or surly Yule	29	1	30
Will or mild nights the new morsels of spring	34		7
His rash-fresh re-winded new-skeined score	35		6
But mothers each new grace	60		22
New Nazareths in us	60		60
New Bethlems and he born	60		63
New self and nobler me	60		69
It melts new lights arise as fair	77		118
Only with us is old and new	81		63
Her finger-long new horns are cappd with black	99		7
Morn does not now new-basilisk his stare	99		17
New love is free love or true love tis not	102	3	20
New love is free love or true love tis not	102	3	27
And feeds new leaves upon the winds of fall	105		10
Met a new shower and saw the rainbow fill	107	3	10
Then often the ears in a new fashion hark	113		7
A mans voice and a new voice speaking near	136		22
Apart wide and new-nestle at heaven most high	149	1	6
Shall new-dapple next year sure as to-morrow morning	152		133
Saying this was yours with her but new one worse	153		10
And she shall child them on the new-world strand	158		4
New-basilisk			
Morn does not now new-basilisk his stare	99		17
New-dapple			
Shall new-dapple next year sure as to-morrow morning	152		133
New-dated			
New-dated from the terms that reappear	12	1	1
New-nestle			
Apart wide and new-nestle at heaven most high	149	1	6
New-skeined			
His rash-fresh re-winded new-skeined score	35		6
New-world			
And she shall child them on the new-world strand	158		4

Word	Poem	Stan.	Line
Newborn			
To newborn prince and royal corse inanimate	1	4	9
Newly			
Where in a newly-drawn green litter	10		5
Which in newly drawn green litter	25		5
Newly-drawn			
Where in a newly-drawn green litter	10		5
News			
News from Belleisle even such a sweetness blows	119		6
But both will share one cell this was good news Gwenvrewi	152		14
Next			
Next morn a peasant from the mountain side	1	14	1
Then next I hungered love when here they say	20		9
He has lost count what came next poor boy	41		71
But each a hands breadth further than the next	91		7
Next to meadows abundant pierced with flowers	98	12	2
Though they took till the seventeenth of next October to read	128		8
Time was next whitest after Marys own	136		4
Next Mary mother of maid and nun	145		43
Next after sweet success I am not left even this	152		92
Shall new-dapple next year sure as tomorrow morning	152		133
Niche			
With the gnarls of the nails in thee niche of the lance his	28	23	3
Nigh			
Gazes aslant his shoulder viewing nigh	1	11	6
Till the lifted clouds were nigh	77		72
Night			
Came midst the drizzle telling how last night	1	14	2
The darkness did not close that night	21		3
Night to a myriad worlds gives birth	23		9
Deep calls to deep and blackest night	23		27
Thou knowest the walls altar and hour and night	28	2	5
But the combs of a smother of sand night drew her	28	14	3
Night roared with the heart-break hearing a heart-broke rabble	28	17	5
Blue-beating and hoary-glow height or night still higher	28	26	5
Read the unshapeable shock night	28	28	3
What was the feast followed the night	28	29	3
Sometimes a lantern moves along the night	40		1
Day and night I deplore	41		85

Word	Poem	Stan.	Line
Now the night come all	54		10
Evening strains to be times vast womb-of-all home-of-all hearse-of-all night	61		2
With our evening is over us our night whelms whelms and will end us	61		8
That night that year	64		14
This night what sights you heart saw ways you went	67		3
Come when night clings to what is hers	77		21
That night the judgment day began	81		90
How looks the night there does not miss a star	98	22	1
The stars were packed so close that night	98	29	1
Nor night is blown with flame-rings everywhere	99		18
Well I know not but all things seem to night	102	1	10
Gilds with some sparky fancies his black night	102	3	30
Gilds with some sparky fancies blinding night	102	3	36
As she lay weeping at the night	109	29	1
Shot lightning to the stifling lid of night	125		56
The stars are packed so thick to-night	135		19
I awoke in the midsummer not-to-call night in the white and the walk of the morning	137		1
With the uproll and the downcarol of day and night delivering	152		118
Nightfall			
And frightful a nightfall folded rueful a day	28	15	5
The times are nightfall look their light grows less	150		1
Nightingale			
You know you said the nightingale	21		22
Miss Ms a nightingale tis well	96	3	1
Nights			
Will or mild nights the new morsels of spring	34		7
With yellowy moisture mild nights blear-all black	46		3
Of rivers lead thro storms and nights	83		4
Nights lantern	98	24	1
Nile			
Not Goshen wasteful wide huge-girthed Nile	5		31
Sure this is Nile I sicken I know not why	5		59
Nimble			
O his nimble finger his gnarled grip	41		80
Nine			
From nine oclock till morning light	21		1
Nine months she then nay years nine years she long	76		5
Nine months she then nay years nine years she long	76		5

Word	Poem	Stan.	Line
Nips			
With draught of thin and pursuant cold so nips	11		6
Nix			
She sour who seems the slighted nix	120		17
When maddest looks the slighted nix	120		19
No			
Frightful sheer no-man-fathomed hold them cheap	65		8
No-man-fathomed			
Frightful sheer no-man-fathomed hold them cheap	65		8
Nobler			
New self and nobler me	60		69
Nobs			
Hoar messmate hobs and nobs with him	29	1	11
Nocturns			
Nocturns I thought were hurried through	81		92
Noise			
I hear a noise of waters drawn away	112		1
A noise of falls I am possessed by	121		1
By there comes a listless stranger beckoned by the noise	159		14
Noises			
On ear and ear two noises too old to end	35		1
None			
Lilies I shew you lilies none	10		7
None in Caesars gardens blow	10		8
None besides me this bye-ways beauty try	12	2	9
See my lilies lilies none	25		7
None in Caesars garden blow	25		8
What none would have known of it only the heart being hard at bay	28	7	8
None but you this her true	28	35	11
And none reck of world after this bids wear	58		13
How to keep is there any any is there none such nowhere known some bow or brooch or braid or brace lace latch or catch or key to keep	59		1
No theres none theres none o no theres none	59		5
No theres none theres none o no theres none	59		5
No theres none theres none o no theres none	59		5
O theres none no no no theres none	59		14
O theres none no no no theres none	59		14
No worst there is none pitched past pitch of grief	65		1
Twas said of none but all men knew	81		91
It might be none of the three	95		7
As void as clouds that house and harbour none	107	1	1
If you are silent that I know of none	125		19
I none can shew	127		6

Word	Poem	Stan.	Line
And other truth is none	133		2
Flung rider and wings away though these were none	136		9
Has shades is nowhere none	148		26
Goes marching thro my mind what sense is this it has none	152		28
What work what harms done there is no harm done none yet	152		39
Theres none but truth can stead you Christ is truth	157		20
Theres none but good can be good both for you	157		21
None good but God a warning waved to	157		23
Nones			
And pelt music till nones to spill nor spend	35		8
Nook			
To the nests nook I balance and buoy	138		43
Noon			
Him morning noon and eve	60		62
There evening noon and morn	60		64
Noonday			
And noonday have a shallow shine	114		4
Nose			
Crisp lips straight nose and tender-slanted cheek	136		16
Nostril			
Her nostril glistens and her wet black eye	99		5
Nostrils			
Your parched nostrils snuff Egyptian air	5		27
Nostrils your careless breath that spend	22		17
Not			
Of us the wimpled-water-dimpled not-by-morning-matched face	59		10
To thy not-staled uncharted memory	117		14
I awoke in the midsummer not-to-call night in the white and the walk of the morning	137		1
This fault-not-found-with good	148		31
Stone palsy cancer cough lung-wasting womb-not-bearing	152		113
Not-by-morning-matched			
Of us the wimpled-water-dimpled not-by-morning-matched face	59		10
Not-staled			
To thy not-staled uncharted memory	117		14
Not-to-call			
I awoke in the midsummer not-to-call night in the white and the walk of the morning	137		1
Note			
From both of whom a changeless note is heard	19		4
Being not forgotten for primroses note	107	3	19
So is it with my friends I note to hear	119		5

Word	Poem	Stan.	Line
Note (cont.)			
Upon this only gambolling and echoing-of-earth note	159		45
Notes			
A simple passage of weak notes	3		13
Or love or pity or all that sweet notes not his might nursle	45		6
A turn of seven notes or five	81		7
Five notes or seven late and few	81		23
He shook with racing notes the standing air	98	38	1
Had been more fertile and had sown with notes	122		5
Or had been effectual to have sown with notes	122		12
Nothing			
With long-superfluous ties for nothing here	12	1	4
Shape nothing lips be lovely-dumb	22		5
Nothing is so beautiful as spring	33		1
Nothing else is like it no not all so strains	48		29
Be beginning since no nothing can be done	59		9
What were worth nothing if all compliment	94		6
Is tasteless nothing and in my degree	117		10
Nourishes			
She inly nourishes a wish to shine	94		12
Nowhere			
How to keep is there any any is there none such nowhere known some bow or brooch or braid or brace lace latch or catch or key to keep	59		1
Nowhere natural hearts ivy patience masks	68		6
Of earths glory earths ease all no one nowhere	70		16
Has shades is nowhere none	148		26
Numb			
Now I grow numb my tongue strikes on the gum	80	7	27
Number			
Five is their number by nature but now	27		40
Numbered			
God three-numbered form	28	9	2
Mid-numbered he in three of the thunder-throne	28	33	5
Is hair of the head numbered	59		21
Numbs			
And numbs and starves as between icy wharves	80	3	6
Nun			
Ears and the call of the tall nun	28	19	7
Thou hadst glory of this nun	28	29	4
Next Mary mother of maid and nun	145		43
Nursing			
And nursing element	60		10

Word	Poem	Stan.	Line
Nursle			
Or love or pity or all that sweet notes not his might nursle	45		6
Nymphs			
Around the water-nymphs in fretted falls	2		50
O			
O should it then be quenched not	10		16
Love o my God to call thee love and love	19		14
O feel-of-primrose hands o feet	22		21
O feel-of-primrose hands o feet	22		21
O no it is the sizing moon	25		20
O this is bringing tears may swarm	25		35
O breath of it bathes great heaven above	27		46
O at lightning and lashed rod	28	2	2
Thy terror o Christ o God	28	2	4
Thy terror o Christ o God	28	2	4
O father not under thy feathers nor ever as guessing	28	12	5
O unteachably after evil but uttering truth	28	18	5
O Deutschland double a desperate name	28	20	3
O world wide of its good	28	20	4
Was calling o Christ Christ come quickly	28	24	7
Finger of a tender of o of a feathery delicacy the breast of the	28	30	6
O where live well your lease of leisure	29	1	3
O look at all the fire-folk sitting in the air	32	1	2
Most o maids child thy choice and worthy the winning	33		14
Complete thy creature dear o where it falls	34		13
Times told lovelier more dangerous o my chevalier	36		10
And hurls for him o half hurls earth for him off under his feet	38		14
The Eurydice it concerned thee o Lord	41		1
Three hundred souls o alas on board	41		2
And you were a liar o blue March day	41		20
O his nimble finger his gnarled grip	41		80
O well wept mother have lost son	41		104
Save my hero o hero savest	41		111
O if we but knew what we do	43		9
Have fair fallen o fair fair have fallen so dear	45		1
Not granted only o on that path you pace	47		13
Run all your race o brace sterner that strain	47		14
O now well work that sealing sacred ointment	48		33
O for now charms arms what bans off bad	48		34
O surely reaving peace my Lord should leave in lieu	51		7
Felix Randal the farrier o is he dead then my duty all ended	53		1
O let them be left wildness and wet	56		15

Word	Poem	Stan.	Line
O (cont.)			
O is there no frowning of these wrinkles ranked wrinkles deep	59		3
No theres none theres none o no theres none	59		5
O theres none no no no theres none	59		14
O then weary then why should we tread o why are we so haggard at the heart so care-coiled care-killed so fagged so fashed so cogged so cumbered	59		26
O then weary then why should we tread o why are we so haggard at the heart so care-coiled care-killed so fagged so fashed so cogged so cumbered	59		26
And makes o marvellous	60		59
O how nay do but stand	60		75
Be thou then o thou dear	60		114
Of Gods love o live air	60		122
Ever so black on it our tale o our oracle let life waned ah let life wind	61		10
To what serves mortal beauty dangerous does set dancing blood the o-seal-that-so feature flung prouder form	62		1
And cry o Christ-done deed so God-made-flesh does too	63		13
But ah but o thou terrible why wouldst thou rude on me	64		5
O in turns of tempest me heaped there me frantic to avoid thee and flee	64		8
Me or me that fought him o which one is it each one	64		13
O the mind mind has mountains cliffs of fall	65		7
England whose honour o all my heart woos wife	66	1	5
What hours o what black hours we have spent	67		2
With perilous o no nor yet plod safe shod sound	70		14
In him all quail to the wallowing o the plough s cheek crimsons curls	71		13
Drowned o pity and indignation manshape that shone	72		13
Wert thou my enemy o thou my friend	74	1	4
Mine o thou Lord of life send my roots rain	74	1	13
O then if in my lagging lines you miss	76		11
I cry o rocks and mountain make me room	80	7	5
O here is the most piteous part	80	7	30
O Lord but I have wrought and striven	81		108
O hideous vice to haggle yet	81		149
Sleep Floris while I rob you tighten o sleep	102	1	18
O Guinevere	102	2	1
O I am the kings son he said	109	5	1
O have you here a foreign lady	109	7	3
O I have here no foreign lady	109	8	1

Word	Poem	Stan.	Line
O what will you now good servingman	109	18	1
O what will you now with me	109	18	2
O where is Lord William my lords she said	109	25	3
O fie that this should be	109	26	4
O why art thou so wan she said	109	31	1
O I will follow thee my true love	109	38	1
Tomorrow meet you o not tomorrow	110		1
O death death he is come	115		1
O grounds of hell make room	115		2
Thy ribbed ports o death	115		5
Make wide thou o Lord of sin	115		6
Lift up your heads o gates	115		8
He sees her o but he must miss	120		9
O what a silence is this wilderness	122		1
O lovely ease in change of place	130		27
O heart have done you beat you beat so high	135		35
O where what can that be	138		2
I am so very o so very glad	138		31
O what a tune the thought	148		3
To make believe my mood was mock O I might think so	152		41
The woeful cradock o the woeful word then what	152		48
O there	152		61
Lord now curb him for ever o daring o deep insight	152		73
Lord now curb him for ever o daring o deep insight	152		73
Despatches with no flinching but will flesh o can flesh	152		77
Second this fiery strain not always o no no	152		78
O now while skies are blue now while seas are salt	152		106
O welcome there their steel or cannon	156		17
O I admire and sorrow the hearts eye grieves	157		1
O but I bear my burning witness though	157		35
O-seal-that-so			
To what serves mortal beauty dangerous does set dancing blood the o-seal-that-so feature flung prouder form	62		1
To what serves mortal beauty dangerous does set dancing blood the o-seal-that-so feature flung prouder form	62		1
Oak			
Felled and furled them the hearts of oak	41		5
Oaks			
And oaks but these were leaved in sharper knots	107	4	8
There was a wood of dwarf and soured oaks	125		2
Oar			
That frocks an oar in Penmaen pool	29	1	36

Word	Poem	Stan.	Line
Oath			
Philip took oath while glory or defeat	1	2	3
Obey			
Maiden could obey so be a bell to ring of it and	28	30	7
To do without take tosses and obey	68		4
To sweep and must obey	148		16
Obscurd			
And silver damasqud plates obscurd in ages crust	1	12	9
Obsolete			
What spirit is that makes stillness obsolete	122		16
Obstruction			
So loading with obstruction that threshold	17		8
Occasion			
Caps occasion with an intellectual fit	143		2
Ocean			
The abysmal ocean hoards of strange and rare	2		55
But when the sun had lapsed to ocean lo	2		136
Stanching quenching ocean of a motionable mind	28	31	5
Oclock			
From nine oclock till morning light	21		1
October			
Though they took till the seventeenth of next October to read	128		8
Oer			
Of forcd persuasion issue oer the free	1	5	7
Marking the spot when they have gurgled oer	2		3
Droopd oer the brows like Hectors casque and swayd	2		42
To mantle-oer the tail such as is shed	2		49
One bound oer dripping gold a turquoise-gemmd	2		60
Which lightening oer the body rosy-pale	2		72
Down that dank rock oer which their lush long tresses weep	2		115
White loomd my rock the water gurgling oer	2		142
Spread oer the swart face of this prodigal earth	5		45
God shall oer-brim the measures you have spent	11		9
Till dimpled joy steals oer its cheeks	23		52
Thy river and oer gives all to rack or wrong	58		8
Were I come oer again cries Christ it should be this	63		14
Mix oer the not unmoved earth	77		130
Breathe oer my bare nerve rather I desire	80	5	5
They swathe and lace the shroud-plaits oer my face	80	5	6

Word	Poem	Stan.	Line
I try the Christus oer again	80	7	11
The fall is oer told off the leaves	81		9
Say oer it hangs a water-cloud	81		56
Oer passes bleak oer perilous bars	83		3
Oer passes bleak oer perilous bars	83		3
Glazed water vaulted oer a drowsy stone	98	39	1
To spill oer fields of lilies so could I	102	1	37
Alone upon the hill-top heaven oer him	107	1	8
And long the trees were colourd but the oer-head	107	4	12
Oer-brim			
God shall oer-brim the measures you have spent	11		9
Oer-head			
And long the trees were colourd but the oer-head	107	4	12
Oertake			
I must oertake thee at once and under heaven	20		15
Of			
O feel-of-primrose hands o feet	22		21
Miracle-in-Mary-of-flame	28	33	4
When drop-of-blood-and-foam-dapple	42		37
The thunder-purple seabeach plumed purple-of-thunder	45		12
Evening strains to be times vast womb-of-all home-of-all hearse-of-all night	61		2
Evening strains to be times vast womb-of-all home-of-all hearse-of-all night	61		2
Evening strains to be times vast womb-of-all home-of-all hearse-of-all night	61		2
Upon this only gambolling and echoing-of-earth note	159		45
Off			
Far off a nereid company and shake	2		75
Or far-off promise of a time to be	13		4
Hovers off the jay-blue heavens appearing	28	26	3
And though the last lights off the black west went	31	1	11
Fetched fresh as I suppose off some sweet wood	34		4
With a flood or a fall low lull-off or all roar	35		3
Left hand off land I hear the lark ascend	35		5
In crisps of curl off wild winch whirl and pour	35		7
In his ecstasy then off off forth on swing	36		4
In his ecstasy then off off forth on swing	36		4
And hurls for him o half hurls earth for him off under his feet	38		14
And flockbells off the aerial	41		6
It hurls hurls off Boniface down	41		31
The riving off that race	41		98

Word	Poem	Stan.	Line
Off (cont.)			
Off him but meaning motion fans fresh our wits with wonder	45		14
O for now charms arms what bans off bad	48		34
Her injurys looks off by both horns of shore	50		3
Down no waving off of these most mournful messengers still messengers sad and stealing messengers of grey	59		4
Off and no way but so	60		33
Off her once skeined stained veined variety upon all on two spools part pen pack	61		11
But these two ware of a world where but these two tell each off the other of a rack	61		13
Worlds loveliest mens selves self flashes off frame and face	62		9
Then lull then leave off fury had shrieked no lingering let me be fell force I must be brief	65		6
You jaded let be call off thoughts awhile	69		10
Sheer off disseveral a star death blots black out nor mark	72		14
Honour is flashed off exploit so we say	73		1
Folds off aloof that signal is and proof	80	6	3
The fall is oer told off the leaves	81		9
Told off their leaves along the piercing gale	98	5	2
The hand draws off the glove the acorn-cup	101		9
But then her tether calls her she falls off	103		12
Lies in her lap which she anon sweeps off	111		9
Dies off in hyacinthed ground	135		33
And after that off the bough	138		39
That here personal tells off these heart-song powerful peals	141		2
Fallow foam-fallow hanks falln off their ranks	144		7
A day off shearing day	144		12
Off trundled timber and scoops of the hill-side ground hollow hollow hollow ground	146		4
And breathes the blots off all with sighs on sighs	151		6
Struck off it has written upon lovely limbs	152		34
Like the thing that never knew the earth never off roots	159		27
Rose here he feasts lovely all is no more off with down he dings	159		28
Fast he opens last he off wrings	159		34
Offend			
Else I am well assured I should offend	14	3	5
No shewn to her it cannot but offend	94		7
Offended			
Tendered to him ah well God rest him all road ever he offended	53		8

Word	Poem	Stan.	Line
Offer			
Returning thanks might offer such array	89		4
Offering			
To offering Mary may	42		36
Your offering with despatch of	49		21
Offerings			
And bring your offerings to a grateful God	5		11
Offspring			
Right offspring of your grimy mother earth	77		2
Oft			
Whence oft I watch but see those mermaids now no more	2		143
Often			
Often when winds impenitent	80	5	1
Things that she likes seems often to despise	94		17
To the often takings of desirous winds	111		3
Then often the ears in a new fashion hark	113		7
Oil			
And they who crush the oil	5		52
With oil of gladness for sackcloth and frieze	11		10
It gathers to a greatness like the ooze of oil	31	1	3
Oils			
Than sewers with sacred oils mankind that mob comes	152		104
Ointment			
O now well work that sealing sacred ointment	48		33
Oit			
To its own best being and its loveliness of youth it is an everlastingness of o it is an all youth	59		13
Old			
He hath abolished the old drouth	8		1
The words are old the purport new	8		5
Chilling remembrance of my days of old	17		5
My national old Egyptian reed gave way	20		7
On ear and ear two noises too old to end	35		1
So God was God of old	60		103
My cries heave herds-long huddle in a main a chief-woe world-sorrow on an age-old anvil wince and sing	65		5
This outer cold my exile from of old	80	1	3
Only with us is old and new	81		63
The lawless honey eaten of old	92		4
What being in rank-old nature should earlier have that breath been	141		1
Of greenery it is old earths groping towards the steep	149	1	10
Of greenery it is old earth gropes for grasps at steep	149	2	6
Older			
Ah as the heart grows older	55		5

Word	Poem	Stan.	Line
Olive			
An olive-branch whence richly reek	77		15
Olive-branch			
An olive-branch whence richly reek	77		15
Once			
Of battle once upon St. Lawrence day	1	2	2
That seed which the good sower once did sow	17		7
Or once or never took loves proper food	20		10
I must oertake thee at once and under heaven	20		15
For he began at once and shook	21		29
That was blest in it once though now it is not	27		9
Whether at once as once at a crash Paul	28	10	5
Whether at once as once at a crash Paul	28	10	5
Wanting which two when they once meet	38		12
Once encounter in here coped and poised powers	44		4
Love-laced what once I well	54		3
What would the world be once bereft	56		13
Off her once skeined stained veined variety upon all on two spools part pen pack	61		11
Those lovely lads once wet-fresh windfalls of wars storm	62		5
I am all at once what Christ is since he was what I am and	72		22
And those strokes once that gashed flesh or galled shield	73		2
Breathes once and quenched faster than it came	76		3
Once it was scarce perceived lent	81		11
Once jostling thick the bluebell sheaves	81		13
At once I struggle with my breath	81		58
Once in a drawer of Indian wood	81		80
Which once were disobedient	93	1	3
To speak so yet Ill speak it for this once	102	1	41
Like scalded banks toppd once with principal flowers	102	2	14
At once the senses give the music back	113		10
At once perceived with excess	118		10
All time at once and span the distant goals	126		4
Upwards at once and win their aureoles	126		8
And sheathe at once his leger wing	130		12
The ruins of rifled once a world of art	153		4
Once I turned from thee and hid	155		9
One once that was found wanting when good weighed	157		24
One			
And scarcely traces where one beauty strays	1	6	7
This was their manner one translucent crest	2		38
One bound oer dripping gold a turquoise-gemmd	2		60
One scarlet feather trailing to the wind	2		81

Word	Poem	Stan.	Line
Slumberd at last in one sweet deep heart-broken close	2		135
Meet in one acre of one land	8		11
Meet in one acre of one land	8		11
We shall be sheaved with one band	8		14
And a quince in hand not one	10		9
The one peculiar of their pleasured eye	12	2	13
I must feed fancy show me any one	14	2	1
One spot and hunger to be there	15		32
This fault in one I found that in another	16		11
And so though each have one while I have all	16		12
You have your wish enter these walls one said	20		17
One word as when a mother speaks	23		50
Quinces look when not one	25		9
Springs one daughter the sweet child may	26		2
Fairer than this one to brighten our day	26		8
For thou as she wert the one fair daughter	26		25
Who can her rose be it could be but one	27		28
One stirred from the rigging to save	28	16	1
Blinds her but she that weather sees one thing one	28	19	5
Blinds her but she that weather sees one thing one	28	19	5
Has one fetch in her she rears herself to divine	28	19	6
Ipse the only one Christ king head	28	27	5
Feast of the one woman without stain	28	29	5
Where she foundered one stroke	41		4
They say who saw one sea-corpse cold	41		72
He was but one like thousands more	41		84
And one but let be let be	41		102
Wept wife wept sweetheart would be one	41		105
Not spared not one	43		5
Mounts then to alight disarming no one dreams	50		13
Each mortal thing does one thing and the same	57		5
Deals out that being indoors each one dwells	57		6
There is one yes I have one hush there	59		2
There is one yes I have one hush there	59		2
Somewhere elsewhere there is ah well where one	59		6
One yes I can tell such a key I do know such a place	59		7
This one work has to do	60		29
In each one and each one	60		70
In each one and each one	60		70
Bloom breathe that one breath more	60		92
Me or me that fought him o which one is it each one	64		13
Me or me that fought him o which one is			

Word	Poem	Stan.	Line
One (cont.)			
it each one	64		13
Of earths glory earths ease all no one nowhere	70		16
By a grey eyes heed steered well one crew fall to	71		5
Times eunuch and not breed one work that wakes	74	1	12
I want the one rapture of an inspiration	76		10
White-faced as one in sad assay to fly	80		8
Does lay men low with one blades sudden blow	80	2	3
And all in one say crucify	80	7	14
I choose one but when I desire	80	7	22
And I shall shape one to my thought	80	7	40
Mercy is left enough for one	81		105
Choose one for hell and one for heaven	81		106
Choose one for hell and one for heaven	81		106
Before the mountain no not one	81		143
See one bow each yet not the same to all	91		6
And hide it though she does one may divine	94		11
We tuned to one key and made their harmonies	98	2	4
Spannd with shadow every one	98	8	3
Catch sunlight and one strain of stupid praise	98	32	2
See on one hand	100		1
Now one word more and then I am gone indeed	102	1	58
Such heathenish misadventure doggd one sin	102	2	15
Such heathenish misadventure dogs one sin	102	2	16
Allow at least it has one term and part	102	3	5
Beyond and one within the lookers eye	102	3	6
One star by daylight from the strong blue air	102	3	10
Yet there came one who sent his flock before him	107	1	7
One and then one along their walks and kept	107	1	12
One and then one along their walks and kept	107	1	12
From one frail horn that crumbled to the plain	107	3	11
One has gone to the kings steward	109	11	1
With one of low degree	109	12	4
It was but one to three	109	13	4
Two made answer in one breath	109	26	1
Have here a true one echoing the sound	116		2
And one to each of us is holy ground	116		3
Will no one show	127		11
The holy three in one	133		4
Young Thecla scanned the dazzling streets one day	136		14
So she one sees that here and there	145		11
How alls to one thing wrought	148		1

Word	Poem	Stan.	Line
And choose for chieftain one	148		28
All is from wreck here there to rescue one	150		6
Let what there needs be done stay with him one companion	152		12
But both will share one cell this was good news Gwenvrewi	152		14
On one that went against me whereas I had warned her	152		37
Now be my pride then perfect all one piece henceforth	152		70
When ts light I quenched its rose times one rich rose my hand	152		82
I all my being have hacked in half with her neck one part	152		93
Deed-bound I am one deed treads all down here cramps all doing what do not yield	152		100
One spell and well that one there ah thereby	153		7
One spell and well that one there ah thereby	153		7
Saying this was yours with her but new one worse	153		10
In one fair fall but for times aftercast	157		7
One once that was found wanting when good weighed	157		24
Let winter wed one sow them in her womb	158		3
Onewhere			
That onewhere curded onewhere sucked or sank	71		7
That onewhere curded onewhere sucked or sank	71		7
Only			
Only with utterance of sweet breath they sung	2		130
And I have only set the same to pen	12	2	14
Which ends those only strains that I approve	19		10
I only feared the wet for you	21		13
Which only makes you eloquent	22		8
What none would have known of it only the heart being hard at bay	28	7	8
Nor rescue only rocket and lightship shone	28	15	6
Ipse the only one Christ king head	28	27	5
Only the inmate does not correspond	34		11
Only the breathing temple and fleet	41		92
Is it only its being brighter	42		9
Ten or twelve only ten or twelve	43		20
Let him oh with his air of angels then lift me lay me only Ill	45		9
Not granted only o on that path you pace	47		13
Recorded only I have put my lips on pleas	48		45
That canst but only be but dost that long	58		4
Only not within seeing of the sun	59		3
Of her who not only	60		17
Only the beakleaved boughs dragonish damask the toolsmooth bleak light black	61		9

Word	Poem	Stan.	Line
Only (cont.)			
Kind love both give and get only what word	67	1	10
Who asks not life but only place to die	80		9
Only with us is old and new	81		63
The rainbow shines but only in the thought	91		2
No Ill not hazard it only his hand	102	1	26
The temperd soil where only her flower is found	102	3	4
For only try by gazing to divide	102	3	9
Only the belled foxgloves lispd together	107	1	6
Only the dahlias blow and all is autumn here	128		10
Christs only charity charmed and chained these two	136		12
What is virtue valour only the heart valiant	152		74
And right only resolution will his will unwavering	152		75
And not from purple Wales only nor from elmy England	152		124
Upon this only gambolling and echoing-of-earth note	159		45
Onyx			
The dainty onyx-coronals deflowers	2		92
Onyx-coronals			
The dainty onyx-coronals deflowers	2		92
Ooze			
It gathers to a greatness like the ooze of oil	31	1	3
Squandering ooze to squeezed dough crust dust stanches starches	72		7
Opal			
Hither bring pearl opal sard	24		3
Ope			
Flowers do ope their heavenward eyes	24		15
Open			
Speard open lustrous gashes crimson-white	2		8
Open wide your hearts that they	24		23
Open the door to me	109	29	4
Said open open to me	109	30	2
Said open open to me	109	30	2
Lay open thine estates	115		7
Cuckoo bird and open ear wells heart-springs delightfully sweet	146		2
Opend			
But opend twice in life and death to state	1	4	8
Shewn to Ezekiels opend sight	77		48
Opening			
Think of an opening page illumined	93	2	1
Opens			
See how spring opens with disabling cold	17		1
Fast he opens last he off wrings	159		34
Opportunest			
Is it opportunest	42		11

Word	Poem	Stan.	Line
Opposition			
Such opposition to the lady-star	14	2	10
Oppressed			
And been in their ruinous reigns oppressed	26		10
Oppression			
Thy impalpable oppression pin him down	102	1	19
Oracle			
Ever so black on it our tale o our oracle let life waned ah let life wind	61		10
Orbd			
To an orbd rose which by hot pantings blown	2		20
Plunge orbd in rainbow arcs and trample and tread	2		78
Orchard			
Is set in any orchard no	25		10
Look look a May-mess like on orchard boughs	31	1	10
Bloom lights the orchard-apple	41		38
Orchard-apple			
Bloom lights the orchard-apple	41		38
Orchards			
In summer are our orchards knopt	124		19
Order			
Dress his days to a dexterous and starlight order	47		20
Orderd			
This was no classic temple orderd round	1	7	1
Organ			
Her jailor with his vigil-organ dead	99		16
Orience			
For orience of the daffodil	81		12
The heightening dawn with milky orience	98	30	2
Original			
Breathe arch and original breath	28	25	2
All things counter original spare strange	36		7
Orinda			
Selvaggia Orinda and Adela and the rest	125		44
Orion			
Gnashed but thou art above thou Orion of light	28	21	5
Ought			
If he suspect that she has ought to sigh at	82		5
Our			
They shrive themselves and cry good service to our God	1	5	9
And planets bud whereer we turn our mazed eyes	2		33
Frost-furred our ivies are and rough	3		3
Drops out and all our day is done	3		32
He hides our corpses dropping by the way	5		5
Egypt the valley of our pleasance there	5		25
Christ our sacrifice is made	6		10
Now in our altar-vessels stored	6		19

Word	Poem	Stan.	Line
Our (cont.)			
Is the sweet vintage of our Lord	6		20
But even our saviours and our blood	6		32
But even our saviours and our blood	6		32
In all our western shires was rare	21		23
That more he shuns our special dale	21		24
God though to thee our psalm we raise	23		1
Our prayer seems lost in desert ways	23		5
Our hymn in the vast silence dies	23		6
Yet know not how our gifts to bring	23		17
Fairer than this one to brighten our day	26		8
The gladdest thing that our eyes have seen	26		18
We all we thro the length of our days	26		34
Thee May-hope of our darkened ways	26		40
Christ Jesus our Lord her God and her Son	27		29
Flesh falls within sight of us we though our flower the same	28	11	6
Our passion-plunged giant risen	28	32	7
Dame at our door	28	34	1
Drowned and among our shoals	28	34	2
Our king back oh upon English souls	28	34	4
Our hearts charitys hearths fire our thoughts chivalrys throngs lord	28	34	8
Our hearts charitys hearths fire our thoughts chivalrys throngs lord	28	34	8
How ring right out our sordid turbid time	35		10
Our make and making break are breaking down	35		13
Down all that glory in the heavens to glean our saviour	38		6
That interests our eyes and who goes there	40		2
They rain against our much-thick and marsh air	40		7
Of the best we boast our sailors are	41		75
I might let bygones be our curse	41		88
Off him but meaning motion fans fresh our wits with wonder	45		14
An our days Gods own Galahad though this childs drift	48		40
Then let the March tread our ears	52		9
Months earlier since I had our sweet reprieve and ransom	53		7
Our boys plays brought on	54		6
Our company thronged the hall	54		11
To thriftless reave both our rich round world bare	58		12
That does now reach our race	60		23
Towards all our ghostly good	60		48
Be Christ our Saviour still	60		54
What must make our daystar	60		106
Sifted to suit our sight	60		113
With our evening is over us our night whelms			

Word	Poem	Stan.	Line
whelms and will end us	61		8
With our evening is over us our night whelms whelms and will end us	61		8
Ever so black on it our tale o our oracle let life waned ah let life wind	61		10
Ever so black on it our tale o our oracle let life waned ah let life wind	61		10
Our law says love what are loves worthiest were all known	62		8
Our redcoats our tars both these being the greater part	63		2
Our redcoats our tars both these being the greater part	63		2
Mark Christ our king he knows war served this soldiering through	63		9
May who neer hung there nor does long our small	65		9
Our ruins of wrecked past purpose there she basks	68		7
We hear our hearts grate on themselves it kills	68		9
Age gasp whose breath is our memento mori	75		7
What bass is our viol for tragic tones	75		8
Now yields you with some sighs our explanation	76		14
I walk towards eve our walks again	81		54
Our swans are now of such remorseless quill	96	2	1
We will charge our flocks that they not feed	98	15	2
Give us our green lots in another mead	98	15	5
Sexing and ranking with our ruder files	102	1	66
Enrolld and sexing with our ruder files	102	1	67
Enrolld and sexed with our ruder files	102	1	68
Like flame they gather on our cliffs at evening	104		7
At morn they come upon our lands like rains	104		8
They plough our vales you see the unsteady flare	104		9
Gave the much music of our Oxford bells	107	2	8
I hope that all the places on our trip	107	4	27
In spring our river-banks are topt	124		17
In summer are our orchards knopt	124		19
Crept all along a hill upon our left	125		3
Of mile-long reaches of our road below us	125		7
And watch until our horses and the men	125		9
I betterd all our path with sanguine eyes	125		17
Our sex should be born in April perhaps or the lily-time	128		13
All slumbered whom our rud red tiles	135		1
Earlier or you fail at our force and lie	153		3
The telling time our task is times some part	153		5

Word	Poem	Stan.	Line
Ours			
That a starlight-wender of ours would say	41		100
Those limbs like ours which are	60		105
Out			
Louder the monks drond out Gregorians slow	1	13	6
Swirling out bloom till all the air is blind	2		89
Drops out and all our day is done	3		32
And out of the swing of the sea	9		8
And other science all gone out of date	19		11
I whirled out wings that spell	28	3	4
Starlight wafting him out of it and	28	5	3
Not out of his bliss	28	6	1
Is out with it oh	28	8	1
Or as Austin a lingering-out sweet skill	28	10	6
Make mercy in all of us out of us all	28	10	7
It will flame out like shining from shook foil	31	1	2
How ring right out our sordid turbid time	35		10
This in drudgery day-labouring-out lifes age	39		4
I cannot and out of sight is out of mind	40		11
I cannot and out of sight is out of mind	40		11
And cast by conscience out spendsavour salt	46		14
Out of hallowed bodies bred	52		4
Bow swung finds tongue to fling out broad its name	57		4
Deals out that being indoors each one dwells	57		6
Master more may than gaze gaze out of countenance	62		4
By him and rips out rockfire homeforth sturdy Dick	70		3
Sheer off disseveral a star death blots black out nor mark	72		14
Earth all out who with trickling increment	73		10
And the tide of ill is out	77		28
Is this from Christ to be shut out	80	1	2
Then I seek out the shadow of stones	80	3	1
And then I choke to tell this out	80	7	16
Vespillo my centurion hacks out	80	7	19
And I cry out for wounded love	81		33
Theyre out of date lent sermons all the year	96	5	2
Out-fleeced bushes like a spaniels ear	98	11	2
Would not put out some tiny golden centre	98	22	6
Drops the fruit out the duct runs dry or breaks	101		10
Piecing the elements out by plan and plot	102	3	18
Come out of space or suddenly engenderd	103		4
And spins her skirts out while her central star	103		7
And then goes out into the cavernous dark	103		16
So I go out my little sweet is done	103		17
They have taken out their long brands	109	14	1
And she came out to see	109	24	2
Flatterys all out of place where praise is true	125		35

Word	Poem	Stan.	Line
Crept trembling out of bed	135		4
That he will out of hand and heartily	140		5
With tears to put her candle out	145		24
Word went she should be crushed out flat	145		38
They had them out and laid them wide	145		49
There rid the dragons root out there the sin	150		10
Hope holds to Christ the minds own mirror out	151		1
Tampering with those sweet bines draws them out strains them strains them	152		21
We cannot live this life out sometimes we must weary	152		79
Not hope not pray despair ay that brazen despair out	152		101
Out on the giant air tell summer no	154		3
From thy hand out swayed about	155		3
With dare and with downdolphinry and bell-bright bodies huddling out	159		17
Out-fleeced			
Out-fleeced bushes like a spaniels ear	98	11	2
Outer			
This outer cold my exile from of old	80	1	3
Outgoings			
The outgoings of the vale does block	92		11
Outline			
He sat and wrought his outline on a cloud	107	1	10
Outrage			
I outrage it with treasonable kissing	102	1	52
Outrides			
With a mercy that outrides	28	32	1
Outright			
Word that heard and kept thee and uttered thee outright	28	29	8
She was a woman upright outright	145		36
Outward			
American-outward-bound	28	12	2
Of the outward sentence low lays him listed to a heresy here	45		4
Unseen the heroic breast not outward-steeled	73		7
Not so far outward in the sea	120		21
Outward-steeled			
Unseen the heroic breast not outward-steeled	73		7
Outwards			
Are measured outwards from my breast	130		2
Outwitted			
And like a self-outwitted blast	81		74
Over			
To be a judge and ruler over us	5		2
Over again I feel thy finger and find thee	28	1	8
With the sea-romp over the wreck	28	17	4
To the men in the tops and the tackle rode over the storms brawling	28	19	8

Word	Poem	Stan.	Line
All the welkin overhead	77		96
No colour in the overhead	81		160
Overspread			
Soon the whole world is overspread	6		25
Overstood			
Fairyland silk-beech scrolled ash packed sycamore wild wychelm hornbeam fretty overstood	159		24
Overtake			
If I shall overtake thee at last above	20		16
Overtaking			
Have at the awful overtaking	41		113
Overvaulted			
Which overvaulted voice	148		20
Overvaults			
Now it overvaults Appledurcombe	41		29
Overworn			
And father be overworn	114		8
Overwrought			
No Atlantic squall overwrought her	41		16
Own			
Each in his own imagining	23		15
What can it be this glee the good you have there of your own	28	18	8
But he scores it in scarlet himself on his own bespoken	28	22	5
Kind but royally reclaiming his own	28	33	7
But his own nest wild nest no prison	39		11
My people and born own nation	41		86
Fast foundering own generation	41		87
Of own of abrupt self there so thrusts on so throngs the ear	45		8
You there are master do your own desire	46		11
To its own fine function wild and self-instressed	47		7
An our days Gods own Galahad though this childs drift	48		40
To own my heart I yield you do come sometimes but	51		4
To his own selfbent so bound so tied to his turn	58		11
To its own best being and its loveliness of youth it is an everlastingness of o it is an all youth	59		13
What do then how meet beauty merely meet it own	62		10
My own heart let me more have pity on let	69		1
You would not house beneath my own	81		4
I own a preference for pride	96	1	4
Sweeter thy kisses my own love	109	38	3
Time was next whitest after Marys own	136		4
Hope holds to Christ the minds own mirror			

Word	Poem	Stan.	Line
Own (cont.)			
out	151		1
Loyal to his own soul laying his own law down no law nor	152		72
Loyal to his own soul laying his own law down no law nor	152		72
His looks the souls own letters see beyond	157		15
Owns			
The shepherds brow fronting forked lightning owns	75		1
Oxeye			
Sunspurge and oxeye	138		28
Oxford			
From Oxford comes the throng and hum of bells	98	3	6
Gave the much music of our Oxford bells	107	2	8
Pace			
Not granted only o on that path you pace	47		13
And millbrook-slips with pretty pace	130		25
Paces			
Teach me the paces that you went	81		125
Pacing			
Turning and pacing so by slips discloses	108		2
Pack			
Off her once skeined stained veined variety upon all on two spools part pen pack	61		11
Packed			
The stars were packed so close that night	98	29	1
The stars are packed so thick to-night	135		19
Fairyland silk-beech scrolled ash packed sycamore wild wychelm hornbeam fretty overstood	159		24
Packs			
Manwolf worse and their packs infest the age	70		20
Pactolus			
A gold-water Pactolus frets	3		27
Page			
Think of an opening page illumined	93	2	1
Pageant			
Some pageant which takes tears and I must foot with feeling that	152		26
Pain			
As poets sing or that it is a pain	2		121
The day that brought my lasting pain	21		10
From all the pain of the pasts unrest	26		12
Well she has thee for the pain for the	28	31	1
My evil words thorny with pain	81		27
You hear nor care of love and pain	81		35
But mine is dreadful leaping pain	81		51
Led Richard with a sweet undoing pain	107	4	17
Take their peculiar thorns and natural pain	123		5
In motion is no weight or pain	130		15

Word	Poem	Stan.	Line
Pained			
Afar in corridors with pained strain	1	13	7
Painful			
Who rising late had missd her painful way	80		5
Pains			
But half the pains he spends upon his boy	97		4
Paint			
How dare I paint Miss Story to Miss May	94		3
Painted			
By rafts and rafts of flake leaves light dealt so painted on the air	159		25
Painting			
With painting gleamd the rich pilasterd walls	1	10	3
Pair			
Shivelights and shadowtackle in long lashes lace lance and pair	72		4
Paird			
She puts in leash her paird lips lest surprise	82		3
Palace			
Hard by a royal palace and a royal tomb	1	1	9
The stretching palace lay as handle fixd	1	4	4
Fell on the palace and the lust of rabble rude	1	14	9
Palate			
Palate the hutch of tasty lust	22		13
Pale			
Which lightening oer the body rosy-pale	2		72
Where liquid heaven sapphire-pale	77		99
The vexd elm-heads are pale with the view	78		1
The lorn moon pale with piteous dismay	80		4
But in pale water frail water wild rash and reeling water	152		120
Bid joy back have at the harvest keep hope pale	154		4
Paling			
The shocks this piece-bright paling shuts the spouse	32	1	13
Palm			
And to my palm the point apply	80	7	49
Into this hollowd palm should moan the blast	90		2
Bring me palm with pearled knops	98	18	2
Palms			
And seventy palms there stand	5		24
Thy unchancelling poising palms were weighing the worth	28	21	6
As struck with rings of sound the close-shut palms	122		10
As might have struck and shook the close-shut palms	122		13
Palmtree			
Ah dip in blood the palmtree pen	25		37
Palmy			
In some broad palmy mead and saintly smiled	1	10	5

Word	Poem	Stan.	Line
Palmy (cont.)			
If a wuthering of his palmy snow-pinions scatter a colossal smile	45		13
Palsy			
Stone palsy cancer cough lung-wasting womb-not-bearing	152		113
Pane			
I steady as a water in a well to a poise to a pane	28	4	5
Pang			
The pang of Tartarus Christians hold	80	1	1
Pangs			
All while her patience morselled into pangs	50		12
More pangs will schooled at forepangs wilder wring	65		2
Pansy			
Their pansy-dark or bronzen locks were strung	2		53
Pansy-dark			
Their pansy-dark or bronzen locks were strung	2		53
Pantings			
To an orbd rose which by hot pantings blown	2		20
Papa			
Bid your papa goodnight sweet exhibition	97		8
Paradisaical			
Or paring of paradisaical fruit lovely in waning but lustreless	137		3
Paradise			
If I were come from paradise	109	32	3
If it were a flower of paradise	109	34	3
If it were a crown of paradise	109	35	3
She has gone with him to paradise	109	39	3
Paradox			
Hear yet my paradox love when all is given	20		13
Parallel			
And straight showers parallel should follow fast	90		4
With parallel shafts as upward-parted ashes	107	4	5
Parapet			
Eclipsing parapet yet above the wall	12	2	7
Parched			
Your parched nostrils snuff Egyptian air	5		27
Parches			
Of yestertempests creases in pool and rutpeel parches	72		6
Pardon			
When waking hearts can pardon much	77		29
And I must take your amends cry pardon and then be dumb	128		20
Pare			
Diamonds are better cut who pare repair	96	7	5

Word	Poem	Stan.	Line
Paring			
Or paring of paradisaical fruit lovely in waning but lustreless	137		3
Paris			
Here in some darkend landscape Paris fair	1	11	1
Park			
This is my park my pleasaunce this to me	12	1	6
The air smells strong of sweetbriar in the park	135		24
Parley			
Your parley was not done and there	25		29
Parlour			
Youve parlour-pastime left and wholl	29	1	34
Parlour-pastime			
Youve parlour-pastime left and wholl	29	1	34
Part			
The winged fowls took part part fell in thorn	7		7
The winged fowls took part part fell in thorn	7		7
Part found no root upon the flinty road	7		9
Part was picked for John	54		7
And plays in grace her part	60		49
Yet no part but what will	60		53
Off her once skeined stained veined variety upon all on two spools part pen pack	61		11
Our redcoats our tars both these being the greater part	63		2
O here is the most piteous part	80	7	30
And with sharp flint will part my feet and dint	80	7	43
And rosing part on part dispenses green	100		3
And rosing part on part dispenses green	100		3
Allow at least it has one term and part	102	3	5
No piece matched those eyes kept most part much cast down	152		57
I all my being have hacked in half with her neck one part	152		93
The telling time our task is times some part	153		5
Parted			
An age is now since passed since parted with the reversal	45		3
With parallel shafts as upward-parted ashes	107	4	5
Of streams and clouds like meshd and parted moss	121		2
Of water clouds like parted moss	121		3
Parted me leaf and leaf divided me eyelid and eyelid of slumber	137		7
Parting			
And thro their parting lids there came and went	2		11
And he my peace my parting sword and strife	66	1	4

Word	Poem	Stan.	Line
Parting (cont.)			
There is no parting or bare interstice	98	22	4
Partless			
You went into the partless air	25		30
Parts			
From parts unlookd for alterd spent	81		24
I knew the brook that parts in two	135		25
Pashed			
Astray or aswarm all throughther in throngs self in self steeped and pashed quite	61		6
Pass			
Thro crimson-golden floods pass swallowd into fire	2		83
That men must wonder as I pass	10		3
Men are amazed to watch me pass	25		3
Low-covered pass and brace the woodland clods	112		6
I have desired desired to pass	130		28
Passage			
A simple passage of weak notes	3		13
In the most murderous passage of his book	14	2	11
Passages			
And passages where we used to meet	81		162
Passd			
Then passd the wind and sobbd with mountain-echod woe	1	13	9
But the spring-tide passd the same	4		24
Passed			
But day passed into day	21		4
An age is now since passed since parted with the reversal	45		3
Passes			
The whole world passes I stand by	15		4
Where whatevers prized and passes of us everything thats fresh and fast flying of us seems to us sweet of us and swiftly away with done away with undone	59		8
Oer passes bleak oer perilous bars	83		3
The wind that passes by so fleet	98	1	1
With waved passes there shall glide	106		2
Passing			
Your passing steps I never heard	21		48
And listen to the passing bell	23		40
Precious passing measure	41		10
Passion			
And let him prove my passion was begun	14	2	4
The dense and the driven passion and frightful sweat	28	7	5
The appealing of the passion is tenderer in prayer apart	28	26	14
Our passion-plunged giant risen	28	32	7
My passion like a foolish wind	81		37

Word	Poem	Stan.	Line
How turn my passion-pastured thought	81		174
Mantling passion in a grandeur crimson grandeur	152		69
That might have spared her were it but for passion-sake	152		86
Passion-pastured			
How turn my passion-pastured thought	81		174
Passion-plunged			
Our passion-plunged giant risen	28	32	7
Passion-sake			
That might have spared her were it but for passion-sake	152		86
Passionflower			
Great Thecla the plumed passionflower	145		42
Passions			
You see that I have come to passions end	14	3	1
Past			
My love is lessened and must soon be past	14	1	1
Two thousands of years are near upon past	27		16
Beyond saying sweet past telling of tongue	28	9	5
Wording it how but by him that present and past	28	28	5
Ground of being and granite of it past all	28	31	6
A vein for the visiting of the past-prayer pent in prison	28	32	5
Waylay her at ebb past Penmaen pool	29	1	24
Have lost that cheer and charm of earths past prime	35		12
He fathers-forth whose beauty is past change	37		10
Time past she has been attempted and pursued	50		5
Two tedious acts were past	54		29
No worst there is none pitched past pitch of grief	65		1
Our ruins of wrecked past purpose there she basks	68		7
The bitterness of death was past	81		120
But the lily is past as I say and the rose is not in its prime	128		14
Past the past no more be seen	129		2
Past the past no more be seen	129		2
And grave past girlhood earnest in her eyes	136		20
Past-prayer			
A vein for the visiting of the past-prayer pent in prison	28	32	5
Pastime			
Youve parlour-pastime left and wholl	29	1	34
Pastoral			
On a pastoral forehead of Wales	28	24	2
Epistles while the running pastoral bleats	107	4	22
Pasts			
From all the pain of the pasts unrest	26		12

Word	Poem	Stan.	Line
Pastured			
How turn my passion-pastured thought	81		174
Pastures			
Raves through Sicilian pastures many a mile	1	11	4
Pipe me to pastures still and be	22		3
Patch			
This Jack joke poor potsherd patch match-wood immortal diamond	72		23
Path			
Not granted only o on that path you pace	47		13
I betterd all our path with sanguine eyes	125		17
Pathless			
Then was discoverd in the pathless sky	80		7
Patience			
Let patience with her chastening wand	23		45
Patience but pity of the rest of them	28	30	2
Buy then bid then what prayer patience alms vows	32	1	9
All while her patience morselled into pangs	50		12
Some good and so he does leave patience exquisite	51		8
Of patience penance prayer	60		123
Patience hard thing the hard thing but to pray	68		1
But bid for patience is patience who asks	68		2
But bid for patience is patience who asks	68		2
Rare patience roots in these and these away	68		5
Nowhere natural hearts ivy patience maks	68		6
Delicious kindness he is patient patience fills	68		13
Patient			
Delicious kindness he is patient patience fills	68		13
Patronize			
And loves a fatal fault to patronize	94		18
Paul			
Whether at once as once at a crash Paul	28	10	5
And Paul is Tarsus true Bellerophon	136		10
She looked she listened Paul taught long that day	136		24
Pauls			
Near by is Pauls free Tarsus fabled where	136		7
Pause			
To pause then from his gurgling Bill	77		83
Paves			
Paves the clouds on the swept azure	78		10
Pay			
So I am victor now I swear to pay	1	2	5
Yea a debt to pay thee yet	155		19
Not the pleasure the pay the plunder	156		6
Pea			
As halves of sweet-pea-blossom are	81		44

Word	Poem	Stan.	Line
Peace			
Peace and food cheered me where four rough ways meet	20		12
A son for king whose name was peace	26		32
Then come who pine for peace or pleasure	30	1	37
He haunted who of all men most sways my spirits to peace	44		11
When will you ever peace wild wooddove shy wings shut	51		1
When when peace will you peace Ill not play hypocrite	51		3
When when peace will you peace Ill not play hypocrite	51		3
That piecemeal peace is poor peace what pure peace allows	51		5
That piecemeal peace is poor peace what pure peace allows	51		5
That piecemeal peace is poor peace what pure peace allows	51		5
O surely reaving peace my Lord should leave in lieu	51		7
That plumes to peace thereafter and when peace here does house	51		9
That plumes to peace thereafter and when peace here does house	51		9
And he my peace my parting sword and strife	66	1	4
Grant that close-folded peace that clad	77		41
Peach			
Yields tender as a pushed peach	48		23
Peacockd			
The peacockd copse were known to fill	81		14
Peacocks			
Mark you how the peacocks eye	86		1
Peak			
Surround the peak from which we gaze	23		26
Peakd			
Sky peakd with tiny flames	98	25	5
Pealed			
Should have pealed with welcome Wales	29		18
Peals			
That here personal tells off these heart-song powerful peals	141		2
Pearl			
Hither bring pearl opal sard	24		3
That swinishly refuses such a pearl	102	3	33
That swinishly refuses such a pearl	102	3	39
Pearled			
With coral shells thick-pearled cords whateer	2		54
Bring me palm with pearled knops	98	18	2

Word	Poem	Stan.	Line
Pearly			
And silver films beneath with pearly mist	2		67
Peartree			
The glassy peartree leaves and blooms they brush	33		6
Peasant			
Next morn a peasant from the mountain side	1	14	1
Pebbly			
Dawn that the pebbly low-down east	98	31	1
Dawn that low-down pebbly east	98	31	4
Pectoral			
And wear it thus a pectoral by my heart	102	1	31
Peculiar			
The one peculiar of their pleasured eye	12	2	13
Take their peculiar thorns and natural pain	123		5
Peeled			
Of pied and peeled May	28	26	4
Peer			
All mine yet common to my every peer	12	1	8
Peers			
When thou at the random grim forge powerful amidst peers	53		13
Pegasus			
Spent Pegasus down the stark-precipitous air	136		8
Pelt			
And pelt music till nones to spill nor spend	35		8
Pelted			
Have an eye to the sakes of him quaint moon-marks to his pelted plumage under	45		10
Pelting			
With rosy foam and pelting blossom and mists	2		90
Pen			
And I have only set the same to pen	12	2	14
Ah dip in blood the palmtree pen	25		37
Off her once skeined stained veined variety upon all on two spools part pen pack	61		11
That will not wear a print that will not stain a pen	152		121
Penance			
Of patience penance prayer	60		123
Penance shall clothe me to the bone	81		135
Pence			
Like that poor pocket of pence poor pence of mine	142		9
Like that poor pocket of pence poor pence of mine	142		9
Pencilled			
And pencilled blue so daintily	3		18
Pendant			
Pendant in formal line from cornice tall	1	12	7
Penetrative			
The penetrative element	81		132

Word	Poem	Stan.	Line
Peril			
Methinks there is more peril from my laughter	102	1	9
Perilous			
In hot sands perilous	5		4
With perilous o no nor yet plod safe shod sound	70		14
Oer passes bleak oer perilous bars	83		3
Methinks my laughter is more perilous	102	1	8
Perishable			
In the lodges of the perishable souls	126		1
Perishd			
Two mazed shepherds perishd in the tide	1	14	3
Perishing			
Woke thee with a we are perishing in the weather of Gennesareth	28	25	6
Permanence			
Nor permanence in the solid world	130		16
Perpetual			
Blot the perpetual festival of day	89		2
Perplexed			
Like a wind-perplexed rose	87		4
Perseus			
Her Perseus linger and leave her to her extremes	50		9
Persistency			
I never promised such persistency	14	1	2
But with a sweet persistency	110		5
Personal			
That here personal tells off these heart-song powerful peals	141		2
Persuasion			
Of forcd persuasion issue oer the free	1	5	7
Petalld			
Apart betwixt ten thousand petalld lips	2		21
Peter			
The Simon Peter of a soul to the blast	28	28	7
Phantasies			
Splendid with phantasies aerial	1	8	2
Phantasy			
Twixt real hue and phantasy	77		122
Pharohs			
Like pharohs ears of windy harvest dry	117		6
Philip			
Philip took oath while glory or defeat	1	2	3
Philip supposing that the gift most meet	1	3	6
Philomel			
It is the way with Philomel	96	3	3
Phoebus			
Where Phoebus weeps for him who Zephyrs guile	1	11	7
Phoebus loosend tresses swim	77		102

Word	Poem	Stan.	Line
Piety (cont.)			
Whence with the scourge of ready piety	1	5	4
The pride of faith and home of sternest piety	1	8	9
Pigeons			
I see the city pigeons veer	15		27
Pilasterd			
With painting gleamd the rich pilasterd walls	1	10	3
Pilates			
Would I could hear the other Pilates shout	80	1	5
Pile			
There is a massy pile above the waste	1	1	1
Piled			
And damasqud arms and foliagd carving piled	1	10	2
Piles			
Tom then Toms fallowbootfellow piles pick	70		2
Pilgrimages			
Here to this holy well shall pilgrimages be	152		123
Pilgrims			
Pilgrims still pilgrims more pilgrims still more poor pilgrims	152		126
Pilgrims still pilgrims more pilgrims still more poor pilgrims	152		126
Pilgrims still pilgrims more pilgrims still more poor pilgrims	152		126
Pilgrims still pilgrims more pilgrims still more poor pilgrims	152		126
Pillars			
With massy pillars of the doric mood	1	7	2
Pillowing			
She pillowing low her lily neck	21		55
Pillows			
Cloud-puffball torn tufts tossed pillows flaunt forth then chevy on an air	72		1
Pillowy			
Pillowy air he treads a time and hangs	50		10
Pin			
Thy impalpable oppression pin him down	102	1	19
Pine			
Then come who pine for peace or pleasure	30	1	37
Whom want could not make pine pine	142		7
Whom want could not make pine pine	142		7
Pines			
In the quick fragrance of tall rolling pines	84		5
And swarter still the rolling pines should cast	90		5
Pining			
Pining pining till time when reason rambled in it and some	53		3
Pining pining till time when reason rambled in it and some	53		3
Pinions			
If a wuthering of his palmy snow-pinions			

Word	Poem	Stan.	Line
scatter a colossal smile	45		13
Pink			
With loops of veins not of an even pink	93	2	4
Pinks			
Or tender pinks with bloody tyrian dye	2		47
Pious			
A pious work with threefold purpose crownd	1	1	5
Pipe			
Pipe me to pastures still and be	22		3
Now I am minded to take pipe in hand	105		1
Pit			
In all her beauty and sunlight to it is a pit den darkness	152		54
Pitch			
No worst there is none pitched past pitch of grief	65		1
Pitchblack			
Of a pool so pitchblack fell-frowning	56		7
Pitched			
He was pitched to his death at a blow	28	16	4
No worst there is none pitched past pitch of grief	65		1
Piteous			
A piteous siren sweetness on the sea	2		127
The lorn moon pale with piteous dismay	80		4
O here is the most piteous part	81	7	30
Pity			
And zeal is flushed and pity bleeds	23		34
Patience but pity of the rest of them	28	30	2
Prayer shall fetch pity eternal	41		119
Or love or pity or all that sweet notes not his might nursle	45		6
My own heart let me more have pity on let	69		1
Drowned o pity and indignation manshape that shone	72		13
The sea took pity it interposed with doom	158		1
Place			
And its place is a secret and shut in the skies	27		4
Find me a place by thee mother of mine	27		7
Does it smell sweet too in that holy place	27		44
Behind where where was a where was a place	28	3	3
One yes I can tell such a key I do know such a place	59		7
Yet found unstinted place for mirth	77		56
Who asks not life but only place to die	80		9
But to be ransomd from this place	80	5	7
But is there a place for tenderness	81		77
No flowers to find no place to halt	81		159
There would not be a whole place in his head	97		6

Word	Poem	Stan.	Line
Place (cont.)			
The place in the east with earliest milky morn	98	30	5
Because its place is known and charted there	102	3	12
No love prescriptive love with place assignd	102	3	13
Which Wordsworth would have dwelt on about the place	107	4	16
Perhaps it was for this she chose the place	111		15
That thrive in the loamy greenness of this place	122		15
Flatterys all out of place where praise is true	125		35
Sees what his place is but for us the rolls	126		5
O lovely ease in change of place	130		27
Beyond Magdalen and by the bridge on a place called there the plain	142		1
And witness in her place would she	145		32
In all her body I say no place was like her eyes	152		56
Placed			
A sombre length of grey four towers placed	1	1	3
Places			
Christ for Christ plays in ten thousand places	57		12
The blue with brighter places not remote	107	3	20
I hope that all the places on our trip	107	4	27
Placid			
Changd to a flower and there with placid eye	1	11	8
Plain			
Is this made plain what have I come across	14	3	10
Or was it Jane she is too plain	95		3
That bead the plain did ever havering church-tower	100		6
And bluer grey the flocks of trees look in the plain	105		8
From one frail horn that crumbled to the plain	107	3	11
Beyond Magdalen and by the bridge on a place called there the plain	142		1
Plaintively			
Then they thus ranged gan make full plaintively	2		126
Plait			
Than fan or hood or strawy plait	120		8
Through the sieve of the straw of the plait	144		18
Plaits			
They swathe and lace the shroud-plaits oer my face	80	5	6
Plan			
But men and masters plan and build	15		6
Piecing the elements out by plan and plot	102	3	18

Word	Poem	Stan.	Line
Plane			
The watery-plated plane-leaves lit	98	17	3
Plane-leaves			
The watery-plated plane-leaves lit	98	17	3
Planets			
And planets bud whereer we turn our mazed eyes	2		33
Amidst the sistering planets till she comes	103		14
Plant			
Come plant the staff by Cadair cliff	30		7
Planted			
The field where he has planted us	6		27
Plants			
Pressed to death he plants the year	145		4
Plash			
Careless of me they sported some would plash	2		102
To plash with cool feet the clay juicy soil	5		50
Plashes			
Plashes amidst the billowy apple-trees	2		87
Plated			
Lighted the watery-plated leaves	98	17	2
The watery-plated plane-leaves lit	98	17	3
Plates			
And silver damasqud plates obscurd in ages crust	1	12	9
Platting			
How soldiers platting thorns around Christs head	7		4
Play			
With light on her face like the waves at play	26		4
When when peace will you peace Ill not play hypocrite	51		3
By meanwhiles making my play	54		15
His powers seemed free to play	148		14
Where is the field I must play the man on	156		16
Playd			
Here playd the virgin mother with her Child	1	10	4
He playd his wings as though for flight	87		1
Plays			
Our boys plays brought on	54		6
Christ for Christ plays in ten thousand places	57		12
And plays in grace her part	60		49
The pupil plays its liquid jet	86		5
Plays to the breeze where now are fled her fears	99		15
Plea			
Oh even for the weakness of the plea	13		8
Thy plea with him who dealt nay does now deal	58		6
Plead			
That I have taken to plead with if the sound	13		9

Word	Poem	Stan.	Line
Plead (cont.)			
To with no tongue to plead no heart to feel	58		3
Me were I pleading plead nor do I I weary of idle a being but by where wars are rife	66	1	7
With thee but sir so what I plead is just	74	1	1
I plead familiarness endears	81		26
I plead and you will give your tears	81		28
I plead and ah how much in vain	81		29
Pleading			
Me were I pleading plead nor do I I weary of idle a being but by where wars are rife	66	1	7
Pleadings			
Of Gods dear pleadings have as yet not moved thee	13		10
Pleas			
Recorded only I have put my lips on pleas	48		45
Pleasance			
Egypt the valley of our pleasance there	5		25
Pleasaunce			
This is my park my pleasaunce this to me	12	1	6
Please			
Will please us so	107	4	28
I do not but to please Valerian	125		39
Pleased			
She pleased the queen and council so	145		34
Pleasurable			
Trying each pleasurable throat that sings	19		6
Pleasure			
Who long for rest who look for pleasure	30		1
Then come who pine for peace or pleasure	30		37
His pleasure to the changing clime	124		6
His pleasure to the changing clime	124		10
Not the pleasure the pay the plunder	156		6
Pleasured			
The one peculiar of their pleasured eye	12	2	13
Pledged			
And pledged purply in a half-lit dell	112		11
Pleiad			
As the last pleiad yea behind	81		46
Plied			
With the sweetest air that said still plied and pressed	47		3
Plight			
To hold me quite fixed in the selfsame plight	81	7	46
Plighted			
Most like the tuft of plighted silver round	102	1	72
Most like the plighted tuft of silver round	102	1	73
Most like the silver plighted tuft about	102	1	74
Plod			
Your hands have borne the tent-poles on you plod	5		7
No wonder of it sheer plod makes plough			

Word	Poem	Stan.	Line
down sillion	36		11
I plod wondering a-wanting just for lack	46		6
With perilous o no nor yet plod safe shod sound	70		14
Plot			
Those whose dry plot for moisture gapes	6		11
Piecing the elements out by plan and plot	102	3	18
And slender element to piece and plot	102	3	25
The slender elements to piece and plot	102	3	26
You spoil the plot I find my true love by	135		36
Plots			
In beds in gardens in thick plots I stand	5		37
Plotted			
Landscape plotted and pieced fold fallow and plough	37		5
With his pulld and plotted leaf	98	18	4
Took primroses their pulld and plotted leaf	107	3	18
Plough			
No wonder of it sheer plod makes plough down sillion	36		11
Landscape plotted and pieced fold fallow and plough	37		5
In him all quail to the wallowing o the plough s cheek crimsons curls	71		13
They plough our vales you see the unsteady flare	104		9
Pluck			
Pluck the harp and breathe the horn	24		11
Plum			
Plum-purple was the west but spikes of light	2		7
Plum-purple			
Plum-purple was the west but spikes of light	2		7
Plumage			
Have an eye to the sakes of him quaint moon-marks to his pelted plumage under	45		10
The shaken plumage of my spirits wings	77		10
Gather the sooty plumage from deaths wings	89		6
Plume			
Brute beauty and valour and act oh air pride plume here	36		8
Plumed			
The thunder-purple seabeach plumed purple-of-thunder	45		12
Great Thecla the plumed passionflower	145		42
Plumes			
Slim-pointed sea-gull plumes and droop behind	2		80
That plumes to peace thereafter and when peace here does house	51		9
Plumy			
To cool his plumy throbbing breast	77		92

Word	Poem	Stan.	Line
Plunder			
Not the pleasure the pay the plunder	156		6
Plunge			
Plunge orbd in rainbow arcs and trample and tread	2		78
Plunged			
Our passion-plunged giant risen	28	32	7
Plunging			
To keep the loaded bolt from plunging back	135		6
Plush			
Word last how a lush-kept plush-capped sloe	28	8	3
Plush-capped			
Word last how a lush-kept plush-capped sloe	28	8	3
Plushy			
That want the yield of plushy sward	22		22
Ply			
By that window what task what fingers ply	46		5
Are still her neck is creased in close-ply rings	99		10
Ply fold on fold across his dangerous eyes	102	1	20
Pocked			
To have havoc-pocked so see the hung-heavenward boughs	157		32
Pocket			
Like that poor pocket of pence poor pence of mine	142		9
Poet			
A boy feels when the poet he pores upon	14	3	13
No what the poet did write ran	147		5
Poetry			
Poetry to it as a tree whose boughs break in the sky	149	1	3
Poets			
As poets sing or that it is a pain	2		121
Point			
The point fast in and my left hand	80	7	44
And to my palm the point apply	80	7	49
To the point of silence in the air	135		32
Pointed			
Slim-pointed sea-gull plumes and droop behind	2		80
Of pointed wing and silver stole	78		12
Pointed with pierced lights and breaks of rays	98	24	2
Pointing			
And foliagd crownals pointing how the ways	1	6	4
Points			
I gather points of lote-flower from an isle	5		33
Poise			
The sumptuous ridge-crest leave to poise and ride	12	2	8
I steady as a water in a well to a poise to a			

Word	Poem	Stan.	Line
pane	28	4	5
Poised			
Once encounter in here coped and poised powers	44		4
He swung to his first poised purport of reply	47		4
Poising			
Thy unchancelling poising palms were weighing the worth	28	21	6
Pole			
Not so far from the pole	88		8
Not so far from the pole	88		12
Poles			
Your hands have borne the tent-poles on you plod	5		7
Pomp			
Than changeful pomp of courts is aye more wonderful	1	15	9
Pompeii			
At red Pompeii on medalliond walls	2		51
Pond			
That still makes counter-roundels in the pond	107	3	5
Ponderous			
To know the dusk depths of the ponderous sea	2		122
Pool			
But here at here at Penmaen pool	30		4
Come swing the sculls on Penmaen pool	30		8
To halve the bowl of Penmaen pool	30		12
In Frank in fairy Penmaen pool	30		16
Shew brighter shaken in Penmaen pool	30		20
Waylay her at ebb past Penmaen pool	30		24
That lace the face of Penmaen pool	30		28
From darksome darksome Penmaen pool	30		32
That frocks an oar in Penmaen pool	30		36
And taste the treats of Penmaen pool	30		40
Of a pool so pitchblack fell-frowning	56		7
Of yestertempests creases in pool and rutpeel parches	72		6
Falling along the breakless pool of air	122		9
That he hies to a pool neighbouring sees it is the best	159		22
Pools			
The sapphire pools are smit with white	78		7
Poor			
Then faild the tongue the poor collapsing frame	1	3	3
For poor loves failure than his hopeless rise	14	3	7
From furrows of the poor and stinting weald	17		13
Reck not what the poor have lost	24		4
Startle the poor sheep back is the shipwrack then a harvest does tempest carry the grain for thee	28	30	8

Word	Poem	Stan.	Line
Poor (cont.)			
Though aloft on turf or perch or poor low stage	39		5
He has lost count what came next poor boy	41		71
That piecemeal peace is poor peace what pure peace allows	51		5
Thy tears that touched my heart child Felix poor Felix Randal	53		11
Soul self come poor jackself I do advise	69		9
This Jack joke poor potsherd patch match-wood immortal diamond	72		23
And the poor corse impale with it and fray	89		7
Some are pretty enough and some are poor indeed	98	15	4
I heard her say poor poor afflicted soul	111		11
I heard her say poor poor afflicted soul	111		11
The country song of willow the poor soul	111		13
Like that poor pocket of pence poor pence of mine	142		9
Like that poor pocket of pence poor pence of mine	142		9
Meantime some tongue cries what teryth what thou poor fond father	152		22
Pilgrims still pilgrims more pilgrims still more poor pilgrims	152		126
Poppies			
As silken garden-poppies do	21		7
And crush-silk poppies aflash	138		21
Pore			
That a quince I pore upon	25		19
Pores			
Unbakes my pores and streams and makes all fresh	5		32
A boy feels when the poet he pores upon	14	3	13
Who lies on grass and pores upon the sky	117		3
Portending			
Us fresh youth fretted in a bloomfall all portending	48		30
Portends			
Are afoot heaven-vault fast purpling portends and what first lightning	152		63
Portholes			
Death teeming in by her portholes	41		38
Portion			
He has his portion God who stretchd apart	126		2
Ports			
Thy ribbed ports o death	115		5
Possessed			
A noise of falls I am possessed by	121		1
Post			
And with the last post over I knew no letter was sent	128		2

Word	Poem	Stan.	Line
Praised			
And every praised sequence of sweet strings	19		7
He praised the lovely lot of continence	136		28
Praises			
Mingle praises prayer and song	24		27
Pranked			
On pranked scale or threads of carmine shot	2		106
Pray			
My prayers I scarcely call to pray	18		4
Patience hard thing the hard thing but to pray	68		1
I pray you tell to me	109	25	4
Not hope not pray despair ay that brazen despair out	152		101
Prayer			
Battling with God is now my prayer	18		16
Our prayer seems lost in desert ways	23		5
Mingle praises prayer and song	24		27
The appealing of the passion is tenderer in prayer apart	28	26	14
A vein for the visiting of the past-prayer pent in prison	28	32	5
Buy then bid then what prayer patience alms vows	32	1	9
And the prayer thou hearst me making	41		112
Prayer shall fetch pity eternal	41		119
Prayer go disregarded	48		47
Of patience penance prayer	60		123
She held her hands to like in prayer	145		48
Prayers			
My prayers must meet a brazen heaven	18		1
My prayers I scarcely call to pray	18		4
Her prayers his providence	60		41
Praying			
Which praying fails to do away	18		12
Prays			
To thee the trembling sinner prays	23		3
Preachings			
Herclots preachings Ill no longer hear	96	5	1
Precedents			
I reckon precedents of love	18		7
Precious			
Five ways the precious branches torn	6		14
Precious passing measure	41		10
And now I get some precious slips	81		84
Though ill-contented precious precious Floris	102	1	56
Though ill-contented precious precious Floris	102	1	56
Precipice			
Or fray a granite from the precipice	80	7	38
Precipitous			
Spent Pegasus down the stark-precipitous air	136		8
Precisely			
Now more precisely touched in light and gloom	98	30	4

Word	Poem	Stan.	Line
Precision			
In more precision now of light and dark	98	30	1
Prediluvian			
Could count on prediluvian age	15		10
Preeminent			
A star most spiritual principal preeminent	98	27	1
Preened			
Boughs being pruned birds preened show more fair	96	7	1
Preference			
I own a preference for pride	96	1	4
Preferred			
And know infallibly which I preferred	19		8
But that sweet sound which I preferred	21		47
Prejudice			
It does no prejudice	60		82
Prenatal			
Love by prenatal serfdom still confined	102	3	15
Prepare			
The very victim would prepare	145		8
Prescriptive			
No love prescriptive love with place assignd	102	3	13
Presence			
Whose presence power is	60		26
Present			
Wording it how but by him that present and past	28	28	5
Appeard not for the present till	92		8
Presented			
This was the prized the desirable sight unsought presented so easily	137		6
Press			
A press of winged things comes down this way	5		15
The wine was racked from the press	6		18
Too proud too proud what a press she bore	41		32
And press it down on either side a bone	80	7	50
Of the press of roses	98	19	8
Of all the golden press	98	27	2
To all the starry press	98	28	6
They seemed to press and stare	98	29	2
They seem to press and droop and stare	135		20
Pressed			
With the sweetest air that said still plied and pressed	46		3
And pressed violets in the folds appear	119		4
Pressed to death he plants the year	145		4
Pressure			
Of the gospel proffer a pressure a principle Christs gift	28	4	8
Pretend			
And Ill pretend the credit given of yore	14	2	3

Word	Poem	Stan.	Line
Pretty			
Some are pretty enough and some are poor indeed	98	15	4
Backward are laid her pretty black-fleeced ears	99		13
And millbrook-slips with pretty pace	130		25
Prey			
Into my hand he gives a host for prey	5		17
And they the prey of the gales	28	24	4
Price			
Here are sweet messes without price or worth	5		47
Priced			
Before-time-taken dearest prized and priced	28	22	6
Prick			
But a prick will make no eye at all	42		15
Prickproof			
Seldomer heartsore that treads through prickproof thick	70		7
Pride			
The pride of faith and home of sternest piety	1	8	9
Upon the stir and keep of pride	22		18
And five-lived and leaved favour and pride	28	23	6
Let him ride her pride in his triumph despatch and have done with his doom there	28	27	8
Pride rose prince hero of us high-priest	28	34	7
Being pure we lifes pride and cared-for crown	34		11
Brute beauty and valour and act oh air pride plume here	35		8
For did she pride her freighted fully on	40		8
This pride of primes enjoyment	48		12
And pride is nerveless and hearts meek	78		38
I own a preference for pride	96	1	4
Now be my pride then perfect all one piece henceforth	152		70
Priest			
Pride rose prince hero of us high-priest	28	34	7
Prime			
I mark the flowers ere the prime	4		14
Have lost that cheer and charm of earths past prime	34		12
But the lily is past as I say and the rose is not in its prime	128		14
Primes			
This pride of primes enjoyment	48		12
Primrose			
O feel-of-primrose hands o feet	22		21
Were eyes of central primrose bluebells ran	98	10	2
And primrose bring and make a sheaf	98	18	3
Primroses			
In lakes of bluebells pieced with primroses	98	9	3

Word	Poem	Stan.	Line
Took primroses their pulld and plotted leaf	107	3	18
Being not forgotten for primroses note	107	3	19
As sure as what is most sure sure as that spring primroses	152		132
Prince			
To newborn prince and royal corse inanimate	1	4	9
Like an Assyrian prince with buds unsheathd	2		62
Pride rose prince hero of us high-priest	28	34	7
Princely			
Now let me see you you large princely hand	102	1	46
Princes			
Princes strong for the sword and slaughter	26		27
Principal			
Waste her earliest stars earlstars stars principal overbend us	61		4
A star most spiritual principal preeminent	98	27	1
Like scalded banks toppd once with principal flowers	102	2	14
Principle			
Of the gospel proffer a pressure a principle Christs gift	28	4	8
Print			
That will not wear a print that will not stain a pen	152		121
Prism			
Most like those hues that in the prism	77		61
Prison			
A vein for the visiting of the past-prayer pent in prison	28	32	5
But his own nest wild nest no prison	39		11
Privacy			
As public is my greater privacy	12	1	7
Prize			
Ah well it is all a purchase all is a prize	32	1	8
Duly dear lord my prize is won	81		109
I must hunt down the prize	88		1
Prized			
Before-time-taken dearest prized and priced	28	22	6
Where whatevers prized and passes of us everything thats fresh and fast flying of us seems to us sweet of us and swiftly away with done away with undone	59		8
This was the prized the desirable sight unsought presented so easily	137		6
Procession			
Warnd by the bright procession of the stars	102	1	59
Proconsul			
Proconsul is Sapricius near	25		41
Prodigal			
Spread oer the swart face of this prodigal earth	5		45

Word	Poem	Stan.	Line
Profess			
Ah surely all who have written will profess	117		8
Proffer			
Of the gospel proffer a pressure a principle Christs gift	28	4	8
Profit			
Thus we shall profit while gold coinage still	96	7	7
Profound			
The miles profound of solid green and be	2		123
Promise			
Or far-off promise of a time to be	13		4
That holds no promise of success	15		34
Which makes so small the promise of that yield	17		11
And the promise of summer within her breast	26		16
Promised			
I never promised such persistency	14	1	2
But is not that my grievance you promised and you forgot	128		6
Promises			
And happy promises fulfilld	15		8
Proof			
No finishd proof was this of Gothic grace	1	6	1
Must you be gorged with proof did ever sand	5		41
Folds off aloof that signal is and proof	80	6	3
Proper			
Or once or never took loves proper food	20		10
The proper sweet re-attributing above	113		11
It is hardly a proper treat for a birthday to rest in her arms	128		12
Prophetess			
A prophetess towered in the tumult a virginal tongue told	28	17	8
Proportion			
That thou hadst borne proportion in my bliss	13		6
Prosper			
Why do sinners ways prosper and why must	74	1	2
Prosperity			
Missing prosperity and praise	133		15
Prosperously			
Ravens for prosperously-boded curses	89		3
Prosperously-boded			
Ravens for prosperously-boded curses	89		3
Proud			
Oh thou proud mother and much proud maiden	26		19
Oh thou proud mother and much proud maiden	26		19
Too proud too proud what a press she bore	41		32
Too proud too proud what a press she bore	41		32
Not mood in him nor meaning proud fire or sacred fear	45		5
Since proud it calls the calling manly gives a guess	63		4

Word	Poem	Stan.	Line
Prouder			
To what serves mortal beauty dangerous does set dancing blood the o-seal-that-so feature flung prouder form	62		1
Proudest			
A cloisterd convent first the proudest home	1	1	6
Prove			
And let him prove my passion was begun	14	2	4
I prove it what then when these lines are dead	117		11
If he would prove	127		16
Proverb			
You have made me quote almost the dismalest proverb I know	128		18
Provide			
And lily-coloured clothes provide	22		27
Providence			
No not uncomforted lovely-felicitous providence	28	30	5
Her prayers his providence	60		41
Prudence			
Prudence she has but wise shell never be	94		24
Pruned			
Boughs being pruned birds preened show more fair	96	7	1
Psalm			
God though to thee our psalm we raise	23		1
Public			
As public is my greater privacy	12	1	7
Puffball			
Cloud-puffball torn tufts tossed pillows flaunt forth then chevy on an air	72		1
Pull			
Did you pull it in the kings garden	109	33	3
I did not pull it in kings garden	109	34	1
The sky is blue and the winds pull	130		22
Pulld			
With his pulld and plotted leaf	98	18	4
Took primroses their pulld and plotted leaf	107	3	18
Pulpit			
While from the pulpit in a heretic land	1	5	1
Punishment			
And the ever-fretting shirt of punishment	11		11
Pupil			
The pupil plays its liquid jet	86		5
Pupils			
She schools the flighty pupils of her eyes	82		1
Purcell			
To me so arch-especial a spirit as heaves in Henry Purcell	45		2
Than Purcell tune lets tread to see it does this keeps warm	62		2
Purchase			
Ah well it is all a purchase all is a prize	32	1	8

Word	Poem	Stan.	Line
Pure			
Pure fasted faces draw unto this feast	11		1
Being pure we lifes pride and cared-for crown	35		11
That piecemeal peace is poor peace what pure peace allows	51		5
Which to pure souls alone may be	77		142
A pure gold lily but by the pure gold lily	98	15	1
A pure gold lily but by the pure gold lily	98	15	1
Make me pure Lord thou are holy	129		6
Purer			
And they are purer but alas not solely	16		5
Purfled			
The satin-purfled smooth to foam and spread	2		79
Purify			
Touch me and purify and shew	77		39
Purple			
And held a cross of flowers in purple bloom	1	10	6
Plum-purple was the west but spikes of light	2		7
The thunder-purple seabeach plumed purple-of-thunder	45		12
The thunder-purple seabeach plumed purple-of-thunder	45		12
Purple eyes and seas of liquid leaves all day	68		8
And not from purple Wales only nor from elmy England	152		124
Purple-of-thunder			
The thunder-purple seabeach plumed purple-of-thunder	45		12
Purpling			
Rounds its still-purpling centreings of cloud	98	30	3
Rounds its still-purpling centre-darks of cloud	98	30	6
Are afoot heaven-vault fast purpling portends and what first lightning	152		63
Purply			
And pledged purply in a half-lit dell	112		11
Purport			
The words are old the purport new	8		5
He swung to his first poised purport of reply	47		4
Purpose			
A pious work with three fold purpose crownd	1	1	5
Our ruins of wrecked past purpose there she basks	68		7
And thy purpose to fulfil	155		18
Pursuant			
With draught of thin and pursuant cold so nips	11		6
Pursud			
What time the baffled frank swept back pursud	1	14	8
Pursued			
Time past she has been attempted and pursued	50		5

Word	Poem	Stan.	Line
Pushed			
Yields tender as a pushed peach	48		23
Pushing			
They said we could not miss a pushing brook	125		5
Put			
He hath put a new song in my mouth	8		4
And put away my sun	21		11
Recorded only I have put my lips on pleas	48		45
And to put graver sins aside	96	1	3
Would not put out some tiny golden centre	98	22	6
What put taught graces on his country lip	107	2	3
It never yet so sweetly was put on	125		29
I put the door to with the bolts unpinned	135		11
With tears to put her candle out	145		24
Puts			
Her reply puts this other	42		14
I muse at how its being puts blissful back	46		2
She puts in leash her paird lips lest surprise	82		3
Python			
Apollo views the smitten python writhe and die	1	11	9
Quail			
In him all quail to the wallowing o the plough s cheek crimsons curls	71		13
Quails			
The gross flock call them quails	5		16
Falling flakes to the throng that catches and quails	28	24	6
Quaint			
Have an eye to the sakes of him quaint moon-marks to his pelted plumage under	45		10
Quarter			
Sitting eastnortheast in cursed quarter the wind	28	13	6
For a quarter of an hour or so	145		59
Quartz			
Quartz-fret or sparks of salt	60		101
Quartz-fret			
Quartz-fret or sparks of salt	60		101
Queen			
Salute thee mother the maid-months queen	26		24
She pleased the queen and council so	145		34
Quell			
The breasts desponding sob I quell	23		38
Those sweet hopes quell whose least me quickenings lift	48		37
Quelled			
My aspens dear whose airy cages quelled	43		1
Quelled or quenched in leaves the leaping sun	43		2
Quench			
But quench her bonniest dearest to her her clearest-selved spark	72		10
To quench the fine-drawn cataract	77		90

Word	Poem	Stan.	Line
Quenchd			
The floating blooms and with tide flowing quenchd	2		139
Quenched			
O should it then be quenched not	10		16
Is it quenched or not	25		16
Quelled or quenched in leaves the leaping sun	43		2
My tongue had taught thee comfort touch had quenched thy tears	53		10
Breathes once and quenched faster than it came	76		3
When ts light I quenched its rose times one rich rose my hand	152		82
Quenching			
Stanching quenching ocean of a motionable mind	28	31	5
Question			
Ere I had further question made	4		16
Question what is spring	42		15
Questioning			
Questioning winds around the hills	77		44
Quests			
All quests save the recital of their greatness	104		3
Quick			
In the quick fragrance of tall rolling pines	84		5
Within her womb the child was quick	145		39
Lifes quick this kind this keen self-feeling	152		96
Quicken			
Now quicken sheathed in the yellow galaxy	98	22	3
Quickenings			
Those sweet hopes quell whose least me quickenings lift	48		37
Quickgold			
The grey lawns cold where gold where quick-gold lies	32	1	5
Quickly			
Was calling o Christ Christ come quickly	28	24	7
Breathe in such ether or the quickly elms	100		7
Quicksilvery			
And the water warbles over into filleted with glassy grassy quicksilvery shives and shoots	159		38
Quiet			
The towers musical quiet-walled grove	12	1	10
Quiet-walled			
The towers musical quiet-walled grove	12	1	10
Quill			
Our swans are now of such remorseless quill	96	2	1
Quills			
With spiked quills all of intensest hue	2		44
Quils			
And on their brittle green quils	98	7	1

Word	Poem	Stan.	Line
Quince			
And a quince in hand not one	10		9
Had she a quince in hand yet gaze	10		19
That a quince I pore upon	25		19
Quinces			
Quinces look when not one	25		9
Quit			
A cusp still clasped him a fluke yet fanged him entagled him not quit utterly	137		5
Quite			
Rich beams till death or distance buys them quite	40		8
Astray or aswarm all throughther in throngs self in self steeped and pashed quite	61		6
To hold me quite fixed in the selfsame plight	80	7	46
His steady wheel quite to the full again	107	3	12
Quite as ladies go	125		27
And these are spent and ended quite	130		21
Quivering			
A quivering pennon then for eye too keen	2		17
Quote			
And taught my lips to quote this word	8		6
You may quote Wordsworth if you like to me	107	3	8
You have made me quote almost the dismalest proverb I know	128		18
Rabble			
Fell on the palace and the lust of rabble rude	1	14	9
Night roared with the heart-break hearing a heart-broke rabble	28	17	5
Brave all and take what comes as here this rabble is come	152		102
Race			
The riving off that race	41		98
Run all your race o brace sterner that strain	47		14
That does now reach our race	60		23
That piece themselves into a race of drops	102	1	36
Or ringlet-race on burling barrow brown	157		12
Raced			
Raced down decks round messes of mortals	41		39
Them broad in bluff hide his frowning feet lashed raced	71		17
Racing			
With richness the racing lambs too have fair their fling	33		8
He shook with racing notes the standing air	98	38	1
Rack			
Hack and rack the growing green	43		11
For wrung all on loves rack	54		17
Thy river and oer gives all to rack or wrong	58		8
But these two ware of a world where but these two tell each off the other of a rack	61		13
Breathed round the rack of ribs the scooped			

Word	Poem	Stan.	Line
Rack (cont.)			
flank lank	71		2
Racked			
The wine was racked from the press	6		18
Cuckoo-echoing bell-swarmed lark-charmed rook-racked river-rounded	44		2
Radiance			
Were limnd about with radiance rare	77		60
Rafts			
By rafts and rafts of flake leaves light dealt so painted on the air	159		25
By rafts and rafts of flake leaves light dealt so painted on the air	159		25
Rage			
Or wring their barriers in bursts of fear or rage	39		8
This by despair bred hangdog dull by rage	70		19
Raging			
His injury shell avenge with raging shame	82		6
Rail			
The flange and the rail flame	28	11	2
Rain			
Adown the clattering gullies swept the rain	1	13	2
Of driving vermeil-rain and as he lists	2		91
But if the rain-blasts be unbound	3		7
A crimson east that bids for rain	21		8
They rain against our much-thick and marsh air	40		7
Mine o thou Lord of life send my roots rain	74	1	13
On the tumblings of the rain	77		104
Then while the rain-born arc glows higher	77		123
My tears are but a cloud of rain	81		36
And ravelld into strings of rain	81		57
Now the rain	98	6	1
While there is neither sun nor rain	105		6
To these Castara is rain or breeze or spring	125		54
Following falls and falls of rain	142		3
Rain-blasts			
But if the rain-blasts be unbound	3		7
Rain-born			
Then while the rain-born arc glows higher	77		123
Rainbow			
Plunge orbd in rainbow arcs and trample and tread	2		78
For a rainbow footing it nor he for his bones risen	39		14
Tresses dippd in rainbow fire	77		14
When the rainbow arching high	77		107
The rainbow shines but only in the thought	91		2
A rainbow also shapes itself beyond	107	3	6
Met a new shower and saw the rainbow fill	107	3	10
Foamfalling is not fresh to it rainbow by it			

Word	Poem	Stan.	Line
not beaming	152		55
Rainbows			
In the ascendancy of rainbows horns	84		2
For who makes rainbows by invention	91		4
Raindrop			
Why raindrop-roundels looped together	30		27
Raindrop-roundels			
Why raindrop-roundels looped together	30		27
Rains			
Wheatfields tumbled with the rains	77		136
At morn they come upon our lands like rains	104		8
No rains shall fresh the flats of sea	114		13
Save in the body of the rains	130		20
While rushy rains shall fall or brooks shall fleet from fountains	152		107
Raisd			
He raisd the convent as a monstrous grate	1	4	1
Raise			
God though to thee our psalm we raise	23		1
Raised			
Lingerd then raised the washing waves and drenchd	2		138
Rambled			
Pining pining till time when reason rambled in it and some	53		3
Rampant			
Legates might rush zeal-rampant fiery	1	5	5
Ramps			
Trench right the tide that ramps against the shore	35		2
Ran			
When the rose ran in crimsonings down the cross-wood	27		35
All hands for themselves the cry ran then	41		41
Ran revel in the elder boy	54		9
Nay roguish ran the vein	54		28
And all into the duomo ran	81		88
Were eyes of central primrose bluebells ran	98	10	2
Ran through it following which we should have sight	125		6
No what the poet did write ran	147		5
It stooped and flashed and fell and ran like water away	152		52
Randal			
Felix Randal the farrier o is he dead then my duty all ended	52		1
Thy tears that touched my heart child Felix poor Felix Randal	52		11
Random			
When thou at the random grim forge powerful amidst peers	52		13

Word	Poem	Stan.	Line
Rangd			
He rangd long corridors and cornicd halls	1	10	1
Blades of Milan in circles rangd grew rust	1	12	8
Range			
I have found the dominant of my range and state	19		13
While all things else may stir and range	130		7
Ranged			
Then they thus ranged gan make full plaintively	2		126
Rank			
Ranters screamd rank rebellion this should be	1	5	2
Of a fresh and following folded rank	43		4
Though as a beechbole firm finds his as at a rollcall rank	71		9
You rank and reeking things	77		5
While the breeze by rank and measure	78		9
What being in rank-old nature should earlier have that breath been	141		1
Whose bloods I reck no more of no more rank with hers	152		103
Rank-old			
What being in rank-old nature should earlier have that breath been	141		1
Ranked			
O is there no frowning of these wrinkles ranked wrinkles deep	59		3
Ranked round the bower	159		51
Ranking			
Sexing and ranking with our ruder files	102	1	66
Rankle			
Disaster there but may he not rankle and roam	48		42
Ranks			
Squander the hell-rook ranks Sally to molest him	48		18
Fallow foam-fallow hanks falln off their ranks	144		7
Ransom			
Their ransom their rescue and first fast last friend	40		14
Months earlier since I had our sweet reprieve and ransom	53		7
Ransomd			
But to be ransomd from this place	80	5	7
Ranters			
Ranters screamd rank rebellion this should be	1	5	2
Rapture			
I want the one rapture of an inspiration	76		10
Rapturous			
Rapturous loves greeting of realer of rounder replies	38		8

Word	Poem	Stan.	Line
Rare			
The abysmal ocean hoards of strange and rare	2		55
Crushes and tears the rare enjewelling	2		85
In all our western shires was rare	21		23
More brightening her rare-dear Britain as his reign rolls	28	34	6
In mould or mind or what not else makes rare	40		6
Rare patience roots in these and these away	68		5
In wide the worlds weal rare gold bold steel bare	70		17
Were limnd about with radiance rare	77		60
Melting into aether rare	77		74
While a subtle spirit and rare	77		127
Their rocky lodges then the weather rare	80	4	5
Rare-dear			
More brightening her rare-dear Britain as his reign rolls	28	34	6
Rarely			
But through black branches rarely drest	3		20
Each hue so rarely wrought that where	77		117
Most rarely see unselfishness	96	1	2
Rarest			
Upon his altar and with rarest store	1	2	8
Of realty the rarest-veined unraveller a not	44		12
Rarest-veined			
Of realty the rarest-veined unraveller a not	44		12
Rash			
The rash smart sloggering brine	28	19	4
His rash-fresh re-winded new-skeined score	35		6
Flame-rash rudred	138		23
But in pale water frail water wild rash and reeling water	152		120
Rash-fresh			
His rash-fresh re-winded new-skeined score	35		6
Rated			
Is statuary rated by its inches	96	7	6
Rather			
I read the story rather	7		3
Rather it is the sizing moon	10		20
Or rather rather then stealing as spring	28	10	3
Or rather rather then stealing as spring	28	10	3
Hand rather my heart lo lapped strength stole joy would laugh cheer	64		11
At God knows when to God knows what whose smiles not wrung see you unforeseen times rather as skies	69		12
Breathe oer my bare nerve rather I desire	80	5	5
These rather are the arc where beauty shines	102	3	3
Rather to ear than eye shews where they stray	112		4

Word	Poem	Stan.	Line
Ration			
Just such slips of soldiery Christs royal ration	48		28
Ravage			
Till fearing ravage worse than in his flight	1	14	7
Rave			
Alas I rave where calm is due	81		70
Ravel			
His locks like all a ravel-ropes-end	144		5
Ravel-ropes-end			
His locks like all a ravel-ropes-end	144		5
Ravelld			
And ravelld into strings of rain	81		57
Ravens			
Ravens for prosperously-boded curses	89		3
Raves			
Raves through Sicilian pastures many a mile	1	11	4
Ravishment			
And carried me with ravishment	81		16
Ray			
And the lessend stars ray not	85		6
Rayd			
In silken undulation spurrd and rayd	2		43
Rays			
With flowing tracery engemming rays	1	6	2
The shearing rays contract me with their blaze	81	2	6
Stars waving their indivisible rays	98	23	1
Pointed with pierced lights and breaks of rays	98	24	2
To fields of light millions of travelling rays	103		9
Re			
His rash-fresh re-winded new-skeined score	35		6
The proper sweet re-attributing above	113		11
That sweetness re-attributing above	113		12
No more than re and mi	148		34
Re-attributing			
The proper sweet re-attributing above	113		11
That sweetness re-attributing above	113		12
Re-winded			
His rash-fresh re-winded new-skeined score	35		6
Reach			
Reach me a fancy come faster	28	27	2
That does now reach our race	60		23
Here at the very furthest reach away	107	4	19
The furthest reach this side on that the bay	107	4	20
And bright iconium eastwards reach my rhymes	136		6
Reachd			
Rowing I reachd a rock the sea was low	2		1
In forty days reachd heaven from earth	6		24
Sounds reachd him Richard came Sylvester smiled	107	4	24

Word	Poem	Stan.	Line
Reaches			
Of mile-long reaches of our road below us	125		7
Read			
I read the story rather	7		3
Read the unshapeable shock night	28	28	3
When you were learner and I read	81		165
I read that the recital of thy sin	102	2	2
The sweetest sonnet five or six times read	117		9
Though they took till the seventeenth of next October to read	128		8
Reading			
Most dented lay Sylvester reading Keats	107	4	21
Readings			
The unquestiond readings of a blotless book	16		6
Reads			
That reads or holds the astrologic lore	14	2	2
Ready			
Whence with the scourge of ready piety	1	5	4
With the ready azure and high carmine think	93	2	2
I find I am as ready with my tears	102	1	34
And bridegroom waits and ready are bower and bed	136		18
Have all things ready in his room	152		10
Real			
Twixt real hue and phantasy	77		122
Realer			
Rapturous loves greeting of realer of rounder replies	38		8
Realize			
Her character she does not realize	94		25
Realm			
Realm both Christ is heir to and there reigns	48		32
Bare the condition of a realm at riot	82		4
Realty			
Of realty the rarest-veined unraveller a not	44		12
Reappear			
New-dated from the terms that reappear	12	1	1
Rearing			
Or rearing billow of the Biscay water	41		17
Rears			
Has one fetch in her she rears herself to divine	28	19	6
The heart rears wings bold and bolder	38		13
Reason			
Her feasts follow reason	42		3
Pining pining till time when reason rambled in it and some	53		3
Reason selfdisposal choice of better or worse way	152		94
Reasond			
I reasond the futility	81		113

Word	Poem	Stan.	Line
Reave			
To thriftless reave both our rich round world bare	58		12
Reaving			
O surely reaving peace my lord should leave in lieu	51		7
Rebel			
Wring thy rebel dogged in den	28	9	3
Head of a rebel	152		33
Rebellion			
Ranters screamd rank rebellion this should be	1	5	2
This royal manhood tis in me rebellion	102	1	40
Rebellious			
To bruise them dearer yet the rebellious wills	68		10
Rebound			
With a ballad with a ballad a rebound	146		3
Rebuff			
The stabbing coldness of rebuff	83		28
Rebuffed			
Rebuffed the big wind my heart in hiding	36		6
Recital			
I read that the recital of thy sin	102	2	2
All quests save the recital of their greatness	104		3
Reck			
Reck not what the poor have lost	24		4
Crushed why do men then now not reck his rod	31	1	4
And none reck of world after this bids wear	58		13
Now her all in two flocks two folds black white right wrong reckon but reck butmind	61		12
Little I reck ho lacklevel in if all had bread	70		9
Whose bloods I reck no more of no more rank with hers	152		103
Reckon			
I reckon precedents of love	18		7
Now her all in two flocks two folds black white right wrong reckon but reck butmind	61		12
Reclaiming			
Kind but royally reclaiming his own	28	33	7
Reconciled			
Father be thou reconciled	155		14
Record			
Thy venerable record virgin is recorded	152		122
Recorded			
That no recorded devilish thing was done	14	2	8
Recorded only I have put my lips on pleas	48		45
Thy venerable record virgin is recorded	152		122
Records			
Monuments of my earnest records of my revenge	152		36

Word	Poem	Stan.	Line
Recover			
Her fame to keep her fame to recover	156		12
Recovery			
The recurb and the recovery of the Gulfs sides	28	31	3
Amongst come-back-again things things with a revival things with a recovery	152		134
Recurb			
The recurb and the recovery of the Gulfs sides	28	31	3
Red			
At red Pompeii on medalliond walls	2		51
Here he knelt then in regimental red	48		9
And seals of red carnation which had each	98	12	4
And each a dinted circle the grass was red	107	4	11
And James shall hate his faded red	114		11
Lined all with silk of juicy red	124		16
What I did ask then was a circle of rose-red sealing-wax	128		15
All slumbered whom our rud red tiles	135		1
No more than red and blue	148		33
Redcoats			
Our redcoats our tars both these being the greater part	63		2
Redeeming			
Not that hell knows redeeming	41		116
Reed			
My national old Egyptian reed gave way	20		7
Reeds			
A moaning voice among the reeds	23		36
Reef			
She struck not a reef or a rock	28	14	2
Reefs			
I see long reefs of violets	3		25
Reek			
An olive-branch whence richly reek	77		15
Reeking			
You rank and reeking things	77		5
Reel			
This ruck and reel which you remark	22		11
Thy lovely dale down thus and thus bids reel	58		7
Reeling			
But in pale water frail water wild rash and reeling water	152		120
Reels			
With a south-westerly wind blustering with a tide rolls reels	141		4
Reeve			
Not vault them the million of rounds of thy mercy not reeve even them in	28	12	8
He of all can reeve a rope best there he bides in bliss	63		10

Word	Poem	Stan.	Line
Refrain			
Refrain	27		5
Refused			
Rhine refused them Thames would ruin them	28	21	3
Refuses			
That swinishly refuses such a pearl	102	3	33
That swinishly refuses such a pearl	102	3	39
Regimen			
It is a regimen on the imperfect wind	102	3	17
Is to give regimen to the imperfect wind	102	3	24
Regimental			
Here he knelt then in regimental red	48		9
Register			
The unchanging register of change	130		5
Regret			
Their fall was fuller of regret	4		30
Regular			
And the sea flint-flake black-backed in the regular blow	28	13	5
Rehearsal			
It is the forged feature finds me it is the rehearsal	45		7
Reign			
More brightening her rare-dear Britain as his reign rolls	28	34	6
Reigns			
And been in their ruinous reigns oppressed	26		10
Realm both Christ is heir to and there reigns	48		32
Rein			
High there how he rung upon the rein of a wimpling wing	36		3
Release			
Yet ah this air I gather and I release	44		9
Released			
A released shower let flash to the shire not a lightning of fire hard-hurled	28	33	8
Relics			
Fair relics too the changeful moor had left	1	8	1
Relief			
Mary mother of us where is your relief	65		4
And each drew bluebells up and for relief	107	3	17
Religious			
Believes herself religious and is not	94		29
Relish			
What relish shall the censers send	22		19
And relish not her loveless kiss	120		11
Remain			
Yet what you are the world would say remain	125		28
Remainder			
Remainder of a miracle	25		34
Remark			
This ruck and reel which you remark	22		11

Word	Poem	Stan.	Line
Remember			
Remember us in the roads the heaven-haven of the reward	28	34	3
I remember a house where all were good	34		1
To remember and exultation	42		47
I would remember love forgive	81		71
As ever I remember in my life	102	1	13
Rememberd			
Rememberd sweetness for my thought	81		139
Remembereth			
Always the time remembereth	81		61
Remembering			
That bird beyond the remembering his free fells	39		3
Weeping even now I curse myself remembering	102	1	44
Remembrance			
Chilling remembrance of my days of old	17		5
Remnants			
The choicest remnants thence such home forlorn	1	15	3
Remorseless			
Our swans are now of such remorseless quill	96	2	1
Remote			
Exiled most remote El Khor	81		47
The blue with brighter places not remote	107	3	20
Remotest			
This to remotest ages was to be	1	8	8
Remove			
Remove not but in all removes I can	66	1	9
Removes			
Remove not but in all removes I can	66	1	9
Renderd			
Must see the eagles bulk renderd in mists	88		3
Rent			
Steel may be melted and rock rent	81		134
Repair			
Or rocks where rockdoves do repair	15		38
Diamonds are better cut who pare repair	96	7	5
Repeat			
Repeat that repeat	146		1
Repeat that repeat	146		1
Repeated			
Rides repeated topsyturvy	29	1	15
Repent			
I did repent I am forgiven	81		110
Are heard that cry she does repent	81		123
Teach me the way I will repent	81		136
Repent he sinned and all his sins be freed	140		6
Any instant falls means me and I do not repent	152		64
I do not and I will not repent not repent	152		65

Word	Poem	Stan.	Line
Repent (cont.)			
I do not and I will not repent not repent	152		65
I repent of what I did	155		12
Replies			
But no forgiving voice replies	23		4
Rapturous loves greeting of realer of rounder replies	38		8
Reply			
And you shall meet me with reply	8		13
Her reply puts this other	42		14
He swung to his first poised purport of reply	47		4
Reprieve			
Months earlier since I had our sweet reprieve and ransom	53		7
Rescue			
Nor rescue only rocket and lightship shone	28	15	6
Their ransom their rescue and first fast last friend	40		14
All is from wreck here there to rescue one	150		6
Resent			
What if my subject seeing this resent	94		5
Residuary			
Fall to the residuary worm worlds wildfire leave but ash	72		20
Resign			
Resign them sign them seal them send them motion them with breath	59		16
Resolution			
And right only resolution will his will unwavering	152		75
Rest			
Looks laid for feasting and for rest	3		24
But I must yield the chase or rest and eat	20		11
To thy breast to thy rest to thy glory divine	27		48
I was under a roof here I was at rest	28	24	3
Patience but pity of the rest of them	28	30	2
Who long for rest who look for pleasure	30		1
Not that the sweet-fowl song-fowl needs no rest	39		9
Doff darkness homing nature knows the rest	47		6
Tendered to him ah well God rest him all road ever he offended	53		8
Birth milk and all the rest	60		21
Lies divinely still at rest	77		98
My thought was there to rest against the trees	125		8
Selvaggia Orinda and Adela and the rest	125		44
It is hardly a proper treat for a birthday to rest in her arms	128		12
At roost and rest they shifted not	135		15
Resurrection			
But vastness blurs and time beats level enough the resurrection	72		16

Word	Poem	Stan.	Line
Retire			
The vital fire does suddenly retire	80	7	24
Retirement			
To canvass the retirement of the lark	113		2
Returning			
Returning thanks might offer such array	89		4
Revel			
Never-eldering revel and river of youth	28	18	7
Ran revel in the elder boy	54		9
Revenge			
In bloody letters lessons of earnest of revenge	152		35
Monuments of my earnest records of my revenge	152		36
Reversal			
An age is now since passed since parted with the reversal	45		3
Reviled			
He where the crownals droopd himself reviled	1	10	7
Revisits			
When life revisits me nerve and vein	80	7	9
Revival			
Amongst come-back-again things things with a revival things with a recovery	152		134
Reward			
Remember us in the roads the heaven-haven of the reward	28	34	3
Rhine			
Rhine refused them Thames would ruin them	28	21	3
Rhyme			
Let the chime of a rhyme	28	35	19
And to their feet the narrow bells gave rhyme	107	1	14
Rhymes			
And bright iconium eastwards reach my rhymes	136		6
Ribbed			
Thy ribbed ports o death	115		5
Ribbon			
No time to think Ill knot it on this ribbon	102	1	30
Ribs			
His charnelhouse-grate ribs between	4		10
Breathed round the rack of ribs the scooped flank lank	71		2
Rich			
With golden fillets and rich blazonry	1	7	6
With painting gleamd the rich pilasterd walls	1	10	3
Rich Titians faded in the straying gleam	1	12	3
From easy runnels the rich-pieced land	5		39
Rich beams till death or distance buys them quite	40		8

Word	Poem	Stan.	Line
Rich (cont.)			
To thriftless reave both our rich round world bare	58		12
Skywards rich rich it laps	60		77
Skywards rich rich it laps	60		77
How when this bloom this honeysuckle that rides the air so rich about thee	152		23
When ts light I quenched its rose times one rich rose my hand	152		82
Or they go rich as roseleaves hence that loathsome came hither	152		129
A juice rides rich through bluebells in vine leaves	157		3
Rich-pieced			
From easy runnels the rich-pieced land	5		39
Richard			
But what drew shepherd Richard from his downs	107	2	1
Led Richard with a sweet undoing pain	107	4	17
Sounds reachd him Richard came Sylvester smiled	107	4	24
Richest			
The richest gift St Lawrence ever bore	1	2	6
Richly			
An olive-branch whence richly reek	77		15
Richness			
With richness the racing lambs too have fair their fling	33		8
Rid			
There rid the dragons root out there the sin	150		10
Riddles			
With riddles and is rife	60		7
Ride			
The sumptuous ridge-crest leave to poise and ride	12	2	8
See love I creep and thou on wings dost ride	20		3
And she beat the bank down with her bows and the ride of her keel	28	14	5
Let him ride her pride in his triumph despatch and have done with his doom there	28	27	8
Would brandle adamantine heaven with ride and jar did	48		46
Rider			
Flung rider and wings away though these were none	136		9
Rides			
But it rides time like riding a river	28	6	7
Rides repeated topsyturvy	29	1	15
How when this bloom this honeysuckle that rides the air so rich about thee	152		23
A juice rides rich through bluebells in vine leaves	157		3

Word	Poem	Stan.	Line
Ridge			
An azure ridge or clouds of violet glowd	2		105
The sumptuous ridge-crest leave to poise and ride	12	2	8
Ridge-crest			
The sumptuous ridge-crest leave to poise and ride	12	2	8
Riding			
But it rides time like riding a river	28	6	7
I caught this morning mornings minion king-dom of daylights dauphin dapple-dawn-drawn falcon in his riding	36		1
Riding there did storms not mingle and	41		25
Rife			
Rife in her wrongs more lawless and more lewd	50		8
With riddles and is rife	60		7
Me were I pleading plead nor do I I weary of idle a being but by where wars are rife	66	1	7
Rifled			
The ruins of rifled once a world of art	153		4
Rigging			
One stirred from the rigging to save	28	16	1
Right			
But further down the valley left and right	1	14	4
Flickering with sunny spokes and left and right	2		77
Ah there was a heart right	28	28	1
Why it seemed of course seemed of right it should	34		8
Trench right the tide that ramps against the shore	35		2
How ring right out our sordid turbid time	35		10
Cheeks right rude of feature	41		49
Disremembering dismembering all now heart you round me right	61		7
Now her all in two flocks two folds black white right wrong reckon but reck butmind	61		12
Thy wring-world right foot rock lay a lion-limb against me scan	64		6
Right offspring of your grimy mother earth	77		2
Lock with my right then knot a barken band	80	7	45
And thus I will thrust in my right	80	7	47
Who knelt were for the lords right hand	81		94
Sees the right thing to do and does not act	94		20
Either left either right	138		8
Right rooting in the bare butts wincing navel in the sight of the sun	143		5
But right must seek a side	148		27
Is neither right nor wrong	148		32
What stroke has Caradocs right arm dealt what done	152		32
And right only resolution will his will un-			

Word	Poem	Stan.	Line
Right (cont.)			
wavering	152		75
Righted			
As half she had righted and hoped to rise	41		37
Righteousness			
Doffs all drives full for righteousness	41		55
Rigour			
With barren rigour and a frigid gloom	1	1	8
Rill			
Let the warbled sweetness rill	77		84
Rilly			
Fit for flowers water-pierced and rilly	98	15	6
Rim			
And slendering to his burning rim	3		30
As tumbled over rim in roundy wells	57		2
And fretted clouds with burnishd rim	77		101
The wrought rim of heavens font	77		112
The rim with ruby fringes dight	77		120
Rime			
With bills of rime the brambles shew	3		4
Rimmon			
No house of rimmon may I take	81		140
Rind			
And ripest under rind	49		18
His ruder-rounded rind	148		40
Rinds			
My eyes hold yet the rinds and bright	25		33
Ring			
On mermaids whether that they ring the knells	2		119
Maiden could obey so be a bell to ring of it and	28	30	7
How ring right out our sordid turbid time	35		10
Stones ring like each tucked string tells each hung bells	57		3
Winks away its ring of green	86		2
My signalling tears might ring up Floris now	102	1	7
Trying on the ring	102	1	28
Round a ring around a ring	138		14
Round a ring around a ring	138		14
The immortals of the eternal ring	145		30
Ringed			
The ringed blindworm hard beside	106		4
Where shake shadow is suns-eye-ringed	138		42
Ringing			
Now ringing clarion-clear to whence it rose	2		134
Ringlet			
Or ringlet-race on burling barrow brown	157		12
Ringlet-race			
Or ringlet-race on burling barrow brown	157		12
Rings			
That shapes in half-light his departing rings	19		3
Are still her neck is creased in close-ply rings	99		10

Word	Poem	Stan.	Line
Nor night is blown with flame-rings everywhere	99		18
As struck with rings of sound the close-shut palms	122		10
Rinse			
Through the echoing timber does so rinse and wring	33		4
Rinsed			
Desire not to be rinsed with wine	22		14
Riot			
Bare the condition of a realm at riot	82		4
And the riot of a rout	159		11
Ripest			
And ripest under rind	49		18
Ripples			
A row of ripples in the brook	21		31
Rips			
By him and rips out rockfire homeforth sturdy Dick	70		3
Rise			
Rise match your strength with monstrous Talmai	5		57
And rise and go about my works again	14	1	9
For poor loves failure than his hopeless rise	14	3	7
For the fallen rise and the stricken spring to thee	26		39
Summer ends now now barbarous in beauty the stooks rise	38		1
As half she had righted and hoped to rise	41		37
The roll the rise the carol the creation	76		12
To rise you bid me with the lark	96	6	1
Risen			
Our passion-plunged giant risen	28	32	7
For a rainbow footing it nor he for his bones risen	39		14
While phosphor risen upon the shallowing dark	98	28	3
The sun just risen	98	34	1
And risen sons yet are the childless free	123		2
Rises			
He rises from the flocks of villages	100		5
Might we not think the sweet and daring rises	122		2
Rising			
All things rising all things sizing	42		25
Who rising late had missd her painful way	80		5
With me tis rising in the dark	96	6	2
Risn			
Risn from the deeps to gaze on sun and heaven	2		35
Rival			
Rivalled insight be rival Italy or Greece	44		13
Rivalled			
Rivalled insight be rival Italy or Greece	44		13

Word	Poem	Stan.	Line
boughs	51		2
Roar			
With a flood or a fall low lull-off or all roar	35		3
By many blows and banes but now hears roar	50		6
Roared			
Night roared with the heart-break hearing a heart-broke rabble	28	17	5
Roaring			
His rollrock highroad roaring down	56		2
Rob			
Sleep Floris while I rob you tighten o sleep	102	1	18
Robberys			
Robberys hand is busy to	41		90
Robe			
She wild web wondrous robe	60		38
Robes			
Earth throws winters robes away	24		17
Robin			
Rough-robin or five-lipped campion clear	144		15
Rock			
Rowing I reachd a rock the sea was low	2		1
From flesh-flowers of the rock but more were wreathd	2		63
So those mermaidens crowded to my rock	2		98
Down that dank rock oer which their lush long tresses weep	2		115
White loomd my rock the water gurgling oer	2		142
Who would drink water from a stony rock	5		20
From wastes of rock he brings	7		11
She struck not a reef or a rock	28	14	2
Now times Andromeda on this rock rude	50		1
Thy wring-world right foot rock lay a lionlimb against me scan	64		6
Before that rock my seat he stands	80	7	15
Steel may be melted and rock rent	81		134
The violet moves and copses rock	98	3	4
Water which keeps thy name for not in rock written	152		119
Mortal my mate bearing my rock-a-heart	153		1
Rock-a-heart			
Mortal my mate bearing my rock-a-heart	153		1
Rockdoves			
Or rocks where rockdoves do repair	15		38
Rocket			
Nor rescue only rocket and lightship shone	28	15	6
Rockfire			
By him and rips out rockfire homeforths sturdy Dick	70		3
Rocks			
Down-splinterd rocks crushd cottages drear sight	1	14	5
Or rocks where rockdoves do repair	15		38

Word	Poem	Stan.	Line
Rocks (cont.)			
I cry o rocks and mountain make me room	80	7	5
Some ice that locks the glacier to the rocks	81	7	20
I know of the bored and bitten rocks	120		20
Roots and rocks is danced and dandled all in froth and waterblowballs down	159		7
Built of chancequarried selfquained hoar-husked rocks	159		37
Rocky			
Their rocky lodges then the weather rare	80	4	5
Rod			
Upon the stubborn fleming and the rod	1	5	6
And fear no iron rod	5		12
I took of vine a cross-barred rod or rood	20		8
O at lightning and lashed rod	28	2	2
Crushed why do men then now not reck his rod	31	1	4
Nay in all that toil that coil since seems I kissed the rod	64		10
They kiss the rod with filial submission	97		9
Rode			
Wherein beneath the cornice horsemen rode	1	7	7
To the men in the tops and the tackle rode over the storms brawling	28	19	8
Rods			
A basket broad of woven white rods	98	19	1
The bluebells up whose crystal-ending rods in their natural sods	112		8
Roguish			
Nay roguish ran the vein	54		28
Roll			
The thick stars round him roll	60		99
The roll the rise the carol the creation	76		12
Must see the waters roll	88		5
Must see the green seas roll	88		9
And lapped in shining hair roll to the banks edge then	152		50
Rollcall			
Though as a beechbole firm finds his as at a rollcall rank	71		9
Rolld			
Has lost its savour and is rolld	92		5
Rolled			
The breakers rolled on her beam with ruinous shock	28	14	6
Crushed them or water and drowned them or rolled	28	17	3
Unchrist all rolled in ruin	41		95
Rolling			
Of the rolling level underneath him steady air and striding	36		2
In the quick fragrance of tall rolling pines	84		5

Word	Poem	Stan.	Line
And swarter still the rolling pines should cast	90		5
Rollrock			
His rollrock highroad roaring down	56		2
Rolls			
More brightening her rare-dear Britain as his reign rolls	28	34	6
Rolls across the labouring willows	78		4
A drop of shade rolls over field and flock	98	3	2
Sees what his place is but for us the rolls	126		5
With a south-westerly wind blustering with a tide rolls reels	141		4
Rome			
How then should Gregory a father have gleaned else from swarmed Rome but God to a nation dealt that days dear chance	62		6
Romp			
With the sea-romp over the wreck	28	17	4
Rood			
I took of vine a cross-barred rod or rood	20		8
Left not a rood with curses unimpregnate	102	2	5
Roof			
The steep-up roof at last behind the small	12	2	6
I was under a roof here I was at rest	28	24	3
Under the cloud-festooned roof	77		66
Whatever time this vapourous roof	80	6	1
Roofd			
Where the upper mill-stone roofd his head	6		7
Rook			
Eye-greeting doves bright-counter to the rook	16		3
Cuckoo-echoing bell-swarmed lark-charmed rook-racked river-rounded	44		2
Squander the hell-rook ranks Sally to molest him	48		18
Rook-racked			
Cuckoo-echoing bell-swarmed lark-charmed rook-racked river-rounded	44		2
Rookery			
The rookery never stirred a wing	135		14
Room			
And bleeding saw thus hung from room to room	1	10	8
And bleeding saw thus hung from room to room	1	10	8
But how shall I make me room there	28	27	1
Elsewhere leave comfort root-room let joy size	69		11
Let incense hang across the room	77		19
I cry o rocks and mountain make me room	80	7	5
O grounds of hell make room	115		2
Have all things ready in his room	152		10
Roost			
At roost and rest they shifted not	135		15
Root			
Part found no root upon the flinty road	7		9
Elsewhere leave comfort root-room let joy size	69		11

Word	Poem	Stan.	Line
Root (cont.)			
My root is dry	127		4
There rid the dragons root out there the sin	150		10
Root-room			
Elsewhere leave comfort root-room let joy size	69		11
Rooted			
But we dream we are rooted in earth dust	28	11	5
Close-rooted in the downward-hollowing fields	107	3	15
Rooting			
Right rooting in the bare butts wincing navel in the sight of the sun	143		5
Roots			
For us was lifted from the roots	6		4
Rare patience roots in these and these away	68		5
Mine o thou Lord of life send my roots rain	74	1	13
He drops his bright roots in the waterd sward	100		2
Roots and rocks is danced and dandled all in froth and waterblowballs down	159		7
Like the thing that never knew the earth never off roots	159		27
Rope			
He of all can reeve a rope best there he bides in bliss	63		10
Rope-over thigh knee-nave and barrelled shank	71		3
Rope-over			
Rope-over thigh knee-nave and barrelled shank	71		3
Roped			
But roped with always all the way down from the tall	28	4	6
Ropes			
With a ropes end round the man handy and brave	28	16	3
Delightfully the bright wind boisterous ropes wrestles beats earth bare	72		5
His locks like all a ravel-ropes-end	144		5
Rose			
To an orbd rose which by hot pantings blown	2		20
The zenith melted to a rose of air	2		23
Now ringing clarion-clear to whence it rose	2		134
The rose in a mystery where is it found	27		1
She is the mystery she is that rose	27		23
Is Mary the rose then Mary the tree	27		26
Who can her rose be it could be but one	27		28
When the rose ran in crimsonings down the cross-wood	27		35
For lettering of the lambs fleece ruddying of the rose-flake	28	22	8
Pride rose prince hero of us high-priest	28	34	7
For rose-moles all in stipple upon trout that swim	37		3

Word	Poem	Stan.	Line
Like a wind-perplexed rose	87		4
Even so my thought the rose and grey dis-poses	108		7
If it be a white rose in his hand	109	22	1
Is it a rose I see	109	33	2
Smells that are sweeter-memoried than the rose	119		3
But the lily is past as I say and the rose is not in its prime	128		14
What I did ask then was a circle of rose-red sealing-wax	128		15
They rose at last and forced her from the spot	136		34
Was a rose or failing that	144		14
When ts light I quenched its rose times one rich rose my hand	152		82
When ts light I quenched its rose times one rich rose my hand	152		82
Rose here he feasts lovely all is no more off with down he dings	159		28
Rose-flake			
For lettering of the lambs fleece ruddying of the rose-flake	28	22	8
Rose-moles			
For rose-moles all in stipple upon trout that swim	37		3
Rose-red			
What I did ask then was a circle of rose-red sealing-wax	128		15
Roseleaves			
Or they go rich as roseleaves hence that loathsome came hither	152		129
Roses			
An isle of roses and another near	2		29
Her choice in roses knows by heart	83		22
Of the press of roses	98	19	8
To colour as smooth and fresh as cheeks of roses	108		4
Rosing			
And rosing part on part dispenses green	100		3
Rosy			
Now all things rosy turnd the west had grown	2		19
The waves were rosy-lippd the crimson glare	2		24
With garnet wreaths and blooms of rosy-budded fire	2		26
With lace of rosy weed were chapleted	2		59
Which lightening oer the body rosy-pale	2		72
With rosy foam and pelting blossom and mists	2		90
Of filmy globes and rosy floating cloud	2		97
The rosy isles so that I stole away	2		140
And count the rosy cross with bannd disastrous things	89		9

Word	Poem	Stan.	Line
Rosy-budded			
With garnet wreaths and blooms of rosy-budded fire	2		26
Rosy-lippd			
The waves were rosy-lippd the crimson glare	2		24
Rosy-pale			
Which lightening oer the body rosy-pale	2		72
Rough			
Frost-furred our ivies are and rough	3		3
Those crooked rough-scored chequers may be pieced	11		4
Peace and food cheered me where four rough ways meet	20		12
Rough-robin or five-lipped campion clear	144		15
Rough-robin			
Rough-robin or five-lipped campion clear	144		15
Rough-scored			
Those crooked rough-scored chequers may be pieced	11		4
Roughcast			
Down roughcast down dazzling whitewash wherever an elm arches	72		3
Round			
At corners flank the stretching compass round	1	1	4
This was no classic temple orderd round	1	7	1
An endless round of deadning solitude	1	14	6
Some carried the sea-fan some round the head	2		58
A stealthy wind crept round seeking to blow	2		137
Many trees and flowers round	4		19
Then find in the horizon-round	15		31
Two hundred souls in the round	28	12	4
With a ropes end round the man handy and brave	28	16	3
What is sound natures round	28	35	3
Toil has shed round your head	28	35	15
Raced down decks round messes of mortals	41		39
Now he shoots short up to the round air	41		64
Your round me roaming end and under be my boughs	51		2
To thriftless reave both our rich round world bare	58		12
With mercy round and round	60		35
With mercy round and round	60		35
Round the four fingergaps	60		78
The thick stars round him roll	60		99
Above me round me lie	60		118
Disremembering dismembering all now heart you round me right	61		7
By groping round my comfortless than blind	69		6
With heavens lights high hung round or mother-ground	70		11
Breathed round the rack of ribs the scooped			

Word	Poem	Stan.	Line
flank lank	71		2
Looks from the zenith round the sky	77		108
Allows the sound of bells in Hamlets round	80	4	6
Acceptance round his mistress mouth	83		8
Towards wastes where round the ice-blocks tilt and fret	88		7
And many standing round a waterfall	91		5
Round this unsexing doublet while I set	102	1	4
Most like the tuft of plighted silver round	102	1	72
Most like the plighted tuft of silver round	102	1	73
Like knocking thunder all round Britains welkin	102	2	3
What taught the humanities and the round of arts	107	2	6
Beyond the river all the meadows round	107	4	10
And all round not to be found	138		5
Round a ring around a ring	138		14
Days and days came round about	145		23
And more and more times laces round and round my heart	152		19
And more and more times laces round and round my heart	152		19
Round and round they came and flashed towards heaven	152		60
Round and round they came and flashed towards heaven	152		60
Ranked round the bower	159		51
Rounded			
Cuckoo-echoing bell-swarmed lark-charmed rook-racked river-rounded	44		2
Rounded it thinning skywards by degrees	107	4	4
His ruder-rounded rind	148		40
Roundels			
Why raindrop-roundels looped together	30		27
That still makes counter-roundels in the pond	107	3	5
Rounder			
Rapturous loves greeting of realer of rounder replies	38		8
Rounding			
Work through a coverd copse whose hollow rounding	112		3
Rounds			
Not vault them the million of rounds of thy mercy not reeve even them in	28	12	8
It rounds and rounds despair to drowning	56		8
It rounds and rounds despair to drowning	56		8
Rounds its still-purpling centreings of cloud	98	30	3
Rounds its still-purpling centre-darks of cloud	98	30	6
Roundy			
As tumbled over rim in roundy wells	56		2
Rout			
And the riot of a rout	159		11

Word	Poem	Stan.	Line
Row			
That was her larkspur row so soon	10		22
A row of ripples in the brook	21		31
Now her mallow-row is gone	25		21
Rowels			
Stars like golden rowels	98	25	4
His gilded rowels	98	26	1
Rowing			
Rowing I reachd a rock the sea was low	2		1
Royal			
Hard by a royal palace and a royal tomb	1	1	9
Hard by a royal palace and a royal tomb	1	1	9
To newborn prince and royal corse inanimate	1	4	9
Since trampled Spain by royal discord torn	1	15	1
Royal and all her royals wore	41		33
Just such slips of soldiery Christs royal ration	48		28
This royal manhood tis in me rebellion	102	1	40
Honouring an uncontrolled royal wrathful nature	152		68
Royally			
Kind but royally reclaiming his own	28	33	7
Royals			
Royal and all her royals wore	41		33
Roysterers			
Built thoroughfare heaven-roysterers in gay-gangs they throng they glitter in marches	72		2
Rubies			
Like shiverd rubies dance or sheen of sapphire hail	2		73
Ruby			
The rim with ruby fringes dight	77		120
Ruck			
This ruck and reel which you remark	22		11
Ruck and wrinkle drooping dying deaths worst winding sheets tombs and worms and tumbling to decay	59		12
Rud			
All slumbered whom our rud red tiles	135		1
Ruddied			
In the ruddied county of the days upbringing	98	28	4
Ruddying			
For lettering of the lambs fleece ruddying of the rose-flake	28	22	8
Rude			
By conqurors rude of honor and not all	1	8	4
Fell on the palace and the lust of rabble rude	1	14	9
Cheeks right rude of feature	41		49
Now times Andromeda on this rock rude	50		1
But ah but o thou terrible why wouldst thou rude on me	64		5

Word	Poem	Stan.	Line
Ruder			
Sexing and ranking with our ruder files	102	1	66
Enrolld and sexing with our ruder files	102	1	67
Enrolld and sexed with our ruder files	102	1	68
His ruder-rounded rind	148		40
Ruder-Rounded			
His ruder-rounded rind	148		40
Rudred			
Flame-rash rudred	138		23
Rueful			
And frightful a nightfall folded rueful a day	28	15	5
Ruin			
Rhine refused them Thames would ruin them	28	21	3
Unchrist all rolled in ruin	41		95
Ruinous			
And been in their ruinous reigns oppressed	26		10
The breakers rolled on her beam with ruinous shock	28	14	6
Of ruinous shrine no hand or worse	41		89
Ruinous heart-beat wandering death	81		53
Ruins			
Our ruins of wrecked past purpose there she basks	68		7
And wreck in ruins of his mother	145		41
The ruins of rifled once a world of art	153		4
Rule			
At tranquil turns by natures rule	30		14
Ruler			
To be a judge and ruler over us	5		2
Run			
The waxen colours weep and run	3		29
And rivers run where all was dry	8		2
I mark the tower swallows run	15		28
While ages and while aeons run	23		20
And the inboard seas run swirling and hawling	28	19	3
Five and twenty years have run	28	35	5
Run all your race o brace sterner that strain	46		14
They breathe not who are late to run	81		148
To not ungentle death now forth I run	103		19
They waste they wither worse they as they run	150		3
Rung			
High there how he rung upon the rein of a wimpling wing	36		3
There the hall rung	54		33
Runnel			
A freezing runnel sobs and dwarfs	80	3	7
Runnels			
From easy runnels the rich-pieced land	5		39
Running			
No running in the river-bed	81		161
Epistles while the running pastoral bleats	107	4	22
Came running over the lea	109	17	4

Word	Poem	Stan.	Line
Running (cont.)			
Rupture running sores what more in brief in burden	152		114
Runs			
The clogged brook runs with choking sound	3		9
Runs his fingers through the wheat	98	1	2
A brittle sheen runs upward like a cliff	98	6	2
As water moulded to the duct it runs in	101		4
Drops the fruit out the duct runs dry or breaks	101		10
Rupture			
Rupture running sores what more in brief in burden	152		114
Rural			
Rural scene a rural scene	43		23
Rural scene a rural scene	43		23
Sweet especial rural scene	43		24
Rural rural keeping folk flocks and flowers	44		8
Rural rural keeping folk flocks and flowers	44		8
Rush			
Legates might rush zeal-rampant fiery	1	5	5
The descending blue that blue is all in a rush	33		7
The hanging snows rush down and bare	80	4	4
Rushy			
While rushy rains shall fall or brooks shall fleet from fountains	152		107
Rust			
Blades of Milan in circles rangd grew rust	1	12	8
Rustle			
When wholesome spirits rustle about	77		27
Rutpeel			
Of yestertempests creases in pool and rutpeel parches	72		6
S			
Sure s bed now low be it lustily he his low lot feel	70		5
In him all quail to the wallowing o the plough s cheek crimsons curls	71		13
Sable			
And that such a sable track	4		21
Sack			
Of silk-sack clouds has wilder wilful-wavier	38		3
Sackcloth			
With oil of gladness for sackcloth and frieze	11		10
Sacred			
Since sacred fountains to the sun	28	35	6
Not mood in him nor meaning proud fire or sacred fear	45		5
O now well work that sealing sacred ointment	48		33
Than sewers with sacred oils mankind that mob comes	152		104
Enough now since the sacred matter that I			

Word	Poem	Stan.	Line
mean	159		43
Sacrifice			
Christ our sacrifice is made	6		10
Talks of self-sacrifice yet cant forgive	94		22
Sacrificed			
And the word of it sacrificed	28	22	4
Sad			
Timed her sad visions with his wreck	21		56
Dancers for sad footsteps slow	24		22
Yet shed what tears sad truelove should	41		107
Down no waving off of these most mournful messengers still messengers sad and stealing messengers of grey	59		4
Me live to my sad self hereafter kind	69		2
Dry were her sad eyes that would fain have streamd	80		2
White-faced as one in sad assay to fly	80		8
And after that sad sorrow	110		4
Saddening			
Think this my birthday falls in saddening time of year	128		9
Sadness			
And a sweet sadness dwelt on everyone	2		117
I knew not why but know that sadness dwells	2		118
I know the sadness but the cause know not	2		125
With fickle spots of sadness accessories	125		47
Safe			
With perilous o no nor yet plod safe shod sound	70		14
Circled the safe flanks of the bulky hills	125		10
Said			
Death said I what do you here	4		12
Although the letter said	7		1
You have your wish enter these walls one said	20		17
You know you said the nightingale	21		22
With the sweetest air that said still plied and pressed	47		3
Twas said of none but all men knew	81		91
They are the goats who stand said I	81		95
I inly said but could not move	81		115
Something I said I swooned and fell	81		118
No let that go I have said goodnight to shame	102	1	45
And said I like this it is almost isled	107	4	25
When are you home my love she said	109	2	1
You may look for me home my love he said	109	2	3
Heaven make the time be short she said	109	3	1
Heaven make it sweet to you she said	109	3	3
And what is your true name she said	109	4	1
How shall I call my love she said	109	4	3
O I am the kings son he said	109	5	1
Said who then is this lowly woman	109	11	3
Said it was not meet the king should wed	109	12	3

Word	Poem	Stan.	Line
And cast by conscience out spendsavour salt	46		14
Theres comfort then theres salt	54		39
Quartz-fret or sparks of salt	60		101
I found the ways were sown with salt	81		155
I dare not taste the thickening salt	120		26
O now while skies are blue now while seas are salt	152		106
Salute			
Salute thee mother the maid-months queen	26		24
Salvation			
See the salvation of the lord	8		9
In God who was her salvation	42		48
Same			
But the spring-tide passd the same	4		24
And I have only set the same to pen	12	2	14
The heart guesses easily is it the same	27		21
Flesh falls within sight of us we though our flower the same	28	11	6
Abel is Cains brother and breasts they have sucked the same	28	20	8
Sorrows springs are the same	55		11
Each mortal thing does one thing and the same	57		5
As if with air the same	60		36
Within her wears bears cares and combs the same	76		6
See one bow each yet not the same to all	91		6
And if you write at last it never can be the same	128		3
Sanctuary			
Along the sanctuary side	22		20
Sand			
Sickend and thickend by the glare and sand	5		19
Must you be gorged with proof did ever sand	5		41
Fresh brooks to salt sand-teasing waters shoaly	16		4
But the combs of a smother of sand night drew her	28	14	3
They have happd him with the sand and stone	109	15	1
Sand-teasing			
Fresh brooks to salt sand-teasing waters shoaly	16		4
Sandal			
Didst fettle for the great grey drayhorse his bright and battering sandal	53		14
And I esteemd the sandal good	81		83
Sandalled			
That dandled a sandalled	43		6
Sandblind			
Are you sandblind slabs of water many a mile	5		35
Sandfield			
After the sandfield and the unveined glare	5		29

Word	Poem	Stan.	Line
Sands			
In hot sands perilous	5		4
And mazy sands all water-wattled	30		23
Sandy			
That his fast-flowing hours with sandy silt	136		1
Sang			
Would it were summer-time anon she sang	111		12
Sanguine			
I betterd all our path with sanguine eyes	125		17
Sank			
Shadow that swam or sank	43		7
That onewhere curded onewhere sucked or sank	71		7
Soared or sank	71		8
Sap			
Has not a charter that its sap shall last	14	1	4
So late there is no force in sap or blood	105		11
My sap is sealed	127		3
Sappd			
Handle the fig suck the full-sappd vine-shoot	5		38
Sapphire			
And was as tho some sapphire molten-blue	2		45
Like shiverd rubies dance or sheen of sapphire hail	2		73
Yet such a sapphire-shot	60		79
From a haze of sapphire light	77		18
Where liquid heaven sapphire-pale	77		99
Sapphire jacinth chrysolite	77		119
The sapphire pools are smit with white	78		7
Sapphire-pale			
Where liquid heaven sapphire-pale	77		99
Sapphire-shot			
Yet such a sapphire-shot	60		79
Sapricious			
Proconsul is Sapricius near	25		41
Sard			
Hither bring pearl opal sard	24		3
Sash			
The ear in milk lush the sash	138		20
Sat			
He sat and wrought his outline on a cloud	107	1	10
Lowly Alice sat in her bower	109	16	1
Like me sat sighing by a sycamore-tree	111		14
The earnest-hearted maiden sat and heard	136		32
Satin			
The satin-purfled smooth to foam and spread	2		79
Satin-purfled			
The satin-purfled smooth to foam and spread	2		79
Saturday			
On Saturday sailed from Bremen	28	12	1
Saturn			
With such a seconding nor Saturn took	14	2	9
Bad Saturn with a swart aspect	83		18

Word	Poem	Stan.	Line
To single Saturn last and solitary	103		15
Save			
Save by two stars more crowding lights arise	2		32
And save by darting accidents forget	14	1	10
No better serves me now save best no other	16		13
Save Christ to Christ I look on Christ I call	16		14
One stirred from the rigging to save	28	16	1
Save my hero o hero savest	41		111
Save where the unvexed west	77		97
Save me and you were standing near	81		103
All quests save the recital of their greatness	104		3
The time save when her tears which still descend	111		5
Save in the body of the rains	130		20
Saved			
The world was saved by virgins made the mark	136		30
Saves			
A schooner sights with another and saves	41		69
Savest			
Save my hero o hero savest	41		111
Saviour			
Down all that glory in the heavens to glean our Saviour	38		6
Be Christ our Saviour still	60		54
Saviours			
But even our saviours and our blood	6		32
Savour			
Has lost its savour and is rolld	92		5
Saw			
And bleeding saw thus hung from room to room	1	10	8
Then saw I sudden from the waters break	2		74
I never saw her so divine	3		19
Then I saw that he had bound	4		18
And soon I saw it shewing new	21		5
When was the summer that saw the bud blow	27		15
They say who saw one sea-corpse cold	41		72
This night what sights you heart saw ways you went	67		3
And saw the men before the flood	93	1	2
Met a new shower and saw the rainbow fill	107	3	10
He saw his brothers three	109	7	2
And there she never saw the king	109	24	3
But saw his brothers three	109	24	4
I never saw those fields whereon their best	119		11
I saw the stars like flash of fire	135		8
Several times I saw them thrice or four times turning	152		59
Say			
Who is this Moses who made him we say	5		1
Who say that had I known I had approved thee	13		12
Then next I hungered love when here they say	20		9

Word	Poem	Stan.	Line
Say (cont.)			
I did say yes	28	2	1
He thought he heard say	41		50
They say who saw one sea-corpse cold	41		72
That a starlight-wender of ours would say	41		100
Much had much to say	42		35
Came I say this day to it to a first communion	48		8
I say more the just man justices	57		9
I say that we are wound	60		34
With witness I speak this but where I say	67		5
Honour is flashed off exploit so we say	73		1
But yet they say Christ comes at the last day	80	1	6
And all in one say crucify	80	7	14
Say oer it hangs a water-cloud	81		56
Who say that angels in your ear	81		122
Hes wedded to his theory they say	97		1
On seeing her children say goodnight to their father	97		7
Did I say but lately	102	1	32
Say beauty lies but in the meet of lines	102	3	21
I heard her say poor poor afflicted soul	111		11
Yet what you are the world would say remain	125		28
Say you do	125		33
Of which I say there is no joy in them	125		53
To say I go because Castara goes	125		60
Yet Id not say it is her face alone	125		61
But the lily is past as I say and the rose is not in its prime	128		14
For a letter comes at last shall I say before Christmas is come	128		19
She high at the housetop sitting as they say	136		13
Say it is ashboughs whether on a December day and furled	149	1	4
In all her body I say no place was like her eyes	152		56
Saying			
Beyond saying sweet past telling of tongue	28	9	5
Saying this was yours with her but new one worse	153		10
Says			
He says his science helps him not to look	14	2	13
Our law says love what are loves worthiest were all known	62		8
Says get you get you a lady to wed	109	9	1
Says are you not Lord Williams love	109	18	3
Which says at least then go while all is fresh	125		64
Says go on then I go on	138		35
But down drop if it says stop	138		37
Scaffold			
But man we scaffold of score brittle bones	75		5

Word	Poem	Stan.	Line
Scarves			
In scarves of silky shot and shine	3		21
Scatter			
And fail or scatter all away	18		2
If a wuthering of his palmy snow-pinions scatter a colossal smile	45		13
Scene			
The sweet especial scene	43		22
Rural scene a rural scene	43		23
Rural scene a rural scene	43		23
Sweet especial rural scene	43		24
Scented			
His lusty hands in gusts of scented wind	2		88
Sceptic			
The sceptic disappointment and the loss	14	3	12
School			
Away from counter court or school	30		2
Away from counter court or school	30		38
Schooled			
More pangs will schooled at forepangs wilder wring	65		2
Schooling			
The vault and scope and schooling	49		15
Schools			
She schools the flighty pupils of her eyes	82		1
Schooner			
A schooner sights with another and saves	41		69
Science			
He says his science helps him not to look	14	2	13
And other science all gone out of date	19		11
Scions			
With lissome scions sweet scions	52		3
With lissome scions sweet scions	52		3
Scoop			
Scoop you from teeming filth some sickly hovel	77		6
Scooped			
Breathed round the rack of ribs the scooped flank lank	71		2
Scoops			
Off trundled timber and scoops of the hillside ground hollow hollow hollow ground	146		4
Scope			
The vault and scope and schooling	49		15
But since I have no scope for benefits	102	1	55
He swept what scope he was	148		15
Score			
His rash-fresh re-winded new-skeined score	35		6
But man we scaffold of score brittle bones	75		5
Scored			
Those crooked rough-scored chequers may be pieced	11		4

Word	Poem	Stan.	Line
Scores			
But he scores it in scarlet himself on his own bespoken	28	22	5
Scorning			
Sweet soul not scorning honest sweat	139		5
Scour			
I can scour thee fresh burnish thee sheathe thee in thy dark lair these drops	152		46
Scourge			
Whence with the scourge of ready piety	1	5	4
The lost are like this and their scourge to be	67		13
Scourged			
Scourged upon the threshing-floor	6		6
Screamd			
Ranters screamd rank rebellion this should be	1	5	2
Screen			
The screen of my captivity	80	6	2
Scroll			
Storm flakes were scroll-leaved flowers lily showers sweet heaven was astrew inthem	28	21	8
Scroll-leaved			
Storm flakes were scroll-leaved flowers lily showers sweet heaven was astrew inthem	28	21	8
Scrolled			
Firm accents strike her fine and scrolled ear	136		21
Fairyland silk-beech scrolled ash packed sycamore wild wychelm hornbeam fretty overstood	159		24
Sculls			
Come swing the sculls on Penmaen pool	30		8
Sculpturd			
The sculpturd image of such faith would be	1	3	7
Scutcheon			
Whose braggart scutcheon whose complaisant crest	98	32	1
Scythe			
The sour scythe cringe and the blear share come	28	11	8
Scythes			
Their harness beams like scythes in morning grass	104		6
Sea			
Rowing I reachd a rock the sea was low	2		1
Some carried the sea-fan some round the head	2		58
Slim-pointed sea-gull plumes and droop behind	2		80
Then like a flock of sea-fowl mounting higher	2		82
Sun-flushd until it seemd their father sea	2		100
Airwards disturbd and the scarce troubled sea	2		110
To know the dusk depths of the ponderous sea	2		122
A piteous siren sweetness on the sea	2		127
And out of the swing of the sea	9		8

Word	Poem	Stan.	Line
Sea (cont.)			
She listened how the sea-gust shook	21		52
Worlds strand sway of the sea	28	1	3
And the sea flint-flake black-backed in the regular blow	28	13	5
With the sea-romp over the wreck	28	17	4
Lend him a lift from the sea-swill	41		63
They say who saw one sea-corpse cold	41		72
And watches change upon the sea	77		32
Around it balances the level sea	98	4	2
Before he went to sea	109	1	4
When are you home from sea	109	2	2
When he is over the sea	109	4	4
When I come home from sea	109	5	4
Come with you from over the sea	109	7	4
Come with me from over the sea	109	8	2
That was beside the sea	109	15	2
Or come from over the sea	109	31	4
Nor yet from over the sea	109	32	2
No rains shall fresh the flats of sea	114		13
Not so far outward in the sea	120		21
The sea took pity it interposed with doom	158		1
Sea-corpse			
They say who saw one sea-corpse cold	41		72
Sea-fan			
Some carried the sea-fan some round the head	2		58
Sea-fowl			
Then like a flock of sea-fowl mounting higher	2		82
Sea-gull			
Slim-pointed sea-gull plumes and droop behind	2		80
Sea-gust			
She listened how the sea-gust shook	21		52
Sea-romp			
With the sea-romp over the wreck	28	17	4
Sea-swill			
Lend him a lift from the sea-swill	41		63
Seabeach			
The thunder-purple seabeach plumed purple-of-thunder	45		12
Seal			
And seal of his seraph-arrival and these thy daughters	28	23	5
Resign them sign them seal them send them motion them with breath	59		16
To what serves mortal beauty dangerous does set dancing blood the o-seal-that-so feature flung prouder form	62		1
To what serves mortal beauty dangerous does set dancing blood the o-seal-that-so feature flung prouder form	62		1
Sealed			
Are sisterly sealed in wild waters	28	23	7

Word	Poem	Stan.	Line
My sap is sealed	127		3
Sealing			
O now well work that sealing sacred ointment	48		33
What I did ask then was a circle of rose-red sealing-wax	128		15
Sealing-wax			
What I did ask then was a circle or rose-red sealing-wax	128		15
Seals			
And seals of red carnation which had each	98	12	4
And seals of live carnation which had each	98	12	5
And seals of vive carnation which had each	98	12	6
Seamanship			
Leagues leagues of seamanship	41		81
Seamark			
Where lies your landmark seamark or souls star	157		19
Seamen			
Of seamen whelmd in chasms of the mid-main	2		120
Take settler and seamen tell men with women	28	12	3
She had come from a cruise training seamen	41		12
Sear			
That struggling should not sear him a gift should cheer him	142		8
Search			
How shall I search who never sought	81		173
And search me through	127		17
Searching			
That dares to cast its searching sight	23		29
Seared			
And all is seared with trade bleared smeared with toil	31	1	6
Seas			
And the inboard seas run swirling and hawling	28	19	3
Burden in winds burly and beat of endragoned seas	28	26	16
Takes to the seas and snows	41		58
Purple eyes and seas of liquid leaves all day	68		8
And keeps the breeze and clears the seas	83		13
Where the seas set	88		6
Must see the green seas roll	88		9
Of crumbling fore-foundering thundering all-surfy seas in seen	141		5
O now while skies are blue now while seas are salt	152		106
But from beyond seas Erin France and Flanders everywhere	152		125
Season			
At this spring season of the year	4		13
What was its season then how long ago	27		14
Dated due to season	42		4
On such a season of the day and year	107	1	4

Word	Poem	Stan.	Line
Seasons			
Into all seasons though no winter cast	14	1	5
Leaves spent new seasons alterd sky	15		2
Had called the seasons changeful moods	23		23
Seat			
Sets up a shadow in thy seat	23		16
Before that rock my seat he stands	80	7	15
Second			
Second this fiery strain not always o no no	152		78
Seconding			
With such a seconding nor Saturn took	14	2	9
Secret			
You striped in secret with breath-taking whips	11		3
And its place is a secret and shut in the skies	27		4
Secrets			
Some of the secrets I would know	77		40
See			
Whence oft I watch but see those mermaids now no more	2		143
I see long reefs of violets	3		25
See the salvation of the lord	8		9
Sphered so fast sweet soul we see	10		23
Where art thou friend whom I shall never see	13		1
You see that I have come to passions end	14	3	1
I see the crowning of their towers	15		7
I see the city pigeons veer	15		27
Knowing them well I can but see the fall	16		10
See how spring opens with disabling cold	17		1
See love I creep and thou on wings dost ride	20		3
To see thee I must see thee to love love	20		14
To see thee I must see thee to love love	20		14
We see the glories of the earth	23		7
See my lilies lilies none	25		7
Sphered so fast sweet soul we see	25		23
Shrewsbury may see others keep	28	35	10
But whats to see in stormy weather	29	1	25
Let me though see no more of him and not disappointment	48		36
See not a hair is not an eyelash not the least lash lost every hair	59		20
Through her we may see him	60		110
Than Purcell tune lets tread to see it does this keeps warm	62		2
Selfyeast of spirit a dull dough sours I see	67		12
At God knows when to God knows what whose smiles not wrung see you unforeseen times rather as skies	69		12
See his wind-lilylocks-laced	71		15
Sir life upon thy cause see banks and brakes	74	1	8
Then may I upwards gaze and see	77		113
Sometimes I see the summit stake	80	4	1
But then I make an eager shift to see	80	6	5

Word	Poem	Stan.	Line
But you so sphered see no more	81		39
You see but with a holier mind	81		40
Must see the eagles bulk renderd in mists	88		3
Must see the waters roll	88		5
Must see the green seas roll	88		9
See one bow each yet not the same to all	91		6
And cannot see at all with others eyes	94		26
Most rarely see unselfishness	96	1	2
We live to see	98	35	1
See on one hand	100		1
Now let me see you you large princely hand	102	1	46
They plough our vales you see the unsteady flare	104		9
The shining slates and houses come and see	107	3	7
Because he should not see	109	13	2
Thy father thou shalt see	109	16	4
And is so fair to see	109	20	4
And she came out to see	109	24	2
Her true love she might see	109	30	4
Is it a rose I see	109	33	2
Shall see the azure turn expressionless	117		4
I see her riving fingers tear	120		5
Have told me I am fair to see	124		24
True madam I am sorry now to see	125		16
But late is better than never you see you have managed so	128		17
For all to see and to admire	131		4
Not of all my eyes see wandering on the world	149	1	1
Work which to see scarce so much as begun	150		7
Spare thou me since I see	155		15
His looks the souls own letters see beyond	157		15
To have havoc-pocked so see the hung-heavenward boughs	157		32
Seed			
That seed which the good sower once did sow	17		7
And tho the silver seed that flits	83		11
Seeing			
That like this sleek and seeing ball	43		14
In scarlet or somewhere of some day seeing	48		38
This seeing the sick endears them to us us too it endears	53		9
Only not within seeing of the sun	59		3
Yes why do we all seeing of a soldier bless him bless	63		1
Now and seeing somewhere some man do all that man can do	63		11
What if my subject seeing this resent	94		5
On seeing her children say goodnight to their father	97		7
On my being and as seeing	155		7

Word	Poem	Stan.	Line
Seek			
Where seek thee with unsandalled feet	23		18
Seek Gods house in happy throng	24		25
Then I seek out the shadow of stones	80	3	1
But right must seek a side	148		27
Seeking			
A stealthy wind crept round seeking to blow	2		137
Seem			
To seem the stranger lies my lot my life	66	1	1
Well I know not but all things seem to-night	102	1	10
They seem to fold the hills with golden capes	104		11
They seem to press and droop and stare	135		20
Seemd			
Fair beds they seemd of water-lily flakes	2		13
Sun-flushd until it seemd their father sea	2		100
It seemd an evening in the spring	4		2
He seemd a dismal mirky stamp	4		8
It seemd so hard and dismal thing	4		31
She stood before a light not hers and seemd	80		3
I dreamd my counterpart it seemd	81		86
Some knelt some stood I seemd to feel	81		93
But all the while it seemd to me	81		112
His sheep seemd to come from it as they stept	107	1	11
Seemed			
Why it seemed of course seemed of right it should	34		8
Why it seemed of course seemed of right it should	34		8
They seemed to press and stare	98	29	2
Of virtue and vice but most it seemed his sense	136		27
His powers seemed free to play	148		14
Seeming			
Unclean and seeming unforgiven	18		3
But for souls sunk in seeming	41		117
Then sweetest seems the seeming bride	120		18
Seems			
It seems for grandeur barren left and dull	1	15	8
Then sweetest seems the houseless shore	15		35
Our prayer seems lost in desert ways	23		5
Seems by a divine doom channelled nor do I cry	48		41
His thoughts on her forsaken that she seems	50		11
Where whatevers prized and passes of us everything thats fresh and fast flying of us seems to us sweet of us and swiftly away with done away with undone	59		8
Nay in all that toil that coil since seems I kissed the rod	64		10
While the upgazing country seems	77		125
Things that she likes seems often to despise	94		17

Word	Poem	Stan.	Line
Then she seems sweet who seems his bride	120		16
Then she seems sweet who seems his bride	120		16
She sour who seems the slighted nix	120		17
Then sweetest seems the seeming bride	120		18
At highest when he seems to brush the clouds	122		4
Wiped I am sure this was it seems not well for still	152		43
Seen			
On the flowers that were seen	4		9
Just seen may be to many unknown men	12	2	12
The gladdest thing that our eyes have seen	26		18
It is even seen times something server	41		52
Scarce worth discovery in some corner seen	103		2
Past the past no more be seen	129		2
Told of the wonders he had seen	131		6
Of crumbling fore-foundering thundering all-surfy seas in seen	141		5
My heart where have we been what have we seen my mind	152		31
What have we seen her head sheared from her shoulders fall	152		49
Sees			
Soft when she sees her infant start	23		51
Blinds her but she that weather sees one thing one	28	19	5
Mary sees sympathising	42		26
When his mellow smile he sees	77		105
Sees the right thing to do and does not act	94		20
He sees her o but he must miss	120		9
Sees what his place is but for us the rolls	126		5
So she one sees that here and there	145		11
Betweenwhiles but she sees herself not him	151		12
Sees the bevy of them how the boys	159		16
That he hies to a pool neighbouring sees it is the best	159		22
Seldom			
That neer need hunger Tom Tom seldom sick	70		6
Seldomer			
Seldomer heartsore that treads through prick-proof thick	70		7
Self			
Of own of abrupt self there so thrusts on so throngs the ear	45		8
To its own fine function wild and self-instressed	47		7
Hies headstrong to its wellbeing of a self-wise self-will	48		24
Hies headstrong to its wellbeing of a self-wise self-will	48		24
Give beauty back beauty beauty beauty back to God beautys self and beautys giver	59		19
The sweet alms self is her	60		43

Word	Poem	Stan.	Line
Self (cont.)			
New self and nobler me	60		69
Astray or aswarm all throughther in throngs self in self steeped and pashed quite	61		6
Astray or aswarm all throughther in throngs self in self steeped and pashed quite	61		6
Worlds loveliest mens selves self flashes off frame and face	62		9
Me live to my sad self hereafter kind	69		2
Soul self come poor jackself I do advise	69		9
And like a self-outwitted blast	81		74
As a self-embraced sweet thought	85		3
As a self-caressd sweet thought	85		4
Talks of self-sacrifice yet cant forgive	94		22
Though self-made bands at last may true love bind	102	3	19
That this is true of tis Castaras self	125		62
Self-sentenced still	127		14
From the self that I have been	129		5
Is corpse now cannot change my other self this soul	152		95
Lifes quick this kind this keen self-feeling	152		96
The selfless self of self most strange most still	157		27
The selfless self of self most strange most still	157		27
Self-caressd			
As a self-caressd sweet thought	85		4
Self-embraced			
As a self-embraced sweet thought	85		3
Self-feeling			
Lifes quick this kind this keen self-feeling	152		96
Self-instressed			
To its own fine function wild and self-instressed	47		7
Self-made			
Though self-made bands at last may true love bind	102	3	19
Self-outwitted			
And like a self-outwitted blast	81		74
Self-sacrifice			
Talks of self-sacrifice yet cant forgive	94		22
Self-sentenced			
Self-sentenced still	127		14
Self-will			
Hies headstrong to its wellbeing of a self-wise self-will	48		24
Self-wise			
Hies headstrong to its wellbeing of a self-wise self-will	48		24
Selfbent			
To his own selfbent so bound so tied to his turn	58		11

Word	Poem	Stan.	Line
Selfdisposal			
Reason selfdisposal choice of better or worse way	152		94
Selfish			
Is slightly selfish in her inmost soul	94		28
Selfless			
The selfless self of self most strange most still	157		27
Selfquained			
Built of chancequarried selfquained hoar-husked rocks	159		37
Selfsame			
To hold me quite fixed in the selfsame plight	80	7	46
Selfstrung			
Where selfwrung selfstrung sheathe-and shelterless thoughts against thoughts in groans grind	61		14
Selfwrung			
Where selfwrung selfstrung sheathe-and shelterless thoughts against thoughts in groans grind	61		14
Selfyeast			
Selfyeast of spirit a dull dough sours I see	67		12
Selvaggia			
Selvaggia Orinda and Adela and the rest	125		44
Selved			
But quench her bonniest dearest to her clearest-selved spark	72		10
Selves			
Selves goes itself myself it speaks and spells	57		7
Worlds lovliest mens selves self flashes off frame and face	62		9
As I am mine their sweating selves but worse	67		14
Send			
But now I am so tired I soon shall send	14	3	8
What relish shall the censers send	22		19
Resign them sign them seal them send them motion them with breath	59		16
Mine o thou Lord of life send my roots rain	74	1	13
For he whom I send forth to crucify	80	7	31
I can send up an Esaus cry	81		126
Spend me or end me what God shall send me	156		13
Sendings			
There and your sweetest sendings ah divine	48		13
Sends			
Heaven comfort sends but harry it away	89		5
Sense			
Oh till thou givest that sense beyond	23		43
His lips moved fast in sense too thick	81		100
With twice as fine a sense to apprehend them	102	1	12
And brought the sense of gentle fellowship	107	2	4
So takes the sister sense can find no mark	113		4

Word	Poem	Stan.	Line
Sense (cont.)			
Of virtue and vice but most it seemed his sense	136		27
Suck any sense from that who can	147		3
Goes marching thro my mind what sense is this it has none	152		28
Senses			
Five like the senses and members of men	27		39
At once the senses give the music back	113		10
Sensitive			
About herself she is most sensitive	94		21
Of the wood-sorrel and all things sensitive	122		11
As the wood-sorrel and all things sensitive	122		14
Sensual			
Hence sensual gross desires	77		1
Sent			
It is the shut the curfew sent	22		6
Flake-doves sent floating forth at a farmyard scare	30	1	7
Is cries countless cries like dead letters sent	67		7
Yet there came one who sent his flock before him	107	1	7
And with the last post over I knew no letter was sent	128		2
Sentence			
Of the outward sentence low lays him listed to a heresy here	45		4
Sentenced			
Self-sentenced still	127		14
Sepulchre			
Before the sepulchre there stood a gate	1	4	6
Sequence			
And every praised sequence of sweet strings	19		7
Sequences			
Or careful-spaced sequences of sound	102	3	2
In careful-spaced sequences of sound	102	3	22
Sequins			
The sky minted into golden sequins	98	25	1
Seraph			
And seal of his seraph-arrival and these thy daughters	28	23	5
The seraph brows of Galahad	77		42
Seraph-arrival			
And seal of his seraph-arrival and these thy daughters	28	23	5
Serfdom			
Love by prenatal serfdom still confined	102	3	15
Serged			
Breathe easter now you serged fellowships	11		7
Sermons			
Theyre out of date lent sermons all the year	96	5	2

Word	Poem	Stan.	Line
Serve			
That here will serve me for comparison	14	3	11
And do serve God to serve to	48		27
And do serve God to serve to	48		27
Served			
Served by messenger	25		28
Mark Christ our king he knows war served this soldiering through	63		9
You cried but I have served thee well	81		107
Server			
It is even seen times something server	41		52
Serves			
No better serves me now save best no other	16		13
To what serves mortal beauty dangerous does set dancing blood the o-seal-that-so feature flung prouder form	62		1
Wretch under a comfort serves in a whirl-wind all	65		11
Ask whom he serves or not	148		23
Serves and what side he takes	148		24
Service			
They shrive themselves and cry good service to our God	1	5	9
His sinew-service where do	71		11
Servingman			
And she was ware of a servingman	109	17	3
O what will you now good servingman	109	18	1
Set			
Is set upon your boughs below	10		10
Not set because their buds not spring	10		11
And I have only set the same to pen	12	2	14
Is set in any orchard no	25		10
Not set because their buds not spring	25		11
Wind-beat whitebeam airy abeles set on a flare	32	1	6
To what serves mortal beauty dangerous does set dancing blood the o-seal-that-so feature flung prouder form	62		1
Is not some little Bela set	81		142
Where the seas set	88		6
Where waters set	88		10
Round this unsexing doublet while I set	102	1	4
Then he set sail in a golden ship	109	6	3
Or ever he set his foot to the land	109	7	1
Ere you set sail the king was dead	109	9	3
Sets			
Sets up a shadow in thy seat	23		16
When tis the confidante that sets the task	94		2
Setting			
And it was at the setting of the day	2		6
Settle			
Will crisp itself or settle and spin	145		10

Word	Poem	Stan.	Line
Settler			
Take settler and seamen tell men with women	28	12	3
Seven			
I gazed unhinderd mermaids six or seven	2		34
And Charless Wain the wondrous seven	30	1	17
The seven or seven times seven	60		87
The seven or seven times seven	60		87
The seven or seven times seven	60		87
Lit with exquisite tints seven	77		109
A turn of seven notes or five	81		7
Five notes or seven late and few	81		23
I think it is seven days she said	109	16	3
And seven ears crown the lodged corn	114		6
Sevenfold			
All a sevenfold-single gem	77		116
Sevenfold-single			
All a sevenfold-single gem	77		116
Seventeenth			
Though they took till the seventeenth of next October to read	128		8
Seventy			
And seventy palms there stand	5		24
Several			
My several moans come distant in their tones	80	3	3
In the first signals of the several drops	84		3
Several times I saw them thrice or four times turning	152		59
Severance			
Then severance and sorrow	110		8
Severe			
Gods counsel columnar-severe	145		1
Sew			
The last thing Margarets fingers sew	145		13
Sewers			
Than sewers with sacred oils mankind that mob comes	152		104
Sex			
Our sex should be born in April perhaps or the lily-time	128		13
Sexed			
Enrolld and sexed with our ruder files	102	1	68
Sexing			
Sexing and ranking with our ruder files	102	1	66
Enrolld and sexing with our ruder files	102	1	67
Shade			
Ye weary come into the shade	6		26
A drop of shade rolls over field and flock	98	3	2
Shades			
More sweetly shades her stolen hair	120		7
Has shades is nowhere none	148		26
Shadow			
Sets up a shadow in thy seat	23		16
Shadow that swam or sank	43		7

Word	Poem	Stan.	Line
Each shape and shadow shows	60		85
Streaks of shadow thistled leas	77		137
Then I seek out the shadow of stones	80	3	1
Spannd with shadow every one	98	8	3
In hollows of her form the shadow clings	99		8
Making the shadow sweeter a spiritual grace	107	4	15
Where shake shadow is suns-eye-ringed	138		42
Shadowiest			
There sweetest freshest shadowiest	159		23
Shadowtackle			
Shivelights and shoadowtackle in long lashes lace lance and pair	72		4
Shafts			
Broad-fluted nor with shafts acanthus-crownd	1	7	3
With parallel shafts as upward-parted ashes	107	4	5
Shake			
Far off a nereid company and shake	2		75
Shall shake her fruit as Libanus	6		28
His fire the sun would shake	60		96
Shake the balanced daffodils	98	7	2
Shake and unset your morticed metaphors	101		8
Where shake shadow is suns-eye-ringed	138		42
Shaken			
Shew brighter shaken in Penmaen pool	30		20
The shaken plumage of my spirits wings	77		10
Shakes			
With fretty Chervil look and fresh wind shakes	74	1	10
Shakes its cocooning mists and so she comes	103		8
Shakespeares			
How Shakespeares England weds with Dantes Italy	98	35	2
Shallow			
How these two shame this shallow and frail town	35		9
The shallow folds of the wood	98	9	1
Covers with shallow silver that unsets	98	31	2
Covers with shallow silver the lock of clouds	98	31	5
And noonday have a shallow shine	114		4
And wonder at her shallow smile	120		12
Shallowing			
While phosphor risen upon the shallowing dark	98	28	3
Shallowy			
The cart road with a shallowy bed	135		26
Shame			
The incapable and cumbrous shame	15		18
How these two shame this shallow and frail town	35		9
For fond love and for shame	54		37
He hand to mouth he lives and voids with shame	75		9
His injury shell avenge with raging shame	82		6
Deep shame it were to be discoverd so	102	1	42

Word	Poem	Stan.	Line
Shame (cont.)			
It is for the shame of the lowly woman	109	14	3
Shank			
Rope-over thigh knee-nave and barrelled shank	71		3
Head and foot shoulder and shank	71		4
Shape			
Of mazy shape and hue but now bereft	1	8	3
Shape nothing lips be lovely-dumb	22		5
Each shape and shadow shows	60		85
And I shall shape one to my thought	80	7	40
Shape on the under side and size and drop	111		7
At last the bird is found a flickering shape and slim	113		9
Shaped			
To grace them spires are shaped with corner squinches	96	7	2
Who shaped these walls has shewn	148		9
Shapen			
The shapen flags and drilled holes of sky	12	2	11
Shapes			
That shapes in half-light his departing rings	19		3
When strangely loom all shapes that be	77		31
Now like the bird that shapes alone	81		6
In gilt and blazon and maild shapes of bronze	102	2	12
A rainbow also shapes itself beyond	107	3	6
It shapes itself in taper skeins	130		18
Sharded			
Nor close the clayfields sharded sores	114		14
Share			
The sour scythe cringe and the blear share come	28	11	8
And men are meant to share	60		44
In both care but share care	70		18
But both will share one cell this was good news Gwenvrewi	152		14
Shares			
And wears mans smudge and shares mans smell the soil	31	1	7
Shares their best gifts surely fall how things will	48		4
Sharp			
To fields where flies no sharp and sided hail	9		3
Sharp with her shorten sail	41		34
And with sharp flint will part my feet and dint	80	7	43
Your comfort is as sharp as swords	81		32
Double as sharp meaning and forcible	102	1	11
Sharper			
And oaks but these were leaved in sharper knots	107	4	8
Sheaf			
When he has sheaved us in his sheaf	6		29
And primrose bring and make a sheaf	98	18	3

Word	Poem	Stan.	Line
And the corn is corded and shoulders its sheaf	138		19
Sheared			
Is all all sheared away thus then I sweat for fear	152		24
What have we seen her head sheared from her shoulders fall	152		49
Shearing			
The shearing rays contract me with their blaze	80	2	6
A day off shearing day	144		12
Sheath			
In sod or sheath or shell	42		24
Sheathe			
Where selfwrung selfstrung sheathe-and shelter-less thoughts against thoughts in groans grind	61		14
And sheathe at once his leger wing	130		12
I can scour thee fresh burnish thee sheathe thee in thy dark lair these drops	152		46
Sheathe-and			
Where selfwrung selfstrung sheathe-and shelterless thoughts against thoughts in groans grind	61		14
Sheathed			
Your scarce-sheathed bones are weary of being bent	11		13
Now quicken sheathed in the yellow galaxy	98	22	3
Sheaved			
Sheaved in cruel bands bruised sore	6		5
When he has sheaved us in his sheaf	6		29
We shall be sheaved with one band	8		14
Of bluebells sheaved in May	144		10
Sheaves			
Once jostling thick the bluebell sheaves	81		13
Shed			
To mantle-oer the tail such as is shed	2		49
Grapes grew and drops of wine were shed	7		5
Food for five thousand on the thorns he shed	7		12
Break the box and shed the nard	24		1
Toil has shed round your head	28	35	15
Yet shed what tears sad truelove should	41		107
From tears shed over childrens graves	123		3
Bud shelling or broad-shed	138		24
Sheen			
Like shiverd rubies dance or sheen of sapphire hail	2		73
A brittle sheen runs upward like a cliff	98	6	2
Sheeny			
While sheeny tears and sunlit mirth	77		129
Her silky coat is sheeny like a hill	99		3
Sheep			
Startle the poor sheep back is the shipwrack			

Word	Poem	Stan.	Line
Sheep (cont.)			
then a harvest does tempest carry the grain for thee	28	30	8
And sheep-flock clouds like worlds of wool	30		18
To hear the sheep-bells dimly die	77		71
His sheep seemd to come from it as they stept	107	1	11
Of sheep from the high fields and other wild	107	4	23
Sheep-bells			
To hear the sheep-bells dimly die	77		71
Sheep-flock			
And sheep-flock clouds like worlds of wool	30		18
Sheer			
No wonder of it sheer plod makes plough down sillion	36		11
As sheer down the ship goes	41		59
Why that my chaff might fly my grain lie sheer and clear	64		9
Frightful sheer no-man-fathomed hold them cheap	65		8
Sheer off disseveral a star death blots black out nor mark	72		14
Sheets			
Ruck and wrinkle drooping dying deaths worst winding sheets tombs and worms and tumbling to decay	59		12
Shell			
Tuggd the bossd smooth-lippd giant strombus-shell	2		57
Or stretchd chords tuneable on turtles shell	2		129
In sod or sheath or shell	42		24
His injury shell avenge with raging shame	82		6
Prudence she has but wise shell never be	94		24
Shelled			
Be shelled eyes with double dark	22		9
Shelling			
Bud shelling or broad-shed	138		24
Shells			
With coral shells thick-pearled cords whateer	2		54
Shelly			
That lick the shelly leaves which floor the copse	84		4
Together as the criss-crossd shelly cup	101		2
Shelter			
A shelter for this flock	5		22
Who would not shelter from the hail	81		76
Her lids half-meshing shelter from the sky	99		6
Then sought such leafy shelter as it yields	107	3	16
Shelterless			
Where selfwrung selfstrung sheathe-and shelterless thoughts against thoughts in groans grind	61		14

Word	Poem	Stan.	Line
Shepherd			
Lead shepherd now we follow shepherd lead	98	15	7
Lead shepherd now we follow shepherd lead	98	15	7
He was a shepherd of the Arcadian mood	107	1	16
But what drew shepherd Richard from his downs	107	2	1
Shepherds			
Two mazed shepherds perishd in the tide	1	14	3
The shepherds brow fronting forked lightning owns	75		1
The shepherds whom I value not	124		23
Shew			
To shew the crimson streams that inward shine	2		71
With bills of rime the brambles shew	3		4
Lilies I shew you lilies none	10		7
Shew me thy son mother mother of mine	27		31
Shew brighter shaken in Penmaen pool	30		20
Touch me and purify and shew	77		39
I none can shew	127		6
Me shew mercy from my heart	155		22
Shewed			
Christ at all hazards fruit hath shewed	7		10
Shewing			
And soon I saw it shewing new	21		5
Shewn			
Love I was shewn upon the mountain-side	20		1
Shewn to Ezekiels opend sight	77		48
No shewn to her it cannot but offend	94		7
Shewn him both gold and fee	109	11	2
Who shaped these walls has shewn	148		9
Yet here he has but shewn	148		39
Shews			
Rather to ear than eye shews where they stray	112		4
Shield			
And those strokes once that gashed flesh or galled shield	73		2
Shift			
But then I make an eager shift to see	80	6	5
Shifted			
At roost and rest they shifted not	135		15
Shilling			
There is the shilling that finds me willing	156		8
Shine			
The motes in ceaseless eddy shine and fall	1	12	4
To shew the crimson streams that inward shine	2		71
In scarves of silky shot and shine	3		21
For all they shine so high in heaven	30		19
Shine and blue-bleak embers ah my dear	36		12
With brine and shine and whirling wind	41		79
She inly nourishes a wish to shine	94		12

Word	Poem	Stan.	Line
Shine (cont.)			
The moonlight-mated glowless glowworms shine	98	36	1
They stand they shine in the sun fame has foregone	104		2
By shine of candles three	109	1	2
And noonday have a shallow shine	114		4
Shines			
The rainbow shines but only in the thought	91		2
These rather are the arc where beauty shines	102	3	3
Shining			
It will flame out like shining from shook foil	31	1	2
With-a-fountains shining-shot furls	71		19
The shining slates and houses come and see	107	3	7
With shining-hilted curves that they may stay	112		7
His cap shall be shining fur	124		13
And lapped in shining hair roll to the banks edge then	152		50
Shining-hilted			
With shining-hilted curves that they may stay	112		7
Shining-shot			
With-a-fountains shining-shot furls	71		19
Ship			
As sheer down the ship goes	41		59
Then he set sail in a golden ship	109	6	3
Shipwrack			
Startle the poor sheep back is the shipwrack then a harvest does tempest carry the grain for thee	28	30	8
Shire			
In starry starry shire it grew	25		17
A released shower let flash to the shire not a lightning of fire hard-hurled	28	33	8
Shires			
In all our western shires was rare	21		23
Shirt			
And the ever-fretting shirt of punishment	11		11
Shivelights			
Shivelights and shadowtackle in long lashes lace lance and pair	72		4
Shiverd			
Like shiverd rubies dance or sheen of sapphire hail	2		73
Shives			
And the water warbles over into filleted with glassy grassy quicksilvery shives and shoots	159		38
Shoal			
The goal was a shoal of a fourth the doom to be drowned	28	12	6
Shoals			
In shoals of bloom as in unpeopled skies	2		31
On tangled shoals that bar the brook a crowd	2		96

Word	Poem	Stan.	Line
Drowned and among our shoals	28	34	2
Shoaly			
Fresh brooks to salt sand-teasing waters shoaly	16		4
Shock			
The breakers rolled on her beam with ruinous shock	28	14	6
Read the unshapeable shock night	28	28	3
I storm and shock you so I fail	81		73
Stand shock and silver-coated	98	13	2
Or like a juicy and jostling shock	144		9
Shocks			
But I shall when the shocks are stored	8		8
The shocks this piece-bright paling shuts the spouse	32	1	13
Like a contented wind or gentle shocks	98	2	2
Shod			
Is bare now nor can foot feel being shod	31	1	8
With perilous o no nor yet plod safe shod sound	70		14
Shone			
Nor rescue only rocket and lightship shone	28	15	6
Drowned o pity and indignation manshape that shone	72		13
Across my foundering deck shone	72		18
Shook			
An intense line of throbbing blood-light shook	2		16
And so my trust confused struck and shook	16		7
For he began at once and shook	21		29
She listened how the sea-gust shook	21		52
To the shrouds they took they shook in the hurling and horrible airs	28	15	8
It will flame out like shining from shook foil	31	1	2
He shook with racing notes the standing air	98	38	1
As might have struck and shook the close-shut palms	122		13
My heart irregularly shook	135		9
No tumbler woke and shook the cot	135		13
Shoot			
Handle the fig suck the full-sappd vine-shoot	5		38
When weeds in wheels shoot long and lovely and lush	33		2
Shoots			
Now he shoots short up to the round air	41		64
And the water warbles over into filleted with glassy grassy quicksilvery shives and shoots	159		38
Shore			
Or weeded landslips of the shore	15		24
Then sweetest seems the houseless shore	15		35
Trench right the tide that ramps against the shore	35		2

Word	Poem	Stan.	Line
Shore (cont.)			
Her injurys looks off by both horns of shore	50		3
Shores			
A mile astern lay the blue shores away	2		5
Short			
Now he shoots short up to the round air	41		64
Crispd up and starchy from a short half-hour	107	3	3
Heaven make the time be short she said	109	3	1
And make it short to me	109	3	4
And why so short with me	109	31	2
Shorten			
Sharp with her shorten sail	41		34
Shorter			
This shorter way	125		12
Shortest			
And then that last and shortest	153		11
Shot			
On pranked scale or threads of carmine shot	2		106
In scarves of silky shot and shine	3		21
Yet such a sapphire-shot	60		79
With-a-fountains shining-shot furls	71		19
And silver-shot with gusty light	78		8
Shot lightning to the stifling lid of night	125		56
Shoulder			
Gazes aslant his shoulder viewing nigh	1	11	6
A tinted fin on either shoulder hung	2		52
And the azurous hung hills are his world-wielding shoulder	38		9
Head heart hand heel and shoulder	49		10
Head and foot shoulder and shank	71		4
Shouldering			
Shouldering down valleys smokes the gloom	80	7	2
Shoulders			
And the corn is corded and shoulders its sheaf	138		19
What have we seen her head sheared from her shoulders fall	152		49
Shout			
We shout with them that tread the grapes	6		12
Would I could hear the other Pilates shout	80	1	5
We are there when we hear a shout	159		8
Show			
I must feed fancy show me any one	14	2	1
To show thee that thou art and near	23		44
Boughs being pruned birds preened show more fair	96	7	1
Will no one show	127		11
And breath immortal thronged that show	145		45
Showd			
Their filmy tails adown whose length there showd	2		104
Shower			
A released shower let flash to the shire not a			

Word	Poem	Stan.	Line
Shrovetide			
When shrovetide two years gone	54		5
Shuns			
That more he shuns our special dale	21		24
Shut			
It is the shut the curfew sent	22		6
And its place is a secret and shut in the skies	27		4
Sprang that but now were shut	28	35	7
When will you ever peace wild wooddove shy wings shut	51		1
Is this from Christ to be shut out	80	1	2
With hope with shut eyes fixedly	80	7	51
Her white weed-bathed knees are shut together	99		2
As struck with rings of sound the close-shut palms	122		10
As might have struck and shook the close-shut palms	122		13
Are shut against the canvassing of art	126		6
Unvalve or shut his vaned tail	130		11
Shuts			
The shocks this piece-bright paling shuts the spouse	32	1	13
Shuttles			
Like shuttles fleet the clouds and after	98	3	1
Shy			
When will you ever peace wild wooddove shy wings shut	51		1
Sicilian			
Raves through Sicilian pastures many a mile	1	11	4
Sick			
This seeing the sick endears them to us us too it endears	53		9
That neer need hunger Tom Tom seldom sick	70		6
When sick men turn and lights are low	77		25
Tho far or sick or heavy or still	81		18
His sick stars falter more he may	83		25
Familiar and so hated by the sick	125		48
Hated and too familiar to the sick	125		49
While sick men shall cast sighs of sweet health all despairing	152		108
Sicken			
Sure this is Nile I sicken I know not why	5		59
Sickend			
Sickend and thickend by the glare and sand	5		19
Sickly			
Scoop you from teeming filth some sickly hovel	77		6
Sickness			
A little sickness in the air	4		3
Sickness broke him impatient he cursed at first but mended	53		5

Word	Poem	Stan.	Line
Side			
Next morn a peasant from the mountain side	1	14	1
Thus I come underneath this chapel-side	12	2	1
Love I was shewn upon the mountain-side	20		1
Along the sanctuary side	22		20
Yet did the dark side of the bay of thy blessing	28	12	7
This side that side hurling a heavyheaded hundredfold	59		24
This side that side hurling a heavyheaded hundredfold	59		24
And press it down on either side a bone	80	7	50
The furthest reach this side on that the bay	107	4	20
Shape on the under side and size and drop	111		7
Serves and what side he takes	148		24
But right must seek a side	148		27
Sided			
To fields where flies no sharp and sided hail	9		3
Sides			
The recurb and the recovery of the gulfs sides	28	31	3
Sidled			
And the sunlight sidled like dewdrops like dandled diamonds	144		17
Siege			
Yields to the sultry siege of melancholy	16		8
Sieve			
Through the sieve of the straw of the plait	144		18
Sift			
I am soft sift	28	4	1
Sifted			
Sifted to suit our sight	60		113
Sigh			
Barely a sigh to thought of hopes forgone	14	3	9
By and by nor spare a sigh	55		7
If he suspect that she has ought to sigh at	82		5
Sighed			
Thus Frances sighed at home while Luke	21		50
Sighing			
Because the sighing wind is low	3		6
Like me sat sighing by a sycamore-tree	111		14
Sighs			
And with sighs soaring soaring sighs deliver	59		17
And with sighs soaring soaring sighs deliver	59		17
Now yields you with some sighs our explanation	76		14
Is anything a milk to the mind so so sighs deep	149	1	2
And breathes the blots off all with sighs on sighs	151		6
And breathes the blots off all with sighs on sighs	151		6
While sick men shall cast sighs of sweet health all despairing	152		108

Word	Poem	Stan.	Line
Sight			
Down-splinterd rocks crushd cottages drear sight	1	14	5
Those Cyclads made that thickend on my sight	2		37
Or sunderd from my sight in the age that is	13		3
Coils keeps and teases simple sight	22		12
That dares to cast its searching sight	23		29
Flesh falls within sight of us we though our flower the same	28	11	6
Thou martyr-master in thy sight	28	21	7
Strike you the sight of it look at it loom there	28	27	3
I cannot and out of sight is out of mind	40		11
Sifted to suit our sight	60		113
Be discoverd to my sight	77		17
Shewn to Ezekiels opend sight	77		48
Thus he ties spiders web across his sight	102	3	28
Such spiders web he ties across his sight	102	3	34
Ran through it following which we should have sight	125		6
To the sight of him who freed me	129		4
This was the prized the desirable sight unsought presented so easily	137		6
Right rooting in the bare butts wincing navel in the sight of the sun	143		5
Sights			
A schooner sights with another and saves	41		69
It will come to such sights colder	55		6
This night what sights you heart saw ways you went	67		3
But when she sights the sun she grows and sizes	103		6
What sights shall be when some that swung wretches on crutches	152		127
Sign			
Resign them sign them seal them send them motion them with breath	59		16
Signal			
Stigma signal cinquefoil token	28	22	7
Folds off aloof that signal is and proof	80	6	3
Your signal when apart we stood	81		17
Signalling			
My signalling tears might ring up Floris now	102	1	7
Signals			
In the first signals of the several drops	84		3
Silence			
And silence and a gulf of air	15		40
Elected silence sing to me	22		1
Our hymn in the vast silence dies	23		6
And still th unbroken silence broods	23		19
Silence holds breath upon her throne	77		33
Who could keep silence tho the smart	77		63
O what a silence is this wilderness	122		1

Word	Poem	Stan.	Line
In copying your sweet silence	125		24
Guilty of silence	125		26
To the point of silence in the air	135		32
Silent			
And thou art silent whilst thy world	23		31
To deaths more silent darker spell	23		42
And when the silent neight were won	77		75
If you are silent that I know of none	125		19
Silk			
Of silk-sack clouds has wilder wilful-wavier	38		3
In silk-ash kept from cooling	50		17
Lined all with silk of juicy red	124		16
She was dressed in silk attire	131		3
And crush-silk poppies aflash	138		21
Fairyland silk-beech scrolled ash packed sycamore wild wychelm hornbeam fretty overstood	159		24
Silk-ash			
In silk-ash kept from cooling	49		17
Silk-beech			
Fairyland silk-beech scrolled ash packed sycamore wild wychelm hornbeam fretty overstood	159		24
Silk-sack			
Of silk-sack clouds has wilder wilful-wavier	38		3
Silken			
In silken undulation spurrd and rayd	2		43
As silken garden-poppies do	21		7
Silky			
In scarves of silky shot and shine	3		21
And bared is the aspens silky skirting	78		6
Her silky coat is sheeny like a hill	99		3
Sillion			
No wonder of it sheer plod makes plough down sillion	36		11
Silt			
That his fast-flowing hours with sandy silt	136		1
Silver			
And silver Damasqud plates obscurd in ages crust	1	12	9
From their white waists a silver skirt was spread	2		48
And silver films beneath with pearly mist	2		67
Thro silver gloomd to a blood-vivid clot	2		107
Makes the silver jubilee	28	35	4
Showering silver jubilee	28	35	8
This her silver jubilee	28	35	12
Silver but for jubilee	28	35	16
Utter silver jubilee	28	35	20
With silver-surfed cherry	42		40
Of pointed wing and silver stole	77		12
Starting the silver rivulet	77		88

Word	Poem	Stan.	Line
Silver (cont.)			
Or if a sudden silver shower	77		93
And silver-shot with gusty light	78		8
And tho the silver seed that flits	83		11
Tingling between dusk and silver	98	1	4
Stand shock and silver-coated	98	13	2
A silver scarce-call-silver gloss	98	17	1
A silver scarce-call-silver gloss	98	17	1
Covers with shallow silver that unsets	98	31	2
Covers with shallow silver the lock of clouds	98	31	5
Whose silver skins lie level and thick in field	102	1	23
Most like the tuft of plighted silver round	102	1	72
Most like the plighted tuft of silver round	102	1	73
Most like the silver plighted tuft about	102	1	74
But many a silver visionary spark	113		5
Silver-coated			
Stand shock and silver-coated	98	13	2
Silver-shot			
And silver-shot with gusty light	78		8
Silver-surfed			
With silver-surfed cherry	42		40
Simile			
Your simile I keep	96	3	2
Simon			
The Simon Peter of a soul to the blast	28	28	7
Simoom			
Most wide ye are who call this gust simoom	5		26
Simple			
A simple passage of weak notes	3		13
Coils keeps and teases simple sight	22		12
To gentle manna and simple bread	81		175
Her sober simple coverlid underplighted	108		3
Sin			
He has a sin of mine he its near brother	16		9
But feel the long success of sin	18		8
To wend and meet no sing	60		117
That shall unglue the crust of sin	81		133
Into the bitterness of sin	92		6
I read that the recital of thy sin	102	2	2
Such heathenish misadventure doggd one sin	102	2	15
Such heathenish misadventure dogs one sin	102	2	16
Make wide thou o lord of sin	115		6
Except for sin	127		7
There rid the dragons root out there the sin	150		10
Since			
Since trampled Spain by royal discord torn	1	15	1
The monks left long ago since which no more	1	15	4
Since its birth and its bloom and its breathing its last	27		17
Since tho he is under the worlds splendour and wonder	28	5	6

Word	Poem	Stan.	Line
Since sacred fountains to the sun	28	35	6
Since country is so tender	43		12
An age is now since passed since parted with the reversal	45		3
An age is now since passed since parted with the reversal	45		3
Months earlier since I had our sweet reprieve and ransom	53		7
Be beginning since no nothing can be done	59		9
Since God has let dispense	60		40
Since proud it calls the calling manly gives a guess	63		4
Nay in all that toil that coil since seems I kissed the rod	64		10
I am all at once what Christ is since he was what I am and	72		22
Since on the face it is unsafe to look	102	1	47
But since I have no scope for benefits	102	1	55
Since all the make of man	148		7
Spare thou me since I see	155		15
Enough now since the sacred matter that I mean	159		43
Sinew			
Bones this sinew and will not waken	41		83
His sinew-service where do	71		11
Sinew-service			
His sinew-service where do	71		11
Sing			
As poets sing or that it is a pain	2		121
Strike timbrels sing eat drink be full of mirth	5		43
With corn that they shall laugh and sing	8		17
Elected silence sing to me	22		1
Wherefore we love thee wherefore we sing to thee	26		33
The ear it strikes like lightnings to hear him sing	33		5
Both sing sometimes the sweetest sweetest spells	39		6
My cries heave herds-long huddle in a main a chief-woe world-sorrow on an age-old anvil wince and sing	65		5
To sing scarce heard and singing fill	77		77
To sing while others sleep	96	3	4
When the wind drops you hear the skylarks sing	98	3	5
But let me sing that which is known to me	116		4
But sing contented as the dove	124		3
And while I sail must listen I sing	138		15
Singeing			
Not within the singeing of the strong sun	59		4
Singing			
A singing bird in morning clear	21		41

Word	Poem	Stan.	Line
Singing (cont.)			
Singing to the Trinity	24		28
To sing scarce heard and singing fill	77		77
Themselves live singing and their hearers kill	96	2	2
Might cover the neighbour downs with a span of singing	98	28	2
Single			
There was single eye	28	28	2
All a sevenfold-single gem	77		116
But single lead a misdirected life	94		32
To single saturn last and solitary	103		15
Sings			
Trying each pleasurable throat that sings	19		6
Sinking			
Westward on his sinking sire	77		124
Sinned			
Repent he sinned and all his sins be freed	140		6
Sow the wind I would I sinned	155		11
Sinner			
To thee the trembling sinner prays	23		3
Sinners			
Why do sinners ways prosper and why must	74	1	2
Sinning			
Before it cloud Christ Lord and sour with sinning	33		12
Sins			
Thou that on sins wages starvest	6		1
Who knowing all the sins and sores	77		53
And to put graver sins aside	96	1	3
Repent he sinned and all his sins be freed	140		6
Sip			
Then would I fling me up to sip	77		131
Sir			
With thee but sir so what I plead is just	74	1	1
Sir life upon thy cause see banks and brakes	74	1	8
Sir Christ against this multitude I strain	80	7	12
You came by Caerwys sir	152		2
Tonight sir	152		8
Help me sir and so I will	155		20
Sire			
Mother to an English sire he	48		3
Sweet fire the sire of muse my soul needs this	76		9
Westward on his sinking sire	77		124
Siren			
A piteous siren sweetness on the sea	2		127
Sister			
Soon as when summer of his sister spring	2		84
When a sister born for each strong month-brother	26		1
Sister a sister calling	28	19	1
Sister a sister calling	28	19	1

Word	Poem	Stan.	Line
So takes the sister sense can find no mark	113		4
As well the sister sits would well the wife	157		14
Sisterhood			
Of a coifed sisterhood	28	20	2
Sistering			
Amidst the sistering planets till she comes	103		14
Sisterly			
Are sisterly sealed in wild waters	28	23	7
Sisters			
Brothers and sisters are in Christ not near	66	1	3
Father mother brothers sisters friends	159		49
Sit			
Come by the flesh-pots you shall sit unshod	5		9
He comes to brood and sit	51		11
The members how they sit	148		2
Sits			
Where yonder crimson fireball sits	3		23
And the beadbonny ash that sits over the burn	56		12
Altho unchallenged where she sits	83		9
Sits without consolation marking not	111		4
Ah no and she who sits beside	120		14
As well the sister sits would well the wife	157		14
Sitting			
Sitting eastnortheast in cursed quarter the wind	28	13	6
O look at all the fire-folk sitting in the air	32	1	2
She high at the housetop sitting as they say	136		13
Six			
I gazed unhinderd mermaids six or seven	2		34
The sweetest sonnet five or six times read	117		9
Size			
Eighth wonder of the earth in size in store	1	15	5
Elsewhere leave comfort root-room let joy size	69		11
Hang of a treble size	88		4
Shape on the under side and size and drop	111		7
Sizes			
But when she sights the sun she grows and sizes	103		6
Sizing			
Rather it is the sizing moon	10		20
O no it is the sizing moon	25		20
All things rising all things sizing	42		25
Skates			
As a skates heel sweeps smooth on a bow-bend the hurl and gliding	36		5
Skeined			
His rash-fresh re-winded new-skeined score	35		6
Off her once skeined stained veined variety upon all on two spools part pen pack	61		11
Skeins			
In skeins about the brakes	98	10	3

Word	Poem	Stan.	Line
Skeins (cont.)			
It shapes itself in taper skeins	130		18
Skies			
In shoals of bloom as in unpeopled skies	2		31
No answering voice comes from the skies	23		2
Gather gladness from the skies	24		13
And its place is a secret and shut in the skies	27		4
Look at the stars look look up at the skies	32	1	1
For skies of couple-colour as a brinded cow	37		2
Meal-drift moulded ever and melted across skies	38		4
At God knows when to God knows what whose smiles not wrung see you unforeseen times rather as skies	69		12
When the fierce skies are blue to black albeit	80	2	5
Not of clear skies but storm to be	80	6	4
When skies are hard as any stone	81		8
Springs in the floating air and the skies swim	113		6
O now while skies are blue now while seas are salt	152		106
Skiff			
Youll dare the alp youll dart the skiff	30		5
Skill			
The skill of dreamy Claude and Titians mellow gloom	1	10	9
That I may win with late-learnt skill uncouth	17		12
Or as Austin a lingering-out sweet skill	28	10	6
With just such sweet potential skill	81		20
Thou Jacinth nor have skill of all thy virtues	102	1	62
Skinned			
And brown-as-dawning-skinned	41		78
Skins			
Whose silver skins lie level and thick in field	102	1	23
Skirt			
From their white waists a silver skirt was spread	2		48
Thou hast a base and brickish skirt there sours	44		5
Skirting			
And bared is the aspens silky skirting	78		6
Skirts			
And spins her skirts out while her central star	103		7
Sky			
So glassy white about the sky	3		16
The shapen flags and drilled holes of sky	12	2	11
Leaves spent new seasons alterd sky	15		2
In tufts of evening sky so soon	25		22
The Deutschland on Sunday and so the sky keeps	28	13	3
Charged steeped sky will not	60		80

Word	Poem	Stan.	Line
With sweet and scarless sky	60		120
Looks from the zenith round the sky	77		108
Then was discoverd in the pathless sky	80		7
They webbd the sky with glassy light	87		2
Sky fleeced with the milky way	98	23	2
The sky minted into golden sequins	98	25	1
Sky peakd with tiny flames	98	25	5
Her lids half-meshing shelter from the sky	99		6
To spread the compass on the all-starrd sky	102	3	8
To turn the compass on the all-starrd sky	102	3	23
Who lies on grass and pores upon the sky	117		3
Attain the windy levels of the sky	121		4
The sky is blue and the winds pull	130		22
To-day the sky is two and two	138		16
Poetry to it as a tree whose boughs break in the sky	149	1	3
Skylark			
As a dare-gale skylark scanted in a dull cage	39		1
Or ever the early stirrings of skylark	98	28	1
Of the flown skylark and his traverse flight	122		3
The skylark is my cousin and he	138		12
Skylarks			
When the wind drops you hear the skylarks sing	98	3	5
Where the stint compass of a skylarks wings	98	22	5
Skywards			
Skywards rich rich it laps	60		77
Rounded it thinning skywards by degrees	107	4	4
Slabby			
The drenched hair of slabby weeds that swung	2		113
Slabs			
Are you sandblind slabs of water many a mile	5		35
Slack			
Not untwist slack they may be these last strands of man	64		2
Her milk-white throat and folded dew-lap slack	99		9
Slake			
This bath of blue and slake	60		95
Slaked			
Dry up the blue and be not slaked thereby	117		7
Slammd			
Doors slammd to the blasts continually more low	1	13	8
Slanted			
Crisp lips straight nose and tender-slanted cheek	136		16
Slates			
The shining slates and houses come and see	107	3	7
Slaty			
And tantalean slaty ashiness	117		5

Word	Poem	Stan.	Line
Slaughter			
Princes strong for the sword and slaughter	26		27
Slay			
Come up arise and slay	5		18
Sleek			
That like this sleek and seeing ball	43		14
Earthless dews on ancles sleek	77		16
Sleep			
I did not mean to sleep but found	21		15
And then lay back to sleep	21		53
Life death does end and each day dies with sleep	65		12
But sleep again ere day be born	77		24
To sing while others sleep	96	3	4
Sleep Floris while I rob you tighten o sleep	102	1	18
Sleep Floris while I rob you tighten o sleep	102	1	18
Slender			
To touch her being so slender	43		13
Who can but barter slender sums	81		146
By slender losses are undone	81		147
And slender element to piece and plot	102	3	25
The slender elements to piece and plot	102	3	26
Bridging the slender difference of two stars	103		3
Slendering			
And slendering to his burning rim	3		30
Slept			
I had slept a little and was chill	21		16
Will have waked and have waxed and have walked with the wind what while we slept	59		23
Slew			
He slew the Egyptian yesterday to-day	5		3
Slight			
With such a violet slight their distanced green	100		8
Slight with such violet their bright-maskd green	100		9
Slighted			
She sour who seems the slighted nix	120		17
When maddest looks the slighted nix	120		19
Slightly			
Is slightly selfish in her inmost soul	94		28
Slim			
Slim-pointed sea-gull plumes and droop behind	2		80
At last the bird is found a flickering shape and slim	113		9
Slim-pointed			
Slim-pointed sea-gull plumes and droop behind	2		80
Slime			
To mans last dust drain fast towards mans first slime	35		14
Mid feverd fumes and slime and caked clot	77		8
Slip			
I am like a slip of comet	103		1

Word	Poem	Stan.	Line
Slips			
Just such slips of soldiery Christs royal ration	48		28
And now I get some precious slips	81		84
Turning and pacing so by slips discloses	108		2
And millbrook-slips with pretty pace	130		25
Slipt			
Somewhere we slipt astray you cannot doubt	125		15
Sloe			
Word last how a lush-kept plush-capped sloe	28	8	3
Sloggering			
The rash smart sloggering brine	28	19	4
Slopd			
Slopd on the galleries upon the wall	1	12	2
Slope			
Great butter-burr leaves floord the slope corpse ground	107	4	9
Sloping			
Now melting upward thro the sloping scale	2		132
Slow			
Louder the monks drond out Gregorians slow	1	13	6
Is it a wonder if the buds are slow	17		3
Dances for sad footsteps slow	24		22
With swift slow sweet sour adazzle dim	37		9
No wonder therefore was not slow	145		19
Slowly			
Into the cooling gloom till slowly all	1	12	5
Slumber			
Slumber in these forsaken	41		82
Parted me leaf and leaf divided me eyelid and eyelid of slumber	137		7
Slumberd			
Slumberd at last in one sweet deep heart-broken close	2		135
Slumbered			
What while we while we slumbered	59		25
All slumbered whom our rud red tiles	135		1
Small			
The Glaucus cleped others small braids enclusterd	2		68
The steep-up roof at last behind the small	12	2	6
Which makes so small the promise of that yield	17		11
May who neer hung there nor does long our small	65		9
Therewith to hanker for the small	81		153
Of small and sugar flints I knew	135		27
Small matter of that then let him smother	145		40
Your will is law in that small commonweal	150		11
Smart			
Are you turned for an exquisite smart	28	18	2
The rash smart sloggering brine	28	19	4
And fain will find as sterling all as all is smart	63		7

Word	Poem	Stan.	Line
Smart (cont.)			
Who could keep silence tho the smart	77		63
Is comforts carol of all or woes worst smart	153		8
Smeared			
And all is seared with trade bleared smeared with toil	31	1	6
Smell			
Does it smell sweet too in that holy place	27		44
And wears mans smudge and shares mans smell the soil	31	1	7
Comforting smell breathed at very entering	34		3
Smells			
Smells that are sweeter-memoried than the rose	119		3
The air smells strong of sweetbriar in the park	135		24
Smile			
Stretches the envied fruit with fatal smile	1	11	2
With eyes that smile thro the tears of the hours	26		14
If a wuthering of his palmy snow-pinions scatter a colossal smile	45		13
When his mellow smile he sees	77		105
He meets her stintless of her smile	83		21
Clings on the stroke of death that I can smile	102	1	2
And wonder at her shallow smile	120		12
Bright-lifting with a little-lasting smile	125		57
Smiled			
In some broad palmy mead and saintly smiled	1	10	5
Smiled blushed and bit his lip	54		19
Sounds reachd him Richard came Sylvester smiled	107	4	24
Smiles			
At God knows when to God knows what whose smiles not wrung see you unforeseen times rather as skies	69		12
They wound their winch of wicked smiles	145		25
Smit			
The sapphire pools are smit with white	78		7
Smitten			
Apollo views the smitten python writhe and die	1	11	9
Smock			
And as she dwindles shreds her smock of gold	103		13
Smokes			
Shouldering down valleys smokes the gloom	80	7	2
Smooth			
Tuggd the bossd smooth-lippd giant strombus-shell	2		57
The satin-purfled smooth to foam and spread	2		79
The languent smooth with dimpling drops and flash	2		103
As a skates heel sweeps smooth on a bow-bend			

Word	Poem	Stan.	Line
the hurl and gliding	36		5
That in smooth spoons spy lifes masque mirrored tame	77		13
To colour as smooth and fresh as cheeks of roses	108		4
Smooth-lippd			
Tuggd the bossd smooth-lippd giant strombus-shell	2		57
Smote			
And like the storm-months smote the earth	26		29
Smother			
But the combs of a smother of sand night drew her	28	14	3
Small matter of that then let him smother	145		40
Smouldering			
The smouldering enormous winter welkin may	149	1	8
The smouldering enormous winter welkin eye	149	2	3
Smudge			
And wears mans smudge and shares mans smell the soil	31	1	7
Snatch			
What hell hopes soon the snatch of	49		20
Snow			
But earth has never felt the snow	3		2
And hunting winds and the long-lying snow	17		2
Wiry and white-fiery and whirlwind-swivelled snow	28	13	7
Surf snow river and earth	28	21	4
If a wuthering of his palmy snow-pinions scatter a colossal smile	45		13
And death falls gently as the snow	77		26
Unchilld I handle stinging snow	80	2	1
Snow-pinions			
If a wuthering of his palmy snow-pinions scatter a colossal smile	45		13
Snowflake			
Snowflake thats fairly mixed	60		6
Snows			
Into the snows she sweeps	28	13	1
Furred snows charged tuft above tuft tower	30		31
Takes to the seas and snows	40		58
The hanging snows rush down and bare	80	4	4
Snowstorm			
Mark makes in the rivelling snowstorm	41		67
Snowwhite			
Mells blue and snowwhite through them a fringe and fray	149	1	9
Mells blue with snowwhite through their fringe and fray	149	2	5
Snowy			
Ebbd back beneath its snowy lids unseen	2		18

Word	Poem	Stan.	Line
Snuff			
Your parched nostrils snuff Egyptian air	5		27
So			
To what serves mortal beauty dangerous does set dancing blood the o-seal-that-so feature flung prouder form	62		1
Soared			
Soared or sank	71		8
Soaring			
And with sighs soaring soaring sighs deliver	59		17
And with sighs soaring soaring sighs deliver	59		17
Sob			
The breasts desponding sob I quell	23		38
Sobbd			
Then passd the wind and sobbd with mountain-echod woe	1	13	9
Sober			
And sober lustres take the gloom	77		20
Her sober simple coverlid underplighted	108		3
Sobs			
A freezing runnel sobs and dwarfs	80	3	7
Sod			
In sod or sheath or shell	42		24
Sodden			
Of the sodden-with-its-sorrowing heart	28	26	12
Sodden-with-its-sorrowing			
Of the sodden-with-its-sorrowing heart	28	26	12
Sods			
The bluebells up whose crystal-ending rods in their natural sods	112		8
Soft			
Soft when she sees her infant start	23		51
I am soft sift	28	4	1
With belled fire and the moth-soft milky way	28	26	6
Or if there does some soft	60		90
Softening			
And hard men feel a softening touch	77		30
Soil			
To plash with cool feet the clay juicy soil	5		50
And wears mans smudge and shares mans smell the soil	31	1	7
The temperd soil where only her flower is found	102	3	4
Soldier			
Yes why do we all seeing of a soldier bless him bless	63		1
Soldiering			
Mark Christ our king he knows war served this soldiering through	63		9
Soldiers			
How soldiers platting thorns around Christs head	7		4

Word	Poem	Stan.	Line
Soldiery			
Just such slips of soldiery Christs royal ration	48		28
Solely			
And they are purer but alas not solely	16		5
Solemn			
Arose in gloom a solemn mockery	1	8	6
Solid			
The miles profound of solid green and be	2		123
Nor permanence in the solid world	130		16
Solitary			
To single Saturn last and solitary	103		15
Solitude			
An endless round of deadning solitude	1	14	6
Affined well to that sweet solitude	107	1	15
Sombre			
A sombre length of grey four towers placed	1	1	3
Some			
In some broad palmy mead and saintly smiled	1	10	5
Here in some darkend landscape parts fair	1	11	1
And was as tho some sapphire molten-blue	2		45
Some traild the nautilus or on the swell	2		56
Some carried the sea-fan some round the head	2		58
Some carried the sea-fan some round the head	2		58
Careless of me they sported some would plash	2		102
Some diving merrily downward drove and gleamd	2		108
Some find me a sword some	28	11	1
Some find me a sword some	28	11	1
Your wealth of life is some way spent	28	35	14
Fetched fresh as I suppose off some sweet wood	34		4
Some asleep unawakened all unwarned eleven fathoms fallen	41		3
Wings so some great stormfowl whenever he has walked his while	45		11
Some candle clear burns somewhere I come by	46		1
In scarlet or somewhere of some day seeing	48		38
Some good and so he does leave patience exquisite	51		8
Pining pining till time when reason rambled in it and some	53		3
Being anointed and all though a heavenlier heart began some	53		6
How to keep is there any any is there none such nowhere known some bow or brooch or braid or brace lace latch or catch or key to keep	59		1
Or if there does some soft	60		90
Now and seeing somewhere some man do all that man can do	63		11
Now yields you with some sighs our explanation	76		14

Word	Poem	Stan.	Line
Some (cont.)			
Scoop you from teeming filth some sickly hovel	77		6
Some of the secrets I would know	77		40
And some of those who stand about	80	7	18
Some ice that locks the glacier to the rocks	80	7	20
And now I get some precious slips	81		84
Some knelt some stood I seemd to feel	81		93
Some knelt some stood I seemd to feel	81		93
Is not some little Bela set	81		142
Some are pretty enough and some are poor indeed	98	15	4
Some are pretty enough and some are poor indeed	98	15	4
Would not put out some tiny golden centre	98	22	6
Gilds with some sparky fancies his black night	102	3	30
Gilds with some sparky fancies blinding night	102	3	36
Scarce worth discovery in some corner seen	103		2
To trace some traceless loss of thought again	107	4	18
Not this some spirits it is told	118		2
Something we guess or know some spirits start	126		7
All over some such words as these though dark	136		29
Or ever did for my sake some good deed	140		2
Some messenger there might have met you from my uncle	152		5
The more some monstrous hand gropes with clammy fingers there	152		20
Meantime some tongue cries what teryth what thou poor fond father	152		22
Some pageant which takes tears and I must foot with feeling that	152		26
What sights shall be when some that swung wretches on crutches	152		127
The telling time our task is times some part	153		5
Of some branchy bunchy bushybowered wood	159		3
Something			
Of something drifting thro delighted air	2		28
It is even seen times something server	41		52
Can something hope wish day come not choose not to be	64		4
Something I said I swooned and fell	81		118
A something in her face of guile	120		10
Something we guess or know some spirits start	126		7
There must be something to supply	133		7
Something of thy holiness	155		8
Sometimes			
Both sing sometimes the sweetest sweetest spells	39		6

Word	Poem	Stan.	Line
Soon (cont.)			
That was her larkspur row so soon	10		22
My love is lessened and must soon be past	14	1	1
But now I am so tired I soon shall send	14	3	8
And soon I saw it shewing new	21		5
In tufts of evening sky so soon	25		22
Death or distance soon consumes them wind	40		9
New boldboys soon to be men	41		13
What hell hopes soon the snatch of	49		20
Undone done with soon done with and yet dearly and dangerously sweet	59		9
Too late or else much much too soon	105		16
Like water soon to be sucked in	145		9
Soon now therefore	152		9
Sooner			
Sooner than their mates and yet	4		29
Soonest			
And flowers finds soonest	42		12
Sooty			
Gather the sooty plumage from deaths wings	89		6
Soppd			
The field is soppd with merciful dew	8		3
Sordid			
How ring right out our sordid turbid time	35		10
Sordidness			
In sordidness of care and crime	133		11
Sore			
Sheaved in cruel bands bruised sore	6		5
That make my eyes sore and cross-colour things	125		46
Sores			
Who knowing all the sins and sores	77		53
Nor close the clayfields sharded sores	114		14
Rupture running sores what more in brief in burden	152		114
Sorrel			
Of the wood-sorrel and all things sensitive	122		11
As the wood-sorrel and all things sensitive	122		14
Sorrow			
We have suffered the sons of winter in sorrow	26		9
My cries heave herds-long huddle in a main a chief-woe world-sorrow on an age-old anvil wince and sing	65		5
And after that sad sorrow	110		4
Then severance and sorrow	110		8
O I admire and sorrow the hearts eye grieves	157		1
Sorrowing			
Of the sodden-with-its-sorrowing heart	28	26	12
Sorrows			
Sorrows springs are the same	55		11
Sorry			
True madam I am sorry now to see	125		16

Word	Poem	Stan.	Line
Sort			
Days after so I in a sort deserve to	48		26
Sorts			
The million sorts of unaccounted motes	98	22	2
Sots			
Defeat thwart me oh the sots and thralls of lust	74	1	6
Sought			
The window-circles these may all be sought	12	1	11
When this is sought trees will be wanting not	80	7	39
How shall I search who never sought	81		173
Then sought such leafy shelter as it yields	107	3	16
Soul			
My soul does loathe it and my spirit fails	5		14
Sphered so fast sweet soul we see	10		23
Giddies the soul with blinding daze	23		28
Sphered so fast sweet soul we see	25		23
The Simon Peter of a soul to the blast	28	28	7
Soul self come poor jackself I do advise	69		9
Sweet fire the sire of muse my soul needs this	76		9
But come thou balm to aching soul	77		11
And soul is subtle and flesh weak	77		37
Is slightly selfish in her inmost soul	94		28
I heard her say poor poor afflicted soul	111		11
The country song of willow the poor soul	111		13
As when a soul laments which hath been blest	119		9
Why theres an interest and sweet soul in beauty	125		41
Sweet soul not scorning honest sweat	139		5
Loyal to his own soul laying his own law down no law nor	152		72
Is corpse now cannot change my other self this soul	152		95
Souls			
Henceforth let your souls alway	24		29
Two hundred souls in the round	28	12	4
Our king back oh upon English souls	28	34	4
God lover of souls swaying considerate scales	34		12
Three hundred souls o alas on board	41		2
But for souls sunk in seeming	41		117
Which to pure souls alone may be	77		142
In the lodges of the perishable souls	126		1
For souls that might have blessed the time	133		9
His looks the souls own letters see beyond	157		15
Where lies your landmark seamark or souls star	157		19
Sound			
The clogged brook runs with choking sound	3		9
That I have taken to plead with if the sound	13		9
And I could hear the tiniest sound	21		17
But that sweet sound which I preferred	21		47
What is sound natures round	28	35	3

Word	Poem	Stan.	Line
Sound (cont.)			
With perilous o no nor yet plod safe shod sound	70		14
Allows the sound of bells in Hamlets round	80	4	6
Or careful-spaced sequences of sound	102	3	2
In careful-spaced sequences of sound	102	3	22
Have here a true one echoing the sound	116		2
As struck with rings of sound the close-shut palms	122		10
And all within the house were sound as posts	135		17
As where the little hurling sound	135		31
The whole landscape flushes on a sudden at a sound	146		5
Sounding			
And headed always downwards with less sounding	112		2
Sounds			
Sounds reachd him Richard came Sylvester smiled	107	4	24
Sour			
Gush flush the man the being with it sour or sweet	28	8	5
The sour scythe cringe and the blear share come	28	11	8
Before it cloud Christ Lord and sour with sinning	33		12
With swift slow sweet sour adazzle dim	37		9
She sour who seems the slighted nix	120		17
When the air was sweet-and-sour of the flown fineflour of	142		4
With dreadful distillation of thoughts sour as blood	152		97
Soured			
There was a wood of dwarf and soured oaks	125		2
Sours			
Thou hast a base and brickish skirt there sours	44		5
Selfyeast of spirit a dull dough sours I see	67		12
South			
But these were found in the east and south	10		13
But they came from the south	25		13
Or fatherd by the sunderd south	83		6
With a south-westerly wind blustering with a tide rolls reels	141		4
South-westerly			
With a south-westerly wind blustering with a tide rolls reels	141		4
Southern			
Southern dean or Lancashire clough or Devon cleave	159		4
Sovereign			
Bathing it is summers sovereign good	159		13

Word	Poem	Stan.	Line
Sovereignty			
Death with a sovereignty that heeds but hides bodes but abides	28	31	8
Sow			
That seed which the good sower once did sow	17		7
Sow the wind I would I sinned	155		11
Let winter wed one sow them in her womb	158		3
Sowed			
Though when the sower sowed	7		6
Sower			
Though when the sower sowed	7		6
That seed which the good sower once did sow	17		7
Sown			
I found the ways were sown with salt	81		155
Had been more fertile and had sown with notes	122		5
Or had been effectual to have sown with notes	122		12
Space			
Come out of space or suddenly engenderd	103		4
Spaced			
Or careful-spaced sequences of sound	102	3	2
In careful-spaced sequences of sound	102	3	22
Spain			
Since trampled Spain by royal discord torn	1	15	1
Spake			
Then up and spake the third brother	109	27	1
Span			
Might cover the neighbour downs with a span of singing	98	28	2
All time at once and span the distant goals	126		4
Spaniels			
Out-fleeced bushes like a spaniels ear	98	11	2
Spannd			
Spannd with shadow every one	98	8	3
Spans			
The river spans it with so deep a hip	107	4	26
Spare			
All things counter original spare strange	37		7
By and by nor spare a sigh	55		7
Spare	59		1
Do in spare hours more thrive than I that spend	74	1	7
Spare thou me since I see	155		15
Spared			
Not spared not one	43		5
That might have spared her were it but for passion-sake	152		86
Spark			
But quench her bonniest dearest to her her clearest-selved spark	72		10
But many a silver visionary spark	113		5

Word	Poem	Stan.	Line
Sparkling			
The thunder brags in joints and sparkling jags	80	7	3
Sparks			
Quartz-fret or sparks of salt	60		101
Sparky			
The sparky air	98	33	1
Gilds with some sparky fancies his black night	102	3	30
Gilds with some sparky fancies blinding night	102	3	36
Spatterd			
Are spatterd we desire the yoke we bore	5		53
Speak			
Speak whisper to my watching heart	23		49
Stir in my ears speak there	60		121
With witness I speak this but where I say	67		5
To speak so yet Ill speak it for this once	102	1	41
To speak so yet Ill speak it for this once	102	1	41
Ah Floris Floris let me speak this little	102	1	53
Speaketh			
Man from the lips of him speaketh and saith	26		5
Speaking			
A mans voice and a new voice speaking near	136		22
Speaks			
One word as when a mother speaks	23		50
Selves goes itself myself it speaks and spells	57		7
Speard			
Speard open lustrous gashes crimson-white	2		8
Special			
Their special-general title to thy love	12	1	14
That more he shuns our special dale	21		24
Special-general			
Their special-general title to thy love	12	1	14
Sped			
That mammocks mighty foot but no way sped	70		12
For all the miles that they were sped	81		158
Speech			
With ear-caressing speech where is the tongue	122		17
By speech so sweetly broken up and gone	125		31
Speechless			
Summoning men from speechless day	23		41
Speeds			
And speeds unchecked her murderous guile	120		30
Spell			
To deaths more silent darker spell	23		42
I whirled out wings that spell	28	3	4
Bars or hells spell thwarts this to hoard unheard	66	1	12
The spell of woe if any could	81		79
One spell and well that one there ah thereby	153		7
Spells			
Both sing sometimes the sweetest sweetest			

Word	Poem	Stan.	Line
spells	39		6
Selves goes itself myself it speaks and spells	57		7
Spend			
My bankrupt heart has no more tears to spend	14	3	4
Nostrils your careless breath that spend	22		17
Spend here your measure of time and treasure	30		39
And pelt music till nones to spill nor spend	35		8
Do in spare hours more thrive than I that spend	74	1	7
Spend me or end me what God shall send me	156		13
Spends			
But half the pains he spends upon his boy	97		4
Spendsavour			
And cast by conscience out spendsavour salt	46		14
Spent			
God shall oer-brim the measures you have spent	11		9
Leaves spent new seasons alterd sky	15		2
The labours I should then have spent	15		11
Your wealth of life is some way spent	28	35	14
And for all this nature is never spent	31	1	9
This needful never spent	60		9
What hours o what black hours we have spent	67		2
Doubtless the voice now falln now spent	81		2
From parts unlookd for alterd spent	81		24
Make it to God I am not spent	81		130
And these are spent and ended quite	130		21
Spent Pegasus down the stark-precipitous air	136		8
Sperses			
That early sperses and high hangs the day	98	31	6
Sphered			
Sphered so fast sweet soul we see	10		23
Sphered so fast sweet soul we see	25		23
But you so sphered see no more	81		39
Spiders			
Thus he ties spiders web across his sight	102	3	28
Such spiders web he ties across his sight	102	3	34
Spiked			
With spiked quills all of intensest hue	2		44
Spikes			
Plum-purple was the west but spikes of light	2		7
Spill			
And pelt music till nones to spill nor spend	35		8
To spill oer fields of lilies so could I	102	1	37
Spin			
Will crisp itself or settle and spin	145		10
Spine			
From crown to tail-fin floating fringed the spine	2		41
Spins			
Spins to the widow-making unchilding unfathering deeps	28	13	8

Word	Poem	Stan.	Line
Spins (cont.)			
And spins her skirts out while her central star	103		7
Spire			
Showerd the cliffs and every fret and spire	2		25
Spires			
To grace them spires are shaped with corner squinches	96	7	2
Spirit			
My soul does loathe it and my spirit fails	5		14
The spirit hovered ere the sun	23		22
Mans mounting spirit in his bone-house mean house dwells	39		2
To me so arch-especial a spirit as heaves in Henry Purcell	45		2
Not flesh but spirit now	60		58
And scarlet wear the spirit of war there express	63		8
Selfyeast of spirit a dull dough sours I see	67		12
My spirit hath a birth	77		3
Who knew the inner spirit that fills	77		43
While a subtle spirit and rare	77		127
What spirit is that makes stillness obsolete	122		16
She was admired the spirit of hell	145		17
Spirits			
The-last-breath penitent spirits the uttermost mark	28	32	6
He haunted who of all men most sways my spirits to peace	44		11
The shaken plumage of my spirits wings	77		10
When wholesome spirits rustle about	77		27
Not this some spirits it is told	118		2
Something we guess or know some spirits start	126		7
Spiritual			
A star most spiritual principal preeminent	98	27	1
Making the shadow sweeter a spiritual grace	107	4	15
Splayd			
Who tread the grapes are splayd with stripes of gore	5		51
Splendid			
Splendid with phantasies aerial	1	8	2
Splendour			
Anon across their swimming splendour strook	2		15
By interchange gaspd splendour and eclipse	2		22
Since tho he is under the worlds splendour and wonder	28	5	6
Splendours			
Does into amber splendours fail	77		100
Splinterd			
Down-splinterd rocks crushd cottages drear sight	1	14	5

Word	Poem	Stan.	Line
Spoil			
You spoil the plot I find my true love by	135		36
Spoke			
The more she askd the more he spoke	109	36	1
The more he told the less she spoke	109	36	3
He spoke of God the Father and his son	136		25
Spokes			
Flickering with sunny spokes and left and right	2		77
Spools			
Off her once skeined stained veined variety upon all on two spools part pen pack	61		11
Spoons			
That in smooth spoons spy lifes masque mirrored tame	75		13
Sport			
Each sport has here its tackle and tool	30		6
Sported			
Careless of me they sported some would plash	2		102
Spot			
Marking the spot when they have gurgled oer	2		3
Where the eye fixd fled the encrimsoning spot	2		9
From the spot where he had been	4		23
One spot and hunger to be there	15		32
But where was it formerly which is the spot	27		8
Who fired France for Mary without spot	44		14
Even to the tillage of the sweetest spot	102	3	16
She loves his face she knows the spot	120		2
They rose at last and forced her from the spot	136		34
So long to this sweet spot this leafy lean-over	152		116
Spots			
In the green spots of that wood	98	10	1
With centres duly touchd and nestlike spots	107	4	7
With fickle spots of sadness accessories	125		47
Spousal			
Wedlock what the water spousal love	159		47
Spouse			
Your spouse not laboured-at nor spun	22		28
The shocks this piece-bright paling shuts the spouse	32	1	13
Sprang			
Sprang that but now were shut	28	35	7
Spray			
With hempen strands in spray	144		6
Sprays			
Their highest sprays were drawn as fine as lashes	107	4	6
Spread			
From their white waists a silver skirt was spread	2		48

Word	Poem	Stan.	Line
Spread (cont.)			
The satin-purfled smooth to foam and spread	2		79
Spread oer the swart face of this prodigal earth	5		45
And with weeping cloud is spread	77		95
To spread the compass on the all-starrd sky	102	3	8
Do cover from the starry spread	135		2
Spreading			
Spreading still its sunned girth	77		70
Spring			
Soon as when summer of his sister spring	2		84
Had gotten him a wreath of sweet spring-broidery	2		101
It seemd an evening in the spring	4		2
At this spring season of the year	4		13
But the spring-tide passd the same	4		24
Death to mark them in the spring	4		32
Not set because their buds not spring	10		11
Spring not cause world is wintering	10		12
See how spring opens with disabling cold	17		1
And a spring-time joy have found	24		16
Not set because their buds not spring	25		11
Spring not for world is wintering	25		12
For the fallen rise and the stricken spring to thee	26		39
Or rather rather then stealing as spring	28	10	3
Nothing is so beautiful as spring	33		1
Will or mild nights the new morsels of spring	34		7
Question what is spring	42		15
Whence spring the jewelld harmonies	77		138
Breaking the air of spring	98	3	7
These should have starvd with the green broods of spring	105		14
In spring our river-banks are topt	124		17
To these Castara is rain or breeze or spring	125		54
Before the spring was done	144		4
As sure as what is most sure sure as that spring primroses	152		132
Spring-broidery			
Had gotten him a wreath of sweet spring-broidery	2		101
Spring-tide			
But the spring-tide passd the same	4		24
Spring-time			
And a spring-time joy have found	24		16
Springs			
Where springs not fail	9		2
Springs one daughter the sweet child May	26		2
Springs the stress felt	28	6	2
Oh morning at the brown brink eastward springs	31	1	12
Springs universal bliss	42		34

Word	Poem	Stan.	Line
Stage			
Though aloft on turf or perch or poor low stage	39		5
Staid			
Her showy leaves staid watchet counterfoiling	108		5
Stain			
Feast of the one woman without stain	28	29	5
Stain light yea mark you this	60		81
That will not wear a print that will not stain a pen	152		121
Stained			
Off her once skeined stained veined variety upon all on two spools part pen pack	61		11
And stained and knots of golden thread	124		14
Stair			
All down the stair-way of the copse	21		45
Stair-way			
All down the stair-way of the copse	21		45
Stake			
Sometimes I see the summit stake	80	4	1
Staled			
To thy not-staled uncharted memory	117		14
Stalk			
With sulphur-colourd lilies brittle in stalk	98	12	3
Stallion			
Majestic as a stallion stalwart very-violet-sweet	38		10
Stalwart			
Majestic as a stallion stalwart very-violet-sweet	38		10
Stamp			
He seemd a dismal mirky stamp	4		8
Stanches			
Squandering ooze to squeezed dough crust dust stanches starches	72		7
Stanching			
Stanching quenching ocean of a motionable mind	28	31	5
Stand			
A fortress of true faith and central stand	1	5	3
And seventy palms there stand	5		24
In beds in gardens in thick plots I stand	5		37
When heavenly vales so thick shall stand	8		16
The whole world passes I stand by	15		4
O how nay do but stand	60		75
Stand at stress each limbs barrowy brawn his thew	71		6
I can stand pent in the monstrous element	80	5	3
They all come here and stand before me clear	80	7	10
And some of those who stand about	80	7	18
Will add a footrest there to stand	80	7	42
They are the goats who stand said I	81		95

Word	Poem	Stan.	Line
I stood but does she stand or kneel	81		96
Stand shock and silver-coated	98	13	2
They stand they shine in the sun fame has foregone	104		2
Now while the full-leaved hursts unalterd stand	105		3
Standing			
Save me and you were standing near	81		103
And many standing round a waterfall	91		5
He shook with racing notes the standing air	98	38	1
Of standing to the blossom-hitting shower	107	3	4
A standing fell	112		9
Stands			
Where stands no host at door or hearth	23		11
Before that rock my seat he stands	80	7	15
Said who is this that stands without	109	30	1
Moonless darkness stands between	129		1
There is a vapour stands in the wind	130		17
Star			
Such opposition to the lady-star	14	2	10
Which is it star or dew	25		18
Star-eyed strawberry-breasted	42		19
Sheer off disseveral a star death blots black out nor mark	72		14
Being a stoled appareld star	81		42
Shall when his star is zenithd find	83		7
How looks the night there does not miss a star	98	22	1
A star most spiritual principal preeminent	98	27	1
One star by daylight from the strong blue air	102	3	10
And spins her skirts out while her central star	103		7
But the Bethlehem star may lead me	129		3
Where lies your landmark seamark or souls star	157		19
Star-eyed			
Star-eyed strawberry-breasted	42		19
Starches			
Squandering ooze to squeezed dough crust dust stanches starches	72		7
Starchy			
Crispd up and starchy from a short half-hour	107	3	3
Stare			
They seemd to press and stare	98	29	2
Morn does not now new-basilisk his stare	99		17
They seem to press and droop and stare	135		20
Staring			
In the staring darkness	132		1
Stark			
Is any of him at all so stark	72		15
Spent Pegasus down the stark-precipitous air	136		8
Stark-precipitous			
Spent Pegasus down the stark-precipitous air	136		8

Word	Poem	Stan.	Line
Starlight			
Starlight wafting him out of it and	28	5	3
That a starlight-wender of ours would say	41		100
Dress his days to a dexterous and starlight order	48		20
Heaven turned its starlight eyes below	145		46
Starlight-wender			
That a starlight-wender of ours would say	41		100
Starrd			
To spread the compass on the all-starrd sky	102	3	8
To turn the compass on the all-starrd sky	102	3	23
Starry			
In starry water-meads they drew	10		17
In starry starry shire it grew	25		17
In starry starry shire it grew	25		17
To all the starry press	98	28	6
Do cover from the starry spread	135		2
Stars			
Save by two stars more crowding lights arise	2		32
These drops which be they stars or dew	10		18
To the stars lovely-asunder	28	5	2
Stroke and a stress that stars and storms deliver	28	6	5
Look at the stars look look up at the skies	32	1	1
The thick stars round him roll	60		99
Waste her earliest stars earlstars stars principal overbend us	61		4
Waste her earliest stars earlstars stars principal overbend us	61		4
And the waked stars are all alone	77		34
The destined lover whom his stars	83		1
His sick stars falter more he may	83		25
And the thin stars tremble not	85		5
And the lessend stars ray not	85		6
Stars float from the borders of the main	98	20	1
The vast of heaven stung with brilliant stars	98	21	2
Stars waving their indivisible rays	98	23	1
Stars like gold tufts	98	25	2
Stars like golden bees	98	25	3
Stars like golden rowels	98	25	4
Now stars of blood	98	26	2
The stars were packed so close that night	98	29	1
Warnd by the bright procession of the stars	102	1	59
Bridging the slender difference of two stars	103		3
Who came from further than the stars	115		3
Or take it thus that the concording stars	122		7
I saw the stars like flash of fire	135		8
The stars are packed so thick to-night	135		19
Hang as still as hawk or hawkmoth as the stars or as the angels there	159		26
Start			
Soft when she sees her infant start	23		51

Word	Poem	Stan.	Line
Why tears is it tears such a melting a madrigal start	28	18	6
Something we guess or know some spirits start	126		7
Starting			
Starting the silver rivulet	77		88
Startle			
Startle the poor sheep back is the shipwrack then a harvest does tempest carry the grain for thee	28	30	8
And learnt her not to startle at his name	82		8
Starvd			
These should have starvd with the green broods of spring	105		14
Starves			
And numbs and starves as between icy wharves	80	3	6
Starvest			
Thou that on sins wages starvest	6		1
State			
Formed bars of stone beyond in stiffend state	1	4	3
But opend twice in life and death to state	1	4	8
I have found the dominant of my range and state	19		13
Statuary			
Is statuary rated by its inches	96	7	6
In gilt and blazon and bronze statuary	102	2	11
Statue			
By any lauded statue nor again	125		30
Staunch			
For that staunch saint still praisd his masters name	1	3	1
Stay			
Then will he keep in this stay	80	1	7
With shining-hilted curves that they may stay	112		7
Let what there needs be done stay with him one companion	152		12
Stays			
Or if I go she stays meanwhile	120		28
Stead			
Theres none but truth can stead you Christ is truth	157		20
Steady			
I steady as a water in a well to a poise to a pane	28	4	5
Of the rolling level underneath him steady air and striding	36		2
His steady wheel quite to the full again	107	3	12
Steal			
Did Helen steal my love from me	95		1
Stealing			
Or rather rather then stealing as spring	28	10	3
Down no waving off of these most mournful			

Word	Poem	Stan.	Line
Stealing (cont.)			
messengers still messengers sad and stealing messengers of grey	59		4
Steals			
Till dimpled joy steals oer its cheeks	23		52
Stealthy			
A stealthy wind crept round seeking to blow	2		137
Steel			
Tom Garlanded with squat and surly steel	70		1
In wide the worlds weal rare gold bold steel bare	70		17
This ice this lead this steel this stone	81		128
Steel may be melted and rock rent	81		134
So be it thou steel thou butcher	152		45
O welcome there their steel or cannon	156		17
Steeled			
Unseen the heroic breast not outward-steeled	73		7
Steep			
The steep-up roof at last behind the small	12	2	6
Durance deal with that steep or deep here creep	65		10
Glimmerd along the square-cut steep	92		1
Beyond the banks wete steep a brush of trees	107	4	3
Of greenery it is old earths groping towards the steep	149	1	10
Of greenery and old earth gropes for grasps at steep	149	2	6
Steep-up			
The steep-up roof at last behind the small	12	2	6
Steeped			
Charged steeped sky will not	60		80
Astray or aswarm all throughther in throngs self in self steeped and pashed quite	61		6
Steered			
By a grey eyes heed steered well one crew fall to	71		5
Stem			
Loose on the stem has done its summering	105		13
Stephen			
The footway Stephen said	135		28
Stepped			
Stepped from the stool drew back from the barrow of dark Maenefa the mountain	137		4
Steps			
Your passing steps I never heard	21		48
Stept			
His sheep seemd to come from it as they stept	107	1	11
Sterling			
And fain will find as sterling all as all is smart	63		7

Word	Poem	Stan.	Line
Sterner			
Run all your race o brace sterner that strain	47		14
Sternest			
The pride of faith and home of sternest piety	1	8	9
Steward			
One has gone to the kings steward	109	11	1
Stick			
With bubbles bugle-eyed struggle and stick	2		95
Stiffend			
Formed bars of stone beyond in stiffend state	1	4	3
Stifling			
Shot lightning to the stifling lid of night	125		56
Stigma			
Stigma signal cinquefoil token	28	22	7
Still			
For that staunch saint still praisd his masters name	1	3	1
And still thou bindst me to fresh fealty	12	1	3
The morning was so still	21		18
Betweens I heard the water still	21		44
Pipe me to pastures still and be	22		3
And still th unbroken silence broods	23		19
And still th abysses infinite	23		25
If still in darkness not in fear	23		48
Through him melt him but master him still	28	10	4
Blue-beating and hoary-glow height or night still higher	28	26	5
With the sweetest air that said still plied and pressed	47		3
Down no waving off of these most mournful messengers still messengers sad and stealing messengers of grey	59		4
Be Christ our Saviour still	60		54
Spreading still its sunned girth	77		70
Lies divinely still at rest	77		98
Tho far or sick or heavy or still	81		18
Heaven and every field are still	85		2
And in grey bands the sun should lie still born	90		3
And swarter still the rolling pines should cast	90		5
But having that believes it greater still	94		10
Thus we shall profit while gold coinage still	96	7	7
Rounds its still-purpling centreings of cloud	98	30	3
Rounds its still-purpling centre-darks of cloud	98	30	6
Forward she leans with hollowing back stock-still	99		1
Are still her neck is creased in close-ply rings	99		10
Love by prenatal serfdom still confined	102	3	15
That still makes counter-roundels in the pond	107	3	5
The time save when her tears which still descend	111		5
Self-sentenced still	127		14

Word	Poem	Stan.	Line
Still (cont.)			
A cusp still clasped him a fluke yet fanged him entangled him not quit utterly	137		5
Wiped I am sure this was it seems not well for still	152		43
Still the scarlet swings and dances on the blade	152		44
Pilgrims still pilgrims more pilgrims still more poor pilgrims	152		126
Pilgrims still pilgrims more pilgrims still more poor pilgrims	152		126
I have life left with me still	155		17
The selfless self of self most strange most still	157		27
Hang as still as hawk or hawkmoth as the stars or as the angels there	159		26
And with heavenfallen freshness down from moorland still brims	159		39
Still-purpling			
Rounds its still-purpling centreings of cloud	98	30	3
Rounds its still-purpling centre-darks of cloud	98	30	6
Stilling			
With levelld lashes stilling their disquiet	82		2
Stillness			
What spirit is that makes stillness obsolete	122		16
Stilly			
As I walkd a stilly wood	4		5
Stinging			
Unchilld I handle stinging snow	81	2	1
Stint			
Where the stint compass of a skylarks wings	98	22	5
Stinting			
From furrows of the poor and stinting weald	17		13
Stintless			
He meets her stintless of her smile	83		21
Stipple			
For rose-moles all in stipple upon trout that swim	37		3
Stir			
Upon the stir and keep of pride	22		18
Stir in my ears speak there	60		121
While all things else may stir and range	130		7
Stirless			
And gaind thro growing dusk the stirless bay	2		141
Stirred			
One stirred from the rigging to save	28	16	1
Stirred for a bird the achieve of the mastery of the thing	36		7
The rookery never stirred a wing	135		14
Stirrings			
Or ever the early stirrings of skylark	98	28	1

Word	Poem	Stan.	Line
Stirs			
Closer because faint morning stirs	77		22
Stock			
Forward she leans with hollowing back stock-still	99		1
Stock-still			
Forward she leans with hollowing back stock-still	99		1
Stole			
The rosy isles so that I stole away	2		140
Hand rather my heart lo lapped strength stole joy would laugh cheer	64		11
Of pointed wing and silver stole	77		12
Stoled			
Being a stoled appareld star	81		42
Stolen			
More sweetly shades her stolen hair	120		7
Stone			
Formed bars of stone beyond in stiffend state	1	4	3
Then laverd founts and posturd stone he mixd	1	4	5
Where the upper mill-stone roofd his head	6		7
To man that needs would worship block or barren stone	62		7
Ill take in hand the blady stone	81	7	48
When skies are hard as any stone	81		8
This ice this lead this steel this stone	81		128
Glazed water vaulted oer a drowsy stone	98	39	1
They have happd him with the sand and stone	109	15	1
Made known though thick through stone	148		11
Stone palsy cancer cough lung-wasting womb-not-bearing	152		113
Stones			
And trees of terebinth and stones	15		39
Stones ring like each tucked string tells each hung bells	57		3
Then I seek out the shadow of stones	80	3	1
And to those stones become akin	80	3	2
Stony			
Who would drink water from a stony rock	5		20
High up the balanced stony air	80	4	2
Which drives the stony air to utterance	122		18
Stood			
Before the sepulchre there stood a gate	1	4	6
Sudden death before me stood	4		6
And danced the balls of dew that stood	21		34
But what a wild flush on the flakes of it stood	27		34
And all in lone air stood the sun	77		76
She stood before a light not hers and seemd	80		3
Your signal when apart we stood	81		17
Some knelt some stood I seemd to feel	81		93
I stood but does she stand or kneel	81		96

Word	Poem	Stan.	Line
Stood (cont.)			
Stood capital eminent gonfalon bearer	98	28	5
She stood before them in the glen	109	25	1
Stooks			
Summer ends now now barbarous in beauty the stooks rise	38		1
Stool			
The triple-hummocked giants stool	30		10
Stepped from the stool drew back from the barrow of dark Maenefa the mountain	137		4
Stooped			
It stooped and flashed and fell and ran like water away	152		52
Stop			
Stop not now to count the cost	24		2
But down drop if it says stop	138		37
Stops			
Kneading the mounded mire that stops	3		10
Yet as he changed his mighty stops	21		43
Store			
Upon his altar and with rarest store	1	2	8
Eighth wonder of the earth in size in store	1	15	5
Stored			
Now in our altar-vessels stored	6		19
But I shall when the shocks are stored	8		8
How she did in her stored	42		31
For learning stored and garnered	81		169
Storm			
The driving storm at hour of vespers beat	1	13	3
And like the storm-months smote the earth	26		29
Mans malice with wrecking and storm	28	9	4
Storm flakes were scroll-leaved flowers lily showers sweet heaven was astrew inthem	28	21	8
The Christ of the father compassionate fetched in the storm of his strides	28	32	8
Those lovely lads once wet-fresh windfalls of wars storm	62		5
Not of clear skies but storm to be	81	6	4
I storm and shock you so I fail	81		73
Jarrd down the balanced storm the bleeding heavens	102	2	4
To hunger and not have yet hope on for to storm and strive and	152		88
Storm-months			
And like the storm-months smote the earth	26		29
Stormfowl			
Wings so some great stormfowl whenever he has walked his while	45		11
Storms			
Where no storms come	9		6
This means you need not fear the storms the cries	14	3	2

Word	Poem	Stan.	Line
Stroke and a stress that stars and storms deliver	28	6	5
And storms bugle his fame	28	11	4
To the men in the tops and the tackle rode over the storms brawling	28	19	8
Riding there did storms not mingle and	41		25
Of rivers lead thro storms and nights	83		4
Stormy			
But whats to see in stormy waether	30		25
Their heads together in a stormy blot	90		6
Story			
They tell its story thus amidst the heat	1	2	1
I read the story rather	7		3
Of it angels fall they are towers from heaven a story	75		3
How dare I paint Miss Story to Miss May	94		3
Miss Story has a moderate power of will	94		9
Storys			
Miss Storys character too much you ask	94		1
Straight			
And straight showers parallel should follow fast	90		4
Crisp lips straight nose and tender-slanted cheek	136		16
Strain			
Afar in corridors with pained strain	1	13	7
Sweld the sweet strain to a melodious wail	2		133
I thought the air must cut and strain	21		36
A strain of the earths sweet being in the beginning	33		10
Run all your race o brace sterner that strain	47		14
His heart up at the strain	54		27
Them birds build but not I build no but strain	74	1	11
To hear his strain descend less loud	77		79
Sir Christ against this multitude I strain	80	7	12
Catch sunlight and one strain of stupid praise	98	32	2
So tiny a trickle of song-strain	138		4
Second this fiery strain not always o no no	152		78
What need I strain my heart beyond my ken	157		34
Strained			
Is strung by duty is strained to beauty	41		77
Strains			
Which ends those only strains that I approve	19		10
Nothing else is like it no not all so strains	48		29
Evening strains to be times vast womb-of-all home-of-all hearse-of-all night	61		2
With white strokes and strains of the blue	138		17
Tampering with those sweet bines draws them out strains them strains them	152		21
Tampering with those sweet bines draws them out strains with strains them	152		21

Word	Poem	Stan.	Line
Strand			
Worlds strand sway of the sea	28	1	3
And she shall child them on the new-world strand	158		4
Stranded			
The stranded keel and kelson warp apart	101		11
Strands			
Not untwist slack they may be these last strands of man	64		2
With hempen strands in spray	144		6
Strange			
The abysmal ocean hoards of strange and rare	2		55
All things counter original spare strange	37		7
From hands now clammy with strange blood	80	7	25
Tho apt to throw it in a strange direction	94		14
The selfless self of self most strange most still	157		27
Strangely			
When strangely loom all shapes that be	77		31
So strangely elemented is my minds weather	102	1	15
Stranger			
To seem the stranger lies my lot my life	66	1	1
By there comes a listless stranger beckoned by the noise	159		14
Strangers			
Among strangers father and mother dear	66	1	2
Straw			
Bring in the glistery straw	5		46
Through the sieve of the straw of the plait	144		18
Strawberry			
Star-eyed strawberry-breasted	42		19
Strawberry-breasted			
Star-eyed strawberry-breasted	42		19
Strawy			
Than fan or hood or strawy plait	120		8
Stray			
Wherein he makes us stray	5		6
Rather to ear than eye shews where they stray	112		4
Straying			
Rich Titians faded in the straying gleam	1	12	3
Strays			
And scarcely traces where one beauty strays	1	6	7
Streakd			
Were veind and streakd with dusk-deep lazuli	2		46
Streaks			
Streaks of shadow thistled leas	77		137
Stream			
Crowd down upon a stream and jostling thick	2		94
Streamd			
With arm and fin the argent bubbles streamd	2		109
Dry were her sad eyes that would fain have			

Word	Poem	Stan.	Line
Strides (cont.)			
in the storm of his strides	28	32	8
Striding			
Of the rolling level underneath him steady air and striding	36		2
Strife			
And he my peace my parting sword and strife	66	1	4
Strike			
Strike timbrels sing eat drink be full of mirth	5		43
Strike you the sight of it look at it loom there	28	27	3
What was it we should strike the road again	125		1
Will on the moulding strike and cling	130		10
Firm accents strike her fine and scrolled ear	136		21
Strike churl hurl cheerless wind then heltering hail	154		1
Strikes			
The ear it strikes like lightnings to hear him sing	33		5
Now I grow numb my tongue strikes on the gum	80	7	27
String			
Stones ring like each tucked string tells each hung bells	57		3
Strings			
And every praised sequence of sweet strings	19		7
And ravelld into strings of rain	81		57
Stringy			
They watched the brush of the swift stringy drops	107	3	13
Striped			
You striped in secret with breath-taking whips	11		3
Stripes			
Who tread the grapes are splayd with stripes of gore	5		51
Strips			
And the flower strips	98	14	2
Strive			
To hunger and not have yet hope on for to storm and strive and	152		88
Striven			
O Lord but I have wrought and striven	81		108
Stroke			
Swings the stroke dealt	28	6	4
Stroke and a stress that stars and storms deliver	28	6	5
Where she foundered one stroke	41		4
Clings on the stroke of death that I can smile	102	1	2
What stroke has Caradocs right arm dealt what done	152		32
Strokes			
Strokes of havoc unselve	43		21
And those strokes once that gashed flesh or			

Word	Poem	Stan.	Line
galled shield	73		2
And marching to false colours those few strokes	102	1	69
With white strokes and strains of the blue	138		17
Strombus			
Tuggd the bossd smooth-lippd giant Strombus-shell	2		57
Strombus-shell			
Tuggd the bossd smooth-lippd giant Strombus-shell	2		57
Strong			
When a sister born for each strong month-brother	26		1
Princes strong for the sword and slaughter	26		27
Thou canst but be but that thou well dost strong	58		5
Not within the singeing of the strong sun	59		4
The fine delight that fathers thought the strong	76		1
Beat heave and the strong mountain tire	80	5	2
The love of women is not so strong	81		48
Knowledge is strong but love is sweet	81		154
Is very capable of strong affection	94		13
One star by daylight from the strong blue air	102	3	10
The air smells strong of sweetbriar in the park	135		24
Strook			
Anon across their swimming splendour strook	2		15
Strove			
Of those who strove Gods gospel to confound	1	1	7
I strove to look I lost the trick	81		97
Struck			
And so my trust confused struck and shook	16		7
She struck not a reef or a rock	28	14	2
As struck with rings of sound the close-shut palms	122		10
As might have struck and shook the close-shut palms	122		13
Struck off it has written upon lovely limbs	152		34
Perhaps we struck no blow Gwenvrewi lives perhaps	152		40
Struggle			
With bubbles bugle-eyed struggle and stick	2		95
And cleaves I struggle and am dumb	80	7	28
At once I struggle with my breath	81		58
Struggling			
That struggling should not sear him a gift should cheer him	142		8
Strung			
Their pansy-dark or bronzen locks were strung	2		53
My head to hear he might have strung	21		30
Is strung by duty is strained to beauty	41		77

Word	Poem	Stan.	Line
Stubborn			
Upon the stubborn fleming and the rod	1	5	6
Stumbling			
And stumbling swears he walks by light of day	102	3	31
And stumbling swears he walks by light of day	102	3	37
Stung			
Because she fears her fingers will be stung	96	4	2
The vast of heaven stung with brilliant stars	98	21	2
Stupendous			
Earnest earthless equal attuneable vaulty voluminous stupendous	61		1
Stupid			
Catch sunlight and one strain of stupid praise	98	32	2
Sturdy			
By him and rips out rockfire homeforth sturdy Dick	70		3
Subject			
What if my subject seeing this resent	94		5
Submission			
They kiss the rod with filial submission	97		9
Subtle			
Of tremulous film more subtle than the vest	2		39
With a subtle web of black	4		20
And soul is subtle and flesh weak	77		37
While a subtle spirit and rare	77		127
Succeed			
Its the day that makes the charm no afterwords could succeed	128		7
Success			
That holds no promise of success	15		34
But feel the long success of sin	18		8
He hung on the imps success	54		24
And I not help nor word now of success	150		5
Next after sweet success I am not left even this	152		92
Such			
The sculpturd image of such faith would be	1	3	7
The choicest remnants thence such home forlorn	1	15	3
More wondrous to have borne such hope before	1	15	7
To mantle-oer the tail such as is shed	2		49
And that such a sable track	4		21
I never promised such persistency	14	1	2
With such malign conjuctions as before	14	2	6
With such a seconding nor Saturn took	14	2	9
Such opposition to the lady-star	14	2	10
Beyond the hurst with such a hue	21		6
Indeed while such a wonders warm	25		36
Why tears is it tears such a melting a madrigal start	28	18	6
To me God knows deserving no such thing	34		2
And he boards her in oh such joy	41		70

Word	Poem	Stan.	Line
Just such slips of soldiery Christs royal ration	48		28
It will come to such sights colder	55		6
Earth brows of such care care and dear concern	58		14
How to keep is there any any is there none such nowhere known some bow or brooch or braid or brace lace latch or catch or key to keep	59		1
One yes I can tell such a key I do know such a place	59		7
One yes I can tell such a key I do know such a place	59		7
Yet such a sapphire-shot	60		79
With just such sweet potential skill	81		20
Returning thanks might offer such array	89		4
Her face was such as being diapered	93	2	3
Our swans are now of such remorseless quill	96	2	1
And I come laden from such floods	98	19	5
Breathe in such ether or the quickly elms	100		7
With such a violet slight their distanced green	100		8
Slight with such violet their bright-maskd green	100		9
Maskd with such violet disallow their green	100		10
Such heathenish misadventure doggd one sin	102	2	15
Such heathenish misadventure dogs one sin	102	2	16
That swinishly refuses such a pearl	102	3	33
Such spiders web he ties across his sight	102	3	34
That swinishly refuses such a pearl	102	3	39
On such a season of the day and year	107	1	4
Then sought such leafy shelter as it yields	107	3	16
News from Belleisle even such a sweetness blows	119		6
Had let such music down without impediment	122		8
All over some such words as these though dark	136		29
I will appear looking such charity	140		3
No man has such a daughter the fathers of the world	152		17
Call no such maiden mine the deeper grows her dearness	152		18
She leans on him with such contentment fond	157		13
Into such a sudden zest	159		20
Suck			
Handle the fig suck the full-sappd vine-shoot	5		38
They draw all coverts cut the fields and suck	104		12
Suck any sense from that who can	147		3
Sucked			
The windpipe when he sucked his breath	21		37
Abel is Cains brother and breasts they have sucked the same	28	20	8
That onewhere curded onewhere sucked or sank	71		7

Word	Poem	Stan.	Line
Sucked (cont.)			
Like water soon to be sucked in	145		9
Sucks			
Sucks close the acorn as the hand and glove	101		3
And sucks the light as full as Gideons fleece	103		11
Sudden			
Then saw I sudden from the waters break	2		74
Sudden death before me stood	4		6
Or if a sudden silver shower	77		93
Does lay men low with one blades sudden blow	80	2	3
Deaths bones fell in with sudden clank	92		12
The whole landscape flushes on a sudden at a sound	146		5
Into such a sudden zest	159		20
Suddenly			
The vital fire does suddenly retire	80	7	24
Come out of space or suddenly engenderd	103		4
Suffer			
I suffer this she said for thee	145		57
Suffered			
We have suffered the sons of winter in sorrow	26		9
Suffering			
And cipher of suffering Christ	28	22	2
Suffers			
Which between ash-tops suffers loss	121		5
Sufficed			
Waking I thought and it sufficed	118		8
Sugar			
Of small and sugar flints I knew	135		27
Suit			
Look foot to forelock how all things suit he	41		76
Sifted to suit our sight	60		113
With yellow flags will suit his brow	124		18
Suiting			
Suiting its grace with him or her	25		26
Suitors			
By other eyes and other suitors move	12	1	12
Sulphur			
With sulphur-colourd lilies brittle in stalk	98	12	3
Sulphur-colourd			
With sulphur-colourd lilies brittle in stalk	98	12	3
Sultry			
Yields to the sultry siege of melancholy	16		8
Sum			
Floris she will not hit thy sum of worth	102	1	61
Summer			
Then through the afternoon the summer beam	1	12	1
Soon as when summer of his sister spring	2		84
Summer was as full of flame	4		25
And the promise of summer within her breast	26		16
When was the summer that saw the bud blow	27		15
Summer ends now now barbarous in beauty			

Word	Poem	Stan.	Line
Sun (cont.)			
I have drawn heat from this contagious sun	103		18
They stand they shine in the sun fame has foregone	104		2
While there is neither sun nor rain	105		6
Right rooting in the bare butts wincing navel in the sight of the sun	143		5
His cheeks the forth-and-flaunting sun	144		2
Sun-flushd			
Sun-flushd until it seemd their father sea	2		100
Sunbeam			
Hued sunbeam will transmit	60		88
Sunday			
The Deutschland on Sunday and so the sky keeps	28	13	3
Sunderd			
Or sunderd from my sight in the age that is	13		3
Or fatherd by the sunderd south	83		6
Sung			
Only with utterance of sweet breath they sung	2		130
So forcibly he sung	21		32
Sunk			
Gurgled where they had sunk melodiously	2		111
But for souls sunk in seeming	41		117
Sunlight			
Catch sunlight and one strain of stupid praise	98	32	2
Anywhere in the sunlight	138		9
And the sunlight sidled like dewdrops like dandled diamonds	144		17
In all her beauty and sunlight to it is a pit den darkness	152		54
Sunlit			
While sheeny tears and sunlit mirth	77		129
Sunned			
Spreading still its sunned girth	77		70
Sunny			
Flickering with sunny spokes and left and right	2		77
And look abroad on sunny clusters	77		134
Suns			
Tall suns tingeing or treacherous the tainting of the earths air	59		5
Where shake shadow is suns-eye-ringed	138		42
Suns-eye-ringed			
Where shake shadow is suns-eye-ringed	138		42
Sunset			
After the sunset I would lie	15		42
In fits of music till sunset	77		87
Has drenchd the molten sunset hour	77		94
Sunspurge			
Sunspurge and oxeye	138		28
Superfluous			
With long-superfluous ties for nothing here	12	1	4

Word	Poem	Stan.	Line
Supplied			
And well supplied with virtues on the whole	94		27
Supply			
There must be something to supply	133		7
Suppose			
Fetched fresh as I suppose off some sweet wood	34		4
Supposing			
Philip supposing that the gift most meet	1	3	6
Surcease			
And fain in the springtime surcease would borrow	26		11
Sure			
Sure this is Nile I sicken I know not why	5		59
Sure s bed now low be it lustily he his low lot feel	70		5
As sure as heaven it is	133		6
Wiped I am sure this was it seems not well for still	152		43
As sure as what is most sure sure as that spring primroses	152		132
As sure as what is most sure sure as that spring primroses	152		132
As sure as what is most sure sure as that spring primroses	152		132
Shall new-dapple next year sure as to-morrow morning	152		133
Surely			
Deeply surely I need to deplore it	41		96
Shares their best gifts surely fall how things will	48		4
O surely reaving peace my lord should leave in lieu	51		7
Ah surely all who have written will profess	117		8
Surf			
Surf snow river and earth	28	21	4
Surfed			
With silver-surfed cherry	42		40
Surfy			
Of crumbling fore-foundering thundering all-surfy seas in seen	141		5
Of New Years month or surly Yule	30		30
Nay what we had lighthanded left in surly the mere mould	59		22
Tom Garlanded with squat and surly steel	70		1
Surprise			
She puts in leash her paird lips lest surprise	82		3
Surrenders			
From there where all surrenders come	22		7
Surround			
Surround the peak from which we gaze	23		26

Word	Poem	Stan.	Line
Survey			
And all the landscape under survey	30		13
Suspect			
If he suspect that she has ought to sigh at	82		5
Suspects			
For Fabian that suspects her not	120		4
Swallow			
The swallow favourite of the gale	130		9
Swallowd			
Thro crimson-golden floods pass swallowd into fire	2		83
Swallowing			
I cannot meet the swallowing main	120		27
Swallows			
I mark the tower swallows run	15		28
Swam			
Shadow that swam or sank	43		7
Swan			
From wings swan-fledged a wheel of watery light	2		76
Swan-fledged			
From wings swan-fledged a wheel of watery light	2		76
Swans			
Our swans are now of such remorseless quill	96	2	1
Sward			
That want the yield of plushy sward	22		22
He drops his bright roots in the waterd sward	100		2
Swarm			
O this is bringing tears may swarm	25		35
Swarmed			
Cuckoo-echoing bell-swarmed lark-charmed rook-racked river-rounded	44		2
How then should Gregory a father have gleaned else from swarmed Rome but God to a nation dealt that days dear chance	62		6
Swart			
Spread oer the swart face of this prodigal earth	5		45
Bad Saturn with a swart aspect	83		18
Swarter			
And swarter still the rolling pines should cast	90		5
Swarthed			
Had swarthed about with lion-brown	144		3
Swathe			
They swathe and lace the shroud-plaits oer my face	80	5	6
Sway			
Worlds strand sway of the sea	28	1	3
Swayd			
Droopd oer the brows like Hectors casque and swayd	2		42
His body swayd upon tiptoes	87		3

Word	Poem	Stan.	Line
Swayed			
From thy hand out swayed about	155		3
Swaying			
Hung in the swaying of the fierce melee	1	2	4
God lover of souls swaying considerate scales	34		12
Sways			
He haunted who of all men most sways my spirits to peace	44		11
And what sways with you maybe this sweet maid	157		22
Swear			
So I am victor now I swear to pay	1	2	5
The turmoil and the torment it has I swear a sweetness	152		90
Swears			
And stumbling swears he walks by light of day	102	3	31
And stumbling swears he walks by light of day	102	3	37
Sweat			
The dense and the driven passion and frightful sweat	28	7	5
Sweet soul not scorning honest sweat	139		5
Is all all sheared away thus then I sweat for fear	152		24
Sweating			
As I am mine their sweating selves but worse	67		14
Sweats			
But here here is a workman from his days task sweats	152		42
Sweep			
The swoon of a heart that the sweep and the hurl of thee trod	28	2	6
To sweep and must obey	148		16
They touch heaven tabour on it how their talons sweep	149	1	7
With talons sweep	149	2	2
Sweeps			
Into the snows she sweeps	28	13	1
As a skates heel sweeps smooth on a bow-bend the hurl and gliding	36		5
Lies in her lap which she anon sweeps off	111		9
Sweet			
Had gotten him a wreath of sweet spring-broidery	2		101
And a sweet sadness dwelt on everyone	2		117
Only with utterance of sweet breath they sung	2		130
Swelld the sweet strain to a melodious wail	2		133
Slumberd at last in one sweet deep heart-broken close	2		135
Here are sweet messes without price or worth	5		47
Is the sweet vintage of our Lord	6		20
Sweet flowers I carry sweets for bitter	10		6
Sphered so fast sweet soul we see	10		23

Word	Poem	Stan.	Line
Sweet (cont.)			
More sweet-familiar grows my love to thee	12	1	2
Grows less and less sweet to him and knows no cause	14	3	14
To the sweet living of my friends I look	16		2
And every praised sequence of sweet strings	19		7
But that sweet sound which I preferred	21		47
The can must be so sweet the crust	22		15
Carries treats of sweet for bitter	25		6
Sphered so fast sweet soul we see	25		23
Springs one daughter the sweet child may	26		2
Does it smell sweet too in that holy place	27		44
Sweet unto God and the sweetness is grace	27		45
Gush flush the man the being with it sour or sweet	28	8	5
Beyond saying sweet past telling of tongue	28	9	5
Or as Austin a lingering-out sweet skill	28	10	6
Storm flakes were scroll-leaved flowers lily showers sweet heaven was astrew in them	28	21	8
A strain of the earths sweet being in the beginning	33		10
Fetched fresh as I suppose off some sweet wood	34		4
With swift slow sweet sour adazzle dim	37		9
Majestic as a stallion stalwart very-violet-sweet	38		10
Not that the sweet-fowl song-fowl needs no rest	39		9
Life this wildworth blown so sweet	41		93
The sweet especial scene	43		22
Sweet especial rural scene	43		24
Or love or pity or all that sweet notes not his might nursle	45		6
Those sweet hopes quell whose least me quickenings lift	48		37
With lissome scions sweet scions	52		3
Months earlier since I had our sweet reprieve and ransom	53		7
Earth sweet earth sweet landscape with leaves throng	58		1
Earth sweet earth sweet landscape with leaves throng	58		1
Where whatevers prized and passes of us everything thats fresh and fast flying of us seem to us sweet of us and swiftly away with done away with undone	59		8
Undone done with soon done with and yet dearly and dangerously sweet	59		9
Winning ways airs innocent maiden manners sweet looks loose locks long locks lovelocks gaygear going gallant girlgrace	59		15
Winning ways airs innocent maiden manners sweet looks loose locks long locks lovelocks			

Word	Poem	Stan.	Line
gaygear going gallant girlgrace	59		15
The sweet alms self is her	60		43
With sweet and scarless sky	60		120
Home at heart heavens sweet gift then leave let that alone	62		11
Sweet fire the sire of muse my soul needs this	76		9
Ending in sweet uncertainty	77		121
Touchd from heaven in sweet dreams	77		126
Ay sweet to taste beside this woe	80	7	7
With just such sweet potential skill	81		20
As halves of sweet-pea-blossom are	81		44
My love and all was sweet and well	81		121
Knowledge is strong but love is sweet	81		154
As a self-embraced sweet thought	85		3
As a self-caressd sweet thought	85		4
Married will make a sweet and matchless wife	94		31
Bid your papa goodnight sweet exhibition	97		8
This sweet deserter lists herself anew	102	1	65
So I go out my little sweet is done	103		17
Affined well to that sweet solitude	107	1	15
Led Richard with a sweet undoing pain	107	4	17
Heaven make it sweet to you she said	109	3	3
But with a sweet persistency	110		5
The proper sweet re-attributing above	113		11
Then she seems sweet who seems his bride	120		16
Might we not think the sweet and daring rises	122		2
In copying your sweet silence	125		24
Why theres an interest and sweet soul in beauty	125		41
And daylight and sweet air	133		14
Should choke sweet virtues glory is times great guilt	136		2
With a sweet joy of a sweet joy	138		44
With a sweet joy of a sweet joy	138		44
Sweet of a sweet of a sweet joy	138		45
Sweet of a sweet of a sweet joy	138		45
Sweet of a sweet of a sweet joy	138		45
Of a sweet a sweet sweet joy	138		46
Of a sweet a sweet sweet joy	138		46
Of a sweet a sweet sweet joy	138		46
As wishing all about us sweet	139		1
Sweet soul not scorning honest sweat	139		5
When the air was sweet-and-sour of the flown fineflour of	142		4
Cuckoo bird and open ear wells heart-springs delightfully sweet	146		2
Or sweet the golden glue	148		35
Tampering with those sweet bines draws them out strains them strains them	152		21
Next after sweet success I am not left even this	152		92
While sick men shall cast sighs of sweet			

Word	Poem	Stan.	Line
Sweet (cont.)			
health all despairing	152		108
So long to this sweet spot this leafy lean-over	152		116
And what sways with you maybe this sweet maid	157		22
Sweet-and-sour			
When the air was sweet-and-sour of the flown fineflour of	142		4
Sweet-familiar			
More sweet-familiar grows my love to thee	12	1	2
Sweet-fowl			
Not that the sweet-fowl song-fowl needs no rest	39		9
Sweet-pea-blossom			
As halves of sweet-pea-blossom are	81		44
Sweetbriar			
The air smells strong of sweetbriar in the park	135		24
Sweeter			
That sweets sweeter ending	48		31
Made sweeter not made dim	60		111
Making the shadow sweeter a spiritual grace	107	4	15
Sweeter thy kisses my own love	109	38	3
Smells that are sweeter-memoried than the rose	119		3
Sweeter-memoried			
Smells that are sweeter-memoried than the rose	119		3
Sweetest			
Then sweetest seems the houseless shore	15		35
Both sing sometimes the sweetest sweetest spells	39		6
Both sing sometimes the sweetest sweetest spells	39		6
With the sweetest air that said still plied and pressed	47		3
There and your sweetest sendings ah divine	48		13
Even to the tillage of the sweetest spot	102	3	16
The sweetest sonnet five or six times read	117		9
Then sweetest seems the seeming bride	120		18
His sweetest nectar hides behind	148		42
There sweetest freshest shadowiest	159		23
Sweetheart			
Wept wife wept sweetheart would be one	41		105
Sweetly			
Sweetly then and of free act	77		89
More sweetly shades her stolen hair	120		7
It never yet so sweetly was put on	125		29
By speech so sweetly broken up and gone	125		31
Sweetness			
A piteous siren sweetness on the sea	2		127
God comes all sweetness to your Lenten lips	11		2

Word	Poem	Stan.	Line
Nor elsewhere can thy sweetness unendear	12	1	5
And minor sweetness scarce made mention of	19		12
Sweet unto God and the sweetness is grace	27		45
Let the warbled sweetness rill	77		84
Sweetness from the hour and dip	77		132
Rememberd sweetness for my thought	81		139
So waste in tears over this bed of sweetness	102	1	38
That sweetness re-attributing above	113		12
News from Belleisle even such a sweetness blows	119		6
The turmoil and the torment it has I swear a sweetness	152		90
Sweets			
Sweet flowers I carry sweets for bitter	10		6
That sweets sweeter ending	48		31
He shall have summer sweets and dress	124		5
And I shall know of sweets for him	124		11
Swell			
Some traild the Nautilus or on the swell	2		56
Where the green swell is in the havens dumb	9		7
And bird and blossom swell	42		23
Swelld			
Swelld the sweet strain to a melodious wail	2		133
Swelling			
Thence the discharge of it there its swelling to be	28	7	6
Swells			
And for the tinklings on the falls and swells	107	2	7
Swept			
Adown the clattering gullies swept the rain	1	13	2
What time the baffled Frank swept back pursud	1	14	8
Paves the clouds on the swept azure	78		10
He swept what scope he was	148		15
Swerver			
In mankinds medley a duty-swerver	41		53
Swift			
With swift slow sweet sour adazzle dim	37		9
They watched the brush of the swift stringy drops	107	3	13
Swiftly			
Where whatevers prized and passes of us everything thats fresh and fast flying of us seems to us sweet of us and swiftly away with done away with undone	59		8
Swill			
Lend him a lift from the sea-swill	41		63
Swim			
For rose-moles all in stipple upon trout that swim	37		3
Phoebus loosend tresses swim	77		102
Springs in the floating air and the skies swim	113		6

Word	Poem	Stan.	Line
Swimming			
Anon across their swimming splendour strook	2		15
Swimming and languishd green upon the deep	2		114
Swims			
Long where we leave him froliclavish while he looks about him laughs swims	159		42
Swing			
And out of the swing of the sea	9		8
Come swing the sculls on Penmaen pool	30		8
In his ecstasy then off off forth on swing	36		4
Swings			
Swings the stroke dealt	28	6	4
Thousands of thorns thoughts swings though commonweal	70		8
Still the scarlet swings and dances on the blade	152		44
Swinishly			
That swinishly refuses such a pearl	102	3	33
That swinishly refuses such a pearl	102	3	39
Swirling			
Swirling out bloom till all the air is blind	2		89
And the inboard seas run swirling and hawling	28	19	3
Swivelled			
Wiry and white-fiery and whirlwind-swivelled snow	28	13	7
Swolln			
Swolln is the wind that in argent billows	78		3
Swoon			
The swoon of a heart that the sweep and the hurl of thee trod	28	2	6
Swooned			
Something I said I swooned and fell	81		118
Sword			
Take Canaan with your sword and with your bow	5		56
Princes strong for the sword and slaughter	26		27
Some find me a sword some	28	11	1
And he my peace my parting sword and strife	66	1	4
Swords			
Your comfort is as sharp as swords	81		32
Swung			
The drenched hair of slabby weeds that swung	2		113
He swung to his first poised purport of reply	47		4
Bow swung finds tongue to fling out broad its name	57		4
Swung down at a disarray	144		8
What sights shall be when some that swung wretches on crutches	152		127
Sycamore			
She by a sycamore	111		1
Like me sat sighing by a sycamore-tree	111		14
Fairyland silk-beech scrolled ash packed sycamore wild wychelm hornbeam fretty			

Word	Poem	Stan.	Line
overstood	159		24
Sycamore-tree			
Like me sat sighing by a sycamore-tree	111		14
Sydney			
Sydney Fletcher Bristol-bred	41		56
Sylvester			
Sylvester come Sylvester you may trust	107	3	1
Sylvester come Sylvester you may trust	107	3	1
Sylvester came they went by Cumnor Hill	107	3	9
Most dented lay Sylvester reading Keats	107	4	21
Sounds reachd him Richard came Sylvester smiled	107	4	24
Sympathising			
Mary sees sympathising	42		26
Table			
Crowded let his table be	24		26
Tabour			
They touch heaven tabour on it how their talons sweep	149	1	7
They touch they tabour on it hover on it here there hurled	149	2	1
Tackle			
To the men in the tops and the tackle rode over the storms brawling	28	19	8
Each sport has here its tackle and tool	30		6
And all trades their gear and tackle and trim	37		6
Tact			
Has wit enough but less than female tact	94		19
Tail			
From crown to tail-fin floating fringed the spine	2		41
To mantle-oer the tail such as is shed	2		49
Unvalve or shut his vaned tail	130		11
Tail-fin			
From crown to tail-fin floating fringed the spine	2		41
Tails			
Their filmy tails adown whose length there showd	2		104
Tainting			
Tall suns tingeing or treacherous the tainting of the earths air	59		5
Take			
Take Canaan with your sword and with your bow	5		56
Take a lesson from the ground	24		14
Take settler and seamen tell men with women	28	12	3
To his youngster take his treat	48		11
Take as for tool not toy meant	49		13
He does take fresh and fresh	60		56
To do without take tosses and obey	68		4
And sober lustres take the gloom	77		20
Take courage this shall need no further art	80	7	33

Word	Poem	Stan.	Line
Take (cont.)			
Ill take in hand the blady stone	80	7	48
No house of rimmon may I take	81		140
But has not learnt to take it gracefully	94		16
Now I am minded to take pipe in hand	105		1
And will not take denial	110		7
Or take it thus that the concording stars	122		7
Take their peculiar thorns and natural pain	123		5
And I must take your amends cry pardon and then be dumb	128		20
To take her while their tongues would go	145		26
To take his lovely likeness more and more	151		2
Brave all and take what comes as here this rabble is come	152		102
Taken			
That I have taken to plead with if the sound	13		9
Before-time-taken dearest prized and priced	28	22	6
They have taken out their long brands	109	14	1
Takes			
Takes to the seas and snows	41		58
So takes the sister sense can find no mark	113		4
Serves and what side he takes	148		24
Some pageant which takes tears and I must foot with feeling that	152		26
Taking			
You striped in secret with breath-taking whips	11		3
Takings			
To the often takings of desirous winds	111		3
Tale			
Give us the tale of bricks as heretofore	5		49
Ever so black on it our tale o our oracle let life waned ah let life wind	61		10
His tale and telling has been given to me	107	1	18
Tales			
Told tales with what hearts stress	54		23
Talks			
Talks of self-sacrifice yet cant forgive	94		22
Tall			
Pendant in formal line from cornice tall	1	12	7
But roped with always all the way down from the tall	28	4	6
Ears and the call of the tall nun	28	19	7
Tall suns tingeing or treacherous the tainting of the earths air	59		5
Veins violets and tall trees makes more and more	73		11
In the quick fragrance of tall rolling pines	84		5
His three brothers are each as tall	109	21	3
I have tall daughters dear that heed my hand	158		2
Talmai			
Rise match your strength with monstrous Talmai	5		57

Word	Poem	Stan.	Line
Talons			
They touch heaven tabour on it how their talons sweep	149	1	7
With talons sweep	149	2	2
Tame			
That in smooth spoons spy lifes masque mirrored tame	75		13
Tampering			
Tampering with those sweet bines draws them out strains them strains them	152		21
Tangled			
On tangled shoals that bar the brook a crowd	2		96
Tatter-tangled and dingle-a-dangled	138		25
Tangles			
And tangles on a down of France	83		14
Tantalean			
And Tantalean slaty ashiness	117		5
Taper			
It shapes itself in taper skeins	130		18
Tapers			
The altar-tapers flard in gusts in vain	1	13	5
Tar			
Every inch a tar	41		74
Tarpeian			
Tarpeian-fast but a blown beacon of light	28	28	8
Tarpeian-fast			
Tarpeian-fast but a blown beacon of light	28	28	8
Tars			
Our redcoats our tars both these being the greater part	63		2
And hate the ill-visaged cursing tars	114		10
Tarsus			
Near by is Pauls free Tarsus fabled where	136		7
And Paul is Tarsus true Bellerophon	136		10
Tartarus			
The pang of Tartarus Christians hold	80	1	1
Task			
By that window what task what fingers ply	46		5
When tis the confidante that sets the task	94		2
But here here is a workman from his days task sweats	152		42
The telling time our task is times some part	153		5
Over finger-teasing task his twiny boots	159		33
Tasking			
Times tasking it is fathers that asking for ease	28	26	11
Tasks			
Wants war wants wounds weary his times his tasks	68		3
Taste			
And taste the treats of Penmaen pool	30		40
Bitter would have me taste my taste was me	67		10

Word	Poem	Stan.	Line
madrigal start	28	18	6
Why tears is it tears such a melting a madrigal start	28	18	6
Yet shed what tears sad truelove should	41		107
I to him turn with tears	52		10
My tongue had taught thee comfort touch had quenched thy tears	53		10
Thy tears that touched my heart child Felix poor Felix Randal	53		11
While sheeny tears and sunlit mirth	77		129
I plead and you will give your tears	81		28
My tears are but a cloud of rain	81		36
Intolerable tears I bleed	81		67
My signalling tears might ring up Floris now	102	1	7
Laughing or tears I think I could do either	102	1	14
That tears and laughter are hung close together	102	1	16
I find I am as ready with my tears	102	1	34
So waste in tears over this bed of sweetness	102	1	38
The time save when her tears which still descend	111		5
From tears shed over childrens graves	123		3
With tears to put her candle out	145		24
Some pageant which takes tears and I must foot with feeling that	152		26
And beautys dearest veriest vein is tears	157		4
Teases			
Coils keeps and teases simple sight	22		12
Teasing			
Fresh brooks to salt sand-teasing waters shoaly	16		4
Over finger-teasing task his twiny boots	159		33
Tedious			
Two tedious acts were past	54		29
Teeming			
If floodtide teeming thrills her full	30		22
Death teeming in by her portholes	41		38
Scoop you from teeming filth some sickly hovel	77		6
Teevo			
Teevo cheevo cheevio chee	138		1
Tell			
They tell its story thus amidst the heat	1	2	1
Which I may tell at autumn-time	4		15
Tell me the name now tell me its name	27		20
Tell me the name now tell me its name	27		20
They multiply multiply who can tell how	27		41
My heart but you were dovewinged I can tell	28	3	6
Take settler and seamen tell men with women	28	12	3
They could tell him for hours dandled the to and fro	28	16	6
But tell me child your choice what shall I buy	47		1
One yes I can tell such a key I do know such a place	59		7

Word	Poem	Stan.	Line
Tell (cont.)			
A care kept where kept do but tell us where kept where	59		30
But these two ware of a world where but these two tell each off the other of a rack	61		13
And then I choke to tell this out	81	7	16
Give him the gift I cannot tell	81		111
And truly tell to me	109	11	4
I pray you tell to me	109	25	4
I know what you will tell me neglectful that you were not	128		5
Why get thee gone then tell thy mother I want her	152		16
Out on the giant air tell summer no	154		3
Telling			
Came midst the drizzle telling how last night	1	14	2
Beyond saying sweet past telling of tongue	28	9	5
His tale and telling has been given to me	107	1	18
Or a jaunting vaunting vaulting assaulting trumpet telling	141		7
The telling time our task is times some part	153		5
Tells			
Tells Mary her mirth till Christs birth	42		46
There boy bugler born he tells me of Irish	48		2
Stones ring like each tucked string tells each hung bells	57		3
That here personal tells off these heart-song powerful peals	141		2
Temperateness			
Controlld them to a grey-green temperateness	107	4	14
Temperd			
The temperd soil where only her flower is found	102	3	4
Tempest			
Startle the poor sheep back is the shipwrack then a harvest does tempest carry the grain for thee	28	30	8
O in turns of tempest me heaped there me frantic to avoid thee and flee	64		8
Tempests			
My tempests there my fire and fever fussy	75		14
Temple			
This was no classic temple orderd round	1	7	1
Only the breathing temple and fleet	41		92
Temples			
Then over his turned temples here	144		13
Tempt			
But if I cannot tempt his thought	124		21
Ten			
Apart betwixt ten thousand petalld lips	2		21
Ten or twelve only ten or twelve	43		20
Ten or twelve only ten or twelve	43		20

Word	Poem	Stan.	Line
Falls light as ten years long taught how to and why	47		8
Christ for Christ plays in ten thousand places	57		12
Tender			
Or tender pinks with bloody Tyrian dye	2		47
Or bat with tender and air-crisping wings	19		2
To thee we tender the beauties all	26		21
Finger of a tender of o of a feathery delicacy the breast of the	28	30	6
Since country is so tender	43		12
Or to-fro tender trambeams truckle at the eye	46		4
Yields tender as a pushed peach	48		23
Turn most on tender byplay	54		16
Crisp lips straight nose and tender-slanted cheek	136		16
Tender-slanted			
Crisp lips straight nose and tender-slanted cheek	136		16
Tendered			
Tendered to him ah well God rest him all road ever he offended	53		8
Tenderer			
The appealing of the passion is tenderer in prayer apart	28	26	14
Tenderest			
Never fleets more fastened with the tenderest truth	59		12
Tenderness			
But is there a place for tenderness	81		77
Tent			
Your hands have borne the tent-poles on you plod	5		7
Tent-poles			
Your hands have borne the tent-poles on you plod	5		7
Terebinth			
And trees of terebinth and stones	15		39
Term			
Allow at least it has one term and part	102	3	5
Terms			
New-dated from the terms that reappear	12	1	1
Terraces			
Upon the mouldring terraces amain	1	13	4
Terrible			
Terrible fruit was on the tree	6		15
To me was terrible to hear	21		42
But ah but o thou terrible why wouldst thou rude on me	64		5
Terror			
Thy terror o Christ o God	28	2	4
Teryth			
Meantime some tongue cries what Teryth what			

Word	Poem	Stan.	Line
Teryth (cont.)			
thou poor fond father	152		22
Tether			
But then her tether calls her she falls off	103		12
Text			
The sun on falling waters writes the text	91		8
These are my very text of discontent	125		50
Th			
And still th unbroken silence broods	23		19
And still th Abysses infinite	23		25
Thames			
Rhine refused them Thames would ruin them	28	21	3
Than			
Till fearing ravage worse than in his flight	1	14	7
Than changeful pomp of courts is aye more wonderful	1	15	9
Of tremulous film more subtle than the vest	2		39
And boasting I have fairer things than these	2		86
Sooner than their mates and yet	4		29
Than treble-fervent more of other men	14	1	13
For poor loves failure than his hopeless rise	14	3	7
More powerless than the blind or lame	15		20
Even than this my thankless lore	15		22
The copse was never more than grey	21		2
Fairer than this one to brighten our day	26		8
Thou heardst me truer than tongue confess	28	2	3
Lower than death and the dark	28	32	4
More more than was will yet be	41		103
Than the most are must delight her	42		10
Well but there was more than this	42		33
Mannerly-hearted more than handsome face	47		9
A wilder beast from west than all were more	50		7
Deep deeper than divined	52		6
Fonder a care kept than we could have kept it kept	59		28
My more than meat and drink	60		11
Nay more than almoner	60		42
Than Purcell tune lets tread to see it does this keeps warm	62		2
Master more may than gaze gaze out of countenance	62		4
By groping round my comfortless than blind	69		6
How wouldst thou worse I wonder than thou dost	74	1	5
Do in spare hours more thrive than I that spend	74	1	7
Breathes once and quenched faster than it came	76		3
Double and higher than his wont	77		111
What have I more than other men	81		168
More golden than the world of lights	83		2
But each a hands breadth further than the next	91		7

Word	Poem	Stan.	Line
Has wit enough but less than female tact	94		19
Worse than when Floris found me in the garden	102	1	43
Yet this could be no others hand than his	102	1	48
Than all the crowns to me	109	38	4
Rather to ear than eye shews where they stray	112		4
Who came from further than the stars	115		3
Than we in the east dare look for buds disclose	119		2
Smells that are sweeter-memoried than the rose	119		3
Than fan or hood or strawy plait	120		8
That has it and she is fairer than Colomb	125		43
But late is better than never you see you have managed so	128		17
Is known to men more than me	138		13
No more than red and blue	148		33
No more than re and mi	148		34
A growing burnish brighter than before	151		4
Than sewers with sacred oils mankind that mob comes	152		104
Thankless			
Even than this my thankless lore	15		22
Thanks			
Returning thanks might offer such array	89		4
That			
To what serves mortal beauty dangerous does set dancing blood the o-seal-that-so feature flung prouder form	62		1
The			
The-last-breath penitent spirits the uttermost mark	28	32	6
Them beauty-in-the-ghost deliver it early now long before death	59		18
The-last-breath			
The-last-breath penitent spirits the uttermost mark	28	32	6
Thecla			
Who thinks of Thecla yet her name was known	136		3
Young Thecla scanned the dazzling streets one day	136		14
Great Thecla the plumed passionflower	145		42
Thence			
The choicest remnants thence such home forlorn	1	15	3
Thence the discharge of it there its swelling to be	28	7	6
Theory			
Hes wedded to his theory they say	97		1
Thereafter			
That plumes to peace thereafter and when peace			

Word	Poem	Stan.	Line
Thereafter (cont.)			
here does house	51		9
Thereby			
Dry up the blue and be not slaked thereby	117		7
One spell and well that one there ah thereby	153		7
Therein			
Their cheeks moved and the bones therein	92		3
Therewith			
Therewith to hanker for the small	81		153
Thew			
For all his dreadnought breast and braids of thew	28	16	5
Both thought and thew now bolder	49		8
Stand at stress each limbs barrowy brawn his thew	71		6
Theyre			
Theyre out of date lent sermons all the year	96	5	2
Thick			
With coral shells thick-pearled cords whateer	2		54
Crowd down upon a stream and jostling thick	2		94
In beds in gardens in thick plots I stand	5		37
When heavenly vales so thick shall stand	8		16
They rain against our much-thick and marsh air	40		7
The thick stars round him roll	60		99
Seldomer heartsore that treads through prick-proof thick	70		7
Now leaved how thick laced they are again	74	1	9
Once jostling thick the bluebell sheaves	81		13
His lips moved fast in sense too thick	81		100
Thick-fleeced bushes like a heifers ear	98	11	1
Whose silver skins lie level and thick in field	102	1	23
The stars are packed so thick to-night	135		19
Made known though thick through stone	148		11
Thick-fleeced			
Thick-fleeced bushes like a heifers ear	98	11	1
Thick-pearled			
With coral shells thick-pearled cords whateer	2		54
Thicken			
And more on each hand thicken and appear	2		30
Thickend			
Those cyclads made that thickend on my sight	2		37
And thickend like that drifted bloom the flock	2		99
Sickend and thickend by the glare and sand	5		19
Thickening			
I dare not taste the thickening salt	120		26
Thickest			
For where the martyrs bones were thickest trod	1	5	8
Thicket			
And thicket and thorp are merry	42		39

Word	Poem	Stan.	Line
Thickly			
She to the black-about air to the breaker the thickly	28	24	5
Thigh			
Rope-over thigh knee-nave and barrelled shank	71		3
Thin			
With a thin floating veil of water hoar	2		4
With draught of thin and pursuant cold so nips	11		6
Cluster of bugle blue eggs thin	41		21
And for that fearful hour life is more thin	80	3	5
And the thin stars tremble not	85		5
Bright hues long lookd at thin dissolve and fly	117		2
Thing			
Of that jacinthine thing that where it lingers	2		65
I had a dream a wondrous thing	4		1
It seemd so hard and dismal thing	4		31
That no recorded devilish thing was done	14	2	8
With not a thing to make me fear	21		40
The gladdest thing that our eyes have seen	26		18
Blinds her but she that weather sees one thing one	28	19	5
Thing that she there then the master	28	27	4
To me God knows deserving no such thing	34		2
All the air thing wear that build this world of wales	34		10
Stirred for a bird the achieve of the mastery of the thing	36		7
Each mortal thing does one thing and the same	57		5
Each mortal thing does one thing and the same	57		5
When the thing we freely forfeit is kept with fonder a care	59		27
Patience hard thing the hard thing but to pray	68		1
Patience hard thing the hard thing but to pray	68		1
A thing that weeps enduring long	81		50
It was a hard thing to undo this knot	91		1
It was a hard thing to undo this knot	91		10
Sees the right thing to do and does not act	94		20
What I do now is but the least least thing	102	1	54
Most ill-content this least least thing I do	102	1	57
The kings friend told the thing that was hid	109	12	1
The last thing Margarets fingers sew	145		13
How alls to one thing wrought	148		1
Like the thing that never knew the earth never off roots	159		27
Things			
Now all things rosy turnd the west had grown	2		19
And boasting I have fairer things than these	2		86
A press of winged things comes down this way	5		15
And would not have that legion of winged things	7		14
There lives the dearest freshness deep down things	31	1	10
Glory be to God for dappled things	37		1
All things counter original spare strange	37		7

Word	Poem	Stan.	Line
Things (cont.)			
These things these things were here and but the beholder	38		11
These things these things were here and but the beholder	38		11
Look foot to forelock how all things suit he	41		76
All things rising all things sizing	42		25
All things rising all things sizing	42		25
Shares their best gifts surely fall how things will	48		4
Leaves like the things of man you	55		3
In every least things life	60		8
On things aloof aloft	60		91
Mens wits to the things that are what good means where a glance	62		3
You rank and reeking things	77		5
And to the mystery of those things	77		47
And count the rosy cross with bannd disastrous things	89		9
Things that she likes seems often to despise	94		17
Well I know not but all things seem to-night	102	1	10
Of the wood-sorrel and all things sensitive	122		11
As the wood-sorrel and all things sensitive	122		14
That make my eyes sore and cross-colour things	125		46
While all things else may stir and range	130		7
Heaven with it whom she childs things by	149	2	7
Have all things ready in his room	152		10
Amongst come-back-again things things with a revival things with a recovery	152		134
Amongst come-back-again things things with a revival things with a recovery	152		134
Amongst come-back-again things things with a revival things with a recovery	152		134
Think			
I think where from and bound I wonder where	40		3
When chill woods wake and think of morn	77		23
Think of an opening page illumined	93	2	1
With the ready azure and high carmine think	93	2	2
Laughing or tears I think I could do either	102	1	14
No time to think Ill knot it on this ribbon	102	1	30
I think it is seven days she said	109	16	3
And every heart think loathingly	114		15
Might we not think the sweet and daring rises	122		2
I think he will not tire of me	124		2
We have come four do you think	125		14
Think this my birthday falls in saddening time of year	128		9
Think you want daffodils and follow as far	135		30
That I do think there is not to be had	138		32
To make believe my mood was mock o I might think so	152		41

Word	Poem	Stan.	Line
Thinking			
And thinking that she thinks has never thought	94		30
Thinks			
And thinking that she thinks has never thought	94		30
Who thinks of Thecla yet her name was known	136		3
Thinly			
Come because then most thinly lies	77		35
Thinned			
The moon dwindled and thinned to the fringe of a fingernail held to the candle	137		2
Thinning			
Rounded it thinning skywards by degrees	107	4	4
Third			
I am in Ireland now now I am at a third	66	1	8
Then up and spake the third brother	109	27	1
He taught another time there and a third	136		31
Thirst			
And never thirst or dearth	5		48
Eyes in their dark can day or thirst can find	69		7
While blind mens eyes shall thirst after day-light draughts of daylight	152		109
Thirsts			
Thirsts all-in-all in all a world of wet	69		8
Thistled			
Streaks of shadow thistled leas	77		137
Thistles			
On thistles that men look not grapes to gather	7		2
Thither			
But she who had housed them thither	41		42
Thongs			
With gorgons gear and barebill thongs and fangs	50		14
Thorn			
For us the vine was fenced with thorn	6		13
The winged fowls took part part fell in thorn	7		7
Or thorn-engaged impaled and pent	81		19
Thorn-engaged			
Or thorn-engaged impaled and pent	81		19
Thorns			
How soldiers platting thorns around Christs head	7		4
Food for five thousand on the thorns he shed	7		12
Thousands of thorns thoughts swings though commonweal	70		8
Take their peculiar thorns and natural pain	123		5
Thorny			
My evil words thorny with pain	81		27
Thorough			
A beetling baldbright cloud thorough England	41		24
Are earthworld airworld waterworld thorough hurled all by turn and turn about	159		18

Word	Poem	Stan.	Line
Thoroughfare			
Built thoroughfare heaven-roysterers in gay-gangs they throng they glitter in marches	72		2
Thorp			
And thicket and thorp are merry	42		39
Thought			
Those charms accepted of my inmost thought	12	1	9
Barely a sigh to thought of hopes forgone	14	3	9
And I had thought so hitherto	21		26
I thought the air must cut and strain	21		36
He thought he heard say	41		50
Both thought and thew now bolder	49		8
To my creating thought would neither hear	66	1	6
The fine delight that fathers thought the strong	76		1
And I shall shape one to my thought	80	7	40
Nocturns I thought were hurried through	81		92
Rememberd sweetness for my thought	81		139
I calld them and I thought them then	81		164
How turn my passion-pastured thought	81		174
As a self-embraced sweet thought	85		3
As a self-caressd sweet thought	85		4
The rainbow shines but only in the thought	91		2
Which yet is in the eye or in the thought	91		9
And thinking that she thinks has never thought	94		30
To trace some traceless loss of thought again	107	4	18
Even so my thought the rose and grey disposes	108		7
And coldly do belie the thought of thee	117		12
Waking I thought and it sufficed	118		8
I thought before I gather strength	118		13
But if I cannot tempt his thought	124		21
My thought was there to rest against the trees	125		8
Doomsday and death whose dateless thought must chart	126		3
I thought that you would have written my birthday came and went	128		1
Or listening thought of linen-winded Ghosts	135		18
To him who ever thought with love of me	140		1
O what a tune the thought	148		3
Hark hearer hear what I do lend a thought now make believe	159		1
Thoughts			
Our hearts charitys hearths fire our thoughts chivalrys throngs lord	28	34	8
His thoughts on her forsaken that she seems	50		11
With your fresh thoughts care for can you	55		4
Where selfwrung selfstrung sheathe-and shelterless thoughts against thoughts in groans grind	61		14
Where selfwrung selfstrung sheathe-and shelterless thoughts against thoughts in groans grind	61		14

Word	Poem	Stan.	Line
You jaded let be call off thoughts awhile	69		10
Thousands of thorns thoughts swings though commonweal	70		8
She kept her love-thoughts on most Lenten diet	82		7
I here forbid my thoughts to fool themselves with fears	152		30
With dreadful distillation of thoughts sour as blood	152		97
Thousand			
Apart betwixt ten thousand petalld lips	2		21
And on a thousand altars laid	6		9
Food for five thousand on the thorns he shed	7		12
Christ for Christ plays in ten thousand places	57		12
Thousands			
Two thousands of years are near upon past	27		16
He was but one like thousands more	41		84
Thousands of thorns thoughts swings though commonweal	70		8
Thralls			
Defeat thwart me oh the sots and thralls of lust	74	1	6
Thread			
A thread of light betrayd the hill	92		9
And stained and knots of golden thread	124		14
Threaded			
Give myrrhy-threaded golden folds of ease	11		12
Threads			
On pranked scale or threads of Carmine shot	2		106
Three			
God three-numbered form	28	9	2
Mid-numbered he in three of the thunder-throne	28	33	5
Three hundred souls o alas on board	41		2
Three rivals throng her garden chair	83		10
It might be none of the three	95		7
But with his other foot three miles beyond	100		4
By shine of candles three	109	1	2
In two years or in three	109	2	4
Although it were years three	109	3	2
For two years and for three	109	6	2
He saw his brothers three	109	7	2
It was but one to three	109	13	4
Beside his brothers three	109	20	2
Beside his brothers three	109	21	2
His three brothers are each as tall	109	21	3
Beside his brothers three	109	22	4
Among his brothers three	109	23	2
But saw his brothers three	109	24	4
No truth between you three	109	28	2
She heard but knockings three	109	29	2
If I give thee kisses three	109	37	2

Word	Poem	Stan.	Line
Three (cont.)			
Give me thy kisses three	109	38	2
Three miles indeed	125		13
The Holy Three in One	133		4
Yet Arthur is a bowman his three-heeled timberll hit	143		3
She caught the crying of those three	145		29
She told his name times-over three	145		56
Three-heeled			
Yet Arthur is a bowman his three-heeled timberll hit	143		3
Three-numbered			
God three-numbered form	28	9	2
Threefold			
A pious work with threefold purpose crownd	1	1	5
Threshing			
Scourged upon the threshing-floor	6		6
Threshing-floor			
Scourged upon the threshing-floor	6		6
Threshold			
So loading with obstruction that threshold	17		8
Threw			
In Josephs garden they threw by	6		21
Thrice			
And thrice and four times and again	98	37	2
Several times I saw them thrice or four times turning	152		59
Thriftless			
To thriftless reave both our rich round world bare	58		12
Thrill			
Through other bars it used to thrill	81		15
Thrills			
If floodtide teeming thrills her full	30		22
Thrive			
Do in spare hours more thrive than I that spend	74	1	7
That thrive in the loamy greenness of this place	122		15
Throat			
Trying each pleasurable throat that sings	19		6
Her milk-white throat and folded dew-lap slack	99		9
Throbbing			
An intense line of throbbing blood-light shook	2		16
To cool his plumy throbbing breast	77		92
Throe			
But here was heart-throe birth of a brain	28	29	7
Throne			
Mid-numbered he in three of the thunder-throne	28	33	5
Silence holds breath upon her throne	77		33

Word	Poem	Stan.	Line
Throned			
Grasp God throned behind	28	31	7
Throng			
Seek Gods house in happy throng	24		25
Falling flakes to the throng that catches and quails	28	24	6
Earth sweet earth sweet landscape with leaves throng	58		1
Built thoroughfare heaven-roysterers in gay-gangs they throng they glitter in marches	72		2
Three rivals throng her garden chair	83		10
From Oxford comes the throng and hum of bells	98	3	6
Thronged			
Our company thronged the hall	54		11
And breath immortal thronged that show	145		45
Throngs			
Our hearts charitys hearths fire our thoughts chivalrys throngs lord	28	34	8
Of own of abrupt self there so thrusts on so throngs the ear	45		8
Astray or aswarm all throughther in throngs self in self steeped and pashed quite	61		6
Throstle			
Throstle above her nested	42		20
Throttled			
The Mawddach how she trips though throttled	30		21
Throughther			
Astray or aswarm all throughther in throngs self in self steeped and pashed quite	61		6
Throw			
Upon Christ throw all away	24		5
Tho apt to throw it in a strange direction	94		14
To the bargain of its hate to throw	145		20
Throws			
Earth throws winters robes away	24		17
Thrush			
Thrushs eggs look little low heavens and thrush	33		3
Thrushs			
Thrushs eggs look little low heavens and thrush	33		3
Thrust			
And thus I will thrust in my right	80	7	47
Thrusts			
Of own of abrupt self there so thrusts on so throngs the ear	45		8
Thunder			
Glow glory in thunder	28	5	4
Mid-numbered he in three of the thunder-throne	28	33	5
But to Christ Lord of thunder	41		108

Word	Poem	Stan.	Line
Thunder (cont.)			
The thunder-purple seabeach plumed purple-of-thunder	45		12
The thunder-purple seabeach plumed purple-of-thunder	45		12
The thunder brags in joints and sparkling jags	80	7	3
Like knocking thunder all round Britains welkin	102	2	3
Thunder-purple			
The thunder-purple seabeach plumed purple-of-thunder	45		12
Thunder-throne			
Mid-numbered he in three of the thunder-throne	28	33	5
Thundering			
Of crumbling fore-foundering thundering all-surfy seas in seen	141		5
Thwart			
Defeat thwart me oh the sots and thralls of lust	74	1	6
Thwarts			
Bars or hells spell thwarts this to hoard unheard	66	1	12
Tide			
Two mazed shepherds perishd in the tide	1	14	3
The floating blooms and with tide flowing quenchd	2		139
But the spring-tide passd the same	4		24
Trench right the tide that ramps against the shore	35		2
And the tide of ill is out	77		28
With a south-westerly wind blustering with a tide rolls reels	141		4
Tides			
Which the tides cover in their overflow	2		2
I admire thee master of the tides	28	31	1
Tied			
And the flowers that he had tied	4		27
To his own selfbent so bound so tied to his turn	58		11
Ties			
With long-superfluous ties for nothing here	12	1	4
Thus he ties spiders web across his sight	102	3	28
Such spiders web he ties across his sight	102	3	34
Tighten			
Sleep Floris while I rob you tighten o sleep	102	1	18
Tiles			
All slumbered whom our rud red tiles	135		1
Till			
Into the cooling gloom till slowly all	1	12	5
Till fearing ravage worse than in his flight	1	14	7
Swirling out bloom till all the air is blind	2		89

Word	Poem	Stan.	Line
By visual compulsion till I hide	12	2	5
From nine oclock till morning light	21		1
Up till that mornings fall of dew	21		27
Oh till thou givest that sense beyond	23		43
Till dimpled joy steals oer its cheeks	23		52
Ill wait till morn eternal breaks	23		54
Till a maid in Davids house had birth	26		30
Till a lioness arose breasting the babble	28	17	7
And pelt music till nones to spill nor spend	35		8
Rich beams till death or distance buys them quite	40		8
Till a lifebelt and Gods will	41		62
Fresh till doomfire burn all	41		118
Tells Mary her mirth till Christs birth	42		46
Pining pining till time when reason rambled in it and some	53		3
Till the lifted clouds were nigh	77		72
In fits of music till sunset	77		87
Appeard not for the present till	92		8
Amidst the sistering planets till she comes	103		14
And they were bedded till daylight	109	1	3
Though they took till the seventeenth of next October to read	128		8
Till the longing is less and the good gone	138		36
Holds till hand aches and wonders what is there	151		8
Till walk the world he can with bare his feet	159		35
Tillage			
Even to the tillage of the sweetest spot	102	3	16
Tilt			
Towards wastes where round the ice-blocks tilt and fret	88		7
Towards those wastes where the ice-blocks tilt and fret	88		11
Timber			
Through the echoing timber does so rinse and wring	33		4
Off trundled timber and scoops of the hillside ground hollow hollow hollow ground	146		4
Timberll			
Yet Arthur is a bowman his three-heeled timberll hit	143		3
Timbrels			
Strike timbrels sing eat drink be full of mirth	5		43
Time			
What time the baffled Frank swept back pursud	1	14	8
Which I may tell at autumn-time	4		15
Autumn-time no earlier came	4		26
Or far-off promise of a time to be	13		4
And a spring-time joy have found	24		16
I shall keep time with thee mother of mine	27		19
But it rides time like riding a river	28	6	7

Word	Poem	Stan.	Line
Time (cont.)			
Before-time-taken dearest prized and priced	28	22	6
Spend here your measure of time and treasure	30		39
How ring right out our sordid turbid time	35		10
So at home time was to his truth and grace	41		99
Time past she has been attempted and pursued	50		5
Pillowy air he treads a time and hangs	50		10
Pining pining till time when reason rambled in it and some	53		3
But vastness blurs and time beats level enough the Resurrection	72		16
Should tongue that time now trumpet now that field	73		3
Whatever time this vapourous roof	80	6	1
Always the time remembereth	81		61
The time was late and the wet yellow woods	98	5	1
Yes for a time they held as well	101		1
No time to think Ill knot it on this ribbon	102	1	30
Their changing feet in flicker all the time	107	1	13
Heaven make the time be short she said	109	3	1
The time save when her tears which still descend	111		5
Would it were summer-time anon she sang	111		12
That shall not fail in winter-time	124		8
That are not less in winter-time	124		12
All time at once and span the distant goals	126		4
Think this my birthday falls in saddening time of year	128		9
Our sex should be born in April perhaps or the lily-time	128		13
For souls that might have blessed the time	133		9
Time was next whitest after Marys own	136		4
He taught another time there and a third	136		31
The telling time our task is times some part	153		5
Timed			
Timed her sad visions with his wreck	21		56
Times			
Times tasking it is fathers that asking for ease	28	26	11
Times told lovelier more dangerous o my chevalier	36		10
It is even seen times something server	41		52
Now times Andromeda on this rock rude	50		1
The seven or seven times seven	60		87
Evening strains to be times vast womb-of-all home-of-all hearse-of-all night	61		2
Wants war wants wounds weary his times his tasks	68		3
At God knows when to God knows what whose smiles not wrung see you unforeseen times rather as skies	69		12
Times eunuch and not breed one work that wakes	74	1	12

Word	Poem	Stan.	Line
And thrice and four times and again	98	37	2
The sweetest sonnet five or six times read	117		9
Should choke sweet virtues glory is times great guilt	136		2
To that first golden age of gospel times	136		5
She told his name times-over three	145		56
The times are nightfall look their light grows less	150		1
The times are winter watch a world undone	150		2
And more and more times laces round and round my heart	152		19
Several times I saw them thrice or four times turning	152		59
Several times I saw them thrice or four times turning	152		59
When ts light I quenched its rose times one rich rose my hand	152		82
The telling time our task is times some part	153		5
In one fair fall but for times aftercast	157		7
Times-over			
She told his name times-over three	145		56
Tingeing			
Tall suns tingeing or treacherous the tainting of the earths air	59		5
Tingling			
Tingling between dusk and silver	98	1	4
Tiniest			
And I could hear the tiniest sound	21		17
Tinklings			
And for the tinklings on the falls and swells	107	2	7
Tinted			
A tinted fin on either shoulder hung	2		52
Twice lovely tinted eastern turned Greek	136		15
Tints			
Lit with exquisite tints seven	77		109
Tiny			
Would not put out some tiny golden centre	98	22	6
Sky peakd with tiny flames	98	25	5
So tiny a trickle of song-strain	138		4
Tiptoes			
His body swayd upon tiptoes	87		3
Tire			
Beat heave and the strong mountain tire	81	5	2
I think he will not tire of me	124		2
Tired			
The trumpet waxes loud tired are your feet	5		8
But now I am so tired I soon shall send	14	3	8
Tires			
The city tires to death	133		12
Titans			
Pourtrayd along the frieze with Titans brood	1	7	4

Word	Poem	Stan.	Line
Titians			
The skill of dreamy Claude and Titians mellow gloom	1	10	9
Rich Titians faded in the straying gleam	1	12	3
Title			
And art and beauty title now too full	1	15	6
Their special-general title to thy love	12	1	14
That forge her title of inheritance	102	1	70
To			
He slew the Egyptian yesterday to-day	5		3
With joy for to-day and hope for to-morrow	26		15
With joy for to-day and hope for to-morrow	26		15
Or to-fro tender trambeams truckle at the eye	46		4
Well I know not but all things seem to-night	102	1	10
The stars are packed so thick to-night	135		19
I awoke in the midsummer not-to-call night in the white and the walk of the morning	137		1
To-day the sky is two and two	138		16
Shall new-dapple next year sure as to-morrow morning	152		133
All lie tumbled-to then with loop-locks	159		31
To-day			
He slew the Egyptian yesterday to-day	5		3
With joy for to-day and hope for to-morrow	26		15
To-day the sky is two and two	138		16
To-fro			
Or to-fro tender trambeams truckle at the eye	46		4
To-morrow			
With joy for to-day and hope for to-morrow	26		15
Shall new-dapple next year sure as to-morrow morning	152		133
To-night			
Well I know not but all things seem to-night	102	1	10
The stars are packed so thick to-night	135		19
Today			
Not today we need lament	28	35	13
Together			
We meet together you and I	8		10
Why raindrop-roundels looped together	30		27
Blast bole and bloom together	41		15
Grass and greenworld all together	42		18
Their heads together in a stormy blot	90		6
Her white weed-bathed knees are shut together	99		2
Together as the criss-crossd shelly cup	101		2
That tears and laughter are hung close together	102	1	16
Only the belled foxgloves lispd together	107	1	6
Toil			
Toil has shed round your head	28	35	15
And all is seared with trade bleared smeared with toil	31	1	6
Nay in all that toil that coil since seems I			

Word	Poem	Stan.	Line
Tongue (cont.)			
Thou heardst me truer than tongue confess	28	2	3
Beyond saying sweet past telling of tongue	28	9	5
A prophetess towered in the tumult a virginal tongue told	28	17	8
Tongue true vaunt-and tauntless	48		15
My tongue had taught thee comfort touch had quenched thy tears	53		10
Dog he did give tongue	54		34
Bow swung finds tongue to fling out broad its name	57		4
To with no tongue to plead no heart to feel	58		3
And what is earths eye tongue or heart else where	58		9
Should tongue that time now trumpet now that field	73		3
Now I grow numb my tongue strikes on the gum	80	7	27
My fast-lodged tongue to her the gift	81		116
You ask why cant Clarissa hold her tongue	96	4	1
With ear-caressing speech where is the tongue	122		17
Must I give tongue again	125		23
Meantime some tongue cries what Teryth what thou poor fond father	152		22
Tongues			
Two tongues like butterflies	98	12	7
To take her while their tongues would go	145		26
Tonight			
Lord Beuno comes tonight	152		7
Tonight sir	152		8
Took			
Philip took oath while glory or defeat	1	2	3
The winged fowls took part part fell in thorn	7		7
With such a seconding nor Saturn took	14	2	9
I took of vine a cross-barred rod or rood	20		8
Or once or never took loves proper food	20		10
To the shrouds they took they shook in the hurling and horrible airs	28	15	8
Of her flesh he took flesh	60		55
Took primroses their pulld and plotted leaf	107	3	18
Though they took till the seventeenth of next October to read	128		8
The sea took pity it interposed with doom	158		1
Tool			
Each sport has here its tackle and tool	30		6
Take as for tool not toy meant	49		13
Toolsmooth			
Only the beakleaved boughs dragonish damask the toolsmooth bleak light black	61		9
Top			
Between the tower-top and the ground	15		29
Alone upon the hill-top heaven oer him	107	1	8

Word	Poem	Stan.	Line
Toppd			
Like scalded banks toppd once with principal flowers	102	2	14
Tops			
To the men in the tops and the tackle rode over the storms brawling	28	19	8
Of wringing tree-tops chalky lanes	77		135
Which between ash-tops suffers loss	121		5
Topsyturvy			
Rides repeated topsyturvy	30		15
Topt			
In Spring our river-banks are topt	124		17
Torment			
The turmoil and the torment it has I swear a sweetness	152		90
Tormented			
Charitable not live this tormented mind	69		3
With this tormented mind tormenting yet	69		4
Tormenting			
With this tormented mind tormenting yet	69		4
Torn			
Since trampled Spain by royal discord torn	1	15	1
Five ways the precious branches torn	6		14
Cloud-puffball torn tufts tossed pillows flaunt forth then chevy on an air	72		1
Tossed			
Cloud-puffball torn tufts tossed pillows flaunt forth then chevy on an air	72		1
Tosses			
To do without take tosses and obey	68		4
Touch			
At the touch of her wandering wondering breath	26		6
Thy doing and dost thou touch me afresh	28	1	7
To touch her being so slender	43		13
My tongue had taught thee comfort touch had quenched thy tears	52		10
And hard men feel a softening touch	77		30
Touch me and purify and shew	77		39
They touch heaven tabour on it how their talons sweep	149	1	7
They touch they tabour on it hover on it here there hurled	149	2	1
Touchd			
Touchd from heaven in sweet dreams	77		126
With centres duly touchd and nestlike spots	107	4	7
Touched			
Ah touched in your bower of bone	28	18	1
Thy tears that touched my heart child Felix poor Felix Randal	52		11
Now more precisely touched in light and gloom	98	30	4

Word	Poem	Stan.	Line
Tower			
I mark the tower swallows run	15		28
Between the tower-top and the ground	15		29
To flash from the flame to the flame then tower from the grace to the grace	28	3	8
Furred snows charged tuft above tuft tower	30		31
And told by nature tower	49		9
That bead the plain did ever havering church-tower	100		6
Tower-top			
Between the tower-top and the ground	15		29
Towered			
A prophetess towered in the tumult a virginal tongue told	28	17	8
Towers			
A sombre length of grey four towers placed	1	1	3
The towers musical quiet-walled grove	12	1	10
I see the crowning of their towers	15		7
Towery city and branchy between towers	44		1
Of it angels fall they are towers from heaven a story	75		3
With potent lips call down cemented towers	104		5
Towery			
Towery city and branchy between towers	44		1
Town			
But Gertrude Lily and Luther are two of a town	28	20	5
How these two shame this shallow and frail town	35		9
Now near by Ventnor town	41		30
The dapple-eared lily below thee that country and town did	44		3
A bell at midnight woke the town	81		87
Of it must be boys from the town	159		12
Towns			
And bred acquaintance of unused towns	107	2	2
Toy			
Take as for tool not toy meant	49		13
Trace			
To trace some traceless loss of thought again	107	4	18
Traced			
Yet when my unset tresses hung loose-traced	102	1	3
There was a meadow level almost you traced	107	4	1
Traceless			
To trace some traceless loss of thought again	107	4	18
Tracery			
With flowing tracery engemming rays	1	6	2
Traces			
And scarcely traces where one beauty strays	1	6	7
Track			
And that such a sable track	4		21

Word	Poem	Stan.	Line
Trade			
And all is seared with trade bleared smeared with toil	31	1	6
Trades			
And all trades their gear and tackle and trim	37		6
Tragic			
What bass is our viol for tragic tones	75		8
Traild			
Some traild the Nautilus or on the swell	2		56
Trailing			
One scarlet feather trailing to the wind	2		81
Training			
She had come from a cruise training seamen	41		12
Trambeams			
Or to-fro tender trambeams truckle at the eye	46		4
Tramp			
I hear the multitude tramp by	80	7	29
Trample			
Plunge orbd in rainbow arcs and trample and tread	2		78
Trampled			
Since trampled Spain by royal discord torn	1	15	1
Tramplers			
Discovering you dark tramplers tyrant years	157		2
Tranquil			
At tranquil turns by natures rule	30		14
Translucent			
This was their manner one translucent crest	2		38
Transmit			
Hued sunbeam will transmit	60		88
Trash			
A beacon an eternal beam flesh fade and mortal trash	72		19
Travelld			
Not furtherd far my travelld feet	81		157
Travelling			
My window shows the travelling clouds	15		1
To fields of light millions of travelling rays	103		9
Traverse			
Of the flown skylark and his traverse flight	122		3
Treacherous			
Tall suns tingeing or treacherous the tainting of the earths air	59		5
Tread			
Plunge orbd in rainbow arcs and trample and tread	2		78
Who tread the grapes are splayd with stripes of gore	5		51
We shout with them that tread the grapes	6		12
Then though I should tread tufts of consolation	48		25
Then let the march tread our ears	52		9
O then weary then why should we tread o why			

Word	Poem	Stan.	Line
Tread (cont.)			
are we so haggard at the heart so care-coiled care-killed so fagged so fashed so cogged so cumbered	59		26
Than Purcell tune lets tread to see it does this keeps warm	62		2
Where you and I were wont to tread	81		156
Treadmire			
Squadroned masks and manmarks treadmire toil there	72		8
Treads			
Pillowy air he treads a time and hangs	50		10
Are the groins of the braes that the brook treads through	56		10
Seldomer heartsore that treads through prick-proof thick	70		7
Deed-bound I am one deed treads all down here cramps all doing what do not yield	152		100
Treasonable			
I outrage it with treasonable kissing	102	1	52
Treasure			
The treasure never eyesight got nor was ever guessed what for the hearing	28	26	8
Spend here your measure of time and treasure	30		39
Lads and men here lade and treasure	41		11
The treasure from all cities	104		13
Treat			
To his youngster take his treat	48		11
It is hardly a proper treat for a birthday to rest in her arms	128		12
Treats			
Carries treats of sweet for bitter	25		6
And taste the treats of Penmaen pool	30		40
Treble			
Than treble-fervent more of other men	14	1	13
Hang of a treble size	88		4
Treble-fervent			
Than treble-fervent more of other men	14	1	13
Tree			
Terrible fruit was on the tree	6		15
On Easter morn the tree was forth	6		23
In its condition no the tropic tree	14	1	3
Who to us are as dew unto grass and tree	26		38
Is Mary the rose then Mary the tree	27		26
Of wringing tree-tops chalky lanes	77		135
Over field and tree	109	17	2
Like me sat sighing by a sycamore-tree	111		14
That comes again to the woodland tree	124		4
Poetry to it as a tree whose boughs break in the sky	149	1	3
Tree-tops			
Of wringing tree-tops chalky lanes	77		135

Word	Poem	Stan.	Line
Trees			
Plashes amidst the billowy apple-trees	2		87
Many trees and flowers round	4		19
And trees of Terebinth and stones	15		39
Veins violets and tall trees makes more and more	73		11
Caught on the dank-ytressed trees	77		106
When this is sought trees will be wanting not	80	7	39
Or else their cooings came from bays of trees	98	2	1
Dappled with diminishd trees	98	8	2
And bluer grey the flocks of trees look in the plain	105		8
Beyond the banks wete steep a brush of trees	107	4	3
And long the trees were colourd but the oer-head	107	4	12
My thought was there to rest against the trees	125		8
Trees by their yield	127		1
Into fairy trees wildflowers woodferns	159		50
Treetop			
To the all-a-leaf of the treetop	138		38
Tremble			
And the thin stars tremble not	85		5
Trembling			
To thee the trembling sinner prays	23		3
Crept trembling out of bed	135		4
Tremulous			
Of tremulous film more subtle than the vest	2		39
Trench			
Trench right the tide that ramps against the shore	35		2
Trenched			
Trenched with tears carved with cares	28	15	3
Tresses			
Down that dank rock oer which their lush long tresses weep	2		115
Tresses dippd in rainbow fire	77		14
Phoebus loosend tresses swim	77		102
Yet when my unset tresses hung loose-traced	102	1	3
Trial			
I would not make the trial	110		2
Trick			
I strove to look I lost the trick	81		97
Tricked			
His tear-tricked cheeks of flame	54		36
Trickle			
So trickle from your hand	5		42
And fainter finer trickle far	77		81
So tiny a trickle of song-strain	138		4
Trickling			
Earth all out who with trickling increment	73		10

Word	Poem	Stan.	Line
Trim			
And all trades their gear and tackle and trim	37		6
He shall have summer goods and trim	124		9
Trinity			
Singing to the Trinity	24		28
Trip			
I hope that all the places on our trip	107	4	27
Triple			
The triple-hummocked giants stool	30		10
Triple-hummocked			
The triple-hummocked giants stool	30		10
Trips			
The mawddach how she trips though throttled	30		21
Triumph			
Triumph of airy grace and perfect harmony	1	7	9
Let him ride her pride in his triumph despatch and have done with his doom there	28	27	8
Deals triumph and immortal years	52		12
Shes framed to triumph in adversity	94		23
Trod			
For where the martyrs bones were thickest trod	1	5	8
The swoon of a heart that the sweep and the hurl of thee trod	28	2	6
Generations have trod have trod have trod	31	1	5
Generations have trod have trod have trod	31	1	5
Generations have trod have trod have trod	31	1	5
Cheer whom though the hero whose heaven-handling flung me foot trod	64		12
Troops			
Clusterd in troops and halod by the light	2		36
Tropes			
And gives for tropes his judgment all away	102	3	29
And gives for tropes his judgment all away	102	3	35
Tropic			
In its condition no the tropic tree	14	1	3
Troubled			
Airwards disturbd and the scarce troubled sea	2		110
Trout			
For rose-moles all in stipple upon trout that swim	37		3
Truckle			
Or to-fro tender trambeams truckle at the eye	46		4
True			
A fortress of true faith and central stand	1	5	3
And now I wish that it were true	21		28
Is it anything true does it grow upon ground	27		2
None but you this her true	28	35	11
Tongue true vaunt-and tauntless	48		15
That should have been true to me	95		9
If that were true it could not live a day	97		2
Tis so conceived in his true lineament	102	1	50

Word	Poem	Stan.	Line
Though self-made bands at last may true love bind	102	3	19
New love is free love or true love tis not	102	3	20
New love is free love or true love tis not	102	3	27
And what is your true name she said	109	4	1
Her true love she might see	109	30	4
Wilt thou follow me my true love	109	37	1
Wilt thou follow me my true love	109	37	3
O I will follow thee my true love	109	38	1
Have here a true one echoing the sound	116		2
True madam I am sorry now to see	125		16
Ill meant yet true I best should flatter then	125		20
Flatterys all out of place where praise is true	125		35
That this is true of tis Castaras self	125		62
The best ideal is the true	133		1
You spoil the plot I find my true love by	135		36
And Paul is Tarsus true Bellerophon	136		10
Truelove			
Yet shed what tears sad truelove should	41		107
Truer			
Thou heardst me truer than tongue confess	28	2	3
Truly			
And truly tell to me	109	11	4
Trumpet			
The trumpet waxes loud tired are your feet	5		8
Forget the waking trumpet the long law	5		44
In a flash at a trumpet crash	72		21
Should tongue that time now trumpet now that field	73		3
Or a jaunting vaunting vaulting assaulting trumpet telling	141		7
Trundled			
Off trundled timber and scoops of the hillside ground hollow hollow hollow ground	146		4
Trust			
And so my trust confused struck and shook	16		7
Sylvester come Sylvester you may trust	107	3	1
I keep my trust	127		15
Truth			
Therefore how bitter and learnt how late the truth	17		14
A warfare of my lips in truth	18		15
And truth is heard with tears impearled	23		35
O unteachably after evil but uttering truth	28	18	5
So at home time was to his truth and grace	41		99
Never fleets more fastened with the tenderest truth	59		12
No truth between you three	109	28	2
And other truth is none	133		2
Theres none but truth can stead you Christ is truth	157		20
Theres none but truth can stead you Christ			

Word	Poem	Stan.	Line
Truth (cont.)			
is truth	157		20
Try			
Is all the winter bird dare try	3		14
None besides me this bye-ways beauty try	12	2	9
Or if they try it I am happier then	12	2	10
I try the Christus oer again	80	7	11
For only try by gazing to divide	102	3	9
Trying			
Trying each pleasurable throat that sings	19		6
Trying on the ring	102	1	28
Ts			
When ts light I quenched its rose times one rich rose my hand	152		82
Tucked			
Stones ring like each tucked string tells each hung bells	57		3
Tuft			
Furred snows charged tuft above tuft tower	30		31
Furred snows charged tuft above tuft tower	30		31
Most like the tuft of plighted silver round	102	1	72
Most like the plighted tuft of silver round	102	1	73
Most like the silver plighted tuft about	102	1	74
Foam-tuft fumitory	138		30
Tufts			
In tufts of evening sky so soon	25		22
Then though I should tread tufts of consolation	48		25
Cloud-puffball torn tufts tossed pillows flaunt forth then chevy on an air	72		1
Stars like gold tufts	98	25	2
Tuggd			
Tuggd the bossd smooth-lippd giant strombus-shell	2		57
Tumbled			
As tumbled over rim in roundy wells	57		2
Wheatfields tumbled with the rains	77		136
All lie tumbled-to then with loop-locks	159		31
Tumbled-to			
All lie tumbled-to then with loop-locks	159		31
Tumbler			
No tumbler woke and shook the cot	135		13
Tumbling			
Ruck and wrinkle drooping dying deaths worst winding sheets tombs and worms and tumbling to decay	59		12
Tumblings			
On the tumblings of the rain	77		104
Tumult			
A prophetess towered in the tumult a virginal tongue told	28	17	8
Tune			
Than Purcell tune lets tread to see it does			

Word	Poem	Stan.	Line
this keeps warm	62		2
Tune it to words of good intent	81		127
O what a tune the thought	148		3
Tuneable			
Or stretchd chords tuneable on turtles shell	2		129
Tuned			
We tuned to one key and made their harmonies	98	2	4
Turbid			
How ring right out our sordid turbid time	35		10
Turf			
Though aloft on turf or perch or poor low stage	39		5
Turmoil			
The turmoil and the torment it has I swear a sweetness	152		90
Turn			
And planets bud whereer we turn our mazed eyes	2		33
And I will turn my looks to you	8		12
I to him turn with tears	52		10
Turn most on tender byplay	54		16
To his own selfbent so bound so tied to his turn	58		11
When sick men turn and lights are low	77		25
A turn of seven notes or five	81		7
How turn my passion-pastured thought	81		174
I must not turn the lantern on his face	102	1	25
To turn the compass on the all-starrd sky	102	3	23
And barley turn to weed and wild	114		5
Shall see the azure turn expressionless	117		4
Ill lay then by and freshly turn instead	117		13
Her hand from heaven to turn a mill	139		4
Are earthworld airworld waterworld thorough hurled all by turn and turn about	159		18
Are earthworld airworld waterworld thorough hurled all by turn and turn about	159		18
Turnd			
Now all things rosy turnd the west had grown	2		19
Abandoned by her saints turnd black and blasted	102	2	13
Turned			
And never turned to corn	7		8
And when he turned it back again	21		38
Are you turned for an exquisite smart	28	18	2
Twice lovely tinted eastern turned Greek	136		15
Then over his turned temples here	144		13
Heaven turned its starlight eyes below	145		46
I told you that she turned her mirror dim	151		11
Once I turned from thee and hid	155		9
Turning			
That with a turning of the wings	77		67
Turning and pacing so by slips discloses	108		2

Word	Poem	Stan.	Line
Turning (cont.)			
Several times I saw them thrice or four times turning	152		59
Turns			
At tranquil turns by natures rule	30		14
Turns and twindles over the broth	56		6
O in turns of tempest me heaped there me frantic to avoid thee and flee	64		8
Turns the lantern on Floris hand	102	1	27
And turns to wash it from her welling eyes	151		5
Turns	159		48
Turquoise			
One bound oer dripping gold a turquoise-gemmd	2		60
Turquoise-gemmd			
One bound oer dripping gold a turquoise-gemmd	2		60
Turtles			
Or stretchd chords tuneable on turtles shell	2		129
Twelve			
Hope was twelve hours gone	28	15	4
Ten or twelve only ten or twelve	43		20
Ten or twelve only ten or twelve	43		20
Twenty			
Five and twenty years have run	28	35	5
Twice			
But opend twice in life and death to state	1	4	8
With twice as fine a sense to apprehend them	102	1	12
Twice lovely tinted eastern turned Greek	136		15
His deacon Dirvan warm twice over must the welcome be	152		13
Twindles			
Turns and twindles over the broth	56		6
Twiny			
Over finger-teasing task his twiny boots	159		33
Twixt			
Twixt real hue and phantasy	77		122
Two			
Two mazed shepherds perishd in the tide	1	14	3
Save by two stars more crowding lights arise	2		32
Two thousands of years are near upon past	27		16
Two hundred souls in the round	28	12	4
But Gertrude Lily and Luther are two of a town	28	20	5
On ear and ear two noises too old to end	35		1
How these two shame this shallow and frail town	35		9
Wanting which two when they once meet	38		12
When Shrovetide two years gone	54		5
Two tedious acts were past	54		29
Off her once skeined stained veined variety upon all on two spools part pen pack	61		11

Word	Poem	Stan.	Line
Unchanging			
The unchanging register of change	130		5
Uncharted			
To thy not-staled uncharted memory	117		14
Unchecked			
And speeds uncheckd her murderous guile	120		30
Unchilding			
Spins to the widow-making unchilding unfathering deeps	28	13	8
Unchilld			
Unchilld I handle stinging snow	80	2	1
Unchrist			
Unchrist all rolled in ruin	41		95
Uncle			
Some messenger there might have met you from my uncle	152		5
Your uncle met the messenger met me and this the message	152		6
Unclean			
Unclean and seeming unforgiven	18		3
Uncomforted			
No not uncomforted lovely-felicitous providence	28	30	5
Unconfessed			
Comfortless unconfessed of them	28	30	4
Uncontrolled			
Honouring an uncontrolled royal wrathful nature	152		68
Uncouth			
That I may win with late-learnt skill uncouth	17		12
Nor tears nor tears this clay uncouth	18		13
Uncreated			
And find the uncreated light	22		10
Uncumbered			
But uncumbered meadow-down is not distressed	39		13
Undenizened			
Undenizened beyond bound	70		15
Under			
His channel under clammy coats	3		11
I must oertake thee at once and under heaven	20		15
Since tho he is under the worlds splendour and wonder	28	5	6
O father not under thy feathers nor ever as guessing	28	12	5
I was under a roof here I was at rest	28	24	3
And all the landscape under survey	30		13
And hurls for him o half hurls earth for him off under his feet	38		14
Now Carisbrook keep goes under in gloom	41		28
All under channel to bury in a beach her	41		48
Crouch lay knee by earth low under	41		109
Have an eye to the sakes of him quaint moonmarks to his pelted plumage under	45		10

Word	Poem	Stan.	Line
Undone (cont.)			
and dangerously sweet	59		9
By slender losses are undone	81		147
The times are winter watch a world undone	150		2
Undulation			
In silken undulation spurrd and rayd	2		43
Unendear			
Nor elsewhere can thy sweetness unendear	12	1	5
Unenduring			
The unenduring fallows of the heaven	122		6
Unespied			
The cold whip-adder unespied	106		1
Unfathering			
Spins to the widow-making unchilding unfathering deeps	28	13	8
Unfathomable			
Both are in an unfathomable all is in an enormous dark	72		12
Unfold			
Or where is strength to make the leaf unfold	17		4
Unforeseen			
At God knows when to God knows what whose smiles not wrung see you unforeseen times rather as skies	69		12
Unforgiven			
Unclean and seeming unforgiven	18		3
Unfurled			
And hosts confront with flags unfurled	23		33
His little Pennon is unfurled	130		14
Ungentle			
To not ungentle death now forth I run	103		19
Ungirdled			
Yet leaves him in ungirdled ease	83		15
Unglue			
That shall unglue the crust of sin	81		133
Unheard			
Bars or hells spell thwarts this to hoard unheard	66	1	12
Unheeded			
Heard unheeded leaves me a lonely began	66	1	13
Unhinderd			
I gazed unhinderd mermaids six or seven	2		34
Unholy			
Myself unholy from myself unholy	16		1
Myself unholy from myself unholy	16		1
Unhouse			
And you unhouse and house the Lord	22		24
Unimperilld			
In unimperilld haven is wreckd	83		20
Unimpregnate			
Left not a rood with curses unimpregnate	102	2	5

Word	Poem	Stan.	Line
Universal			
Springs universal bliss	42		34
Unkind			
For the infinite air is unkind	28	13	4
Unknown			
An antique chaunt and in an unknown tongue	2		131
Just seen may be to many unknown men	12	2	12
Unleaving			
Over goldengrove unleaving	55		2
Unlookd			
From parts unlookd for alterd spent	81		24
Unlovely			
Fairer these are the flaring shows unlovely	125		45
Unmade			
And after it almost unmade what with dread	28	1	6
Unmindful			
Unmindful of their grace the Escorial	1	8	5
Unmoved			
Mix oer the not unmoved earth	77		130
Unpalateable			
Unpalateable fruits to eat	81		167
Unpassiond			
Even your unpassiond eyelids might be wet	14	1	14
Unpeopled			
In shoals of bloom as in unpeopled skies	2		31
Unpinned			
I put the door to with the bolts unpinned	135		11
Unquestiond			
The unquestiond readings of a blotless book	16		6
Unraveller			
Of realty the rarest-veined unraveller a not	44		12
Unrest			
From all the pain of the pasts unrest	26		12
Unreticent			
It is the waste done in unreticent youth	17		10
Unsafe			
Since on the face it is unsafe to look	102	1	47
Unsandalled			
Where seek thee with unsandalled feet	23		18
Unseen			
Ebbd back beneath its snowy lids unseen	2		18
We guess we clothe thee unseen king	23		13
Unseen the heroic breast not outward-steeled	73		7
He drops towards the river unseen	159		15
Unselfishness			
Most rarely see unselfishness	96	1	2
Unselve			
Strokes of havoc unselve	43		21
Unset			
Shake and unset your morticed metaphors	101		8
Yet when my unset tresses hung loose-traced	102	1	3

Word	Poem	Stan.	Line
Unsets			
Covers with shallow silver that unsets	98	31	2
Unsexing			
Round this unsexing doublet while I set	102	1	4
Unshapeable			
Read the unshapeable shock night	28	28	3
Unsheathd			
Like an Assyrian prince with buds unsheathd	2		62
Unshod			
Come by the flesh-pots you shall sit unshod	5		9
Unsought			
This was the prized the desirable sight unsought presented so easily	137		6
Unsteady			
They plough our vales you see the unsteady flare	104		9
Unstinted			
Yet found unstinted place for mirth	77		56
Unswerving			
Unswerving through the firmament	77		50
Untainted			
During the Eastering of untainted morns	84		1
Untaught			
I who was wise would be untaught	81		171
Unteachably			
O unteachably after evil but uttering truth	28	18	5
Until			
Sun-flushd until it seemd their father sea	2		100
In wandering until broad light of day	80		6
And watch until our horses and the men	125		9
Unto			
Pure fasted faces draw unto this feast	11		1
That was unto Judah as May and brought her	26		31
Who to us are as dew unto grass and tree	26		38
Sweet unto God and the sweetness is grace	27		45
The crown should be unto her head	109	10	3
Fie she said unto them all	109	28	1
Untwist			
Not untwist slack they may be these last strands of man	64		2
Unused			
And bred acquaintance of unused towns	107	2	2
Unvalve			
Unvalve or shut his vaned tail	130		11
Unveined			
After the sandfield and the unveined glare	5		29
Unvexed			
Save where the unvexed west	77		97
Unvisited			
Dress hoar-hallowed shrines unvisited	41		91
Unwarned			
Some asleep unawakened all unwarned eleven			

Word	Poem	Stan.	Line
fathoms fallen	41		3
Unwavering			
And right only resolution will his will unwavering	152		75
Unwet			
And there she waits with locks unwet	120		3
Unworthiness			
My hopes and my unworthiness	118		9
Up			
Come up arise and slay	5		18
The steep-up roof at last behind the small	12	2	6
Up till that mornings fall of dew	21		27
Sets up a shadow in thy seat	23		16
Look at the stars look look up at the skies	32	1	1
Around up above what wind-walks what lovely behaviour	38		2
I walk I lift up I lift up heart eyes	38		5
I walk I lift up I lift up heart eyes	38		5
Now he shoots short up to the round air	41		64
His heart up at the strain	54		27
Then would I fling me up to sip	77		131
High up the balanced stony air	80	4	2
Cuckoo calls cuckoo up the wood	81		22
I can send up an Esaus cry	81		126
At last up the blue element	87		6
Leaps up before my vision thou art gone	98	33	2
My signalling tears might ring up Floris now	102	1	7
No they are come their horn is lifted up	104		1
Crispd up and starchy from a short half-hour	107	3	3
And each drew bluebells up and for relief	107	3	17
Then up and spake the third brother	109	27	1
Whose all-belated leaves yield up themselves	111		2
The bluebells up whose crystal-ending rods in their natural sods	112		8
Lift up your heads o gates	115		8
Be ye lift up ye everlasting doors	115		9
Dry up the blue and be not slaked thereby	117		7
By speech so sweetly broken up and gone	125		31
Upbringing			
In the ruddied county of the days upbringing	98	28	4
Upgazing			
While the upgazing country seems	77		125
Uplands			
To where the listening uplands are	77		82
Upon			
Of battle once upon St Lawrence day	1	2	2
Upon his altar and with rarest store	1	2	8
Upon the stubborn fleming and the rod	1	5	6
Slopd on the galleries upon the wall	1	12	2
Upon the mouldring terraces amain	1	13	4
Crowd down upon a stream and jostling thick	2		94
Swimming and languishd green upon the deep	2		114

Word	Poem	Stan.	Line
Upon (cont.)			
Scourged upon the threshing-floor	6		6
Part found no root upon the flinty road	7		9
Is set upon your boughs below	10		10
A boy feels when the poet he pores upon	14	3	13
Love I was shewn upon the mountain-side	20		1
The mist upon the leaves have strewed	21		33
And beat upon my whorled ear	22		2
Upon the stir and keep of pride	22		18
As erst upon chaotic floods	23		21
My hand upon my lips I lay	23		37
Upon Christ throw all away	24		5
That a quince I pore upon	25		19
Is it anything true does it grow upon ground	27		2
And broke into bloom upon Nazareth hill	27		11
Two thousands of years are near upon past	27		16
Our king back oh upon English souls	28	34	4
High there how he rung upon the rein of a wimpling wing	36		3
For rose-moles all in stipple upon trout that swim	37		3
Why fasten that upon her	42		7
Off her once skeined stained veined variety upon all on two spools part pen pack	61		11
Sir life upon thy cause see banks and brakes	74	1	8
And watches change upon the sea	77		32
Silence holds breath upon her throne	77		33
Most dead-alive upon those days	80	2	7
Upon you dreamed	81		85
He meets upon midsummer day	83		27
His body swayd upon tiptoes	87		3
But half the pains he spends upon his boy	97		4
The breaking leaves of gold are curld upon her lips	98	14	3
While phosphor risen upon the shallowing dark	98	28	3
The knot of feathery locks upon her head	99		14
This downy counterfeit upon my lip	102	1	5
Pierce her she hangs upon the flame-cased sun	103		10
At morn they come upon our lands like rains	104		8
And feeds new leaves upon the winds of fall	105		10
Whose gaps and hollows are not browzed upon	107	1	2
Alone upon the hill-top heaven oer him	107	1	8
If he wear the crown upon his head	109	23	1
If he wear a crown upon his head	109	23	3
She kneeled upon her knee	109	25	2
Down upon ground fell she	109	39	2
Her barred fingers claspd upon her eyes	111		6
Who lies on grass and pores upon the sky	117		3
Crept all along a hill upon our left	125		3
And breath upon it that is her face is this	125		58
He drops upon the wind again	130		13

Word	Poem	Stan.	Line
As it fell upon a day	131		1
Upon my forehead hit the burly wind	135		12
Struck off it has written upon lovely limbs	152		34
Or deaf ears shall desire that lipmusic thats lost upon them	152		110
Upon this only gambolling and echoing-of-earth note	159		45
Upper			
Where the upper mill-stone roofd his head	6		7
In breezy belts of upper air	77		73
To manhood on the upper lip they lookd	102	1	71
Upraisd			
Upraisd an emblem of that fiery constancy	1	3	8
Upright			
She was a woman upright outright	145		36
Uproll			
With the uproll and the downcarol of day and night delivering	152		118
Upward			
Now melting upward thro the sloping scale	2		132
A brittle sheen runs upward like a cliff	98	6	2
With parallel shafts as upward-parted ashes	107	4	5
Upward-parted			
With parallel shafts as upward-parted ashes	107	4	5
Upwards			
Then may I upwards gaze and see	77		113
Upwards at once and win their aureoles	126		8
Us			
To be a judge and ruler over us	5		2
Wherein he makes us stray	5		6
Give us the tale of bricks as heretofore	5		49
For us was gatherd the first-fruits	6		3
For us was lifted from the roots	6		4
For us the vine was fenced with thorn	6		13
For us by Calvarys distress	6		17
The field where he has planted us	6		27
When he has sheaved us in his sheaf	6		29
When he has made us bear his leaf	6		30
The praise of the lips and the hearts of us bring to thee	26		35
Who to us are as dew unto grass and tree	26		38
Make mercy in all of us out of us all	28	10	7
Make mercy in all of us out of us all	28	10	7
Flesh falls within sight of us we though our flower the same	28	11	6
Remember us in the roads the heaven-haven of the reward	28	34	3
Let him Easter in us be a dayspring to the dimness of us be a crimson-cressetedeast	28	34	5
Let him Easter in us be a dayspring to the dimness of us be a crimson-cressetedeast	28	34	5
Pride rose prince hero of us high-priest	28	34	7

Word	Poem	Stan.	Line
Us (cont.)			
This very very day came down to us after a boon he on	48		5
Us fresh youth fretted in a bloomfall all portending	48		30
This seeing the sick endears them to us us too it endears	53		9
This seeing the sick endears them to us us too it endears	53		9
Where whatevers prized and passes of us everything thats fresh and fast flying of us seems to us sweet of us and swiftly away with done away with undone	59		8
Where whatevers prized and passes of us everything thats fresh and fast flying of us seems to us sweet of us and swiftly away with done away with undone	59		8
Where whatevers prized and passes of us everything thats fresh and fast flying of us seems to us sweet of us and swiftly away with done away with undone	59		8
Where whatevers prized and passes of us everything thats fresh and fast flying of us seems to us sweet of us and swiftly away with done away with undone	59		8
Of us the wimpled-water-dimpled not-by-morning-matched face	59		10
A care kept where kept do but tell us where kept where	59		30
New Nazareths in us	60		60
Waste her earliest stars earlstars stars principal overbend us	61		4
With our evening is over us our night whelms whelms and will end us	61		8
With our evening is over us our night whelms whelms and will end us	61		8
Mary mother of us where is your relief	65		4
Of us we do bid God bend to him even so	68		11
What country is honour enough in all us lordly head	70		10
Only with us is old and new	81		63
The angel lifted us above	81		119
Give us our green lots in another mead	98	15	5
Will please us so	107	4	28
And one to each of us is holy ground	116		3
Of mile-long reaches of our road below us	125		7
Which makes us eye-attentive to the eye	125		42
Sees what his place is but for us the rolls	126		5
As wishing all about us sweet	139		1
Heaven whom she childs us by	149	1	11
Used			
Through other bars it used to thrill	81		15

Word	Poem	Stan.	Line
And passages where we used to meet	81		162
Utter			
Utter silver jubilee	28	35	20
Utterance			
Only with utterance of sweet breath they sung	2		130
Which drives the stony air to utterance	122		18
Uttered			
Word that heard and kept thee and uttered thee outright	28	29	8
The utterer uttered uttering	145		31
Utterer			
The utterer uttered uttering	145		31
Uttering			
O unteachably after evil but uttering truth	28	18	5
The utterer uttered uttering	145		31
Utterly			
Of a mastering heaven utterly blue	78		2
A cusp still clasped him a fluke yet fanged him entangled him not quit utterly	137		5
Uttermost			
The-last-breath penitent spirits the uttermost mark	28	32	6
V			
Through the velvety wind v-winged	138		41
V-winged			
Through the velvety wind v-winged	138		41
Vacant			
Vacant creations lamps appal	23		12
On beings dread and vacant maze	23		30
Vain			
The altar-tapers flard in gusts in vain	1	13	5
I plead and ah how much in vain	81		29
Vale			
The outgoings of the vale does block	92		11
Valerian			
Good Valerian I will come	125		37
I do not but to please Valerian	125		39
Vales			
When heavenly vales so thick shall stand	8		16
Then for her whose velvet vales	28	35	17
Lovely the woods waters meadows combes vales	34		9
They plough our vales you see the unsteady flare	104		9
Valiant			
What is virtue valour only the heart valiant	152		74
Valley			
But further down the valley left and right	1	14	4
Egypt the valley of our pleasance there	5		25
Valleys			
Shouldering down valleys smokes the gloom	80	7	2

Word	Poem	Stan.	Line
Valour			
Brute beauty and valour and act oh air pride plume here	36		8
What is virtue valour only the heart valiant	152		74
Value			
The shepherds whom I value not	124		23
Van			
In the van between Ffestiniog and Bala	96	1	5
Vaned			
Unvalve or shut his vaned tail	130		11
Vanishd			
Death was vanishd from the glade	4		17
Vanishing			
Back beauty keep it beauty beauty beauty from vanishing away	59		2
Vantage			
That gave you vantage when you would despise	14	3	3
Vapour			
There is a vapour stands in the wind	130		17
Vapourous			
Whatever time this vapourous roof	80	6	1
Variety			
Off her once skeined stained veined variety upon all on two spools part pen pack	61		11
Various			
Her hues a various brown with creamy lakes	99		11
Vast			
Our hymn in the vast silence dies	23		6
Evening strains to be times vast womb-of-all home-of-all hearse-of-all night	61		2
The sun whose vast afflictive heat	80	2	2
The vast of heaven stung with brilliant stars	98	21	2
Vastness			
But vastness blurs and time beats level enough the Resurrection	72		16
Vasty			
In grimy vasty vault	60		102
Vault			
Not vault them the million of rounds of thy mercy not reeve even them in	28	12	8
Mend first and vital candle in close hearts vault	46		10
The vault and scope and schooling	49		15
In grimy vasty vault	60		102
Are afoot heaven-vault fast purpling portends and what first lightning	152		63
Vaulted			
Glazed water vaulted oer a drowsy stone	98	39	1
Vaulting			
Or a jaunting vaunting vaulting assaulting trumpet telling	141		7
Denis whose motionable alert most vaulting wit	143		1

Word	Poem	Stan.	Line
Vaulty			
Earnest earthless equal attuneable vaulty voluminous stupendous	61		1
Vaunt			
Tongue true vaunt-and tauntless	48		15
Vaunt-and			
Tongue true vaunt-and tauntless	48		15
Vaunting			
Or a jaunting vaunting vaulting assaulting trumpet telling	141		7
Veer			
I see the city pigeons veer	15		27
And leaves the blades whereer he will veer	98	1	3
Veil			
With a thin floating veil of water hoar	2		4
The veil that covers mysteries	77		36
Vein			
Fells or flanks of the voel a vein	28	4	7
Heart go and bleed at a bitterer vein for the	28	30	3
A vein for the visiting of the past-prayer pent in prison	28	32	5
Beautys bearing or muse of mounting vein	47		10
Nay roguish ran the vein	54		28
When life revisits me nerve and vein	80	7	9
And beautys dearest veriest vein is tears	157		4
Veind			
Were veind and streakd with dusk-deep Lazuli	2		46
Veined			
Of realty the rarest-veined unraveller a not	44		12
Off her once skeined stained veined variety upon all on two spools part pen pack	61		11
Veins			
Thou hast bound bones and veins in me fastened me flesh	28	1	5
Veins violets and tall trees makes more and more	73		11
With loops of veins not of an even pink	93	2	4
Velvet			
Then for her whose velvet vales	28	35	17
Velvety			
Through the velvety wind v-winged	138		41
Venerable			
Thy venerable record virgin is recorded	152		122
Vengeances			
There they did appeal therefore airy vengeances	152		62
Ventnor			
Now near by Ventnor town	41		30
Venus			
Fronts Venus his ill-launched hope	83		19
Veriest			
And beautys dearest veriest vein is tears	157		4

Word	Poem	Stan.	Line
Vermeil			
Of driving vermeil-rain and as he lists	2		91
Vermeil-rain			
Of driving vermeil-rain and as he lists	2		91
Vermilion			
Fall Gall themselves and gash gold-vermilion	36		13
Verse			
A bad verse in the middle then	95		5
Very			
Comforting smell breathed at very entering	34		3
Majestic as a stallion stalwart very-violet-sweet	38		10
This very very day came down to us after a boon he on	48		5
This very very day came down to us after a boon he on	48		5
His very looks in other years	81		62
Is very capable of strong affection	94		13
Here at the very furthest reach away	107	4	19
These are my very text of discontent	125		50
There was a lady very gay	131		2
And Im very glad	132		5
I am so very o so very glad	138		31
I am so very o so very glad	138		31
The very victim would prepare	145		8
Very-violet-sweet			
Majestic as a stallion stalwart very-violet-sweet	38		10
Vespers			
The driving storm at hour of vespers beat	1	13	3
Vespillo			
Vespillo my centurion hacks out	80	7	19
Vessels			
Now in our altar-vessels stored	6		19
Vest			
Of tremulous film more subtle than the vest	2		39
Vexd			
The vexd elm-heads are pale with the view	79		1
Vice			
O hideous vice to haggle yet	81		149
Of virtue and vice but most it seemed his sense	136		27
Victim			
The very victim would prepare	145		8
Victor			
So I am victor now I swear to pay	1	2	5
View			
The vexd elm-heads are pale with the view	79		1
Viewing			
Gazes aslant his shoulder viewing nigh	1	11	6
Views			
Apollo views the smitten python writhe and die	1	11	9

Word	Poem	Stan.	Line
Vigil			
You vigil-keepers with low flames decreased	11		8
Her jailor with his vigil-organ dead	99		16
Vigil-keepers			
You vigil-keepers with low flames decreased	11		8
Vigil-organ			
Her jailor with his vigil-organ dead	99		16
Vigorous			
The vigorous horizontals each way fall	12	2	3
Villages			
He rises from the flocks of villages	100		5
Vine			
Handle the fig suck the full-sappd vine-shoot	5		38
For us the vine was fenced with thorn	6		13
The rivn vine leafless lifeless dry	6		22
I took of vine a cross-barred rod or rood	20		8
A juice rides rich through bluebells in vine leaves	157		3
Vine-shoot			
Handle the fig suck the full-sappd vine-shoot	5		38
Vines			
Under the cloister-light of greenhouse vines	84		6
Vintage			
Is the sweet vintage of our Lord	6		20
Viol			
What bass is our viol for tragic tones	75		8
Violent			
The blame bear who aroused me what I have done violent	152		66
Violet			
An azure ridge or clouds of violet glowd	2		105
Majestic as a stallion stalwart very-violet-sweet	38		10
To win a look of violet	86		6
The violet moves and copses rock	98	3	4
With such a violet slight their distanced green	100		8
Slight with such violet their bright-maskd green	100		9
Maskd with such violet disallow their green	100		10
The mouthed centre of a violet	102	1	75
Violets			
I see long reefs of violets	3		25
Veins violets and tall trees makes more and more	73		11
And pressed violets in the folds appear	119		4
Virgin			
Here playd the virgin mother with her child	1	10	4
Mary the Virgin well the heart knows	27		22
And favouring virgin freshness yet	139		6
Thy venerable record virgin is recorded	152		122
Virginal			
Of the month by men called virginal	26		22

Word	Poem	Stan.	Line
Virginal (cont.)			
A prophetess towered in the tumult a virginal tongue told	28	17	8
Virgins			
The world was saved by virgins made the mark	136		30
Virtue			
Of virtue and vice but most it seemed his sense	136		27
Being to her virtue clinching-blind	145		18
What is virtue valour only the heart valiant	152		74
Virtues			
And for those virtues I in thee have found	13		11
For these make all the virtues to abound	13		13
And well supplied with virtues on the whole	94		27
Of virtues I most warmly bless	96	1	1
Thou Jacinth nor have skill of all thy virtues	102	1	62
Where all the virtues were illustrated	102	2	9
Should choke sweet virtues glory is times great guilt	136		2
Visaged			
And hate the ill-visaged cursing tars	114		10
Vision			
Fair but of fairness as a vision dreamd	80		1
Leaps up before my vision thou art gone	98	33	2
Visionary			
But many a silver visionary spark	113		5
Visions			
Timed her sad visions with his wreck	21		56
Visiting			
A vein for the visiting of the past-prayer pent in prison	28	32	5
How it does my heart good visiting at that bleak hill	48		21
Visual			
By visual compulsion till I hide	12	2	5
Vital			
Mend first and vital candle in close hearts vault	46		10
The vital fire does suddenly retire	80	7	24
Vive			
And seals of vive carnation which had each	98	12	6
Vivid			
Thro silver gloomd to a blood-vivid clot	2		107
Voel			
Fells or flanks of the voel a vein	28	4	7
Voice			
No answering voice comes from the skies	23		2
But no forgiving voice replies	23		4
A moaning voice among the reeds	23		36
In whose dead lake even a voice may make	80	4	3

Word	Poem	Stan.	Line
At last I hear the voice well known	81		1
Doubtless the voice now falln now spent	81		2
At last I hear the voice I knew	81		25
A mans voice and a new voice speaking near	136		22
A mans voice and a new voice speaking near	136		22
Which overvaulted voice	148		20
Void			
As void as clouds that house and harbour none	107	1	1
As void as those the gentle downs appear	107	1	3
Voids			
He hand to mouth he lives and voids with shame	75		9
Voluminous			
Earnest earthless equal attuneable vaulty voluminous stupendous	61		1
Vows			
Buy then bid then what prayer patience alms vows	32	1	9
Wading			
With all down darkness wide his wading light	40		4
Waft			
Idle for ever to waft her or wind her with these she endured	28	14	8
Wafting			
Starlight wafting him out of it and	28	5	3
Wag			
Wag or crossbridle in a wind lifted windlaced	71		14
Wages			
Thou that on sins wages starvest	6		1
Wail			
Swelld the sweet strain to a melodious wail	2		133
Wailing			
The womans wailing the crying of child without check	28	17	6
Wain			
And Charless wain the wondrous seven	30		17
Waist			
He leans to it harry bends look back elbow and liquid waist	71		12
The river wound about it as a waist	107	4	2
Waists			
From their white waists a silver skirt was spread	2		48
Wait			
Ill wait till morn eternal breaks	23		54
Waits			
And there she waits with locks unwet	120		3
And bridegroom waits and ready are bower and bed	136		18

Word	Poem	Stan.	Line
Wake			
I wake and feel the fell of dark not day	67		1
When chill woods wake and think of morn	77		23
Waked			
Will have waked and have waxed and have walked with the wind what while we slept	59		23
And the waked stars are all alone	77		34
Waken			
Bones this sinew and will not waken	41		83
Wakes			
Times eunuch and not breed one work that wakes	74	1	12
Waking			
Forget the waking trumpet the long law	5		44
When waking hearts can pardon much	77		29
Waking I thought and it sufficed	118		8
Wales			
On a pastoral forehead of Wales	28	24	2
Should have pealed with welcome Wales	28	35	18
All the air thing wear that build this world of Wales	34		10
And not from purple Wales only nor from elmy England	152		124
Walk			
I walk my breezy belvedere	15		25
But you shall walk the golden street	22		23
I walk I lift up I lift up heart eyes	38		5
I walk towards eve our walks again	81		54
I awoke in the midsummer not-to-call night in the white and the walk of the morning	137		1
Till walk the world he can with bare his feet	159		35
Walkd			
As I walkd a stilly wood	4		5
Walked			
Wings so some great stormfowl whenever he was walked his while	45		11
Will have waked and have waxed and have walked with the wind what while we slept	59		23
Walks			
Around up above what wind-walks what lovely behaviour	38		2
I walk towards eve our walks again	81		54
And stumbling swears he walks by light of day	102	3	31
And stumbling swears he walks by light of day	102	3	37
One and then one along their walks and kept	107	1	12
Wall			
Slopd on the galleries upon the wall	1	12	2
Eclipsing parapet yet above the wall	12	2	7
In an hourglass at the wall	28	4	2
The girth of it and the wharf of it and the wall	28	31	4
Henry by the wall	54		12
The fruit against the wall	105		12

Word	Poem	Stan.	Line
Walled			
The towers musical quiet-walled grove	12	1	10
Wallow			
His charge through the champ-white water-in-a-wallow	41		47
Wallowing			
In him all quail to the wallowing o the plough s cheek crimsons curls	71		13
Walls			
With painting gleamd the rich pilasterd walls	1	10	3
At red Pompeii on medalliond walls	2		51
You have your wish enter these walls one said	20		17
Thou knowest the walls altar and hour and night	28	2	5
He lived on these weeds and waters these walls are what	44		10
Who shaped these walls has shewn	148		9
Who built these walls made known	148		37
Walnut			
A branch of walnut leaves and that	120		6
Walsingham			
The marvellous milk was Walsingham way	41		101
Wan			
O why art thou so wan she said	109	31	1
Wand			
Let patience with her chastening wand	23		45
More will wear this wand and then	25		39
Wandering			
At the touch of her wandering wondering breath	26		6
On meadow and river and wind-wandering weed-winding bank	43		8
In wandering until broad light of day	80		6
Ruinous heart-beat wandering death	81		53
Not of all my eyes see wandering on the world	149	1	1
Waned			
It waned into the world of light	25		31
Ever so black on it our tale o our oracle let life waned ah let life wind	61		10
The wanner waned she	109	36	4
Waning			
Or paring of paradisaical fruit lovely in waning but lustreless	137		3
Wanner			
The wanner waned she	109	36	4
Want			
That want the yield of plushy sward	22		22
I want the one rapture of an inspiration	76		10
Think you want daffodils and follow as far	135		30
Whom want could not make pine pine	142		7
Why get thee gone then tell thy mother I			

Word	Poem	Stan.	Line
Want (cont.)			
want her	152		16
Wanted			
Grace that day Grace was wanted	41		115
Wanting			
Never ask if meaning it wanting it warned of it men go	28	8	8
Wanting which two when they once meet	38		12
I plod wondering a-wanting just for lack	46		6
Of answer the eagerer a-wanting Jessy or Jack	46		7
When this is sought trees will be wanting not	80	7	39
One once that was found wanting when good weighed	157		24
Wanton			
A glorious wanton all the wrecks in showers	2		93
Against the wild and wanton work of men	157		36
Wants			
There eyes them heart wants care haunts foot follows kind	40		13
Wants war wants wounds weary his times his tasks	68		3
Wants war wants wounds weary his times his tasks	68		3
Wanwood			
Though worlds of wanwood leafmeal lie	55		8
War			
And scarlet wear the spirit of war there express	63		8
Mark Christ our King he knows war served this soldiering through	63		9
Wants war wants wounds weary his times his tasks	68		3
But be the war within the brand we wield	73		6
Warbled			
Let the warbled sweetness rill	77		84
Warbles			
And the water warbles over into filleted with glassy grassy quicksilvery shives and shoots	159		38
Warbling			
For warbling of the warbling bird	21		49
For warbling of the warbling bird	21		49
Warder			
Frowning and forefending angel-warder	48		17
Warding			
Fruit-cloistering Hyacinth-warding woods	81		163
Ware			
Then looking on the waters I was ware	2		27
But these two ware of a world where but these two tell each off the other of a rack	61		13
And she was ware of a servingman	109	17	3

Word	Poem	Stan.	Line
Wars (cont.)			
Alarms of wars the daunting wars the death of it	51		6
Those lovely lads once wet-fresh windfalls of wars storm	62		5
Me were I pleading plead nor do I I weary of idle a being but by where wars are rife	66	1	7
Grown wicked in the wicked wars	114		12
Wash			
Wood banks and brakes wash wet like lakes	42		42
To wash before the multitude	80	7	23
And turns to wash it from her welling eyes	151		5
Washing			
Lingerd then raised the washing waves and drenchd	2		138
While he was washing from on deck	21		54
And lives at last were washing away	28	15	7
Waste			
There is a massy pile above the waste	1	1	1
They do not waste their meted hours	15		5
It is the waste done in unreticent youth	17		10
Christs Lily and beast of the waste wood	28	20	6
Waste her earliest stars earlstars stars principal overbend us	61		4
Are waste and had no wholesome foods	81		166
So waste in tears over this bed of sweetness	102	1	38
They waste they wither worse they as they run	150		3
Wasted			
That warring wasted the lands increase	26		28
Wasteful			
Not Goshen wasteful wide huge-girthed Nile	5		31
Wastes			
From wastes of rock he brings	7		11
Towards wastes where round the ice-blocks tilt and fret	88		7
Towards those wastes where the ice-blocks tilt and fret	88		11
Wasting			
Stone palsy cancer cough lung-wasting womb-not-bearing	152		113
Watch			
Whence oft I watch but see those mermaids now no more	2		143
To watch the low or levant sun	15		26
Men are amazed to watch me pass	25		3
And watch until our horses and the men	125		9
The times are winter watch a world undone	150		2
Watchd			
But most in a half-circle watchd the sun	2		116
Watched			
Who have watched his mould of man big-boned and hardy-handsome	53		2

Word	Poem	Stan.	Line
Water (cont.)			
But in pale water frail water wild rash and reeling water	152		120
And the water warbles over into filleted with glassy grassy quicksilvery shives and shoots	159		38
Wedlock what the water spousal love	159		47
Water-cloud			
Say oer it hangs a water-cloud	81		56
Water-in-a-wallow			
His charge through the champ-white water-in-a-wallow	41		47
Water-lily			
Fair beds they seemd of water-lily flakes	2		13
Water-meads			
In starry water-meads they drew	10		17
Water-nymphs			
Around the water-nymphs in fretted falls	2		50
Water-pierced			
Fit for flowers water-pierced and rilly	98	15	6
Water-wattled			
And mazy sands all water-wattled	30		23
Waterblowballs			
Roots and rocks is danced and dandled all in froth and waterblowballs down	159		7
Waterd			
With the warmd and the waterd buds	98	19	7
He drops his bright roots in the waterd sward	100		2
Waterfall			
And many standing round a waterfall	91		5
Waterfalls			
Down the beetling banks like water in waterfalls	152		51
Waterfearers			
Fallers in dreadful frothpits waterfearers wild	152		112
Waters			
Then looking on the waters I was ware	2		27
Then saw I sudden from the waters break	2		74
Fresh brooks to salt sand-teasing waters shoaly	16		4
Are sisterly sealed in wild waters	28	23	7
Lovely the woods waters meadows combes vales	34		9
He lived on these weeds and waters these walls are what	44		10
Must see the waters roll	88		5
Where waters set	88		10
The sun on falling waters writes the text	91		8
I hear a noise of waters drawn away	112		1
Waterworld			
Are earthworld airworld waterworld thorough			

Word	Poem	Stan.	Line
hurled all by turn and turn about	159		18
Watery			
From wings swan-fledged a wheel of watery light	2		76
The webbed and the watery west	3		22
Low lie his mates now on watery bed	41		57
Lighted the watery-plated leaves	98	17	2
The watery-plated plane-leaves lit	98	17	3
Watery-plated			
Lighted the watery-plated leaves	98	17	2
The watery-plated plane-leaves lit	98	17	3
Wattled			
And mazy sands all water-wattled	29	1	23
Wave			
Wave with the meadow forget that there must	28	11	7
With the burl of the fountains of air buck and the flood of the wave	28	16	8
Waved			
With waved passes there shall glide	106		2
None good but God a warning waved to	157		23
Waver			
And here the faithful waver the faithless fable and miss	28	6	8
Waves			
The waves were rosy-lippd the crimson glare	2		24
Lingerd then raised the washing waves and drenchd	2		138
With light on her face like the waves at play	26		4
Him after an hour of wintry waves	41		68
Wavier			
Of silk-sack clouds has wilder wilful-wavier	38		3
Waving			
Down no waving off of these most mournful messengers still messengers sad and stealing messengers of grey	59		4
Stars waving their indivisible rays	98	23	1
Wax			
What I did ask then was a circle of rose-red sealing-wax	128		15
Waxed			
Will have waked and have waxed and have walked with the wind what while we slept	59		23
The fairer waxed he	109	36	2
Waxen			
The waxen colours weep and run	3		29
And pierce the yellow waxen light	15		43
Waxes			
The trumpet waxes loud tired are your feet	5		8
Way			
He hides our corpses dropping by the way	5		5
A press of winged things comes down this way	5		15
The vigorous horizontals each way fall	12	2	3

Word	Poem	Stan.	Line
Way (cont.)			
My national old Egyptian reed gave way	20		7
All down the stair-way of the copse	21		45
I move along lifes tomb-decked way	23		39
But roped with always all the way down from the tall	28	4	6
With belled fire and the moth-soft milky way	28	26	6
Your wealth of life is some way spent	28	35	14
Her commander and thou too and thou this way	41		51
The marvellous milk was Walsingham way	41		101
Off and no way but so	60		33
That mammocks mighty foot but no way sped	70		12
Who rising late had missd her painful way	80		5
Lifts them a little way above	81		38
Teach me the way I will repent	81		136
It is the way with Philomel	96	3	3
Sky fleeced with the milky way	98	23	2
Bids him this way his gazes fix	120		15
And how long was the way	125		11
This shorter way	125		12
The words came from a court across the way	136		23
She mends the way she means to go	145		12
Reason selfdisposal choice of better or worse way	152		94
Waylay			
Waylay her at ebb past Penmaen pool	30		24
Ways			
And foliagd crownals pointing how the ways	1	6	4
Five ways the precious branches torn	6		14
Lo linked heavens with milky ways	10		21
None besides me this bye-ways beauty try	12	2	9
Peace and food cheered me where four rough ways meet	20		12
Our prayer seems lost in desert ways	23		5
Thee may-hope of our darkened ways	26		40
Come then your ways and airs and looks locks maidengear gallantry and gaiety and grace	59		14
Winning ways airs innocent maiden manners sweet looks loose locks long locks love-locks gaygear going gallant girlgrace	59		15
Minds me in many ways	60		16
This night what sights you heart saw ways you went	67		3
His crisp combs and that comes those ways we know	68		14
Why do sinners ways prosper and why must	74	1	2
I found the ways were sown with salt	81		155
Withal her mien is modest ways are wise	136		19
We			
And planets bud whereer we turn our mazed eyes	2		33
Who is this Moses who made him we say	5		1

Word	Poem	Stan.	Line
Are spatterd we desire the yoke we bore	5		53
Are spatterd we desire the yoke we bore	5		53
Behold we have the joy in harvest	6		2
At morn we found the heavenly bread	6		8
We shout with them that tread the grapes	6		12
We scarcely call that banquet food	6		31
We are so grafted on his wood	6		33
We meet together you and I	8		10
We shall be sheaved with one band	8		14
Sphered so fast sweet soul we see	10		23
God though to thee our psalm we raise	23		1
We see the glories of the earth	23		7
We guess we clothe thee unseen king	23		13
We guess we clothe thee unseen king	23		13
With attributes we deem are meet	23		14
Surround the peak from which we gaze	23		26
Sphered so fast sweet soul we see	25		23
The warped world we shall undo	25		40
We have suffered the sons of winter in sorrow	26		9
And we that joy in this month joy-laden	26		17
To thee we tender the beauties all	26		21
Wherefore we love thee wherefore we sing to thee	26		33
Wherefore we love thee wherefore we sing to thee	26		33
We all we thro the length of our days	26		34
We all we thro the length of our days	26		34
We lash with the best or worst	28	8	2
But we dream we are rooted in earth dust	28	11	5
But we dream we are rooted in earth dust	28	11	5
Flesh falls within sight of us we though our flower the same	28	11	6
Woke thee with a we are perishing in the weather of Gennesareth	28	25	6
Feasts when we shall fall asleep	28	35	9
Not today we need lament	28	35	13
Being pure we lifes pride and cared-for crown	35		11
Of the best we boast our sailors are	41		75
O if we but knew what we do	43		9
O if we but knew what we do	43		9
When we delve or hew	43		10
Where we even where we mean	43		16
Where we even where we mean	43		16
To mend her we end her	43		17
When we hew or delve	43		18
Nay what we had lighthanded left in surly the mere mould	59		22
Will have waked and have waxed and have walked with the wind what while we slept	59		23
What while we while we slumbered	59		25
What while we while we slumbered	59		25

Word	Poem	Stan.	Line
We (cont.)			
O then weary then why should we tread o why are we so haggard at the heart so care-coiled care-killed so fagged so fashed so cogged so cumbered	59		26
O then weary then why should we tread o why are we so haggard at the heart so care-coiled care-killed so fagged so fashed so cogged so cumbered	59		26
When the thing we freely forfeit is kept with fonder a care	59		27
Fonder a care kept than we could have kept it kept	59		28
Far with fonder a care and we we should have lost it finer fonder	59		29
Far with fonder a care and we we should have lost it finer fonder	59		29
Yonder what high as that we follow now we follow	59		31
Yonder what high as that we follow now we follow	59		31
I say that we are wound	60		34
Through her we may see him	60		110
Yes why do we all seeing of a soldier bless him bless	63		1
What hours o what black hours we have spent	67		2
We hear our hearts grate on themselves it kills	68		9
Of us we do bid God bend to him even so	68		11
His crisp combs and that comes those ways we know	68		14
Honour is flashed off exploit so we say	73		1
But be the war within the brand we wield	73		6
But man we scaffold of score brittle bones	76		5
Your signal when apart we stood	81		17
And passages where we used to meet	81		162
Thus we shall profit while gold coinage still	96	7	7
We tuned to one key and made their harmonies	98	2	4
We found were dabbled with a colouring growth	98	9	2
We will charge our flocks that they not feed	98	15	2
Lead shepherd now we follow shepherd lead	98	15	7
We live to see	98	35	1
Bellisle that is a fabling name but we	116		1
Than we in the east dare look for buds disclose	119		2
Might we not think the sweet and daring rises	122		2
What was it we should strike the road again	125		1
They said we could not miss a pushing brook	125		5
Ran through it following which we should have sight	125		6

Word	Poem	Stan.	Line
Wear (cont.)			
express	63		8
And wear it thus a pectoral by my heart	102	1	31
If he wear the crown upon his head	109	23	1
If he wear a crown upon his head	109	23	3
That will not wear a print that will not stain a pen	152		121
His bleached both and woolwoven wear	159		29
Weariest			
Then even in weariest wintry hour	30		29
Wears			
And wears mans smudge and shares mans smell the soil	31	1	7
Within her wears bears cares and combs the same	76		6
Weary			
Ye weary come into the shade	6		26
Your scarce-sheathed bones are weary of being bent	11		13
O then weary then why should we tread o why are we so haggard at the heart so care-coiled care-killed so fagged so fashed so cogged so cumbered	59		26
O then weary then why should we tread o why are we so haggard at the heart so care-coiled care-killed so fagged so fashed so cogged so cumbered	59		26
In me or most weary cry I can no more I can	64		3
Me were I pleading plead nor do I I weary of idle a being but by where wars are rife	66	1	7
Wants war wants wounds weary his times his tasks	68		3
This weary Martinmas would it were summer	111		10
We cannot live this life out sometimes we must weary	152		79
Weather			
Blinds her but she that weather sees one thing one	28	19	5
Woke thee with a we are perishing in the weather of Gennesareth	28	25	6
But whats to see in stormy weather	30		25
Must it worst weather	41		14
Their rocky lodges then the weather rare	81	4	5
Gold gallant flowers much looked at in April weather	98	16	2
Gem-fleeced at morn so brilliant is the weather	99		4
So strangely elemented is my minds weather	102	1	15
Web			
With a subtle web of black	4		20
She wild web wondrous robe	60		38
Thus he ties spiders web across his sight	102	3	28
Such spiders web he ties across his sight	102	3	34

Word	Poem	Stan.	Line
Webbd			
They webbd the sky with glassy light	87		2
Webbed			
The webbed and the watery west	3		22
Webs			
Of those gilt webs that languishd in a fall	1	8	7
Wed			
Then will you wed with an English lady	109	8	3
Says get you get you a lady to wed	109	9	1
And if I chose a love to wed	109	10	1
Said it was not meet the king should wed	109	12	3
Who means to wed or means to kill	120		29
Her weeds all mark her maiden though to wed	136		17
Let winter wed one sow them in her womb	158		3
Wedded			
Hes wedded to his theory they say	97		1
They were wedded at midnight	109	1	1
As wedded you must be	109	8	4
Wedlock			
Who to wedlock his wonder wedlock	52		11
Who to wedlock his wonder wedlock	52		11
Wedlock what the water spousal love	159		47
Weds			
How Shakespeares England weds with Dantes Italy	98	35	2
Weed			
With lace of rosy weed were chapleted	2		59
On meadow and river and wind-wandering weed-winding bank	43		8
I fall I tear and shower the weed	81		64
Her white weed-bathed knees are shut together	99		2
And barley turn to weed and wild	114		5
Weed-bathed			
Her white weed-bathed knees are shut together	99		2
Weed-winding			
On meadow and river and wind-wandering weed-winding bank	43		8
Weeded			
Or weeded landslips of the shore	15		24
Weedio			
Weedio-weedio there again	138		3
Weedio-weedio there again	138		3
Weedio-weedio			
Weedio-weedio there again	138		3
Weeds			
The drenched hair of slabby weeds that swung	2		113
When weeds in wheels shoot long and lovely and lush	33		2
He lived on these weeds and waters these walls			

Word	Poem	Stan.	Line
Weeds (cont.)			
are what	44		10
Long live the weeds and the wilderness yet	56		16
Her weeds all mark her maiden though to wed	136		17
Week			
You may depend that ere a week was fled	97		5
Weeks			
Late in the green weeks of April	81		21
The weighty weeks without hands grow	145		5
Weep			
Down that dank rock oer which their lush long tresses weep	2		115
The waxen colours weep and run	3		29
And yet you will weep and know why	55		9
Maidens shall weep at merry morn	114		1
Weeping			
And with weeping cloud is spread	77		95
Weeping even now I curse myself remembering	102	1	44
As she lay weeping at the night	109	29	1
Weepings			
With fiercer weepings of these desperate eyes	14	3	6
Weeps			
Where Phoebus weeps for him whom Zephyrs guile	1	11	7
A thing that weeps enduring long	81		50
Weigh			
But why then should Castara weigh with me	125		40
Weighed			
One once that was found wanting when good weighed	157		24
Weighing			
Thy unchancelling poising palms were weighing the worth	28	21	6
Weight			
In motion is no weight or pain	130		15
Weights			
When she felt the kill-weights crush	145		55
Weighty			
The weighty weeks without hands grow	145		5
Welcome			
Should have pealed with welcome Wales	28	35	18
Welcome in womb and breast	60		20
Makes welcome death does dear forgetfulness	150		8
His deacon Dirvan warm twice over must the welcome be	152		13
O welcome there their steel or cannon	156		17
Welkin			
And down the welkin gushing free	77		85
All the welkin overhead	77		96
Like knocking thunder all round Britains welkin	102	2	3
The smouldering enormous winter welkin may	149	1	8

Word	Poem	Stan.	Line
The smouldering enormous winter welkin eye	149	2	3
Well			
Else I am well assured I should offend	14	3	5
Knowing them well I can but see the fall	16		10
Yet made its market here as well	25		32
Mary the Virgin well the heart knows	27		22
I steady as a water in a well to a poise to a pane	28	4	5
Well she has thee for the pain for the	28	30	1
O where live well your lease of leisure	30		3
Ah well it is all a purchase all is a prize	32	1	8
O well wept mother have lost son	41		104
Well but there was more than this	42		33
O now well work that sealing sacred ointment	48		33
Tendered to him ah well God rest him all road ever he offended	53		8
Love-laced what once I well	54		3
Thou canst but be but that thou well dost strong	58		5
Somewhere elsewhere there is ah well where one	59		6
By a grey eyes heed steered well one crew fall to	71		5
At last I hear the voice well known	81		1
You cried but I have served thee well	81		107
My love and all was sweet and well	81		121
And well supplied with virtues on the whole	94		27
Miss Ms a nightingale tis well	96	3	1
Yes for a time they held as well	101		1
Well I know not but all things seem to-night	102	1	10
Blindness a learned fool and well-bred churl	102	3	32
A learned fool indeed and well-bred churl	102	3	38
Affined well to that sweet solitude	107	1	15
In copying well what you have best begun	125		21
Well after all ah but hark	138		10
Her mould of features mated well	145		16
It will not well so she would bring about	151		3
Warned her well she knew I warned her of this work	152		38
Wiped I am sure this was it seems not well for still	152		43
Here to this holy well shall pilgrimages be	152		123
One spell and well that one there ah thereby	153		7
As well the sister sits would well the wife	157		14
As well the sister sits would well the wife	157		14
Well-bred			
Blindness a learned fool and well-bred churl	102	3	32
A learned fool indeed and well-bred churl	102	3	38
Wellbeing			
Hies headstrong to its wellbeing of a self-wise self-will	48		24

Word	Poem	Stan.	Line
Welling			
And turns to wash it from her welling eyes	151		5
Wells			
Behold at Elim wells on every hand	5		23
As tumbled over rim in roundy wells	57		2
Cuckoo bird and open ear wells heart-springs delightfully sweet	146		2
Wend			
Frequenting there while moon shall wear and wend	35		4
To wend and meet no sin	60		117
Wender			
That a starlight-wender of ours would say	41		100
Went			
And thro their parting lids there came and went	2		11
You went into the partless air	25		30
It was made of earths mould but it went from mens eyes	27		3
And though the last lights off the black west went	31	1	11
This night what sights you heart saw ways you went	67		3
Could crowd career with conquest while there went	73		12
On Chebars banks and why they went	77		49
Went forth to compass mysteries	77		52
To alien eaves you fled and went	81		5
Teach me the paces that you went	81		125
In eddies of the wind he went	87		5
Sylvester came they went by Cumnor hill	107	3	9
Before he went to sea	109	1	4
I thought that you would have written my birthday came and went	128		1
Word went she should be crushed out flat	145		38
On one that went against me whereas I had warned her	152		37
Wept			
O well wept mother have lost son	41		104
Wept wife wept sweetheart would be one	41		105
Wept wife wept sweetheart would be one	41		105
West			
Plum-purple was the west but spikes of light	2		7
Now all things rosy turnd the west had grown	2		19
The webbed and the watery west	3		22
Kiss my hand to the dappled-with-damson west	28	5	5
Away in the loveable west	28	24	1
And though the last lights off the black west went	31	1	11
A wilder beast from west than all were more	50		7
Her fond yellow hornlight wound to the west her wild hollow hoarlight hung to the height	61		3

Word	Poem	Stan.	Line
Wheel			
From wings swan-fledged a wheel of watery light	2		76
And canvas and compass the whorl and the wheel	28	14	7
His steady wheel quite to the full again	107	3	12
Wheels			
When weeds in wheels shoot long and lovely and lush	33		2
Whelmd			
Of seamen whelmd in chasms of the mid-main	2		120
Whelms			
With our evening is over us our night whelms whelms and will end us	61		8
With our evening is over us our night whelms whelms and will end us	61		8
Whence			
Whence with the scourge of ready piety	1	5	4
Now ringing clarion-clear to whence it rose	2		134
Whence oft I watch but see those mermaids now no more	2		143
An olive-branch whence richly reek	77		15
Whence spring the jewelld harmonies	77		138
Whereas			
Whereas did air not make	60		94
On one that went against me whereas I had warned her	152		37
Wherefore			
Wherefore we love thee wherefore we sing to thee	26		33
Wherefore we love thee wherefore we sing to thee	26		33
Wherein			
Wherein beneath the cornice horsemen rode	1	7	7
Wherein he makes us stray	5		6
My happier world wherein	60		116
Whereon			
I never saw those fields whereon their best	119		11
While			
Philip took oath while glory or defeat	1	2	3
While his crackd flesh lay hissing on the grate	1	3	2
While from the pulpit in a heretic land	1	5	1
But hapless youth Antinous the while	1	11	5
Blaze for him all this while	5		36
And so though each have one while I have all	16		12
But watching while the colour grew	21		12
Thus Frances sighed at home while Luke	21		50
While he was washing from on deck	21		54
While ages and while Aeons run	23		20
While ages and while Aeons run	23		20
Where winter-while is all forgot	25		14
Indeed while such a wonders warm	25		36

Word	Poem	Stan.	Line
Frequenting there while moon shall wear and wend	35		4
Wings so some great stormfowl whenever he has walked his while	45		11
Give God while worth consuming	49		7
All while her patience morselled into pangs	50		12
Will have waked and have waxed and have walked with the wind what while we slept	59		23
What while we while we slumbered	59		25
What while we while we slumbered	59		25
Could crowd career with conquest while there went	73		12
While the sun streams forth amain	77		103
Then while the rain-born arc glows higher	77		123
While the upgazing country seems	77		125
While a subtle spirit and rare	77		127
While sheeny tears and sunlit mirth	77		129
While the breeze by rank and measure	79		9
But all the while it seemd to me	81		112
Has danced with her and all the while	83		23
To sing while others sleep	96	3	4
Thus we shall profit while gold coinage still	96	7	7
While phosphor risen upon the shallowing dark	98	28	3
Round this unsexing doublet while I set	102	1	4
Sleep Floris while I rob you tighten o sleep	102	1	18
And spins her skirts out while her central star	103		7
Now while the full-leaved hursts unalterd stand	105		3
While there is neither sun nor rain	105		6
Epistles while the running pastoral bleats	107	4	22
Which says at least then go while all is fresh	125		64
While all things else may stir and range	130		7
And while I sail must listen I sing	138		15
To take her while their tongues would go	145		26
O now while skies are blue now while seas are salt	152		106
O now while skies are blue now while seas are salt	152		106
While rushy rains shall fall or brooks shall fleet from fountains	152		107
While sick men shall cast sighs of sweet health all despairing	152		108
While blind mens eyes shall thirst after day-light draughts of daylight	152		109
While cripples are while lepers dancers in dismal limbdance	152		111
While cripples are while lepers dancers in dismal limbdance	152		111
Long where we leave him froliclavish while he looks about him laughs swims	159		42

Word	Poem	Stan.	Line
Whilst			
And thou art silent whilst thy world	23		31
Whip			
The cold whip-adder unespied	106		1
Whip-adder			
The cold whip-adder unespied	106		1
Whips			
You striped in secret with breath-taking whips	11		3
Whirl			
In crisps of curl off wild winch whirl and pour	35		7
All else may whirl or dive or fly	130		8
Whirled			
I whirled out wings that spell	28	3	4
Whirling			
With brine and shine and whirling wind	41		79
Whirlwind			
Wiry and white-fiery and whirlwing-swivelled snow	28	13	7
Wretch under a comfort serves in a whirlwind all	65		11
Whirlwind-swivelled			
Wiry and white-fiery and whirlwind-swivelled snow	28	13	7
Whisper			
Speak whisper to my watching heart	23		49
Whispers			
Whispers if thou have warmth at heart	80	7	32
White			
Speard open lustrous gashes crimson-white	2		8
From their white waists a silver skirt was spread	2		48
Others with fingers white would comb among	2		112
White loomd my rock the water gurgling oer	2		142
So glassy white about the sky	3		16
White to begin with immaculate white	27		33
White to begin with immaculate white	27		33
Wiry and white-fiery and whirlwind-swivelled snow	28	13	7
His charge through the champ-white water-in-a-wallow	41		47
Now her all in two flocks two folds black white right wrong reckon but reck but mind	61		12
The sapphire pools are smit with white	79		7
White-faced as one in sad assay to fly	80		8
A basket broad of woven white rods	98	19	1
Her white weed-bathed knees are shut together	99		2
Her milk-white throat and folded dew-lap slack	99		9
If it be a white rose in his hand	109	22	1
With green-white apples on the bough	124		20
And a few leaves not lily-white but charactered over with blacks	128		16
Their clouds with breathing edges white	130		23

Word	Poem	Stan.	Line
I awoke in the midsummer not-to-call night in the white and the walk of the morning	137		1
With white strokes and strains of the blue	138		17
White-faced			
White-faced as one in sad assay to fly	80		8
White-fiery			
Wiry and white-fiery and whirlwind-swivelled snow	28	13	7
Whitebeam			
Wind-beat whitebeam airy abeles set on a flare	32	1	6
Whitest			
Time was next whitest after Marys own	136		4
Whitewash			
Down roughcast down dazzling whitewash wherever an elm arches	72		3
Whole			
Soon the whole world is overspread	6		25
The whole world passes I stand by	15		4
And well supplied with virtues on the whole	94		27
There would not be a whole place in his head	97		6
The whole landscape flushes on a sudden at a sound	146		5
Wholesome			
When wholesome spirits rustle about	77		27
Are waste and had no wholesome foods	81		166
Wholl			
Youve parlour-pastime left and wholl	30		34
Wholly			
Or wholly winds him to her will	120		31
Whorl			
And canvas and compass the whorl and the wheel	28	14	7
Whorled			
And beat upon my whorled ear	22		2
Wicked			
Grown wicked in the wicked wars	114		12
Grown wicked in the wicked wars	114		12
They wound their winch of wicked smiles	145		25
Wicket			
Fling to the convent wicket fast	81		75
Wide			
Most wide ye are who call this gust Simoom	5		26
Not Goshen wasteful wide huge-girthed Nile	5		31
Open wide your hearts that they	24		23
O world wide of its good	28	20	4
With all down darkness wide his wading light	40		4
In wide the worlds weal rare gold bold steel bare	70		17
When she had made the door wide	109	30	3
Make wide thou o Lord of sin	115		6
They had them out and laid them wide	145		49
For good grows wild and wide	148		25

Word	Poem	Stan.	Line
Wide (cont.)			
Apart wide and new-nestle at heaven most high	149	1	6
In a wide world of defiance Caradoc lives alone	152		71
Widow			
Spins to the widow-making unchilding unfathering deeps	28	13	8
The widow of an insight lost she lives with aim	76		7
Widow-making			
Spins to the widow-making unchilding unfathering deeps	28	13	8
Wield			
But be the war within the brand we wield	73		6
Wielding			
And the azurous hung hills are his world-wielding shoulder	38		9
Wife			
Wept wife wept sweetheart would be one	41		105
England whose honour o all my heart woos wife	66	1	5
Married will make a sweet and matchless wife	94		31
As well the sister sits would well the wife	157		14
Wild			
But what a wild flush on the flakes of it stood	27		34
The wild woman-kind below	28	16	2
Are sisterly sealed in wild waters	28	23	7
The cross to her she calls Christ to her christens her wild-worst	28	24	8
In crisps of curl off wild winch whirl and pour	35		7
But his own nest wild nest no prison	39		11
To its own fine function wild and self-instressed	47		7
When will you ever peace wild wooddove shy wings shut	51		1
Wild air world-mothering air	60		1
She wild web wondrous robe	60		38
World-mothering air air wild	60		124
Her fond yellow hornlight wound to the west her wild hollow hoarlight hung to the height	61		3
Of sheep from the high fields and other wild	107	4	23
And barley turn to weed and wild	114		5
How can he be the words are wild	147		2
How can he be the words are wild	147		8
For good grows wild and wide	148		25
Fallers in dreadful frothpits waterfearers wild	152		112
But in pale water frail water wild rash and reeling water	152		120
Mays beauty massacre and wisped wild clouds grow	154		2

Word	Poem	Stan.	Line
Will (cont.)			
When will you ever peace wild wooddove shy wings shut	51		1
When when peace will you peace Ill not play hypocrite	51		3
It will come to such sights colder	55		6
And yet you will weep and know why	55		9
Will have waked and have waxed and have walked with the wind what while we slept	59		23
Yet no part but what will	60		53
Charged steeped sky will not	60		80
Hued sunbeam will transmit	60		88
With our evening is over us our night whelms whelms and will end us	61		8
And fain will find as sterling all as all is smart	63		7
More pangs will schooled at forepangs wilder wring	65		2
The airy empire at his will	77		78
Then will he keep in this stay	80	1	7
I will break free from the Jews company	80	7	36
When this is sought trees will be wanting not	80	7	39
Will add a footrest there to stand	80	7	42
And with sharp flint will part my feet and dint	80	7	43
And thus I will thrust in my right	80	7	47
I plead and you will give your tears	81		28
Teach me the way I will repent	81		136
As wrecks of mined embers will	92		13
Miss Story has a moderate power of will	94		9
Married will make a sweet and matchless wife	94		31
Because she fears her fingers will be stung	96	4	2
And leaves the blades whereer he will veer	98	1	3
We will charge our flocks that they not feed	98	15	2
My cousin will not love you as I love	102	1	60
Floris she will not hit thy sum of worth	102	1	61
And find it will not therefore be descried	102	3	11
Will please us so	107	4	28
Then will you wed with an English lady	109	8	3
O what will you now good servingman	109	18	1
O what will you now with me	109	18	2
And he will come to thee	109	19	4
But how will you Lord William know	109	20	1
Yet how will you Lord William know	109	21	1
O I will follow thee my true love	109	38	1
And will not take denial	110		7
The king of glory will come in	115		10
Confirmed beauty will not bear a stress	117		1
Ah surely all who have written will profess	117		8
Or wholly winds him to her will	120		31
I think he will not tire of me	124		2
With yellow flags will suit his brow	124		18
Good Valerian I will come	125		37

Word	Poem	Stan.	Line
But this distemperd court will change it all	125		63
Will no one show	127		11
I know what you will tell me neglectful that you were not	128		5
Will on the moulding strike and cling	130		10
She lends in aid of work and will	139		3
I will appear looking such charity	140		3
That he will out of hand and heartily	140		5
Will crisp itself or settle and spin	145		10
Her will was bent at God for that	145		37
Your will is law in that small commonweal	150		11
It will not well so she would bring about	151		3
But both will share one cell this was good news Gwenvrewi	152		14
I do not and I will not repent not repent	152		65
And right only resolution will his will unwavering	152		75
And right only resolution will his will unwavering	152		75
Despatches with no flinching but will flesh o can flesh	152		77
That will not wear a print that will not stain a pen	152		121
That will not wear a print that will not stain a pen	152		121
Help me sir and so I will	155		20
Man lives that list that leaning in the will	157		25
Worst will the best what worm was here we cry	157		31
Dark or daylight on and on here he will then here he will the fleet	159		40
Dark or daylight on and on here he will then here he will the fleet	159		40
Willd			
Have willd to be disparadised	118		3
William			
Lord William they call me	109	5	2
Lord William comes hunting tomorrow morning	109	19	3
But how will you Lord William know	109	20	1
Yet how will you Lord William know	109	21	1
O where is Lord William my lords she said	109	25	3
Fie you are not Lord William she said	109	26	3
Lord William is king of all this land	109	27	3
Williams			
Says are you not Lord Williams love	109	18	3
I am Lord Williams love she said	109	19	1
Willing			
There is the shilling that finds me willing	156		8
Willow			
The country song of willow the poor soul	111		13
Willows			
Rolls across the labouring willows	79		4

Word	Poem	Stan.	Line
With brine and shine and whirling wind	41		79
On meadow and river and wind-wandering weed-winding bank	43		8
Will have waked and have waxed and have walked with the wind what while we slept	59		23
Ever so black on it our tale o our oracle let life waned ah let life wind	61		10
Wag or crossbridle in a wind lifted windlaced	71		14
See his wind-lilylocks-laced	71		15
Delightfully the bright wind boisterous ropes wrestles beats earth bare	72		5
With fretty Chervil look and fresh wind shakes	75	1	10
Swolln is the wind that in argent billows	79		3
My passion like a foolish wind	81		37
The light was so the wind so loud	81		59
Like a wind-perplexed rose	87		4
In eddies of the wind he went	87		5
The wind that passes by so fleet	98	1	1
Like a contented wind or gentle shocks	98	2	2
The wind comes breaking here and there with laughter	98	3	3
When the wind drops you hear the skylarks sing	98	3	5
It is a regimen on the imperfect wind	102	3	17
Is to give regimen to the imperfect wind	102	3	24
He drops upon the wind again	130		13
There is a vapour stands in the wind	130		17
Of the cold wind blowing	132		3
Upon my forehead hit the burly wind	135		12
Through the velvety wind v-winged	138		41
With a south-westerly wind blustering with a tide rolls reels	141		4
Or wind-long fleeces on the flock	144		11
Strike churl hurl cheerless wind then heltering hail	154		1
Sow the wind I would I sinned	155		11
Wind-beat			
Wind-beat whitebeam airy Abeles set on a flare	32	1	6
Wind-lilylocks-laced			
See his wind-lilylocks-laced	71		15
Wind-long			
Or wind-long fleeces on the flock	144		11
Wind-perplexed			
Like a wind-perplexed rose	87		4
Wind-walks			
Around up above what wind-walks what lovely behaviour	38		2
Wind-wandering			
On meadow and river and wind-wandering weed-winding bank	43		8

Word	Poem	Stan.	Line
Winded			
His rash-fresh re-winded new-skeined score	35		6
Or listening thought of linen-winded ghosts	135		18
Windfalls			
Those lovely lads once wet-fresh windfalls of wars storm	62		5
Winding			
On meadow and river and wind-wandering weed-winding bank	43		8
Ruck and wrinkle drooping dying deaths worst winding sheets tombs and worms and tumbling to decay	59		12
Windlaced			
Wag or crossbridle in a wind lifted windlaced	71		14
Window			
The window-circles these may all be sought	12	1	11
My window shows the travelling clouds	15		1
By that window what task what fingers ply	46		5
Window-circles			
The window-circles these may all be sought	12	1	11
Windpipe			
The windpipe when he sucked his breath	21		37
Windpuff			
A windpuff-bonnet of fawn-froth	56		5
Windpuff-bonnet			
A windpuff-bonnet of fawn-froth	56		5
Winds			
And hunting winds and the long-lying snow	17		2
Burden in winds burly and beat of endragoned seas	28	26	16
Questioning winds around the hills	77		44
Often when winds impenitent	80	5	1
And feeds new leaves upon the winds of fall	105		10
To the often takings of desirous winds	111		3
And John shall lie where winds are dead	114		9
Or wholly winds him to her will	120		31
The sky is blue and the winds pull	130		22
Windy			
Like Pharohs ears of windy harvest dry	117		6
Attain the windy levels of the sky	121		4
Wine			
The wine was racked from the press	6		18
Grapes grew and drops of wine were shed	7		5
Desire not to be rinsed with wine	22		14
Ye have kept your choicest wine	24		9
Wing			
All over as a bevy of eggs the mothering wing	34		6
High there how he rung upon the rein of a wimpling wing	36		3
Of pointed wing and silver stole	77		12
And sheathe at once his leger wing	130		12
The rookery never stirred a wing	135		14

Word	Poem	Stan.	Line
Winged			
A press of winged things comes down this way	5		15
The winged fowls took part part fell in thorn	7		7
And would not have that legion of winged things	7		14
Through the velvety wind v-winged	138		41
Wings			
From wings swan-fledged a wheel of watery light	2		76
Bear him to heaven on easeful wings	7		15
Or bat with tender and air-crisping wings	19		2
See love I creep and thou on wings dost ride	20		3
The bats wings lisping as they flew	21		19
I whirled out wings that spell	28	3	4
World broods with warm breast and with ah bright wings	31	1	14
Fresh-firecoal chestnut-falls finches wings	37		4
The heart rears wings bold and bolder	38		13
Wings so some great stormfowl whenever he has walked his while	45		11
When will you ever peace wild wooddove shy wings shut	51		1
The shaken plumage of my spirits wings	77		10
That with a turning of the wings	77		67
Caught from angels wings in heaven	77		110
He playd his wings as though for flight	87		1
Gather the sooty plumage from deaths wings	89		6
Where the stint compass of a skylarks wings	98	22	5
Flung rider and wings away though these were none	136		9
Wink			
My meal at every wink	60		12
Winks			
Winks away its ring of green	86		2
Winning			
Most o maids child thy choice and worthy the winning	33		14
Winning ways airs innocent maiden manners sweet looks loose locks long locks lovelocks gaygear going gallant girlgrace	59		15
Winter			
Is all the winter bird dare try	3		14
Where winter is the clime forgot	10		14
Into all seasons though no winter cast	14	1	5
Where winter-while is all forgot	25		14
We have suffered the sons of winter in sorrow	26		9
Thou art lightning and love I found it a winter and warm	28	9	6
My winter world that scarcely breathes that bliss	76		13
That shall not fail in winter-time	124		8
That are not less in winter-time	124		12
The smouldering enormous winter welkin may	149	1	8

Word	Poem	Stan.	Line
Winter (cont.)			
The smouldering enormous winter welkin eye	149	2	3
The times are winter watch a world undone	150		2
Hideous dashed down leaving earth a winter withering	152		84
Let winter wed one sow them in her womb	158		3
Winter-time			
That shall not fail in winter-time	124		8
That are not less in winter-time	124		12
Winter-while			
Where winter-while is all forgot	25		14
Wintering			
Spring not cause world is wintering	10		12
Spring not for world is wintering	25		12
Winters			
Earth throws winters robes away	24		17
Wintry			
Then even in weariest wintry hour	30		29
Him after an hour of wintry waves	41		68
Wiped			
Wiped I am sure this was it seems not well for still	152		43
Wiry			
Wiry and white-fiery and whirlwind-swivelled snow	28	13	7
Wiry heathpacks flitches of fern	56		11
Wisdom			
And wisdom is early to despair	59		8
No wisdom can forecast by gauge or guess	157		26
Wise			
Hies headstrong to its wellbeing of a self-wise self-will	48		24
I who was wise would be untaught	81		171
Prudence she has but wise shell never be	94		24
In this wise you may know your lord	109	22	3
Withal her mien is modest ways are wise	136		19
Wisest			
Wisest my heart breeds dark heavens baffling ban	66	1	11
Wish			
You have your wish enter these walls one said	20		17
And now I wish that it were true	21		28
Yea wish that though wish all Gods better beauty grace	62		12
Yea wish that though wish all Gods better beauty grace	62		12
Can something hope wish day come not choose not to be	64		4
She inly nourishes a wish to shine	94		12
Wishing			
As wishing all about us sweet	139		1

Word	Poem	Stan.	Line
Wisp			
The gold-wisp the airy-grey	49		3
Careless these in coloured wisp	159		30
Wisped			
Mays beauty massacre and wisped wild clouds grow	154		2
Wit			
Has wit enough but less than female tact	94		19
She never had the wit	95		2
Denis whose motionable alert most vaulting wit	143		1
Witch			
There lives the witch shall win my locks	120		22
With			
Kiss my hand to the dappled-with-damson west	28	5	5
Of the sodden-with-its-sorrowing heart	28	26	12
Look march-bloom like on mealed-with-yellow sallows	32	1	11
With-a-fountains shining-shot furls	71		19
This fault-not-found-with good	148		31
With-a-fountains			
With-a-fountains shining-shot furls	71		19
Withal			
Withal her mien is modest ways are wise	136		19
Wither			
They waste they wither worse they as they run	150		3
Withering			
Hideous dashed down leaving earth a winter withering	152		84
Within			
And the promise of summer within her breast	26		16
Flesh falls within sight of us we though our flower the same	28	11	6
Forms and warms the life within	42		22
Only not within seeing of the sun	59		3
Not within the singeing of the strong sun	59		4
But be the war within the brand we wield	73		6
Within her wears bears cares and combs the same	76		6
That nest within close-barred doors	77		54
As though they were not from within	80	3	4
So far but I have yet within	81		131
Beyond and one within the lookers eye	102	3	6
If life within	127		5
And all within the house were sound as posts	135		17
Cheevio when the cry within	138		34
Within her womb the child was quick	145		39
The man within that makes	148		22
Or what is else there is your world within	150		9
Withindoors			
These are indeed the barn withindoors house	32	1	12
Without			
Here are sweet messes without price or worth	5		47

Word	Poem	Stan.	Line
Without (cont.)			
The womans wailing the crying of child without check	28	17	6
Feast of the one woman without stain	28	29	5
Who fired France for Mary without spot	44		14
To do without take tosses and obey	68		4
Those years and years by of world without event	73		13
Who could forgive without grudge after	77		57
It is as cold as death without	109	29	3
Said who is this that stands without	109	30	1
Sits without consolation marking not	111		4
Had let such music down without impediment	122		8
The weighty weeks without hands grow	145		5
Withouten			
Withouten instrument or conch or bell	2		128
Witness			
With witness I speak this but where I say	67		5
And witness in her place would she	145		32
O but I bear my burning witness though	157		35
Witnessed			
Witnessed so fortune fell	54		4
Wits			
Off him but meaning motion fans fresh our wits with wonder	45		14
Mens wits to the things that are what good means where a glance	62		3
Witted			
Carrier-witted I am bold to boast	28	3	7
Woe			
Then passd the wind and sobbd with mountain-echod woe	1	13	9
Perfumes for the garb of woe	24		20
My cries heave herds-long huddle in a main a chief-woe world-sorrow on an age-old anvil wince and sing	65		5
My cries heave herds-long huddle in a main a chief-woe world-sorrow on an age-old anvil wince and sing	65		5
Ay sweet to taste beside this woe	80	7	7
The spell of woe if any could	81		79
She was with the choke of woe	145		60
Enough corruption was the worlds first woe	157		33
Woeful			
The woeful cradock o the woeful word then what	152		48
The woeful cradock o the woeful word then what	152		48
Woes			
But droppd its coil of woes Arthurs Britain	102	2	7
Is comforts carol of all or woes worst smart	153		8

Word	Poem	Stan.	Line
Woke			
Woke thee with a we are perishing in the weather of Gennesareth	28	25	6
A bell at midnight woke the town	81		87
No tumbler woke and shook the cot	135		13
Wolfsnow			
Heavengravel wolfsnow worlds of it wind there	41		27
Woman			
The wild woman-kind below	28	16	2
Feast of the one woman without stain	28	29	5
Merely a woman yet	60		25
Said who then is this lowly woman	109	11	3
It is for the shame of the lowly woman	109	14	3
She was a woman upright outright	145		36
Woman-kind			
The wild woman-kind below	28	16	2
Womans			
The womans wailing the crying of child without check	28	17	6
Womb			
Warm-laid grave of a womb-life grey	28	7	3
Welcome in womb and breast	60		20
Evening strains to be times vast womb-of-all home-of-all hearse-of-all night	61		2
Within her womb the child was quick	145		39
Stone palsy cancer cough lung-wasting womb-not-bearing	152		113
Let winter wed one sow them in her womb	158		3
Womb-life			
Warm-laid grave of a womb-life grey	28	7	3
Womb-not-bearing			
Stone palsy cancer cough lung-wasting womb-not-bearing	152		113
Womb-of-all			
Evening strains to be times vast womb-of-all home-of-all hearse-of-all night	61		2
Women			
Take settler and seamen tell men with women	28	12	3
The love of women is not so strong	81		48
Won			
And lifes first germs from death had won	23		24
And when the silent neight were won	77		75
Duly dear Lord my prize is won	81		109
Of world made marred and mended lost and won	136		26
Wonder			
Eighth wonder of the earth in size in store	1	15	5
That men must wonder as I pass	10		3
Is it a wonder if the buds are slow	17		3
Since tho he is under the worlds splendour and wonder	28	5	6
No wonder of it sheer plod makes plough down			

Word	Poem	Stan.	Line
Wood-sorrel			
Of the wood-sorrel and all things sensitive	122		11
As the wood-sorrel and all things sensitive	122		14
Wooddove			
When will you ever peace wild wooddove shy wings shut	51		1
Woodferns			
Into fairy trees wildflowers woodferns	159		50
Woodland			
Low-covered pass and brace the woodland clods	112		6
That comes again to the woodland tree	124		4
Woodlark			
I am the little woodlark	138		11
Woods			
Down in dim woods the diamond delves the elves-eyes	32	1	4
Lovely the woods waters meadows combes vales	34		9
When chill woods wake and think of morn	77		23
Fruit-cloistering hyacinth-warding woods	81		163
The time was late and the wet yellow woods	98	5	1
Wool			
And sheep-flock clouds like worlds of wool	30		18
Woolwoven			
His bleached both and woolwoven wear	159		29
Woos			
England whose honour o all my heart woos wife	66	1	5
Word			
And taught my lips to quote this word	8		6
I have found my music in a common word	19		5
One word as when a mother speaks	23		50
Word last how a lush-kept plush-capped sloe	28	8	3
And the word of it sacrificed	28	22	4
Heaven and earth are word of worded by	28	28	6
Word that heard and kept thee and uttered thee outright	28	29	8
Kind love both give and get only what word	66	1	10
Now one word more and then I am gone indeed	102	1	58
Word went she should be crushed out flat	145		38
And I not help nor word now of success	150		5
The woeful cradock o the woeful word then what	152		48
Worded			
Heaven and earth are word of worded by	28	28	6
Wording			
Wording it how but by him that present and past	28	28	5
Words			
The words are old the purport new	8		5
Have you make words break from me here all alone	28	18	3

Word	Poem	Stan.	Line
And thou art silent whilst thy world	23		31
Spring not for world is wintering	25		12
It waned into the world of light	25		31
The warped world we shall undo	25		40
O world wide of its good	28	20	4
Now burn new born to the world	28	33	1
The world is charged with the grandeur of God	31	1	1
World broods with warm breast and with ah bright wings	31	1	14
All the air thing wear that build this world of Wales	34		10
And the azurous hung hills are his world-wielding shoulder	38		9
With that world of good	42		27
What would the world be once bereft	56		13
To thriftless reave both our rich round world bare	58		12
And none reck of world after this bids wear	58		13
Wild air world-mothering air	60		1
My happier world wherein	60		116
World-mothering air air wild	60		124
But these two ware of a world where but these two tell each off the other of a rack	61		13
Thy wring-world right foot rock lay a lionlimb against me scan	64		6
My cries heave herds-long huddle in a main a chief-woe world-sorrow on an age-old anvil wince and sing	65		5
Thirsts all-in-all in all a world of wet	69		8
Those years and years by of world without event	73		13
My winter world that scarcely breathes that bliss	76		13
More golden than the world of lights	83		2
Yet what you are the world would say remain	125		28
Nor permanence in the solid world	130		16
Beyond the world the streams are full	130		24
Of world made marred and mended lost and won	136		26
The world was saved by virgins made the mark	136		30
Not of all my eyes see wandering on the world	149	1	1
The times are winter watch a world undone	150		2
Or what is else there is your world within	150		9
No man has such a daughter the fathers of the world	152		17
In a wide world of defiance Caradoc lives alone	152		71
And in this darksome world what comfort can I find	152		80
Down this darksome world comfort where can			

Word	Poem	Stan.	Line
World (cont.)			
I find	152		81
The ruins of rifled once a world of art	153		4
And she shall child them on the new-world strand	158		4
Till walk the world he can with bare his feet	159		35
World-mothering			
Wild air world-mothering air	60		1
World-mothering air air wild	60		124
World-sorrow			
My cries heave herds-long huddle in a main a chief-woe world-sorrow on an age-old anvil wince and sing	65		5
My cries heave herds-long huddle in a main a chief-woe world-sorrow on an age-old anvil wince and sing	65		5
World-wielding			
And the azurous hung hills are his world-wielding shoulder	38		9
Worlds			
Night to a myriad worlds gives birth	23		9
Worlds strand sway of the sea	28	1	3
Since tho he is under the worlds splendour and wonder	28	5	6
And sheep-flock clouds like worlds of wool	30		18
Heavengravel wolfsnow worlds of it wind there	41		27
Though worlds of wanwood leafmeal lie	55		8
Worlds loveliest mens selves self flashes off frame and face	62		9
In wide the worlds weal rare gold bold steel bare	70		17
Fall to the residuary worm worlds wildfire leave but ash	72		20
Enough corruption was the worlds first woe	157		33
Worm			
Fall to the residuary worm worlds wildfire leave but ash	72		20
Worst will the best what worm was here we cry	157		31
Worms			
Ruck and wrinkle drooping dying deaths worst winding sheets tombs and worms and tumbling to decay	59		12
Worse			
Till fearing ravage worse than in his flight	1	14	7
Of ruinous shrine no hand or worse	41		89
As I am mine their sweating selves but worse	67		14
Manwolf worse and their packs infest the age	70		20
How wouldst thou worse I wonder than thou dost	74	1	5
Worse than when Floris found me in the garden	102	1	43

Word	Poem	Stan.	Line
Wound (cont.)			
The river wound about it as a waist	107	4	2
They wound their winch of wicked smiles	145		25
Wounded			
And I cry out for wounded love	81		33
Wounds			
I shall worship his wounds with thee mother of mine	27		37
Wants war wants wounds weary his times his tasks	68		3
Woven			
A basket broad of woven white rods	98	19	1
Wrapped			
Kept to her care-drowned and wrapped in	41		45
Wrathful			
Honouring an uncontrolled royal wrathful nature	152		68
Wreath			
Had gotten him a wreath of sweet spring-broidery	2		101
Wreathd			
From flesh-flowers of the rock but more were wreathd	2		63
Wreaths			
With garnet wreaths and blooms of rosy-budded fire	2		26
Wreck			
Hung like a wreck that flames not billows beat	1	3	4
Timed her sad visions with his wreck	21		56
With the sea-romp over the wreck	28	17	4
And wreck in ruins of his mother	145		41
All is from wreck here there to rescue one	150		6
Wreckd			
In unimperilld haven is wreckd	83		20
Wrecked			
But what black boreas wrecked her he	41		22
Our ruins of wrecked past purpose there she basks	68		7
Wrecking			
Mans malice with wrecking and storm	28	9	4
Wrecks			
A glorious wanton all the wrecks in showers	2		93
As wrecks of mined embers will	92		13
Wrestles			
Delightfully the bright wind boisterous ropes wrestles beats earth bare	72		5
Wrestling			
Of now done darkness I wretch lay wrestling with my God my God	64		15
Wretch			
Of now done darkness I wretch lay wrestling with my God my God	64		15

Word	Poem	Stan.	Line
Wretch under a comfort serves in a whirlwind all	65		11
Wretches			
What sights shall be when some that swung wretches on crutches	152		127
Wring			
And from dank feathers wring the drops	3		8
Wring thy rebel dogged in den	28	9	3
Through the echoing timber does so rinse and wring	33		4
Or wring their barriers in bursts of fear or rage	39		8
Thy wring-world right foot rock lay a lionlimb against me scan	64		6
More pangs will schooled at forepangs wilder wring	65		2
Wring-world			
Thy wring-world right foot rock lay a lionlimb against me scan	64		6
Wringing			
Of wringing tree-tops chalky lanes	77		135
Wrings			
Now he wrings for breath with the deathgush brown	41		61
Fast he opens last he off wrings	159		34
Wrinkle			
Ruck and wrinkle drooping dying deaths worst winding sheets tombs and worms and tumbling to decay	59		12
Wrinkles			
O is there no frowning of these wrinkles ranked wrinkles deep	59		3
O is there no frowning of these wrinkles ranked wrinkles deep	59		3
Writ			
Dorothea or was your writ	25		27
Write			
And if you write at last it never can be the same	128		3
No what the poet did write ran	147		5
Writes			
The sun on falling waters writes the text	91		8
Writhe			
Apollo views the smitten python writhe and die	1	11	9
Written			
Ah surely all who have written will profess	117		8
I thought that you would have written my birthday came and went	128		1
Struck off it has written upon lovely limbs	152		34
Water which keeps thy name for not in rock written	152		119

Word	Poem	Stan.	Line
Wrong			
Thy river and oer gives all to rack or wrong	58		8
Now her all in two flocks two folds black white right wrong reckon but reck but mind	61		12
Now known and hand at work now never wrong	76		8
Is neither right nor wrong	148		32
Wrongd			
I have wrongd it of its coronet and now	102	1	51
Wronging			
I should be wronging longer leaving it to float	159		44
Wrongs			
Rife in her wrongs more lawless and more lewd	50		8
Wrought			
But not the hand that wrought them all	23		8
The wrought rim of heavens font	77		112
Each hue so rarely wrought that where	77		117
O Lord but I have wrought and striven	81		108
He sat and wrought his outline on a cloud	107	1	10
How alls to one thing wrought	148		1
Wrung			
Father and fondler of heart thou hast wrung	28	9	7
For wrung all on loves rack	54		17
At God knows when to God knows what whose smiles not wrung see you unforeseen times rather as skies	69		12
Wuthering			
If a wuthering of his palmy snow-pinions scatter a colossal smile	45		13
Wychelm			
Fairyland silk-beech scrolled ash packed sycamore wild wychelm hornbeam fretty overstood	159		24
Yawnd			
Yawnd like long furrow in the heart	77		64
Yea			
Yea iron is mingled with my clay	18		10
Stain light yea mark you this	60		81
Yea wish that though wish all Gods better beauty grace	62		12
As the last pleiad yea behind	81		46
Yea to myself I answer make	81		145
Yea crushd my heart and made me dumb	118		12
Yea a debt to pay thee yet	155		19
Year			
At this spring season of the year	4		13
Lies in the breast of the young year-mother	26		3
That night that year	64		14
There is a day of all the year	80	7	8
Theyre out of date Lent sermons all the year	96	5	2
And yield a song to the decaying year	105		2
On such a season of the day and year	107	1	4

Word	Poem	Stan.	Line
As Devonshire letters earlier in the year	119		1
Think this my birthday falls in saddening time of year	128		9
Pressed to death he plants the year	145		4
Shall new-dapple next year sure as to-morrow morning	152		133
Year-mother			
Lies in the breast of the young year-mother	26		3
Yearnd			
He yearnd he yearnd to have his love	109	6	1
He yearnd he yearnd to have his love	109	6	1
Years			
Two thousands of years are near upon past	27		16
Of the yore-flood of the years fall	28	31	2
Five and twenty years have run	28	35	5
Of New Years month or surly Yule	30		30
Falls light as ten years long taught how to and why	47		8
Deals triumph and immortal years	52		12
How far from then forethought of all thy more boisterous years	53		12
When shrovetide two years gone	54		5
Hours I mean years mean life and my lament	67		6
Those years and years by of world without event	73		13
Those years and years by of world without event	73		13
Nine months she then nay years nine years she long	76		5
Nine months she then nay years nine years she long	76		5
His very looks in other years	81		62
In two years or in three	109	2	4
Although it were years three	109	3	2
For two years and for three	109	6	2
With a two years child at her knee	109	16	2
Discovering you dark tramplers tyrant years	157		2
Yellow			
Its brindled wharves and yellow brim	3		28
And pierce the yellow waxen light	15		43
Look March-bloom like on mealed-with-yellow sallows	32	1	11
Her fond yellow hornlight wound to the west her wild hollow hoarlight hung to the height	61		3
When lily-yellow is the west	81		55
The time was late and the wet yellow woods	98	5	1
Now quicken sheathed in the yellow galaxy	98	22	3
The autumn yellow feather in the boughs	105		5
With yellow flags will suit his brow	124		18
Yellowy			
With yellowy moisture mild nights blear-all black	46		3

Word	Poem	Stan.	Line
Yes			
I did say yes	28	2	1
At downright no or yes	41		54
There is one yes I have one hush there	59		2
One yes I can tell such a key I do know such a place	59		7
Yonder yes yonder yonder	59		32
Yes why do we all seeing of a soldier bless him bless	63		1
Yes for a time they held as well	101		1
Ah yes	152		15
Yes	152		87
Fast furled and all foredrawn to no or yes	157		28
Yesterday			
He slew the Egyptian yesterday to-day	5		3
Yestertempests			
Of yestertempests creases in pool and rutpeel parches	72		6
Yet			
Sooner than their mates and yet	4		29
Had she a quince in hand yet gaze	10		19
All mine yet common to my every peer	12	1	8
Eclipsing parapet yet above the wall	12	2	7
Of Gods dear pleadings have as yet not moved thee	13		10
That less is heavens higher even yet	14	1	12
Yet it is now too late to heal	15		17
Afflicts no less what yet I hope may blow	17		6
Hear yet my paradox love when all is given	20		13
Yet as he changed his mighty stops	21		43
Yet like a lighted empty hall	23		10
Yet know not how our gifts to bring	23		17
Yet made its market here as well	25		32
My eyes hold yet the rinds and bright	25		33
Maid yet mother as may hath been	26		20
Though felt before though in high flood yet	28	7	7
Yet did the dark side of the bay of thy blessing	28	12	7
And eyes heart what looks what lips yet gave you a	38		7
Yet both droop deadly sometimes in their cells	39		7
More more than was will yet be	41		103
Yet shed what tears sad truelove should	41		107
Yet ah this air I gather and I release	44		9
What hinders are you beam-blind yet to a fault	46		12
And yet you will weep and know why	55		9
Long live the weeds and the wilderness yet	56		16
Undone done with soon done with and yet dearly and dangerously sweet	59		9
Merely a woman yet	60		25
Yet no part but what will	60		53

Word	Poem	Stan.	Line
Where she shall yet conceive	60		61
Yet such a sapphire-shot	60		79
And more must in yet longer lights delay	67		4
To bruise them dearer yet the rebellious wills	68		10
With this tormented mind tormenting yet	69		4
With perilous o no nor yet plod safe shod sound	70		14
Yet God that hews mountain and continent	73		9
Leaves yet the mind a mother of immortal song	76		4
Yet found unstinted place for mirth	77		56
But yet they say Christ comes at the last day	80	1	6
And yet I know it would be better so	80	7	6
Tis marvel she is yet alive	81		10
So far but I have yet within	81		131
O hideous vice to haggle yet	81		149
Yet leaves him in ungirdled ease	83		15
Of him that looks yet not in that alone	91		3
See one bow each yet not the same to all	91		6
Which yet is in the eye or in the thought	91		9
Talks of self-sacrifice yet cant forgive	94		22
Yet when my unset tresses hung loose-traced	102	1	3
Lodge his eyes fast but yet as easy and light	102	1	21
To speak so yet Ill speak it for this once	102	1	41
Yet this could be no others hand than his	102	1	48
Yet there came one who sent his flock before him	107	1	7
Yet how will you Lord William know	109	21	1
Nor yet from over the sea	109	32	2
He dallies yet and yet with me	110		6
He dallies yet and yet with me	110		6
And risen sons yet are the childless free	123		2
Ill meant yet true I best should flatter then	125		20
Yet what you are the world would say remain	125		28
It never yet so sweetly was put on	125		29
Yet Id not say it is her face alone	125		61
What yet there must	127		19
Who thinks of Thecla yet her name was known	136		3
A cusp still clasped him a fluke yet fanged him entangled him not quit utterly	137		5
And favouring virgin freshness yet	139		6
Yet Arthur is a bowman his three-heeled timberll hit	143		3
Yet here he has but shewn	148		39
Or else a funeral and yet tis not a funeral	152		25
What work what harms done there is no harm done none yet	152		39
To hunger and not have yet hope on for to storm and strive and	152		88
Bad I am but yet thy child	155		13
Yea a debt to pay thee yet	155		19

Word	Poem	Stan.	Line
Yield			
Which makes so small the promise of that yield	17		11
But I must yield the chase or rest and eat	20		11
That want the yield of plushy sward	22		22
Though grief yield them no good	41		106
To own my heart I yield you do come sometimes but	51		4
I yield I would have cried at last	81		117
And yield a song to the decaying year	105		2
Whose all-belated leaves yield up themselves	111		2
Trees by their yield	127		1
Deed-bound I am one deed treads all down here cramps all doing what do not yield	152		100
Yields			
Yields to the sultry siege of melancholy	16		8
Yields tender as a pushed peach	48		23
Now yields you with some sighs our explanation	76		14
Then sought such leafy shelter as it yields	107	3	16
Yoke			
Are spatterd we desire the yoke we bore	5		53
Yonder			
Where yonder crimson fireball sits	3		23
Whats yonder grizzled dyphwys dim	30		9
Yonder what high as that we follow now we follow	59		31
Yonder yes yonder yonder	59		32
Yonder yes yonder yonder	59		32
Yonder yes yonder yonder	59		32
Yonder	59		33
Yore			
The easy burden of yore	5		54
And Ill pretend the credit given of yore	14	2	3
Of the yore-flood of the years fall	28	31	2
Yore-flood			
Of the yore-flood of the years fall	28	31	2
Youll			
Youll dare the Alp youll dart the skiff	30		5
Youll dare the Alp youll dart the skiff	30		5
Young			
Lies in the breast of the young year-mother	26		3
Young John then fear then joy	54		8
Young Thecla scanned the dazzling streets one day	136		14
Their young delightful hour do feature down	157		10
Youngster			
To his youngster take his treat	48		11
Youth			
But hapless youth Antinous the while	1	11	5
It is the waste done in unreticent youth	17		10
Never-eldering revel and river of youth	28	18	7

Word*	Poem	Stan.	Line
When limber liquid youth that to all I teach	48		22
Us fresh youth fretted in a bloomfall all portending	48		30
To its own best being and its loveliness of youth it is an everlastingness of o it is an all youth	59		13
To its own best being and its loveliness of youth it is an everlastingness of o it is an all youth	59		13
To its own best being and its loveliness of youth it is an everlastingness of o it is an all youth	59		13
Of favoured make and mind and health and youth	157		18
Youve			
Youve parlour-pastime left and wholl	30		34
Ytressed			
Caught on the dank-ytressed trees	77		106
Yule			
Of New Years month or surly Yule	30		30
Zeal			
Legates might rush zeal-rampant fiery	1	5	5
And zeal is flushed and pity bleeds	23		34
Zeal-rampant			
Legates might rush zeal-rampant fiery	1	5	5
Zenith			
The zenith melted to a rose of air	2		23
Looks from the zenith round the sky	77		108
Zenithd			
Shall when his star is zenithd find	83		7
Zephyrs			
Where Phoebus weeps for him whom Zephyrs guile	1	11	7
Zest			
Keeps a kind of joy in it a zest an edge an ecstasy	152		91
Into such a sudden zest	159		20
Zone			
I am the midst of every zone	130		3
8000			
8000 furlongs in advance	83		16

Appendix I
Alphabetized List of Words and the Frequency of Their Appearance

Word	Frequency
A	7
A-wanting	2
Abandoned	1
Abel	1
Abeles	1
Abide	1
Abides	1
Abject	1
Abode	1
Abolished	1
Abound	1
About	23
Above	21
Abreast	1
Abroad	2
Abrupt	1
Abundant	1
Abysmal	1
Abysses	1
Acanthus	1
Acanthus-crownd	1
Accents	1
Accept	1
Acceptance	1
Accepted	1
Accepting	1
Accessories	1
Accidents	1
Accumulated	1
Aches	1
Achieve	1
Aching	1
Acknowledging	1
Acorn	2
Acorn-cup	1
Acquaintance	1
Acre	3
Acres	1
Across	12
Act	3
Acts	2
Adamantine	1
Adazzle	1
Add	1
Adder	1
Adela	1
Admire	3
Admired	1
Adored	3
Adown	2
Advance	1
Adversity	1
Advise	1
Aeolis	1
Aeons	1
Aerial	2
Aether	1
Afar	1
Affection	1
Affined	1
Afflicted	1
Afflictive	1
Afflicts	1
Aflash	1
Afoot	1
Afresh	1
After	22
After-comers	1
After-words	1
Aftercast	1
Afterdraught	1
Afternoon	1
Again	1
Against	10
Age	9
Age-old	1
Ages	4
Aggrandise	1
Ago	3
Aid	1
Aidenn	1
Aim	1
Air	64
Air-blended	1
Air-crisping	1
Airs	4
Airwards	1
Airworld	1
Airy	6
Airy-grey	1
Akin	1
Alarms	1
Alas	6
Albeit	1

Appendix I

Ale........................ 1
Alert 1
Alfonso.................. 1
Alice 3
Alien 3
Alight 1
Alighted 1
Alive.....................3
All.....................245
All-a-leaf 1
All-accepting............ 1
All-belated 1
All-fire 1
All-heal 1
All-in-all................ 1
All-starrd 2
All-surfy 1
Allow.................... 1
Allows................... 2
Alls...................... 2
Almoner 1
Almost 4
Alms 2
Aloft 2
Alone 11
Along 14
Aloof.................... 3
Alp 1
Altar.....................4
Altar-tapers 1
Altar-vessels............ 1
Altars....................1
Alter 1
Alterd 3
Altogether............... 1
Alway.................... 2
Always................... 6
Amain....................2
Amansstrength 1
Amaze....................1
Amazed 1
Amber.................... 2
Amend 1
Amends 1
American 1
American-outward-bound....1
Amethyst 1
Amidst...................5
Amiss....................1
Among....................7
Amongst 2
Ancient.................. 1
Ancles................... 1
And 5
Andromeda 1
Anew 1
Angel 4
Angel-warder 1
Angels 7
Anointed 1
Anon 3
Answer 4
Answering................1
Antinous 1
Antipodes 1
Antique 1
Anvil....................2
Anvil-ding............... 1
Any..................... 16
Anything 2
Anywhere 2
Apart 7
Apollo 1
Appal.................... 1
Appareld 1
Appeal................... 2
Appealing................1
Appear................... 5
Appeard 1
Appearing................1
Apple.................... 2
Apple-trees 1
Appledurcombe 1
Apples...................1
Apply....................1
Apprehend 1
Approve 1
Approved 2
April.................... 4
April-weather 1
Apt. 2
Arba 1
Arc 2
Arcadia 1
Arcadian 1
Arch 2
Arch-especial.............1
Arched 1
Arches 1
Arching 1
Arcs 1
Argent 2

Argued 1
Arise 3
Ark 1
Arm 2
Arms 4
Arose 2
Around 7
Aroused 1
Array 1
Arrival 1
Art 21
Arthur 1
Arthurs 1
Artist 1
Arts 1
As 167
Ascend 1
Ascendancy 1
Ascribed 1
Ash 5
Ash-tops 1
Ashboughs 1
Ashes 2
Ashiness 1
Aside 1
Ask 6
Askd 3
Asked 1
Asking 1
Asks 2
Aslant 1
Asleep 2
Aspect 1
Aspens 2
Assault 1
Assaulting 1
Assay 1
Assignd 1
Assured 1
Assyrian 1
Astern 1
Astrain 1
Astral 1
Astray 2
Astrew 1
Astrologic 1
Asunder 1
Aswarm 1
At 2
Atlantic 1
Atmosphere 1
Attain 2
Attempted 1
Attentive 1
Attire 1
Attributes 1
Attributing 2
Attuneable 1
Attuning 1
Aureoles 1
Austin 1
Authentic 1
Autumn 5
Autumn-time 2
Avenge 1
Avoid 1
Avow 1
Away 28
Awful 1
Awhile 1
Awoke 1
Ay 3
Aye 1
Azure 5
Azured 1
Azuring 1
Azuring-over 1
Azurous 1
Babble 2
Babes 1
Babyhood 1
Back 17
Backed 1
Backward 1
Backwheels 1
Bad 5
Baffle 1
Baffled 1
Baffling 1
Bala 2
Balance 1
Balanced 4
Balances 1
Bald 1
Baldbright 1
Bales 1
Ball 3
Ballad 2
Balls 1
Balm 1
Ban 1
Band 2

Word	Count
Bands	5
Banes	2
Bank	2
Bankrupt	1
Banks	9
Bannd	1
Banned	1
Banner	9
Banquet	1
Bans	1
Bar	1
Barbarous	1
Bare	12
Barebill	1
Bared	1
Barely	2
Bargain	1
Barken	1
Barley	1
Barn	1
Barrack	1
Barrd	1
Barred	3
Barrel	1
Barrelled	1
Barren	3
Barrens	1
Barriers	1
Barrow	2
Barrowy	1
Bars	4
Barter	1
Barterd	1
Base	2
Basilisk	1
Basket	5
Basks	1
Bason	1
Bass	1
Bat	1
Bath	2
Bathe	1
Bathed	2
Bathes	1
Bathing	1
Bats	1
Battering	1
Battle	1
Battled	1
Battling	1
Bay	6
Bays	1
Beach	1
Beacon	2
Bead	2
Beadbonny	1
Beakleaved	1
Beam	4
Beam-blind	1
Beaming	1
Beams	3
Bean	1
Bear	10
Bearer	1
Bearing	4
Bears	1
Beast	2
Beat	15
Beating	2
Beats	2
Beauties	1
Beautiful	2
Beauty	37
Beauty-bow	1
Beauty-in-the-ghost	1
Beautys	5
Beckoned	2
Become	1
Bed	9
Bedded	1
Beds	2
Bee	1
Beech	1
Beechbole	1
Bees	1
Beetle	1
Beetle-browed	1
Beetling	2
Befal	1
Befall	1
Before	26
Before-time-taken	1
Began	4
Begged	1
Begin	3
Beginning	6
Begun	6
Behaviour	1
Behind	12
Behold	3
Beholder	1
Being	32

Beings 2
Bela 1
Belated 1
Belie 1
Believe 2
Believes 2
Bell 5
Bell-swarmed 1
Bellbright 1
Belled 2
Belleisle 1
Bellerophon 1
Bellisle 1
Bellows 1
Bells 7
Belong 1
Below 6
Belts 1
Belvedere 1
Bend 2
Bends 1
Beneath 5
Benediction 1
Benefits 1
Bent 4
Bereft 2
Berg 1
Beryl 2
Beryl-covered 1
Beside 11
Besides 1
Bespoken 1
Best 18
Bestowing 1
Bethlehem 1
Bethlem 1
Bethlems 1
Betimes 1
Betray 1
Betrayd 1
Better 6
Betterd 1
Between 10
Betweenpie 1
Betweens 1
Betweenwhiles 1
Betwixt 3
Beuno 1
Bevy 2
Beyond 16
Bid 7
Bides 1
Bids 4
Bidst 1
Big 2
Big-boned 1
Bill 2
Billion 1
Billow 2
Billows 2
Billowy 1
Bills 1
Bind 2
Bindst 1
Bines 1
Bird 10
Birds 2
Birth 8
Birthday 5
Biscay 1
Bit 1
Bite 1
Bitten 1
Bitter 4
Bitterer 1
Bitterness 1
Black 19
Black-about 1
Black-backed 1
Black-fleeced 1
Blackest 1
Blackness 1
Blacks 1
Blade 2
Blade-gash 1
Blades 3
Blady 1
Blame 1
Blast 5
Blasted 1
Blasts 2
Blaze 2
Blazon 4
Blazoned 2
Blazonry 1
Bleached 1
Bleak 4
Blear 3
Blear-all 1
Bleared 1
Bleat 2
Bleats 1

Bleed ... 2
Bleeding ... 3
Bleeds ... 1
Blended ... 1
Bless ... 5
Blessed ... 3
Blessing ... 1
Blest ... 4
Blight ... 1
Blind ... 9
Blindfold ... 1
Blinding ... 3
Blindness ... 1
Blinds ... 1
Blindworm ... 1
Blinking ... 1
Bliss ... 6
Blissful ... 1
Block ... 3
Blocks ... 4
Blood ... 13
Blood-gush ... 1
Blood-light ... 1
Blood-vivid ... 1
Bloods ... 1
Bloody ... 3
Bloom ... 14
Bloomfall ... 1
Blooming ... 1
Blooms ... 4
Blossom ... 7
Blossom-hitting ... 1
Blot ... 2
Blotless ... 1
Blots ... 2
Blow ... 13
Blowing ... 1
Blown ... 4
Blowpipe ... 1
Blows ... 2
Blue ... 30
Blue-beating ... 1
Blue-bleak ... 1
Bluebell ... 1
Bluebells ... 6
Bluer ... 1
Bluff ... 1
Blurrd ... 1
Blurs ... 1
Blushed ... 1
Blustering ... 1
Board ... 1
Boards ... 1
Boast ... 3
Boasting ... 1
Boatman ... 1
Boded ... 1
Bodes ... 1
Bodies ... 2
Body ... 6
Boisterous ... 2
Boisterously ... 1
Bold ... 8
Boldboys ... 1
Bolder ... 2
Bole ... 1
Bolt ... 1
Bolts ... 1
Bone ... 4
Bone-house ... 1
Boned ... 1
Bones ... 11
Bonfire ... 1
Boniface ... 1
Bonnet ... 1
Bonniest ... 1
Book ... 2
Boon ... 3
Boons ... 1
Boots ... 1
Borders ... 1
Bore ... 6
Boreas ... 1
Bored ... 1
Bores ... 1
Born ... 12
Borne ... 3
Boroughs ... 1
Borrow ... 1
Bossd ... 1
Bough ... 3
Boughs ... 10
Bound ... 19
Bounden ... 1
Bow ... 9
Bow-bend ... 1
Bowd ... 2
Bower ... 4
Bowl ... 1
Bowman ... 1
Bows ... 2
Box ... 1

Boy 8
Boys 3
Brace 3
Braes 1
Braggart 2
Brags 1
Braid. 1
Braids. 2
Brain. 3
Brains 1
Brakes 4
Brambles 1
Branch 2
Branches 2
Branchy 2
Brand 1
Brandle 1
Brands 1
Brass 2
Brass-bold 1
Brave 2
Bravest. 1
Brawling. 1
Brawn 1
Brazen. 2
Bread 5
Breadth 1
Break 11
Breaker. 1
Breakers 1
Breaking 5
Breakless. 1
Breaks 6
Breast 11
Breasted 1
Breasting. 1
Breasts 2
Breath. 21
Breath-taking 1
Breathe 12
Breathed. 3
Breathes 4
Breathing. 4
Bred. 7
Breed 1
Breeds 1
Breeze 4
Breezy 2
Bremen 1
Brickish 1
Bricks 1
Bride. 4
Bridegroom 1
Bridge 1
Bridging. 1
Brief 2
Brier 1
Bright 20
Bright-counter 1
Bright-lifting. 1
Bright-maskd 1
Brighten 1
Brightening 1
Brighter 4
Brightest 1
Brightness 1
Brilliance. 1
Brilliant 3
Brilliant-hued 1
Brim 3
Brimmed 1
Brims 2
Brinded 1
Brindled 1
Brine. 2
Bring 10
Bringing 2
Brings 3
Brink 1
Bristol 1
Bristol-bred 1
Britain 2
Britains 1
Brittle 4
Broad 7
Broad-fluted 1
Broad-shed 1
Broiders 1
Broidery 1
Broke 3
Broken 2
Bronze 3
Bronzen 1
Brooch 1
Brood 2
Broods 3
Brook 6
Brooks 2
Broth 2
Brother 5
Brothers 10
Brought 5

Brow 6
Browed 2
Brown 8
Brown-as-dawning-skinned . . 1
Brows 3
Browzed 1
Bruise 1
Bruised 2
Brush 4
Brute 1
Bubbles 2
Buck 1
Buckle 1
Bud 4
Budded 1
Buds 8
Bugle 4
Bugle-eyed 1
Bugler 2
Bugles 1
Build 5
Built 5
Bulk 1
Bulky 1
Bullion 1
Bunchy 1
Buoy 2
Burden 4
Burial 1
Burl 1
Burling 1
Burly 3
Burn 4
Burning 2
Burnish 2
Burnishd 1
Burns 3
Burr 1
Burst 2
Bursts 1
Bury 1
Bush 1
Bush-browed 1
Bushes 3
Bushybowered 1
Business 1
Busy 1
Butcher 1
Butmind 1
Butter 1
Butter-burr 1
Butterflies 1
Butts 1
Buy 4
Buys 1
By 1
Bye 1
Bye-ways 1
Bygones 1
Byplay 1
Cadair 1
Cadence 1
Caerwys 2
Caesars 2
Cage 1
Cages 1
Cains 1
Caked 1
Call 18
Calld 2
Called 6
Calling 3
Calls 7
Calm 2
Calvary 1
Calvarys 1
Came 37
Campion 1
Canaan 1
Cancer 1
Candle 4
Candlemas 1
Candles 1
Candour 1
Candycoloured 1
Cannon 1
Cant 2
Canvas 1
Canvass 1
Canvassing 1
Cap 1
Capable 1
Capes 1
Capital 1
Cappd 1
Capped 1
Caps 2
Capsize 1
Captain 1
Capitivity 1
Caradoc 1
Caradocs 1

Care 16
Care-coiled 1
Care-drowned 1
Care-killed 1
Cared 1
Cared-for 1
Career 1
Careful 2
Careful-spaced 2
Careless 3
Cares 2
Caressd 1
Caressing. 1
Carisbrook 1
Carmine 2
Carnation 3
Carol 2
Carouse 1
Carried 3
Carrier 1
Carrier-witted 1
Carriers. 1
Carries 1
Carrion 1
Carry 2
Cart 2
Carved 1
Carving 1
Case 1
Cased 1
Casements 1
Casque 1
Cast 10
Castara 6
Castaras 1
Castilian 1
Cataract 1
Catch 4
Catches 1
Caught. 4
Cause 7
Cavernous 1
Cease 2
Ceaseless 1
Cell 1
Cells 1
Cemented 1
Censers 1
Central 3
Centre. 4
Centre-darks 1
Centreings 1
Centres 2
Centurion 1
Ceres 1
Certainty 1
Chaff 1
Chained 1
Chair 1
Chalky. 1
Chamferd 1
Champ 1
Champ-white 1
Chance 1
Chancequarried 1
Changd. 1
Change 6
Changed 3
Changeful 3
Changeless 1
Changing 3
Channel 2
Channelled 1
Chaotic 1
Chapel 1
Chapel-side 1
Chapleted 1
C haplets 1
Chaptered 1
Character 2
Charactered 1
Charge 2
Charged 3
Charitable 1
Charity 7
Charitys 1
Charless 1
Charm 3
Charmed 2
Charms 3
Charnelhouse 1
Charnelhouse-grate 1
Chart. 1
Charted. 1
Charter 1
Chase 1
Chasms 1
Chastening 1
Chastity 1
Chaunt 1
Cheap .1
Chebars 1

Check 1
Chee 1
Cheek 3
Cheeks 6
Cheer 5
Cheered 1
Cheering 1
Cheerless 1
Cheers 1
Cheevio 2
Cheevo 1
Chequers 1
Cherry 1
Chervil 1
Chestnut 4
Chestnut-falls 1
Chestnut-fans 1
Chevalier 1
Chevy 1
Chewd 1
Chief 2
Chief-woe 1
Chiefs 1
Chieftain 1
Child 19
Child-like 1
Childless 1
Children 2
Childrens 1
Childs 3
Chill 2
Chilling 1
Chime 2
Chips 1
Chivalry 1
Chilvarys 1
Choice 5
Choicest 2
Choir 1
Choke 3
Choking 1
Choose 4
Chords 2
Chose 2
Chrism 1
Christ 40
Christ-done 1
Christ-ed 1
Christens 1
Christian 1
Christians 1
Christmas 2
Christs 10
Christus 1
Chrysolite 1
Church 2
Church-tower 1
Churl 3
Churlsgrace 1
Churning 1
Cield 1
Cinquefoil 1
Cipher 1
Circle 4
Circle-citadels 1
Circled 2
Circles 2
Circlet 1
Circling 1
Citadels 1
Cite 1
Cithern 1
Cities 1
City 4
Clad 2
Clammy 4
Clammish 1
Clank 1
Clarion 2
Clarion-clear 1
Clarions 1
Clarissa 1
Claspd 1
Clasped 2
Classic 1
Clattering 1
Claude 1
Clay 5
Clayfields 1
Clear 9
Clearest 1
Clearest-selved 1
Clears 2
Cleave 1
Cleaves 2
Cleped 1
Clicking 1
Cliff 3
Cliffs 3
Clime 3
Clinches 1
Clinching 1

Clinching-blind .1
Cling 1
Clings 3
Clitheroe 8
Clods 1
Clogged 1
Cloister 1
Cloister-light 1
Cloisterd 1
Cloistering 1
Cloisters 1
Close 14
Close-barred 1
Close-folded 1
Close-ply 1
Close-rooted 1
Close-shut 2
Closer 1
Closes 1
Clot 2
Clothe 2
Clothes 1
Cloud 13
Cloud-festooned 1
Cloud-puffball 1
Clouds 18
Clough 1
Cloy 1
Cluster 2
Clusterd 1
Clustering 1
Clusters 1
Clutched 1
Coal 1
Coast 1
Coat 1
Coated 1
Coats 1
Cobbled 1
Cocooning 1
Coffer 1
Coffin 1
Coffin-black 1
Cogged 1
Coifed 1
Coil 2
Coiled 1
Coils 1
Coinage 1
Cold 16
Colder 1
Coldly 1
Coldness 1
Collapsing 1
Colomb 1
Colossal 1
Colour 8
Colourd 2
Coloured 2
Colouring 1
Colours 2
Columnar 1
Columnar-severe 1
Columns 1
Comb 2
Combating 1
Combes 1
Combs 5
Come 69
Come-back-again 1
Comers 1
Comes 23
Comet 1
Comfort 12
Comfortable 1
Comforter 1
Comforting 2
Comfortless 2
Comforts 1
Coming 2
Commander 1
Commands 1
Common 3
Commonweal 2
Communion 1
Companion 1
Company 5
Comparison 1
Compass 7
Compassion 1
Compassionate 1
Complaisant 1
Complete 1
Compliment 1
Compulsion 1
Comrade 1
Concavity 1
Conceive 3
Conceived 3
Conceiving 1
Concern 1
Concerned 1

Conch 1
Concording 1
Condition 2
Confess 1
Confidante 1
Confidence 1
Confined 1
Confirmed 1
Confound 1
Confounded 1
Confront 1
Confused 1
Conjecture 1
Conjuctions 1
Conquest 1
Conqurors 1
Conscience 1
Considerate 1
Considered 1
Consolation 2
Constancy 1
Consumes 1
Consuming 1
Contagious 1
Contend 1
Contended 1
Contends 1
Content 1
Contented 4
Contentment 1
Continence 1
Continent 1
Continually 1
Contract 1
Controlld 1
Convent 3
Coo. 2
Cooings 1
Cool 3
Cooling 2
Coop 1
Coped 1
Copse 8
Copses 1
Copying 3
Coral 1
Corded 1
Cordial 1
Cords 1
Corn 4
Corner 2
Corners 2
Cornicd 1
Cornice 2
Coronals 1
Coronet 1
Corpse 3
Corpses 1
Correspond 1
Corridors 2
Corruption 1
Corse 2
Cost 1
Cot 1
Cottages 1
Cough 1
Council 1
Counsel 1
Count 4
Countenance 1
Counter 5
Counter-roundels 1
Counterfeit 1
Counterfoiling 1
Counterpart 2
Countervail 1
Counting 1
Countless 1
Country 8
County 1
Couple 1
Couple-colour 1
Courage 1
Course 1
Courses 1
Court 4
Courtesies 1
Courts 2
Cousin 2
Cover 5
Coverd 1
Covered 2
Coverlid 1
Covers 3
Coverts 1
Cow 1
Crackd 1
Cradock 1
Cragiron 1
Crags 1
Cramps 1
Crash 2

Crawl 1
Creamy 1
Crease 1
Creased 2
Creases 1
Creating 1
Creation 1
Creations 1
Creature 1
Creatures 1
Credit 1
Creeds 1
Creep 3
Crept 3
Cressetedeast 1
Crest 3
Crew 3
Cried 4
Cries 6
Crime 1
Crimson 8
Crimson-cressetedeast 1
Crimson-golden 1
Crimson-white 1
Crimsonings 1
Crimsons 1
Cringe 1
Cripples 1
Crisp 5
Crispd 1
Crisping 1
Crisps 1
Criss 1
Criss-crossd 1
Crocodiles 1
Crooked 1
Cross 7
Cross-barred 1
Cross-colour 1
Cross-wood 1
Crossbridle 1
Crossd 2
Crosses 1
Crouch 1
Crowd 3
Crowded 2
Crowding 1
Crowds 2
Crown 14
Crownals 2
Crownd 2
Crowned 1
Crowning 2
Crowns 1
Crucified 3
Crucify 3
Cruel 1
Cruise 1
Crumbled 1
Crumbling 1
Crush 3
Crush-silk 1
Crushd 2
Crushed 3
Crushes 1
Crust 4
Crutches 2
Cry 15
Crying 3
Crystal 1
Crystal-ending 1
Crystalline 1
Cuckoo 5
Cuckoo-echoing 1
Cuckoocall 1
Cud 1
Cue 1
Cullys 1
Cumber 1
Cumbered 1
Cumbrous 1
Cumnor 1
Cup 2
Cupboard 1
Cuppd 1
Curb 1
Curded 1
Cure 1
Curfew 1
Curl 1
Curld 1
Curls 1
Current 2
Curse 4
Cursed 2
Curses 2
Cursing 1
Curves 1
Cusp 1
Customary 1
Cut 4
Cyclads 1

Cypris 1
Dabbled 1
Daffodil 1
Daffodillies 1
Daffodils 3
Dahlias 1
Daintily 1
Dainty 3
Dainty-delicate 1
Daisies 1
Dale 2
Dallies 1
Damask 1
Damaskd 1
Damasqud 2
Dame 1
Damp 1
Damson 1
Dance 1
Danced 3
Dancers 1
Dances 2
Dancing 1
Dandled 4
Dandy 1
Dandy-hung 1
Danger 1
Dangerous 3
Dangerously 1
Dangled 1
Dank 3
Dank-ytressed 1
Dantes 1
Daphnis 1
Dapple 5
Dapple-dawn-drawn 1
Dapple-eared 1
Dappled 5
Dappled-with-damson 1
Dare 7
Dare-gale 1
Dared 2
Daredeaths 1
Dares 1
Daring 2
Dark 25
Darkend 1
Darkened 1
Darker 2
Darkles 1
Darkness 11
Darks 1
Darksome 6
Darling 1
Dart 1
Darting 1
Dashed 1
Date 2
Dated 2
Dateless 1
Dates 1
Daughter 4
Daughters 2
Daunting 1
Dauntless 1
Dauphin 1
Davids 1
Dawn 7
Dawning 1
Day 62
Day-dissolved 1
Day-labouring-out 1
Daylight 14
Daylights 1
Days 17
Dayspring 1
Daystar 1
Daze 1
Dazzle 1
Dazzling 2
Deacon 1
Dead 13
Dead-alive 1
Deadly 2
Deadly-electric 1
Deadning 1
Deaf 1
Deal 5
Deals 2
Dealt 5
Dean 3
Dear 18
Dearer 3
Dearest 7
Dearly 5
Dearness 1
Dears 1
Dearth 2
Death 37
Deathdance 1
Deathgush 1
Deaths 5

Debt . . . 2
Decay . . . 1
Decaying . . . 1
December . . . 1
Deck . . . 5
Decked . . . 1
Decks . . . 2
Decreased . . . 1
Decree . . . 1
Deed . . . 5
Deed-bound . . . 1
Deem . . . 1
Deemed . . . 1
Deems . . . 1
Deep . . . 17
Deep-groved . . . 1
Deepening . . . 1
Deeper . . . 3
Deeply . . . 2
Deeps . . . 2
Defeat . . . 2
Defiance . . . 1
Deflowers . . . 1
Deft . . . 1
Deft-handed . . . 1
Degged . . . 1
Degree . . . 7
Degrees . . . 1
Dejection . . . 1
Delay . . . 1
Delicacy . . . 1
Delicate . . . 1
Delicious . . . 1
Delight . . . 3
Delighted . . . 1
Delightful . . . 3
Delightfully . . . 2
Deliver . . . 3
Delivering . . . 1
Dell . . . 1
Delve . . . 2
Delves . . . 1
Den . . . 2
Denial . . . 1
Denis . . . 1
Dense . . . 1
Dented . . . 1
Departed . . . 1
Departing . . . 2
Depend . . . 1
Deplore . . . 2
Depths . . . 1
Descend . . . 2
Descending . . . 3
Descried . . . 1
Desert . . . 1
Deserter . . . 1
Deserve . . . 1
Deserving . . . 1
Desirable . . . 1
Desire . . . 9
Desired . . . 3
Desires . . . 1
Desirous . . . 1
Despair . . . 13
Despairing . . . 1
Despatch . . . 2
Despatches . . . 1
Desperate . . . 2
Despise . . . 2
Desponding . . . 1
Destined . . . 1
Deutschland . . . 2
Device . . . 1
Devilish . . . 1
Devon . . . 1
Devonshire . . . 1
Devouring . . . 1
Dew . . . 10
Dew-lap . . . 1
Dewbell . . . 1
Dewdrop . . . 1
Dewdrops . . . 1
Dews . . . 2
Dewy . . . 2
Dexterous . . . 1
Diadem . . . 1
Diademd . . . 1
Diamond . . . 3
Diamonds . . . 2
Diapered . . . 1
Diapers . . . 1
Dick . . . 1
Die . . . 12
Die-away . . . 1
Died . . . 2
Dies . . . 3
Diet . . . 1
Difference . . . 1
Dight . . . 1
Dim . . . 6
Diminishd . . . 1

Diminishes 1
Dimly 1
Dimmd 1
Dimness 1
Dimpled 2
Dimpling...................1
Din 1
Ding 1
Dingle......................1
Dingle-a-dangled...........1
Dings 1
Dint........................1
Dinted 1
Dintless 1
Dip.........................3
Dippd 1
Direction 1
Directly 1
Dirvan......................1
Disabling 1
Disallow...................1
Disappointed...............1
Disappointment............3
Disarming 1
Disarray 1
Disaster 1
Disastrous 1
Discharge 1
Discharging 1
Disclose 1
Discloses..................1
Discontent 1
Discord 1
Discoverd..................5
Discovered 1
Discovering 1
Discovery...................1
Dishevelled................1
Dismal 4
Dismalest...................1
Dismay.....................1
Dismembering 1
Disobedient...............1
Disorders 1
Disparadised.............. 1
Dispel 1
Dispense 1
Dispenses 1
Disposes 1
Disquiet 1
Disregarded 1
Disremembering............1
Disseveral 1
Dissolve 1
Dissolved...................1
Distance....................3
Distanced 1
Distant 2
Distemperd.................1
Distillation 1
Distills 1
Distinction 1
Distress 2
Distressed.................1
Disturbd 1
Dither 1
Dive 1
Divers 1
Divide 1
Divided 1
Divine 17
Divined 1
Divinely 1
Diving 1
Dizzy 1
Doff 1
Doffs 1
Dog 1
Dogeared 1
Doggd 1
Dogged 2
Dogrose 1
Dogs 1
Doing 3
Domain 1
Dominant 1
Done 27
Doom 5
Doomed 2
Doomfire 1
Dooms 1
Dooms-day 1
Doomsday..................1
Door 7
Doors 3
Doric 1
Dorothea 1
Dorothy 2
Double.................... 6
Double-musical 1
Double-natured............1
Doublet 1

Doubt	3
Doubtless	2
Dough	2
Dove	2
Doves	2
Dovewinged	1
Down	64
Down-dugged	1
Down-splinterd	1
Downcarol	1
Downdolphinry	1
Downright	1
Downs	4
Downward	2
Downward-hollowing	1
Downwards	1
Downy	1
Dragon	1
Dragonflies	1
Dragonish	1
Dragons	1
Drain	1
Draining	1
Draught	2
Draughts	1
Draw	7
Drawer	1
Drawn	9
Draws	2
Drayhorse	1
Dread	2
Dreaded	1
Dreadful	3
Dreadnought	1
Dream	3
Dreamd	2
Dreamed	2
Dreams	3
Dreamy	1
Drear	1
Drenchd	2
Drenched	1
Dress	4
Dressed	1
Drest	1
Drew	5
Drift	4
Drifted	1
Drifting	1
Drilled	1
Drink	4
Drinks	1
Dripping	1
Driven	2
Drives	2
Driving	2
Drizzle	1
Drond	1
Droop	3
Droopd	2
Drooping	2
Drop	6
Drop-of-blood-and-foam-dapple	1
Droppd	1
Dropped	1
Dropping	1
Drops	14
Drouth	1
Drove	3
Drowned	5
Drowning	1
Drowsy	1
Drudgery	1
Drum	3
Dry	13
Duct	2
Due	2
Dugged	1
Dull	4
Duly	2
Dumb	6
Duomo	1
Durance	1
During	1
Dusk	4
Dusk-deep	1
Dust	5
Duty	4
Duty-swerver	1
Dwarf	1
Dwarfs	1
Dwellest	1
Dwells	3
Dwelt	2
Dwindled	2
Dwindles	1
Dwindling	1
Dye	2
Dying	1
Dyphwys	1
Eager	1

Eagerer....1
Eagles....1
Ear....13
Ear-caressing....1
Eared....1
Earlier....5
Earliest....2
Earlstars....1
Early....4
Earnest....6
Earnest-hearted....1
Ears....8
Earth....34
Earthless....2
Earths....8
Earthworld....1
Ease....6
Easeful....1
Easily....2
East....8
Easter....8
Eastering....1
Eastern....1
Eastnortheast....1
Eastward....1
Eastwards....1
Easy....3
Eat....3
Eaten....1
Eaves....2
Ebb....1
Ebbd....1
Echod....1
Echoing....4
Echoing-of-earth....1
Eclipse....1
Eclipsing....1
Ecstacy....2
Ecstasy....3
Ed....1
Eddies....1
Eddy....1
Eden....1
Edge....2
Edged....1
Edges....1
Effectual....1
Eggs....3
Egypt....1
Egyptian....3
Eighth....1
El....1
Elbow....1
Elder....2
Eldering....1
Elected....1
Electric....1
Electrical....1
Element....6
Elemented....1
Elements....3
Eleven....1
Elim....1
Elm....2
Elm-heads....1
Elms....1
Elmy....1
Eloquent....1
Else....15
Else-minded....1
Elsewhere....3
Elves....1
Elves-eyes....1
Embers....2
Emblem....1
Embraced....1
Eminent....1
Empire....1
Employment....1
Empty....2
Enclusterd....1
Encounter....1
Encrimsoning....1
End....13
Endears....3
Endeavour....1
Ended....2
Ending....3
Endless....1
Endlessly....1
Endragoned....1
Ends....3
Endured....1
Enduring....1
Enemy....1
Enforced....1
Engaged....1
Engemming....1
Engenderd....1
England....4
Englands....1
English....5

Enjewelling 1
Enjoy 1
Enjoyment 1
Enormous 3
Enough 10
Enriched 1
Enrolld 2
Entangled 1
Enter 1
Entering 1
Entrance 1
Entrancingly 1
Envied 1
Epistles 1
Equal 3
Equipped 1
Ere 9
Erin 1
Erst 1
Esaus 1
Escape 1
Escorial 1
Especial 3
Espial 1
Essence 1
Estates 1
Esteemd 1
Etc 1
Eternal 4
Ether 1
Eucharist 1
Eunuch 1
Eurydice 1
Eve 2
Even 18
Evening 7
Event 1
Ever 22
Ever-fretting 1
Everlasting 1
Everlastingness 1
Evermore 1
Every 17
Everyone 2
Everything 3
Everywhere 7
Evil 3
Evil-heavend 1
Evils 1
Ewe 1
Except 1
Excess 1
Exhibition 1
Exile 1
Exiled 1
Explanation 1
Exploit 1
Express 1
Expressed 1
Expressionless 1
Exquisite 3
Extremes 1
Extremity 1
Exultation 1
Eye 29
Eye-attentive 1
Eye-greeting 1
Eyed 3
Eyelash 2
Eyelid 2
Eyelids 1
Eyes 44
Eyesight 1
Ezekiels 1
Fabian 2
Fable 1
Fabled 1
Fabling 1
Face 17
Faced 1
Faces 4
Fade 1
Faded 2
Fading 1
Fagged 1
Fail 7
Faild 1
Failing 1
Fails 3
Failure 1
Fain 5
Faint 2
Fainter 1
Fair 20
Fairer 6
Fairly 1
Fairness 1
Fairy 3
Fairyland 1
Faith 3
Faithful 2
Faithless 1

Falcon 1
Fall 28
Fall-gold 1
Fallen 5
Fallers 1
Falling 5
Falln 2
Fallow 3
Fallowbootfellow 1
Fallows 1
Falls 13
False 1
Falsely 1
Falsified 1
Falter 1
Fame 4
Fames 1
Familiar 3
Familiarness 1
Fan 3
Fancied 1
Fancies 3
Fanciful 1
Fancy 2
Fang 2
Fanged 1
Fangs 1
Fans 3
Fantastic 1
Far 19
Far-off 1
Farmyard 1
Farrier 1
Fashed 1
Fashion 1
Fast 26
Fast-flowing 1
Fast-lodged 1
Fasted 1
Fasten 1
Fastened 2
Faster 2
Fasts 1
Fatal 3
Father 23
Fatherd 1
Fathers 4
Fathers-forth 1
Fathomed 1
Fathoms 1
Fault 6
Fault-not-found-with 1
Favour 1
Favourable 1
Favoured 1
Favouring 1
Favourite 1
Fawn 1
Fawn-froth 1
Fawning 2
Fealty 1
Fear 9
Feard 1
Feared 1
Fearful 1
Fearing 1
Fears 3
Feast 6
Feasting 2
Feasts 3
Feather 3
Feathers 2
Feathery 2
Feature 4
Features 3
Featuring 1
Fed 1
Fee 3
Feeble 1
Feed 3
Feeds 2
Feel 10
Feel-of-primrose 1
Feelers 1
Feeling 3
Feels 1
Feet 16
Feigns 1
Felicitous 1
Felix 3
Fell 15
Fell-frowning 1
Felled 4
Fellowship 2
Fellowships 1
Fells 2
Felt 4
Female 1
Fenced 1
Fens 1
Fern 1
Fertile 1

Word	Count
Fervent	1
Festival	1
Festconed	1
Fetch	2
Fetched	3
Fettle	1
Fever	1
Feverd	1
Few	6
Ffestiniog	1
Fickle	2
Fie	3
Field	12
Field-flowers	1
Field-flown	1
Fields	10
Fierce	2
Fiercer	1
Fiercest	1
Fiery	5
Fig	1
Fight	2
Fighter	1
Files	3
Filial	1
Fill	5
Filld	1
Filled	1
Filleted	1
Fillets	1
Fills	3
Film	1
Films	1
Filmy	2
Filth	1
Fin	3
Finches	1
Find	21
Finding	1
Finds	6
Fine	12
Fine-drawn	1
Fineflour	1
Finer	2
Finger	5
Finger-long	1
Finger-teasing	1
Fingergaps	1
Fingering	1
Fingernail	1
Fingers	9
Finishd	2
Fire	21
Fire-featuring	1
Fire-folk	1
Fireball	1
Firecoal	1
Fired	1
Firedint	1
Fires	2
Firm	2
Firmament	2
First	18
First-fruits	1
Fishes	1
Fit	3
Fits	1
Five	13
Five-lipped	1
Five-lived	1
Fix	1
Fixd	3
Fixed	2
Fixedly	1
Flag	2
Flags	3
Flake	4
Flake-doves	1
Flakes	4
Flame	14
Flame-cased	1
Flame-rash	1
Flame-rings	1
Flames	3
Flanders	1
Flange	1
Flank	3
Flanks	2
Flard	1
Flare	2
Flares	1
Flaring	1
Flash	6
Flashed	3
Flashes	2
Flashing	1
Flat	2
Flats	1
Flatter	1
Flattery	2
Flatterys	1
Flaunt	1

Flaunting 1
Flawed 1
Flecks 1
Fled....................... 6
Fledged 1
Flee....................... 1
Fleece 6
Fleeced.................... 6
Fleeces 1
Fleeciest 1
Fleet.......................6
Fleeted 1
Fleets..................... 1
Fleming 1
Flesh......................20
Flesh-bound 1
Flesh-burst 1
Flesh-flowers 1
Flesh-pots..................1
Fleshed.................... 2
Fletcher 1
Flew....................... 1
Flicker 1
Flickering 2
Flies...................... 1
Flight......................3
Flighty 1
Flinching.................. 1
Fling...................... 5
Flings..................... 1
Flint 3
Flint-flake.................1
Flints..................... 1
Flinty 2
Flirting 1
Flitches 1
Flits 1
Flixed 1
Float.......................3
Floated 1
Floating 6
Floats..................... 1
Flock 9
Flockbells 1
Flocks 5
Flood...................... 7
Floods 3
Floodtide 1
Floor...................... 2
Floord..................... 1
Floris.....................10
Flow 3
Flower.....................10
Flowerets.................. 1
Flowers 20
Flowing 3
Flown 3
Flue 1
Fluke 1
Flung 6
Flush 3
Flushd 1
Flushed 2
Flushes.................... 1
Fluted......................1
Flutes......................1
Fly 5
Flying 2
Foam 8
Foam-fallow 1
Foam-fleece 1
Foam-tuft 1
Foamfalling.................1
Foil........................1
Foiled 1
Foiling 1
Fold........................7
Folded 6
Folds 5
Foliagd 2
Foliage.................... 1
Folk 2
Follow.................... 14
Followed 1
Following.................. 3
Follows 1
Fond........................7
Fonder 4
Fondler.....................1
Font 1
Food 5
Foods 1
Fool....................... 3
Foolish.....................2
Foot 11
Footfretted 1
Footing.................... 2
Footrest 1
Footsteps 1
Footway 1
For 1
Forbid..................... 2

Word	Count
Forcd	1
Force	3
Forced	1
Forcible	1
Forcibly	1
Fore	1
Fore-foundering	1
Forecast	2
Foredrawn	1
Forefalls	1
Forefending	1
Foregone	1
Forehead	3
Foreign	2
Foreknown	1
Forelock	2
Forepangs	1
Forethought	1
Forfeit	1
Forge	5
Forged	1
Forget	3
Forgetfulness	1
Forgive	3
Forgiven	1
Forgives	1
Forgiving	1
Forgone	1
Forgot	4
Forgotten	2
Forked	1
Forlorn	2
Form	4
Formal	1
Formed	1
Formerly	1
Forms	1
Forsaken	2
Forsook	1
Forth	16
Forth-and-flaunting	1
Forth-driven	1
Fortress	1
Fortune	1
Forty	1
Forward	4
Forward-like	1
Fought	2
Foul	2
Fouled	1
Found	23
Foundered	1
Foundering	3
Fountain	1
Fountains	4
Founts	1
Four	7
Fourth	1
Fowl	3
Fowls	1
Foxgloves	1
Fragrance	2
Frail	4
Frailest	1
Frailest-flixed	1
Frailty	1
Frame	2
Framed	3
France	3
Frances	1
Francis	1
Frank	2
Frantic	1
Fray	5
Freckled	1
Free	13
Freed	2
Freely	2
Freeze	1
Freezing	1
Freighted	1
Frenzied	1
Frequenting	1
Fresh	25
Fresh-firecoal	1
Fresh-leaved	1
Freshest	1
Freshly	1
Freshness	4
Fret	4
Fretful	1
Frets	1
Fretted	4
Fretting	1
Fretty	2
Friend	5
Friends	3
Frieze	2
Frigate	1
Frightful	3
Frigid	1
Fringe	4

Fringed....................1
Fringes 1
Fro.......................2
Frocks....................1
Froliclavish..............1
Fronting..................2
Fronts....................1
Frost.....................1
Frost-furred..............1
Froth.....................2
Frothpits.................1
Frothy....................1
Froward...................1
Frown.....................1
Frowning..................5
Fruit....................11
Fruit-cloistering.........1
Fruits....................2
Fueled....................1
Fulfil....................1
Fulfilld..................1
Full.....................13
Full-leaved...............1
Full-sappd................1
Fuller....................1
Fully.....................1
Fumes.....................1
Fuming....................1
Fumitory..................1
Function..................1
Funeral...................2
Fur.......................2
Furl......................1
Furled....................4
Furlongs..................1
Furls.....................2
Furnace...................1
Furred....................2
Furrow....................3
Furrows...................1
Further...................7
Furtherd..................1
Furthest..................2
Fury......................1
Fussy.....................1
Futility..................1
Gaiety....................1
Gain......................1
Gaind.....................1
Gainings..................1
Galahad...................2
Galaxy....................1
Gale......................4
Gales.....................1
Galilee...................1
Galilees..................1
Gall......................2
Gallant...................2
Gallantry.................1
Galled....................1
Galleries.................1
Gallop....................1
Gambol....................1
Gambolling................1
Gan.......................1
Gangs.....................1
Gapes.....................1
Gaps......................1
Garb......................1
Garden....................8
Garden-poppies............1
Gardens...................9
Garland...................1
Garlanded.................2
Garnered..................1
Garnering.................1
Garnet....................1
Gash......................2
Gashed....................1
Gashes....................1
Gasp......................1
Gaspd.....................1
Gasping...................1
Gasps.....................1
Gate......................1
Gates.....................1
Gather...................12
Gatherd...................1
Gathering.................1
Gathers...................1
Gauge.....................1
Gave......................7
Gay.......................2
Gay-gangs.................1
Gaygear...................1
Gaylinks..................1
Gaze......................9
Gazed.....................1
Gazes.....................3
Gazing....................1
Gear......................2
Gem.......................2

Gem-fleeced . . . 1
Gemmd. . . . 1
General . . . 1
Generation . . . 1
Generations . . . 1
Gennesareth. . . . 1
Gentle . . . 5
Gently . . . 1
Germs . . . 1
Gertrude . . . 1
Get . . . 7
Gethsemane . . . 1
Ghost . . . 3
Ghostly . . . 1
Ghosts . . . 1
Giant . . . 4
Giants . . . 1
Giddies . . . 1
Gideons . . . 1
Gift . . . 7
Gifts . . . 3
Gilded . . . 1
Gilds . . . 2
Gilt . . . 4
Girder . . . 1
Girdled . . . 1
Girdles . . . 1
Girl . . . 3
Girlgrace . . . 1
Girlhood . . . 1
Girth . . . 2
Girthed . . . 1
Give . . . 17
Given . . . 4
Giver . . . 2
Gives . . . 7
Givest . . . 1
Glacier . . . 1
Glad . . . 2
Gladdest . . . 1
Glade. . . . 1
Gladness . . . 2
Glance . . . 1
Glances . . . 1
Glare. . . . 3
Glass . . . 3
Glass-blue . . . 1
Glassy . . . 6
Glassy-clear . . . 1
Glaucus . . . 1
Glazed . . . 1
Gleam . . . 1
Gleamd . . . 2
Glean. . . . 1
Gleaned . . . 1
Glee . . . 1
Glen. . . . 1
Glens . . . 1
Glide . . . 2
Glides. . . . 1
Gliding . . . 1
Glimmerd . . . 1
Glimpses . . . 1
Glistens . . . 1
Glistery . . . 1
Glitter . . . 1
Globe . . . 1
Globes . . . 1
Gloom . . . 9
Gloomd . . . 1
Glories . . . 1
Glorify . . . 1
Glorious . . . 3
Glory. . . . 15
Gloss . . . 1
Glove . . . 2
Glow . . . 4
Glowd . . . 1
Glowless . . . 1
Glows . . . 2
Glowworms . . . 1
Glue . . . 1
Gluegold . . . 1
Gluegold-brown . . . 1
Gnarled . . . 1
Gnarls . . . 1
Gnashed . . . 1
Go . . . 24
Goal . . . 1
Goals . . . 1
Goats . . . 1
God . . . 55
God-made-flesh . . . 1
Goddess. . . . 1
Godhead . . . 1
Godless . . . 1
Gods . . . 20
Goes . . . 12
Going . . . 2
Goings . . . 1
Gold . . . 20
Gold-vermilion . . . 1

Word	Count
Gold-water	1
Gold-wisp	1
Golden	17
Golden-girdled	1
Goldengrove	1
Goldish	1
Goldnails	1
Goldy	1
Gone	16
Gonfalon	1
Good	29
Goodnight	3
Goods	1
Gore	1
Gorged	1
Gorgons	1
Gorse	1
Goshen	2
Gospel	3
Gossamer	1
Gossamers	1
Got	2
Gothic	1
Gotten	1
Grace	24
Gracefully	1
Graceless	1
Graces	2
Grafted	1
Grain	2
Grains	1
Grandeur	4
Granite	2
Grant	2
Granted	2
Grapes	4
Grasp	1
Grasps	1
Grass	9
Grasses	1
Grassy	1
Grate	4
Grateful	1
Grave	2
Graver	1
Graves	1
Great	8
Greater	4
Greatness	2
Greece	1
Greek	1
Green	26
Green-white	1
Greenery	2
Greenest	1
Greenhouse	1
Greenness	1
Greenworld	1
Greet	1
Greeting	2
Gregorians	1
Gregory	1
Grew	5
Grey	18
Grey-green	1
Greybell	1
Grief	3
Griefs	1
Grievance	1
Grieves	1
Grieving	1
Grim	1
Grimy	2
Grind	2
Grip	1
Grizzled	1
Groans	2
Groins	2
Groom	1
Gropes	2
Groping	2
Gross	3
Ground	14
Ground-hugged	1
Grounded	1
Groundlong	1
Grounds	1
Grove	2
Groved	1
Grovel	1
Grow	4
Growing	3
Grown	4
Grows	8
Growth	4
Growths	1
Grudge	1
Guard	1
Guardedly	1
Guess	5
Guessed	2
Guesses	1

Word	Count
Guessing	1
Guile	3
Guilt	2
Guilty	2
Guinevere	1
Gulf	1
Gulfs	1
Gull	1
Gullies	2
Gum	1
Gurgled	2
Gurgling	2
Gush	2
Gushing	1
Gust	2
Gusts	3
Gusty	1
Gwen	1
Gwenvrewi	3
Hack	1
Hacked	1
Hacks	1
Haemony	1
Haggard	1
Haggle	1
Hail	4
Hailropes	1
Hair	10
Hair-bound	1
Hairs	1
Half	11
Half-circle	1
Half-hour	1
Half-light	1
Half-lit	1
Half-meshing	1
Hall	3
Hallowed	2
Hallowing	1
Hallows	1
Halls	1
Halod	1
Halt	2
Halve	1
Halves	1
Hamlets	1
Hampstead	1
Hand	42
Handed	1
Handle	3
Handling	1
Hands	14
Handsome	2
Handy	1
Hang	5
Hangdog	1
Hanging	2
Hangs	6
Hanker	1
Hanks	1
Hapless	1
Happd	1
Happier	3
Happiness	1
Happy	4
Harbour	2
Hard	17
Hard-hurled	1
Hardend	1
Hardest	1
Hardly	1
Hardy	1
Hardy-handsome	1
Hare	1
Hark	4
Harm	2
Harmonies	2
Harmony	1
Harms	1
Harness	1
Harp	1
Harry	3
Harshness	1
Harvest	5
Hastend	1
Hat	1
Hate	4
Hated	3
Hatred	1
Haunt	1
Haunted	1
Haunts	1
Haven	4
Havens	1
Havering	1
Having	2
Havoc	3
Havoc-pocked	1
Hawk	1
Hawkmoth	1
Hawling	1
Hazard	2

Word	Count
Hazards	1
Haze	1
Hazels	1
Head	25
Headed	1
Heads	4
Headstrong	1
Headway	1
Heady	1
Heal	2
Health	2
Heaped	1
Hear	29
Heard	18
Heardst	1
Hearer	1
Hearers	1
Hearing	3
Hears	2
Hearse	1
Hearse-of-all	1
Hearses	1
Hearst	1
Heart	76
Heart-at-ease	1
Heart-beat	1
Heart-break	1
Heart-broke	1
Heart-broken	1
Heart-fleshed	1
Heart-forsook	1
Heart-song	1
Heart-springs	1
Heart-throe	1
Heartburn	1
Hearted	2
Hearth	1
Hearths	1
Heartily	1
Hearts	17
Hearts-clarion	1
Heartsore	1
Heat	4
Heathenish	2
Heathpacks	1
Heave	2
Heaved	1
Heaven	53
Heaven-enforced	1
Heaven-flung	1
Heaven-handling	1
Heaven-haven	1
Heaven-roysterers	1
Heaven-vault	1
Heavend	1
Heavenfallen	1
Heavengravel	1
Heavenlier	1
Heavenly	7
Heavens	11
Heavenward	2
Heaves	1
Heaving	1
Heavy	1
Heavyheaded	1
Hectors	1
Hedge	1
Hedgerow	1
Hedges	2
Heed	3
Heeds	1
Heel	2
Heeled	1
Heels	1
Heft	1
Heifers	1
Height	4
Heightening	1
Heightens	1
Heights	1
Heir	2
Held	5
Helen	2
Hell	8
Hell-rook	1
Hells	1
Help	2
Helpd	1
Helps	1
Heltering	1
Hempen	1
Hence	3
Henceforth	2
Henry	3
Herclots	1
Herds	1
Herds-long	1
Hereafter	1
Heresy	1
Heretic	1
Heretofore	1
Heritage	2

Hero 5
Heroic 1
Hew 2
Hews 1
Hid 3
Hide 3
Hideous 2
Hides 3
Hiding 1
Hies 2
High 23
High-hung 1
High-priest 1
Higher 5
Highest 2
Highroad 1
Hill 9
Hill-top 1
Hills 5
Hillside 1
Hilted 1
Hinders 1
Hindrance 1
Hip 1
Hissing 2
Hit 3
Hither 3
Hitherto 1
Hitting 1
Ho 1
Hoar 6
Hoar-hallowed 1
Hoar-husked 1
Hoard 2
Hoards 1
Hoarlight 1
Hoarse 1
Hoary 2
Hoary-glow 1
Hobs 1
Hold 8
Holds 6
Holes 1
Holier 1
Holiest 1
Holiness 1
Hollow 6
Hollowd 1
Hollowing 2
Hollows 3
Holy 6
Home 23
Home-of-all 1
Homeforth 1
Homes 1
Homing 1
Honest 1
Honey 1
Honeysuck 1
Honeysuckle 1
Honor 1
Honour 15
Honouring 1
Hood 3
Hope 18
Hoped 1
Hopeless 2
Hopes 6
Horizon 1
Horizon-round 1
Horizontals 1
Horn 3
Hornbeam 1
Hornlight 1
Horns 3
Horoscope 1
Horrible 1
Horror 3
Horseback 1
Horsemen 1
Horses 1
Host 3
Hosts 1
Hot 2
Hour 13
Hourglass 1
Hours 9
House 13
Housed 1
Housel 1
Houseless 1
Houses 2
Housetop 1
Hovel 1
Hover 4
Hover-float 1
Hovered 1
Hoverings 1
Hovers 1
Huddle 1
Huddling 1
Hue 5

Hued 2
Hues 4
Huge 2
Huge-girthed 1
Hugged 1
Hum 1
Humanities 1
Hummocked 1
Hundred 2
Hundredfold 1
Hundredweights 1
Hung 15
Hung-heavenward 1
Hunger 3
Hungered 1
Hunt 2
Hunters 1
Hunting 2
Hurdle 1
Hurdles 2
Hurl 3
Hurled 3
Hurling 4
Hurls 5
Hurried 1
Hurst 1
Hursts 1
Hurt 1
Hurtle 2
Hush 2
Hushd 1
Hushed 1
Husked 1
Hussy 1
Hustle 1
Hutch 1
Hyacinth 1
Hyacinth-warding 1
Hyacinthed 1
Hyacinths 1
Hyaline 1
Hymn 1
Hypocrite 1
I 505
Ice 6
Ice-blocks 2
Iconium 1
Icy 1
Id 1
Ideal 1
Idle 2
Ignorantly 1
Ill 23
Ill-balanced 1
Ill-content 1
Ill-contented 1
Ill-launched 1
Ill-visaged 1
Illumined 1
Illustrated 1
Im 2
Image 1
Images 1
Imagining 1
Immaculate 2
Immortal 8
Immortals 1
Impale 1
Impaled 1
Impalpable 1
Impatient 1
Impeached 1
Impearled 1
Impediment 1
Impenitent 1
Imperfect 2
Imps 1
In 4
Inanimate 1
Inboard 1
Incapable 1
Incense 1
Inch 1
Inches 1
Increase 1
Increment 1
Indeed 9
Indian 1
Indiferrence 1
Indignation 1
Indivisible 1
Indoors 2
Inexplicably 1
Infallibly 1
Infancy 1
Infant 1
Infest 1
Infinite 2
Infinitely 1
Infinity 1
Influential 1
Inheritance 1

Word	Count
Initiate	1
Injury	1
Injurys	1
Inly	2
Inmate	1
Inmost	2
Inner	3
Innocent	2
Insight	4
Inspiration	1
Instant	1
Instead	2
Instressed	2
Instrument	2
Insufficiencies	1
Int	1
Intellectual	1
Intense	1
Intensest	1
Intensity	1
Intent	2
Interchange	1
Interest	3
Interests	1
Interposed	1
Interstice	1
Inthem	1
Intolerable	1
Invention	1
Inward	1
Ipse	1
Ireland	1
Irish	1
Iron	3
Irregularly	1
Island	1
Isle	2
Isled	2
Isles	1
Issue	1
Italy	2
Its	1
Ive	1
Ivies	1
Ivy	1
Jacinth	2
Jacinthine	1
Jack	4
Jacks	1
Jackself	1
Jaded	1
Jading	1
Jagged	1
Jags	1
Jailor	1
James	1
Jane	2
Jar	2
Jarrd	1
Jaunting	1
Jay	1
Jay-blue	1
Jessy	1
Jesu	2
Jesus	4
Jet	1
Jewelld	1
Jews	2
John	3
Joints	1
Joke	1
Jolt	1
Josephs	1
Jostling	3
Joy	22
Joy-laden	1
Joyless	1
Joys	1
Jubilee	5
Judah	1
Judge	1
Judgment	4
Juice	2
Juicy	3
Just	12
Justices	1
Justify	1
Kate	1
Keats	1
Keel	3
Keen	4
Keener	1
Keep	15
Keepers	1
Keeping	1
Keeps	8
Kelson	2
Ken	2
Kentish	1
Kept	15
Key	3
Khor	1

Kill 3
Kill-weights 1
Killed 2
Kills 1
Kind. 16
Kindcold 1
Kindness 1
Kindred 1
Kine 1
King 12
Kingdom 1
Kingfishers. 1
Kings 7
Kirjath 1
Kirjath-arba 1
Kiss 6
Kissed 1
Kisses 4
Kissing. 1
Kneading 1
Knee 6
Knee-nave 1
Kneel 2
Kneeled 1
Knees 3
Knells 1
Knelt 3
Knew 14
Knock 1
Knocking 1
Knockings 1
Knops 1
Knopt 1
Knot 5
Knots 2
Know 31
Knowest 1
Knowing 4
Knowledge 1
Known 16
Knows 12
Laboured 1
Laboured-at 1
Labouring. 2
Labours 1
Lace 6
Lace-leaved 1
Laced 5
Laces 1
Lack 2
Lacklevel 1
Lad 2
Lade 1
Laden 2
Ladies 1
Lads 2
Lady 8
Lady-star 1
Lag 1
Lagging 1
Laid 6
Lair 1
Lake 3
Lakes 4
Lambs. 2
Lame 1
Lament 2
Lamentable 1
Laments 1
Lamps 1
Lancashire 1
Lance 2
Lanced 1
Lancing 1
Land 15
Landmark 2
Lands 2
Landscape 5
Landslips 1
Lanes 1
Languent 1
Languishd 2
Lank 1
Lantern 4
Lap 2
Lapped 2
Laps 1
Lapsed 1
Large 2
Lark 5
Lark-charmed 1
Larkspur 1
Larkspurs 1
Lash 2
Lashed 2
Lashes 3
Lashtender 1
Last 35
Lasting 2
Latch 2
Latched 1
Late 18

Late-found 1
Late-learnt 1
Lately 2
Lauded 1
Laugh 2
Laughing 1
Laughs 1
Laughter 6
Launched 1
Laverd 1
Law 6
Lawless 2
Lawns 1
Lawrence 2
Laws 1
Lay 17
Laying 2
Lays 1
Lazuli 1
Lea 1
Lead 7
Leaf 9
Leaf-light 1
Leafing 1
Leafless 1
Leafmeal 1
Leafwhelmed 1
Leafy 2
Leagues 2
Lean 1
Lean-over 1
Leaning 2
Leans 5
Leap 1
Leaping 2
Leaps 1
Learn 1
Learned 2
Learner 1
Learning 1
Learnt 4
Leas 1
Lease 1
Leash 1
Least 9
Leave 11
Leaved 7
Leaves 31
Leaving 2
Led 3
Ledges 1
Leeward 1
Left 18
Legates 1
Leger 1
Legion 1
Leisure 2
Lend 2
Lends 1
Length 4
Lent 2
Lenten 2
Lepers 1
Less 16
Lessend 2
Lessened 1
Lesson 1
Lessons 1
Lest 1
Let 43
Lets 1
Letter 4
Lettering 1
Letters 4
Levant 1
Level 5
Levelld 1
Levels 2
Lewd 1
Liar 2
Libanus 1
Liberties 2
Lick 1
Lid 1
Lids 3
Lie 13
Lies 10
Lieu 1
Life 26
Lifebelt 1
Lifeless 1
Lifes 9
Lift 8
Lifted 6
Lifting 1
Lifts 2
Light 41
Lighted 2
Lighten 1
Lightening 1
Lighthanded 1
Lightning 6

Lightnings . . . 2
Lights . . . 10
Lightship . . . 1
Like . . . 99
Likeness . . . 1
Likes . . . 1
Likest . . . 1
Lilies . . . 9
Lily . . . 16
Lily-buds . . . 1
Lily-coloured . . . 1
Lily-time . . . 1
Lily-white . . . 1
Lily-yellow . . . 1
Lilylocks . . . 1
Limbdance . . . 1
Limber . . . 1
Limbs . . . 5
Lime . . . 1
Limnd . . . 1
Line . . . 3
Lineament . . . 2
Lined . . . 4
Linen . . . 1
Linen-winded . . . 1
Lines . . . 4
Linger . . . 1
Lingerd . . . 1
Lingerer . . . 1
Lingering . . . 2
Lingering-out . . . 1
Lingers . . . 1
Linked . . . 1
Lion . . . 2
Lion-brown . . . 1
Lioness . . . 1
Lionlike . . . 1
Lionlimb . . . 1
Lip . . . 5
Lipmusic . . . 1
Lippd . . . 2
Lipped . . . 1
Lips . . . 17
Liquid . . . 5
Lispd . . . 1
Lisping . . . 1
Lissome . . . 1
List . . . 1
Listed . . . 1
Listen . . . 3
Listened . . . 2
Listening . . . 2
Listenr . . . 1
Listless . . . 1
Lists . . . 3
Lit . . . 3
Litter . . . 3
Little . . . 15
Little-lasting . . . 1
Live . . . 18
Lived . . . 3
Lives . . . 9
Living . . . 3
Lo . . . 5
Loaded . . . 1
Loading . . . 1
Loamy . . . 1
Loathd . . . 1
Loathe . . . 1
Loathed . . . 1
Loathingly . . . 1
Loathsome . . . 1
Lock . . . 3
Locks . . . 13
Lodge . . . 1
Lodged . . . 2
Lodges . . . 3
Loins . . . 1
Lone . . . 1
Lonely . . . 1
Long . . . 40
Long-lying . . . 1
Long-superfluous . . . 1
Longer . . . 4
Longing . . . 1
Lock . . . 31
Lookd . . . 3
Looked . . . 2
Lookers . . . 1
Looking . . . 3
Looks . . . 14
Loom . . . 2
Loomd . . . 1
Loop . . . 1
Loop-locks . . . 1
Looped . . . 1
Loops . . . 1
Loose . . . 3
Loose-traced . . . 1
Loosely . . . 1
Loosend . . . 1
Lord . . . 33

Lordly 2
Lords 2
Lore 3
Lorn 1
Lose 1
Loss 3
Losses 1
Lost 16
Lot 4
Lote 1
Lote-flower 1
Lots 1
Louched 1
Loud 4
Louder 2
Love 80
Love-laced 1
Love-thoughts 1
Loveable 1
Loved 1
Loveless 2
Lovelier 1
Loveliest 2
Loveliness 2
Lovelocks 1
Lovely 22
Lovely-asunder 1
Lovely-dumb 1
Lovely-felicitous 1
Lover 4
Loves 9
Lovescape 1
Low 28
Low-covered 1
Low-down 2
Low-latched 1
Lower 1
Lowly 5
Loyal 1
Luke 1
Lull 2
Lull-off 1
Lung 2
Lung-wasting 1
Lurch 1
Lush 5
Lush-kept 1
Lust 3
Lustily 1
Lustred 1
Lustreless 1
Lustres 2
Lustrous 1
Lusty 1
Luther 1
Lying 1
Madam 1
Maddest 1
Made 26
Madrid 1
Madrigal 1
Maenefa 1
Maentwrog 2
Magdalen 1
Magic 1
Magnify 1
Magnifying 1
Maid 5
Maid-months 1
Maiden 8
Maiden-furled 1
Maidengear 1
Maidens 2
Maids 2
Maild 1
Maim 1
Main 5
Mainstrength 1
Majestic 1
Majestical 1
Majesty 3
Majorca 1
Make 39
Makes 23
Makesbelieve 1
Making 7
Malice 1
Malign 1
Mallow 1
Mallow-row 1
Mallows 1
Mammocks 1
Man 32
Managed 1
Manger 1
Manhood 2
Mankind 2
Mankinds 1
Manly 2
Manmarks 1
Manna 3
Manna-bushes 1

Word	Count
Manner	1
Mannerly	1
Mannerly-hearted	1
Manners	1
Mans	13
Mansex	1
Manshape	1
Mantle	1
Mantle-oer	1
Mantles	1
Mantling	1
Manwolf	1
Many	13
Mar	2
Marbled	1
March	5
March-bloom	1
Marches	1
Marching	2
Marcus	1
Margaret	10
Margarets	1
Mark	16
Markd	2
Market	1
Marking	2
Marred	1
Marriage	1
Married	1
Marsh	1
Martinmas	1
Martyr	2
Martyr-master	1
Martyrs	1
Marvel	1
Marvellous	2
Mary	12
Marys	3
Maskd	2
Masks	2
Masons	1
Masque	1
Massacre	1
Massy	2
Master	10
Masterhood	1
Mastering	2
Masters	2
Mastery	3
Match	1
Matched	2
Matchless	1
Matchwood	1
Mate	3
Mated	2
Mates	2
Matter	3
Mawddach	1
May	2
May-hope	1
May-mess	1
Maybe	1
Mayday	1
Mays	1
Maze	2
Mazed	2
Mazy	2
Me	171
Mead	2
Meadow	5
Meadow-down	1
Meadows	4
Meads	1
Meal	3
Meal-drift	1
Mealed	1
Mealed-with-yellow	1
Mealtime	1
Mean	8
Meaning	4
Means	6
Meant	4
Meantime	1
Meanwhile	2
Meanwhiles	1
Measure	5
Measured	2
Measures	1
Meat	2
Medalliond	1
Medley	1
Meek	2
Meet	19
Meets	2
Melancholy	1
Melee	1
Mellow	2
Mells	2
Melodious	1
Melodiously	1
Melody	1
Melt	3

Melted 4
Melting 4
Melts 2
Members 2
Memento 1
Memoried 1
Memory 1
Men 38
Mend 2
Mended 2
Mends 1
Mens 5
Mention 1
Mercies 1
Merciful 3
Mercy 6
Mere 1
Merely 2
Mermaidens 1
Mermaids 3
Merrily 1
Merry 2
Meshd 1
Meshing 1
Mess 1
Message 1
Messenger 3
Messengers 3
Messes 2
Messmate 1
Met 6
Metal 1
Metal-lustred 1
Metaphors 1
Meted 1
Methinks 2
Mi 1
Michaelmas 1
Mid 4
Mid-air 1
Mid-main 1
Mid-numbered 1
Middle 1
Midnight 2
Midriff 1
Midst 2
Midsummer 2
Mien 1
Might 20
Mighty 5
Milan 1
Mild 3
Mile 5
Mile-long 1
Miles 4
Milk 6
Milk-white 1
Milky 6
Mill 4
Mill-stone 1
Millbrook 1
Millbrook-slips 1
Million 3
Million-fueled 1
Millions 1
Mind 24
Minded 2
Minds 5
Mine 18
Mined 2
Mingle 2
Mingled 1
Minion 1
Miniver 1
Minor 1
Mint 1
Minted 1
Miracle 2
Miracle-in-Mary-of-flame . . 1
Mire 1
Mirky 1
Mirror 2
Mirrored 1
Mirth 5
Misadventure 2
Misdirected 1
Misery 1
Mislike 1
Miss 12
Missd 1
Missing 1
Mist 3
Mistress 1
Mists 3
Mix 1
Mixd 1
Mixed 1
Moan 1
Moaning 1
Moans 1
Mob 1
Mock 1

Mockery 1
Mocks 1
Moderate 1
Modest 1
Moist 1
Moisture 2
Moles 1
Molest 1
Molten 3
Molten-blue 1
Monarchs 1
Monition 1
Monks 2
Monstrous 5
Month 6
Month-brother 1
Months 4
Monuments 1
Mood 4
Moods 1
Moon 7
Moonless 1
Moonlight 2
Moonlight-mated 1
Moonmarks 1
Moor 1
Moorland 1
More 89
Mori 1
Morn 14
Morning 15
Mornings 2
Morns 1
Morrow 3
Morselled 1
Morsels 2
Mortal 5
Mortals 1
Morticed 1
Moses 1
Moss 2
Most 42
Mote 1
Mote-like 1
Motes 2
Moth 2
Moth-soft 1
Mother 34
Mother-ground 1
Motherhood 2
Mothering 4
Mothers 2
Motion 5
Motionable 2
Mould 8
Moulded 2
Moulding 1
Mouldring 1
Mounded 1
Mounds 1
Mountain 10
Mountain-bound 1
Mountain-echod 1
Mountain-side 1
Mountains 2
Mounting 3
Mounts 1
Mourn 1
Mournful 1
Mourning 2
Mouth 6
Mouthed 2
Move 3
Moved 3
Moves 2
Ms 1
Much 20
Much-dreaded 1
Much-thick 1
Multiply 2
Multitude 4
Murder 2
Murderous 2
Muse 4
Music 11
Musical 3
My 239
Myriad 2
Myrrhy 1
Myrrhy-threaded 1
Myself 5
Mysteries 2
Mysterious 1
Mystery 5
Nadir 1
Nadir-fires 1
Nails 1
Name 21
Names 1
Nard 1
Narrow 1
Nation 2

National 1
Natural 3
Nature 11
Natured 1
Natures 5
Nautilus 1
Nave 1
Navel 1
Navvy 1
Nay 10
Nazareth 2
Nazareths 1
Near 15
Nearest 2
Nearness 1
Neck 4
Nectar 1
Need 9
Needed 1
Needful 1
Needs 6
Neer 3
Neglectful 1
Neighbour 3
Neighbour-nature 1
Neighbouring 1
Neighbours 1
Neight 1
Nereid 1
Nerve 3
Nerveless 1
Nest 5
Nested 1
Nestle 1
Nestlike 1
Nestling 1
Nests 1
Nets 1
Never 37
Never-eldering 1
Never-needed 1
New 27
New-basilisk 1
New-dapple 1
New-dated 1
New-nestle 1
New-skeined 1
New-world 1
Newborn 1
Newly 2
Newly-drawn 1
News 2
Next 10
Niche 1
Nigh 2
Night 30
Nightfall 2
Nightingale 2
Nights 4
Nile 2
Nimble 1
Nine 3
Nips 1
Nix 2
No 1
No-man-fathomed 1
Nobler 1
Nobs 1
Nocturns 1
Noise 3
Noises 1
None 28
Nones 1
Nook 1
Noon 2
Noonday 1
Nose 1
Nostril 1
Nostrils 2
Not 5
Not-by-morning-matched . 1
Not-staled 1
Not-to-call 1
Note 4
Notes 7
Nothing 7
Nourishes 1
Nowhere 4
Numb 1
Number 1
Numbered 3
Numbs 1
Nun 3
Nursing 1
Nursle 1
Nymphs 1
O 100
O-seal-that-so 1
Oak 1
Oaks 2
Oar 1
Oath 1

Obey 3
Obscurd 1
Obsolete 1
Obstruction 1
Occasion 1
Ocean 3
Oclock 1
October 1
Oer 25
Oer-brim 1
Oer-head 1
Oertake 1
Of 8
Off 43
Offend 2
Offended 1
Offer 1
Offering 2
Offerings 1
Offspring 1
Oft 1
Often 4
Oil 3
Oils 1
Ointment 1
Oit 1
Old 13
Older 1
Olive 1
Olive-branch 1
Once 32
One 101
Onewhere 2
Only 33
Onyx 1
Onyx-coronals 1
Ooze 2
Opal 1
Ope 1
Open 7
Opend 2
Opening 1
Opens 2
Opportunest 1
Opposition 1
Oppressed 1
Oppression 1
Oracle 1
Orbd 2
Orchard 3
Orchard-apple 1
Orchards 1
Order 1
Orderd 1
Organ 1
Orience 2
Original 2
Orinda 1
Orion 1
Ought 1
Our 84
Ours 2
Out 55
Out-fleeced 1
Outer 1
Outgoings 1
Outline 1
Outrage 1
Outrides 1
Outright 2
Outward 4
Outward-steeled 1
Outwards 1
Outwitted 1
Over 34
Overbend 1
Overflow 2
Overflowing 1
Overhead 3
Overspread 1
Overstood 1
Overtake 1
Overtaking 1
Overvaulted 1
Overvaults 1
Overworn 1
Overwrought 1
Own 24
Owns 1
Oxeye 1
Oxford 2
Pace 2
Paces 1
Pacing 1
Pack 1
Packed 3
Packs 1
Pactolus 1
Pace 1
Pageant 1
Pain 10
Pained 1

Painful 1
Pains 1
Paint 1
Painted 1
Painting 1
Pair 1
Paird 1
Palace 3
Palate 1
Pale 6
Paling 1
Palm 3
Palms 4
Palmtree 1
Palmy 2
Palsy 1
Pane 1
Pang 1
Pangs 2
Pansy 1
Pansy-dark 1
Pantings 1
Papa 1
Paradisaical 1
Paradise 4
Paradox 1
Parallel 2
Parapet 1
Parched 1
Parches 1
Pardon 2
Pare 1
Paring 1
Paris 1
Park 2
Parley 1
Parlour 1
Parlour-pastime 1
Part 16
Parted 5
Parting 3
Partless 1
Parts 2
Pashed 1
Pass 5
Passage 2
Passages 1
Passd 2
Passed 2
Passes 5
Passing 3
Passion 8
Passion-pastured 1
Passion-plunged 1
Passion-sake 1
Passionflower 1
Passions 1
Past 18
Past-prayer 1
Pastime 1
Pastoral 2
Pasts 1
Pastured 1
Pastures 2
Patch 1
Path 2
Pathless 1
Patience 12
Patient 1
Patronize 1
Paul 3
Pauls 1
Pause 1
Paves 1
Pay 3
Pea 1
Peace 15
Peach 1
Peacockd 1
Peacocks 1
Peak 1
Peakd 1
Pealed 1
Peals 1
Pearl 3
Pearled 2
Pearly 1
Peartree 1
Peasant 1
Pebbly 2
Pectoral 1
Peculiar 2
Peeled 1
Peer 1
Peers 1
Pegasus 1
Pelt 1
Pelted 1
Pelting 1
Pen 4
Penance 2
Pence 2

Word	Count
Pencilled	1
Pendant	1
Penetrative	1
Penitence	1
Penitent	1
Penmaen	10
Pennon	2
Pent	3
People	2
Perceived	2
Perch	1
Perfect	5
Perfumes	1
Perhaps	5
Peril	1
Perilous	4
Perishable	1
Perishd	1
Perishing	1
Permanence	1
Perpetual	1
Perplexed	1
Perseus	1
Persistency	2
Personal	1
Persuasion	1
Petalld	1
Peter	1
Phantasies	1
Phantasy	1
Pharohs	1
Philip	2
Philomel	1
Phoebus	2
Phosphor	1
Phrenzy	1
Pick	1
Picked	1
Piece	9
Piece-bright	1
Pieced	4
Piecemeal	1
Piecing	1
Pied	1
Pierce	2
Pierced	3
Piercing	1
Piety	3
Pigeons	1
Pilasterd	1
Pilates	1
Pile	1
Piled	1
Piles	1
Pilgrimages	1
Pilgrims	4
Pillars	1
Pillowing	1
Pillows	1
Pillowy	1
Pin	1
Pine	3
Pines	2
Pining	2
Pinions	1
Pink	1
Pinks	1
Pious	1
Pipe	2
Pit	1
Pitch	1
Pitchblack	1
Pitched	2
Piteous	3
Pity	7
Place	23
Placed	1
Places	3
Placid	1
Plain	6
Plaintively	1
Plait	2
Plaits	1
Plan	2
Plane	1
Plane-leaves	1
Planets	2
Plant	1
Planted	1
Plants	1
Plash	2
Plashes	1
Plated	2
Plates	1
Platting	1
Play	5
Playd	2
Plays	5
Plea	2
Plead	7
Pleading	1
Pleadings	1

Word	Count
Pleas	1
Pleasance	1
Pleasaunce	1
Please	2
Pleased	1
Pleasurable	1
Pleasure	5
Pleasured	1
Pledged	1
Pleiad	1
Plied	1
Plight	1
Plighted	3
Plod	4
Plot	5
Plots	1
Plotted	3
Plough	4
Pluck	1
Plum	1
Plum-purple	1
Plumage	3
Plume	1
Plumed	2
Plumes	2
Plumy	1
Plunder	1
Plunge	1
Plunged	1
Plunging	1
Plush	1
Plush-capped	1
Plushy	1
Ply	3
Pocked	1
Pocket	1
Poet	2
Poetry	1
Poets	1
Point	3
Pointed	3
Pointing	1
Points	1
Poise	2
Poised	2
Poising	1
Pole	2
Poles	1
Pomp	1
Pompeii	1
Pond	1
Ponderous	1
Pool	14
Pools	1
Poor	20
Poppies	2
Pore	1
Pores	3
Portending	1
Portends	1
Portholes	1
Portion	1
Ports	1
Possessed	1
Post	1
Posts	2
Posturd	1
Pot	1
Potent	1
Potential	1
Pots	1
Potsherd	1
Pour	1
Pourtrayd	1
Poverty	1
Power	3
Powerful	2
Powerless	1
Powers	2
Praisd	1
Praise	7
Praised	2
Praises	1
Pranked	1
Pray	4
Prayer	11
Prayers	3
Praying	1
Prays	1
Preachings	1
Precedents	1
Precious	5
Precipice	1
Precipitous	1
Precisely	1
Precision	1
Prediluvian	1
Preeminent	1
Preened	1
Preference	1
Preferred	2
Prejudice	1

Prenatal....................1
Prepare....................1
Prescriptive................1
Presence...................1
Present....................2
Presented..................1
Press......................9
Pressed....................3
Pressure...................1
Pretend....................1
Pretty.....................3
Prey.......................2
Price......................1
Priced.....................1
Prick......................1
Prickproof.................1
Pride......................12
Priest.....................1
Prime......................3
Primes.....................1
Primrose...................3
Primroses..................4
Prince.....................3
Princely...................1
Princes....................1
Principal..................3
Principle..................1
Print......................1
Prism......................1
Prison.....................2
Privacy....................1
Prize......................3
Prized.....................3
Procession.................1
Proconsul..................1
Prodigal...................1
Profess....................1
Proffer....................1
Profit.....................1
Profound...................1
Promise....................4
Promised...................2
Promises...................1
Proof......................3
Proper.....................3
Prophetess.................1
Proportion.................1
Prosper....................1
Prosperity.................1
Prosperously...............1
Prosperously-boded.........1
Proud......................6
Prouder....................1
Proudest...................1
Prove......................3
Proverb....................1
Provide....................1
Providence.................2
Prudence...................1
Pruned.....................1
Psalm......................1
Public.....................1
Puffball...................1
Pull.......................3
Pulld......................2
Pulpit.....................1
Punishment.................1
Pupil......................1
Pupils.....................1
Purcell....................2
Purchase...................1
Pure.......................7
Purer......................1
Purfled....................1
Purify.....................1
Purple.....................6
Purple-of-thunder..........1
Purpling...................3
Purply.....................1
Purport....................2
Purpose....................3
Pursuant...................1
Pursud.....................1
Pursued....................1
Pushed.....................1
Pushing....................1
Put........................9
Puts.......................3
Python.....................1
Quail......................1
Quails.....................2
Quaint.....................1
Quarter....................2
Quartz.....................1
Quartz-fret................1
Queen......................2
Quell......................2
Quelled....................2
Quench.....................2
Quenchd....................1
Quenched...................6
Quenching..................1

Question 2
Questioning 1
Quests 1
Quick 3
Quicken 1
Quickenings 1
Quickgold 1
Quickly 2
Quicksilvery 1
Quiet 1
Quiet-walled 1
Quill 1
Quills 1
Quils 1
Quince 3
Quinces 1
Quit 1
Quite 6
Quivering 1
Quote 3
Rabble 3
Race 5
Raced 2
Racing 2
Rack 5
Racked 2
Radiance 1
Rafts 2
Rage 2
Raging 1
Rail 1
Rain 14
Rain-blasts 1
Rain-born 1
Rainbow 8
Rainbows 2
Raindrop 1
Raindrop-roundels 1
Rains 5
Raisd 1
Raise 1
Raised 1
Rambled 1
Rampant 1
Ramps 1
Ran 9
Randal 2
Random 1
Rangd 2
Range 2
Ranged 1
Rank 7
Rank-old 1
Ranked 2
Ranking 1
Rankle 1
Ranks 2
Ransom 2
Ransomd 1
Ranters 1
Rapture 1
Rapturous 1
Rare 11
Rare-dear 1
Rarely 3
Rarest 2
Rarest-veined 1
Rash 4
Rash-fresh 1
Rated 1
Rather 9
Ration 1
Ravage 1
Rave 1
Ravel 1
Ravel-ropes-end 1
Ravelld 1
Ravens 1
Raves 1
Ravishment 1
Ray 1
Rayd 1
Rays 5
Re 4
Re-attributing 2
Re-winded 1
Reach 5
Reachd 3
Reaches 1
Read 6
Reading 1
Readings 1
Reads 1
Ready 5
Real 1
Realer 1
Realize 1
Realm 2
Realty 1
Reappear 1
Rearing 1
Rears 2

Reason 3
Reasond 1
Reave 1
Reaving 1
Rebel 2
Rebellion 2
Rebellious 1
Rebound 1
Rebuff 1
Rebuffed 1
Recital 2
Reck 6
Reckon 2
Reclaiming 1
Reconciled 1
Record 1
Recorded 3
Records 1
Recover 1
Recovery 2
Recurb 1
Red 9
Redcoats 1
Redeeming 1
Reed 1
Reeds 1
Reef 1
Reefs 1
Reek 1
Reeking 1
Reel 2
Reeling 1
Reels 1
Reeve 2
Refrain 1
Refused 1
Refuses 2
Regimen 2
Regimental 1
Register 1
Regret 1
Regular 1
Rehearsal 1
Reign 1
Reigns 2
Rein 1
Release 1
Released 1
Relics 1
Relief 2
Religious 1
Relish 2
Remain 1
Remainder 1
Remark 1
Remember 5
Rememberd 1
Remembereth 1
Remembering 2
Remembrance 1
Remnants 1
Remorseless 1
Remote 2
Remotest 1
Remove 1
Removes 1
Renderd 1
Rent 1
Repair 2
Repeat 2
Repeated 1
Repent 8
Replies 2
Reply 3
Reprieve 1
Rescue 3
Resent 1
Residuary 1
Resign 1
Resolution 1
Rest 15
Resurrection 1
Retire 1
Retirement 1
Returning 1
Revel 2
Revenge 2
Reversal 1
Reviled 1
Revisits 1
Revival 1
Reward 1
Rhine 1
Rhyme 2
Rhymes 1
Ribbed 1
Ribbon 1
Ribs 2
Rich 12
Rich-pieced 1
Richard 3
Richest 1

Word	Count
Richly	1
Richness	1
Rid	1
Riddles	1
Ride	5
Rider	1
Rides	4
Ridge	2
Ridge-crest	1
Riding	3
Rife	3
Rifled	1
Rigging	1
Right	21
Righted	1
Righteousness	1
Rigour	1
Rill	1
Rilly	1
Rim	5
Rime	1
Rimmon	1
Rind	2
Rinds	1
Ring	10
Ringed	2
Ringing	1
Ringlet	1
Ringlet-race	1
Rings	4
Rinse	1
Rinsed	1
Riot	2
Ripest	1
Ripples	1
Rips	1
Rise	8
Risen	5
Rises	2
Rising	3
Risn	1
Rival	1
Rivalled	1
Rivals	1
Rivelling	1
River	13
River-banks	1
River-bed	1
River-rounded	1
Rivers	2
Riving	2
Rivn	1
Rivulet	1
Road	5
Roads	1
Roam	1
Roaming	1
Roar	2
Roared	1
Roaring	1
Rob	1
Robberys	1
Robe	1
Robes	1
Robin	1
Rock	15
Rock-a-heart	1
Rockdoves	1
Rocket	1
Rockfire	1
Rocks	7
Rocky	1
Rod	7
Rode	2
Rods	2
Roguish	1
Roll	5
Rollcall	1
Rolld	1
Rolled	3
Rolling	3
Rollrock	1
Rolls	5
Rome	1
Romp	1
Rood	2
Roof	4
Roofd	1
Rook	3
Rook-racked	1
Rookery	1
Room	8
Roost	1
Root	4
Root-room	1
Rooted	2
Rooting	1
Roots	6
Rope	2
Rope-over	1
Roped	1
Ropes	3

Rose . . . 23
Rose-flake . . . 1
Rose-moles . . . 1
Rose-red . . . 1
Roseleaves . . . 1
Roses . . . 4
Rosing . . . 1
Rosy . . . 9
Rosy-budded . . . 1
Rosy-lippd . . . 1
Rosy-pale . . . 1
Rough . . . 4
Rough-robin . . . 1
Rough-scored . . . 1
Roughcast . . . 1
Round . . . 43
Rounded . . . 3
Roundels . . . 2
Rounder . . . 1
Rounding . . . 1
Rounds . . . 5
Roundy . . . 1
Rout . . . 1
Row . . . 3
Rowels . . . 2
Rowing . . . 1
Royal . . . 8
Royally . . . 1
Royals . . . 1
Roysterers . . . 1
Rubies . . . 1
Ruby . . . 1
Ruck . . . 2
Rud . . . 1
Ruddied . . . 1
Ruddying . . . 1
Rude . . . 5
Ruder . . . 4
Ruder-rounded . . . 1
Rudred . . . 1
Rueful . . . 1
Ruin . . . 2
Ruinous . . . 4
Ruins . . . 3
Rule . . . 1
Ruler . . . 1
Run . . . 10
Rung . . . 2
Runnel . . . 1
Runnels . . . 1
Running . . . 4
Runs . . . 5
Rupture . . . 1
Rural . . . 5
Rush . . . 3
Rushy . . . 1
Rust . . . 1
Rustle . . . 1
Rutpeel . . . 1
S . . . 2
Sable . . . 1
Sack . . . 1
Sackcloth . . . 1
Sacred . . . 5
Sacrifice . . . 2
Sacrificed . . . 1
Sad . . . 8
Saddening . . . 1
Sadness . . . 4
Safe . . . 2
Said . . . 35
Sail . . . 4
Sailed . . . 1
Sailors . . . 1
Saint . . . 2
Saintly . . . 1
Saints . . . 1
Saith . . . 1
Sake . . . 3
Sakes . . . 1
Sallows . . . 1
Sally . . . 1
Salt . . . 7
Salute . . . 1
Salvation . . . 2
Same . . . 11
Sanctuary . . . 1
Sand . . . 5
Sand-teasing . . . 1
Sandal . . . 2
Sandalled . . . 1
Sandblind . . . 1
Sandfield . . . 1
Sands . . . 2
Sandy . . . 1
Sang . . . 1
Sanguine . . . 1
Sank . . . 3
Sap . . . 3
Sappd . . . 1
Sapphire . . . 7
Sapphire-pale . . . 1

Word	Count
Sapphire-shot	1
Sapricius	1
Sard	1
Sash	1
Sat	4
Satin	1
Satin-purfled	1
Saturday	1
Saturn	3
Save	11
Saved	1
Saves	1
Savest	1
Saviour	2
Saviours	1
Savour	1
Saw	16
Say	32
Saying	2
Says	7
Scaffold	1
Scalded	1
Scale	2
Scales	1
Scan	1
Scanned	1
Scanted	1
Scarce	8
Scarce-call-silver	1
Scarce-sheathed	1
Scarcely	5
Scare	1
Scarless	1
Scarlet	5
Scarves	1
Scatter	2
Scene	4
Scented	1
Sceptic	1
School	2
Schooled	1
Schooling	1
Schools	1
Schooner	1
Science	2
Scions	2
Scoop	1
Scooped	1
Scoops	1
Scope	3
Score	2
Scored	1
Scores	1
Scorning	1
Scour	1
Scourge	2
Scourged	1
Screamd	1
Screen	1
Scroll	1
Scroll-leaved	1
Scrolled	2
Sculls	1
Sculpturd	1
Scutcheon	1
Scythe	1
Scythes	1
Sea	29
Sea-corpse	1
Sea-fan	1
Sea-fowl	1
Sea-gull	1
Sea-gust	1
Sea-romp	1
Sea-swill	1
Seabeach	1
Seal	3
Sealed	2
Sealing	2
Sealing-wax	1
Seals	3
Seamanship	1
Seamark	1
Seamen	3
Sear	1
Search	2
Searching	1
Seared	1
Seas	10
Season	4
Seasons	3
Seat	2
Second	1
Seconding	1
Secret	2
Secrets	1
See	59
Seed	2
Seeing	9
Seek	4
Seeking	1
Seem	4

Seemd 10
Seemed 5
Seeming 3
Seems 15
Seen 10
Sees 11
Seldom 1
Seldomer 1
Self 24
Self-caressd 1
Self-embraced 1
Self-feeling 1
Self-instressed 1
Self-made 1
Self-outwitted 1
Self-sacrifice 1
Self-sentenced 1
Self-will 1
Self-wise 1
Selfbent 1
Selfdisposal 1
Selfish 1
Selfless 1
Selfquained 1
Selfsame 1
Selfstrung 1
Selfwrung 1
Selfyeast 1
Selvaggia 1
Selved 1
Selves 3
Send 7
Sendings 1
Sends 1
Sense 8
Senses 2
Sensitive 3
Sensual 1
Sent 5
Sentence 1
Sentenced 1
Sepulchre 1
Sequence 1
Sequences 2
Sequins 1
Seraph 2
Seraph-arrival 1
Serfdom 1
Serged 1
Sermons 1
Serve 3
Served 3
Serves 5
Service 2
Servingman 2
Set 14
Sets 2
Setting 1
Settle 1
Settler 1
Seven 10
Sevenfold 1
Sevenfold-single 1
Seventeenth 1
Seventy 1
Several 3
Severance 1
Severe 1
Sew 1
Sewers 1
Sex 1
Sexed 1
Sexing 2
Shade 2
Shades 2
Shadow 9
Shadowiest 1
Shadowtackle 1
Shafts 2
Shake 6
Shaken 2
Shakes 2
Shakespeares 1
Shallow 6
Shallowing 1
Shallowy 1
Shame 8
Shank 2
Shape 6
Shaped 2
Shapen 1
Shapes 6
Sharded 1
Share 4
Shares 2
Sharp 5
Sharper 1
Sheaf 3
Sheared 2
Shearing 2
Sheath 1
Sheathe 3

Sheathe-and 1
Sheathed 2
Sheaved 4
Sheaves 1
Shed 8
Sheen 2
Sheeny 2
Sheep 5
Sheep-bells 1
Sheep-flock 1
Sheer 5
Sheets 1
Shell 5
Shelled 1
Shelling 1
Shells 1
Shelly 2
Shelter 4
Shelterless 1
Shepherd 4
Shepherds 3
Shew 8
Shewed 1
Shewing 1
Shewn 6
Shews 1
Shield 1
Shift 1
Shifted 1
Shilling 1
Shine 11
Shines 2
Shining 6
Shining-hilted 1
Shining-shot 1
Ship 2
Shipwrack 1
Shire 2
Shires 1
Shirt 1
Shivelights 1
Shiverd 1
Shives 1
Shoal 1
Shoals 3
Shoaly 1
Shock 5
Shocks 3
Shod 2
Shone 3
Shook 10
Shoot 2
Shoots 2
Shore 4
Shores 1
Short 5
Shorten 1
Shorter 1
Shortest 1
Shot 6
Shoulder 5
Shouldering 1
Shoulders 2
Shout 3
Show 5
Showd 1
Shower 5
Showerd 1
Showering 1
Showers 4
Shows 3
Showy 2
Shreds 1
Shrewsbury 1
Shrieked 1
Shrine 2
Shrines 1
Shrive 1
Shroud 3
Shroud-plaits 1
Shrouds 1
Shrovetide 1
Shuns 1
Shut 11
Shuts 1
Shuttles 1
Shy 1
Sicilian 1
Sick 8
Sicken 1
Sickend 1
Sickly 1
Sickness 2
Side 12
Sided 1
Sides 1
Sidled 1
Siege 1
Sieve 1
Sift 1
Sifted 1
Sigh 3

Sighed 1
Sighing 2
Sighs 7
Sight 18
Sights 5
Sign 1
Signal 3
Signalling 1
Signals 1
Silence 10
Silent 4
Silk 6
Silk-ash 1
Silk-beech 1
Silk-sack 1
Silken 2
Silky 3
Sillion 1
Silt 1
Silver 26
Silver-coated 1
Silver-shot 1
Silver-surfed 1
Simile 1
Simon 1
Simoom 1
Simple 4
Sin 11
Since 19
Sinew 2
Sinew-service 1
Sing 14
Singeing 1
Singing 5
Single 4
Sings 1
Sinking 1
Sinned 2
Sinner 1
Sinners 1
Sinning 1
Sins 4
Sip 1
Sir 6
Sire 3
Siren 1
Sister 6
Sisterhood 1
Sistering 1
Sisterly 1
Sisters 2
Sit 3
Sits 6
Sitting 3
Six 2
Size 4
Sizes 1
Sizing 3
Skates 1
Skeined 2
Skeins 2
Skies 13
Skiff 1
Skill 5
Skinned 1
Skins 1
Skirt 2
Skirting 1
Skirts 1
Sky 21
Skylark 4
Skylarks 2
Skywards 2
Slabby 1
Slabs 1
Slack 2
Slake 1
Slaked 1
Slammd 1
Slanted 1
Slates 1
Slaty 1
Slaughter 1
Slay 1
Sleek 2
Sleep 7
Slender 6
Slendering 1
Slept 2
Slew 1
Slight 2
Slighted 2
Slightly 1
Slim 2
Slim-pointed 1
Slime 2
Slip 1
Slips 4
Slipt 1
Sloe 1
Sloggering 1
Slopd 1

Slope 1
Sloping 1
Slow 5
Slowly 1
Slumber 2
Slumberd 1
Slumbered 2
Small 8
Smart 5
Smeared 1
Smell 3
Smells 2
Smile 8
Smiled 3
Smiles 2
Smit 1
Smitten 1
Smock 1
Smokes 1
Smooth 6
Smooth-lippd 1
Smote 1
Smother 2
Smouldering 2
Smudge 1
Snatch 1
Snow 7
Snow-pinions 1
Snowflake 1
Snows 4
Snowstorm 1
Snowwhite 2
Snowy 1
Snuff 1
So 1
Soared 1
Soaring 2
Sob 1
Sobbd 1
Sober 2
Sobs 1
Sod 1
Sodden 1
Sodden-with-its-sorrowing. . . . 1
Sods 1
Soft 4
Softening 1
Soil 3
Soldier 1
Soldiering 1
Soldiers 1
Soldiery 1
Solely 1
Solemn 1
Solid 2
Solitary 1
Solitude 2
Sombre 1
Some 49
Something 8
Sometimes 6
Somewhere 6
Son 9
Song 9
Song-fowl 1
Song-strain 1
Sonnet 1
Sons 2
Soon 14
Sooner 1
Soonest 1
Sooty 1
Soppd 1
Sordid 1
Sordidness 1
Sore 2
Sores 3
Sorrel 2
Sorrow 5
Sorrowing 1
Sorrows 1
Sorry 1
Sort 1
Sorts 1
Sots 1
Sought 4
Soul 17
Souls 11
Sound 14
Sounding 1
Sounds 1
Sour 7
Soured 1
Sours 2
South 4
South-westerly 1
Southern 1
Sovereign 1
Sovereignty 1
Sow 3
Sowed 1
Sower 2

Sown 3
Space 1
Spaced 2
Spain 1
Spake 1
Span 2
Spaniels 1
Spannd 1
Spans 1
Spare 5
Spared 2
Spark 2
Sparkling 1
Sparks 1
Sparky 3
Spatterd 1
Speak 6
Speaketh 1
Speaking 1
Speaks 2
Speard 1
Special 2
Special-general 1
Sped 2
Speech 2
Speechless 1
Speeds 1
Spell 5
Spells 2
Spend 6
Spends 1
Spendsavour 1
Spent 12
Sperses 1
Sphered 3
Spiders 2
Spiked 1
Spikes 1
Spill 2
Spin 1
Spine 1
Spins 2
Spire 1
Spires 1
Spirit 12
Spirits 6
Spiritual 2
Splayd 1
Splendid 1
Splendour 3
Splendours 1
Splinterd 1
Spoil 1
Spoke 3
Spokes 1
Spools 1
Spoons 1
Sport 1
Sported 1
Spot 10
Spots 3
Spousal 1
Spouse 2
Sprang 1
Spray 1
Sprays 1
Spread 6
Spreading 1
Spring 24
Spring-broidery 1
Spring-tide 1
Spring-time 1
Springs 8
Springtime 1
Sprit 1
Spun 1
Spur 1
Spurrd 1
Spy 2
Squadroned 1
Squall 1
Squander 1
Squandering 1
Square 1
Square-cut 1
Squared 1
Squat 1
Squeezed 1
Squinches 1
St 2
Stabbing 1
Staff 1
Stage 1
Staid 1
Stain 3
Stained 2
Stair 1
Stair-way 1
Stake 1
Staled 1
Stalk 1
Stallion 1

Stalwart 1
Stamp 1
Stanches 1
Stanching 1
Stand..................... 16
Standing.................... 5
Stands 5
Star...................... 12
Star-eyed.................... 1
Starches 1
Starchy 1
Stare 3
Staring 1
Stark..................... 2
Stark-precipitous 1
Starlight 4
Starlight-wender............. 1
Starrd 2
Starry 5
Stars 28
Start 3
Starting.................... 1
Startle 2
Starvd 1
Starves 1
Starvest 1
State 3
Statuary.................... 2
Statue 1
Staunch 1
Stay 3
Stays 1
Stead 1
Steady 3
Steal 1
Stealing.................... 2
Steals 1
Stealthy 1
Steel 6
Steeled 1
Steep 6
Steep-up 1
Steeped 2
Steered 1
Stem 1
Stephen 1
Stepped 1
Steps 1
Stept 1
Sterling 1
Sterner 1
Sternest 1
Steward 1
Stick 1
Stiffend 1
Stifling 1
Stigma 1
Still 38
Still-purpling 2
Stilling 1
Stillness 1
Stilly 1
Stinging................ 1
Stint 1
Stinting 1
Stintless 1
Stipple 1
Stir 3
Stirless 1
Stirred 3
Stirrings 1
Stirs 1
Stock 1
Stock-still 1
Stole 3
Stoled 1
Stolen 1
Stone 11
Stones 4
Stony 3
Stood 11
Stooks 1
Stool 2
Stooped 1
Stop 2
Stops 2
Store 2
Stored 4
Storm 10
Storm-months 1
Stormfowl 1
Storms 7
Stormy 2
Story 5
Storys 1
Straight................ 2
Strain 13
Strained 1
Strains 6
Strand 2
Stranded............... 1
Strands 2

Strange 5
Strangely 2
Stranger.....................2
Strangers....................1
Straw........................2
Strawberry...................1
Strawberry-breasted 1
Strawy 1
Stray........................2
Straying.................... 1
Strays 1
Streakd......................1
Streaks 1
Stream 1
Streamd 2
Streams 5
Street 1
Streets 1
Strength 4
Strengthen 1
Stress.......................8
Stressed.....................1
Stretchd 2
Stretches....................1
Stretching...................2
Strewed 1
Stricken 1
Strides 1
Striding 1
Strife.......................1
Strike...................... 6
Strikes 2
String 1
Strings 2
Stringy 1
Striped 1
Stripes 1
Strips 1
Strive 1
Striven 1
Stroke...................... 5
Strokes..................... 4
Strombus 1
Strombus-shell.............. 1
Strong......................11
Strook...................... 1
Strove...................... 2
Struck 6
Struggle 3
Struggling...................1
Strung.......................3
Stubborn 1
Stumbling 2
Stung........................2
Stupendous...................1
Stupid.................... 1
Sturdy.......................1
Subject 1
Submission...................1
Subtle 4
Succeed 1
Success 5
Such 45
Suck 3
Sucked 4
Sucks 2
Sudden 7
Suddenly.....................2
Suffer 1
Suffered 1
Suffering 1
Suffers......................1
Sufficed 1
Sugar 1
Suit 3
Suiting......................1
Suitors................... 1
Sulphur 1
Sulphur-colourd 1
Sultry.................... 1
Sum 1
Summer.................... 13
Summer-time.............. 1
Summering 1
Summers................... 1
Summertime 2
Summit.......................1
Summoning 1
Sumptuous 1
Sums 1
Sun 29
Sun-flushd 1
Sunbeam......................1
Sunday.......................1
Sunderd 2
Sung 2
Sunk 2
Sunlight 4
Sunlit 1
Sunned.......................1
Sunny 2
Suns 2

Suns-eye-ringed 1
Sunset 3
Sunspurge 1
Superfluous 1
Supplied 1
Supply 1
Suppose 1
Supposing 1
Surcease 1
Sure 8
Surely 4
Surf 1
Surfed 1
Surfy 1
Surly 3
Surprise 1
Surrenders 1
Surround 1
Survey 1
Suspect 1
Suspects 1
Swallow 1
Swallowd 1
Swallowing 1
Swallows 1
Swam 1
Swan 1
Swan-fledged 1
Swans 1
Sward 2
Swarm 1
Swarmed 2
Swart 2
Swarter 1
Swarthed 1
Swathe 1
Sway 1
Swayd 2
Swayed 1
Swaying 2
Sways 2
Swear 2
Swears 2
Sweat 3
Sweating 1
Sweats 1
Sweep 4
Sweeps 3
Sweet 87
Sweet-and-sour 1
Sweet-familiar 1
Sweet-fowl 1
Sweet-pea-blossom 1
Sweetbriar 1
Sweeter 5
Sweeter-memoried 1
Sweetest 10
Sweetheart 1
Sweetly 4
Sweetness 12
Sweets 4
Swell 3
Swelld 1
Swelling 1
Swells 1
Swept 4
Swerver 1
Swift 2
Swiftly 1
Swill 1
Swim 3
Swimming 2
Swims 1
Swing 3
Swings 3
Swinishly 2
Swirling 2
Swivelled 1
Swolln 1
Swoon 1
Swooned 1
Sword 4
Swords 1
Swung 5
Sycamore 3
Sycamore-tree 1
Sydney 1
Sylvester 5
Sympathising 1
Table 1
Tabour 2
Tackle 3
Tact 1
Tail 3
Tail-fin 1
Tails 1
Tainting 1
Take 20
Taken 3
Takes 4
Taking 1
Takings 1

Tale 3
Tales 1
Talks 1
Tall 8
Talmai 1
Talons 2
Tame 1
Tampering 1
Tangled 2
Tangles 1
Tantalean 1
Taper 1
Tapers 1
Tar 1
Tarpeian 1
Tarpeian-fast 1
Tars 2
Tarsus 2
Tartarus 1
Task 5
Tasking 1
Tasks 1
Taste 6
Tasteless 1
Tasty 1
Tatter 1
Tatter-tangled 1
Taught 7
Tauntless 1
Teach 4
Tear 4
Tear-tricked 1
Tears 29
Teases 1
Teasing 2
Tedious 1
Teeming 3
Teevo 1
Tell 19
Telling 5
Tells 4
Temperateness 1
Temperd 1
Tempest 2
Tempests 1
Temple 2
Temples 1
Tempt 1
Ten 5
Tender 9
Tender-slanted 1
Tendered 1
Tenderer 1
Tenderest 1
Tenderness 1
Tent 1
Tent-poles 1
Terebinth 1
Term 1
Terms 1
Terraces 1
Terrible 3
Terror 1
Teryth 1
Tether 1
Text 2
Th 2
Thames 1
Than 48
Thankless 1
Thanks 1
That 1
The 2
The-last-breath 1
Thecla 3
Thence 2
Theory 1
Thereafter 1
Thereby 2
Therein 1
Therewith 1
Thew 3
Theyre 1
Thick 14
Thick-fleeced 1
Thick-pearled 1
Thicken 1
Thickend 3
Thickening 1
Thickest 1
Thicket 1
Thickly 1
Thigh 1
Thin 6
Thing 25
Things 31
Think 15
Thinking 1
Thinks 2
Thinly 1
Thinned 1
Thinning 1

Third 3
Thirst 3
Thirsts 1
Thistled 1
Thistles 1
Thither 1
Thongs 1
Thorn 3
Thorn-engaged 1
Thorns 4
Thorny 1
Thorough 2
Thoroughfare 1
Thorp 1
Thought 31
Thoughts 10
Thousand 4
Thousands 3
Thralls 1
Thread 2
Threaded 1
Threads 1
Three 27
Three-heeled 1
Three-numbered 1
Threefold 1
Threshing 1
Threshing-floor 1
Threshold 1
Threw 1
Thrice 2
Thriftless 1
Thrill 1
Thrills 1
Thrive 2
Throat 2
Throbbing 2
Throe 1
Throne 2
Throned 1
Throng 6
Thronged 2
Throngs 3
Throstle 1
Throttled 1
Throughther 1
Throw 3
Throws 1
Thrush 1
Thrushs 1
Thrust 1
Thrusts 1
Thunder 7
Thunder-purple 1
Thunder-throne 1
Thundering 1
Thwart 1
Thwarts 1
Tide 6
Tides 2
Tied 2
Ties 3
Tighten 1
Tiles 1
Till 26
Tillage 1
Tilt 2
Timber 2
Timberll 1
Timbrels 1
Time 34
Timed 1
Times 22
Times-over 1
Tingeing 1
Tingling 1
Tiniest 1
Tinklings 1
Tinted 2
Tints 1
Tiny 3
Tiptoes 1
Tire 2
Tired 2
Tires 1
Titans 1
Titians 2
Title 3
To 10
To-day 3
To-fro 1
To-morrow 2
To-night 2
Today 1
Together 9
Toil 4
Token 1
Told 13
Tom 6
Tomb 2
Tomb-decked 1
Tombs 1

Word	Count
Tomorrow	3
Toms	1
Tones	2
Tongue	18
Tongues	2
Tonight	2
Took	10
Tool	2
Toolsmooth	1
Top	2
Toppd	1
Tops	3
Topsyturvy	1
Topt	1
Torment	1
Tormented	2
Tormenting	1
Torn	3
Tossed	1
Tosses	1
Touch	8
Touchd	2
Touched	3
Tower	6
Tower-top	1
Towered	1
Towers	6
Towery	1
Town	6
Towns	1
Toy	1
Trace	1
Traced	2
Traceless	1
Tracery	1
Traces	1
Track	1
Trade	1
Trades	1
Tragic	1
Traild	1
Trailing	1
Training	1
Trambeams	1
Tramp	1
Trample	1
Trampled	1
Tramplers	1
Tranquil	1
Translucent	1
Transmit	1
Trash	1
Travelld	1
Travelling	2
Traverse	1
Treacherous	1
Tread	8
Treadmire	1
Treads	4
Treasonable	1
Treasure	4
Treat	2
Treats	2
Treble	2
Treble-fervent	1
Tree	10
Tree-tops	1
Trees	14
Treetop	1
Tremble	1
Trembling	2
Tremulous	1
Trench	1
Trenched	1
Tresses	4
Trial	1
Trick	1
Tricked	1
Trickle	3
Trickling	1
Trim	2
Trinity	1
Trip	1
Triple	1
Triple-hummocked	1
Trips	1
Triumph	4
Trod	6
Troops	1
Tropes	2
Tropic	1
Troubled	1
Trout	1
Truckle	1
True	24
Truelove	1
Truer	1
Truly	1
Trumpet	5
Trundled	1
Trust	3
Truth	10

Word	Count
Try	5
Trying	2
Ts	1
Tucked	1
Tuft	6
Tufts	4
Tuggd	1
Tumbled	3
Tumbled-to	1
Tumbler	1
Tumbling	1
Tumblings	1
Tumult	1
Tune	3
Tuneable	1
Tuned	1
Turbid	1
Turf	1
Turmoil	1
Turn	16
Turnd	2
Turned	8
Turning	3
Turns	6
Turquoise	1
Turquoise-gemmd	1
Turtles	1
Twelve	3
Twenty	1
Twice	4
Twindles	1
Twiny	1
Twixt	1
Two	26
Tyrant	1
Tyrian	1
Unaccounted	1
Unalterd	1
Unawakened	1
Unaware	1
Unbakes	1
Unblown	1
Unbound	2
Unbroken	1
Uncertainty	1
Unchallenged	1
Unchancelling	1
Unchanging	1
Uncharted	1
Uncheckd	1
Unchilding	1
Unchilld	1
Unchrist	1
Uncle	2
Unclean	1
Uncomforted	1
Unconfessed	1
Uncontrolled	1
Uncouth	2
Uncreated	1
Uncumbered	1
Undenizened	1
Under	27
Underground	1
Underneath	4
Underplighted	1
Understand	2
Understood	2
Underwing	1
Undivulged	1
Undo	3
Undoing	1
Undone	4
Undulation	1
Unendear	1
Unenduring	1
Unespied	1
Unfathering	1
Unfathomable	1
Unfold	1
Unforeseen	1
Unforgiven	1
Unfurled	2
Ungentle	1
Ungirdled	1
Unglue	1
Unheard	1
Unheeded	1
Unhinderd	1
Unholy	2
Unhouse	1
Unimperilld	1
Unimpregnate	1
Universal	1
Unkind	1
Unknown	2
Unleaving	1
Unlookd	1
Unlovely	1
Unmade	1
Unmindful	1
Unmoved	1

Unpalateable 1
Unpassiond 1
Unpeopled 1
Unpinned 1
Unquestiond 1
Unraveller 1
Unrest 1
Unreticent 1
Unsafe 1
Unsandalled 1
Unseen 4
Unselfishness 1
Unselve 1
Unset 2
Unsets 1
Unsexing 1
Unshapeable 1
Unsheathd 1
Unshod 1
Unsought 1
Unsteady 1
Unstinted 1
Unswerving 1
Untainted 1
Untaught 1
Unteachably 1
Until 3
Unto 6
Untwist 1
Unused 1
Unvalve 1
Unveined 1
Unvexed 1
Unvisited 1
Unwarned 1
Unwavering 1
Unwet 1
Unworthiness 1
Up 27
Uperinging 1
Upgazing 1
Uplands 1
Upon 58
Upper 3
Upraisd 1
Upright 1
Uproll 1
Upward 3
Upward-parted 1
Upwards 2
Us 46
Used 2
Utter 1
Utterance 2
Uttered 2
Utterer 1
Uttering 2
Utterly 2
Uttermost 1
V 1
V-winged 1
Vacant 2
Vain 2
Vale 1
Valerian 2
Vales 4
Valiant 1
Valley 2
Valleys 1
Valour 2
Value 1
Van 1
Vaned 1
Vanishd 1
Vanishing 1
Vantage 1
Vapour 1
Vapourous 1
Variety 1
Various 1
Vast 4
Vastness 1
Vasty 1
Vault 5
Vaulted 1
Vaulting 2
Vaulty 1
Vaunt 1
Vaunt-and 1
Vaunting 1
Veer 2
Veil 2
Vein 7
Veind 1
Veined 2
Veins 3
Velvet 1
Velvety 1
Venerable 1
Vengeances 1
Ventnor 1
Venus 1

Veriest 1
Vermeil 1
Vermeil-rain 1
Vermilion 1
Verse 1
Very 13
Very-violet-sweet 1
Vespers 1
Vespillo 1
Vessels 1
Vest 1
Vexd 1
Vice 2
Victim 1
Victor 1
View 1
Viewing 1
Views 1
Vigil 2
Vigil-keepers 1
Vigil-organ 1
Vigorous 1
Villages 1
Vine 5
Vine-shoot 1
Vines 1
Vintage 1
Viol 1
Violent 1
Violet 8
Violets 3
Virgin 4
Virginal 2
Virgins 1
Virtue 3
Virtues 7
Visaged 1
Vision 2
Visionary 1
Visions 1
Visiting 2
Visual 1
Vital 2
Vive 1
Vivid 1
Voel 1
Voice 10
Void 2
Voids 1
Voluminous 1
Vows 1

Wading 1
Waether 1
Waft 1
Wafting 1
Wag 1
Wages 1
Wail 1
Wailing 1
Wain 1
Waist 2
Waists 1
Wait 1
Waits 2
Wake 2
Waked 2
Waken 1
Wakes 1
Waking 3
Wales 4
Walk 6
Walkd 1
Walked 2
Walks 5
Wall 6
Walled 1
Wallow 1
Wallowing 1
Walls 7
Walnut 1
Walsingham 1
Wan 1
Wand 2
Wandering 5
Waned 3
Waning 1
Wanner 1
Want 5
Wanted 1
Wanting 6
Wanton 2
Wants 3
Wanwood 1
War 4
Warbled 1
Warbles 1
Warbling 2
Warder 1
Warding 1
Ware 3
Warfare 1
Warm 10

Warm-laid 1
Warmd 1
Warmly 2
Warms 1
Warmth 1
Warnd 1
Warned 4
Warning 1
Warp 1
Warped 1
Warrants 1
Warring 1
Wars 5
Wash 3
Washing 3
Waste 8
Wasted 1
Wasteful 1
Wastes 3
Wasting 1
Watch 5
Watchd 1
Watched 3
Watches 1
Watchet 2
Watching 2
Water 34
Water-cloud 1
Water-in-a-wallow 1
Water-lily 1
Water-meads 1
Water-nymphs 1
Water-pierced 1
Water-wattled 1
Waterblowballs 1
Waterd 2
Waterfall 1
Waterfalls 1
Waterfearers 1
Waters 10
Waterworld 1
Watery 5
Watery-plated 2
Wattled 1
Wave 2
Waved 2
Waver 1
Waves 4
Wavier 1
Waving 2
Wax 1

Waxed 2
Waxen 2
Waxes 1
Way 24
Waylay 1
Ways 15
We 99
Weak 2
Weakness 1
Weal 1
Weald 1
Wealth 2
Wear 11
Weariest 1
Wears 2
Weary 8
Weather 8
Web 4
Webbd 1
Webbed 1
Webs 1
Wed 7
Wedded 3
Wedlock 3
Weds 1
Weed 5
Weed-bathed 1
Weed-winding 1
Weeded 1
Weedio 2
Weedio-weedio 1
Weeds 5
Week 1
Weeks 2
Weep 4
Weeping 3
Weepings 1
Weeps 2
Weigh 1
Weighed 1
Weighing 1
Weight 1
Weights 1
Weighty 1
Welcome 5
Welkin 5
Well 36
Well-bred 2
Wellbeing 1
Welling 1
Wells 3

Wend 2
Wender 1
Went 16
Wept 3
West 12
Westerd 1
Westerly 1
Western 1
Westward 1
Wet 10
Wet-fresh 1
Wete 1
Wether 1
Wharf 1
Wharves 2
Whatevers 1
Wheat 2
Wheat-acre 1
Wheatfields 1
Wheel 3
Wheels 1
Whelmd 1
Whelms 2
Whence 5
Whereas 2
Wherefore 2
Wherein 3
Whereon 1
While 50
Whilst 1
Whip 1
Whip-adder 1
Whips 1
Whirl 2
Whirled 1
Whirling 1
Whirlwind 2
Whirlwind-swivelled 1
Whisper 1
Whispers 1
White 21
White-faced 1
White-fiery 1
Whitebeam 1
Whitest 1
Whitewash 1
Whole 5
Wholesome 2
Wholl 1
Wholly 1
Whorl 1
Whorled 1
Wicked 3
Wicket 1
Wide 12
Widow 2
Widow-making 1
Wield 1
Wielding 1
Wife 4
Wild 22
Wild-worst 1
Wilder 3
Wilderness 4
Wildfire 1
Wildflowers 1
Wildness 2
Wildworth 1
Wiles 1
Wilful 1
Wilful-wavier 1
Will 83
Willd 1
William 7
Williams 2
Willing 1
Willow 1
Willows 1
Wills 1
Wilt 2
Wimpled 2
Wimpled-water-dimpled 1
Wimpling 1
Win 8
Wince 1
Winch 2
Wincing 1
Wind 40
Wind-beat 1
Wind-lilylocks-laced 1
Wind-long 1
Wind-perplexed 1
Wind-walks 1
Wind-wandering 1
Winded 2
Windfalls 1
Winding 2
Windlaced 1
Window 3
Window-circles 1
Windpipe 1
Windpuff 1

Windpuff-bonnet 1
Winds 9
Windy 2
Wine 4
Wing 5
Winged 4
Wings 18
Wink 1
Winks 1
Winning 2
Winter 14
Winter-time 2
Winter-while 1
Wintering 2
Winters 1
Wintry 2
Wiped 1
Wiry 2
Wisdom 2
Wise 5
Wisest 1
Wish 6
Wishing 1
Wisp 2
Wisped 1
Wit 3
Witch 1
With 5
With-a-fountains 1
Withal 1
Wither 1
Withering 1
Within 17
Withindoors 1
Without 12
Withouten 1
Witness 3
Witnessed 1
Wits 2
Witted 1
Woe 7
Woeful 2
Woes 2
Woke 3
Wolfsnow 1
Woman 6
Woman-kind 1
Womans 1
Womb 6
Womb-life 1
Womb-not-bearing 1
Womb-of-all 1
Women 2
Won 4
Wonder 13
Wonderful 1
Wondering 3
Wonders 3
Wondrous 4
Wont 2
Wood 16
Wood-sorrel 2
Wooddove 1
Woodferns 1
Woodland 2
Woodlark 1
Woods 5
Wool 1
Woolwoven 1
Woos 1
Word 12
Worded 1
Wording 1
Words 10
Wordsworth 2
Wordy 1
Wore 2
Work 14
Working 1
Workman 1
Works 1
World 42
World-mothering 2
World-sorrow 1
World-wielding 1
Worlds 10
Worm 2
Worms 1
Worse 10
Worship 3
Worst 8
Worth 8
Worthiest 1
Worthy 2
Wound 6
Wounded 1
Wounds 2
Woven 1
Wrapped 1
Wrathful 1
Wreath 1
Wreathd 1

Word	Count
Wreaths	1
Wreck	5
Wreckd	1
Wrecked	2
Wrecking	1
Wrecks	2
Wrestles	1
Wrestling	1
Wretch	2
Wretches	1
Wring	6
Wring-world	1
Wringing	1
Wrings	2
Wrinkle	1
Wrinkles	2
Writ	1
Write	2
Writes	1
Writhe	1
Written	4
Wrong	4
Wrongd	1
Wronging	1
Wrongs	1
Wrought	6
Wrung	3
Wuthering	1
Wychelm	1
Yawnd	1
Yea	7
Year	11
Year-mother	1
Yearnd	2
Years	19
Yellow	9
Yellowy	1
Yes	10
Yesterday	1
Yestertempests	1
Yet	72
Yield	10
Yields	4
Yoke	1
Yonder	7
Yore	3
Yore-flood	1
Youll	2
Young	4
Youngster	1
Youth	8
Youve	1
Ytressed	1
Yule	1
Zeal	2
Zeal-rampant	1
Zenith	2
Zenithd	1
Zephyrs	1
Zest	2
Zone	1
8000	1

Appendix II
Words in Order of Their Frequency of Appearance

ONCE

Abandoned
Abel
Abeles
Abide
Abides
Abject
Abode
Abolished
Abound
Abreast
Abrupt
Abundant
Abysmal
Abysses
Acanthus
Acanthus-crownd
Accents
Accept
Acceptance
Accepted
Accepting
Accessories
Accidents
Accumulated
Aches
Achieve
Aching
Acknowledging
Acorn-cup
Acquaintance
Acres
Adamantine
Adazzle
Add
Adder
Adela
Admired
Advance
Adversity
Advise
Aeolis
Aeons
Aether
Afar
Affection
Affined
Afflicted
Afflictive
Afflicts
Aflash
Afoot
Afresh
After-comers
After-words
Aftercast
Afterdraught
Afternoon
Again
Age-old
Aggrandise
Aid
Aidenn
Aim
Air-blended
Air-crisping
Airwards
Airworld
Airy-grey
Akin
Alarms
Albeit
Ale
Alert
Alfonso
Alight
Alighted
All-a-leaf
All-accepting
All-belated
All-fire
All-heal
All-in-all
All-surfy
Allow
Almoner
Alp
Altar-tapers
Altar-vessels
Altars
Alter
Altogether
Amansstrength
Amaze
Amazed
Amend
Amends
American
American-outward-bound
Amethyst
Amiss
Ancient
Ancles
Andromeda
Anew
Angel-warder
Anointed
Answering
Antinous
Antipodes
Antique
Anvil-ding
Apollo
Appal
Appareld
Appealing
Appeard
Appearing
Apple-trees
Appledurcombe
Apples
Apply
Apprehend
Approve
April-weather
Arba
Arcadia
Arcadian
Arch-especial
Arched
Arches
Arching
Arcs
Argued
Ark
Aroused
Array
Arrival
Arthur
Arthurs
Artist
Arts
Ascend
Ascendancy
Ascribed
Ash-tops
Ashboughs
Ashiness

Aside
Asked
Asking
Aslant
Aspect
Assault
Assaulting
Assay
Assignd
Assured
Assyrian
Astern
Astrain
Astral
Astrew
Astrologic
Asunder
Aswarm
Atlantic
Atmosphere
Attempted
Attentive
Attire
Attributes
Attuneable
Attuning
Aureoles
Austin
Authentic
Avenge
Avoid
Avow
Awful
Awhile
Awoke
Aye
Azured
Azuring
Azuring-over
Azurous
Babes
Babyhood
Backed
Backward
Backwheels
Baffle
Baffled
Baffling
Balance
Balances
Bald
Baldbright
Bales
Balls
Balm
Ban
Bankrupt
Bannd
Banned
Banquet
Bans
Bar
Barbarous
Barebill
Bared
Bargain
Barken
Barley
Barn
Barrack
Barrd
Barrel
Barrelled
Barrens
Barriers
Barrowy
Barter
Barterd
Basilisk
Basks
Bason
Bass
Bat
Bathe
Bathes
Bathing
Bats
Battering
Battle
Battled
Battling
Bays
Beach
Beadbonny
Beakleaved
Beam-blind
Beaming
Bean
Bearer
Bears
Beauties
Beauty-bow
Beauty-in-the-ghost
Become
Bedded
Bee
Beech
Beechbole
Bees
Beetle
Beetle-browed
Befal
Befall
Before-time-taken
Begged
Behaviour
Beholder
Bela
Belated
Belie
Bell-swarmed
Bellbright
Belleisle
Bellerophon
Bellisle
Bellows
Belong
Belts
Belvedere
Bends
Benediction
Benefits
Berg
Beryl-covered
Besides
Bespoken
Bestowing
Bethlehem
Bethlem
Bethlems
Betimes
Betray
Betrayd
Betterd
Betweenpie
Betweens
Betweenwhiles
Beuno
Bides
Bidst
Big-boned
Billion
Billowy

Bills
Bindst
Bines
Biscay
Bit
Bite
Bitten
Bitterer
Black-about
Black-backed
Black-fleeced
Blackest
Blackness
Blacks
Blade-gash
Blady
Blame
Blasted
Blazonry
Bleached
Blear-all
Bleared
Bleats
Bleeds
Blended
Blessing
Blight
Blindfold
Blindness
Blinds
Blindworm
Blinking
Blissful
Blood-gush
Blood-light
Blood-vivid
Bloods
Bloomfall
Blooming
Blossom-hitting
Blotless
Blowing
Blowpipe
Blue-beating
Blue-bleak
Bluebell
Bluer
Bluff
Blurrd
Blurs
Blushed
Blustering
Board
Boards
Boasting
Boatman
Boded
Bodes
Boisterously
Boldboys
Bole
Bolt
Bolts
Bone-house
Boned
Bonfire
Boniface
Bonnet
Bonniest
Boons
Boots
Borders
Boreas
Bored
Bores
Boroughs
Borrow
Bossd
Bounden
Bow-bend
Bowl
Bowman
Box
Braes
Brags
Braid
Brains
Brambles
Brand
Brandle
Brands
Brass-bold
Bravest
Brawling
Brawn
Breadth
Breaker
Breakers
Breakless
Breasted
Breasting
Breath-taking
Breed
Breeds
Bremen
Brickish
Bricks
Bridegroom
Bridge
Bridging
Brier
Bright-counter
Bright-lifting
Bright-maskd
Brighten
Brightening
Brightest
Brightness
Brilliance
Brilliant-hued
Brimmed
Brinded
Brindled
Brink
Bristol
Bristol-bred
Britains
Broad-fluted
Broad-shed
Broiders
Broidery
Bronzen
Brooch
Brown-as-dawning-skinned
Browzed
Bruise
Brute
Buck
Buckle
Budded
Bugle-eyed
Bugles
Bulk
Bulky
Bullion
Bunchy
Burial
Burl
Burling
Burnishd
Burr
Bursts

Bury
Bush
Bush-browed
Bushybowered
Business
Busy
Butcher
Butmind
Butter
Butter-burr
Butterflies
Butts
Buys
By
Bye
Bye-ways
Bygones
Byplay
Cadair
Cadence
Cage
Cages
Cains
Caked
Calvary
Calvarys
Campion
Canaan
Cancer
Candlemas
Candles
Candour
Candycoloured
Cannon
Canvas
Canvass
Canvassing
Cap
Capable
Capes
Capital
Cappd
Capped
Capsize
Captain
Captivity
Caradoc
Caradocs
Care-coiled
Care-drowned
Care-killed
Cared
Cared-for
Career
Caressd
Caressing
Carisbrook
Carouse
Carrier
Carrier-witted
Carriers
Carries
Carrion
Carved
Carving
Case
Cased
Casements
Casque
Castaras
Castilian
Cataract
Catches
Cavernous
Ceaseless
Cell
Cells
Cemented
Censers
Centre-darks
Centreings
Centurion
Ceres
Certainty
Chaff
Chained
Chair
Chalky
Chamferd
Champ
Champ-white
Chance
Chancequarried
Changd
Changeless
Channelled
Chaotic
Chapel
Chapel-side
Chapleted
Chaplets
Chaptered
Charactered
Charitable
Charitys
Charless
Charnelhouse
Charnelhouse-grate
Chart
Charted
Charter
Chase
Chasms
Chastening
Chastity
Chaunt
Cheap
Chebars
Check
Chee
Cheered
Cheering
Cheerless
Cheers
Cheevo
Chequers
Cherry
Chervil
Chestnut-falls
Chestnut-fans
Chevalier
Chevy
Chewd
Chief-woe
Chiefs
Chieftain
Child-like
Childless
Childrens
Chilling
Chips
Chivalry
Chivalrys
Choir
Choking
Chrism
Christ-done
Christ-ed
Christens
Christian
Christians
Christus
Chrysolite

Church-tower
Churlsgrace
Churning
Cield
Cinquefoil
Cipher
Circle-citadels
Circlet
Circling
Citadels
Cite
Cithern
Cities
Clammyish
Clank
Clarion-clear
Clarions
Clarissa
Claspd
Classic
Clattering
Claude
Clayfields
Clearest
Clearest-selved
Cleave
Cleped
Clicking
Clinches
Clinching
Clinching-blind
Cling
Clods
Clogged
Cloister
Cloister-light
Cloisterd
Cloistering
Cloisters
Close-barred
Close-folded
Close-ply
Close-rooted
Closer
Closes
Clothes
Cloud-festooned
Cloud-puffball
Clough
Cloy
Clusterd
Clustering
Clusters
Clutched
Coal
Coast
Coat
Coated
Coats
Cobbled
Cocooning
Coffer
Coffin
Coffin-black
Cogged
Coifed
Coiled
Coils
Coinage
Colder
Coldly
Coldness
Collapsing
Colomb
Colossal
Colouring
Columnar
Columnar-severe
Columns
Combating
Combes
Come-back-again
Comers
Comet
Comfortable
Comforter
Comforts
Commander
Commands
Communion
Companion
Comparison
Compassion
Compassionate
Complaisant
Complete
Compliment
Compulsion
Comrade
Concavity
Conceiving
Concern
Concerned
Conch
Concording
Confess
Confidante
Confidence
Confined
Confirmed
Confound
Confounded
Confront
Confused
Conjecture
Conjuctions
Conquest
Conqurors
Conscience
Considerate
Considered
Constancy
Consumes
Consuming
Contagious
Contend
Contended
Contends
Content
Contentment
Continence
Continent
Continually
Contract
Controlld
Cooings
Coop
Coped
Copses
Coral
Corded
Cordial
Cords
Cornicd
Coronals
Coronet
Corpses
Correspond
Corruption
Cost
Cot
Cottages
Cough

Council
Counsel
Countenance
Counter-roundels
Counterfeit
Counterfoiling
Countervail
Counting
Countless
County
Couple
Couple-colour
Courage
Course
Courses
Courtesies
Coverd
Coverlid
Coverts
Cow
Crackd
Craddock
Cragiron
Crags
Cramps
Crawl
Creamy
Crease
Creases
Creating
Creation
Creations
Creature
Creatures
Credit
Creeds
Cressetedeast
Crime
Crimson-cressetedeast
Crimson-golden
Crimson-white
Crimsonings
Crimsons
Cringe
Cripples
Crispd
Crisping
Crisps
Criss
Criss-crossd
Crocodiles
Crooked
Cross-barred
Cross-colour
Cross-wood
Crossbridle
Crosses
Crouch
Crowding
Crowned
Crowns
Cruel
Cruise
Crumbled
Crumbling
Crush-silk
Crushes
Crystal
Crystal-ending
Crystalline
Cuckoo-echoing
Cuckoocall
Cud
Cue
Cullys
Cumber
Cumbered
Cumbrous
Cumnor
Cupboard
Cuppd
Curb
Curded
Cure
Curfew
Curl
Curld
Curls
Cursing
Curves
Cusp
Customary
Cyclads
Cypris
Dabbled
Daffodil
Daffodillies
Dahlias
Daintily
Dainty-delicate
Daisies
Dallies
Damask
Damaskd
Dame
Damp
Damson
Dance
Dancers
Dancing
Dandy
Dandy-hung
Danger
Dangerously
Dangled
Dank-ytressed
Dantes
Daphnis
Dapple-dawn-drawn
Dapple-eared
Dappled-with-damson
Dare-gale
Daredeaths
Dares
Darkend
Darkened
Darkles
Darks
Darling
Dart
Darting
Dashed
Dateless
Dates
Daunting
Dauntless
Dauphin
Davids
Dawning
Day-dissolved
Day-labouring-out
Daylights
Dayspring
Daystar
Daze
Dazzle
Deacon
Dead-alive
Deadly-electric
Deadning
Deaf
Dearness
Dears

Deathdance
Deathgush
Decay
Decaying
December
Decked
Decreased
Decree
Deed-bound
Deem
Deemed
Deems
Deep-groved
Deepening
Defiance
Deflowers
Deft
Deft-handed
Degged
Degrees
Dejection
Delay
Delicacy
Delicate
Delicious
Delighted
Delivering
Dell
Delves
Denial
Denis
Dense
Dented
Departed
Depend
Depths
Describd
Desert
Deserter
Deserve
Deserving
Desirable
Desires
Desirous
Despairing
Despatches
Desponding
Destined
Device
Devilish
Devon

Devonshire
Devouring
Dew-lap
Dewbell
Dewdrop
Dewdrops
Dexterous
Diadem
Diademd
Diapered
Diapers
Dick
Die-away
Diet
Difference
Dight
Diminishd
Diminishes
Dimly
Dimmd
Dimness
Dimpling
Din
Ding
Dingle
Dingle-a-dangled
Dings
Dint
Dinted
Dintless
Dippd
Direction
Directly
Dirvan
Disabling
Disallow
Disappointed
Disarming
Disarray
Disaster
Disastrous
Discharge
Discharging
Disclose
Discloses
Discontent
Discord
Discovered
Discovering
Discovery
Dishevelled

Dismalest
Dismay
Dismembering
Disobedient
Disorders
Disparadised
Dispel
Dispense
Dispenses
Disposes
Disquiet
Disregarded
Disremembering
Disseveral
Dissolve
Dissolved
Distanced
Distemperd
Distillation
Distills
Distinction
Distressed
Disturbd
Dither
Dive
Divers
Divide
Divided
Divined
Divinely
Diving
Dizzy
Doff
Doffs
Dog
Dogeared
Doggd
Dogrose
Dogs
Domain
Dominant
Doomfire
Dooms
Dooms-day
Doomsday
Doric
Dorothea
Double-musical
Double-natured
Doublet
Dovewinged

Down-dugged
Down-splinterd
Downcarol
Downdolphinry
Downright
Downward-hollowing
Downwards
Downy
Dragon
Dragonflies
Dragonish
Dragons
Drain
Draining
Draughts
Drawer
Drayhorse
Dreaded
Dreadnought
Dreamy
Drear
Drenched
Dressed
Drest
Drifted
Drifting
Drilled
Drinks
Dripping
Drizzle
Drond
Drop-of-blood-and-foam-dapple
Droppd
Dropped
Dropping
Drouth
Drowning
Drowsy
Drudgery
Dugged
Duomo
Durance
During
Dusk-deep
Duty-swerver
Dwarf
Dwarfs
Dwellest
Dwindles
Dwindling
Dying
Dyphwys
Eager
Eagerer
Eagles
Ear-caressing
Eared
Earlstars
Earnest-hearted
Earthworld
Easeful
Eastering
Eastern
Eastnortheast
Eastward
Eastwards
Eaten
Ebb
Ebbd
Echod
Echoing-of-earth
Eclipse
Eclipsing
Ed
Eddies
Eddy
Eden
Edged
Edges
Effectual
Egypt
Eighth
El
Elbow
Eldering
Elected
Electric
Electrical
Elemented
Eleven
Elim
Elm-heads
Elms
Elmy
Eloquent
Else-minded
Elves
Elves-eyes
Emblem
Embraced
Eminent
Empire
Employment
Enclusterd
Encounter
Encrimsoning
Endeavour
Endless
Endlessly
Endragoned
Endured
Enduring
Enemy
Enforced
Engaged
Engemming
Engenderd
Englands
Enjewelling
Enjoy
Enjoyment
Enriched
Entangled
Enter
Entering
Entrance
Entrancingly
Envied
Epistles
Equipped
Erin
Erst
Esaus
Escape
Escorial
Espial
Essence
Estates
Esteemd
Etc
Ether
Eucharist
Eunuch
Eurydice
Event
Ever-fretting
Everlasting
Everlastingness
Evermore
Evil-heavend
Evils
Ewe

Except
Excess
Exhibition
Exile
Exiled
Explanation
Exploit
Express
Expressed
Expressionless
Extremes
Extremity
Exultation
Eye-attentive
Eye-greeting
Eyelids
Eyesight
Ezekiels
Fable
Fabled
Fabling
Faced
Fade
Fading
Fagged
Faild
Failing
Failure
Fainter
Fairly
Fairness
Fairyland
Faithless
Falcon
Fall-gold
Fallers
Fallowbootfellow
Fallows
False
Falsely
Falsified
Falter
Fames
Familiarness
Fancied
Fanciful
Fanged
Fangs
Fantastic
Far-off
Farmyard
Farrier
Fashed
Fashion
Fast-flowing
Fast-lodged
Fasted
Fasten
Fasts
Fatherd
Fathers-forth
Fathomed
Fathoms
Fault-not-found- with
Favour
Favourable
Favoured
Favouring
Favourite
Fawn
Fawn-froth
Fealty
Feard
Feared
Fearful
Fearing
Featuring
Fed
Feeble
Feel-of-primrose
Feelers
Feels
Feigns
Felicitous
Fell-frowning
Fellowships
Female
Fenced
Fens
Fern
Fertile
Fervent
Festival
Festooned
Fettle
Fever
Feverd
Ffestiniog
Field-flowers
Field-flown
Fiercer
Fiercest
Fig
Fighter
Filial
Filld
Filled
Filleted
Fillets
Film
Films
Filth
Finches
Finding
Fine-drawn
Fineflour
Finger-long
Finger-teasing
Fingergaps
Fingering
Fingernail
Fire-featuring
Fire-folk
Fireball
Firecoal
Fired
Firedint
First-fruits
Fishes
Fits
Five-lipped
Five-lived
Fix
Fixedly
Flake-doves
Flame-cased
Flame-rash
Flame-rings
Flanders
Flange
Flard
Flares
Flaring
Flashing
Flats
Flatter
Flatterys
Flaunt
Flaunting
Flawed
Flecks
Fledged
Flee

Fleeces
Fleeciest
Fleeted
Fleets
Fleming
Flesh-bound
Flesh-burst
Flesh-flowers
Flesh-pots
Fletcher
Flew
Flicker
Flies
Flighty
Flinching
Flings
Flint-flake
Flints
Flirting
Flitches
Flits
Flixed
Floated
Floats
Flockbells
Floodtide
Floord
Flowerets
Flue
Fluke
Flushd
Flushes
Fluted
Flutes
Foam-fallow
Foam-fleece
Foam-tuft
Foamfalling
Foil
Foiled
Foiling
Foliage
Followed
Follows
Fondler
Font
Foods
Footfretted
Footrest
Footsteps
Footway
For
Forcd
Forced
Forcible
Forcibly
Fore
Fore-foundering
Foredrawn
Forefalls
Forefending
Foregone
Foreknown
Forepangs
Forethought
Forfeit
Forged
Forgetfulness
Forgiven
Forgives
Forgiving
Forgone
Forked
Formal
Formed
Formerly
Forms
Forsook
Forth-and-flaunting
Forth-driven
Fortress
Fortune
Forty
Forward-like
Fouled
Foundered
Fountain
Founts
Fourth
Fowls
Foxgloves
Frailest
Frailest-flixed
Frailty
Frances
Francis
Frantic
Freckled
Freeze
Freezing
Freighted
Frenzied
Frequenting
Fresh-firecoal
Fresh-leaved
Freshest
Freshly
Fretful
Frets
Fretting
Frigate
Frigid
Fringed
Fringes
Frocks
Froliclavish
Fronts
Frost
Frost-furred
Frothpits
Frothy
Froward
Frown
Fruit-cloistering
Fueled
Fulfil
Fulfilld
Full-leaved
Full-sappd
Fuller
Fully
Fumes
Fuming
Fumitory
Function
Furl
Furlongs
Furnace
Furrows
Furtherd
Fury
Fussy
Futility
Gaiety
Gain
Gaind
Gainings
Galaxy
Gales
Galilee
Galilees
Gallantry
Galled

Galleries
Gallop
Gambol
Gambolling
Gan
Gangs
Gapes
Gaps
Garb
Garden-poppies
Garland
Garnered
Garnering
Garnet
Gashed
Gashes
Gasp
Gaspd
Gasping
Gasps
Gate
Gates
Gatherd
Gathering
Gathers
Gauge
Gay-gangs
Gaygear
Gaylinks
Gazed
Gazing
Gem-fleeced
Gemmd
General
Generation
Generations
Gennesareth
Gently
Germs
Gertrude
Gethsemane
Ghostly
Ghosts
Giants
Giddies
Gideons
Gilded
Girder
Girdled
Girdles
Girlgrace
Girlhood
Girthed
Givest
Glacier
Gladdest
Glade
Glance
Glances
Glass-blue
Glassy-clear
Glaucus
Glazed
Gleam
Glean
Gleaned
Glee
Glen
Glens
Glides
Gliding
Glimmerd
Glimpses
Glistens
Glistery
Glitter
Globe
Globes
Gloomd
Glories
Glorify
Gloss
Glowd
Glowless
Glowworms
Glue
Gluegold
Gluegold-brown
Gnarled
Gnarls
Gnashed
Goal
Goals
Goats
God-made-flesh
Goddesss
Godhead
Godless
Goings
Gold-vermilion
Gold-water
Gold-wisp
Golden-girdled
Goldengrove
Goldish
Goldnails
Goldy
Gonfalon
Goods
Gore
Gorged
Gorgons
Gorse
Gossamer
Gossamers
Gothic
Gotten
Gracefully
Graceless
Grafted
Grains
Grasp
Grasps
Grasses
Grassy
Grateful
Graver
Graves
Greece
Greek
Green-white
Greenest
Greenhouse
Greenness
Greenworld
Greet
Gregorians
Gregory
Grey-green
Greybell
Griefs
Grievance
Grieves
Grieving
Grim
Grip
Grizzled
Groom
Ground-hugged
Grounded
Groundlong
Grounds
Groved

Grovel
Growths
Grudge
Guard
Guardedly
Guesses
Guessing
Guinevere
Gulf
Gulfs
Gull
Gum
Gushing
Gusty
Gwen
Hack
Hacked
Hacks
Haemony
Haggard
Haggle
Hailropes
Hair-bound
Hairs
Half-circle
Half-hour
Half-light
Half-lit
Half-meshing
Hallowing
Hallows
Halls
Halod
Halve
Halves
Hamlets
Hampstead
Handed
Handling
Handy
Hangdog
Hanker
Hanks
Hapless
Happd
Happiness
Hard-hurled
Hardend
Hardest
Hardly
Hardy
Hardy-handsome
Hare
Harmony
Harms
Harness
Harp
Harshness
Hastend
Hat
Hatred
Haunt
Haunted
Haunts
Havens
Havering
Havoc-pocked
Hawk
Hawkmoth
Hawling
Hazards
Haze
Hazels
Headed
Headstrong
Headway
Heady
Heaped
Heardst
Hearer
Hearers
Hearse
Hearse-of-all
Hearses
Hearst
Heart-at-ease
Heart-beat
Heart-break
Heart-broke
Heart-broken
Heart-fleshed
Heart-forsook
Heart-song
Heart-springs
Heart-throe
Heartburn
Hearth
Hearths
Heartily
Hearts-clarion
Heartsore
Heathpacks
Heaved
Heaven-enforced
Heaven-flung
Heaven-handling
Heaven-haven
Heaven-roysterers
Heaven-vault
Heavend
Heavenfallen
Heavengravel
Heavenlier
Heaves
Heaving
Heavy
Heavyheaded
Hectors
Hedge
Hedgerow
Heeds
Heeled
Heels
Heft
Heifers
Heightening
Heightens
Heights
Hell-rook
Hells
Helpd
Helps
Heltering
Hempen
Herclots
Herds
Herds-long
Hereafter
Heresy
Heretic
Heretofore
Heroic
Hews
Hiding
High-hung
High-priest
Highroad
Hill-top
Hillside
Hilted
Hinders
Hindrance
Hip

Hitherto
Hitting
Ho
Hoar-hallowed
Hoar-hushed
Hoards
Hoarlight
Hoarse
Hoary-glow
Hobs
Holes
Holier
Holiest
Holiness
Hollowd
Home-of-all
Homeforth
Homes
Homing
Honest
Honey
Honeysuck
Honeysuckle
Honor
Honouring
Hoped
Horizon
Horizon-round
Horizontals
Hornbeam
Hornlight
Horoscope
Horrible
Horseback
Horsemen
Horses
Hosts
Hourglass
Housed
Housel
Houseless
Housetop
Hovel
Hover-float
Hovered
Hoverings
Hovers
Huddle
Huddling
Huge-girthed
Hugged
Hum
Humanities
Hummocked
Hundredfold
Hundredweights
Hung-heavenward
Hungered
Hunters
Hurdle
Hurried
Hurst
Hursts
Hurt
Hushd
Hushed
Husked
Hussy
Hustle
Hutch
Hyacinth
Hyacinth-warding
Hyacinthed
Hyacinths
Hyaline
Hymn
Hypocrite
Iconium
Icy
Id
Ideal
Ignorantly
Ill-balanced
Ill-content
Ill-contented
Ill-launched
Ill-visaged
Illumined
Illustrated
Image
Images
Imagining
Immortals
Impale
Impaled
Impalpable
Impatient
Impeached
Impearled
Impediment
Impenitent
Imps
Inanimate
Inboard
Incapable
Incense
Inch
Inches
Increase
Increment
Indian
Indifference
Indignation
Indivisible
Inexplicably
Infallibly
Infancy
Infant
Infest
Infinitely
Infinity
Influential
Inheritance
Initiate
Injury
Injurys
Inmate
Inspiration
Instant
Insufficiencies
Int
Intellectual
Intense
Intensest
Intensity
Interchange
Interests
Interposed
Interstice
Inthem
Intolerable
Invention
Inward
Ipse
Ireland
Irish
Irregularly
Island
Isles
Issue
Its
Ive
Ivies

Ivy
Jacinthine
Jacks
Jackself
Jaded
Jading
Jagged
Jags
Jailor
James
Jarrd
Jaunting
Jay
Jay-blue
Jessy
Jet
Jewelld
Joints
Joke
Jolt
Josephs
Joy-laden
Joyless
Joys
Judah
Judge
Justices
Justify
Kate
Keats
Keener
Keepers
Keeping
Kentish
Khor
Kill-weights
Kills
Kindcold
Kindness
Kindred
Kine
Kingdom
Kingfishers
Kirjath
Kirjath-arba
Kissed
Kissing
Kneading
Knee-nave
Kneeled
Knells

Knock
Knocking
Knockings
Knops
Knopt
Knowest
Knowledge
Laboured
Laboured-at
Labours
Lace-leaved
Laces
Lacklevel
Lade
Ladies
Lady-star
Lag
Lagging
Lair
Lame
Lamentable
Laments
Lamps
Lancashire
Lanced
Lancing
Landslips
Lanes
Languent
Lank
Laps
Lapsed
Lark-charmed
Larkspur
Larkspurs
Lashtender
Latched
Late-found
Late-learnt
Lauded
Laughing
Laughs
Launched
Laverd
Lawns
Laws
Lays
Lazuli
Lea
Leaf-light
Leafing

Leafless
Leafmeal
Leafwhelmed
Lean
Lean-over
Leap
Leaps
Learn
Learner
Learning
Leas
Lease
Leash
Ledges
Leeward
Legates
Leger
Legion
Lends
Lepers
Lessened
Lesson
Lessons
Lest
Lets
Lettering
Levant
Levelld
Lewd
Libanus
Lick
Lid
Lieu
Lifebelt
Lifeless
Lifting
Lighten
Lightening
Lighthanded
Lightship
Likeness
Likes
Likest
Lily-buds
Lily-coloured
Lily-time
Lily-white
Lily-yellow
Lilylocks
Limbdance
Limber

Lime
Limnd
Linen
Linen-winded
Linger
Lingerd
Lingerer
Lingering-out
Lingers
Linked
Lion-brown
Lioness
Lionlike
Lionlimb
Lipmusic
Lipped
Lispd
Lisping
Lissome
List
Listed
Listenr
Listless
Little-lasting
Loaded
Loading
Loamy
Loathd
Loathe
Loathed
Loathingly
Loathsome
Lodge
Loins
Lone
Lonely
Long-lying
Long-superfluous
Longing
Lookers
Loomd
Loop
Loop-locks
Looped
Loops
Loose-traced
Loosely
Loosend
Lorn
Lose
Losses
Lote
Lote-flower
Lots
Louched
Love-laced
Love-thoughts
Loveable
Loved
Lovelier
Lovelocks
Lovely-asunder
Lovely-dumb
Lovely-felicitous
Lovescape
Low-covered
Low-latched
Lower
Loyal
Luke
Lull-off
Lung-wasting
Lurch
Lush-kept
Lustily
Lustred
Lustreless
Lustrous
Lusty
Luther
Lying
Madam
Maddest
Madrid
Madrigal
Maenefa
Magdalen
Magic
Magnify
Magnifying
Maid-months
Maiden-furled
Maidengear
Maild
Maim
Mainstrength
Majestic
Majestical
Majorca
Makesbelieve
Malice
Malign
Mallow
Mallow-row
Mallows
Mammocks
Managed
Manger
Mankinds
Manmarks
Manna-bushes
Manner
Mannerly
Mannerly-hearted
Manners
Mansex
Manshape
Mantle
Mantle-oer
Mantles
Mantling
Manwolf
Marbled
March-bloom
Marches
Marcus
Margarets
Market
Marred
Marriage
Married
Marsh
Martinmas
Martyr-master
Martyrs
Marvel
Masons
Masque
Massacre
Masterhood
Match
Matchless
Matchwood
Mawddach
May-hope
May-mess
Maybe
Mayday
Mays
Meadow-down
Meads
Meal-drift
Mealed

Mealed-with-yellow
Mealtime
Meantime
Meanwhiles
Measures
Medalliond
Medley
Melancholy
Melee
Melodious
Melodiously
Melody
Memento
Memoried
Memory
Mends
Mention
Mercies
Mere
Mermaidens
Merrily
Meshd
Meshing
Mess
Message
Messmate
Metal
Metal-lustred
Metaphors
Meted
Mi
Michaelmas
Mid-air
Mid-main
Mid-numbered
Middle
Midriff
Mien
Milan
Mile-long
Milk-white
Mill-stone
Millbrook
Millbrook-slips
Million-fueled
Millions
Mingled
Minion
Miniver
Minor
Mint
Minted
Miracle-in-mary-of-flame
Mire
Mirky
Mirrored
Misdirected
Misery
Mislike
Missd
Missing
Mistress
Mix
Mixd
Mixed
Moan
Moaning
Moans
Mob
Mock
Mockery
Mocks
Moderate
Modest
Moist
Moles
Molest
Molten-blue
Monarchs
Monition
Month-brother
Monuments
Moods
Moonless
Moonlight-mated
Moonmarks
Moor
Moorland
Mori
Morns
Morselled
Mortals
Morticed
Moses
Mote
Mote-like
Moth-soft
Mother-ground
Moulding
Mouldring
Mounded
Mounds
Mountain-bound
Mountain-echod
Mountain-side
Mounts
Mourn
Mournful
Ms
Much-dreaded
Much-thick
Myrrhy
Myrrhy-threaded
Mysterious
Nadir
Nadir-fires
Nails
Names
Nard
Narrow
National
Natured
Nautilus
Nave
Navel
Navvy
Nazareths
Nearness
Nectar
Needed
Needful
Neglectful
Neighbour-nature
Neighbouring
Neighbours
Neight
Nereid
Nerveless
Nested
Nestle
Nestlike
Nestling
Nests
Nets
Never-eldering
Never-needed
New-basilisk
New-dapple
New-dated
New-nestle
New-skeined
New-world

Newborn
Newly-drawn
Niche
Nimble
Nips
No
No-man-fathomed
Nobler
Nobs
Nocturns
Noises
Nones
Nook
Noonday
Nose
Nostril
Not-by-morning-matched
Not-staled
Not-to-call
Nourishes
Numb
Number
Numbs
Nursing
Nursle
Nymphs
O-seal-that-so
Oak
Oar
Oath
Obscurd
Obsolete
Obstruction
Occasion
Oclock
October
Oer-brim
Oer-head
Oertake
Offended
Offer
Offerings
Offspring
Oft
Oils
Ointment
Oit
Older
Olive
Olive-branch
Onyx
Onyx-coronals
Opal
Ope
Opening
Opportunest
Opposition
Oppressed
Oppression
Oracle
Orchard-apple
Orchards
Order
Orderd
Organ
Orinda
Orion
Ought
Out-fleeced
Outer
Outgoings
Outline
Outrage
Outrides
Outward-steeled
Outwards
Outwitted
Overbend
Overflowing
Overspread
Overstood
Overtake
Overtaking
Overvaulted
Overvaults
Overworn
Overwrought
Owns
Oxeye
Paces
Pacing
Pack
Packs
Pactolus
Page
Pageant
Pained
Painful
Pains
Paint
Painted
Painting
Pair
Paird
Palate
Paling
Palmtree
Palsy
Pane
Pang
Pansy
Pansy-dark
Pantings
Papa
Paradisaical
Paradox
Parapet
Parched
Parches
Pare
Paring
Paris
Parley
Parlour
Parlour-pastime
Partless
Pashed
Passages
Passion-pastured
Passion-plunged
Passion-sake
Passionflower
Passions
Past-prayer
Pastime
Pasts
Pastured
Patch
Pathless
Patient
Patronize
Pauls
Pause
Paves
Pea
Peach
Peacockd
Peacocks
Peak
Peakd
Pealed
Peals
Pearly

Peartree
Peasant
Pectoral
Peeled
Peer
Peers
Pegasus
Pelt
Pelted
Pelting
Pencilled
Pendant
Penetrative
Penitence
Penitent
Perch
Perfumes
Peril
Perishable
Perishd
Perishing
Permanence
Perpetual
Perplexed
Perseus
Personal
Persuasion
Petalld
Peter
Phantasies
Phantasy
Pharohs
Philomel
Phosphor
Phrenzy
Pick
Picked
Piece-bright
Piecemeal
Piecing
Pied
Piercing
Pigeons
Pilasterd
Pilates
Pile
Piled
Piles
Pilgrimages
Pillars
Pillowing
Pillows
Pillowy
Pin
Pinions
Pink
Pinks
Pious
Pit
Pitch
Pitchblack
Placed
Placid
Plaintively
Plaits
Plane
Plane-leaves
Plant
Planted
Plants
Plashes
Plates
Platting
Pleading
Pleadings
Pleas
Pleasance
Pleasaunce
Pleased
Pleasurable
Pleasured
Pledged
Pleiad
Plied
Plight
Plots
Pluck
Plum
Plum-purple
Plume
Plumy
Plunder
Plunge
Plunged
Plunging
Plush
Plush-capped
Plushy
Pocked
Pocket
Poetry
Poets
Pointing
Points
Poising
Poles
Pomp
Pompeii
Pond
Ponderous
Pools
Pore
Portending
Portends
Portholes
Portion
Ports
Possessed
Post
Posturd
Pot
Potent
Potential
Pots
Potsherd
Pour
Pourtrayd
Poverty
Powerless
Praisd
Praises
Pranked
Praying
Prays
Preachings
Precedents
Precipice
Precipitous
Precisely
Precision
Prediluvian
Preeminent
Preened
Preference
Prejudice
Prenatal
Prepare
Prescriptive
Presence
Presented
Pressure
Pretend
Price

Priced
Prick
Prickproof
Priest
Primes
Princely
Princes
Principle
Print
Prism
Privacy
Procession
Proconsul
Prodigal
Profess
Proffer
Profit
Profound
Promises
Prophetess
Proportion
Prosper
Prosperity
Prosperously
Prosperously-boded
Prouder
Proudest
Proverb
Provide
Prudence
Pruned
Psalm
Public
Puffball
Pulpit
Punishment
Pupil
Pupils
Purchase
Purer
Purfled
Purify
Purple-of-thunder
Purply
Pursuant
Pursud
Pursued
Pushed
Pushing
Python
Quail

Quaint
Quartz
Quartz-fret
Quenchd
Quenching
Questioning
Quests
Quicken
Quickenings
Quickgold
Quicksilvery
Quiet
Quiet-walled
Quill
Quills
Quils
Quinces
Quit
Quivering
Radiance
Raging
Rail
Rain-blasts
Rain-born
Raindrop
Raindrop-roundels
Raisd
Raise
Raised
Rambled
Rampant
Ramps
Random
Ranged
Rank-old
Ranking
Rankle
Ransomd
Ranters
Rapture
Rapturous
Rare-dear
Rarest-veined
Rash-fresh
Rated
Ration
Ravage
Rave
Ravel
Ravel-ropes-end
Ravelld

Ravens
Raves
Ravishment
Ray
Rayd
Re-winded
Reaches
Reading
Readings
Reads
Real
Realer
Realize
Realty
Reappear
Rearing
Reasond
Reave
Reaving
Rebellious
Rebound
Rebuff
Rebuffed
Reclaiming
Reconciled
Record
Records
Recover
Recurb
Redcoats
Redeeming
Reed
Reeds
Reef
Reefs
Reek
Reeking
Reeling
Reels
Refrain
Refused
Regimental
Register
Regret
Regular
Rehearsal
Reign
Rein
Release
Released
Relics

Religious
Remain
Remainder
Remark
Rememberd
Remembereth
Remembrance
Remnants
Remorseless
Remotest
Remove
Removes
Renderd
Rent
Repeated
Reprieve
Resent
Residuary
Resign
Resolution
Resurrection
Retire
Retirement
Returning
Reversal
Reviled
Revisits
Revival
Reward
Rhine
Rhymes
Ribbed
Ribbon
Rich-pieced
Richest
Richly
Richness
Rid
Riddles
Rider
Ridge-crest
Rifled
Rigging
Righted
Righteousness
Rigour
Rill
Rilly
Rime
Rimmon
Rinds
Ringing
Ringlet
Ringlet-race
Rinse
Rinsed
Ripest
Ripples
Rips
Risn
Rival
Rivalled
Rivals
Rivelling
River-banks
River-bed
River-rounded
Rivn
Rivulet
Roads
Roam
Roaming
Roared
Roaring
Rob
Robberys
Robe
Robes
Robin
Rock-a-heart
Rockdoves
Rocket
Rockfire
Rocky
Roguish
Rollcall
Rolld
Rollrock
Rome
Romp
Roofd
Rook-racked
Rookery
Roost
Root-room
Rooting
Rope-over
Roped
Rose-flake
Rose-moles
Rose-red
Roseleaves
Rosing
Rosy-budded
Rosy-lippd
Rosy-pale
Rough-robin
Rough-scored
Roughcast
Rounder
Rounding
Roundy
Rout
Rowing
Royally
Royals
Roysterers
Rubies
Ruby
Rud
Ruddied
Ruddying
Ruder-rounded
Rudred
Rueful
Rule
Ruler
Runnel
Runnels
Rupture
Rushy
Rust
Rustle
Rutpeel
Sable
Sack
Sackcloth
Sacrificed
Saddening
Sailed
Sailors
Saintly
Saints
Saith
Sakes
Sallows
Sally
Salute
Sanctuary
Sand-teasing
Sandalled
Sandblind
Sandfield

Sandy
Sang
Sanguine
Sappd
Sapphire-pale
Sapphire-shot
Sapricius
Sard
Sash
Satin
Satin-purfled
Saturday
Saved
Saves
Savest
Saviours
Savour
Scaffold
Scalded
Scales
Scan
Scanned
Scanted
Scarce-call-silver
Scarce-sheathed
Scare
Scarless
Scarves
Scented
Sceptic
Schooled
Schooling
Schools
Schooner
Scoop
Scooped
Scoops
Scored
Scores
Scorning
Scour
Scourged
Screamd
Screen
Scroll
Scroll-leaved
Sculls
Sculpturd
Scutcheon
Scythe
Scythes
Sea-corpse
Sea-fan
Sea-fowl
Sea-gull
Sea-gust
Sea-romp
Sea-swill
Seabeach
Sealing-wax
Seamanship
Seamark
Sear
Searching
Seared
Second
Seconding
Secrets
Seeking
Seldom
Seldomer
Self-caressd
Self-embraced
Self-feeling
Self-instressed
Self-made
Self-outwitted
Self-sacrifice
Self-sentenced
Self-will
Self- wise
Selfbent
Selfdisposal
Selfish
Selfless
Selfquained
Selfsame
Selfstrung
Selfwrung
Selfyeast
Selvaggia
Selved
Sendings
Sends
Sensual
Sentence
Sentenced
Sepulchre
Sequence
Sequins
Seraph-arrival
Serfdom
Serged
Sermons
Server
Setting
Settle
Settler
Sevenfold
Sevenfold-single
Seventeenth
Seventy
Severance
Severe
Sew
Sewers
Sex
Sexed
Shadowiest
Shadowtackle
Shakespeares
Shallowing
Shallowy
Shapen
Sharded
Sharper
Sheath
Sheathe-and
Sheaves
Sheep-bells
Sheep-flock
Sheets
Shelled
Shelling
Shells
Shelterless
Shewed
Shewing
Shews
Shield
Shift
Shifted
Shilling
Shining-hilted
Shining-shot
Shipwrack
Shires
Shirt
Shivelights
Shiverd
Shives
Shoal
Shoaly

Shores
Shorten
Shorter
Shortest
Shouldering
Showd
Showerd
Showering
Shreds
Shrewsbury
Shrieked
Shrines
Shrive
Shroud-plaits
Shrouds
Shrovetide
Shuns
Shuts
Shuttles
Shy
Sicilian
Sicken
Sickend
Sickly
Sided
Sides
Sidled
Siege
Sieve
Sift
Sifted
Sighed
Sign
Signalling
Signals
Silk-ash
Silk-beech
Silk-sack
Sillion
Silt
Silver-coated
Silver-shot
Silver-surfed
Simile
Simon
Simoom
Sinew-service
Singeing
Sings
Sinking
Sinner

Sinners
Sinning
Sip
Siren
Sisterhood
Sistering
Sisterly
Sizes
Skates
Skiff
Skinned
Skins
Skirting
Skirts
Slabby
Slabs
Slake
Slaked
Slammd
Slanted
Slates
Slaty
Slaughter
Slay
Slendering
Slew
Slightly
Slim-pointed
Slip
Slipt
Sloe
Sloggering
Slopd
Slope
Sloping
Slowly
Slumberd
Smeared
Smit
Smitten
Smock
Smokes
Smooth-lippd
Smote
Smudge
Snatch
Snow-pinions
Snowflake
Snowstorm
Snowy
Snuff

So
Soared
Sob
Sobbd
Sobs
Sod
Sodden
Sodden-with-its-sorrowing
Sods
Softening
Soldier
Soldiering
Soldiers
Soldiery
Solely
Solemn
Solitary
Sombre
Song-fowl
Song-strain
Sonnet
Sooner
Soonest
Sooty
Soppd
Sordid
Sordidness
Sorrowing
Sorrows
Sorry
Sort
Sorts
Sots
Sounding
Sounds
Soured
South-westerly
Southern
Sovereign
Sovereignty
Sowed
Space
Spain
Spake
Spaniels
Spannd
Spans
Sparkling
Sparks
Spatterd

Speaketh
Speaking
Speard
Special-general
Speechless
Speeds
Spends
Spendsavour
Sperses
Spiked
Spikes
Spin
Spine
Spire
Spires
Splayd
Splendid
Splendours
Splinterd
Spoil
Spokes
Spools
Spoons
Sport
Sported
Sousal
Sprang
Spray
Sprays
Spreading
Spring-broidery
Spring-tide
Spring-time
Springtime
Sprit
Spun
Spur
Spurrd
Squadroned
Squall
Squander
Squandering
Square
Square-cut
Squared
Squat
Squeezed
Squinches
Stabbing
Staff
Stage
Staid
Stair
Stair-way
Stake
Staled
Stalk
Stallion
Stalwart
Stamp
Stanches
Stanching
Star-eyed
Starches
Starchy
Staring
Stark-precipitous
Starlight-wender
Starting
Starvd
Starves
Starvest
Statue
Staunch
Stays
Stead
Steal
Steals
Stealthy
Steeled
Steep-up
Steered
Stem
Stephen
Stepped
Steps
Stept
Sterling
Sterner
Sternest
Steward
Stick
Stiffend
Stifling
Stigma
Stilling
Stillness
Stilly
Stinging
Stint
Stinting
Stintless
Stipple
Stirless
Stirrings
Stirs
Stock
Stock-still
Stoled
Stolen
Stooks
Stooped
Storm-months
Stormfowl
Storys
Strained
Stranded
Strangers
Strawberry
Strawberry-breasted
Strawy
Straying
Strays
Streakd
Streaks
Stream
Street
Streets
Strengthen
Stressed
Stretches
Strewed
Stricken
Strides
Striding
Strife
String
Stringy
Striped
Stripes
Strips
Strive
Striven
Strombus
Strombus-shell
Strook
Struggling
Stubborn
Stupendous
Stupid
Sturdy
Subject
Submission

Succeed
Suffer
Suffered
Suffering
Suffers
Sufficed
Sugar
Suiting
Suitors
Sulphur
Sulphur-colourd
Sultry
Sum
Summer-time
Summering
Summers
Summit
Summoning
Sumptuous
Sums
Sun-flushd
Sunbeam
Sunday
Sunlit
Sunned
Suns-eye-ringed
Sunspurge
Superfluous
Supplied
Supply
Suppose
Supposing
Surcease
Surf
Surfed
Surfy
Surprise
Surrenders
Surround
Survey
Suspect
Suspects
Swallow
Swallowd
Swallowing
Swallows
Swam
Swan
Swan-fledged
Swans
Swarm
Swarter
Swarthed
Swathe
Sway
Swayed
Sweating
Sweats
Sweet-and-sour
Sweet-familiar
Sweet-fowl
Sweet-pea-blossom
Sweetbriar
Sweeter-memoried
Sweetheart
Swelld
Swelling
Swells
Swerver
Swiftly
Swill
Swims
Swivelled
Swolln
Swoon
Swooned
Swords
Sycamore-tree
Sydney
Sympathising
Table
Tact
Tail-fin
Tails
Tainting
Taking
Takings
Tales
Talks
Talmai
Tame
Tampering
Tangles
Tantalean
Taper
Tapers
Tar
Tarpeian
Tarpeian-fast
Tartarus
Tasking
Tasks
Tasteless
Tasty
Tatter
Tatter-tangled
Tauntless
Tear-tricked
Teases
Tedious
Teevo
Temperateness
Temperd
Tempests
Temples
Tempt
Tender-slanted
Tendered
Tenderer
Tenderest
Tenderness
Tent
Tent-poles
Terebinth
Term
Terms
Terraces
Terror
Teryth
Tether
Thames
Thankless
Thanks
That
The-last-breath
Theory
Thereafter
Therein
Therewith
Theyre
Thick-fleeced
Thick-pearled
Thicken
Thickening
Thickest
Thicket
Thickly
Thigh
Thinking
Thinly
Thinned
Thinning
Thirsts

Thistled
Thistles
Thither
Thongs
Thorn-engaged
Thorny
Thoroughfare
Thorp
Thralls
Threaded
Threads
Three-heeled
Three-numbered
Threefold
Threshing
Threshing-floor
Threshold
Threw
Thriftless
Thrill
Thrills
Throe
Throned
Throstle
Throttled
Throughther
Throws
Thrush
Thrushs
Thrust
Thrusts
Thunder-purple
Thunder-throne
Thundering
Thwart
Thwarts
Tighten
Tiles
Tillage
Timberll
Timbrels
Timed
Times-over
Tingeing
Tingling
Tiniest
Tinklings
Tints
Tiptoes
Tires
Titans

To-fro
Today
Token
Tomb-decked
Tombs
Toms
Toolsmooth
Toppd
Topsyturvy
Topt
Torment
Tormenting
Tossed
Tosses
Tower-top
Towered
Towery
Towns
Toy
Trace
Traceless
Tracery
Traces
Track
Trade
Trades
Tragic
Traild
Trailing
Training
Trambeams
Tramp
Trample
Trampled
Tramplers
Tranquil
Translucent
Transmit
Trash
Travelld
Traverse
Treacherous
Treadmire
Treasonable
Treble-fervent
Tree-tops
Treetop
Tremble
Tremulous
Trench
Trenched

Trial
Trick
Tricked
Trickling
Trinity
Trip
Triple
Triple-hummocked
Trips
Troops
Tropic
Troubled
Trout
Truckle
Truelove
Truer
Truly
Trundled
Ts
Tucked
Tuggd
Tumbled-to
Tumbler
Tumbling
Tumblings
Tumult
Tuneable
Tuned
Turbid
Turf
Turmoil
Turquoise
Turquoise-gemmd
Turtles
Twenty
Twindles
Twiny
Twixt
Tyrant
Unaccounted
Unalterd
Unawakened
Unaware
Unbakes
Unblown
Unbroken
Uncertainty
Unchallenged
Unchancelling
Unchanging
Uncharted

Uncheckd
Unchilding
Unchilld
Unchrist
Unclean
Uncomforted
Unconfessed
Uncontrolled
Uncreated
Uncumbered
Undenizened
Underground
Underplighted
Underwing
Undivulged
Undoing
Undulation
Unendear
Unenduring
Unespied
Unfathering
Unfathomable
Unfold
Unforeseen
Unforgiven
Ungentle
Ungirdled
Unglue
Unheard
Unheeded
Unhinderd
Unhouse
Unimperilld
Unimpregnate
Universal
Unkind
Unleaving
Unlookd
Unlovely
Unmade
Unmindful
Unmoved
Unpalateable
Unpassiond
Unpeopled
Unpinned
Unquestiond
Unraveller
Unrest
Unreticent
Unsafe
Unsandalled
Unselfishness
Unselve
Unsets
Unsexing
Unshapeable
Unsheathd
Unshod
Unsought
Unsteady
Unstinted
Unswerving
Untainted
Untaught
Unteachably
Untwist
Unused
Unvalve
Unveined
Unvexed
Unvisited
Unwarned
Unwavering
Unwet
Unworthiness
Upbringing
Upgazing
Uplands
Upraisd
Upright
Uproll
Upward-parted
Utter
Utterer
Uttermost
V
V-winged
Vale
Valiant
Valleys
Value
Van
Vaned
Vanishd
Vanishing
Vantage
Vapour
Vapourous
Variety
Various
Vastness
Vasty
Vaulted
Vaulty
Vaunt
Vaunt-and
Vaunting
Veind
Velvet
Velvety
Venerable
Vengeances
Ventnor
Venus
Veriest
Vermeil
Vermeil-rain
Vermilion
Verse
Very-violet-sweet
Vespers
Vespillo
Vessels
Vest
Vexd
Victim
Victor
View
Viewing
Views
Vigil-keepers
Vigil-organ
Vigorous
Villages
Vine-shoot
Vines
Vintage
Viol
Violent
Virgins
Visaged
Visionary
Visions
Visual
Vive
Vivid
Voel
Voids
Voluminous
Vows
Wading
Waether

Waft
Wafting
Wag
Wages
Wail
Wailing
Wain
Waists
Wait
Waken
Wakes
Walkd
Walled
Wallow
Wallowing
Walnut
Walsingham
Wan
Waning
Wanner
Wanted
Wanwood
Warbled
Warbles
Warder
Warding
Warfare
Warm-laid
Warmd
Warms
Warmth
Warnd
Warning
Warp
Warped
Warrants
Warring
Wasted
Wasteful
Wasting
Watchd
Watches
Water-cloud
Water-in-a-wallow
Water-lily
Water-meads
Water-nymphs
Water-pierced
Water-wattled
Waterblowballs
Waterfall
Waterfalls
Waterfearers
Waterworld
Wattled
Waver
Wavier
Wax
Waxes
Waylay
Weakness
Weal
Weald
Weariest
Webbd
Webbed
Webs
Weds
Weed-bathed
Weed-winding
Weeded
Weedio-weedio
Week
Weepings
Weigh
Weighed
Weighing
Weight
Weights
Weighty
Wellbeing
Welling
Wender
Westerd
Westerly
Western
Westward
Wet-fresh
Wete
Wether
Wharf
Whatevers
Wheat-acre
Wheatfields
Wheels
Whelmd
Whereon
Whilst
Whip
Whip-adder
Whips
Whirled
Whirling
Whirlwind-swivelled
Whisper
Whispers
White-faced
White-fiery
Whitebeam
Whitest
Whitewash
Wholl
Wholly
Whorl
Whorled
Wicket
Widow-making
Wield
Wielding
Wild-worst
Wildfire
Wildflowers
Wildworth
Wiles
Wilful
Wilful-wavier
Willd
Willing
Willow
Willows
Wills
Wimpled-water-dimpled
Wimpling
Wince
Wincing
Wind-beat
Wind-lilylocks-laced
Wind-long
Wind-perplexed
Wind-walks
Wind-wandering
Windfalls
Windlaced
Window-circles
Windpipe
Windpuff
Windpuff-bonnet
Wink
Winks
Winter-while
Winters
Wiped

Wisest
Wishing
Wisped
Witch
With-a-fountains
Withal
Wither
Withering
Withindoors
Withouten
Witnessed
Witted
Wolfsnow
Woman-kind
Womans
Womb-life
Womb-not-bearing
Womb-of-all
Wonderful
Wooddove
Woodferns
Woodlark
Wool
Woolwoven
Woos
Worded
Wording
Wordy
Working
Workman
Works
World-sorrow
World-wielding
Worms
Worthiest
Wounded
Woven
Wrapped
Wrathful
Wreath
Wreathd
Wreaths
Wreckd
Wrecking
Wrestles
Wrestling
Wretches
Wring-world
Wringing
Wrinkle
Writ
Writes
Writhe
Wrongd
Wronging
Wrongs
Wuthering
Wychelm
Yawnd
Year-mother
Yellowy
Yesterday
Yestertempests
Yoke
Yore-flood
Youngster
Youve
Ytressed
Yule
Zeal-rampant
Zenithd
Zephyrs
Zone
8000

TWICE

A—wanting
Abroad
Acorn
Acts
Adown
Aerial
All-starrd
Allows
Alls
Alms
Aloft
Alway
Amain
Amber
Amongst
Anvil
Anything
Anywhere
Appeal
Apple
Approved
Apt
Arc
Arch
Argent
Arm
Arose
Ashes
Asks
Asleep
Aspens
Astray
At
Attain
Attributing
Autumn-time
Babble
Bala
Ballad
Band
Banes
Bank
Barely
Barrow
Base
Bath
Bathed
Beacon
Bead
Beast
Beating
Beats
Beautiful
Beckoned
Beds
Beetling
Beings
Believe
Believes
Belled
Bend
Bereft
Beryl
Bevy
Big
Bill
Billow
Billows
Bind
Birds
Bitterness
Blade
Blasts
Blaze
Blazoned
Bleat

Bleed
Blot
Blots
Blows
Bodies
Boisterous
Bolder
Book
Bowd
Bows
Braggart
Braids
Branch
Branches
Branchy
Brass
Brave
Brazen
Breasts
Breezy
Brief
Brims
Brine
Bringing
Britain
Broken
Brood
Brooks
Broth
Browed
Bruised
Bubbles
Bugler
Buoy
Burning
Burnish
Burst
Caerwys
Caesars
Calld
Calm
Cant
Caps
Careful
Careful-spaced
Cares
Carmine
Carol
Carry
Cart
Cease
Centres
Channel
Character
Charge
Charmed
Cheevio
Chief
Children
Chill
Chime
Choicest
Chords
Chose
Christmas
Church
Circled
Circles
Clad
Clarion
Clasped
Clears
Cleaves
Close-shut
Clot
Clothe
Cluster
Coil
Colourd
Coloured
Colours
Comb
Comforting
Comfortless
Coming
Commonweal
Condition
Consolation
Coo
Cooling
Corner
Corners
Cornice
Corridors
Corse
Counterpart
Courts
Cousin
Covered
Crash
Creased
Crossd
Crowded
Crowds
Crownals
Crownd
Crowning
Crushd
Crutches
Cup
Current
Cursed
Curses
Dale
Damasqud
Dances
Dared
Daring
Darker
Date
Dated
Daughters
Dazzling
Deadly
Deals
Dearth
Debt
Decks
Deeply
Deeps
Defeat
Delightfully
Delve
Den
Departing
Deplore
Descend
Despatch
Desperate
Despise
Deutschland
Dews
Dewy
Diamonds
Died
Dimpled
Distant
Distress
Dogged
Doomed
Dorothy
Doubtless
Dough

Dove
Doves
Downward
Draught
Draws
Dread
Dreamd
Dreamed
Drenchd
Driven
Drives
Driving
Droopd
Drooping
Duct
Due
Duly
Dwelt
Dwindled
Dye
Earliest
Earthless
Easily
Eaves
Ecstacy
Edge
Elder
Elm
Embers
Empty
Ended
Enrolld
Eve
Everyone
Eyelash
Eyelid
Fabian
Faded
Faint
Faithful
Falln
Fancy
Fang
Fastened
Faster
Fawning
Feasting
Feathers
Feathery
Feeds
Fellowship
Fells
Fetch
Fickle
Fierce
Fight
Filmy
Finer
Finishd
Fires
Firm
Firmament
Fixed
Flag
Flanks
Flare
Flashes
Flat
Flattery
Fleshed
Flickering
Flinty
Floor
Flushed
Flying
Foliagd
Folk
Foolish
Footing
Forbid
Forecast
Foreign
Forelock
Forgotten
Forlorn
Forsaken
Fought
Foul
Fragrance
Frame
Frank
Freed
Freely
Fretty
Frieze
Fro
Fronting
Froth
Fruits
Funeral
Fur
Furls
Furred
Furthest
Galahad
Gall
Gallant
Garlanded
Gash
Gay
Gear
Gem
Gilds
Girth
Giver
Glad
Gladness
Gleamd
Glide
Glove
Glows
Going
Goshen
Got
Graces
Grain
Granite
Grant
Granted
Grave
Greatness
Greenery
Greeting
Grimy
Grind
Groans
Groins
Gropes
Groping
Grove
Guessed
Guilt
Guilty
Gullies
Gurgled
Gurgling
Gush
Gust
Hallowed
Halt
Handsome
Hanging
Harbour

Harm
Harmonies
Having
Hazard
Heal
Health
Hears
Hearted
Heathenish
Heave
Heavenward
Hedges
Heel
Heir
Helen
Help
Henceforth
Heritage
Hew
Hideous
Hies
Highest
Hissing
Hoard
Hoary
Hollowing
Hopeless
Hot
Houses
Hued
Huge
Hundred
Hunt
Hunting
Hurdles
Hurtle
Hush
Ice-blocks
Idle
Im
Immaculate
Imperfect
Indoors
Infinite
Inly
Inmost
Innocent
Instead
Instressed
Instrument
Intent
Isle
Isled
Italy
Jacinth
Jane
Jar
Jesu
Jews
Juice
Kelson
Ken
Killed
Kneel
Knots
Labouring
Lack
Lad
Laden
Lads
Lambs
Lament
Lance
Landmark
Lands
Languishd
Lap
Lapped
Large
Lash
Lashed
Lasting
Latch
Lately
Laugh
Lawless
Lawrence
Laying
Leafy
Leagues
Leaning
Leaping
Learned
Leaving
Leisure
Lend
Lent
Lenten
Lessend
Levels
Liar
Liberties
Lifts
Lighted
Lightnings
Lineament
Lingering
Lion
Lippd
Listened
Listening
Lodged
Looked
Loom
Lordly
Lords
Louder
Loveless
Loveliest
Loveliness
Low-down
Lull
Lung
Lustres
Maentwrog
Maidens
Maids
Manhood
Mankind
Manly
Mar
Marching
Markd
Marking
Martyr
Marvellous
Maskd
Masks
Massy
Mastering
Matched
Mated
Mates
May
Maze
Mazed
Mazy
Mead
Meanwhile
Measured
Meat
Meek
Meets

Mellow
Mells
Melts
Members
Mend
Mended
Merely
Merry
Messes
Methinks
Midnight
Midst
Midsummer
Minded
Mined
Mingle
Miracle
Mirror
Misadventure
Moisture
Monks
Moonlight
Mornings
Morsels
Moss
Motes
Moth
Motherhood
Mothers
Motionable
Moulded
Mountains
Mourning
Mouthed
Moves
Multiply
Murder
Murderous
Myriad
Mysteries
Nation
Nazareth
Nearest
Newly
News
Nigh
Nightfall
Nightingale
Nile
Nix
Noon
Nostrils
Oaks
Offend
Offering
Onewhere
Ooze
Opend
Opens
Orbd
Orience
Original
Ours
Outright
Overflow
Oxford
Pace
Palmy
Pangs
Parallel
Pardon
Park
Parts
Passage
Passd
Passed
Pastoral
Pastures
Path
Pearled
Pebbly
Peculiar
Penance
Pence
Pennon
People
Perceived
Persistency
Philip
Phoebus
Pierce
Pines
Pining
Pipe
Pitched
Plait
Plan
Planets
Plash
Plated
Playd
Plea
Please
Plumed
Plumes
Poet
Poise
Poised
Pole
Poppies
Posts
Powerful
Powers
Praised
Preferred
Present
Prey
Prison
Promised
Providence
Pulld
Purcell
Purport
Quails
Quarter
Queen
Quell
Quelled
Quench
Question
Quickly
Raced
Racing
Racked
Rafts
Rage
Rainbows
Randal
Rangd
Range
Ranked
Ranks
Ransom
Rarest
Re-attributing
Realm
Rears
Rebel
Rebellion
Recital
Reckon
Recovery
Reel

Reeve
Refuses
Regimen
Reigns
Relief
Relish
Remembering
Remote
Repair
Repeat
Replies
Revel
Revenge
Rhyme
Ribs
Ridge
Rind
Ringed
Riot
Rises
Rivers
Riving
Roar
Rode
Rods
Rood
Rooted
Rope
Roundels
Rowels
Ruck
Ruin
Rung
S
Sacrifice
Safe
Saint
Salvation
Sandal
Sands
Saviour
Saying
Scale
Scatter
School
Science
Scicns
Score
Scourge
Scrolled
Sealed
Sealing
Search
Seat
Secret
Seed
Senses
Sequences
Seraph
Service
Servingman
Sets
Sexing
Shade
Shades
Shafts
Shaken
Shakes
Shank
Shaped
Shares
Sheared
Shearing
Sheathed
Sheen
Sheeny
Shelly
Shines
Ship
Shire
Shod
Shoot
Shoots
Shoulders
Showy
Shrine
Sickness
Sighing
Silken
Sinew
Sinned
Sisters
Six
Skeined
Skeins
Skirt
Skylarks
Skywards
Slack
Sleek
Slept
Slight
Slighted
Slim
Slime
Slumber
Slumbered
Smells
Smiles
Smother
Smouldering
Snowwhite
Soaring
Sober
Solid
Solitude
Sons
Sore
Sorrel
Sours
Sower
Spaced
Span
Spared
Spark
Speaks
Special
Sped
Speech
Spells
Spiders
Spill
Spins
Spiritual
Spouse
Spy
St
Stained
Stark
Starrd
Startle
Statuary
Stealing
Steeped
Still-purpling
Stool
Stop
Stops
Store
Stormy
Straight
Strand
Strands

Strangely
Stranger
Straw
Stray
Streamd
Stretchd
Stretching
Strikes
Strings
Strove
Stumbling
Stung
Sucks
Suddenly
Summertime
Sunderd
Sung
Sunk
Sunny
Suns
Sward
Swarmed
Swart
Swayd
Swaying
Sways
Swear
Swears
Swift
Swimming
Swinishly
Swirling
Tabour
Talons
Tangled
Tars
Tarsus
Teasing
Tempest
Temple
Text
Th
The
Thence
Thereby
Thinks
Thorough
Thread
Thrice
Thrive
Throat
Throbbing
Throne
Thronged
Tides
Tied
Tilt
Timber
Tinted
Tire
Tired
Titians
To-morrow
To-night
Tomb
Tones
Tongues
Tonight
Tool
Top
Tormented
Touchd
Traced
Travelling
Treat
Treats
Treble
Trembling
Trim
Tropes
Trying
Turnd
Unbound
Uncle
Uncouth
Understand
Understood
Unfurled
Unholy
Unknown
Unset
Upwards
Used
Utterance
Uttered
Uttering
Utterly
Vacant
Vain
Valerian
Valley
Valour
Vaulting
Veer
Veil
Veined
Vice
Vigil
Virginal
Vision
Visiting
Vital
Void
Waist
Waits
Wake
Waked
Walked
Wand
Wanton
Warbling
Warmly
Watchet
Watching
Waterd
Watery-plated
Wave
Waved
Waving
Waxed
Waxen
Weak
Wealth
Wears
Weedio
Weeks
Weeps
Well-bred
Wend
Wharves
Wheat
Whelms
Whereas
Wherefore
Whirl
Whirlwind
Wholesome
Widow
Wildness
Williams
Wilt
Wimpled
Winch

Winded
Winding
Windy
Winning
Winter-time
Wintering
Wintry
Wiry
Wisdom
Wisp
Wits
Woeful
Woes
Women
Wont
Wood-sorrel
Woodland
Wordsworth
Wore
World-mothering
Worm
Worthy
Wounds
Wrecked
Wrecks
Wretch
Wrings
Wrinkles
Write
Yearnd
Youll
Zeal
Zenith
Zest

THREE TIMES

Acre
Act
Admire
Adored
Ago
Alice
Alien
Alive
Aloof
Alterd
Anon
Arise
Askd
Ay
Ball
Barred
Barren
Beams
Begin
Behold
Betwixt
Blades
Blear
Bleeding
Blessed
Blinding
Block
Bloody
Boast
Boon
Borne
Bough
Boys
Brace
Brain
Breathed
Brilliant
Brim
Brings
Broke
Bronze
Broods
Brows
Burly
Burns
Bushes
Calling
Careless
Carnation
Carried
Central
Changed
Changeful
Changing
Charged
Charm
Charms
Cheek
Childs
Choke
Churl
Cliff
Cliffs
Clime
Clings
Common
Conceive
Conceived
Convent
Cool
Copying
Corpse
Covers
Creep
Crept
Crest
Crew
Crowd
Crucified
Crucify
Crush
Crushed
Crying
Daffodils
Dainty
Danced
Dangerous
Dank
Dean
Dearer
Deeper
Delight
Delightful
Deliver
Descending
Desired
Diamond
Dies
Dip
Disappointment
Distance
Doing
Doors
Doubt
Dreadful
Dream
Dreams
Droop
Drove
Drum
Dwells
Easy
Eat
Ecstasy
Eggs
Egyptian

Elements
Elsewhere
Endears
Ending
Ends
Enormous
Equal
Especial
Everything
Evil
Exquisite
Eyed
Fails
Fairy
Faith
Fallow
Familiar
Fan
Fancies
Fans
Fatal
Fears
Feasts
Feather
Features
Fee
Feed
Feeling
Felix
Fetched
Fie
Files
Fills
Fin
Fit
Fixd
Flags
Flames
Flank
Flashed
Flight
Flint
Float
Floods
Flow
Flowing
Flown
Flush
Following
Fool
Force

Forehead
Forget
Forgive
Foundering
Fowl
Framed
France
Friends
Frightful
Furrow
Gazes
Ghost
Gifts
Girl
Glare
Glass
Glorious
Goodnight
Gospel
Grief
Gross
Growing
Guile
Gusts
Gwenvrewi
Hall
Handle
Happier
Harry
Hated
Havoc
Hearing
Heed
Hence
Henry
Hid
Hide
Hides
Hit
Hither
Hollows
Hood
Horn
Horns
Horror
Host
Hunger
Hurl
Hurled
Inner
Interest

Iron
John
Jostling
Juicy
Keel
Key
Kill
Knees
Knelt
Lake
Lashes
Led
Lids
Line
Listen
Lists
Lit
Litter
Lived
Living
Lock
Lodges
Lookd
Looking
Loose
Lore
Loss
Lust
Majesty
Manna
Marys
Masters
Mastery
Mate
Matter
Meal
Melt
Merciful
Mermaids
Messenger
Messengers
Mild
Million
Mist
Mists
Molten
Morrow
Mounting
Move
Moved
Musical

Natural
Neer
Neighbour
Nerve
Nine
Noise
Numbered
Nun
Obey
Ocean
Oil
Orchard
Overhead
Packed
Palace
Palm
Parting
Passing
Paul
Pay
Pearl
Pent
Pierced
Piety
Pine
Piteous
Places
Plighted
Plotted
Plumage
Ply
Point
Pointed
Pores
Power
Prayers
Pressed
Pretty
Prime
Primrose
Prince
Principal
Prize
Prized
Proof
Proper
Prove
Pull
Purpling
Purpose
Puts
Quick
Quince
Quote
Rabble
Rarely
Reachd
Reason
Recorded
Reply
Rescue
Richard
Riding
Rife
Rising
Rolled
Rolling
Rook
Ropes
Rounded
Row
Ruins
Rush
Sake
Sank
Sap
Saturn
Scope
Seal
Seals
Seamen
Seasons
Seeming
Selves
Sensitive
Serve
Served
Several
Sheaf
Sheathe
Shepherds
Shoals
Shocks
Shone
Shout
Shows
Shroud
Sigh
Signal
Silky
Sire
Sit
Sitting
Sizing
Smell
Smiled
Soil
Sores
Sow
Sown
Sparky
Sphered
Splendour
Spoke
Spots
Stain
Stare
Start
State
Stay
Steady
Stir
Stirred
Stole
Stony
Struggle
Strung
Suck
Suit
Sunset
Surly
Sweat
Sweeps
Swell
Swim
Swing
Swings
Sycamore
Tackle
Tail
Taken
Tale
Teeming
Terrible
Thecla
Thew
Thickend
Third
Thirst
Thorn
Thousands
Throngs
Throw

Ties
Tiny
Title
To-day
Tomorrow
Tops
Torn
Touched
Trickle
Trust
Tumbled
Tune
Turning
Twelve
Undo
Until
Upper
Upward
Veins
Violets
Virtue
Waking
Waned
Wants
Ware
Wash
Washing
Wastes
Watched
Wedded
Wedlock
Weeping
Wells
Wept
Wheel
Wherein
Wicked
Wilder
Window
Wit
Witness
Woke
Wondering
Wonders
Worship
Wrung
Yore

FOUR TIMES

Ages
Airs
Almost
Altar
Angel
Answer
April
Arms
Balanced
Bars
Beam
Bearing
Began
Bent
Bids
Bitter
Blazon
Bleak
Blest
Blocks
Blooms
Blown
Bone
Bower
Brakes
Breathes
Breathing
Breeze
Bride
Brighter
Brittle
Brush
Bud
Bugle
Burden
Burn
Buy
Candle
Catch
Caught
Centre
Chestnut
Choose
Circle
City
Clammy
Contented
Corn
Count

Court
Cried
Crust
Curse
Cut
Dandled
Daughter
Dismal
Downs
Dress
Drift
Drink
Dull
Dusk
Duty
Early
Echoing
England
Eternal
Faces
Fame
Fathers
Feature
Felled
Felt
Flake
Flakes
Fonder
Forgot
Form
Forward
Fountains
Frail
Freshness
Fret
Fretted
Fringe
Furled
Gale
Giant
Gilt
Given
Glow
Grandeur
Grapes
Grate
Greater
Grow
Grown
Growth
Hail

Happy
Hark
Hate
Haven
Heads
Heat
Height
Hover
Hues
Hurling
In
Insight
Jack
Jesus
Judgment
Keen
Kisses
Knowing
Lakes
Lantern
Learnt
Length
Letter
Letters
Lined
Lines
Longer
Lot
Loud
Lover
Meadows
Meaning
Meant
Melted
Melting
Mid
Miles
Mill
Months
Mood
Mothering
Multitude
Muse
Neck
Nights
Note
Nowhere
Often
Outward
Palms
Paradise

Pen
Perilous
Pieced
Pilgrims
Plod
Plough
Pray
Primroses
Promise
Rash
Re
Rides
Rings
Roof
Root
Roses
Rough
Ruder
Ruinous
Running
Sadness
Sail
Sat
Scene
Season
Seek
Seem
Share
Sheaved
Shelter
Shepherd
Shore
Showers
Silent
Simple
Single
Sins
Size
Skylark
Slips
Snows
Soft
Sought
South
Starlight
Stones
Stored
Strength
Strokes
Subtle
Sucked

Sunlight
Surely
Sweep
Sweetly
Sweets
Swept
Sword
Takes
Teach
Tear
Tells
Thorns
Thousand
Toil
Treads
Treasure
Tresses
Triumph
Tufts
Twice
Underneath
Undone
Unseen
Vales
Vast
Virgin
Wales
War
Warned
Waves
Web
Weep
Wife
Wilderness
Wine
Winged
Won
Wondrous
Written
Wrong
Yields
Young

FIVE TIMES

Amidst
And
Appear
Ash
Autumn
Azure

Bad
Bands
Basket
Beautys
Bell
Beneath
Birthday
Blast
Bless
Bread
Breaking
Brother
Brought
Build
Built
Cheer
Choice
Clay
Combs
Company
Counter
Cover
Crisp
Cuckoo
Dapple
Dappled
Deal
Dealt
Dearly
Deaths
Deck
Deed
Discovered
Doom
Drew
Drowned
Dust
Earlier
English
Fain
Fallen
Falling
Fiery
Fill
Finger
Fling
Flocks
Fly
Folds
Food
Forge
Fray
Friend
Frowning
Gentle
Grew
Guess
Hang
Harvest
Held
Hero
Higher
Hills
Hue
Hurls
Jubilee
Knot
Laced
Landscape
Lark
Leans
Level
Limbs
Lip
Liquid
Lo
Lowly
Lush
Maid
Main
March
Meadow
Measure
Mens
Mighty
Mile
Minds
Mirth
Monstrous
Mortal
Motion
Myself
Mystery
Natures
Nest
Not
Parted
Pass
Passes
Perfect
Perhaps
Play
Plays
Pleasure
Plot
Precious
Race
Rack
Rains
Rays
Reach
Ready
Remember
Ride
Rim
Risen
Road
Roll
Rolls
Rounds
Rude
Runs
Rural
Sacred
Sand
Scarcely
Scarlet
Seemed
Sent
Serves
Sharp
Sheep
Sheer
Shell
Shock
Short
Shoulder
Show
Shower
Sights
Singing
Skill
Slow
Smart
Sorrow
Spare
Spell
Standing
Stands
Starry
Story
Strange
Streams

Stroke
Success
Sweeter
Swung
Sylvester
Task
Telling
Ten
Trumpet
Try
Vault
Vine
Walks
Wandering
Want
Wars
Watch
Watery
Weed
Weeds
Welcome
Welkin
Whence
Whole
Wing
Wise
With
Woods
Wreck

SIX TIMES

Airy
Alas
Always
Ask
Bay
Beginning
Begun
Below
Better
Bliss
Bluebells
Body
Bore
Breaks
Brook
Brow
Called
Castara
Change
Cheeks
Cries
Darksome
Dim
Double
Drop
Dumb
Earnest
Ease
Element
Fairer
Fault
Feast
Few
Finds
Flash
Fled
Fleece
Fleeced
Fleet
Floating
Flung
Folded
Glassy
Hangs
Hoar
Holds
Hollow
Holy
Hopes
Ice
Kiss
Knee
Lace
Laid
Laughter
Law
Lifted
Lightning
Means
Mercy
Met
Milk
Milky
Month
Mouth
Needs
Pale
Plain
Proud
Purple
Quenched
Quite
Read
Reck
Roots
Shake
Shallow
Shape
Shapes
Shewn
Shining
Shot
Silk
Sir
Sister
Sits
Slender
Smooth
Sometimes
Somewhere
Speak
Spend
Spirits
Spread
Steel
Steep
Strains
Strike
Struck
Taste
Thin
Throng
Tide
Tom
Tower
Towers
Town
Trod
Tuft
Turns
Unto
Walk
Wall
Wanting
Wish
Woman
Womb
Wound
Wring
Wrought

SEVEN TIMES

A
Among
Angels
Apart
Around
Bells
Bid
Blossom
Bred
Broad
Calls
Cause
Charity
Compass
Cross
Dare
Dawn
Dearest
Degree
Door
Draw
Evening
Everywhere
Fail
Flood
Fold
Fond
Four
Further
Gave
Get
Gift
Gives
Heavenly
Kings
Lead
Leaved
Making
Moon
Notes
Nothing
Open
Pity
Plead
Praise
Pure
Rank
Rocks
Rod
Salt
Sapphire
Says
Send
Sighs
Sleep
Snow
Sour
Storms
Sudden
Taught
Thunder
Vein
Virtues
Walls
Weather
Wed
William
Woe
Yea
Yonder

EIGHT TIMES

Birth
Bold
Boy
Brown
Buds
Clitheroe
Colour
Copse
Country
Crimson
Ears
Earths
East
Easter
Foam
Garden
Great
Grows
Hell
Hold
Immortal
Keeps
Lady
Lift
Maiden
Mean
Mould
Of
Passion
Rainbow
Repent
Rise
Room
Royal
Sad
Scarce
Sense
Shame
Shed
Shew
Sick
Small
Smile
Something
Springs
Stress
Sure
Tall
Touch
Tread
Turned
Violet
Waste
Weary
Win
Worst
Worth
Youth

NINE TIMES

Age
Banks
Banner
Bed
Blind
Bow
Clear
Desire
Drawn
Ere
Fear
Fingers
Flock
Gardens
Gaze
Gloom
Grass
Hill

Hours
Indeed
Leaf
Least
Lifes
Lilies
Lives
Loves
Need
Piece
Press
Put
Ran
Rather
Red
Rosy
Seeing
Shadow
Son
Song
Tender
Together
Winds
Yellow

TEN TIMES

Against
Bear
Between
Bird
Boughs
Bring
Brothers
Cast
Christs
Dew
Enough
Feel
Fields
Floris
Flower
Hair
Lies
Lights
Margaret
Master
Mountain
Nay
Next
Pain

Penmaen
Ring
Run
Seas
Seemd
Seen
Seven
Shook
Silence
Spot
Storm
Sweetest
Thoughts
To
Took
Tree
Truth
Voice
Warm
Waters
Wet
Words
Worlds
Worse
Yes
Yield

ELEVEN TIMES

Alone
Beside
Bones
Break
Breast
Darkness
Foot
Fruit
Half
Heavens
Leave
Music
Nature
Prayer
Rare
Same
Save
Sees
Shine
Shut
Sin
Souls

Stone
Stood
Strong
Wear
Year

TWELVE TIMES

Across
Bare
Behind
Born
Breathe
Comfort
Die
Field
Fine
Gather
Goes
Just
King
Knows
Mary
Miss
Patience
Pride
Rich
Side
Spent
Spirit
Star
Sweetness
West
Wide
Without
Word

THIRTEEN TIMES

Blood
Blow
Cloud
Dead
Despair
Dry
Ear
End
Falls
Five
Free
Full

Hour
House
Lie
Locks
Mans
Many
Old
River
Skies
Strain
Summer
Told
Very
Wonder

FOURTEEN TIMES

Along
Bloom
Close
Crown
Daylight
Drops
Flame
Follow
Ground
Hands
Knew
Locks
Morn
Pool
Rain
Set
Sing
Soon
Sound
Thick
Trees
Winter
Work

FIFTEEN TIMES

Beat
Cry
Else
Fell
Glory
Honour
Hung
Keep
Kept
Land
Little
Morning
Near
Peace
Rest
Rock
Seems
Think
Ways

SIXTEEN TIMES

Any
Beyond
Care
Cold
Feet
Forth
Gone
Kind
Known
Less
Lily
Lost
Mark
Part
Saw
Stand
Turn
Went
Wood

SEVENTEEN TIMES

Back
Days
Deep
Divine
Every
Face
Give
Golden
Hard
Hearts
Lay
Lips
Soul
Within

EIGHTEEN TIMES

Best
Call
Clouds
Dear
Even
First
Grey
Heard
Hope
Late
Left
Live
Mine
Past
Sight
Tongue
Wings

NINETEEN TIMES

Black
Bound
Child
Far
Meet
Since
Tell
Years

TWENTY TIMES AND UP

Bright
Fair
Flesh
Flowers
Gods
Gold
Might
Much
Poor
Take

21

Above
Art
Breath
Find
Fire
Name
Right
Sky
White

22

After
Ever
Joy

22 (cont.)

Lovely
Times
Wild

23

About
Comes
Father
Found
High
Home
Ill
Makes
Place
Rose

24

Go
Grace
Mind
Own
Self
Spring
True
Way

25

Dark
Fresh
Head
Oer
Thing

26

Before
Fast
Green
Life
Made
Silver
Till
Two

27

Done
New
Three
Under
Up

28

Away
Fall
Low
None
Stars

29

Eye
Good
Hear
Sea
Sun
Tears

30

Blue
Night

31

Know
Leaves
Look
Things
Thought

32

Being
Man
Once
Say

33

Lord
Only

34

Earth
Mother
Over
Time
Water

35

Last
Said

36

Well

37

Beauty
Came
Death
Never

38

Men
Still

39

Make

40

Christ
Long
Wind

41

Light

42

Hand
Most
World

43

Let
Off
Round

44

Eyes

45

Such

46

Us

48

Than

49

Some

50

While

53

Heaven

55

God
Out

58

Upon

59

See

62

Day

64

Air
Down

69

Come

72

Yet

76

Heart

80

Love

83

Will

84

Our

87

Sweet

89

More

99

Like
We

100

O

101

One

167

As

171

Me

239

My

245

All

505

I

Appendix III
Omitted Words

a
again
ah
also
altho
although
am
an
and
are
at
another
be
because
been
both
but
by
can
cannot
canst
could
dost
did
didst
do
each
either
for
from
had
hadst
has
hast
hath
have
he
her
here
hers
herself
hes
him
himself
his
how
however
if
in
into
is
it
its
itself
may
must
neither
no
nor
not
now
of
oh
on
or
other
others
shall
shalt
she
shes
should
so
that
thats
the
thee
their
them
themselves
then
there
therefore
theres
these
they
thine
this
tho
those
thou
though
thro
through
thus
thy
tis
to
too
towards
towrds
twas
was
were
wert
what
whateer
whatever
whats
when
whenever
where
whereer
wherever
whether
which
who
whom
whose
why
with
would
wouldst
ye
you
your
yours